ARMY HISTORICAL SERIES

AMERICAN MILITARY HISTORY

VOLUME II

THE UNITED STATES ARMY

IN A

GLOBAL ERA, 1917–2008

Second Edition

Richard W. Stewart
General Editor

MILITARY INSTRVCTION

Center of Military History
United States Army
Washington, D.C., 2010

Library of Congress Cataloging-in-Publication Data

American military history / Richard W. Stewart, general editor. — 2nd ed.
   p. cm. — (Army historical series)
  Includes bibliographical references and index.
  1. United States—History, Military. 2. United States. Army—History. I. Stewart,
Richard W. (Richard Winship), 1951– II. Center of Military History. III. Title. IV.
Series.

E181.A44 2009
355'.00973—dc22   2009011595

Revised Edition—First Printed 2005—CMH Pub 30–22

For sale by the Superintendent of Documents, U.S. Government Printing Office
Internet: bookstore.gpo.gov   Phone: toll free (866) 512-1800; DC area (202) 512-1800
Fax: (202) 512-2104 Mail: Stop IDCC, Washington, DC 20402-0001

ISBN 978-0-16-084184-2

Army Historical Series

Advisory Committee
(As of October 2009)

U.S. *Army Center of Military History*

Jeffrey J. Clarke, Chief of Military History

CONTENTS

Charts

Maps

Illustrations

Illustrations courtesy of the following: cover illustration by Elzie R. Golden; 3, 217, 316, U.S. Air Force; 8, Harry S. Truman Presidential Museum and Library; 11, 20, 27, 31, 33, 50, 56, 57, 68, 80, 81, 84, 87, 91, 93, 94 (*bottom*), 114, 135, 147, 148, 154, 159 (*top*), 163, 164, 179, 198, 204, 205, 215, 245, 268, 269 (*top*), National Archives; 14, Fort George G. Meade Museum; 44, Virginia Military Institute; 65, Bettman/Corbis Archives; 66, 306, Library of Congress; 86, *Illustrated London News*; 171, U.S. Navy; 75, 258, Smithsonian Institution; 260, National Park Service; 270, Corbis; 339, Lt. Col. Ernest I. Gruber, U.S. Army; 344, Department of Defense; 348, University of California–Berkley, Indochina Center; 377, 378, 385, 386, 396, 399, 401, 402 (*top*), 417, 418, 421, 426, 427, 433, 434, 438 (*bottom*), 439, 446, 464, 465, 466, 474, 491, 494, 497, Defense Visual Information Center; 395, 407, *Soldiers* magazine; 488 (*top*), U.S. Marine Corps. Other illustrations from Department of the Army files.

FOREWORD

American Military History provides the United States Army—in particular, its young officers, NCOs, and cadets—with a comprehensive but brief account of its past. The Center of Military History first published this work in 1956 as a textbook for senior ROTC courses. Since then it has gone through a number of updates and revisions, but the primary intent has remained the same. Support for military history education has always been a principal mission of the Center, and this new edition of an invaluable history furthers that purpose.

The history of an active organization tends to expand rapidly as the organization grows larger and more complex. The period since the Vietnam War, at which point the most recent edition ended, has been a significant one for the Army, a busy period of expanding roles and missions and of fundamental organizational changes. In particular, the explosion of missions and deployments since 11 September 2001 has necessitated the creation of additional, open-ended chapters in the story of the U.S. Army in action.

The first volume covers the Army's history from its birth in 1775 to the eve of World War I. By 1917, the United States was already a world power. The Army had sent large expeditionary forces beyond the American hemisphere, and at the beginning of the new century Secretary of War Elihu Root had proposed changes and reforms that within a generation would shape the Army of the future. But world war—global war—was still to come. This second volume of the new edition takes up that story and extends it into the twenty-first century and the early years of the war on terrorism.

The Center of Military History has continued to refine the new design for these volumes to reflect the highly visual nature of contemporary textbooks. This work's primary audience is still the young officer and NCO; but by adopting a more illustrated format, it also hopes to promote a greater awareness of the Army's history within the American public. In so doing, its authors remain mindful of the Center's responsibility to publish an accurate and objective account that reflects the highest professional historical standards. The Center owes no less to the soldier and the veteran, to the student and the teacher, and to those pursuing a personal interest in learning more about the Army's campaigns—and about its role in the larger history of the nation.

Washington, D.C.
24 September 2009

JEFFREY J. CLARKE
Chief of Military History

PREFACE

The story of the United States Army is always growing and changing. Historians constantly seek to reinterpret the past while accumulating new facts as America's Army continues to be challenged on new foreign battlefields. Nor does the Army, as an institution, ever stand still. It necessarily changes its organization, materiel, doctrine, and composition to cope with an ever-changing world of current conflict and potential danger. Thus, the Center of Military History is committed to preparing new editions of *American Military History* as we seek to correct past mistakes, reinterpret new facts, and bring the Army's story up to date. This new edition of that textbook, an important element in soldier and officer education since 1956, seeks to do just that.

This edition of *American Military History* builds on the previous edition, published in 2005, and expands its coverage to include an analysis of the wars in Afghanistan and Iraq up to January 2009. This expanded section is necessarily only an initial survey of the first eight years of the war on terrorism; it is far from the final word on the subject. It may take an additional decade or more to collect sufficient documents, interviews, memoirs, and other sources to know the details of military and political planning, the implementation of those plans on the global battlefield, and the impact on the Army as an institution and on the nation. The events of the past eight years are more like current events than they are history. History—the detailed telling of a story over time based upon all the extant evidence—requires more time to find and analyze the documents and facts and bring to bear on that evidence the insight that comes only from perspective. However, today's soldiers need their story told. The events in which they participate and in which they are such important elements need to be given some form and order, no matter how tentative. The Army continues to be the nation's servant, and the soldiers that make up that Army deserve their recognition. They continue to protect our freedom at great personal risk to themselves and incalculable cost to their loved ones. This is their continuing story.

Washington, D.C.   RICHARD W. STEWART
24 September 2009   Chief Historian

PREFACE TO THE 2005 EDITION

Despite the popular image of the solitary historian immured in the stacks of a library or archives, history is very much a collective enterprise. This is true not only in philosophical terms (all historians stand on the shoulders of previous generations of scholars) but also in the practical sense that historians rely heavily on the work of many others when they attempt to weave a narrative that covers centuries of history. *American Military History* is truly such a collaborative work.

Over the years numerous military historians have contributed to the earlier versions of this textbook published in 1956, 1969, and 1989. In this latest telling of the story of the U.S. Army, additional scholars inside and outside the Center of Military History have conducted research, written or revised chapters and inserts, or reviewed the texts of others. Other experts have edited text, proofed bibliographies, prepared maps, and located photographs to bring this book together.

It is important to highlight those historians and other professionals who have helped make this book a reality. Indeed, there were so many contributors that I hasten to beg forgiveness in advance if I have inadvertently left someone off this list. First, I wish to thank those many scholars outside the Center of Military History who voluntarily gave of their time to review chapters of this book and provide their expertise to ensure that the latest scholarship and sources were included. These scholars include: John Shy, Don Higginbotham, Robert Wright, John Mahon, William Skelton, Joseph Dawson, Joseph Glathaar, Gary Gallagher, Carol Reardon, Mark Grimsley, Perry Jamieson, Robert Wooster, Brian Linn, Timothy Nenninger, Edward Coffman, David Johnson, Stanley Falk, Mark Stoler, Gerhard Weinberg, Edward Drea, Steve Reardon, Allan R. Millett, Charles Kirkpatrick, and Eric Bergerud. Their careful reviews and suggested additions to the manuscript enriched the story immeasurably and saved me from numerous errors in interpretation and fact. Within the Center of Military History, of course, we have a number of outstanding historians of our own to draw upon. The Center is, I believe, as rich in talent in military history as anywhere else in the country; and I was able to take advantage of that fact. In particular, I would like to thank the following historians from the Histories Division for their writing and reviewing skills: Andrew J. Birtle, Jeffrey A. Charlston, David W. Hogan, Edgar F. Raines, Stephen A. Carney, William M. Donnelly, William M. Hammond, and Joel D. Meyerson. Within the division, every member participated in writing the short inserts that appear throughout the text. In addition to the names previously listed, I would be remiss if I did not also thank Stephen J. Lofgren, William J. Webb, Dale Andrade, Gary A. Trogdon, James L. Yarrison, William A. Dobak, Mark D. Sherry, Bianka J. Adams, W. Blair Haworth, Terrence J. Gough, William A. Stivers, Erik B. Villard, Charles E. White, Shane Story, and Mark J. Reardon. Whether they have been in the division for one year or twenty, their contributions to this work and to the history of the U.S. Army are deeply appreciated.

I particularly wish to thank the Chief of Military History, Brig. Gen. John Sloan Brown, for his patience and encouragement as he reviewed all of the text to provide his own insightful comments. He also found time, despite his busy schedule, to write the final two chapters of the second volume to bring the story of the U.S. Army nearly up to the present day. Also, I wish to thank Michael Bigelow, the Center's Executive Officer, for his contribution. In addition, I would like to note the support and guidance that I received from the Chief Historian of the Army, Jeffrey J. Clarke, and the Editor in Chief, John W. Elsberg. Their experience and wisdom is always valued. I wish to thank the outstanding editor of *American Military History*, Diane M. Donovan, who corrected my ramblings, tightened my prose, and brought consistency to the grammar and style. Her patience and skilled work made this a much finer book. I also wish to thank those who worked on the graphics, photographs, and maps that helped make this book so interesting and attractive. This book would not have been possible without the diligence and hard work of the Army Museum System Staff, as well as Beth MacKenzie, Keith Tidman, Sherry Dowdy, Teresa Jameson, Julia Simon, and Dennis McGrath. Their eye for detail and persistence in tracking down just the right piece of artwork or artifact or providing the highest quality map was of tremendous value.

Although countless historians have added to this text over the years, I know that any attempt to write a survey text on the history of the U.S. Army will undoubtedly make many errors of commission and omission. I take full responsibility for them and will endeavor, when informed, to correct them as best I can in future editions. In conclusion, I wish to dedicate this book to the finest soldiers in the world, to the men and women who have fought and died in service to the United States over two centuries and those who continue to serve to protect our freedom. They have built America into what it is today, and they continue to defend the principles upon which our great country was founded. This is their story.

Washington, D.C.
14 June 2004

RICHARD W. STEWART
Chief, Histories Division

PROLOGUE
THE WAR IN EUROPE
1914–1917

The event that set off war in Europe came in late June 1914 at Sarajevo, when a fanatical Serbian nationalist assassinated Archduke Francis Ferdinand, the heir to the Austro-Hungarian throne. In other times and under different conditions, this act might not have been enough to catapult the world into the most widespread and costly conflict man had yet known, one that would eventually put under arms 65 million men from thirty countries representing every continent. Yet as matters stood that summer of 1914, Europe was a tinderbox awaiting a spark, an armed camp with two rival power blocs. There was at first the Triple Alliance composed of Germany, Austria, and Italy. On the other side, the Entente Cordiale between Britain and France gradually merged with the Dual Alliance of France and Russia to become the Triple Entente. With the defection of Italy, Germany and Austria became the Central Powers, which Bulgaria and Turkey eventually joined. The Triple Entente became, with the addition of Italy, the nucleus of the Allied Powers.

Despite some halfhearted efforts to localize the dispute over the assassinated prince, since Russia backed Serbia and Kaiser Wilhelm II of Germany promised Austria full support, the only real question was when the war was to begin. The answer to that came on July 28, when Austria declared war on Serbia. As Russia began its ponderous mobilization process to back the Serbs, Germany rushed to strike first.

Germany's location between Russia and France dictated for the Germans a two-front war. To meet this contingency, the German General Staff had laid plans to defeat France swiftly before the Russians with their ponderous masses could fully mobilize, then to shift forces rapidly to the east and destroy the Russians at will.

The maneuver designed to defeat the French was the handiwork of Germany's gifted former Chief of Staff, Count Alfred von Schlieffen, who lent his name to the plan. Deducing that the French would attack in Alsace and Lorraine, Schlieffen proposed to trap them in a massive single envelopment, a great scythe-like movement through the Low Countries and into northern France, then west and south of Paris. Schlieffen was prepared to give ground on his left wing in Alsace-Lorraine to keep the French armies occupied until a powerful right wing—the tip of the scythe—could complete the envelopment. (*See Map 1.*)

The German staff modified the Schlieffen Plan continually between its creation and the start of the war, but one of the plan's major faults was in the area of logistics. Such a massive movement of troops and horses quickly moved beyond available railroad support and could not be sustained. The troops at the tip of the spearhead would have to slow down due to supply problems before they would be able to encircle Paris. Yet the maneuver achieved such surprise that by late August the French and British armies were in full retreat and the threat to Paris was so real that the French government abandoned the city. Only a hastily arranged French counterattack against an exposed German flank saved Paris. That action afforded time for main British and French forces to turn, halt the Germans at the Marne River east of Paris, and drive them back to the Aisne River, forty miles to the north.

As stalemate developed along the Aisne, each side tried to envelop the northern flank of the other in successive battles that by October had extended the opposing lines all the way to the Belgian coast. Allied and German armies alike went to ground. The landscape from Switzerland to the sea soon was scarred with opposing systems of zigzag, timber-revetted trenches, fronted by tangles of barbed wire sometimes more than 150 feet wide and featured here and there by covered dugouts providing shelter for troops and horses and by observation posts in log bunkers or concrete turrets. Out beyond the trenches and the barbed wire was a muddy desert called No-Man's-Land, where artillery fire had eliminated habitation and vegetation alike, where men in nighttime listening posts strained to hear what the enemy was about, and where rival patrols clashed.

Eventually both sides would realize that they had miscalculated, that the newly developed machine gun and improved indirect-fire artillery had bolstered not the offense but the defense. This development had been presaged—but ignored—in the U.S. Civil War. Principles of war such as maneuver, economy of force, and surprise were seemingly subordinated to the critical principle of mass: masses of men (nearly 2 million Germans and 3 million Allied troops); masses of artillery (barrages lasted days and even weeks before an offensive); and masses of casualties (the British and French in 1915 lost 1.5 million men killed, wounded, and missing). Yet through it all the opposing lines stood much as they had at the start. For more than two years they would vary less than ten miles in either direction.

To meet the high cost of the long, deadly struggle, the opposing powers turned more than ever before in history to the concept of the nation in arms. Even Britain, for so many years operating on the theory of a powerful navy and only a small (though highly professional) army, resorted to conscription and sent massive new armies to the continent.

The landscape from Switzerland to the sea soon was scarred with opposing systems of zigzag, timber-revetted trenches, fronted by tangles of barbed wire.

To appease the appetite of the vast armies for munitions, equipment, and supplies, the nations harnessed their mines, factories, and railroads to war production; levied high income taxes; froze wages and prices; and rationed food and other commodities. It was industrialized war on a vast scale never before seen.

On the battlefield, commanders persisted in a vain hope that somehow the stalemate might be ended and breakthrough and exploitation achieved. In April 1915 the Germans released clouds of chlorine gas against a French colonial division on the British sector of the front. The colonials broke, but the Germans were unprepared to exploit the advantage. The first use of poison gas thus was a strategic blunder, wasting total surprise for nothing more than local gains.

The British similarly blundered the next year, when they also introduced a new weapon prematurely. The tank, an ungainly, ponderous offspring of a marriage of armor with the caterpillar tractor, owed its name to British attempts to deceive the Germans that the vehicle was a water-storage device. In the tank's first commitment in September 1916, thirty-four tanks helped the British infantry advance a painful mile and a half. There would be other attacks in later months involving tanks in strengths close to five hundred, but the critical element of surprise already had passed. Tanks later would prove sufficient to achieve the penetration everybody sought, but they were initially too slow and too subject to mechanical failure to fill the horse cavalry's former role as the tool of exploitation.

For all the lack of decision, both poison gas and tank soon were established weapons, although the Germans were slow to make use of the tank. Another weapon, the airplane, meanwhile found full acceptance on both sides. Used at first primarily for reconnaissance, then as a counterreconnaissance weapon to fight the enemy's planes, and finally as an offensive weapon to attack ground troops, by the time the war ended aircraft had engaged in strategic missions against railroads, factories, and cities, presaging the mass destruction that was to follow in another great war.

THE U.S. ARMY SIGNAL CORPS AND AVIATION

The Aviation Section of the U.S. Army Signal Corps for almost its first decade of existence consisted of one airplane and one pilot, Lt. Benjamin Foulois. Foulois did not know how to fly: he had to learn through trial-and-error and written instruction from the Wright brothers. He later remarked that he was the only person to obtain his pilot's license by correspondence course. Although the Aviation Section had grown to twenty-seven aircraft and fifty-eight pilots by May 1916, it remained minuscule compared to the large and technically superior European aerial fleets engaged in World War I.

Lt. Benjamin Foulois

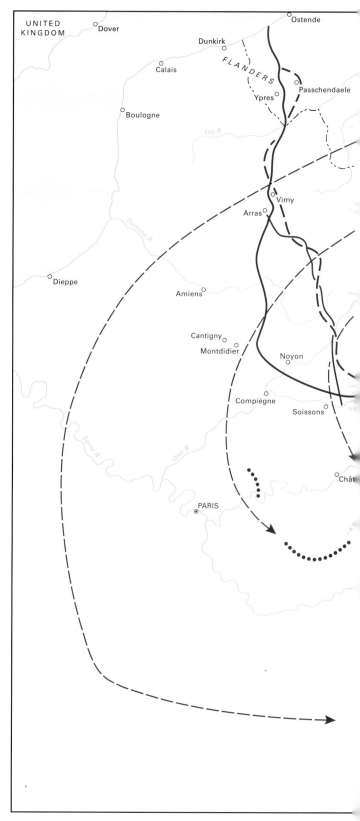

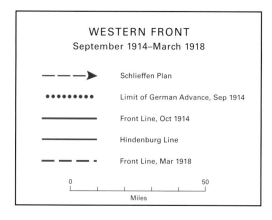

WESTERN FRONT
September 1914–March 1918

– – – – ▶	Schlieffen Plan
●●●●●●●●●	Limit of German Advance, Sep 1914
————	Front Line, Oct 1914
————	Hindenburg Line
– – – – –	Front Line, Mar 1918

0   50
Miles

Map 1

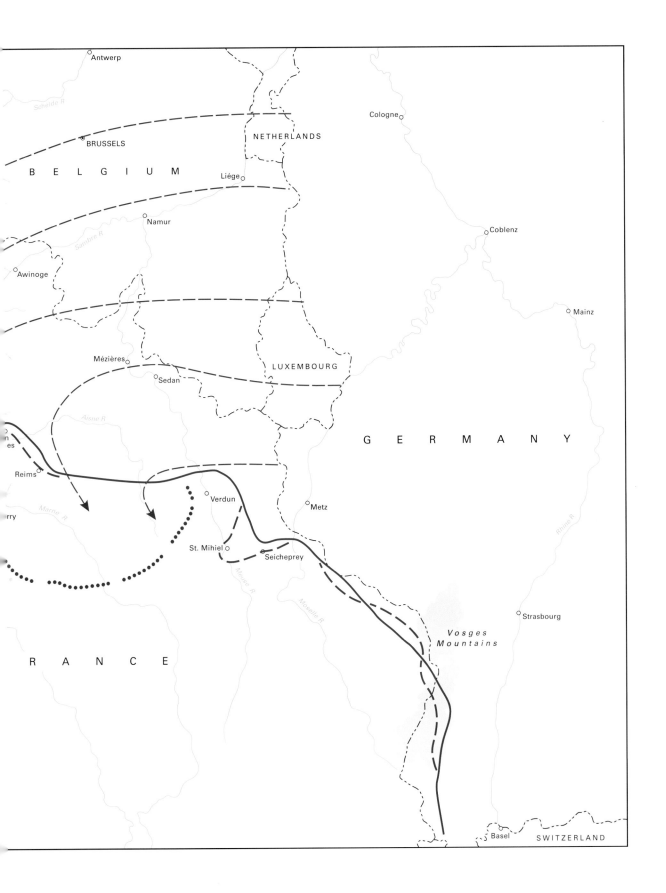

Bloody battle followed bloody battle in quick succession in 1915, 1916, and 1917. The names of the battles would echo throughout the ages as symbols of slaughter: Verdun (750,000 casualties), the Somme (1.3 million casualties), Passchendale (350,000 casualties).

By early 1917 bloody stalemate on the Western Front continued and the collapse of the Russians on the Eastern Front threatened to free up millions of Germans for service in the west. In Russia, a spontaneous revolution had erupted in March, prompting the czar to abdicate and initiating a struggle for power between moderate Socialists and the hard-core revolutionaries, the Bolsheviks. The Bolsheviks seized power in the October Revolution and immediately sued for peace. Only the slowness of the negotiations prevented the immediate release to the west of huge numbers of German soldiers.

The worst was still to come. In 1917, after yet another failed French offensive, mutiny broke out in one French regiment and spread swiftly through fifty-four divisions. Many of the French soldiers swore that they would continue to defend their homeland, but they would no longer take part in offensive operations.

More disastrous still were the results of an Austrian offensive launched with German assistance in Italy in the fall. In what became known as the Battle of Caporetto, the Italians in one blow lost 305,000 men; 275,000 of them surrendered as the Italian Army fell back a hundred miles in panic. British and French divisions had to be rushed to Italy to keep the Italians in the war. By the time America was forced to enter the war in April 1917, the disasters on all the fronts had brought the Allies close to collapse.

1

THE U.S. ARMY IN
WORLD WAR I, 1917–1918

On April 2, 1917, President Woodrow Wilson addressed Congress, asking for a declaration of war against Germany. Just over two months earlier, on January 31, the German government had announced its resumption of "unrestricted submarine warfare." With the announcement, German U-boats would without warning attempt to sink *all* ships traveling to or from British or French ports. Under the new strategy, U-boats had sunk three American merchant ships with a heavy loss of American life in March 1917. Two days after Wilson's speech, the Senate overwhelmingly declared that a state of war existed between Germany and the United States. Two days later the House of Representatives followed suit. The United States had entered "the Great War."

Since the United States went to war over the limited issue of Germany's submarine warfare, the Wilson administration conceivably could have taken only a naval role against the German submarines. That role, however, never received fervent support from the Allied or the U.S. Army's leadership. Pressure from both the British and French leaders urged Wilson to reinforce the Western Front that stretched from Belgium to Switzerland. Despite the carnage, the Army's military leaders and planners saw the Western Front as the only place that the United States could play a decisive role in defeating Germany. That participation in the decisive theater would give Wilson a larger role and greater leverage in deciding the peace that followed. Thus it would be on the battlefields and in the trenches of France that the U.S. Army would fight in 1917 and 1918.

The United States had joined a war that was entering into its fourth bitter year by the summer of 1917. After the opening battles of August 1914, the British and French armies and their German foes had settled into an almost continuous line of elaborate entrenchments from the English Channel to Switzerland that became known as the Western Front. To break this stalemate, each side sought to rupture the other's

President Wilson

lines, using huge infantry armies supported by increasingly massive and sophisticated artillery fire, as well as poison gas. Nevertheless, against the barbed wire and interlocking machine guns of the trenches, compounded by the mud churned up by massive artillery barrages, these attempts floundered and failed to make meaningful penetrations. Into this stalemate the U.S. Army would throw a force of over 2 million men by the end of the war. Half of these men fought in the trenches of northern France, mostly in the last six months of the war. It would prove to be the military weight needed to tip the strategic balance in the favor of the Allies.

The U.S. Army Arrives in Europe

In the latter part of April 1917 the French and British governments sent delegations to the United States to coordinate assistance and offer advice on the form of American involvement. Foreign Minister Arthur Balfour, Maj. Gen. G. M. T. Bridges, and the rest of the British mission arrived first; a few days later the French mission followed, led by former French Premier René Viviani and Marshal Joseph Joffre. Characteristic of the lack of planning and unity between the two Allies, the missions had devised no common plan for American participation, nor had they even held joint sessions before meeting with the Americans. Public ceremonies were well coordinated and presented a common, unified front; in private, each delegation pressed its own national interests and viewpoints.

After obtaining American loans for their depleted war chests, the French and British officials proposed ways to best make use of American manpower. Neither of the Allies believed that the United States would be able to raise, train, and equip a large army quickly. Marshal Joffre, the former French Army Commander and victor of the 1914 Battle of the Marne, offered his proposal first. To bolster sagging morale, the Frenchman suggested that an American division be sent to France to symbolize American participation. He proffered French help with the

CAPTAIN HARRY S. TRUMAN (1884–1972)

In April 1917, 33-year-old Harry Truman rejoined the Missouri National Guard in which he had served during 1905–1911. He was promptly elected a first lieutenant in the 2d Missouri Field Artillery. Two months after debarking in France as part of the 35th Division, Truman was promoted to captain and commander of Battery D. Instinctively grasping the best way to treat citizen-soldiers, Truman quickly turned his battery into an operationally skilled unit. The long-term importance of this command experience for Truman is difficult to overstate: psychologically, he proved himself a success for the first time in his life, even as he acquired a bias against "West Pointers" and their perceived disdain for citizen-soldiers.

training of the American units, but he was careful to point out that the United States should eventually have its own army.

The British had their own solution to use American manpower. General Bridges, a distinguished divisional commander, proposed the rapid mobilization of 500,000 Americans to ship to England, where they would be trained, equipped, and incorporated into the British Army. This proposal would be the first of many schemes to integrate American battalions and regiments into one of the Allied armies.

Amalgamation, as the general concept of placing American soldiers into British or French units became known, had the advantage of expanding the existing military system rather than establishing an entirely new one. If the United States decided to build a separate force, it would have to start at the ground level and create the entire framework for a modern army and then ship it overseas. That endeavor would require more shipping and more time, both of which were in short supply in 1917. Conversely, using American troops in foreign armies would be an affront to national pride and a slur especially on the professionalism of the American officer corps. Furthermore, amalgamation would decrease the visibility of the American contribution and lessen the role American leadership would be able to play in the war and in the peace that followed. For these political and patriotic reasons, President Wilson rejected the proposal of having American troops serve under the British flag; however, he did agree to Joffre's recommendation to send a division to France immediately.

With the decision to send a division overseas, Maj. Gen. Hugh L. Scott, the Chief of Staff, directed the General Staff to study a divisional structure of two infantry brigades, each consisting of two infantry regiments. In consultation with Joffre's staff, the Army planners, headed by Maj. John M. Palmer, developed a division organization with four regiments of 17,700 men, of which 11,000 were infantrymen. After adding more men, Maj. Gen. Tasker H. Bliss, Scott's deputy, approved this "square" organization—four regiments in two brigades—for the initial division deploying to France.

At the same time that Palmer's committee worked on its study, Scott asked Maj. Gen. John J. Pershing, commander of the Army's Southern Department at Fort Sam Houston, Texas, to select four infantry regiments and a field artillery regiment for overseas service. Pershing chose the 6th Field Artillery and the 16th, 18th, 26th, and 28th Infantries. Although these regiments were among the most ready in the Regular Army, they all needed an infusion of recruits to reach full strength. By the time the regiments left for France, they were composed of about two-thirds raw recruits. Nevertheless, on June 8, Brig. Gen William L. Sibert assumed command of the 1st Expeditionary Division and four days later sailed for France. The division would provide the nucleus of a larger American force in France.

Secretary of War Newton D. Baker selected General Pershing to command the larger expeditionary force. Ultimately, there was little doubt of the selection, even though Pershing was junior to five other major generals, including former Chief of Staff Maj. Gen. Leonard Wood. Wood and the other candidates were quickly ruled out from active field command because of health or age, while Pershing was at fifty-six vigorous and robust. In addition, Pershing's record throughout

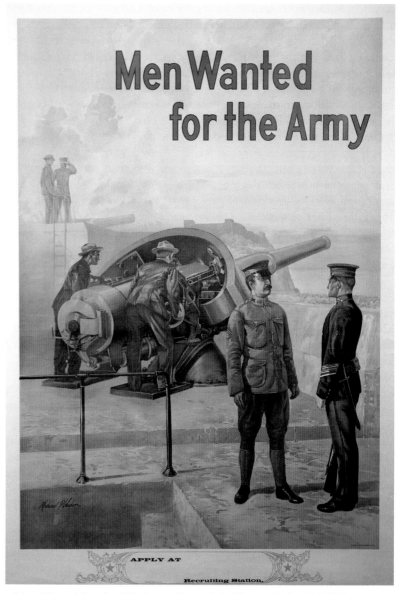

Men Wanted for the U.S. Army (Coastal Artillery), *Michael P. Whelan, 1909*

Pershing demonstrated that he would remain loyal to the administration's policies, although he might personally disagree with them.

his three decades of military service had been exceptional. By 1917 he had proven himself as a tough, experienced, and loyal commander. In particular, his command of the Punitive Expedition made a favorable impression on Secretary Baker. In addition to having gained recent command experience in the field, Pershing demonstrated that he would remain loyal to the administration's policies, although he might personally disagree with them. In early May Pershing was told to report to Washington, D.C.

Shortly after Pershing arrived in Washington, he learned of his appointment as the American Expeditionary Forces (AEF) commander. In turn he began selecting members of his headquarters staff. Pershing first chose resourceful and energetic Maj. James G. Harbord, a fellow cavalryman of long acquaintance, as the AEF Chief of Staff. Together, they settled on thirty other officers, including Maj. Fox Conner, who would end the war as the AEF's Chief of Operations (G–3), and Capt. Hugh Drum, who would later become the Chief of Staff of the U.S. First Army. As the staff prepared to depart for France, Pershing reviewed the organization of the 1st Division, discussed the munitions situation, and went over the embarkation plans. He met with both Secretary Baker and President Wilson. On May 28, 1917, Pershing and his headquarters staff of 191 set sail for Europe.

Pershing and his staff began much of the preliminary planning on the nature, scope, and objectives for the future AEF while en route to Europe. First in England and later in France, the group met their Allied counterparts, coordinated with the staffs, and assessed the conditions of wartime Europe. One staff committee inspected ports and railroads to begin arranging for the American lines of communications. Amid ceremonies and celebrations, the blueprints for the future AEF slowly took shape.

On June 26 the advance elements of the 1st Division joined Pershing and his staff in France. From St. Nazaire, the port of debarkation, the division traveled to the Gondrecourt area in Lorraine, about 120 miles southwest of Paris. There, the division would undergo badly needed training. Not only had the War Department brought its regiments up to strength with new recruits, but it had also siphoned off many of their long-service, well-trained regulars to provide the nucleus for the new divisions forming in the United States.

As the bulk of the division settled into its new home to learn the basics of soldiering, the French authorities persuaded Pershing to allow a battalion of the 16th Infantry to march through Paris on the Fourth of July to encourage the French people with the appearance of American troops. The parade culminated at Picpus Cemetery, burial place of Gilbert du Montier, the Marquis de Lafayette. At the tomb of the American Revolution hero, on behalf of Pershing, Col. Charles E. Stanton, a quartermaster officer fluent in French, gave a rousing speech, ending with the words "Lafayette, we are here!" Mistakenly attributed to Pershing, the words nevertheless captured the sentiments of many Americans: repaying an old debt.

A young soldier bids his family farewell in 1917.

Organizing the American Expeditionary Forces

Before Pershing departed for France, Secretary Baker told him: "I will give you only two orders, one to go to France and the other to come home. In the meantime, your authority in France will be supreme." Baker thus had given Pershing a free hand to make basic decisions and plan for the shape and form of the American ground contribution to the war in Europe. Consequently, during the summer of 1917, Pershing and his small staff went about building the AEF's foundations.

In late June 1917 the most crucial decision that Pershing needed to make concerned the location of the American zone of operations. With the advanced elements of the 1st Division due to arrive in France by the end of the month, it was essential that the staff lay out the training areas. Moreover, the selection of supply lines and depots all hinged on the establishment of the AEF's sector. Accordingly, Pershing ordered his staff to make a reconnaissance of the Lorraine region, south and southwest of Nancy. For the American commander, the prime consideration in exploring this area was its potential for development and employment of a large, independent AEF in a decisive offensive. On June 21 the staff officers departed on a four-day tour of a number of villages and possible training areas in Lorraine.

When the team returned, they recommended that the AEF assume the section of the Allied line from St. Mihiel to Belfort. They considered the training areas in the region adequate. With the greatest concentration of training grounds in the area of Gondrecourt and Neufchâteau, they further proposed that the American training effort be centered there. Yet the suitability of the region's training areas was not the major reason to select the Lorraine region as the American zone. Instead, Pershing's staff believed that the area offered important military objectives (coal and iron mines and vital railroads) within reasonable striking distance.

The recommendation of the Lorraine sector of the Western Front as the American zone of operations, however, was not especially imaginative. Even before Pershing left Washington, the French had advised the Americans to place their troops somewhere in the eastern half of the Allied line. By the time the inspection team visited the area, the French had made considerable progress in preparing training areas for the AEF. In so doing, they simply took a realistic and practical view of the situation.

With the massive armies of Germany, France, and Great Britain stalemated in the trenches of northern Europe since 1914, there was little chance of the Americans' exercising much strategic judgment in choosing their zone of operations. On the Allied northern flank, the British Expeditionary Forces guarded the English Channel ports that provided their logistical link with Great Britain and provided an escape route from Europe in case the Western Front collapsed. To the British right, nationalism compelled the French armies to cover the approaches to Paris, the French capital. Moreover, the Allied armies were already straining the supply lines of northern France, especially the overburdened Paris railroad network. Any attempt to place a large American army north of Verdun would not only disrupt the British and French armies and limit any independent American activity, but it would also risk a complete breakdown of the supply system. These considerations left Lorraine as the only real choice for the American sector.

Although the military situation of 1917 had determined that the American sector would be on the Allied southern flank, neither Pershing nor his staff lamented the circumstance. On the contrary, they believed that Lorraine was ideally suited to deploy a large, independent AEF. Logisticians supplying an American army in Lorraine would avoid the congested northern logistical facilities by using the railroads of central France that stretched back to the ports along the southwestern French coast. Furthermore, the Americans could move into the region with relative ease and without disturbing any major Allied forces, since only a relative few French troops occupied Lorraine. Once there, the AEF could settle down to the task of training its inexperienced soldiers and

With the massive armies of Germany, France, and Great Britain stalemated in the trenches of northern Europe since 1914, there was little chance of the Americans' exercising much strategic judgment in choosing their zone of operations.

developing itself into a fighting force in the relative calm of a sector quiet since 1915.

Once Pershing had organized and trained the AEF, it would be ready to attempt a major offensive. His planners believed that the area to the west of Lorraine offered excellent operational objectives. If the American forces could penetrate the German lines and carry the advance into German territory, they could deprive Germany of the important Longwy-Briey iron fields and coal deposits of the Saar. More important, an American offensive would threaten a strategic railroad that Germans used to supply their armies to the west. Cutting the vital railroad would seriously hamper German operations and might even cause a withdrawal of some forces along the southern portion of the German line. Nevertheless, it was perhaps an exaggeration when some of the AEF staff noted that these logistical and economical objectives were at least as important to the Germans as Paris and the channel ports were to the Allies.

On June 26, the day after Pershing accepted his officers' recommendation, he met with General Henri Philippe Petain, the hero of Verdun and now overall commander of French forces. Petain readily agreed to the Americans' taking the Lorraine portion of the Western Front. By the end of June elements of the 1st Division began to move into the training areas near Gondrecourt. Within three months three more American divisions would join the 1st Division.

With the decision to situate the AEF in Lorraine, Pershing and his staff turned their attention to the next order of business: a tactical organization for the AEF. Pershing himself wanted the AEF to be employed in decisive offensive operations that would drive the Germans from their trenches and then defeat them in a war of movement. That the AEF would fight in primarily offensive operations would be the guiding principle for the American planners, headed by Lt. Col. Fox Conner and Maj. Hugh Drum. As they developed their organizational schemes, they relied heavily on the General Staff's provisional organization of May 1917 and consulted with both their French and British counterparts. Before finalizing their recommendations, they met with another American group, under Col. Chauncey Baker, which the War Department had commissioned to study the proper tactical organization for the U.S. Army. The result of the AEF staff's studies and planning was the General Organization Project, which guided the AEF's organization throughout the war.

The General Organization Project outlined a million-man field army comprising five corps of thirty divisions. While the infantry division remained the primary combined-arms unit and standard building block of combat power, the AEF planners helped bring the modern concepts of operational corps and field armies to the U.S. Army. The organizational scheme was based on two principles: both the corps and division would have a "square" structure, and the division would contain a large amount of riflemen adequately supported by large numbers of artillery and machine guns.

Rather than mobile units that moved quickly to the battlefield, the AEF's proposed corps and division organizations emphasized staying power for prolonged combat. In a war of masses and protected flanks, the AEF planners believed that success would come with powerful

Above: *World War I Helmet, 2d Division, 1917.* Below: *World War I Enlisted Service Coat, 91st Division.*

THE MACHINE GUN

The machine gun quickly became the most important direct-fire infantry weapon of World War I, and its importance only grew. A British infantry division was organized with 18,000 men and 24 heavy machine guns at the beginning of the war. By the end of the war, a division was much smaller in manpower but had 64 heavy and 192 light machine guns down to the platoon level. Though a number of Americans had been closely associated with the development of the machine gun, the U.S. Army had been slow to adopt the new weapon. Combined with the sudden shift from neutrality to mobilization, this policy left the AEF heavily dependent on an assortment of French and British designs to provide the 260 heavy and 768 light machine guns each 28,000-man U.S. infantry division required. By the Armistice, however, a variety of American weapons were entering service, most designed by John M. Browning.

Colt "Potato Digger" Machine Gun

blows of depth. This depth of attacking forces could be achieved with units of a square organization—corps of four divisions and divisions of four regiments. This square organization would permit the division to attack on a frontage of two brigades with the four regiments in two brigade columns. Similarly, a corps could attack with a phalanx of two divisions on line and two divisions in reserve. In these formations, once the strength of the attack was drained from losses or sheer exhaustion, the lead units could be relieved easily and quickly by units advancing from behind. The fresh units would then continue the attack. Thus the depth of the formations would allow the AEF to sustain constant pressure on the enemy.

To maintain divisional effectiveness in the trenches of the Western Front, the General Organization Project enlarged the division to a strength of 25,484, about twice the size of Allied divisions. Increasing both the number and the size of the rifle companies accounted for more than three-quarters of this expansion. The project added one company to each of the division's twelve rifle battalions and increased the size of a rifle company by fifty men for a total strength of 256. Three artillery battalions of seventy-two artillery pieces each would support the division's four regiments of over 12,000 riflemen and fourteen machine-gun companies with 240 heavy machine guns.

The AEF's organizational plan also created modern corps and armies. In the past, the Army's corps and field armies were little more than small headquarters to command their subordinate units. The General Organization Project created an army and several corps that each had headquarters to command, control, and coordinate the increasing large and complex subordinate echelons. The project's field army had a headquarters of about 150 officers and men, while the corps had one of 350 officers and men. Moreover, both echelons of command had a significant amount of their own dedicated combat power outside the attached divisions. Ideally, the corps in the AEF would have a brigade of heavy artillery and an engineer regiment as well as cavalry, antiaircraft, signal, and support units. The field army had a massive artillery organization of twenty-four regiments as well as large numbers of engineer, military police, and supply units. A corps would have about 19,000 such supporting troops, while an army would have 120,000.

Consistent with the AEF planners' emphasis on sustained combat over a period of time, they also created a system to feed trained replacements into the units at the front. In addition to four attached combat divisions, each corps contained two base divisions organized to coordinate the AEF's replacement system. These divisions would feed replacements to the combat divisions, first from their own ranks and later from replacement battalions sent from the United States. With little need for a full complement of support units, artillery and engineer units would be detached from the replacement divisions and attached to the corps headquarters. The losses from the future American campaigns would fully test this system.

In August the War Department incorporated the AEF's proposed divisional organization in its table of organization. It also approved the six-division corps and the five-corps army.

With the AEF's organization settled by the end of August, Pershing only needed to decide where to aim this formidable force when it became ready. In September the AEF's operational staff presented a comprehensive strategic study that outlined the long-range prospects for the war in Europe and laid the groundwork for an American offensive toward Metz in 1919. Although the planners recognized the logistical realities of having the AEF in Lorraine, they based their study on an analysis of the geopolitical situation of late 1917 and their own views of operational theory. The major premise behind the study was Pershing's guiding principle to use the AEF as a separate army in a decisive offensive operation.

The study noted that only the possible collapse of Russia would constitute a significant change in the military situation. Germany could then transfer forces from the Eastern Front and use them to strike a decisive blow on the Italian or Western Front. While the Italian Front offered Germany the best chance for local success, any long-term results would come from successful operations against the French or British armies on the Western Front. Believing that it would be difficult to defeat the British forces, the AEF planners predicted a German spring offensive against the French, probably in the central portion of the Allied line.

On the Allied side, the great losses suffered in 1917 offensives precluded the British and French from undertaking any major offensive in 1918. Nor would the AEF be able to make any serious offensive in 1918: there would not be enough American troops in France until early 1919. Allied activity in 1918, therefore, would have to be restricted to meeting the predicted German offensive and to carrying out limited operations. One of those limited operations, the planners recommended, would be the first employment of the American army—the reduction of the St. Mihiel salient in the spring of 1918. (*See Map 2.*) The Germans had held the salient since the end of 1914, and its reduction would seize key terrain for future advances, free a critical French railroad, and train

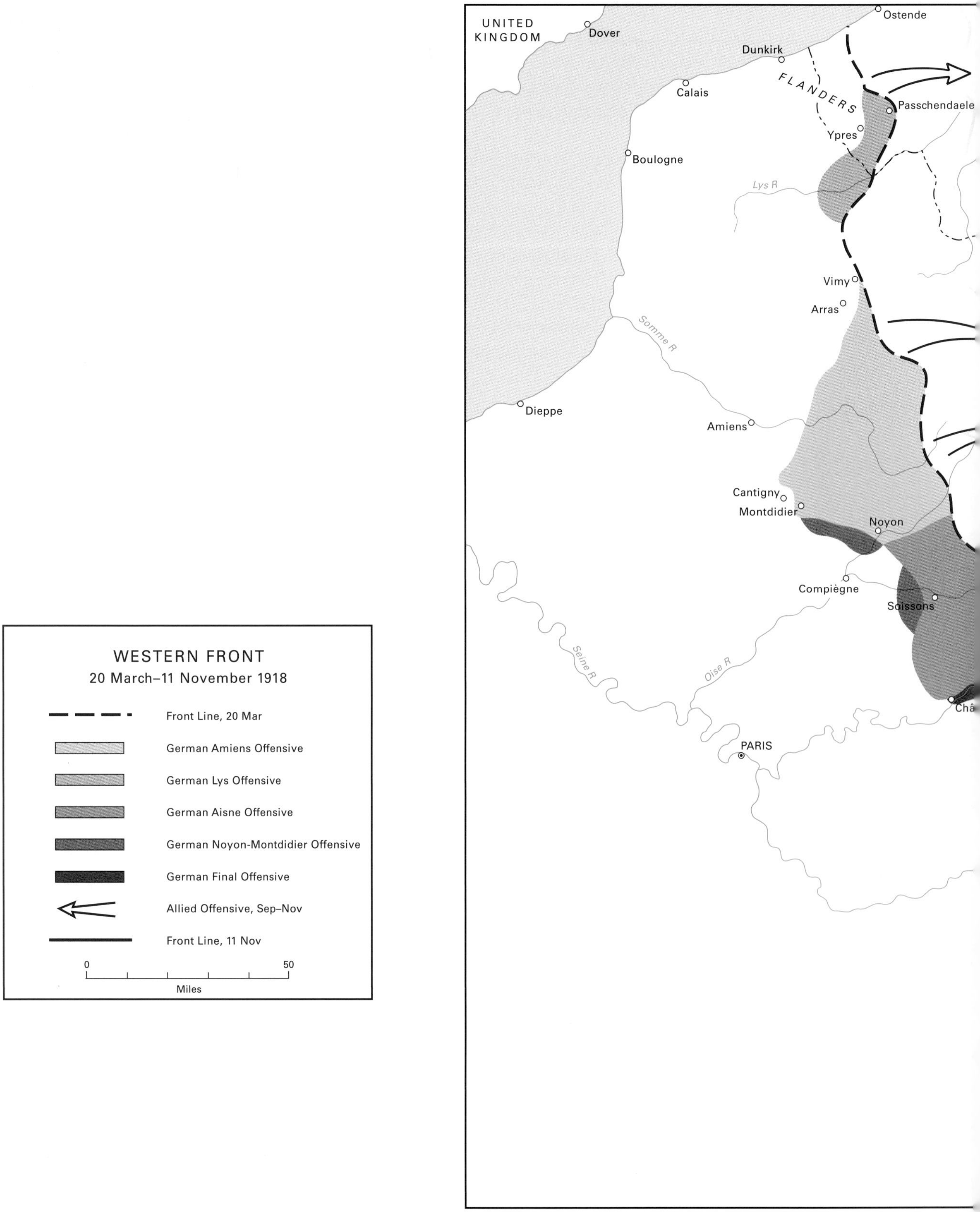

WESTERN FRONT
20 March–11 November 1918
Front Line, 20 Mar
German Amiens Offensive
German Lys Offensive
German Aisne Offensive
German Noyon-Montdidier Offensive
German Final Offensive
Allied Offensive, Sep–Nov
Front Line, 11 Nov
0
50
Miles
UNITED KINGDOM
Dover
Ostende
Dunkirk
Calais
FLANDERS
Passchendaele
Ypres
Boulogne
Lys R
Vimy
Arras
Somme R
Dieppe
Amiens
Cantigny
Montdidier
Noyon
Compiègne
Soissons
Seine R
Oise R
PARIS

Map 2

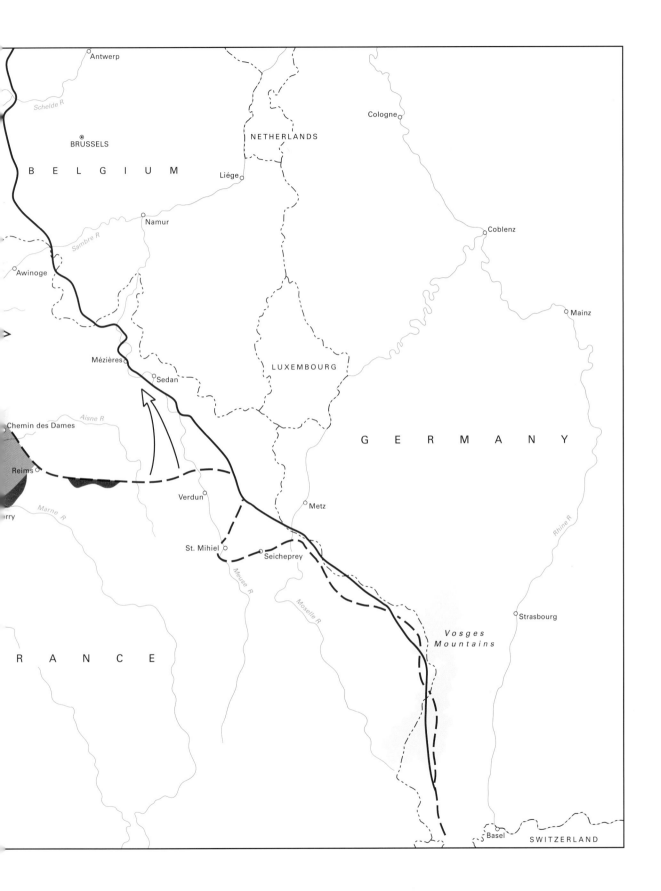

American units and commanders. Likewise, the British 1918 operations should be made in preparation for the more substantial offensives planned for 1919.

For 1919 the American planners argued for a grand offensive involving concurrent operations along the entire Western Front, preventing the Germans from shuttling forces from one threatened point to another. While the British and French attacked toward vital German communication and economic objectives in the north, the now-ready American ground forces would advance northeast from Lorraine along the Metz-Saarbrücken axis. A 45-mile advance northeast from Nancy would cut the two railroads running from Strasbourg to Metz and to Thionville. Together with the French interdiction of the rail lines to the north of Metz, this action would sever the German armies from the vital resources of Lorraine and the German left wing from the right and would precipitate the Germans to withdraw from some if not all of their lines from Belgium and France. This advance would provide General Pershing with the decisive offensive he desired.

Over the summer and early fall of 1917, Pershing and his small headquarters laid the groundwork for a large American force deployed to the Western Front. This foundation helped shape every aspect of the AEF's operation and organization, from training and tactics to troop strength and shipping. Moreover, until the armistice a year later, Pershing's steadfast belief in the envisioned American advance toward Metz would influence his stubborn resistance against American forces' serving under French or British flags and his equally stubborn insistence on the development of an independent American army.

The War Effort in the United States

Despite the efforts of Pershing and his staff to organize the AEF and develop its strategic designs, as they well knew, in the summer of 1917 the U.S. Army was in no position to make its weight felt. In April 1917 the Regular Army had an aggregate strength of 127,588 officers and men; the National Guard could count another 80,446. Together, the total, little over 208,000 men, was minute compared to the armies already fighting in Europe. The small Army barely had enough artillery and machine guns to support itself, and before the formation of the 1st Division not a single unit of division size existed. Although service in the Philippines and Mexico had given many of the officers and men of the small Regular Army important field skills and experience, it had done little to prepare them for the large-scale planning, maneuvering of divisions and corps, and other logistical and administrative knowledge necessary for this new war. The task of managing the Army's necessary expansion into a large, modern force fell largely to Newton Baker, the Secretary of War.

Secretary Baker seemed out of place heading America's war effort. Small and unassuming, he looked more at home on a university campus than in the War Department. A longtime friend of Woodrow Wilson, Baker had been appointed Secretary of War in the spring of 1916, despite his pacifistic attitudes. Although as the mayor of Cleveland he had changed that city's government into an efficient organization, as Secretary of War he would often stay on the moderate, uncontroversial course rather than strike out on a new path. Yet in the bureaucratic chaos that ensued after the

Pershing's steadfast belief in the envisioned American advance toward Metz would influence his stubborn resistance against American forces' serving under French or British flags and his equally stubborn insistence on the development of an independent American army.

United States' entry into the war, Baker proved an unflappable leader who was flexible enough to force change if he had the correct tools.

In the spring of 1917 Baker did not have the correct tools. The Army's General Staff was a small war-planning agency rather than a coordinating staff for the War Department and its staff bureaus. The National Defense Act of 1916 had limited the number of General Staff officers that could be stationed in Washington to fewer than twenty, less than a tenth of England's staff when it entered the war in 1914. Once the war broke out many of the talented officers left Washington for overseas or commands, while the staff had to undergo a massive expansion. Without a strong coordination agency to provide oversight, the staff bureaus ran amok. By July more than 150 War Department purchasing committees competed against each other on the open market, often cornering the market for scarce items and making them unavailable for the Army at large. While the General Staff at least established troop movement and training schedules, no one established industrial and transportation priorities. To a large degree the problem was that Baker did not have a strong Chief of Staff to control the General Staff and manage the bureaus. Both General Scott and his successor, General Bliss, were very near retirement and distracted by special assignments. Secretary Baker did little to alleviate these problems until late 1917.

By then the situation had become a crisis. Responding to pressure from Congress and recommendations from the General Staff, Baker took action to centralize and streamline the supply activities. First, in November, he appointed industrialist Benedict Crowell, a firm believer in centralized control, as the Assistant Secretary of War; later Crowell would also assume duties as Director of Munitions. On the military side, Baker called back from retirement Maj. Gen. George W. Goethals, who had coordinated the construction of the Panama Canal. First appointed Acting Quartermaster General in December, Goethals quickly assumed the mantle of the Army's Chief Supply Officer. Eliminating red tape and consolidating supply functions, especially the purchasing agencies, he also brought in talented administrators from both the military and the civilian sector to run the supply system.

In the meantime, the Secretary of War was beginning to reorganize the General Staff. Congress had increased the size of the staff's authorization, but it wasn't until Maj. Gen. Peyton C. March became the Chief of Staff in March of 1918 that the General Staff gained a firm, guiding hand. Over his thirty years of service, the 53-year-old March had gained an experience well balanced between line and staff. He had been cited for gallantry for actions as a junior officer in the War with Spain and in the Philippine Insurrection. He also served tours of duty with the Office of the Adjutant General. Forceful and brilliant, March was unafraid of making decisions. At the time of his appointment as Chief of Staff, March had been Pershing's artillery chief in France.

March's overarching goal was to get as many men as possible to Europe and into the AEF to win the war. To achieve this, he wanted to establish effectiveness and efficiency in the General Staff and the War Department. He quickly went about clearing bureaucratic logjams, streamlining operations, and ousting ineffective officers. In May 1918 he was aided immeasurably by the Overman Act, which granted the President authority to reorganize executive agencies during the war emergency. Moreover, he received the additional authority of the rank of four-star general. March quickly decreed that the powerful bureau chiefs were subordinate to the General Staff and were to report to the Secretary of War only through the Chief of Staff.

In August 1918 March drastically reorganized the General Staff. He created four main divisions: Operations; Military Intelligence; Purchase, Storage, and Traffic; and War Plans. The divisions' titles fairly well explained their functions. Notably, with the creation of the Purchase, Storage, and Traffic Division, for the first time the Army had centralized control over logistics. Under this reorganization, the total military and civilian strength of the General Staff increased to just over a thousand. In the process the General Staff had become an active, not merely a supervisory, operating agency.

By the end of the summer of 1918, Generals March and Goethals and their talented military and civilian subordinates had engineered a managerial revolution in the War Department. Inefficiency, pigeon-holes, and snarled actions were replaced by centralized control and decentralized operations.

Yet even before General March formed an efficient and effective staff, the War Department had taken steps in the right direction. On May 18, 1917, as Pershing was preparing to sail for Europe, Congress passed the Selective Service Act to raise the necessary manpower for the war. With this act the United States experienced none of the difficulties and inequities with conscription that the Union had during the Civil War: the General Staff had studied those problems and carefully sought to avoid them as it prepared the draft for the legislation. The result was a model system. Based on the principle of universal obligation, it eliminated substitutes, most exemptions, and bounties and assured that conscripts would serve for the duration of the emergency. Initially, all males between the ages of 21 and 30 had to register; later

THE DRAFT

Having declared war on Germany, Congress in April 1917 was debating what would become the Selective Service Act. In the Office of the Judge Advocate General, Capt. Hugh S. Johnson learned that registration of draft-eligible men could not begin for a month after the act's passage: it would take that long to print the 30 million registration forms. Fearing the possible consequences of the delay, Johnson risked court-martial by illegally ordering the forms printed in advance.

Secretary Baker chooses the first number for the Second Draft.

The act was passed on May 18, and the registration process began on June 5. At some 4,000 local draft boards, registrants were issued numbers that would determine the order in which they were called into military service. In Washington, on July 21 Secretary Baker held the First Draft, randomly choosing numbers that corresponded to those the draft boards had issued. A Second Draft on June 27, 1918, applied to men who had turned twenty-one since the First Draft and thus were eligible to be drafted. The draft brought more than 2.7 million men to the colors during the war.

the range included males from 18 to 45. At the national level, the Office of the Provost Marshal General under Maj. Gen. Enoch Crowder established policy and issued general directives. The administration of the draft, however, was left to local boards composed of local citizens; these local civilians could grant selective exemptions based on essential occupations and family obligations.

The Selective Service Act was hugely successful. The Army's prewar strength of a little over 200,000 men grew to almost 3.7 million by November 1918. About two-thirds of this number was raised through conscription. The Selective Service process proved so successful at satisfying the Army's needs while ensuring that essential civilian occupations remained filled that voluntary enlistments ended in August 1918. For the rest of the war, conscription remained the sole means of filling the Army's ranks.

The act also established the broad framework for the Army's structure. It outlined three components of the Army: the Regular Army, the National Guard, and the National Army. As Pershing's forces became more actively involved in the war, much of these identities disappeared as new soldiers were absorbed into units of all three elements. By mid-1918 the War Department changed the designation of all land forces to one "United States Army." Nevertheless, the three components continued to manifest themselves in the numerical designations. For example, the Regular Army divisions were numbered from 1 to 25. Numbers 26 through 75 were reserved for the National Guard and higher numbers for divisions of the National Army.

Just how large an army the United States needed depended in large measure on General Pershing's plans and recommendations to meet the operational situation in France. In the General Organization Project of July 1917, Pershing and his staff called for a field army of about 1 million men to be sent to France before the end of 1918. The War Department in turn translated Pershing's proposal into a plan to send 30 divisions with supporting services—almost 1.4 million men—to Europe by 1919. As the Germans launched their spring offensives and the AEF began more active operations, Pershing increased his estimates. In June 1918 he would ask for 3 million men with 66 divisions in France by May 1919. He quickly raised this estimate to 80 divisions by April 1919, followed shortly (under pressure from the Allies) by a request for 100 divisions by July of the same year. Although the War Department questioned whether 100 divisions could be sent to France by mid-1919 and even whether that many would be needed, it produced plans to raise 98 divisions, with 80 of them to be in France by the summer of 1919. These plans increased the original goal for divisions in France by the end of 1918 from 30 to 52. In the end the Army actually would form 62 divisions, of which 43 were sent overseas. Consequently, when the war ended in November 1918 the Army was running close to its projected goal of 52 divisions in France by 1919.

To train these divisions the Army would eventually establish thirty-two camps or cantonments throughout the United States. How much training incoming soldiers needed before going overseas had long been a matter of debate, but in 1917 the War Department settled on four months. It established a sixteen-week program that emphasized training soldiers by military specialty, e.g., riflemen, artillery gunners, supply or

THE PLATTSBURG MOVEMENT

After the defeat of a Universal Military Training Program, during the summer of 1913 Army Chief of Staff Maj. Gen. Leonard Wood created two military training camps for college students. The program, reflecting Progressive-era social theory, expanded and developed into a popular movement promoting health and the social benefits of military training, citizenship responsibilities, and national unity. By 1916 the movement included a businessman's training course at Plattsburg, New York, a camp that lent its name to the movement. Attendees, 16,000 in 1916 alone, paid out of their own pockets to receive the equivalent of four months' military instruction in a few short weeks. The camps and their graduates became valuable resources in the World War I mobilization effort, when the camps became officer candidate schools and many of their alumni entered uniformed service.

personnel clerks, or medical specialists. Division commanders at the cantonments would train their men progressively from individual to battalion level but only within each battalion's specialty fields. Within the four-month period, the War Department policy gave the divisional commanders latitude to vary the content and duration of the specialty training. Initially, much to the dismay of Pershing and his staff in France, this training only emphasized trench, or positional, warfare and excluded rifle marksmanship and other elements of a more open and mobile warfare. Moreover, with the entire training period dedicated to the development of individual and small-unit skills, the larger units never came together to train as combined-arms teams. Until the end of the war, the training managers at the War Department had various degrees of success as the department worked to establish a consistent training regime and to move away from the sole emphasis on trench warfare. The Army, however, was never able to implement an effective method for combined-arms training at the regiment and division levels before the units deployed. It would remain for the AEF in France to either complete the training of the incoming divisions or send them into combat not fully prepared.

The training of replacements also remained problematic throughout the war. As early as the late summer of 1917, Pershing knew that sooner or later he would have to deal with the problem of replacing combat losses in his divisions. He complained to the War Department that he did not have the resources—especially time—to train replacements and instead recommended that a stateside division be assigned the mission of providing training replacements to each of his corps in France. The War Department did not act on his proposal and did little on its own to resolve the problem until early 1918. A major obstacle to a replacement training system was the Wilson administration's concern that the establishment of replacement training centers would imply that the government anticipated wholesale American losses. Nevertheless, General March was able to establish several centers to train infantry, artillery, and machine-gun replacements in April 1918. Though the Army continued to make progress on creating a viable program, the press from replacements overwhelmed the nascent system; again, it was left up to the deployed forces to deal with the problem.

The mobilization of manpower and the training of that manpower had been the major concern of a century of American military thought; but in World War I, the demands of arming, equipping, and supplying a 3-million-man Army meant that American industry also had to be mobilized. The National Defense Act of 1916 had to a degree anticipated this need with the creation of the Council of National Defense to provide a central point for the coordination of military industrial needs. Even before America's entry into the war, the council had created the Munitions Standards Board to establish industry standards for the production of ordnance. Soon, however, it became apparent that the enormous materiel requirements of war would need careful management; thus the Munitions Standards Board grew in stages to become the War Industries Board. With both civilian and military representatives, the board had broad powers to coordinate all purchasing by the Army and Navy, to establish production priorities, to create new plants and convert existing plants to priority uses, and to coordinate the activities of various civilian war agencies. Under the vigorous leadership of industrialist Bernard Baruch, the War Industries Board would become the chief agency of economic and industrial mobilization for the war.

The Army's representative on the War Industries Board, Brig. Gen. Hugh Johnson, would later use his experiences with industrial coordination as the head of the New Deal's National Recovery Administration in the 1930s. In general, the Army's liaison with civilian mobilization agencies was coordinated through Baruch's board; however, it maintained separate liaison with the administration's Shipping and Railway War Boards. To secure the Army's industrial and transportation requirements, Goethals and Johnson coordinated with one of the civilian boards for the appropriate allotments of available resources and services.

Even with these efforts, the demand for arms was so immense and immediate and the time required for contracts to be let and industry to retool so lengthy that the Army had to depend heavily on Allied, especially French, weapons. For the AEF's Air Service, the United States had 2,698 planes in service, of which 667, less than one-fourth, were of American manufacture. Of the almost 3,500 artillery pieces the AEF had in France, only 477 were of American manufacture and only 130 of those were used in combat. Despite possessing the world's largest automotive industry, the United States had to rely on French tanks for the operations of the AEF's Tank Corps; in some instances British and French tank battalions supported U.S. troops.

American industry had better success with the infantry weapons. Almost 900,000 rifles were on hand for the Army's use when the war broke out. Two Army arsenals were producing the excellent Model 1903 Springfield and could step up production. Three private companies were producing the Lee-Enfield rifle for the British; when they completed their contract, they began turning out Enfields modified for American ammunition. Since the Army had not purchased a large number of machine guns in the prewar period, the AEF was armed almost exclusively with French machine guns and automatic rifles until July 1918. American industry, however, was able to recover relatively quickly and by the end of the war had produced excellent results. By the late summer of 1918 new American units were armed with superb Browning machine guns and the famous Browning Automatic Rifle (BAR); these weapons were the among the best of their kind in the world.

Industry also did well in terms of the soldier's personal needs. The Army worked closely with the War Food Administration to avoid the food scandals of earlier wars. Inductions had to be slowed briefly until sufficient uniforms could be accumulated, and shortages in some items persisted; but this resulted less from industry's failures than from a cumbersome Quartermaster contracting system, which was eventually corrected.

The AEF Settles In

As the War Department struggled with the complexities of manpower and economic mobilization, Pershing went about organizing and training his forces. To provide logistical support, he created a Commander of the Line of Communications, subsequently renamed Services of Supply, responsible directly to him. After a series of short-term commanders, Maj. Gen. Francis J. Kernan, a capable administrator, headed the Services of Supply; Kernan would be followed by Maj. Gen. James G. Harbord, Pershing's first Chief of Staff. Headquartered in Tours along the Loire River, the supply organization was divided into several base sections built around the French ports, an intermediate section for storage and classification of supplies, and an advance section for distribution to the zone of operations. Once the AEF entered combat, the advance section's depots loaded supplies onto trains that moved forward to division railheads, whence the divisions pushed the supplies to the front in wagons and trucks. Like Goethals' supply organization in the United States, Kernan and Harbord relied heavily on businessmen temporarily in uniform, like Charles G. Dawes, a Chicago banker who acted as the AEF's General Purchasing Agent in Europe, and William W. Atterbury, a Vice President of the Pennsylvania Railroad, who supervised the AEF's transportation system.

Pershing also established his own General Staff in France. Reflecting the French system, Pershing's AEF staff ultimately included a Chief of Staff, a Deputy Chief, and five Assistant Chiefs supervising five sections: G–1 (Personnel), G–2 (Intelligence), G–3 (Operations), G–4 (Supply), and G–5 (Training). Under the commander's watchful eye, the staff developed into a confident, competent, and loyal team that understood his goals and standards. As the war progressed, the staff officers could and did increasingly act and speak for Pershing without waiting for his personal approval. This practice would sometime raise the ire of subordinate commanders, who were more accustomed to direct contact with their commanding officer than receiving directives and guidance through staff officers. Nevertheless, Pershing's staff officers freed him of the details of intricate planning and administration and allowed him to coordinate on strategic matters with the allies, confer with his subordinate commanders, and inspect and inspire his troops.

One advantage that many of Pershing's staff officers shared was their training at Fort Leavenworth's service schools. A component of the Root reforms at the turn of the century, these schools provided comprehensive training in the tactics, administration, and employment of large-scale units. Eight of the twelve officers to serve as AEF principal staff officers had Leavenworth training. In addition, a great majority of the division, corps, and army chiefs of staff had been educated at Leavenworth. Because of their common educational experience, this group was called, somewhat disparagingly, the Leavenworth Clique. There is little question, however, that this common background and doctrinal training served the officers well as they coordinated the massive movement of American troops.

Pershing placed great value in the benefits of a Leavenworth education. Its graduates knew how to move large concentrations of men and equipment to battle, how to write clear and precise operation orders, and how to coordinate the staff and line to effect these operations. An unexpected windfall was the officers' great familiarity with the Metz area by virtue of Leavenworth's reliance on German maps—rather than inferior American maps—for map exercises and terrain analysis. The officers' common Leavenworth experience, moreover, permitted the AEF staff to speak the same language and to approach strategic and tactical situations in a similar manner. "Except for an ominous rumble to the north of us," one graduate noted in the fall of 1918, "I might have thought that we were back at Leavenworth ... the technique and the talk were the same."

In September 1917 Pershing moved his General Headquarters (GHQ) to Chaumont, about 150 miles southeast of Paris. Perhaps symbolic of the growing autonomy—at least in thought—of the American leaders in France, Chaumont was also centrally located to the prospective American front lines and to the American training areas in Lorraine. From Chaumont, Pershing and his staff would oversee the training of the AEF divisions.

With the massive infusion of new recruits into the Army, the AEF Commander knew that all American units were badly in need of training. His training staff outlined an extensive regime for the incoming divisions, divided into three phases: The first phase emphasized basic soldier skills and unit training at platoon, company, and battalion levels; the second phase had battalions join French regiments in a quiet sector to gain front-line experience; in the third phase, the division's infantry and artillery would join for field training to begin to work as a combined team. Throughout the phases, regiment, brigade, and division staffs would conduct tactical command post exercises. Then the divisions would be ready for actual, independent combat operations.

By the fall of 1917 Pershing had four divisions to train. The 1st Division had been in France since late June 1917. It was joined by the 2d Division, with a brigade of soldiers and a brigade of marines; the 26th Division of the New England National Guard; and the 42d Division, called the Rainbow Division because it was a composite of guardsmen from many states. As with the 1st Division, many of these divisions' men were new recruits. Only in mid-January 1918, six months after the 1st Division's arrival in France, did Pershing consider it ready to move as a unit into a quiet sector of the trenches. The other three divisions would follow later in 1918.

For training in trench warfare, Pershing gratefully accepted the help of experienced Allied, especially French, instructors. For its training,

> The officers' common Leavenworth experience ... permitted the AEF staff to speak the same language and to approach strategic and tactical situations in a similar manner.

GAS IN WORLD WAR I

The Western Front had seen extensive chemical operations since April 1915; but in mid-July 1917, 12,000 newly arrived U.S. soldiers found themselves stationed within thirty miles of the front without gas masks. The United States entered World War I with its troops essentially unprepared for chemical warfare, which had to be remedied before the AEF could add its combat power to that of the Allies. The U.S. Army and Marine Corps had to rely heavily on French and British expertise for chemical training, doctrine, and materiel. Building on this imported knowledge base, the U.S. forces devoted substantial resources to defensive and offensive chemical warfare. The Army eventually established a separate Chemical Warfare Service to coordinate the offensive, defensive, and supply problems involved. Gas inflicted over a quarter of all AEF casualties: one of each U.S. division's four field hospitals had to be dedicated to treatment of gas injuries.

Typical World War I Gas Mask

the 1st Division was paired with the crack French 47th *Chasseur Alpin* Division. The AEF also followed the Allied system of setting up special training centers and schools to teach subjects such as gas warfare, demolitions, and the use of the hand grenade and the mortar. Pershing, however, believed that the French and British had become too imbued with trench warfare to the exclusion of the open warfare. Since Pershing strongly held that the victory could come only after driving the Germans from their trenches and defeating them in open warfare, he insisted on additional training in offensive tactics, including detailed work in rifle marksmanship and use of the bayonet.

Ideally, the divisions would go through their training cycle in three or four months. Unfortunately, the situation was rarely ideal. Soldiers and units arrived from the United States without many basic skills or training. Also, the regimental and divisional officers and men were too often sent away from their units to attend schools or perform labor details. Moreover, due to the German offensives in the spring of 1918, divisions were pressed into line service before they completed the full training regime.

Wanting to ensure that the Americans would not stumble in taking their first step, Pershing waited until late October 1917 to allow the 1st Division to have its first trial experience in the line. One battalion at a time from each regiment spent ten days with a French division. In early November one of these deployments resulted in the first U.S. Army casualties of the war when the Germans staged a trench raid against the same battalion that had paraded in Paris. With a loss of 3 men, the Germans captured 11 Americans and killed 3: Cpl. James B. Gresham, Pvt. Thomas F. Enright, and Pvt. Merle D. Hay.

German Offensives and the AEF's First Battles

By late 1917, as the AEF methodically pursued its training program, the Allied situation on the Western Front had reached low ebb. The French armies were still recovering from the disastrous Nivelle Offensive of April 1917 and subsequent mutinies in which the French soldiers told their officers that they would defend France but would no longer attack. The British armies, under Field Marshal Sir Douglas Haig, suffered shocking losses in the Passchendaele campaign. As a consequence of this offensive, British Prime Minister David Lloyd George withheld replacements to assure that Haig would have to remain on the defensive. The Allies appeared to have no alternative for 1918 but to grimly hold on until enough American troops arrived to assure the numerical superiority essential to victory.

While the Allies were smarting from their losses, Germany triumphed on its other fronts. In Russia, the Bolshevik Revolution ended the war on the Eastern Front in October. Using forces freed from the Eastern Front, the Germans spearheaded an Austro-German offensive against the Italians along the Isonzo River in late October. By November the Italians had been defeated and thrown back over sixty miles. What had been a three-front war for the Germans in the spring of 1917 was now essentially a single front. The Germans could concentrate their forces on the Western Front for offensive operations.

Against this strategic backdrop, the Allies pressed Pershing to abandon his plans to wait for 1919 to make a large-scale commitment of American forces. With Pershing unwilling to discard the objective of an independent American army, the questions over amalgamation surfaced anew at the end of 1917. The Allies had experienced commanders and units and the necessary artillery, aviation, and tank support; but they lacked men. Meanwhile, the American situation was the reverse. Amalgamation would permit American manpower to be quickly brought to bear to hasten the victory. Toward this end, the British opened the next round of the debate by going directly to the American leadership in Washington.

In late 1917 Lloyd George approached "Colonel" Edward House, President Wilson's close adviser, on the possibility of American companies' training and fighting, if necessary, as part of British units. President Wilson and Secretary Baker deferred the decision to Pershing, who stubbornly refused. The issue arose again early in 1918, when the British offered to transport 150 battalions of riflemen and machine gunners, which would be used to temporarily fill out British divisions. Pershing again refused but made a counterproposal for the British to ship six complete American divisions instead of only infantry battalions. These units would train with the British, although their artillery would train with the French. Once the training was over, the battalions and regiments would be formed into divisions under their own American officers. The British reluctantly consented to this six-division agreement. For the French, Pershing made additional agreements to have the four American divisions then in France to serve under the French in Lorraine. In addition, Pershing agreed to transfer the four African-American infantry regiments of the 93d Division to the French Army, where they were eventually incorporated into French divisions.

*Gas Masks for Man and Horse
ca. 1917–1918*

In opposing the amalgamation of the American troops into Allied commands, Pershing was not callous to the Allied situation. While he appreciated the threat of a German attack, neither he nor his staff shared the Allied pessimism of the threat. Pershing's operational staff believed that the British and French could withstand the potential German offensive and that neither was at the brink of collapse. Moreover, Pershing steadfastly held to his objective of an independent American Army. Although he personally believed strongly in such a force, he was also following his instruction from Washington to create "a separate and distinct force." Amalgamation would squander American forces in the present, instead of looking toward the future, when the United States would provide a bulk of the Allied forces, a bulk not to be used under foreign flags. To Secretary Baker Pershing explained that men were not pawns to be shoved from one army to another, that Allied training methods differed, and, most important, that once the American troops were put into Allied units they would be hard to retrieve. For the time being, the debate over amalgamation had subsided.

As the Allies debated, the German high command planned a series of spring offensives to end the war. With the collapse of Russia and the victory at Caporetto over the Italians, Germany was able to achieve numerical superiority on the Western Front. Strategically, however, Germany's manpower reservoir was shrinking, its economy was stretched to the limit, and its population faced starvation. To achieve victory, the German Army needed to act before the strategic difficulties overcame the battlefield advantages. With new tactics for massing artillery and infiltrating infantry through weaknesses in the Allied lines, the German military leaders believed they could strike decisive blows before American manpower and resources could weigh in for the Allies.

On March 21, 1918, the first German blow fell on the British along the Somme. After a massive artillery barrage, sixty-two German divisions smashed the British line and achieved a penetration along a fifty-mile front. They were heading toward Amiens, a communications hub on the Somme that in German hands would effectively split the French and British armies. (*See Map 2.*) British forces rallied to prevent the capture of Amiens, and by the end of March the German offensive had bogged down. The Germans nevertheless had achieved a brilliant

HUTIER TACTICS

Named for General Oskar von Hutier, German Eighth Army commander on the Eastern Front in 1917, Hutier Tactics employed rolling and box artillery barrages to enable infantry to bypass strong points and penetrate enemy positions deeply enough to envelop adjacent Russian defenses. Their greatest success occurred during the 1917 German capture of Riga; and this success at the operational level brought the favorable notice of the General Staff and Chief of Staff as well as General Erich von Ludendorff's decision to employ them with storm troops during the spring 1918 Western Front offensive. Germany began developing infantry storm-troop units and tactics on the Western Front as early as 1915, as maneuver there stagnated. The General Staff supported developing special units, tactics, and weapons to enable local penetrations of enemy weak points to permit envelopment of bypassed enemy forces and strong points.

tactical victory: an advance of forty miles in eight days, 70,000 prisoners and 200,000 other Allied casualties. Strategically, the result was empty. The Germans had failed to destroy the British armies or separate them from the French.

Operationally, at this point, the Americans could do little materially to assist the British. On March 25 Pershing offered General Petain any AEF division that could be of service and postponed the idea of fielding American divisions under the American I Corps. Appreciating the offer, Petain preferred for the Americans to replace French divisions in quiet sectors, freeing the more experienced French divisions for action against the Germans. Field Marshal Haig specifically asked Pershing for any available heavy artillery or engineer units. Pershing had no heavy artillery available but sent three engineer regiments north.

The German offensives also jarred the Allied leadership into building a stronger joint command structure. After the Italian defeat at Caporetto in November 1917, the British and French leaders agreed to the creation of the Supreme War Council to coordinate actions and strategy on the Western Front. In addition to political leaders, the council provided for a committee of military advisers; General Bliss, the former Chief of Staff, more than ably served as the American representative. Although the council provided a useful forum for the Allies, committees are rarely able to provide firm direction. Consequently, when the German attack fell on the Somme, the Allies saw the need to coordinate the British and French responses to the attack. They chose General Ferdinand Foch, both respected and capable, to coordinate the forces around the Amiens salient. Later, he was charged with coordination of all Allied land forces. Although Foch never had the full authority to command the Allied forces, through persuasion and force of character, he was able to successfully orchestrate the other strong-willed Allied commanders, including General Pershing.

In April the Germans launched another attack on the British lines. This time the attack was aimed along the Lys River, to the north of the Amiens salient. Once again the Germans achieved tactical victory but operationally only created another salient in the Western Front.

With the German advances in March and April, the Allied leadership again pressed Pershing for the service of American troops with their armies. At the end of March the Supreme War Council had drafted Joint Note No. 18, which recommended that priority of shipping go to American infantry. To the British, this looked to nullify the six-division agreement of January; they wanted to ship just riflemen and machine gunners for the next four months (April–July). Pershing stubbornly refused. Over the next few weeks, in a series of confused and often contradicting negotiations in London, Washington, and France, the Allies and the Americans bickered over American manpower. At the end of April Pershing and Lord Alfred Milner, the new British War Minister, agreed to a modified six-division agreement: British shipping would transport six American divisions to train with Haig's armies, but Pershing agreed to have all the infantry and machine gunners shipped first.

At the May summit of Allied and American leaders (only President Wilson was absent) at Abbeville, France, the Allies, led by French Premier George Clemenceau, again brought up the issue of amalgamation.

Over the two-day conference, virtually all the Allied leaders pressed Pershing to bring over American infantry at the expense of the rest of the divisional elements throughout the summer of 1918. At one point, General Foch asked Pershing in exasperation, "You are willing to risk our being driven back to the Loire?" The American replied: "Yes, I am willing to take the risk. Moreover, the time may come when the American Army will have to stand the brunt of this war, and it is not wise to fritter away our resources in this manner." Pershing continued to believe that the Allies were overestimating the effect of the German offensives and exploiting the situation to recruit American soldiers for their armies.

Finally, after two days of acrimonious debate, Pershing proposed to continue the agreement with Milner for both May and June. Discussion of troop shipments in July would be delayed for the time being. The Allies unhappily accepted this arrangement. The Abbeville Agreement held that 130,000 Americans were to be transported in British shipping in May 1918 and 150,000 in June. American shipping would be used to ship artillery, engineer, and other support and service troops to build a separate American army.

In the meantime AEF divisions fought their first two engagements, albeit in only local operations. In late April Maj. Gen. Clarence Edwards' 26th (Yankee) Division held a quiet sector near St. Mihiel. On April 20 the quiet erupted with a heavy German bombardment followed by a regiment-size German attack to seize the village of Seicheprey. Boxing in the defenders with artillery, the German attackers overwhelmed two American companies and seized the trench line. The American division botched the counterattacks; when it finally advanced, the Americans found that the enemy had withdrawn. The Germans left behind 160 dead, but they took over 100 prisoners and inflicted over 650 casualties. Pershing was infuriated. In the midst of the debate over amalgamation, he did not need a humiliating setback that would raise questions about the American ability to handle divisions—or higher units. Much more satisfying to Pershing and the American leadership was the 1st Division's attack at Cantigny.

In mid-April the 1st Division went north in response to the German Lys offensive. Petain had selected its sector near Montdidier, along the line where the Germans had been stopped in front of Amiens. Once in line, the division's new commander, Maj. Gen. Robert L. Bullard, an aggressive, long-time regular, urged his French corps commander for an offensive mission. Finally, Petain himself agreed that Bullard's men should attack to seize the village of Cantigny on commanding ground near the tip of the salient. Even after careful preparations and rehearsals, the regiment-size American attack was not a sure thing: twice before, the French had taken and lost the key piece of terrain.

On the morning of May 28 Col. Hanson Ely's 28th Regiment, well supported by American and French artillery and by French tanks, took the village in a well-executed assault. The difficulty came in holding the town against German counterattacks. To help deal with the enemy attacks, the Americans could rely only on their own organic artillery after the supporting French guns withdrew to deal with another large German offensive. The American gunners, however, proved up to the task and assisted in breaking up several actual or potential

An antiaircraft machine gun of the 101st Field Artillery fires on a German observation plane at Plateau Chemin des Dames, France, in March 1918.

counterattacks. When the German counterattacks came, they were poorly coordinated with their own artillery; Ely's men repulsed them. Altogether, the Americans would repulse six counterattacks. After three days of counterattacks and constant artillery shelling, Ely and his regiment were replaced by the 18th Regiment. During their efforts in taking and holding Cantigny, the Americans lost almost 200 men killed and suffered another 800 casualties. Yet for the Americans, this local operation was only the first step.

Americans Help Stem the Tide, May–July 1918

To bleed off reserves from the north, on May 27 the German high command launched its third spring offensive at the French lines in the Chemin des Dames area northeast of Paris. By the end of the first day the attackers had driven the French over the Aisne River, the second defensive line. By the next day they were across the Vesle River and driving toward the Marne. When the offensive eventually ground to a halt, German troops were within fifty miles of Paris, almost as close as they had come in 1914.

The offensive had caught the Allies flatfooted. With most of the reserves in the north, Foch and Petain struggled to scrape up enough reserves to form a new line. To the west, the American 1st Division extended its lines to free a French division for redeployment. Moreover, two large American divisions (Maj. Gen. Omar Bundy's 2d Division and Maj. Gen. Joseph T. Dickman's 3d Division) entered the line near Château-Thierry on the Marne. Of the five American divisions almost ready for battle, Bundy's and Dickman's were closest to the path of the Germans. On May 30 they had been ordered forward to feed into the French line under French command.

Loaded on trucks, troops of the 3d Division's 7th Machine Gun Battalion arrived on the Marne first and were in position to help French troops hold the main bridge site over the river on May 31. The next day Dickman's infantry arrived. For the next week, the division repulsed the

Army Camp, *George Harding, 1917*

limited German attacks in its sector. On June 6 the division assisted the French 10th Colonial Division in an attack to Hill 204 overlooking the Marne. The 3d Division held an eight-mile stretch of ground along the Marne for the next month.

On June 1 Bundy's 2d Division had assumed defensive positions astride the Paris-Metz highway west of Château-Thierry. In 1918 the 2d Division had a distinctive organization: it had a brigade of Army regulars and a brigade of marines. Bundy placed the two brigades abreast with the marines to the west and the regulars to the east. As the Americans settled into their positions, the French troops withdrew through the 2d Division's lines. Across from Bundy's lines, the Germans moved into Belleau Wood and the surrounding area while their artillery shelled the American positions. Nevertheless, the German advance had shot its bolt and the Americans had no difficulty holding their position.

Once the German advance was stopped, the 2d Division was ordered to seize Belleau Wood and the villages of Bouresches and Vaux to the east. The attack began on June 6. Over the next month the infantrymen and marines fought a bloody, toe-to-toe fight against four German divisions. The struggle for Belleau Wood was particularly hard fought. The fight became a test of wills, with the Germans checking the mettle of the Americans. By June 17 the marines had taken Bouresches. Six days later they cleared Belleau Wood, and on July 1 the infantrymen captured Vaux. Though the Americans had gained their objectives and inflicted over 10,000 casualties on the Germans, the price was reciprocally steep. Bundy's division suffered over 9,777 casualties, including 1,811 dead. One of the opposing German commanders noted that the division "must be considered a very good one and may even be reckoned as storm troops." The AEF had proved itself in battle.

While the 2d Division continued its battle in the tangled forest of Belleau Wood, the Germans launched their fourth offensive. One German army attacked southwesterly from the Amiens salient, while another launched a westward attack from the Marne salient. The German high command hoped to shorten their lines and ease their logistical difficulties by joining the two bulges in their lines. The French, however, having been forewarned of the offensive, launched a vigorous artillery strike on the German assault troops and disrupted the force of the attack. By June 13 both attacks were halted after only limited gains.

With these meager gains, the German high command planned yet another offensive against the French. Once again the Germans wanted to use two converging attacks to shorten their lines and draw off reserves from the British sector, thus setting the conditions for their future operations in Flanders. On July 15 one German army attacked south from positions east of Reims while another attacked southeast from the Marne salient. Again, the Allies were tipped off about the attack and sent a counterbarrage against the Germans. Moreover, the allied forces, including the U.S. 42d Division and the three African-American infantry regiments of the 93d Division, withdrew from the forward lines, leaving the German artillery and infantry assaults to hit an empty bag. By the time the Germans reached the French and American main defensive line, their attack was played out.

Officers of the "Buffalos," 367th Infantry, 92d Division, in France, ca. 1918

In front of the German attack against the Marne, the French commanders did not want to allow the enemy a foothold over the river and maintained the forward positions. The Germans thus were able to make greater headway, up to five miles beyond the Marne at some points. On the eastern flank of the French line, however, the U.S. 3d Division prevented the Germans from crossing the Marne. Dickman's men had been in the area since early June. Initially, Dickman had deployed them in depth with two regiments forward and two in reserve. But since the division was required to defend a lot of ground, he had to spread the defenses more thinly across the front. By mid-July the division was defending a ten-mile front with four infantry regiments abreast. Nevertheless, Dickman established as much of an echelon defense as he could: an outpost line of rifle pits along the Marne River (backed by the main defensive line along the forward slopes of the hill line about 1,500 yards from the river) and a reserve line about 3,000 yards beyond that.

On the early morning hours of July 15 the Germans began their attack against the 3d Division with a creeping barrage followed shortly by an assault-crossing of the Marne. The weight of the attack came against Col. Edmund Butts' 30th Infantry and Col. Ulysses Grant McAlexander's 38th Infantry. After heavy fighting in the morning, when the 30th Infantry inflicted horrendous casualties on the Germans, Butts' men were forced back to a line along the hills where they had stopped the Germans. McAlexander faced a more precarious position when the adjacent French division hastily retreated, leaving the 38th Infantry's right flank exposed. Turning some of the regiment to defend that flank, McAlexander also had to deal with a penetration of his main line. Although fighting on three sides, the riflemen and machine gunners of the 38th Infantry held, earning the sobriquet Rock of the Marne. By the end of the day the German attack against the 3d Division had been stopped. Between the 30th and 38th Infantries the Americans had defeated six regiments from two German divisions. One German 1,700-man regiment was so badly cut up that the German leaders could only find 150 survivors at nightfall on July 15.

The AEF's combat along the Marne carried an unfortunate note. Four rifle companies of the 28th Division from the Pennsylvania National Guard had been attached to the French division to the east of

ROCK OF THE MARNE

On July 15, 1918, the 38th Infantry of the 3d Infantry Division successfully defended its position on the Paris-Metz railroad, 200 yards from the River Marne, against six German attacks. It was the last great offensive of the German Army and the first fight of the 38th Infantry in World War I. Initially, the Germans succeeded in driving a wedge 4,000 yards deep into the 38th Infantry's front while the U.S. 30th Infantry on its left and the French 125th Division on its right withdrew under heavy pressure. With the situation desperate, the regiment stood and fought. The two flanks of the 38th Infantry moved toward the river, squeezing the German spearhead between them and exposing it to heavy shelling by the 3d Division artillery. The German Army's offensive failed. With this brave stand the 38th Infantry earned its *nom de guerre* Rock of the Marne. General John J. Pershing declared its stand "one of the most brilliant pages in our military annals."

the 38th Infantry. When the French retreated, they neglected to inform the Pennsylvanians; the riflemen became surrounded. Most of them were killed or captured; only a few fought their way to the south. By the time the survivors made it back to friendly lines, they found their division in line against the Germans.

The Growing AEF

Prior to March 1918 Pershing's efforts to create a distinct American ground combat force had been checked by the shortage of transportation available for troops and the objectives and demands of the Allies. In December 1917 only 183,000 American soldiers were in France, comprising parts of five divisions and performing various service support functions. During the first three months of 1918 the number of Americans doubled, but only an additional two combat divisions had arrived. However, after April 1918 the various shipping arrangements with the Allies, especially the British, had begun to pay dividends; American troops began to pour into Europe. At the end of June over 900,000 Americans had arrived in France, with 10,000 arriving daily.

In early July the AEF had reached the million-man mark, with twenty-three combat divisions (an equivalent of almost fifty Allied divisions). Six of the AEF's divisions had seen combat over the previous two months: two of those were holding segments of active front lines; four were in reserve positions. The 4th Division joined those in reserve. Six other divisions were training in the American sector around Chaumont, and another five were training with the British behind the front lines in the north. Four more were brigaded with French divisions for training along quiet sectors of the line, while the regiments of the 93d Division served with French divisions.

Since late 1917 Pershing had envisioned as the next step in establishing an independent American army the creation of American corps organizations with tactical command over American divisions. Toward this end he had established I Corps in January 1918 under the command of the unassuming but extremely capable Maj. Gen. Hunter Liggett. Over the next six months Liggett held administrative control over four American divisions, overseeing their training and interceding on their behalf with the French commanders. With the assistance of his effective Chief of Staff, Col. Malin Craig, he also ensured that his corps staff and headquarters were trained. The I Corps spent much of its time collocated with the French XXXII Corps in the Pont-à-Mousson region north of Toul.

By the end of June the AEF had formed three more corps headquarters. In late February 1918 the II Corps assumed administrative control of the American troops training with the British. In June Maj. Gen. George W. Read took command; until that time the corps staff had reported directly to GHQ. During the late spring the III and IV Corps were formed to manage Americans unit-training with the French Seventh and Eighth Armies, respectively. Eventually, General Bullard would assume command of the III Corps, while General Dickman would take over the IV Corps.

At the same time the AEF was organizing its first corps, Pershing was eyeing the front north of Toul, along the St. Mihiel salient, as the

Pershing had envisioned as the next step in establishing an independent American army the creation of American corps organizations with tactical command over American divisions.

sector to employ them. Ever since the 1st Division initially occupied a sector north of Toul in early 1918, the AEF staff had planned to expand that sector into an area of operations first for an American corps, then for an American army. In May, once the military situation stabilized after the failure of the German offensives in March and April, General Foch proposed concentrating available U.S. divisions to establish a separate AEF sector and left it to Petain and Pershing to work out the details. Subsequently, the two national commanders agreed that once four American divisions were in line along the Toul front, the sector would be turned over to the AEF. The AEF headquarters began to make arrangements to move units into the region, then the Germans struck with their Marne offensive on May 27. The available U.S. divisions were sent northward to help stem the tide along the Marne.

By June the better part of five American divisions was positioned in the Château-Thierry area. Forgoing the Toul sector for the time being, Pershing decided to use this concentration of American divisions for the first tactical employment of an AEF corps. In mid-June, with General Petain's permission, the AEF's GHQ notified General Liggett and his I Corps to prepare to move to the Château-Thierry region. As the I Corps prepared to move north, the AEF made an important shift in its doctrine for the employment of corps. Initially, the GHQ had followed the policy of assigning 6 divisions (4 combat, 1 base, and 1 depot divisions) permanently to each corps headquarters. The reaction to the German offensives, however, meant that the corps' assigned divisions were strewn individually over the recent battle zones. With the AEF corps' divisions scattered, it seemed unlikely that it would be in position to take tactical control of the divisions. Consequently, the AEF announced that divisions and special troops would be assigned temporarily to the corps. Organically, the corps itself would consist of only a headquarters and some artillery, aviation, engineer, and technical units. The change also reflected the French system for a more flexible corps organization that could be adapted to a particular mission.

Liggett and his I Corps staff arrived at La Ferte-sous-Jouarre, southwest of Château-Thierry, on June 21. There, the I Corps assumed administrative control over the 1st, 2d, 3d, 4th, and 28th Divisions. More important, the corps began to work with the French III Corps that was holding the sector just west of Château-Thierry. A little less than two weeks later the I Corps took tactical control of the sector with the French 167th Division and the U.S. 26th Division. Perhaps fittingly, the corps assumed command on the American Independence Day, July 4, 1918. Fourteen days later the I Corps would provide the pivot for the first large-scale Allied counteroffensive in 1918.

The AEF in the Aisne-Marne Campaign July–August 1918

Even as the Germans launched their June and July offensives, General Foch had been looking for an opportunity to strike a counterblow. The Marne salient presented an excellent prospect: the salient was inherently weak as the German forces relied on a single railroad through Soissons for the majority of their supplies. The Germans had failed to improve the situation with their June offensive. In mid-June Foch directed Petain to begin making plans for an attack against Soissons; Petain and his commanders completed the plans by the end of June. After French intelligence had warned him of the German attack east of Chateau-Thierry that would begin on July 15, Foch set the date for his counterattack as the eighteenth. Consequently, as the Germans were attacking on the eastern flank of the salient, the Allies would be attacking against their exposed western flank.

The Allied attack plan called for two French armies to attack on July 18 toward Braine on the Vesle River. In the north, the French Tenth Army would conduct the main attack between the Aisne and the Ourcq Rivers; in the south, the French Sixth Army would attack between the Ourcq and the Marne. Their mission was to cut the German lines of communications in the salient. The French Fifth and Ninth Armies on the eastern flank would join the attack after defeating the German offensive. Foch expected the reduction of the Marne salient to follow.

Under the cover of the forest of Villers-Cotterêts, the assault forces for the French Tenth Army gathered efficiently and secretly in the three days prior to the attack. Against the German defenders along the western flank of the salient, Foch had been able the gather twenty-three first-class divisions. Among them were the 1st and 2d Divisions assigned to the French XX Corps. Administratively the two U.S. divisions fell under General Bullard's III Corps, which had been rushed

Storming Machine Gun, *George Harding, 1918*

to the sector. Pershing had wanted Bullard to command the American troops; but Bullard arrived in the assembly areas too late to properly exercise tactical command, and he was instead attached to the XX Corps as an assistant commander. In addition to the two U.S. divisions with the Tenth Army, three more American divisions would take part in the initial days of the operation. In the French Sixth Army area, the U.S. 4th Division supported two French corps with an infantry brigade apiece, while Liggett's I Corps with the 26th Division held the eastern flank of that army. Meanwhile, the 3d Division supported the French Ninth Army.

On July 18 the Franco-American attack came as a tactical and operational surprise to the Germans. To preserve secrecy the Allies had made no artillery preparation of any kind prior to the attack. Instead the infantry attack was supported by over 550 tanks; short but intensive preparatory fires preceded a rolling barrage. Moreover, many of the assault units had moved into attack positions during the night before the attack. Darkness, heavy rain, and mud hampered the American divisions' movements to the front; and some of the 2d Division's infantry reached their jump-off point with only minutes to spare.

Spearheading the Tenth Army's attack, the XX Corps began a dawn assault to seize the high ground to the south of Soissons and cut the key rail lines. It attacked on a three-division front: Maj. Gen. Charles Summerall's 1st Division on the northern flank, General Harbord's 2d Division on the southern, and the Moroccan 1st Division in the center. On July 18 both American divisions made remarkable progress, advancing over three miles and achieving their objectives by 8:00 A.M. The next day the corps renewed its attack. The Germans, however, had been heavily reinforced with machine guns and artillery during the night; the French and American infantry found the advance slower and more costly. After a day of hard fighting, Harbord asked for the relief of his division; it was replaced by a French division. In two days the 2d Division had advanced more than eight miles and captured 3,000 prisoners and sixty-six field guns, at a cost of almost 4,000 men. Summerall's division remained in line for another three days and cut the Soissons–Château-Thierry highway and the Villers-Cotterêts railroad and held the ground that dominated Soissons. In its five-day battle the 1st Division captured 3,800 prisoners and seventy guns from the seven German divisions used against it. For these gains, the division paid a heavy price: 7,000 casualties (1,000 killed and a 73 percent casualty rate among the infantry's field officers).

Despite the high cost, the XX Corps' attack was an operational success. To counter the Allied attack south of Soissons, the German high command halted its offensive east of Château-Thierry and withdrew from its footholds over the Marne. Furthermore, the allied interdiction of the supply line through Soissons made the Marne salient untenable and the Germans began to withdraw.

To the south of the Tenth Army, the Sixth Army also attacked on July 18. Among the attacking units was Maj. Gen. George H. Cameron's 4th Division, which supported the French II and VII Corps. From July 18–20 Cameron's division advanced about four miles in two separate sectors. More significantly, Liggett's I Corps advanced up the spine of the Marne salient for four weeks. With the American 26th

Pulling Caisson Uphill, *George Harding, 1918*

Division and the French 167th Division, I Corps pushed beyond the old Belleau Wood battlegrounds and advanced about ten miles from July 18–25. For the next three weeks the corps made steady gains against the tenacious German defenders. Advancing with the 42d Division from July 25–August 3 and then the 4th Division from August 3–12, the American corps crossed the Ourcq and then the Vesle, a distance of almost fifteen miles. On August 12 Liggett and his headquarters were withdrawn to the Toul sector in preparation for the next offensive.

To the east of Château-Thierry, the AEF troops also played a significant role. The 3d Division had been a mainstay of this portion of the Marne line since early June. Initially, its role was to pin down German forces as the Sixth and Tenth Armies advanced. After July 20, as part of the French XXXVIII Corps, the division crossed the Marne, cleared the northern bank, and pursued the Germans as they withdrew. The division pushed forward until relieved by the 32d Division on July 29. The 32d Division continued the advance until it reached the Vesle. On August 1 Bullard's III Corps arrived and assumed tactical control of the 32d, 28th, and 3d Divisions from the French XXXVIII Corps. Thus for a few days the American I and III Corps stood side by side on the front lines.

At the end of the first week of August, the Aisne-Marne Campaign came to a close. The campaign successfully removed the threat against Paris and freed several important railroads for Allied use. It also eliminated the German high command's plans for another offensive against the British in Flanders. More important, the campaign effectively seized the initiative from the Germans and gave it to Foch and his national commanders. With the initiative passing to the Allies, so too passed the chance for Germany to defeat Britain and France before the United States could intervene in force.

To maintain pressure on the Germans, Foch had Petain continue the advance beyond the Vesle. From mid-August to mid-September this advance included troops from the American III Corps before they withdrew southward to join the new American First Army. From August 28–September 1 Maj. Gen. William G. Haan's 32d Division attacked north of Soissons, seizing the key town of Juvigny and making a two-and-a-half-mile penetration of the German lines. In early September, the 28th and the 77th Divisions attacked northward, almost reaching the Aisne River by September 16.

An American Army and St. Mihiel, September 1918

Shortly after the dramatic advance of the 1st and 2d Divisions south of Soissons, Pershing renewed his efforts for an independent American field army. On July 21 he approached Petain about organizing an army and establishing its own distinct area of operations. Pershing wanted one sector in the active Marne front and another in a more quiet sector, the Toul area, where he could send exhausted units to rest and refit. He wanted to form the American First Army in the active sector and take command himself. Petain agreed in principle to Pershing's plans, and together they met with Foch. Foch was favorably disposed to the plan but made no firm commitment.

Three days later, as the Allied forces were approaching the Ourcq River, Foch called a meeting of his senior military commanders to lay out his plan to maintain the initiative on the Western Front. He envisioned a set of immediate limited offensives aimed at freeing important railroads and key resources. Beside the ongoing Marne Campaign, these included operations to reduce the Lys and Amiens salients in the north and the St. Mihiel salient in the south. The latter was to be an American operation. Upon completion of these limited operations, Foch wanted a general offensive along the entire front, pushing to end the war in the summer of 1919.

On the same day Pershing officially announced the formation of the American First Army, with an effective date of August 10, 1918. When on August 4 the I and III Corps assumed adjacent sectors south of the Vesle, arrangements were made to extend both their fronts to cover the entire French Sixth Army's sector. By August 8 the two corps held a front of eight miles and had control of six American and two French divisions. Petain's headquarters issued orders affecting the relief of the Sixth Army by the American First. On August 10 Pershing achieved one of his major objectives for the AEF, the formation of an independent American army that combined American corps and American divisions.

These arrangements were quickly overtaken by events. By the time Petain and Pershing could establish a sector for an American army, the situation along the Vesle had stabilized. With no need or desire to occupy an inactive sector, Pershing arranged with Petain to begin moving his army headquarters southward to prepare for operations against the St. Mihiel salient. Leaving Petain with the American III Corps of three divisions, Pershing began shifting other American units to the St. Mihiel region. American troops from the Vesle region, the Vosges, the training areas around Chaumont, and the British sector were concentrated along the salient. Initially, the forces available to the American First Army were three American corps of fourteen divisions and a French corps of three divisions.

Just as the concentration of American forces was making headway, Foch, newly promoted to Marshal of France, came to Pershing's headquarters on August 30. Pershing and his staff had been planning to achieve Foch's desire to reduce the St. Mihiel salient and then push the Germans back along the whole front as stated at the July 24 conference. But now, several weeks later, Foch had reconsidered the need for the St. Mihiel operation. Based on a suggestion from Field Marshal Haig, the British commander, Foch wanted to launch a series of converging attacks against the Germans' lateral lines of communications. This plan called for British forces to attack southeasterly and the Franco-American forces to attack northward from the Meuse-Argonne region in a vast double envelopment against the German Army. With the northward attack, a full reduction of the St. Mihiel salient would be unnecessary. Foch further complicated the situation by proposing to divide the American army into two pieces on either side of the Meuse-Argonne, separated by a French army. He made his proposal even more uninviting to the AEF by detailing two French generals to "assist" the Americans.

Not surprisingly, Pershing fervently objected to the suggestion of dividing the American forces. He offered counterproposals, which Foch dismissed as impractical. Quickly, the tempers of the two commanders flared. Foch demanded to know if the American commander wanted to go into battle. Pershing replied, "Most assuredly, but as an American Army." Having reached an impasse, Foch departed.

Once again Pershing turned to his friend Petain for assistance. Petain wanted American support and cooperation and believed that a strong AEF with its own sector of the front was in the best interest of the French Army. Together, Petain and Pershing met with Foch on September 2. Supported by Petain, Pershing offered to assume the entire sector of the front from Pont-à-Mousson through the Meuse valley to the Argonne Forest, a length of about ninety miles. The AEF commander contended that the attack against the St. Mihiel salient could begin within two weeks and that it offered operational advantages to Foch's desired attack along the Meuse as well as the potential to build confidence and experience in the American First Army. Foch insisted that the operation be limited to simply reducing the salient and that the Americans would have to attack northward by the end of the month. Pershing noted that after his Army had eliminated the salient it could pivot and still launch its offensive against the Meuse-Argonne on schedule. Finally, the three commanders agreed to two distinct American operations supported by French troops and equipment: the elimination of the St. Mihiel salient beginning about September 10 and the larger offensive along the west bank of the Meuse starting between September 20–25.

BARBED WIRE

Barbed wire was invented in the United States in 1873 as agricultural fencing. By the outbreak of World War I it had become an important element of field fortifications. Barbed-wire entanglements tens of meters deep combined with trenches and machine guns to make the Western Front essentially impassable to large bodies of troops. A substantial fraction of artillery rounds were spent for the sole purpose of cutting the wire in front of attacking infantry. The emplacement, maintenance, and removal of barbed wire entanglements consumed the bulk of infantry patrols and much of the combat-engineering effort. New tactics and the introduction of improved equipment such as tanks and bangalore torpedoes reduced, but by no means eliminated, barbed wire as a battlefield obstruction.

With approval to proceed with the St. Mihiel offensive, the AEF staff began the final planning for the operation. Resulting from a German offensive in September 1914, the St. Mihiel salient was a 200-square-mile triangle jutting fourteen miles into the Allied lines between the Moselle and Meuse rivers. Bounded by Pont-à-Mousson to the south, St. Mihiel to the west, and the Verdun area to the north, the terrain was mostly rolling plain, heavily wooded in spots. After three years of occupation, the Germans had turned the area into a fortress with heavy bands of barbed wire and strong artillery and machine-gun emplacements. Eight divisions defended the salient, with five more in reserve.

The Americans planned to make near-simultaneous attacks against the two flanks of the salient. While an attached French corps of three divisions pressed the apex of the salient, the three divisions of the newly formed V Corps would attack southeasterly toward Vigneulles. General Cameron, who had impressed Pershing in the July operations, commanded the corps. Cameron's men would link up with the three divisions of the IV Corps, now under General Dickman who had fought so well along the Marne. To the right, the experienced I Corps of four divisions would push to the base of the salient. The I and IV Corps were to attack at 5:00 A.M., the French corps an hour later, and the V Corps at 8:00.

Pershing was determined not to fail in his first operation as an army commander. To support his 11 divisions (7 American and 4 French), he arranged for the use of over 3,000 guns, 1,400 planes, and 267 tanks. The British and the French provided the vast majority of artillery, planes, and tanks, though a large number of the planes and some of the tanks were manned by Americans. Initially, to maintain the element of surprise, Pershing was going to have little to no artillery fire before the attack; but in the end he decided to use a four-hour bombardment along the southern flank and a seven-hour one along the western flank. In addition, Pershing, at the suggestion of Petain, developed an elaborate scheme to deceive the Germans into thinking that the American first blow would come to the south near Belfort; the scheme worked well enough to get the Germans to move three divisions into that sector.

At 1:00 on the morning of September 12 the artillery began its bombardments. As planned, four hours later the infantry and tanks of the I and IV Corps attacked on a twelve-mile front. Pivoting on the I Corps, Dickman's infantrymen swept ahead over five miles. Meanwhile, the V Corps kicked off its attack at 8:00, also making good progress. The Germans put up a determined defense long enough to retreat in good order. (They had been ordered to withdraw from the salient on September 8 but had been slow in executing the order.) By the end of the day the 1st Division, advancing from the south, was within striking distance of Vigneulles and ten miles from the advancing columns of the V Corps' 26th Division.

On the afternoon of September 12 Pershing learned that columns of Germans were retreating on roads from Vigneulles and urged both the 1st and 26th Divisions to continue their attacks through the night. Despite having made a very deliberate advance during the day, the 26th Division moved quickly throughout the night; one regiment captured Vigneulles by 2:30 on the morning of the thirteenth. At dawn a brigade of the 1st Division had made contact with the New Englanders. With the capture of Vigneulles and the linkup of the two converging American columns, the critical part of operation was over. By the end of September 13 the First Army had taken practically all its objectives.

In two days the American soldiers had cleared a salient that had remained virtually undisturbed for three years. While suffering 7,000 casualties, the American army inflicted over 17,000 casualties, mostly prisoners, on the German defenders as well as seizing 450 cannon and a large amount of war stores. Although the defenders had planned to leave the salient, the attack's timing came as a surprise and hurried their withdrawal. The operation freed the Paris-Nancy railroad and secured the American rear for the upcoming northward thrust. More important, the battle had given Pershing and his First Army staff experience in directing a battle of several corps supported by tanks and aircraft. It would be needed for the much larger and complex operation along the Meuse.

The Meuse-Argonne Campaign
September–November 1918

Though local operations to improve the defensive positions and aggressive patrolling continued along the St. Mihiel front, the main effort of Pershing and the AEF shifted forty miles to the northwest along the west bank of the Meuse. Over the next two weeks, the AEF now executed a complex and massive movement of troops, artillery, and supplies to its new battleground. This movement was completed over only three roads capable of heavy traffic and confined to the hours of darkness to maintain secrecy. Over 820,000 men were transferred in the region: 220,000 French and Italian troops left the area, and about 600,000 Americans entered. Of the 15 American divisions that took over the sector, 7 had been involved in the St. Mihiel operation, 3 came from the Vesle sector, 3 from the area of Soissons, 1 near Bar-le-Duc, and 1 from a training area. That this movement went off without a serious setback was largely attributable to the careful planning of a young staff officer on Pershing's First Army staff, Col. George C. Marshall.

The AEF's attack into the Meuse-Argonne region was part of Foch's larger general offensive against the Germans. Together with

GEORGE C. MARSHALL, JR.
(1880–1959)

Col. George C. Marshall, Jr., made his reputation during World War I while serving as operations officer for the U.S. First Army. Marshal Ferdinand Foch insisted that the First Army break off its long-planned attack south and west of Verdun on the St. Mihiel salient and instead attack north through the Argonne Forest. Marshall directed the team that planned the shift in the axis of attack and then successfully supervised the movement of 600,000 troops, 3,000 guns, and 40,000 tons of supplies to the new sector in ten days. The American attack commenced on schedule, due in no small measure to Marshall's planning expertise.

the concentric attacks of the British toward Mons and the Americans toward Mézières, the French would attack in the center, as well as supporting both of their allies in their operations. This broad-front campaign would force the Germans to defend the entire front. Foch's objective was to cut the enemy's vital lateral rail lines and compel the Germans to retire inside their own frontier before the end of 1918. For this grand offensive, Foch had 220 divisions, of which forty-two were the big divisions of the AEF.

The American First Army would attack northward in conjunction with the French Fourth Army. Its main objective was the rail line between Carignan-Sedan-Mézières, an artery of the important rail system running through Luxembourg, Thionville, and Metz. (*See Map 3.*) That objective was about thirty miles from the jump-off line east of Verdun. In addition, by attacking east of the Argonne Forest, the First Army's offensive would outflank the German forces along the Aisne, in front of their French counterparts to the west.

The American army's area of operations was fifteen to twenty miles wide, bounded by the unfordable Meuse River on the east and the dense Argonne Forest and the Aire River on the west. The heights of the Meuse dominated the east side of the American sector, while the Argonne sat on high ground that commanded the western side. Between the river and the forest, a hogback ridge ran southeast and northwest from Montfaucon, Cunel, and Barricourt. A series of three lateral hill lines presented barriers to a northward advance. In addition to the Argonne, the area was dotted with various woods that presented even more obstacles to the American advance.

For their defense of the area, the Germans took full advantage of the region's rugged terrain. The high ground on either flank gave them excellent observation points from which to rain artillery on the American advance. Moreover, like the St. Mihiel salient, the Germans had occupied the area for several years and had developed an elaborate defensive system of four fortified lines featuring a dense network of wire entanglements, machine-gun positions with interlocking fires, and concrete fighting posts. In between these trench lines, the Germans had developed a series of intermediate strong points in the numerous woods and knolls. The German defensive system was about fifteen miles deep with five divisions on line and another seven in immediate reserve. Petain believed that the German defenses were so strong that the Americans would do well if they captured Montfaucon, on the second line, before winter.

Against this imposing defense, the American First Army mustered over 600,000 men. It would attack with nine divisions on line and another five in reserve. These were divided among the three attacking corps: Bullard's III Corps on the east, Cameron's V Corps in the center, and Liggett's I Corps on the west. The American infantrymen were supported by 2,700 pieces of artillery, 189 tanks, and 821 aircraft.

Pershing and his staff envisioned the offensive in two stages. During the first stage U.S. forces would penetrate the third German line, advancing about ten miles and clearing the Argonne Forest to link up with the French Fourth Army at Grandpré. The second stage would consist of a further advance of ten miles to outflank the enemy positions along the Aisne and prepare for further attacks toward Sedan and Mézières on the Meuse River. Additional operations were planned to clear the heights along the east bank of the Meuse.

The first attacks would kick off on September 26. Initially, the operations plan called for two thrusts on either side of the high ground around Montfaucon, with a linkup achieved before the Germans could bring in additional reinforcements. The V Corps would make the main attack, taking Montfaucon and penetrating the second German line. On its flanks, the I and III Corps would advance to protect both the army's and the V Corps' flanks. In addition, their corps artillery was charged with suppressing the German artillery on the flanks. Pershing wanted to seize Cunel and, to its west, Romagne, by the end of the second day.

At 5:30 A.M., after a three-hour artillery bombardment, the three corps launched their attacks in the Meuse-Argonne. Despite a heavy fog, the rugged terrain, and the network of barbed wire, the weight of the American onslaught quickly overran the Germans' forward positions. On both flanks, the corps made good progress. In the III Corps sector, Maj. Gen. John Hines' 4th Division pushed ahead about four miles, penetrated the German second line, and defeated several counterattacks in the process. On the western flank, Liggett's corps reached its objectives, advancing three miles on the open ground to the east of the Argonne. Maj. Gen. Robert Alexander's 77th Division made lesser gains in the Argonne itself. In the center, however, the V Corps experienced problems and was checked to the south of Montfaucon; it was not until the next day that Cameron's men were able to seize the position.

Throughout the remainder of September, the First Army slowly plodded forward. Heavy rains on September 27–28 bogged down the few tanks that had not already succumbed to mechanical failure. The rains also interfered with the forward movement of the supporting artillery and the resupply efforts as the already congested roads became muddy. Moreover, the Germans had used the delay in front of Montfaucon to rush local reserves to the strong positions in the center of their line, south of Cunel and Romagne. As the American battalions and companies encountered German machine-gun positions in depth, the advance slowed further. Once the American infantry silenced the

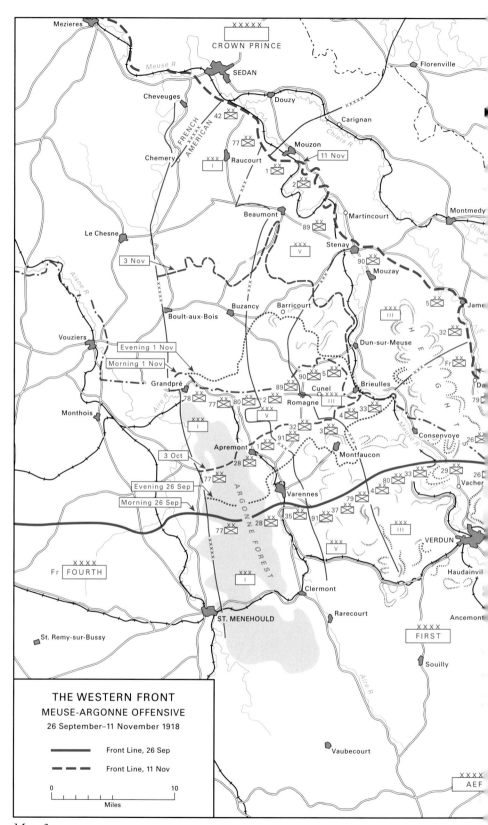

Mezieres

XXXXX
CROWN PRINCE

Meuse R

SEDAN

Florenville

Cheveuges

Douzy

Carignan

42 ⊠

FRENCH
XXXXX
AMERICAN

77 ⊠

Mouzon

Chiers R

11 Nov

Chemery

XXX
I Raucourt

1 ⊠

Montmedy

Beaumont

2 ⊠

Martincourt

89 ⊠

Le Chesne

XXX
V

Stenay

90 ⊠

Mouzay

3 Nov

Aisne R

Buzancy

XXX
III

5 ⊠

Jame

32 ⊠

Boult-aux-Bois

HEIGHTS

Vouziers

Evening 1 Nov

Dun-sur-Meuse

Fr

79

Morning 1 Nov

90 5 ⊠

Da

Aire R

Grandpré

89 ⊠

Cunel

Brieulles

78 ⊠

77 ⊠ 80 ⊠ =2 ⊠

Romagne

XXX
III

Monthois

XXX
V

4 ⊠ 33 ⊠

Consenvoye

26

XXX
I

32 ⊠

3 ⊠

91 ⊠

Apremont

1 ⊠

Montfaucon

28 ⊠

3 Oct

29 ⊠

26

80 ⊠ 33 ⊠

Vacher

Evening 26 Sep

77 ⊠

Varennes

79 ⊠

4 ⊠

Morning 26 Sep

ARGONNE FOREST

28 ⊠

35 ⊠ 91 ⊠ 37 ⊠

XXX
III

VERDUN

77 ⊠

XXX
V

Haudainvil

Fr XXXX
FOURTH

XXX
I

Clermont

Rarecourt

Ancemont

St. Remy-sur-Bussy

XXXX
FIRST

ST. MENEHOULD

Souilly

Aire R

THE WESTERN FRONT
MEUSE-ARGONNE OFFENSIVE
26 September–11 November 1918

——————— Front Line, 26 Sep

– – – – – – Front Line, 11 Nov

Vaubecourt

0 ————————————— 10
Miles

XXXX
AEF

Map 3

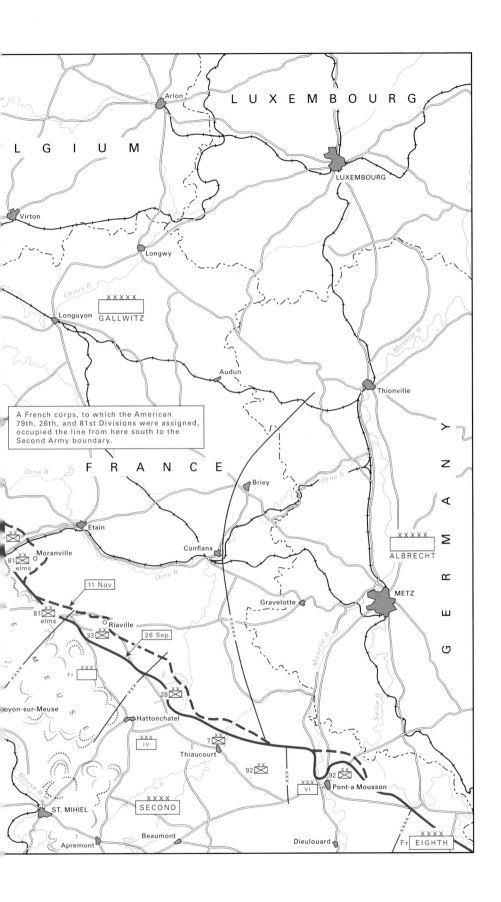

LUXEMBOURG

Arlon

LUXEMBOURG

BELGIUM

Virton

Longwy

Chiers R

Longuyon

XXXXX
GALLWITZ

Audun

Moselle R

Thionville

A French corps, to which the American
79th, 26th, and 81st Divisions were assigned,
occupied the line from here south to the
Second Army boundary.

FRANCE

Orne R

Briey

Orne R

Etain

Moranville

81 elms

XXXXX
ALBRECHT

GERMANY

Conflans

Orne R

81 elms

11 Nov

Riaville

26 Sep

33

Gravelotte

METZ

Moselle R

MEUSE

Fr XXX

Seille R

...oyon-sur-Meuse

28

Hattonchatel

XXX
IV

7

Thiaucourt

92

XXX

Moselle R

92

VI Pont-a-Mousson

MEUSE R

ST. MIHIEL

XXXX
SECOND

Beaumont

Dieulouard

Fr EIGHTH

Apremont

CODE TALKERS

As a means to secure radio communications, the U.S. Army in World War I used Choctaw Indians with their unique language to rapidly and securely transmit information across the airwaves. This experiment was a success, and the Army would later turn to several tribes of American Indians in World War II (Comanche and Sioux among others) to use their native tongues in that conflict. Although often overshadowed by the more celebrated Navajo code talkers of the U.S. Marine Corps, the Choctaws of the U.S. Army pioneered the code-talker concept in World War I.

forward positions, supporting guns to the rear opened fire. In addition, the German artillery poured enfilading fire onto the attackers from the heights of the Meuse and the Argonne Forest. The advance had become a continuous series of bloody, hard-fought engagements.

Nor were all the First Army's difficulties from the enemy or weather. Of the nine divisions in the initial assault, only three (the 4th, 28th, and 77th) had significant combat experience. The 79th Division, which had the critical mission to take Montfaucon, had been in France for only seven weeks. The heavy fog and rain and the broken terrain exacerbated the situation for the inexperienced troops. Many divisions suffered from a lack of coordination among their own units and liaison with adjoining and higher units. Teamwork between the infantry and their supporting artillery often proved awkward and ineffective, especially in those divisions that had to rely on artillery brigades from other divisions since their own brigades were unavailable.

Overcoming these problems, the First Army advanced eight miles into the German lines by the end of September. Remarkably, it had fought through some of the strongest positions on the Western Front and captured 9,000 prisoners and a large amount of war supplies, including 100 guns. With the severity of the fighting and the intermingling of units in the twisted terrain, Pershing had little choice but to pause to reorganize.

Elsewhere on the Western Front, the remainder of Foch's general offensive had also slowed. The effort in Flanders had bogged down in the rain and mud, while the French armies in the center of the Allied line had not yet begun their attacks. Along the Somme, Haig's British armies did make a penetration of the German Hindenburg Line, with the help of the 27th and 30th Divisions of the AEF's II Corps. The British expanded the penetration to create a gap all the way through the German fortifications; but at the beginning of October, the British had to pause to improve their own lines of communications.

During the first days of October Pershing took advantage of the pause to rotate three battle-hardened divisions (the 3d, 32d, and 1st) into the line, relieving some of the less experienced (the 37th, 79th, and 35th). As the First Army reorganized its line, the Germans also strengthened their position with six new divisions brought into the area for a total of eleven. The numerical odds were beginning to even.

At 5:30 A.M. on October 4 the First Army renewed its general attack. The III and V Corps were to take the heights around Cunel and Romagne, respectively. Meanwhile, the I Corps was to neutralize the enemy's flanking fire from the Argonne and gain some room to maneuver around the forest. The fighting was especially severe. The American infantry launched a series of frontal attacks to penetrate the German lines and then to exploit the exposed enemy flanks. Progress was slow. The III and V Corps made some gains against their objectives, but the Cunel and Romagne heights remained in German hands. On the west, the 1st Division gained three miles and the I Corps captured an important ridge on the east edge of the Argonne. As new American divisions were rotated into line, the Germans continued their reinforcement efforts; and by October 6 they had twenty-seven divisions in the area.

As the two corps on the east continued their fight for high ground in the center of the First Army sector, Liggett's I Corps executed an effective flanking operation. On October 7, as the 77th Division attacked northward in the Argonne, Liggett sent the 82d Division almost due west into the rear of the German positions. By noon the Germans were withdrawing from the forest. By the tenth, the I Corps had cleared the forest.

With the divisions of First Army fighting in the Meuse-Argonne region, other American divisions were providing crucial assistance to the French and British advances. To the north, two divisions of General Read's II Corps continued to support the British advance. With the French Fourth Army on the First Army's western flank, the 2d Division (now commanded by Maj. Gen. John A. Lejeune of the Marine Corps) captured Mont Blanc Ridge, which provided the only natural defensive line south of the Aisne River, in a hard-fought battle from October 2–4. On October 10 the 36th Division relieved the 2d Division and advanced to the Aisne River by the thirteenth. The advance to the Aisne River brought the French Fourth Army on line with the American First Army.

On October 8 Pershing had the French XVII Corps attack across the Meuse near Brabant, due east of Montfaucon. The corps' two French and two American divisions advanced two miles and captured 3,000 prisoners and several important observation points. This limited operation also forced the Germans to divert divisions away from the main battleground between the Meuse and the Argonne.

On October 14 the First Army launched a general assault all along the German lines. The III and V Corps once again aimed at taking the fortified hills and forests of the Cunel-Romagne front. Over the next four days the 3d, 5th, and 32d Divisions battled for and captured the vital strong points. On the western flank, the I Corps advanced to the southern half of Grandpré on October 16. By the third week in October the First Army had reached most of the objectives of the first phase of the campaign: penetration of the third German line and clearing of the Argonne.

By mid-October Pershing realized that too much of the operational and tactical direction of the war was concentrated in his hands. As AEF commander, he was the American theater commander responsible for the administration, training, and supplying of the American troops in France as well as coordination with the other national commanders. In addition, he was the field commander for three corps of fourteen divisions in a desperate fight over rough terrain. Moreover, the First Army had become unwieldy, with over a million men along an 83-mile front.

Sgt. Alvin C. York (1887–1964)

On October 8 some doughboys of the 82d Infantry Division ("All American") were attacking westward into the Argonne Forest to outflank the strong German positions. Among the attackers was a lean backwoodsman from Tennessee, Acting Sgt. Alvin York. When heavy enemy fire slowed his regiment's attack, York and a patrol were sent to suppress the machine-gun positions. Working its way behind the German lines, the patrol surprised an enemy battalion headquarters and forced its surrender. Shortly after, German machine guns and rifles opened on the doughboys, wounding over half the patrol. York single-handedly silenced the German fire, killing around twenty of the enemy in the process. York and the remainder of the patrol led 132 prisoners back to American lines.

On October 12 Pershing organized the Second Army and named Bullard its commander. Bullard and his army assumed control over thirty-four miles of the front—the quiet sector between the Meuse and the Moselle south of Verdun. The active Meuse-Argonne sector remained the First Army's responsibility, and on October 16 General Liggett assumed command of that army. Pershing could now focus his attention on the larger strategic issues of theater command.

After visiting the First Army's corps and divisions, Liggett discovered that the Army was in deplorable shape after weeks of continuous and bitter fighting. Several divisions were combat ineffective, having less than 25 percent of their authorized strength. Liggett estimated that there were over 100,000 stragglers, which drained the army's strength. A lack of draft animals immobilized the army's artillery. The army needed to rest and refit, so for the next two weeks Liggett allowed it to do just that and resisted pressure to do more than local attacks.

More important, however, Liggett retooled and remodeled the First Army. He took particular care in retraining his infantry and artillery. Some infantry received special training in techniques for attacking strong points, while the rest were trained to bypass these defenses. Artillery batteries laid out supporting plans to use interdicting fires to isolate infantry objectives and to conduct counterbattery fires against German artillery. In his commanders Liggett instilled the need to maximize supporting fires and gas to suppress enemy defenses.

To prepare for the second phase of the offensive, Liggett ordered a series of limited attacks aimed at securing a suitable line of departure. Both III Corps, now under General Hines, and V Corps, now under General Summerall, launched local attacks to clear forests and seize hills in the center of the line. Some of these attacks involved heavy and hard fighting, but the bloodiest of the local operations was the I Corps' ten-day battle to capture Grandpré, which fell on the twenty-seventh. Meanwhile, Liggett and his army staff ensured that supplies were stockpiled and roads repaired. By the end of October the First Army was ready for the next general attack.

On November 1 Liggett's First Army attacked north, toward the Meuse River. The main objective was the Barricourt Ridge in the center, a realistic advance of five miles. Only once the ridgeline was secured would the army thrust west to maneuver around the Bourgogne Forest, link up with the French Fourth Army, then thrust northeast to drive to Sedan and the Meuse River. On the first day of the attack Summerall's corps, in the center, easily gained control of the ridgeline. Hines' corps, in the east, kept pace and advanced to the Meuse River. Only Dickman's corps, in the west, failed to make much progress. On the following day, however, the I Corps made excellent progress and cleared the flank of the French Fourth Army. Over the next several days, Liggett's army continued to advance as fast as it could displace its artillery and supplies forward. At one point the advance was so rapid that it ran off the AEF headquarters' maps. By November 4 the First Army had elements along the heights overlooking the Meuse and brought the railroad from Sedan to Mézières under artillery fire. The Americans had achieved their objective.

Liggett's careful preparation of the First Army paid off. Infantry and artillery coordination was superb. Troops pushed through and around German strong points, while special assault troops reduced them. Improved staff work and coordination afforded the First Army the flexibility to bypass German defenses. Unlike former attacks that made strong first-day gains followed by increasingly smaller ones, this attack was different: the advance on the third day exceeded those of the first. Under Liggett's tutelage, the American units had finally developed into a well-trained, well-organized fighting force.

A week after Liggett's forces reached the Meuse, the Armistice was signed. The fighting ended at the eleventh hour of the eleventh day of the eleventh month—November 11, 1918.

When it ended, the Meuse-Argonne Campaign was the greatest battle that the U.S. Army had fought in its history. Almost 1.25 million American troops had participated during the course of the 47-day campaign. American casualties were high—over 117,000—but the results were impressive. The American First Army had driven forty-three German divisions back about thirty miles over some of the most difficult terrain and most heavily fortified positions on the Western Front. It had inflicted over 120,000 casualties on the Germans and captured 468 guns.

The American Army and the Great War

When the war ended, the American participants were convinced that the AEF had played a decisive role in the defeat of Germany. In 200 days of fighting the AEF had captured about 49,000 Germans and 1,400 guns. Over 1 million American soldiers in 29 divisions saw active operations. The AEF lost over 320,000 casualties, of which 50,280 were killed and another 200,600 were wounded in action. In October the Americans held over 101 miles, or 23 percent, of the Western Front; in November, as the front contracted with the German retreat, the AEF held over 80 miles, or one-fifth of the line.

> Improved staff work and coordination afforded the First Army the flexibility to bypass German defenses.

The French and British helped train and transport the American soldiers and supplied much of the artillery, tanks, and airplanes for the AEF.

Obviously, some of these numbers paled in comparison to those of the rest of the Allies. For example, the French fought for four years with over 1.35 million men killed. Also, from July to November 1918, the French armies captured 139,000 Germans and 1,880 guns. Moreover, the AEF achievements would not have been possible without Allied assistance. The French and British helped train and transport the American soldiers and supplied much of the artillery, tanks, and airplanes for the AEF. The French especially engendered the cooperation of the American army. General Petain himself often intervened on behalf of Pershing and the AEF to establish the independent American army fighting on his own sector of the front. More than other Allied leaders, Petain seemed to understand what the AEF meant to the Allied cause.

More than its achievements on the battlefield, the 2-million-man AEF helped the Allied cause by its mere presence. Throughout 1918, while Germany grew progressively weaker, the Allied military strength grew stronger by virtue of the growing AEF. Besides the sheer weight of numbers, the Americans also helped rejuvenate flagging Allied spirits, both on and off the battlefield. In short, the AEF provided sufficient advantage to assure victory for the Allied side.

Pershing's AEF was the first modern American army. It had deployed to Europe and fought alongside the Allies in a mass, industrialized war. It never lacked élan—from Soissons to the banks of the Meuse, the AEF aggressively attacked its enemy. Although at the beginning of active operations the American soldiers showed more courage than skill, they and their leaders learned quickly. Within the span of several months, the best American divisions showed considerable tactical skill in their battles in October and November 1918. Leaders like Hunter Liggett and John Hines proved able tacticians and understood the conditions on the Western Front. At the higher levels, the AEF staffs proved the equal of their Allied counterparts.

For the U.S. Army, the ground forces of World War II would be direct descendants of the AEF of 1918. Many World War II generals had been captains, majors, and colonels in the AEF, learning their tactics and trade on the fields and forests of France. World War II battles were planned and coordinated by staffs organized and operated based on the precedents of the general staffs of the AEF's armies, corps, and divisions. In both wars, combat divisions were the means of projecting and measuring combat power. Like the AEF the American armies of 1944 were built around divisions grouped in corps and supported by corps and army troops. A harbinger of the future, the American army of World War I was more similar to those that followed than those that came before. The U.S. Army was seemingly ready to assume its place in the world as one of the great armies of a great power.

Discussion Questions

1. In what ways was America prepared or unprepared for war in 1917? How successfully did the U.S. Army overcome its initial problems?

2. How much strategic or operational flexibility did the American Army have when the United States entered the war?

3. Why did Pershing disagree with the concept of amalgamation? Was he correct? Discuss the viewpoints of the French and the British.

4. What role did the U.S. Army play in the operations of the Aisne-Marne and St. Mihiel? Why were these operations important to the Army's development?

5. What did the Army learn from the Meuse-Argonne Campaign? What should it have learned?

6. How did World War I change the Army?

Recommended Readings

Barbeau, Arthur E., and Florette Henri. *The Unknown Soldiers: African American Troops in World War I.* New York: Da Capo Press, 1996.

Beaver, Daniel R. *Newton D. Baker and the American War Effort, 1917–1919.* Lincoln: University of Nebraska Press, 1966.

Braim, Paul F. *The Test of Battle: The American Expeditionary Forces in the Meuse-Argonne Campaign.* Shippensburg, Pa.: White Mane Books, 1998.

Coffman, Edward M. *The Hilt of the Sword: The Career of Peyton C. March.* Madison: University of Wisconsin Press, 1966.

———. *The War To End All Wars: The American Military Experience in World War I.* Lexington: University Press of Kentucky, 1998.

Eisenhower, John S. D. *Yanks: The Epic Story of the American Army in World War I.* New York: Free Press, 2001.

Johnson, Douglas V., and Rolfe L. Hillman, Jr. *Soissons 1918.* College Station: Texas A&M University Press, 1999.

Smythe, Donald. *Pershing: General of the Armies.* Bloomington: Indiana University Press, 1986.

Other Readings

American Battle Monuments Commission. *American Armies and Battlefields in Europe: A History, Guide, and Reference Book.* Washington, D.C.: U.S. Marine Corps, 1989.

Asprey, Robert B. *At Belleau Wood.* Denton: University of North Texas Press, 1996.

Bruce, Robert B. *A Fraternity of Arms: America & France in the Great War.* Lawrence: University Press of Kansas, 2003.

DeWeerd, Harvey A. *President Wilson Fights His War: World War I and the American Intervention.* New York: Macmillan, 1968.

Hallas, James H. *Squandered Victory: The American First Army at St. Mihiel.* Westport, Conn.: Praeger, 1995.

Marshall, George C. *Memoirs of My Services in the World War, 1917–1918.* Boston: Houghton Mifflin, 1976.

Trask, David F. *The United States in the Supreme War Council: American War Aims and Inter-Allied Strategy, 1917–1918.* Westport, Conn.: Greenwood Press, 1978.

Triplet, William S. *A Youth in the Meuse-Argonne: A Memoir, 1917–1918,* ed. Robert H. Ferrell. Columbia: University of Missouri Press, 2000.

Wilson, John B. *Maneuver and Firepower: The Evolution of Divisions and Separate Brigades.* Army Lineage Series. Washington, D.C.: U.S. Army Center of Military History, 1998.

Zimmerman, Phyllis A. *The Neck of the Bottle: George W. Goethals and the Reorganization of the U.S. Army Supply System, 1917–1918.* College Station: Texas A&M University Press, 1992.

2

BETWEEN
WORLD WARS

Soon after the Armistice of November 1918, the War Department urged Congress to authorize the establishment of a permanent Regular Army of roughly 500,000 and a three-month universal training system that would permit quick expansion of this force to meet the demands of any new major war. Congress and American public opinion rejected these proposals. It was hard to believe that the defeat of Germany and the exhaustion of the other European powers did not guarantee there would be no major war on land for years to come. Although American leaders recognized the possibility of war with Japan, they assumed that such a war, if it came, would be primarily naval in character. Reliance on the Navy as the first line of national defense remained a cornerstone of U.S. military policy for the next two decades.

Another factor that determined the Army's character between the world wars was the United States' decision not to join the League of Nations, thus rejecting a chance to participate in an international security system. In keeping with a traditional distrust of foreign alliances and large military establishments, the American people also proved unwilling to support an Army in being any larger than required to defend the Continental United States and its overseas territories and possessions, to sustain knowledge of the military arts, and to train inexpensive and voluntary reserve components. The Army between the wars was thus a small "mobilization army," focusing much of its time and energy on planning and preparing for future expansion to meet contingencies. As threats seemed to diminish around the world, the interest in funding for even that small army began to wane. And since the Army had huge stocks of materiel left over from its belated production for World War I, there was no push for funding to modernize that small force. Thus the principal concern of the War Department until the 1930s was simply maintaining the manpower to fulfill those peacetime missions.

Troops Arriving Home from France, 1919

Demobilization

Planning for demobilization had begun less than a month before the Armistice, since few in the United States had expected the war to end so quickly. Almost all officers and men in the Army became eligible for discharge when the fighting in Europe stopped. The War Department had to determine how to muster out these men as rapidly and equitably as possible, without unduly disrupting the national economy, while maintaining an effective force for occupation and other postwar duties. It decided that the traditional method of demobilizing by units was most likely to achieve those goals. Units in the United States relocated to thirty demobilization centers around the country so their personnel could be outprocessed and discharged near their homes. Overseas units returned as quickly as shipping space could be found for them, processed through debarkation centers operated by the Transportation Service, and moved to the demobilization centers for deactivation and discharge. In practice the unit system was supplemented by a great many individual discharges and by the release of certain occupational groups, such as railroad workers and anthracite coal miners.

In the first full month of demobilization the Army released approximately 650,000 officers and men, and within nine months it had demobilized nearly 3.25 million without seriously disturbing the American economy. Demobilization of war industries and disposal of surplus materiel paralleled the release of soldiers, but the War Department kept a large reserve of weapons and materiel for peacetime or new emergency use. Despite the lack of advance planning, the demobilization process worked reasonably well.

The Army faced one major concern as the process unfolded. Reflecting its lack of planning for the conclusion of hostilities and return to a peacetime posture, the Army had no authority to enlist men to replace those being discharged. On February 28, 1919, Congress ended that dilemma by authorizing enlistments in the Regular Army for either one or three years. By the end of the year the Active Army, reduced to about 19,000 officers and 205,000 enlisted men, was again a regular volunteer force.

Immediate Duties

Regular Army units continued to guard the Mexican border during 1919 and 1920 due to the ongoing revolutionary disturbances in that country. Because the National Guard had not yet been reorganized, the Regular Army also had to supply troops on numerous occasions through the summer of 1921 to help suppress domestic disorders arising out of labor disputes and race conflicts in a restless postwar America.

American soldiers remained in Europe for some time as the demobilization continued, guarding against renewed hostilities. A newly activated Third Army crossed the French border into Germany on December 1, 1918, to occupy the region around Koblenz, between Luxembourg and the Rhine River. Eight U.S. divisions organized into three corps participated in the occupation of Germany. Similarly, an Army regiment sent to Italy before the end of hostilities spent four

OCCUPATION OF THE RHINELAND

Luxembourgers Greeting the American Army of Occupation, 1918

Pursuant to the terms of the Armistice ending Western Front hostilities on November 11, 1918, the Allies (Belgium, France, Great Britain, and the United States) constituted forces that would occupy the German Rhineland. British forces occupied the area on its left, with French forces on its right. The Third Army entered Luxembourg on November 20 and was surprised by the warm reception from the German-speaking Luxembourgers. Proceeding to the Rhine, Third Army forces entered Germany on December 1 and again were greeted with some warmth by most Germans, who for the most part were relieved not to be under the sway of the French. The American occupation of German territory proceeded largely without incident, though German attitudes toward the occupiers cooled after the Peace Conference at Versailles. Political disagreements between the American and French commanders led General Pershing to comply willingly with U.S. government desires to return American forces to the United States as rapidly as possible. The last U.S. troops on the Rhine departed for home in January 1923.

months participating in the occupation of Austria. American occupation troops encountered no unusual difficulties with the populace, and their numbers were rapidly reduced after the Paris Peace Conference ended in May 1919. They numbered only about 15,000 by the beginning of 1920. After rejecting the Treaty of Versailles that resulted from the peace conference, the United States technically remained at war with Germany until a separate peace was signed in the summer of 1921. Occupying forces gradually withdrew after that, until the last thousand troops departed on January 24, 1923.

After the Armistice, Army units continued to serve elsewhere in the world, including two generally unsuccessful expeditions into revolution-torn Russia. In August 1918 the chaos in Russia resulting from the Bolshevik seizure of power induced President Woodrow Wilson to order the Army to join Allied forces in expeditions into Russian territory. Multinational forces penetrated the Murmansk-Archangel region of European Russia and entered Siberia via Vladivostok to safeguard various interests, and support anti-Bolshevik forces. The European Russia force, containing about 5,000 American troops under British command, suffered heavy casualties while guarding Allied war supplies meant for the Tsarist forces and communication lines before withdrawing in June 1919. The Siberian force of about 10,000, under Maj. Gen. William S. Graves, encountered many difficulties in its attempts to rescue Czech troops, captured soldiers of the newly collapsed Austro-Hungarian empire trapped by the deteriorating Russian situation, and to curb Japanese expansionist tendencies in the region between August 1918 and April 1920. Together these two forces incurred about 500 combat casualties. While seen in the West as only a footnote to World War I, the American and Allied intervention into the Russian civil war was deeply resented by the eventually triumphant Reds and continued to foster suspicion of American intentions in the minds of the leaders of the new Soviet Union for years to come.

Between 1923 and 1941, the only Army forces stationed on foreign soil were the garrison of about 1,000 maintained at Tientsin, China, from 1912 until 1938 and a force of similar strength dispatched from the Philippines to Shanghai for five months' duty in 1932. The Marine Corps provided the other small foreign garrisons and expeditionary forces that U.S. policy required after World War I, particularly in the Caribbean area. There remained, of course, the large American garrison

THE SIBERIAN EXPEDITION

In August 1918, as a civil war raged in Russia, the War Department ordered American troops to the Siberian port of Vladivostok. A major aim of this action was to constrain the territorial ambitions of Japan, ostensibly a partner in the intervention. Wisely, the American commander refused to involve U.S. forces in hostilities on behalf of Russian "White" counterrevolutionaries. In January 1920, in view of the ground commander's assessment that the Whites were doomed, the War Department withdrew the American troops. When the last forces left on April 1, the ill-starred episode had created a memory the Russians never forgot and left the graves of 192 Americans in the frozen wastes of Siberia.

in the Philippines with the mission of guarding those islands as part of the American empire and another major garrison in the Panama Canal Zone protecting that vital waterway. We should not discount the importance of these forces in the careers of thousands of officers and men in the interwar period. It was the principal "real world" mission of a large proportion of the Regular Army throughout the 1920s and 1930s. Nevertheless, the main challenges that confronted the U.S. Army between the Armistice that ended World War I and renewed hostilities in Europe in 1939 were not operational in nature but rather organizational and financial.

Reorganization under the National Defense Act of 1920

After many months of careful consideration, Congress passed a sweeping amendment to the National Defense Act of 1916. The National Defense Act of June 4, 1920, governed the organization and regulation of the Army until 1950 as one of the most constructive pieces of military legislation ever adopted in the United States. It rejected the theory of an expansible Regular Army that Army leaders had urged since the days of John C. Calhoun. In its place the new defense act established the Army of the United States as an organization of three components: the standing Regular Army, the National Guard, and the Organized Reserves. That component consisted of the Officers' Reserve Corps and the Enlisted Reserve Corps, two distinct organizations. Each of the three Army components was to be so regulated in peacetime that it could contribute its appropriate share of troops in a war emergency.

The act acknowledged and authorized the historical practice of the United States: a standing peacetime Army too small to be expanded to meet the needs of a large war and reliance on a new force of citizen-soldiers when large-scale mobilizations were necessary. In contrast to earlier practice, training the National Guard and Organized Reserves became a major peacetime task of the Regular Army. To fulfill that mission Congress authorized a maximum Regular Army officer strength of 17,726 officers, more than three times the prewar number. At least half the new career officers were to be chosen from among nonregulars who had served during the war. The act also required that officer promotions, except for doctors and chaplains, be made from a single list. That policy equalized opportunities for advancement throughout most of the Army. Congress authorized a maximum Regular Army enlisted strength of 280,000 men, but the actual enlisted and officer strengths would depend on the amount of money appropriated annually.

The new defense act also authorized the addition of three new branches to the arm and service branches established before 1917. The new branches were the Air Service and the Chemical Warfare Service, reflecting new combat techniques demonstrated during the war, and the Finance Department. The Tank Corps that emerged during World War I, representing another new combat technique, was absorbed into the Infantry.

The National Defense Act of 1920 specifically charged the War Department with mobilization planning and preparation for the event of war, assigning the planning and supervision of industrial procurement to the Assistant Secretary of War and the military aspects of that responsibility to the Chief of Staff and the General Staff. The World War I experience had greatly strengthened the position and authority of the General Staff in both Washington and Paris. When General John J. Pershing became Chief of Staff in 1921 he reorganized the War Department General Staff on the model of his wartime General Headquarters staff in France. The reorganized staff included five divisions: G–1, Personnel; G–2, Intelligence; G–3, Training and Operations; G–4, Supply; and a new War Plans Division that dealt with strategic planning and related preparations for war. The War Plans Division eventually helped to draft color-coded plans for the event of war with individual nations, such as War Plan ORANGE for Japan; it would also serve as the nucleus for any new wartime General Headquarters established to direct operations. The General Staff divisions assisted the Chief of Staff in his supervision of the military branches of the War Department and of the field forces. The only major change in this organizational framework during the 1920s came in 1926, when the Air Corps was established as an equal combat arm.

Nine geographic corps areas of approximately equal population assumed command and administrative responsibilities for the field forces in the Continental United States; departments with similar authority directed forces overseas in Panama, Hawaii, and the Philippines. The division, rather than the regiment, became the basic unit of the interwar Army, particularly for mobilization planning. Each corps area was allocated 6 infantry divisions: 1 Regular Army, 2 National Guard, and 3 Organized Reserve. In addition, a cavalry division patrolled the Mexican border; in Pacific outposts, Army mobile units were organized as separate Hawaiian and Philippine Divisions. The defense act had contemplated a higher organization of divisions into corps and armies, but no such organizations existed in fact for many years.

Education for and within the Army between the world wars received far greater attention than ever before. This reflected the National Defense Act's emphasis on peacetime preparedness and the increasing complexity of modern warfare. The U.S. Military Academy and the Reserve Officers' Training Corps (ROTC) program furnished most of the basic schooling for new officers. Thirty-one special service schools provided branch training. These branch schools trained officers and enlisted men of the National Guard and Organized Reserves in addition to the Regular Army, utilizing extension courses to supplement their residential programs. Three general service schools formed the capstone of the Army educational system. The oldest, located at Fort Leavenworth, Kansas, and known from 1922 to 1947 as the Command and General Staff School, provided officers with the requisite training for divisional command and General Staff positions. In Washington, the Army War College and, after 1924, the Army Industrial College prepared senior officers of demonstrated ability for the most responsible command and staff positions and assisted in the development of war plans. By establishing the Industrial College, the Army acknowledged the high importance of industrial mobilization and logistical training for the conduct of modern warfare.

Regular Army Strength and Support

When the National Defense Act was adopted in June 1920, the Regular Army contained about 200,000 soldiers, roughly two-thirds

By establishing the Industrial College, the Army acknowledged the high importance of industrial mobilization and logistical training for the conduct of modern warfare.

the maximum authorized strength. In January 1921 Congress directed a prompt reduction in enlisted strength to 175,000 and in June 1921 decreased that figure to 150,000. A year later Congress limited the Regular Army to 12,000 commissioned officers and 125,000 enlisted men, not including the 7,000 or so in the Philippine Scouts; Army strength stabilized at about that level until 1936.

Appropriations for the military expenses of the War Department also stabilized after the early 1920s at roughly $300 million per year. This was about half the estimated cost of fully implementing the force structure authorized in the National Defense Act. During this period the United States spent less on its Army than on its Navy, in accordance with the national policy of depending on the Navy as the first line of defense. War Department officials, especially in the early 1920s, repeatedly expressed alarm over Congress' failure to fully fund the force structure described in the National Defense Act. They believed that U.S. strategy required a minimum Regular Army enlisted strength of 150,000, a figure that grew to 165,000 after the Air Corps Act of 1926. From his position as Chief of Staff, General Douglas MacArthur pointed out that in 1933 the active strength of the Army ranked only seventeenth in the world.

Despite its limited size, the Regular Army still deserved international respect. Foreign observers rated its recently established, newly equipped Air Corps second or third in actual power. But the Air Corps' small inventory of modern equipment offered a marked contrast to the rest of the Army, where ground units had to get along as best they could for almost two decades with weapons left over from World War I. The Army was well aware that these old weapons were becoming increasingly obsolete. In 1933 General MacArthur described the Army's tanks, with the exception of a dozen experimental models, as completely useless for employment against any modern unit on the battlefield.

During the interwar era the Army focused its limited resources on maintaining personnel strength rather than on procuring new equipment. Army arsenals and laboratories were consequently handicapped by small budgets. Despite that obstacle they worked continuously to devise new items and to improve old ones, capitalizing on the rapid technological advances of the 1920s and 1930s. Service boards, acting as links between branch schools and headquarters, tested prototypes and determined doctrines for their employment so they could be incorporated into training manuals. Little new equipment was forthcoming for ground units until Army appropriations began to rise in 1936, but the emphasis on maintaining force levels meant that the acquisition of such equipment did not consume scarce resources in a period of rapid obsolescence.

For a number of years only about a quarter of the officers and half of the enlisted men of the Regular Army were available for assignment to tactical units in the Continental United States. Many units existed only on paper; almost all had only skeleton strength. The Regular Army's nine infantry divisions possessed the combined strength of only three full divisions. In May 1927 one of those undermanned infantry divisions, a cavalry brigade, and 200 aircraft participated in a combined-arms maneuver in Texas; but for the most part Regular Army units had to train as battalions or companies.

The continued dispersion of understrength divisions, brigades, and regiments among a large number of posts, many of them relics of the Indian Wars, was a serious hindrance to training Regular Army soldiers; though it was helpful in training the reserve components. Efforts to abandon small posts continued to meet stubborn opposition from local interests and their elected representatives in Congress. In the Infantry, for example, in 1932 the twenty-four regiments available in the United States for field service were spread among forty-five posts, thirty-four of them hosting a battalion or smaller unit.

Most of the organic transportation of field units was of World War I vintage, and the Army did not have the money to concentrate them for training by other means. Nor were there large posts in which to house them if transportation became possible. The best training of larger units occurred overseas in the fairly sizable garrisons the Army maintained in Hawaii, the Philippines, and Panama. Cuts in appropriations and pay in the early 1930s as a result of the Great Depression made travel and training all the more difficult, further reducing the readiness of Army units.

The Reserve Components

Promoting the integration of the Regular Army, National Guard, and Organized Reserves by establishing uniformity in training and professional standards was one of the major purposes of the National Defense Act of 1920. While falling considerably short of fully realizing that goal, the new Army structure did foster an unprecedented amount of military training for the reserve components. This training brought the regular out of his traditional isolation from the civilian community and acquainted large numbers of National Guard and Organized Reserve personnel with the problems and views of professional soldiers. Reserve component units and the groups in training that contributed to their ranks had an average strength of about 400,000 between the wars. The Reserve Component Training Program would result in an orderly and effective mobilization of the National Guard and Organized Reserve into the Active Army during 1940 and 1941.

The absorption of the National Guard into the Regular Army during World War I originally left the states without any Guard units after the Armistice. The National Defense Act of 1920 contemplated a National Guard of 436,000, but its actual interwar strength stabilized at about 180,000. This force relieved the Regular Army of any duty in curbing domestic disturbances within the states from the summer of 1921 until 1941 and stood ready for immediate induction into the Active Army whenever necessary. The War Department, in addition to supplying regular training officers and large quantities of surplus World War I materiel, applied about one-tenth of its military budget to the support of the Guard in the years between the wars. Guardsmen engaged in forty-eight armory drills and fifteen days of field training each year. Though not comparable to Regular Army units in readiness for war, by 1939 the increasingly federalized Guard was better trained than it had been when mobilized for duty on the Mexican border in 1916. Numerically, the National Guard was the largest component of the Army of the United States between 1922 and 1939.

In addition to the Guard, the civilian community contained a large number of trained officers and enlisted men after World War I, which provided a reservoir of manpower for the Army. Few enlisted men joined the Enlisted Reserve Corps to participate in the Organized Reserves after their wartime service. In contrast, large numbers of officers maintained their commissions by serving in the Officers' Reserve Corps (ORC). ORC strength remained fairly consistent during the interwar period at about 100,000 officers, but its composition gradually changed as war veterans were replaced by men commissioned through the ROTC or the Citizens' Military Training Camp (CMTC) programs.

University training programs to prepare citizens for military service had a long history. It can be said to have begun in 1819, when Norwich University in Vermont established the first such program. Soon other military colleges were established and military training gained prominence in the state land-grant schools set up under the Morrill Act of 1862. ROTC was formally established in the Defense Act of 1916. The CMTC program was more recent and limited, emerging from the Plattsburg movement just before World War I and the citizens' training camps it fostered.

For several decades before World War I the Army had provided equipment and annually detailed up to one hundred regular officers to support college military training through ROTC programs, but until the defense acts of 1916 and 1920 the program was only loosely associated with the Army's own needs. The new dependence on the National Guard and Organized Reserves for Army expansion, and the establishment of the Officers' Reserve Corps as a vehicle to retain college men in the Army of the United States after graduation, gave impetus to a greatly enlarged and better regulated ROTC program after 1920. By 1928 there were ROTC units in 325 schools enrolling 85,000 college and university students. Officers detailed as professors of military science instructed these units, and about 6,000 graduates were commissioned in the ORC each year. Thousands of other college graduates received at least some military training through the inexpensive program, which paid rich dividends in 1940 and 1941, when the nation began mobilizing to meet the threat of war.

The Army's CMTC program, a very modest alternative to the system of universal military training proposed in 1919, provided about 30,000 young volunteers with four weeks of military training in summer camps each year between 1921 and 1941. Those who completed three, later four, years of CMTC training and related home-study courses became eligible for commissions in the Officers' Reserve Corps. The CMTC thus provided another source of leadership for the Organized Reserves. Although relatively few officers emerged directly from the program, a substantial number of CMTC participants later attended West Point, entered ROTC programs, or received commissions during World War II.

The Army Air Corps

The airplane and the tank both came to symbolize the changing face of warfare during Word War I. But U.S. aviation programs retained their vitality after the war, while the tank fell captive to the conservatism of existing service branches after the National Defense Act of 1920's dissolution of the Tank Corps. The glamour of flight had captured the public imagination, and champions of air power insisted that the new technology could change the face of warfare. Strategic bombing, according to Italy's Giulio Douhet and other theorists, could replace traditional land and naval actions as the dominant form of warfare by directly targeting an enemy nation's population and industrial base, hence its will and capacity to wage war.

Advocates of strategic bombing disagreed with the Army's prevailing view of the airplane as a vehicle for reconnaissance and fire support, producing a split within both the Army and the Air Service itself. Brig. Gen. (Acting) William "Billy" Mitchell emerged from the war as the leading U.S. champion of strategic air power, demonstrating the potential of heavy bombers in a series of tests against obsolete warships during 1921 and 1923. Mitchell's outspoken behavior and open criticism of prevailing aerial doctrine resulted in his 1925 reduction to the permanent rank of colonel, 1926 court-martial for insubordination, and subsequent resignation from the Army.

The debate over the proper role of air power continued into World War II. As late as 1940 the Army General Staff largely disagreed with the decision of Maj. Gen. Frank M. Andrews, Commander, General Headquarters Air Force, to purchase the B–17 heavy bomber. The decision was referred to as Andrews' Folly, but it marked the culmination of two decades of effort to produce an effective strategic bomber. Dissent extended into the proper structure for the use of air power, as champions of strategic bombing sought to free aerial operations from those of the Army and Navy. In December 1925 a report from a House of Representatives committee chaired by Congressman Florian Lampert called for an independent Air Force combining all Army and Navy aircraft and a Department of Defense to coordinate the three services. A board President Calvin Coolidge established under the leadership of Dwight W. Morrow concluded that a separate air arm and a defense department were not necessary. In the Air Corps Act of 1926, Congress accepted the Morrow Board's recommendation to establish an Assistant Secretary of War for Air Affairs, to rename the Air Service the Air Corps, and to represent the Air Corps on the General Staff.

The Morrow Board's compromise plan provided a greater degree of independence for the advocates of strategic air power, but it also guaranteed that the War and Navy Departments could continue to harness the airplane as a tactical vehicle. Army Aviation pursued both potentials during the interwar period, substantially benefiting from dedicated funding and rapidly advancing technologies. But, despite precedence over many other Army priorities, even the Army Air Corps suffered from limited budgets; and the goals of the five-year expansion program authorized by the Air Corps Act were not met until the United States began preparing for war.

Domestic Employment

The most notable domestic use of regular troops in the twenty years of peace that followed World War I happened in the nation's capital during the summer of 1932. Several thousand "Bonus Marchers" remained in Washington after the adjournment of Congress dashed their hopes for immediate payment of a bonus for military service in the war. On July 28 marshals and police tried to evict one group encamped near the Capitol, and the ensuing riot produced some bloodshed. President Herbert C. Hoover directed the Army to intervene. A force of about 600 cavalrymen and infantrymen with a few tanks advanced to the scene under the personal leadership of Chief of Staff MacArthur. The troops cleared the Bonus Marchers from the Capitol and eventually evicted them from the District of Columbia, burning their shantytown in the process. The Army had performed an unpleasant task in an efficient manner; but the public largely viewed the use of military force against civilians, most of them veterans, as heavy-handed. The incident tarnished the Army's public image and helped to defeat the administration in the next election.

Aside from the Bonus Marchers incident, the most conspicuous employment of the Army within the United States after World War I was in a variety of nonmilitary tasks that fell to it because no other institution possessed the necessary organization or resources. After large-scale natural disasters the Army often provided the first substantial relief effort. The Army, especially the National Guard, was used extensively in a variety of humanitarian relief efforts after floods, storms, and fires, following a long tradition of

General MacArthur and Maj. Dwight D. Eisenhower stand among troops in Anacostia Flats.

such operations. Army Engineers expanded their work on rivers and harbors for the improvement of navigation and flood control; and for four months in 1934 the Air Corps, on orders from President Franklin D. Roosevelt, took over airmail shipment for the Post Office Department. That endeavor had tragic consequences, as the unprepared Air Corps struggled to meet the challenge during a period of unusually poor weather. Twelve pilots lost their lives in the first few weeks of the operation.

The Army's most important and immediately disruptive nonmilitary peacetime operation began in 1933, after Congress passed the Emergency Conservation Work Act in response to the Great Depression. The relief legislation put large numbers of jobless young men into reforestation and other reclamation work under the aegis of the Civilian Conservation Corps (CCC) it created. Despite MacArthur's strenuous protestations that running the CCC would have an adverse effect on Army readiness, President Roosevelt directed him to mobilize the CCC and run its camps without in any way making the program a covert military project.

Within seven weeks the Army mobilized 310,000 men into 1,315 camps more rapidly and orderly than any other mobilization in the Army's history. For more than a year the War Department had to keep about 3,000 regular officers and many noncommissioned officers assigned to this task; in order to do so the Army had to strip tactical units of their leadership. Unit training came to a halt, and the Army's

CCC CAMPS

By March of 1933, 13.6 million people were unemployed in the United States. President Franklin Roosevelt, only two days after his inauguration, called a meeting to create a Civilian Conservation Corps. The CCC would put more than 3 million young men to work improving public lands. Rather than create a new bureaucracy, the President used existing governmental departments. The U.S. Army's primary function for the CCC was to organize and administer the camps. This was a major logistical undertaking in that each state normally had as many as several dozen camps in operation at one time. A typical camp consisted of a dozen or more barracks, a post exchange, recreational building, mess hall, classroom, dispensary, officers' quarters, blacksmith shop, garage, bathhouse, supply room, green house, and storage buildings. Many Army officers, who otherwise would not have had an opportunity to construct and administer an installation or supervise large numbers of men during the interwar years, significantly benefited from this experience.

CCC Camp in Granite County, Montana

readiness for immediate military employment was nearly destroyed. In the second half of 1934 the War Department called a large number of reserve officers to active duty as replacements for the regulars, and by August 1935 about 9,300 reserve officers not counted in Active Army strength were serving with the CCC. A good many of them continued in this service until 1941.

The Army never wanted to insert military training into the work program, in part because the CCC camps were small and isolated enough to make that task quite difficult. But despite its initial serious interference with normal Army operations and deliberate nonmilitary nature, the CCC program eventually improved the country's military preparedness. It furnished many thousands of reserve officers with valuable experience and gave nonmilitary but disciplined training to over 3 million men, many of whom would serve in the military during World War II.

National and Military Policy

For fifteen years, from 1921 to 1936, American policy accepted the premise that future wars with other major powers, except possibly Japan, could be avoided. National decision makers pursued that goal by maintaining a minimum of defensive military strength, avoiding entangling commitments with Old World nations, and using American good offices to promote international peace and the limitation of armaments. Reacting to a widely held belief that an arms race had contributed to the outbreak of World War I, that the arms race might continue, and that such a contest would prove costly, in 1921 the United States called for an international conference to consider the limitation of major types of armaments, especially capital ships such as battleships and aircraft carriers.

The treaties that emerged from the Washington Naval Conference in 1922 temporarily checked the race for naval supremacy. Their provisions froze new capital-ship construction in the United States, Great Britain, Japan, and other signatory nations for ten years. Limitations on individual capital-ship size and armament and a 5:5:3 ratio in the total permissible capital-ship tonnage of the United States, Great Britain, and Japan guaranteed that none of the three great naval powers could successfully launch a Pacific offensive as long as the powers respected the treaty provisions. Separate provisions froze the construction of new fortifications or naval facilities in the western Pacific. The treaties made a U.S. defense of the Philippines against a Japanese attack nearly impossible, but the general agreement to maintain the status quo in the Pacific and in China offered fair assurance against a Japanese war of aggression as long as the Western powers did not themselves become embroiled in the European-Atlantic area.

During 1928 the United States and France joined in drafting the Pact of Paris, through which many nations renounced war as an instrument of national policy. Thereafter the United States proclaimed that, if other powers did likewise, it would limit its armed forces to those necessary to maintain internal order and defend its national territory against aggression and invasion. In 1931 the Chief of the Army's War Plans Division advised the Chief of Staff that the defense of frontiers was precisely the cardinal task for which the Army had been organized, equipped, and trained. There was no real conflict between national policy and the Army's conception of its mission during the 1920s and early 1930s. But, in the Army's opinion, the government and the American public in their antipathy to war failed to support even the minimum needs for national defense.

The clouds of war began to form again in 1931, when the Japanese seized Manchuria and defied the diplomatic efforts of the League of Nations and the United States to end the occupation. Japan left the League in 1933 and a year later announced that it would not be bound by the postwar system of arms control treaties that had begun with the Washington Naval Conference after the last of its obligations under that system expired in 1936. In Europe, Adolf Hitler came to power in Germany during 1933, denounced the Treaty of Versailles, embarked on rearmament, and occupied the demilitarized Rhineland by 1936. Italy's Benito Mussolini launched his own war of aggression by attacking Ethiopia in 1935. Spain's 1936 revolution produced a third dictatorship and an extended civil war that became a proving ground for weapons and tactics used later in World War II.

In response to these developments the U.S. Congress passed a series of neutrality acts between 1935 and 1937, hoping to avoid entanglement in another European conflict. The United States tried to strengthen its international position in other ways by opening diplomatic relations with the Soviet Union in 1933, by promising eventual independence to the Philippines in 1934, and by liquidating its protectorates in the Caribbean area and generally pursuing the policy of the good neighbor toward Latin America.

No quick changes in American military policy followed. But beginning in 1935 the armed forces began receiving larger appropriations that allowed them to improve their readiness for action. Changes in

Hitler and Mussolini in Munich, ca. June 1940

the Army over the next three years reflected the increasingly critical international situation and the careful planning of the War Department during General MacArthur's 1930–1935 tour as Chief of Staff. His recommendations led to a reorganization of the combat forces and a modest increase in their size, accompanied by more realistic planning for using the manpower and industrial might of the United States for war if it should become necessary.

The Army Strengthened

The central objective of the Chief of Staff's recommendations was strategic mobility, using the Army's limited resources to replace horses as a means of transportation and to create a small, hard-hitting force ready for emergency use. In pursuit of those objectives the Army wanted to mechanize and motorize its regular combat units as soon as possible and bring them to full strength so they could be trained effectively. The Army also needed new organizations to control the training of larger ground and air units and combined-arms teams and to command them if war came. Between 1932 and 1935 the War Department created four army headquarters and a General Headquarters Air Force in the Continental United States for those purposes. Under these headquarters, beginning in the summer of 1935, regular and National Guard divisions and other units started training together in summer maneuvers and other exercises, including joint exercises with the Navy. In the same year Congress authorized the Regular Army to increase its enlisted strength to the long-sought goal of 165,000. Substantial increases in equipment and housing budgets followed, so that by 1938 the Regular Army enjoyed greater combat strength and improved readiness. The strength and readiness of foreign armies had been increasing even more rapidly.

The slow improvement in Army readiness by the end of the 1930s highlights the fact that the Army was more prepared for war than many of its critics, arguing from the vantage of hindsight after World War II was over, have been willing to admit. In many ways, the Army was as prepared as it could be to fight the war that the civilian and military leadership of the country expected it to fight, a war focusing on the defense of the western hemisphere—"Fortress America"—rather than the war that finally arrived in 1941. When America was forced into war in a very different strategic world of 1941, a world that saw the fall of France and the near collapse of both the USSR and the British Empire, it was forced to prepare large expeditionary forces for overseas combat on a grand scale for a global, two-front war. None of this was foreseen in the 1930s.

The Army in the 1920s and 1930s, responding as always to the strategic needs of the nation as formulated by the civilian leadership and short on personnel, equipment, and funding, had to focus on its primary assigned mission of hemispheric defense. Most of the modernization funds of the Army were absorbed in the rapid expansion of the new Army Air Corps that was seen as one of the Army's principal contributions to that mission.

The second priority of the Army was the defense of the nation's seaports. To accomplish this, the Army poured huge sums into the modernization of the coastal fortifications at eighteen major seaports, increasing the number and caliber of the coast artillery guns and improving the defenses of their emplacements. Almost one-third of the Army's manpower, over 50,000 soldiers, was tied up in the coast artillery mission as the logical backstop to the Navy and Air Corps defensive belts. The Army even retained a separate coast artillery branch until 1950. In the 1930s the Army was relatively prepared for war but not for the war that came.

During the slow rebuilding of the 1930s the Army began to concentrate, when resources allowed, on equipping and training its combat units for mobile operations rather than for the static warfare that had characterized the Western Front in World War I. It managed to develop some new weapons and equipment that promised improved fire power and mobility once they could be obtained in quantity. Such projects included the mobile 105-mm. howitzer that became the principal divisional artillery piece of World War II and light and medium tanks that were much faster than the lumbering models of World War I. The Army's tanks still reflected their design origins in the Infantry and Cavalry. Infantry tanks were designed to support infantry assaults, and cavalry tanks were developed as "iron horses" to support traditional cavalry missions. Consequently, Army tanks would not compare favorably in firepower, one on one, to World War II German and Russian models. However, many American tanks, such as the fabled M4 Sherman, would be so mechanically reliable and were produced in such great numbers that they proved highly competitive in support of vast infantry formations in mobile warfare.

In terms of infantry weapons, the Army proved highly innovative, adopting the Garand semiautomatic rifle in 1936 as a replacement

In many ways, the Army was as prepared as it could be to fight the war that the civilian and military leadership of the country expected it to fight, a war focusing on the defense of the western hemisphere.

THE TRIANGULAR DIVISION

The World War I square division consisted of about 25,000 men. It had considerable hitting and staying power but lacked flexibility. During the 1930s, the Army tested a triangular configuration in which each level of command from the rifle company through the division had three subordinate maneuver elements and a fire support element. This organization permitted a commander to maneuver two units, retain a third in reserve, and bring organic fire to bear. Adopted in 1940, the new infantry division also minimized support elements to slim down to 15,000 men, which made it easier to transport. Corps and army commands each had pools of units, such as tank battalions, to attach to divisions when they needed more capability. This flexible configuration was both powerful and maneuverable and would soon prove its worth, not only on the battlefields of Europe and the Pacific but also in the postwar Army.

for the 1903 Springfield. This gave the U.S. soldier a marked advantage over his World War II German or Russian counterparts who still employed bolt-action rifles. The infantryman was also assisted by the comparatively rapid motorization of the Army. Horsepower yielded to motor power as quickly as vehicles could be acquired, although horse cavalry retained a hold on Army thinking and tactics for years. After successful field tests the Army decided to improve the mobility of its regular infantry divisions by reducing them from four to three infantry regiments. The new "triangular" divisions would employ only motor transport, decreasing their overall size to little more than half that of their World War I counterparts but enhancing their mobility and combat power.

The complexities of mobilizing for industrialized warfare required careful planning. The Army's Industrial Mobilization Plan of 1930 established the basic principles for harnessing the nation's economic strength to war needs, and continued revisions of the plan through 1939 improved its provisions. Manpower planning followed a similar process and culminated in the Protective Mobilization Plan of 1937. Under that plan, the first step in a general mobilization would be the induction of the National Guard into federal service, providing the Army an initial protective force of about 400,000. The Navy and this defensive force would then protect the nation while the Army engaged in an orderly expansion to planned strengths of 1, 2, or 4 million, as necessary. The Army's manpower planning included, for the first time prior to actual war, a definite training plan that specified the location, size, and schedules of replacement training centers, unit training centers, and schools. It also incorporated the details of unit and individual training programs and the production of a variety of training manuals.

While these plans eventually helped to guide the mobilization that began in the summer of 1940, they had their faults. Planners set their sights too low. They assumed a maximum mobilization of World War I dimensions, but the Army mobilized more than twice as many men for World War II and required an even greater comparative industrial effort to meet their needs. Until 1939 planners also assumed that mobilization for war would come more or less suddenly, instead of relatively slowly during many months of nominal peace. The Protective Mobilization Plan standardized many existing weapons designs to facilitate procurement and stockpiling, an understandable decision given the Army's poor equipment state and the ominous international situation. But standardization, in combination with the Army's earlier emphasis on funding personnel strength at the expense of research and development, impeded weapons programs in an era of rapidly advancing military technology. As a result the Army entered World War II with weapons designs from the mid-1930s, many of them already obsolete.

The Beginnings of World War II

The German annexation of Austria in March 1938 and the Czech crisis in September of the same year awakened the United States and the other democratic nations to the imminence of another great world conflict. In retrospect that new conflict had already begun with Japan's 1937 invasion of China. When Germany seized Czechoslovakia in March 1939, war in Europe became a near certainty since Hitler apparently had no intention of stopping his eastward expansion and Great Britain and France had decided that they must fight rather than acquiesce to further German aggression. In August Germany made a deal with the Soviet Union that provided for a partition of Poland and gave Joseph Stalin a free hand in Finland and the northern Baltic states. On September 1, 1939, Germany invaded Poland. France and Great Britain responded by declaring war on Germany but provided little direct assistance. An overwhelming majority of the American people wanted to stay out of the new war if they could, and this sentiment necessarily governed the initial U.S. response to the perilous international situation.

President Roosevelt and his advisers, fully aware of the danger, had launched a limited preparedness campaign at the beginning of 1939. By that date improvements in aircraft technology and the unproven but intriguing theories of strategic bombing had introduced a new factor into the military calculations of the United States. It would soon be technically feasible for a hostile European power to establish air bases in the western hemisphere from which to attack the Panama Canal (the key to American defense) or the Continental United States itself. Such an act would negate the oceanic security that the United States had traditionally enjoyed. Increasing the power of the Army Air Corps to counter that aerial threat became a key goal of defense planners as Europe braced for war.

Army and Navy officers began drafting a new series of war plans for facing a hostile coalition as the preparedness campaign began. Students at the Army War College had started researching such coalition plans during 1934, working in close cooperation with the General Staff. The RAINBOW plans would be the successors to existing plans that used colors to symbolize potential adversaries, e.g., War Plan ORANGE for a war against Japan. The new plans incorporated aspects of both War College research and the older color plans. A month after the European war began, the President, by formally approving the RAINBOW I plan, changed the avowed national military policy from one of guarding only the United States and its possessions to one of hemispheric defense, a policy that guided Army plans and actions until the end of 1940.

The Army concentrated on making its regular force ready for emergency action by providing it with full and modern equipment as quickly as possible and by conducting in April 1940 the first genuine corps and army training maneuvers in American military history.

Immediately after the European war started, the President proclaimed a limited national emergency and authorized increases in Regular Army and National Guard enlisted strengths to 227,000 and 235,000, respectively. He also proclaimed American neutrality, but at his urging Congress soon gave indirect support to the Western democracies by ending the prohibition on munitions sales to nations at war embodied in the Neutrality Act of 1937. British and French orders for munitions in turn helped to prepare American industry for the large-scale war production that was to come. When the quick destruction of Poland was followed by a lull in the war, the tempo of America's own defense preparations decreased. The Army concentrated on making its regular force ready for emergency action by providing it with full and modern equipment as quickly as possible and by conducting in April 1940 the first genuine corps and army training maneuvers in American military history.

These maneuvers were followed the next year by some of the largest maneuvers in Army history, in Louisiana and North Carolina. The Louisiana Maneuvers in particular were important testing grounds for new doctrine and equipment as well as for the expanded officer corps. Armies, corps, and divisions conducted massive motorized and armored movements in a series of "force on force" mock battles.

The adequacy of the Army's preparations depended on the fate of France and Great Britain. Germany's April 1940 conquest of Denmark and Norway, the subsequent defeat of the Low Countries and France, and the grave threat Great Britain faced by June forced the United States to adopt a new and greatly enlarged program for defense during that month. Before the summer of 1940 had truly begun, it appeared that the United States might eventually have to face the aggressors of the Old World almost alone.

The Prewar Mobilization

Under the leadership of Chief of Staff General George C. Marshall and, after July, of Secretary of War Henry L. Stimson, the Army initiated a large expansion designed to protect the United States and the rest of the western hemisphere from any hostile forces that might be unleashed from the European conflict. The Army expansion was matched by a naval program designed to give the United States a two-ocean Navy strong enough to deal simultaneously with the Japanese in the Pacific and Germany and its new war partner, Italy, in the Atlantic (if they defeated Great Britain). Both expansion programs had the overwhelming support of the American people, who were now convinced that the danger to the United States was very real but remained strongly opposed to entering the war. Congressional appropriations between May and October 1940 reflected the threat. The Army received more than $8 billion for its needs during the following year, a greater sum than it had received to support its activities over the preceding twenty years. The munitions program approved for the Army on June 30, 1940, called for the procurement of all items needed to equip and maintain a 1.2-million-man force by October 1941, including a greatly enlarged and modernized Army Air Corps. By September the War Department was planning to create an Army of 1.5 million soldiers as soon as possible.

PARACHUTE TEST PLATOON

The Army had considered organizing an "air infantry" as early as May 1939 in light of German air-landed forces' 1938 seizure of the Vienna airport. In January 1940 the Army decided to study the feasibility of air infantry and the air transport of ground troops. Germany's use of airborne troops in their May 1940 invasion of the Low Countries gave these studies added impetus. On June 25 the War Department directed the Infantry School to organize a parachute test platoon. Two officers and 49 enlisted men were selected from over 200 volunteers, and the platoon undertook a rigorous course of physical training and small-unit tactics, with classes on parachute packing and parachuting. The first platoon member jumped from an aircraft on August 16. The first mass jump occurred on August 29; in September the War Department authorized constitution of the 1st Parachute Battalion, marking the Army's entry into this new form of warfare.

On August 27, 1940, Congress approved the induction of the National Guard into federal service and the activation of the Organized Reserves to fill the ranks of this new Army. It also approved in the Selective Service and Training Act of September 14 the first peacetime draft of untrained civilian manpower in the nation's history. Units of the National Guard, draftees, members of the Enlisted Reserve Corps, and the reserve officers required to train them all entered active service as rapidly as the Army could construct camps to house them. During the last six months of 1940 the Active Army more than doubled in strength, and by mid-1941 it achieved its planned strength of 1.5 million officers and men.

A new organization, the General Headquarters, took charge of training the Army in July 1940. During the same month the Army established a separate Armored Force and subsequently the Antiaircraft and Tank Destroyer Commands that with the Infantry, Field Artillery, Coast Artillery, and Cavalry increased the number of ground combat arms to seven. The Infantry's tank units and the Cavalry's mechanized brigade combined to form the Armored Force, over the objections of the Chiefs of the Infantry and Cavalry branches. Chief of Staff Marshall believed that he had to take this drastic step in light of the reluctance of those conservative branches to pursue a role for armor greater than supporting the infantry and performing traditional cavalry missions. He also saw the startling success of German blitzkrieg operations in the opening days of the war in Europe.

During 1940 and 1941 the existing branch schools and a new Armored Force School concentrated their efforts on improving the fitness of National Guard and reserve officers for active duty, and in early 1941 the War Department established officer candidate schools to train men selected from the ranks for junior leadership positions. In October 1940 the four armies assumed command of ground units in the Continental United States and thereafter trained them under the supervision of the General Headquarters. The corps area commands became administrative and service organizations. Major overseas garrisons were strengthened; and the Army established new commands to supervise the garrisoning of Puerto Rico and Alaska, where there had been almost no Regular Army troops for many years. In June 1941 the War Department established the

THE FATHER OF AMERICAN ARMOR

Adna R. Chaffee, Jr. (1884–1941), son of the second Chief of Staff of the Army Adna R. Chaffee, Sr., struggled to mechanize the Army for fourteen years, beginning as a major on the General Staff in 1927 and culminating in his command of U.S. Armored Forces (1940–1941). One of the first American cavalrymen to recognize that the tank must supplant the horse on the battlefield, Chaffee also understood that armored warfare would require the participation of all the branches and services. His constant advocacy of this concept ensured that the U.S. Army, unlike the British Army, was spared a controversy between "all-tank" and combined-arms advocates. Though his command of the Armored Force would be cut short when he died of a brain tumor in 1941, his role as Father of American Armor was secure.

Army Air Forces to train and administer air units in the United States. In July it began the transformation of General Headquarters into an operational post for General Marshall as Commanding General of the Field Forces. By the autumn of 1941 the Army had 27 infantry, 5 armored, and 2 cavalry divisions; 35 air groups; and a host of supporting units in training within the Continental United States. But most of these units were still unready for action, in part because the United States had shared so much of its old and new military equipment with the nations actively fighting the Axis triumvirate of Germany, Italy, and Japan.

Toward War

On the eve of France's defeat in June 1940, President Roosevelt had directed the transfer or diversion of large stocks of World War I weapons, ammunition, and aircraft to both France and Great Britain. After France fell, these munitions helped to replace Britain's losses from the evacuation of its expeditionary force at Dunkerque. Additional aid to Britain materialized in September, when the United States agreed to exchange fifty over-age destroyers for offshore Atlantic bases and the President announced that future U.S. production of heavy bombers would be shared equally with the British. Open collaboration with Canada from August 1940 provided strong support for the Canadian war effort (Canada had followed Great Britain to war in September 1939). These foreign aid activities culminated in the Lend-Lease Act of March 1941 that swept away the pretense of American neutrality by openly avowing the intention of the United States to become an "arsenal of democracy" against aggression. Prewar foreign aid was largely a self-defense measure; its fundamental purpose was to help contain the military might of the Axis powers until the United States could complete its own protective mobilization.

Thus by early 1941 the focus of American policy had shifted from hemispheric defense to limited participation in the war. Indeed, by then it appeared to Army and Navy leaders and to President Roosevelt that the United States might be drawn into full participation in the not-too-distant future. Assuming the probability of simultaneous operations in the Pacific and the Atlantic, they agreed that Germany was the greater menace and that if the United States did enter the war it ought to concentrate first on the defeat of Germany. This principle was established as shared policy in staff conversations between American and British military representatives in Washington ending on March 29.

After those conversations the Army and Navy began adjusting the most comprehensive of the existing war plans, RAINBOW 5, to correspond with ongoing military preparations and actions. During the following months the trend moved steadily toward American participation in the war against Germany. In April the President authorized an active naval patrol of the western half of the Atlantic Ocean in response to German submarine warfare. In May the United States accepted responsibility for the development and operation of military air routes across the North Atlantic via Greenland and across the South Atlantic via Brazil. During that month it appeared to the President and his military advisers that a German drive through Spain and Portugal to northwestern Africa and its adjacent islands might be imminent. This prospect, together with German naval activity in the North Atlantic, caused the President to proclaim an unlimited national emergency and direct the Army and Navy to prepare an expeditionary force to be sent to the Azores as a step toward blocking any German advance toward the South Atlantic. Then, in early June, the President learned that Hitler was preparing to attack the Soviet Union. That offensive would divert German military power away from the Atlantic for some time.

The Germans did invade the Soviet Union on June 22, 1941; three days later U.S. Army troops landed in Greenland to protect the island from German attack and to build bases for the air ferry route across the North Atlantic. The Army units and nearby Coast Guard elements quickly captured several German weather teams in the Greenland area, highlighting the strategic importance of the region. Earlier that month President Roosevelt had decided that Americans should relieve British troops guarding another critical outpost in the North Atlantic, Iceland, and the first contingent of U.S. forces reached that island nation in early July. A sizable Army expeditionary force followed in September. In August the President and British Prime Minister Winston Churchill met in Newfoundland and drafted the Atlantic Charter, which defined the general terms of a just peace for the world. By October the U.S. Navy was fully engaged in convoy-escort duties

I Want You for the U.S. Army
James Montgomery Flagg, 1941

"OHIO"

By mid-1941, with no attack on the United States, National Guardsmen and draftees whose congressionally mandated twelve months of active service had begun in the fall of 1940 were growing restless. Although inadequate training facilities and equipment were improving, morale dipped as lengthy political debate over an extension of service proceeded. In the camps, the hand-lettered acronym "OHIO" (for Over the Hill in October, the end of the mandated year) appeared on walls, weapons, and vehicles. Congress, by a one-vote margin in the House in August 1941, precluded a disastrous disruption in the building of the Army by extending the period of service by six months.

in the western reaches of the North Atlantic and its ships, with some assistance from Army aircraft, were joining British and Canadian forces in their struggle against German submarines. In November Congress voted to repeal prohibitions against the arming of American merchant vessels and their entry into combat zones. The stage was set, as Prime Minister Churchill noted on November 9, for "constant fighting in the Atlantic between German and American ships."

These overt moves toward involvement in the war had solid backing in the American public opinion. Only an increasingly small, though vociferous, minority criticized the President for the nation's departure from neutrality. But the American people were still not prepared for an open declaration of war against Germany.

American policy toward Japan stiffened as the United States moved toward war in the Atlantic. Although the United States wanted to avoid a two-front war, it was not ready to do so by surrendering vital areas or interests to the Japanese as the price of peace. When the Japanese moved large forces into southern French Indochina in late July 1941, the United States responded by cutting off oil shipments and freezing Japanese assets. At the same time the War Department recalled General MacArthur from his retirement and position as Field Marshal of the Philippine Army to serve as Commander of both U.S. and Philippine Army forces in the Far East. It also decided to send Army reinforcements to the Philippines, including heavy bombers intended to dissuade the Japanese from making any more southward moves.

For their part, the Japanese, while continuing to negotiate with the United States, tentatively decided in September to embark on a war of conquest in Southeast Asia and the Indies as soon as possible. The plan called for immobilizing American naval opposition through an initial air strike against the U.S. Fleet stationed at the great naval base of Pearl Harbor in Hawaii. When intensive last-minute negotiations in November failed to produce any accommodation, the Japanese made their decision for war irrevocable.

The United States should not, perhaps, have been as surprised as it was by Japanese attacks on Hawaii and the Philippines on December 7, 1941. Japan's expansion aims by then were quite obvious, and the United States was the only major obstacle in its path. When Roosevelt

MacArthur and the Philippines

Upon stepping down as U.S. Army Chief of Staff in 1935, Douglas MacArthur (1880–1964) led a military mission to the Philippine Islands and became military adviser to the nascent commonwealth. Focusing on his task "to survey the military needs of the Philippine commonwealth," General MacArthur sought to create a defense force that could defend the Philippines after independence. He encountered numerous obstacles: financial demands that outpaced available funds, the War Department's reluctance to provide tangible support, unexpectedly high training requirements for Filipinos (who had high illiteracy rates and spoke numerous dialects), lagging conscription numbers, and the growing Filipino fear of Japan. In late 1940 War Department policy changed, and full-scale mobilization of the Philippines began in mid-1941. However, time was about to run out.

cut off U.S. shipments of oil to Japan, the situation grew even more critical. Despite this evidence and the benefit of superb U.S. code-breaking efforts against Japanese naval and diplomatic codes (MAGIC intercepts) similar to British successes against the Germans (code-named ULTRA), America was caught militarily and psychologically unprepared for war.

The Japanese attacks on Pearl Harbor and the Philippines immediately ended the remaining division of American opinion on participation in the war, and the United States officially entered hostilities with a unanimity of popular support that was unprecedented in its military history. This was also the first time that the United States entered a war with a large force in being and an industrial system partially retooled for hostilities. The Army stood ready to defend the western hemisphere against invasion with a force of 1,643,477 soldiers. This is the mission for which it was prepared. Yet, on many levels, it was not ready to take part in a very different type of war, a war of large-scale expeditionary forces launched to conduct complex combined and joint operations across the huge expanses of two oceans. Many months would pass before the United States could begin even limited offensives against the well-prepared, battle-hardened forces of the Axis powers.

DISCUSSION QUESTIONS

1. Some commentators have described U.S. policy as isolationist in the interwar era. What impact did this policy have on the Army in the interwar period, and how did this affect national security policy?

2. Interwar military policy emphasized maintaining force levels over procuring state-of-the-art equipment. Why did the War Department make that decision, and how ready was the Army for war in this period?

3. Describe the U.S. Army school system during the interwar period. What was its role, and how well did it perform that role? What was its impact on the Army?

4. During the late 1930s the United States began to rearm and eventually abandoned its policy of strict neutrality to support France and Great Britain. How did the President implement this policy shift? Could neutrality and a continued policy of defending only U.S. territory have served the nation's interests better than supporting the allies?

5. What roles, missions, and operations did the Army perform during the interwar period? How successful was the Army, and did these missions or operations enhance or detract from its ability to perform its wartime missions?

6. To what extent did the outbreak of European hostilities in 1939 find the Army operating with outdated doctrine or organizations? How did this compare with prior experience, especially from World War I? What lessons can we learn?

RECOMMENDED READINGS

Cline, Ray S. *Washington Command Post: The Operations Division*. U.S. Army in World War II. Washington, D.C.: Department of the Army, 1951, chs. 1–4.

Gabel, Christopher R. *The U.S. Army GHQ Maneuvers of 1941.* Washington, D.C.: U.S. Army Center of Military History, 1991.

Gole, Henry G. *The Road to Rainbow: Army Planning for Global War, 1934–1940.* Annapolis: Naval Institute Press, 2003.

Griffith, Robert K. *Men Wanted for the U.S. Army: America's Experience with an All-Volunteer Army between the World Wars.* Westport, Conn.: Greenwood Press, 1982.

Johnson, David E. *Fast Tanks and Heavy Bombers: Innovation in the U.S. Army, 1917–1945.* Ithaca, N.Y.: Cornell University Press, 1998.

Matloff, Maurice, and Edwin M. Snell. *Strategic Planning for Coalition Warfare, 1941–1942.* U.S. Army in World War II. Washington, D.C.: U.S. Army Center of Military History, 1999, chs. 1–4.

Murray, Williamson, and Allan R. Millett, eds. *Military Innovation in the Interwar Period.* Cambridge: Cambridge University Press, 1996, chs. 3–4, 7–10.

Winton, Harold R., and David R. Mets, eds. *The Challenge of Change: Military Institutions and New Realities, 1918–1941.* Lincoln: University of Nebraska Press, 2000, chs. 5–6.

Other Readings

Dallek, Robert. *Franklin Roosevelt and American Foreign Policy, 1932–1945.* New York: Oxford University Press, 1995.

English, John A., and Bruce I. Gudmundsson. *On Infantry,* rev. ed. Westport, Conn.: Praeger Publishing, 1994, ch. 3.

Huntington, Samuel P. *The Soldier and the State: The Theory and Politics of Civil-Military Relations.* Cambridge: Harvard University Press, 1957, ch. 11.

Hurley, Alfred F. *Billy Mitchell: Crusader for Air Power,* rev. ed. Bloomington: Indiana University Press, 1975.

Killigrew, John W. *The Impact of the Great Depression on the Army.* New York: Garland, 1979.

Kington, Donald M. *Forgotten Summers: The Story of the Citizen's Military Training Camps, 1921–1940.* San Francisco, Calif.: Two Decades Publishing, 1995.

Koistinen, Paul A. C. *Planning War, Pursuing Peace: The Political Economy of American Warfare, 1920–1939.* Lawrence: University Press of Kansas, 1998.

Kreidberg, Marvin A., and Merton G. Henry. *History of Military Mobilization in the United States Army, 1775–1945.* Westport, Conn.: Greenwood Press, 1975, chs. 12–15.

Lisio, Donald J. *The President and Protest: Hoover, MacArthur, and the Bonus Riot.* New York: Fordham University Press, 1994.

Maurer, Maurer. *Aviation in the U.S. Army, 1919–1939.* Washington, D.C.: U.S. Air Force, 1987.

Odom, William O. *After the Trenches: The Transformation of U.S. Army Doctrine, 1918–1939.* College Station: Texas A&M University Press, 1999.

3

WORLD WAR II
THE DEFENSIVE PHASE

The news came as a shock, even as the attack itself had come. About one o'clock in Washington on the afternoon of December 7, 1941, the first news of the Japanese attack on Pearl Harbor, Hawaii, reached the War Department. It caught by surprise not only the American people at large, who learned of the attack a short while later, but also their leaders, including the very officers who had earlier been so much concerned over the possibility of just such an attack. These officers and their political superiors had expected the Japanese momentarily to use all their forces against weakly held British and Dutch positions in the Far East (and probably, but not certainly, against the Philippines). But without warning in the early morning of December 7, powerful carrier-borne air forces had smashed the U.S. Pacific Fleet at anchor in Pearl Harbor. The same day, about noon on December 8 in the Philippines, the Japanese Air Force targeted U.S. assets in central Luzon. Formosa-based warplanes virtually destroyed the bulk of the U.S. Far East Air Force lined up on the Clark and Iba airfields not far from Manila. For the second time within a quarter-century, Americans found themselves fully involved in a war they had not sought and, although they had had ample warning, one for which they were still woefully unprepared.

The Outbreak of War: Action and Reaction

The Japanese attack on Pearl Harbor was one of the most brilliant tactical feats of the war. From six carriers that had advanced undetected to a position just 200 miles north of Oahu, some 350 aircraft came in through the morning mist, achieving complete tactical surprise. They bombed and strafed the neatly aligned Army planes on Hickam and Wheeler Fields, as well as Navy and Marine Corps aircraft; they carefully singled out as targets major units of the Navy's battle force at anchor in the harbor. Fortunately, the fleet's three carriers were away at the time

The sinking of the USS Arizona *came to symbolize the devastation of the attack and the American determination to avenge "a day that will live in infamy."*

and the attackers failed to hit the oil tanks and naval repair shops on shore. But the blow was devastating enough. About 170 aircraft were destroyed and 102 damaged; all eight battleships were sunk or badly damaged along with other vessels; and total casualties came to about 3,400, including 2,402 service men and civilians killed. Japanese losses were about forty-nine aircraft and five midget submarines. In an astonishing achievement, the enemy managed to apply in one shattering operation a combination of the principles of surprise, objective, mass, security, and maneuver. In its larger strategic context, the Pearl Harbor attack also exemplifies the principles of the offensive and economy of force. The joint congressional committee investigating the attack justly called it the "greatest military and naval disaster in our Nation's history."

These two attacks, on Pearl Harbor and on the Philippines, effectively crippled American striking power in the Pacific. The Philippines and other American possessions in the western Pacific were isolated, their loss a foregone conclusion. The Hawaiian Islands and Alaska lay open to invasion; the Panama Canal and the cities, factories, and shipyards of the West Coast were vulnerable to raids from the sea and air. Months would pass before the United States could regain a capacity for even the most limited kind of offensive action against its Pacific enemy. As Japanese forces moved swiftly southward against the Philippines, Malaya, and the Netherlands Indies, Japan's Axis partners, Germany and Italy, promptly declared war on the United States, thus ending the uncertainty as to whether the United States would become a full-fledged belligerent in the European war. For the first time in its history, the United States had embarked upon an all-out, two-front war.

Meanwhile, Britain was battling to maintain its hold on the eastern Mediterranean region that lay athwart its historic lifeline to its empire in the Far East. Late in 1940 small British forces based in Egypt gained important successes against Italian armies in Libya, and the Greeks in the winter of 1940–1941 resoundingly defeated an invading Italian army and chased it back into Albania. But German armies quickly came to the aid of their ally. In April 1941 the famous panzer divisions, supported by overwhelming air power, swept through the Balkans, crushing the Yugoslav and Greek armies and a British expeditionary force hastily dispatched to aid the latter. The following month German airborne forces descended on the island of Crete and swamped British and Greek defenders in a spectacular, though costly, attack. In Libya, a powerful German-Italian army under General Erwin Rommel drove the British back across the Egyptian border, isolating a large garrison in Tobruk and threatening the Nile Delta. Against these disasters Britain could count only the final expulsion of the Italians from the Red Sea area and of the Vichy French from Syria, the suppression of pro-German uprisings in Iraq, and the achievement of a precarious naval ascendancy in the eastern and western portions of the Mediterranean. During the remainder of 1941 the British gradually built up strength in eastern Libya, and late in the year they succeeded in relieving Tobruk and pushing Rommel back to his original starting point at El Agheila.

Since mid-1940 the military fortunes of the anti-Axis powers had declined as the European war expanded. Germany had crushed all its continental European opponents in the west and then attempted to destroy Britain's air forces as a prelude to an invasion across the English Channel. During the air battles over Britain in August and September 1940, the Royal Air Force had won a brilliant but close-run victory. During the following winter and spring the waning threat of invasion had been replaced by the equally deadly and more persistent menace of economic strangulation. German aircraft pulverized Britain's ports and inland cities, while U-boats, surface raiders, and mines decimated shipping. By 1941 the imports on which the United Kingdom depended for existence had dwindled to less than two-thirds of their prewar volume, and the British people faced the prospect of outright starvation.

By June 1941, however, the storm center of the war had moved elsewhere. Only slightly delayed by the conquest of the Balkans, Hitler on June 22, 1941, hurled German might against the Soviet Union, the only remaining power on the European continent capable of challenging his dominance. By early December, when the onset of winter and stiffening Soviet resistance finally brought the advance to a halt, the German armies had driven to the suburbs of Moscow, inflicted huge losses on the Red Army, and occupied a vast expanse of European Russia embracing its most densely populated and industrialized regions. This, as it turned out, was the high tide of German success in World War II; Hitler, like Napoleon, was to meet disaster on the wind-swept plains of Russia. But in December 1941 few were willing to predict this outcome. British and American leaders assembling in Washington at the end of that month to make plans for dealing with the crisis had to reckon with the probability that in the year to come, unless the Western Allies could somehow force Germany to divert substantial forces from the Eastern Front, the German steamroller would complete the destruction of the Soviet armies. Hitler would then be able, with the resources and enslaved peoples of all Europe at his feet, to throw his full power against the West.

American military leaders had already given thought to this grim prospect and to the implications it held for America's role in the war. In the Victory Program, which the Army and Navy drew up at the President's behest during the summer of 1941, the leaders of the two services had set forth in some detail the strategy and the means they considered necessary to win ultimate victory if, as they expected, Soviet Russia

A B–17C Aircraft at Hickam Air Force Base, Hawaii, After the Attack on Pearl Harbor

THE PERSIAN CORRIDOR

In order to ensure that the Soviet Union stayed in the war, the United States and Britain moved troops into Persia (present-day Iran) and established rail and road supply routes into the southern Soviet Union. Huge truck convoys delivered supplies and vehicles to the Soviets, but the majority of the materiel flowed in by train. Only the naval supply route through the Pacific to the Soviet Far East succeeded in delivering more to the Soviets. In third place was the sprint past the Germans in the North Atlantic and around Norway to Murmansk and Archangel. In all, American shipments of aircraft, tanks, trucks, oil, and other Lend-Lease cargo through Iraq and Iran from July 1941 to the end of the war were enough, according to one U.S. Army estimate, to keep sixty Soviet divisions in the fight.

succumbed to the Axis onslaught. The strategy was the one laid down in the RAINBOW 5 war plan: wearing Germany down by bombing, blockade, subversion, and limited offensives while mobilizing the strength needed to invade the European continent and to defeat Germany on its own ground. Japan, meanwhile, would be contained by air and sea power, local defense forces, China's inexhaustible manpower, and the Soviet Union's Siberian divisions. With Germany out of the running, Japan's defeat or collapse would soon follow.

As for the means, the United States would have to provide them in large part, for the British were already weary and their resources limited. The United States would serve not merely, to use the President's catchy phrase, as the "arsenal of democracy," supplying weapons to arm its Allies, but also as the main source of the armies without which no wars, above all this war, could be won. U.S. Army leaders envisaged the eventual mobilization of 215 divisions, 61 of them armored, and 239 combat air groups, requiring a grand total, with supporting forces, of 8.8 million men. Five million of these would be hurled against the European Axis. Victory over the Axis powers would require a maximum military effort and full mobilization of America's immense industrial resources.

Yet the Victory Program was merely an expression of professional military views, not a statement of national military policy. That policy, on the eve of Pearl Harbor, ostensibly was still hemisphere defense. Much of the Army's resources were focused on coastal artillery defenses and the establishment of air bases to defend the Panama Canal and the coasts of America. Much of America's plans and resources throughout the 1930s had focused on this mission and not on a mission of preparing for expeditionary warfare in Europe or the Pacific. The pace of rearmament and mobilization in the summer and fall of 1941 was actually slowing. Signs pointed to a policy of making the American contribution to the defeat of the Axis, as columnist Walter Lippmann put it, one "basically of Navy, Air, and manufacturing," something a great deal less than the all-out effort envisaged in the Victory Program. Public and congressional sentiment, moreover, still clung to the hope that an immediate showdown with the Axis powers could be avoided and that the country would not be forced into full belligerent participation in the war, as evidenced by a near defeat of the bill to extend Selective Service, continuation of a prohibition against sending selectees outside

Public and congressional sentiment, moreover, still clung to the hope that an immediate showdown with the Axis powers could be avoided and that the country would not be forced into full belligerent participation in the war.

the Western Hemisphere, and apathetic public response to submarine attacks on American destroyers escorting convoys to Britain in September and October.

The Japanese attack on Pearl Harbor and the Philippines changed the picture. A wave of patriotic indignation over Japanese duplicity and brutality swept the country. Isolationism virtually evaporated as a public issue, and all parties closed ranks in support of the war effort. Indeed, in retrospect, despite the immediate tactical success the Japanese achieved at Pearl Harbor, that attack proved to be a great blunder for them politically and strategically.

President Franklin D. Roosevelt took one of the first tangible steps toward equipping America to fight the new war the month after Pearl Harbor. Early in January he dramatized the magnitude of the effort now demanded by proclaiming a new set of production goals: 60,000 airplanes in 1942 and 125,000 in 1943; 45,000 tanks in 1942 and 75,000 in 1943; 20,000 antiaircraft guns in 1942 and 35,000 in 1943; 0.5 million machine guns in 1942 and as many more in 1943; and 8 million deadweight tons of merchant shipping in 1942 and 10 million in 1943. Vanished were the two illusions that America could serve only as an arsenal of democracy, contributing weapons without the men to wield them, or, conversely, that the nation could rely solely on its own fighting forces, leaving other anti-Axis nations to shift for themselves. "We must not only provide munitions for our own fighting forces," Roosevelt advised Secretary of War Henry L. Stimson, "but vast quantities to be used against the enemy in every appropriate theater of war." A new Victory Program boosted the Army's ultimate mobilization goal to 10 million men; and the War Department planned to have seventy-one divisions and 115 combat air groups organized by the end of 1942, with a total of 3.6 million men under arms. As an Army planner had predicted back in the spring of 1941, the United States now seemed destined to become "the final reserve of the democracies both in manpower and munitions."

Medium Tanks on an American Assembly Line

One of the more unpleasant side effects of the Japanese attack on Pearl Harbor was the growing clamor on the West Coast for the immediate internment of all persons of Japanese ancestry. In this public fear, racism doubtless played a role. The Japanese, even those born in America and thus citizens, were characterized as not being "real Americans" and of being a dangerous "fifth column" of potential spies and traitors. The fact that there was little to no evidence behind these fears did not seem to matter in the panic immediately after December 7.

The War Department had plans in place for the internment of all aliens of potentially belligerent states including Italy, Germany, and Japan. There were 40,869 Japanese aliens and about 58,000 Italian and 22,000 German aliens in the three Pacific states. In addition, there were 71,484 American-born, American citizens of Japanese ancestry in that region of the country. Initial plans thus only addressed the necessity of detaining aliens, not citizens, from the West Coast and removing them to the Zone of the Interior. During time of war this was a common practice under international law. Numerous Italian and German citizens living in America were also targeted for detention, and hundreds were arrested and interned for a time. Such a program of internment would ensure that there was no chance for such persons who technically were loyal to a foreign government to engage in sabotage or intelligence activities. The main controversy, however, was when this program was extended to U.S. citizens, specifically against U.S. citizens of Japanese ancestry.

The Army was to some degree caught in the middle of this problem. The commander of the Western Defense Command, Lt. Gen. John L. DeWitt, at first opposed any evacuation of U.S. citizens regardless of their ancestry. However, strong pressure from California congressional delegations and an approval of a more draconian evacuation plan by President Roosevelt changed the situation. By February 20 DeWitt and his staff had planned for the forced movement and internment of *all* people of Japanese ancestry, citizens and noncitizens, out of coastal "security" areas. Similar plans to include large numbers of German and Italian aliens in this internment program were in effect scuttled when the War Department decreed first that Italians would be evacuated only with the express permission of the Secretary of War and only on an individual basis. "Bona fide" German refugees would also be exempted. This had the effect of preventing any large-scale internment of Italian or German aliens, although some 187 Germans had been apprehended as security risks by early 1942.

After the President's Executive Order 9066 of February 19 and the implementing War Department directives of February 20,

President Roosevelt signs the declaration of war on Japan, December 8, 1941.

the mass evacuation of persons of Japanese ancestry—citizens and noncitizens—began. The Army, FBI, and other agencies coordinated the evacuation. Despite the lack of any hard evidence of spying activities or intention to commit sabotage, over 110,000 Japanese Americans were rounded up and interned in camps ("Relocation Centers") away from the Pacific coast. What little justification was possible for interning noncitizens was not available for interning native-born American citizens, and the program was attacked both at the time and for decades thereafter. It was not until 1988 that this injustice was officially addressed and compensation provided for those who suffered this indignity.

The degree to which such draconian measures were unnecessary can be highlighted by how the military and civilian leadership in Hawaii handled their Japanese American "problem." There were over 159,000 Japanese Americans in Hawaii, about 30 percent of the population, and military commanders had feared extensive sabotage by these individuals in the event of war with Japan. On December 7 the Air Corps planes at Hickam Field were parked wing tip to wing tip to keep them close together and make them easier to protect from sabotage. (This made them sitting ducks for the Japanese bombers.)

Immediately after December 7 American counterintelligence and FBI agents rounded up 736 individual Japanese aliens; by the end of January 1942 that total had reached about 1,300. Yet no massive internment of Japanese American citizens was seriously contemplated or executed. They were deemed vital to the war effort, and military necessity in this instance overrode all concerns. The results of this very different policy in Hawaii led Japanese Americans to flock to the colors to form labor battalions and infantry units. Two of the most decorated units in the American Army in World War II were the 100th Infantry Battalion and the 442d Infantry Regimental Combat Team, both recruited from Japanese Americans. Nineteen individuals in these units were awarded the nation's highest decoration, the Medal of Honor, in 2000 as a belated recognition of their loyalty and bravery.

Strategic Decisions

Late in December 1941 President Roosevelt and Prime Minister Winston Churchill met with their advisers in Washington (the ARCADIA Conference) to establish the bases of coalition strategy and to concert immediate measures to meet the military crisis. They faced an agonizing dilemma. Prompt steps had to be taken to stem the spreading tide of Japanese conquest. On the other hand, it seemed likely that the coming year might see the collapse of Soviet resistance and of the British position in the Middle East. In this difficult situation the Allied leaders made a far-reaching decision that shaped the whole course of the war. Reaffirming the principle laid down in Anglo-American staff conversations in Washington ten months earlier, they agreed that the first and main effort must go into defeating Germany, the more formidable enemy. Japan's turn would come later. Defeating Germany would involve a prolonged process of "closing and tightening the ring" about Fortress Europe. Operations in 1942 would have to be defensive and preparatory, though limited offensives might be undertaken if the opportunity presented itself. Not until 1943 at the earliest could the Allies contemplate a return

GERMANY FIRST

At the December 1941 Arcadia Conference in Washington, Britain and the United States agreed to put the war in the Pacific second to victory in Europe—even if that meant a U.S. withdrawal from the Philippines and its other possessions in the Pacific. Admiral Harold R. Stark, Chief of Naval Operations in 1940, had argued when contemplating such an eventuality, "If Britain wins decisively against Germany we could win everywhere, but ... if she loses, the problems confronting us would be very great; ... we might, possibly, not *win* anywhere." This policy was not popular with the many Americans thirsting for revenge against the Japanese for Pearl Harbor, but it was realistic. As U.S. Commander in the Southwest Pacific, General MacArthur would also argue vehemently against the approach; but it remained U.S. policy until Germany surrendered in 1945.

Churchill and Roosevelt at the Arcadia Conference, 1941

to the European continent "across the Mediterranean, from Turkey into the Balkans, or by landings in Western Europe."

Another important action taken at the Arcadia Conference was the establishment of the Combined Chiefs of Staff (CCS). This staff element consisted of the professional military chiefs of both countries and answered to the President and Prime Minister for planning and directing the grand strategy of the coalition. Its American members were the Army Chief of Staff, General George C. Marshall; the Chief of Naval Operations, Admiral Harold R. Stark (replaced early in 1942 by Admiral Ernest J. King); and the Chief (later Commanding General) of the Army Air Forces, Lt. Gen. Henry H. "Hap" Arnold. In July a fourth member was added, the President's personal Chief of Staff, Admiral William D. Leahy. Since the CCS normally sat in Washington, the British Chiefs of Staff, making up its British component, attended in person only at important conferences with the heads of state. In the intervals they were represented in Washington by the four senior members of the permanent British Joint Staff Mission, headed until late in 1944 by Field Marshal Sir John Dill, the former Chief of the British Imperial General Staff. Under the CCS grew a system of primarily military subordinate committees specifically designated to handle such matters as strategic and logistical planning, transportation, and communications.

By February 1942 the Joint Chiefs of Staff (JCS), consisting of the U.S. members of the CCS, had emerged as the highest authority in the U.S. military hierarchy, though never formally chartered as such, responsible directly to the President. Like the CCS, the JCS in time developed a machinery of planning and working committees, the most important of which were the Joint Staff Planners, the Joint Strategic Survey Committee, and the Joint Logistics Committee. No executive machinery was created at either the CCS or JCS level. The CCS ordinarily named either the British Chiefs or the U.S. Joint Chiefs to act as its executive agent, and these in turn employed the established machinery of the service departments.

In the spring of 1942 Britain and the United States agreed on a worldwide division of strategic responsibility. The U.S. Joint Chiefs of Staff were to have primary responsibility for the war in the Pacific and the British Chiefs for the Middle East–Indian Ocean region, while the European-Mediterranean-Atlantic area would be a combined responsibility of both staffs. China was designated a separate theater commanded by its chief of state, Generalissimo Chiang Kai-shek, though within the United States' sphere of responsibility. In the Pacific, the Joint Chiefs established two main theaters, the Southwest Pacific Area (SWPA) and the Pacific Ocean Area (POA), the former under General Douglas MacArthur, the latter under Admiral Chester W. Nimitz. The POA was further subdivided into North, Central, and South Pacific areas,

Generalissimo and Madame Chiang Kai-shek with General Stilwell

the first two directly controlled by Nimitz, the third by Rear Adm. Robert L. Ghormley. Later in 1942 the U.S. air and service troops operating in China, India, and northern Burma were organized as U.S. Army Forces, China-Burma-India (CBI), under Lt. Gen. Joseph W. Stilwell. On various other far-flung lines of communications, U.S. Army forces, mostly air and service troops during 1942, were organized under similar theater commands. In June Maj. Gen. Dwight D. Eisenhower arrived in England to take command of the newly established European Theater of Operations; after the landings in North Africa late in the year, a new U.S. theater was organized in that region.

The British and the Americans had decided at the ARCADIA Conference that Allied forces in each overseas theater would operate as much as possible under a single commander, and this principle was subsequently applied in most theaters. Within theaters, subordinate unified commands were created, in some cases for Allied ground, naval, or air forces and most frequently for task forces formed to carry out a specific operation or campaign. The authority of Allied theater commanders over national forces was always restricted with respect to areas and missions; as a last resort, senior national commanders in each theater could appeal to their own governments against specific orders or policies of the theater commander. In practice, this right of appeal was rarely invoked.

In essence, unified command at the Allied level gave the commander control of certain specific forces for operational purposes, rather than jurisdiction over a given geographical area. Administration of national forces and the allocation of resources were usually handled through separate national channels. In certain cases, interallied boards or committees responsible to the Allied theater commander controlled the common use of critical resources (such as petroleum products) or facilities (such as railways and shipping) within a theater. Administration of U.S. forces overseas also generally followed separate Army and Navy channels, except in the Pacific, where from 1943 on supply, transportation, and certain other services were jointly administered to a limited degree.

Even before Pearl Harbor, Army leaders had realized that the peacetime organization of the War Department General Staff, dating back to 1921, was an inadequate instrument for directing a major war effort. Originally, a small coordinating and planning body, the General Staff, and especially its War Plans and Supply Divisions, rapidly expanded during the emergency period into a large operating organization increasingly immersed in the details of supervision to the detriment of its planning and policymaking functions. The Chief of Staff, to whom some sixty-one officers and agencies had direct access, carried an especially heavy burden.

Three additional features of the organization demanded remedy. One, the continued subordination of the Army Air Forces to General Staff supervision, conflicted with the Air Forces' drive for autonomy. Another was the anomalous position of the General Headquarters (GHQ), whose role as command post for the field forces and responsibilities in the fields of training and logistics clashed with the authority of the General Staff at many points. Finally, the division of supply responsibilities between the Supply Division (G–4) and the Office of the Under Secretary of War (with requirements and distribution assigned to the former and procurement to the latter) was breaking down under the pressure of mobilization.

Spurred by the Pearl Harbor disaster, which seemed to accentuate the need for better staff coordination in Washington, on March 9, 1942, General Marshall put into effect a sweeping reorganization of the War Department. Under the new plan, which underwent little change during the war years, the General Staff, except for the War Plans and Intelligence Divisions, was drastically whittled down and limited in function to broad planning and policy guidance. An expanded War Plans Division, soon renamed the Operations Division (OPD), became General Marshall's command post and in effect a superior general staff for the direction of overseas operations. The Army Air Forces had virtually complete control of the development of its special weapon—the airplane. Administering its own personnel and training, it organized and supported the combat air forces to be employed in theaters of operations and came also to exercise considerable influence over both strategic and operational planning. The groundwork was even then being laid for the Army Air Forces' rise to the status of a separate service after the war.

The reorganization of March 9 created two new commands: the Army Ground Forces (AGF) and the Services of Supply, later renamed the Army Service Forces (ASF). The former, headed by Lt. Gen. Lesley J. McNair, took over the training mission of GHQ, now abolished, and absorbed the ground combat arms. To the ASF, commanded by Lt. Gen. Brehon B. Somervell, were subordinated the supply (renamed technical) and administrative services, the nine corps areas, and most of the Army posts and installations throughout the United States, including the ports of embarkation through which troops and supplies flowed to the forces overseas. In supply matters, Somervell now reported to two masters, the

LESLEY J. MCNAIR
(1883–1944)

McNair built a strong reputation as a trainer during World War I and became a close friend of Col. George C. Marshall, Jr. During World War II, General Marshall made him the chief trainer of the U.S. Army, first as Chief of Staff of General Headquarters (1940–1942) and then as Commanding General of the Army Ground Forces (1942–1944). McNair oversaw the development of a systematic training and testing program for the ninety divisions that the Army mobilized during the war. He was killed by a misdirected American bomb while observing operations near St. Lô, France, on July 25, 1944.

General McNair (left) *and Maj. Gen. George S. Patton, Jr., Studying a Map*

Chief of Staff for requirements and distribution and the Under Secretary of War, Mr. Robert P. Patterson, for procurement. His subordination to the latter was, in reality, only nominal since most of Patterson's organization was transferred bodily to Somervell's headquarters. Except for equipment peculiar to the Army Air Forces, the ASF thus became the Army's central agency for supply in the United States. It drew up the Army's "shopping list" of requirements, the Army Supply Program. Through the seven technical services (Quartermaster, Ordnance, Signal, Chemical, Engineer, Medical, and Transportation), the ASF procured most of the Army's supplies and equipment and distributed these materials to the Army at home and abroad, as well as to Allies under Lend-Lease. Finally, it operated the Army's fleet of transports and it trained specialists and service units to perform various specialized jobs. General Somervell himself became General Marshall's principal logistical adviser.

All this looked to the future. In the first few weeks after Pearl Harbor, while the Navy was salvaging what it could from the wreckage at Pearl Harbor and striving to combat German submarines in the western Atlantic, the War Department made desperate efforts to bolster the defenses of Hawaii, the Philippines, the Panama Canal, Alaska, and the U.S. West Coast. By the end of December, the danger of an attack on the Hawaii-Alaska-Panama triangle seemed to have waned, and the emphasis shifted to measures to stave off further disasters in the Far East. The British and Americans decided at ARCADIA that the Allies would attempt to hold the Japanese north and east of the line of the Malay Peninsula and the Netherlands Indies and to reestablish communications with the Philippines to the north. To coordinate operations in this vast theater, the Allied leaders created the ABDA (American-British-Dutch-Australian) Command, including the Netherlands Indies (present-day Indonesia), Malaya, Burma, and the Philippines; although

General Brehon B. Somervell
(1892–1955)

Somervell was a hard-driving engineer officer who made things happen. Heading the huge federal Works Progress Administration in New York City during the Great Depression, he orchestrated the construction of La Guardia Airport. As the Army expanded in the year before Pearl Harbor, he reorganized the Quartermaster Corps' Construction Division to meet the urgent need for new facilities. Somervell took command in March 1942 of what would become the Army Service Forces, an organization of more than 2 million soldiers and civilians. An innovative, decisive, and tough manager, Somervell directed the massive supply operations that were crucial to Allied victory.

in the latter case MacArthur continued reporting directly to Washington. British Lt. Gen. Sir Archibald P. Wavell was placed in overall command of ABDA. Through India from the west and Australia from the east, the Allies hoped in a short time to build up a shield of air power stout enough to blunt the Japanese threat.

For a time it seemed as though nothing could stop the Japanese juggernaut. In less than three weeks after Pearl Harbor, the isolated American outposts of Wake Island and Guam fell to the invaders; the British garrison of Hong Kong was overwhelmed; and powerful land, sea, and air forces were converging on Malaya and the Netherlands Indies. Picked, jungle-trained Japanese troops drove down the Malay Peninsula toward the great fortress of Singapore, infiltrating and outflanking successive British positions. Two of the most formidable warships in the British Navy, the battleship *Prince of Wales* and the battle cruiser *Repulse*, sailing without air cover, were sunk by Japanese torpedo planes off the east coast of Malaya, a loss that destroyed the Allies' last hope of effectively opposing Japan's naval power in the Far East. Attacked from the land side, Singapore and its British force of over 80,000 troops surrendered on February 15, 1942, in the greatest single defeat in British history.

Meanwhile, the Japanese had invaded the Netherlands Indies from the north, west, and east. In a series of actions during January and February, the weak Dutch and Australian naval forces, joined by the U.S. Asiatic Fleet withdrawing from the Philippines, were destroyed piecemeal; only four American destroyers escaped south to Australia. On March 9 the last Allied ground and air forces in the Netherlands Indies, almost 100,000 men (mostly native troops, but including one U.S. National Guard field artillery battalion on Java) surrendered to the invaders.

In Burma, the day before, the British had been forced under heavy bombing to evacuate Rangoon and retreat northward. Before the end of April the Japanese had completed the occupation of Burma, driving the British westward into India and the bulk of General Stilwell's Chinese forces back into China. Stilwell and the remnants of other

Chinese units retreated to India, where, living up to his nickname of Vinegar Joe, he announced to the world that his units had taken "a hell of a beating." In the process the Japanese had won possession of a huge section of the Burma Road, the only viable land route between China and India. Henceforth and until late in the war, communication between China and its allies was to be limited to an air ferry from India over the "hump" of the Himalayan Mountains. During the late spring strong Japanese naval forces reached the coastal cities of India and even attacked Britain's naval base on Ceylon.

By the end of April 1942 the Japanese had thus gained control of Burma, Malaya, Thailand, French Indochina, the Netherlands Indies, and the Malay Archipelago; farther to the east, they had won strong lodgments on the islands of New Guinea, New Britain, and in the Solomons.

An Army B–25 takes off from the USS Hornet *to participate in the Doolittle Raid on Japan, April 1942.*

They were in a position to flank the approaches to Australia and New Zealand and cut them off from the United States. The Japanese had won this immense empire at remarkably little cost through an effective combination of superior air and sea power and only a handful of well-trained ground divisions. The Japanese had seized and held the initiative while keeping their opponents off balance. They had concentrated their strength for the capture of key objectives such as airfields and road junctions and for the destruction of major enemy forces, while diverting only minimum forces on secondary missions, thus giving an impression of overwhelming numerical strength. They had frequently gained the advantage of surprise and had baffled their enemies by their speed and skill in maneuver. The whole whirlwind campaign, in short, had provided Japan's enemies with a capsule course of instruction in the principles of war. The Americans were able to launch only a few carrier and submarine attacks on the Japanese, including the Doolittle bomber raid on Tokyo on April 18. These operations, while having a major impact on American morale, were militarily insignificant and failed to slow the Japanese. Only the stubborn defense of the Philippines had significantly disrupted Japanese plans.

The Fall of the Philippines

Only in the Philippines, almost on Japan's southern doorstep, was the timetable of conquest delayed. When the Japanese struck, the defending forces in the islands numbered more than 130,000, including the Philippine Army, which, though mobilized to a strength of ten divisions, was ill trained and ill equipped. Of the U.S. Army contingent of 31,000, more than a third consisted of the Philippine Scouts, most of whom were part of the Regular Army Philippine Division, the core of the mobile defense forces. The Far East Air Force before the Japanese attack had a total of 277 aircraft of all types, mostly obsolescent but including 35 new heavy bombers. The Asiatic Fleet, based in the Philippines, consisted of 3 cruisers, 13 old destroyers, 6 gunboats, 6 motor torpedo boats, 32 patrol bombers, and 29 submarines. A regiment of marines, withdrawn from Shanghai, also joined the defending forces late in November 1941. Before the end of December, however, American air and naval power in the Philippines had virtually ceased to exist. The handful of bombers surviving the early attacks had been evacuated to Australia; the bulk of the Asiatic Fleet, its base facilities in ruins, had withdrawn southward to help in the defense of the Netherlands Indies.

The main Japanese invasion of the Philippines, following preliminary landings, began on December 22, 1941. While numerically inferior to the defenders, the invading force of two divisions with supporting units was well trained and equipped and enjoyed complete mastery of the air and on the sea. The attack centered on Luzon, the northernmost and largest island of the archipelago, where all but a small fraction of the defending forces was concentrated. The main landings were made on the beaches of Lingayen Gulf in the northwest and Lamon Bay in the southeast. General MacArthur planned to meet and destroy the invaders on the beaches, but his troops were unable to prevent the enemy from gaining secure lodgments. On December 23 MacArthur ordered a general withdrawal into the mountainous Bataan Peninsula, across Manila Bay from the capital city. Manila itself was occupied by the Japanese without resistance. The retreat into Bataan was a complex operation, involving converging movements over difficult terrain into a cramped assembly area from which only two roads led into the peninsula itself. Under constant enemy attack, the maneuver was executed with consummate skill and at considerable cost to the attackers. Yet American and Filipino losses were heavy, and MacArthur's ill-advised abandonment of large stocks of supplies foredoomed the defenders of Bataan to ultimate defeat in the siege that followed.

By January 7, 1942, General MacArthur's forces held hastily prepared defensive positions across the upper part of the Bataan Peninsula. Their presence there and on Corregidor and its satellite island fortresses guarding the entrance to Manila Bay denied the enemy the use of the bay throughout the siege. In the first major enemy offensive, launched early in January, the "battling bastards of Bataan" were outflanked and forced to give ground back to a final line halfway down the peninsula. Thereafter combat operations paused until April while the Japanese brought in reinforcements. The defenders of Bataan were, however, too weak to seize the initiative themselves.

General Wainwright broadcasts surrender instructions to U.S. forces in the Philippines.

BATAAN AND CORREGIDOR

One day after the Japanese landings in Lingayen Gulf and Lamon Bay on December 23, 1941, General MacArthur decided he would have to fall back to the Bataan Peninsula and fight a delaying action there until a relief force from the United States arrived in the Philippines. Two corps of the Philippine Army, including seven Filipino infantry divisions, two regiments of Filipino Scouts, and a regiment of U.S. Infantry, defended Bataan against furious assaults launched by elements of the Japanese 14th Army. The attackers, possessing a tremendous superiority in air power, artillery, and armor, finally forced the Americans and Filipinos to surrender on April 9, 1942. The remaining American bastion in the Philippines, the heavily fortified island of Corregidor in Manila Bay, succumbed after a 25-day-long intensive aerial

Surrender of U.S. Troops at Corregidor, May 1942

and artillery preparatory barrage followed by an amphibious assault by the Japanese 4th Infantry Division on May 4–5. Corregidor remained in enemy hands until the American 11th Airborne Division liberated the island in February 1945.

Meanwhile, the President ordered General MacArthur to leave his post and go to Australia to take command of Allied operations against the Japanese in the Southwest Pacific. In mid-March he and a small party made their way through the Japanese lines by motor torpedo boat to Mindanao and from there flew to Australia. Command of the forces in the Philippines devolved upon Lt. Gen. Jonathan M. Wainwright.

By April the troops on Bataan were subsisting on about fifteen ounces of food daily, less than a quarter of the peacetime ration. Their diet, mostly rice supplemented by carabao, mule, monkey, or lizard meat, was gravely deficient in vitamins and provided less than 1,000 calories a day, barely enough to sustain life. Weakened by hunger and poor diet, thousands succumbed to malaria, dengue, scurvy, beriberi, and amoebic dysentery, made impossible to control by the shortage of medical supplies, especially quinine. The U.S. Navy made desperate efforts to send food, medicine, ammunition, and other supplies through the Japanese blockade to the beleaguered forces. But during the early weeks, before the enemy cordon had tightened, it proved impossible, despite promises of lavish pay and bonuses, to

The Chaplain in World War II, *Ken Riley, 1975*

Prisoners of War Forced To Participate in the Infamous Bataan Death March from Bataan to Cabanatuan

muster the necessary ships and crews. Only about 4,000 tons of rations ever reached Manila Bay.

At the beginning of April the Japanese, behind a pulverizing artillery barrage, attacked again. The American lines crumpled, and in a few days the defending forces virtually disintegrated. On April 9 Maj. Gen. Edward P. King, Jr., commanding the forces on Bataan, surrendered. For almost another month the garrison on Corregidor, including some 2,000 refugees who reached the island from Bataan when forces there surrendered, held out under air bombardment and almost continuous plunging fire from heavy artillery massed on adjacent shores and heights—one of the most intense artillery bombardments, for so small a target, of the entire war. On the night of May 5, after a final terrible barrage, Japanese assault troops won a foothold on Corregidor; the following night, when it became apparent that further resistance was useless, General Wainwright surrendered unconditionally. Under his orders, which the Japanese forced him to broadcast, other American commanders in the Philippines capitulated one by one. By early June, except for scattered guerrilla detachments in the hills, some composed of American officers and men who disobeyed the surrender order, all organized resistance on the islands had ceased.

THE VICTORY PLAN

In May 1941 the United States lacked an up-to-date plan for its potential requirements if it were involved in a war in Europe. Maj. Albert C. Wedemeyer, a planner on the War Department General Staff, was assigned to develop a plan within ninety days—an extremely difficult task, since lack of a national consensus on the war had precluded firm strategic guidance from civilian authorities. Wedemeyer, thoroughly prepared by extensive strategic reading and attendance at the German *Kriegsakademie*, determined that the United States would be fighting a two-front war with Germany and Japan and required mechanized and armored forces with a powerful air arm to defeat the enemy. Although slightly overestimating the size and structure of the required land force, his projected Army of 8.7 million troops was presciently close to the actual peak strength of 8.1 million. Wedemeyer's plan (often called the Victory Plan or Victory Program), a wise and essential meshing of politico-military considerations, was used to guide the nation in a war only months away.

Deploying American Military Strength

After more than a year and a half of rearming, the United States in December 1941 was still in no position to carry the war to its enemies. On December 7 the Army numbered some 1,644,000 men (including about 120,000 officers), organized into 4 armies, 37 divisions (30 infantry, 5 armored, 2 cavalry), and over 40 combat air groups. Three of the divisions were overseas (2 in Hawaii, 1 in the Philippines), with other garrison forces totaling fewer than 200,000. By spreading equipment and ammunition thin, the War Department might have put a substantial force into the field to repel an attack on the Continental United States. Seventeen of the divisions at home were rated as technically ready for combat but lacked the supporting units and the training necessary to weld them into corps and armies. More serious still, they were inadequately equipped with many weapons that recent operations in Europe had proven indispensable (e.g., tank and antitank guns, antiaircraft artillery, radios, and radar); and some of these shortages were aggravated by lack of auxiliary equipment like fire-control mechanisms.

Above all, ammunition of all kinds was so scarce that the War Department was unwilling to commit more than one division and a single antiaircraft regiment for service in any theater where combat operations seemed imminent. In fact, only one division-size task force was sent to the far Pacific before April 1942. Against air attacks, too, the country's defenses were meager. Along the Pacific coast, the Army had only forty-five modern fighter planes ready to fly and only twelve 3-inch antiaircraft guns to defend the whole Los Angeles area. On the East Coast, there were only fifty-four Army fighter planes ready for action. While the coastal air forces, primarily training commands, could be reinforced by airlift, in the interior of the country, the total number of modern fighter aircraft available was less than 1,000. Fortunately, there was no real threat of an invasion in force, and the rapidly expanding output of munitions from American factories promised to remedy some of these weaknesses within a few months. Furthermore, temporary diversions of Lend-Lease equipment, especially aircraft, helped to bolster the overall defense posture within the first few weeks after Pearl Harbor. The Army hoped by April to have as many as thirteen divisions equipped and supplied with ammunition for combat.

The training of combat-ready divisions was also slowed by the nation's fears about internal security, homeland defense, and factory sabotage. After Pearl Harbor, legitimate concerns about such matters ballooned into a near panic. After the Japanese attack the War Department implemented its plans for continental defense. The President and the Army Chief of Staff quickly assigned nineteen of the thirty-four divisions then undergoing training to the Eastern and Western Defense Commands. Those commands dispersed units to patrol the coastline and guard key defense plants, bridges, and dams. In doing so, these units were removed from their training programs for months.

As the continental defense assignments dragged on with no signs of invasion or sabotage, General McNair, head of Army Ground Forces, argued for returning ground tactical units to their training cycles to prepare them for deployment overseas. When Army Chief of Staff General Marshall undertook the comprehensive War Department reorganization in March 1942, he approved McNair's recommendation and returned most ground forces to training missions under Army Ground Forces command. However, many units suffered from a four-to-six-month interruption of their training due to this diversion. Homeland security and preparations for taking the war to the enemy always pull the nation's leaders in two different directions.

Once the divisions were ready to deploy, U.S. planners faced another dilemma. Although the U.S. Merchant Marine ranked second only to Great Britain's and the country possessed an immense shipbuilding capacity, the process of chartering, assembling, and preparing shipping for the movement of troops and military cargo took time. Time was also needed to schedule and organize convoys; and, owing to the desperate shortage of escort vessels, troop movements had to be widely spaced. Convoying and evasive routing greatly reduced the effective capacity of shipping. Moreover, vast distances separated U.S. ports from the areas threatened by Japan, and to these areas went the bulk of the forces deployed overseas during the months immediately following Pearl Harbor. Through March 1942, as a result, the outflow of troops to overseas bases averaged only about 50,000 per month, as compared with upwards of 250,000 during 1944, when shipping was fully mobilized and plentiful and the sea lanes were secure.

There seemed a real danger early in 1942, however, that German U-boats might succeed in reducing transatlantic deployment to a trickle—not so much by attacking troop transports, most of which could outrun their attackers, as by sinking the slow cargo ships upon which the forces overseas depended for support. Soon after Germany's declaration of war, the U-boats struck at the virtually unprotected shipping lanes in the western Atlantic and subsequently extended their attacks to the Gulf of Mexico and Caribbean areas and the mouth of the St. Lawrence. During the spring of 1942 tankers and freighters were torpedoed in plain view of vacationers on East Coast beaches, and coastal cities dimmed or extinguished their lights that ships might not provide silhouetted targets for the U-boats. The Navy lacked the

Homeland security and preparations for taking the war to the enemy always pull the nation's leaders in two different directions.

means to cope with the peril. In late December 1941 it had only twenty assorted surface vessels and about a hundred aircraft to protect the whole North Atlantic coastal frontier. During the winter and spring these were supplemented by another hundred Army planes of longer range, several armed British trawlers, and as many improvised craft as could be pressed into service.

But the toll of ship sinkings increased. In March 788,000 dead-weight tons of Allied and neutral dry cargo shipping were lost, in June 936,000 tons. Tanker losses reached an all-time peak of 375,000 tons in March, which led to a temporary suspension of coastal tanker movements and to gasoline rationing in the seaboard states. During the first six months of 1942, losses of Allied shipping were almost as heavy as during the whole of 1941 and exceeded new construction by almost 2.8 million deadweight tons. The United States was able by May to balance its own current losses by building new ships; Britain and other Allied countries continued until the following August to lose more than they could build, and another year passed before new construction offset cumulative losses.

Slowly and with many setbacks a system of countermeasures was developed. Convoying of coastal shipping, with ships sailing only by day, began in the spring of 1942. North-south traffic between U.S. and Caribbean and South American ports was also convoyed, on schedules interlocked with those of the transatlantic convoys. The latter, during 1942, were protected in the western half of the Atlantic by the U.S. and Canadian Navies, in the eastern half by the British. Troops were transported across the Atlantic either without escort in large, speedy liners like the *Queen Elizabeth* and the *Queen Mary* (between them, they carried almost a quarter of all U.S. troops sent to Europe) or in heavily escorted convoys. Throughout the war, not a single loaded troop transport was sunk on the United Kingdom run. The slow merchant ships were convoyed in large groups according to speed.

But with responsibility for U.S. antisubmarine operations divided between the Navy and Army Air Forces, effective cooperation was hampered by sharp disagreement over organization and methods and available resources throughout 1942 were inadequate. The U-boats, meanwhile, were operating with deadly effect and in growing numbers. Late in the year they began to hunt in packs, resupplied at sea by large cargo submarines ("milch cows"). The Allied convoys to Murmansk and other northern Soviet ports suffered especially heavy losses on their long passage around the top of the Scandinavian Peninsula. In November shipping losses from all causes soared above 1.1 million deadweight tons—the peak, as it turned out, for the entire war, but few at the time dared so to predict.

In the Pacific, fortunately, the principal barriers to deployment of U.S. forces were distance and lack of prepared bases, not enemy submarines. Japan's fleet of undersea craft made little effort to prey on the Allied sea lanes and probably over the vast reaches of the Pacific could not have inflicted serious damage in any case. The chief goal of American deployment to the Pacific during most of 1942, following the initial reinforcement of Hawaii and the Panama Canal, was to build up a base in Australia and secure the chain of islands leading to it. Australia was a vast, thinly populated and, except in its southeastern portion, a largely undeveloped island continent, 7,000 miles and almost a month's sail from the U.S. West Coast. It had provided a haven for some 4,000 American troops who on December 7 had been at sea bound for the Philippines. In January a task force of division size (POPPY Force) was hastily assembled and dispatched to New Caledonia to guard its eastern approaches. During the first few weeks the main effort of the small American forces went into sending relief supplies to the Philippines and aircraft and troops to Java to stem the Japanese invasion. Beginning in March, as the futility of these efforts became evident and coincident with the arrival of General MacArthur to assume command of all Allied forces in the Southwest Pacific, the construction of base facilities and the buildup of balanced air and ground forces got under way in earnest.

This buildup had as its first object the defense of Australia itself, for at the end of January the Japanese had occupied Rabaul on New Britain Island, thus posing an immediate threat to Port Moresby, the weakly held Australian base in southeastern New Guinea. In February President Roosevelt pledged American help in countering this threat, and in March and April two infantry divisions (the 41st and 32d) left the United States for the Southwest Pacific. At the same time, construction of air and refueling bases was being rushed to completion in the South Pacific islands that formed steppingstones along the ocean routes to Australia and New Zealand. After the western anchor of this chain, New Caledonia, was secured by the POPPY Force, Army and Marine garrisons and reinforcements were sent to various other islands along the line, culminating with the arrival of the 37th Division in the Fiji Islands in June.

These moves came none too soon: during the spring and summer the Japanese, after occupying Rabaul, pushed into the southern Solomons, within easy striking distance of the American bases on Espíritu Santo and New Caledonia. They also sent forces to establish bases along the northeastern coast of New Guinea, just across the narrow Papuan peninsula from Port Moresby, which the Americans and Australians were developing into a major advanced base in preparation for an eventual offensive northward. The stage was thus set for a major test of strength in the Pacific: American forces were spread thinly along an immense arc from Hawaii to Australia with outposts far to the north in Alaska; the Japanese had secured the vast areas north and west of the arc and with the advantage of interior lines could strike in force at any point.

The first test came in May, when the Japanese made an attempt from the sea to take Port Moresby. This was successfully countered in the carrier battle of the Coral Sea. Thereupon the Japanese struck eastward, hoping to destroy the U.S. Pacific Fleet and to seize Midway in a bid for naval supremacy in the Pacific. A diversionary attack on Dutch Harbor, the most forward U.S. base in Alaska, caused considerable damage; and the Japanese were able to occupy the islands of Kiska and Attu in the foggy Aleutian chain. But the main Japanese forces, far to the south, were crushingly defeated, with especially heavy losses in irreplaceable carriers, aircraft, and trained pilots. The Battle of Midway in June 1942 was one of the truly decisive engagements of the war. By seriously weakening Japan's mobile striking forces, Midway left the Japanese virtually helpless to prevent the consolidation of American

Midway left the Japanese virtually helpless to prevent the consolidation of American positions and the eventual development of overwhelming military supremacy throughout the Pacific.

positions and the eventual development of overwhelming military supremacy throughout the Pacific. Only two months later, in fact, American forces took the first step on the long "road back" by landing on Guadalcanal in the southern Solomons.

Although the RAINBOW 5 plan was put into effect immediately after Pearl Harbor, the desperate situation in the Pacific and Far East and the shortage of shipping and escorts ruled out most of the scheduled Atlantic, Caribbean, and South American deployments. In January reinforcements were sent to Iceland and a token force to Northern Ireland. By June two full divisions (the 34th Infantry and the 1st Armored) had reached Ireland, while the remainder of the 5th Infantry had arrived in Iceland, completing the relief of the U.S. Marine brigade and most of the British garrison on that island. No more divisions sailed eastward until August. Meanwhile, garrisons in the Atlantic and the Caribbean were building up to war strength. But plans to occupy the Azores, the Canaries, and Cape Verdes and to capture Dakar on the west African coast went by the board, primarily for lack of shipping. Also abandoned after lengthy discussion was Project GYMNAST, which Prime Minister Churchill had proposed at the ARCADIA Conference, for an Anglo-American occupation of French North Africa.

Thus, despite the reaffirmation of the "Germany first" strategy at ARCADIA, the great bulk of American forces sent overseas during the first half of 1942 went to the theaters of war against Japan. Of the eight Army divisions that left the country before August, five went to the Pacific. Including two more already in Hawaii and a Marine division at sea bound for New Zealand (eventually for the landings on Guadalcanal in August), eight divisions were deployed against Japan in July 1942. Of the approximately 520,000 Army troops in overseas bases, 60 percent was in the Pacific (including Alaska) and the newly established China-Burma-India Theater; the remainder was almost entirely in Caribbean and western Atlantic garrisons. Of 2,200 Army aircraft overseas, about 1,300 were in the Pacific (including Alaska) and the Far East, 900 in the western Atlantic and Latin America. Not until August did the U.S. Army Air Forces in the British Isles attain sufficient strength to fly a single independent bombing mission over northern France.

Planning for a Cross-Channel Invasion

The Army's leaders and planners, schooled in a tradition that emphasized the principles of mass and offensive, had been fretting over the scale of deployment to the Pacific since early in the year. Late in January, then Brig. Gen. Dwight D. Eisenhower, a War Department staff officer whom General Marshall had assigned to handle the crisis in the Pacific, noted, "We've got to go to Europe and fight—and we've got to quit wasting resources all over the world." In the joint committees Army planners urged that as soon as the situation could be stabilized in the Southwest Pacific, U.S. forces should begin to concentrate in the British Isles for an offensive against Germany. Secretary Stimson and others were pressing the same views on the President. In the middle of March the Joint Chiefs of Staff approved this course of action; in April, at the President's order, General Marshall and Harry Hopkins, the President's personal representative, went to London to seek British approval.

Logistical considerations heavily favored both the general strategy of concentration against Germany and the specific plan of invading northwestern Europe from a base in the British Isles. Because the target area was close to the main sources of British and American power, two to three times as many forces could be hurled against northwestern Europe (with a given amount of shipping) as could be supported in operations against Japan. Britain itself was a highly industrialized country, fully mobilized after two-and-a-half years of war and well shielded by air and naval power—a ready-made base for a land invasion and air attacks on Germany's vitals. While invasion forces were assembling, moreover, they would serve to garrison the British Isles. Finally, an attack across the English Channel would use the only short water crossing to the Continent from a base already available and would thrust directly at the heart of Fortress Europe by the main historic invasion routes.

Even so, the plan was a desperate gamble. If northwestern Europe offered the Allies a position of strength, the Germans also would be strong there, close to their own heartland, served by the superb rail and road nets of western and central Europe and shielded by submarines based along the entire length of Europe's Atlantic front. The limited range of fighter aircraft based in southern England narrowly restricted the choice of landing areas. Much hinged on the USSR, where for the present the bulk of Germany's land forces was pinned down. If the Soviet Union collapsed, an invasion from the west would be a suicidal venture. The invasion therefore had to be launched before the Soviet armies were crushed and, moreover, in sufficient strength to draw substantial German forces away from the Eastern Front and avert that very catastrophe.

On the face of it, these two requirements seemed to cancel each other. Allied planners had little hope that the Russians could stand up under another summer's onslaught; it was obvious, in view of the scarcity of shipping, that any attack the Western Allies could mount by the coming summer or early fall would be hardly more than a pinprick. The best solution General Marshall's planners could offer to this dilemma was to set the invasion (ROUNDUP) for the spring of 1943. Until then, through air bombardment of Germany and a continued flow of materiel to the Soviet Union, the Allies hoped to help the Soviet armies stave off defeat. If these measures should fail, and Soviet resistance seemed about to collapse, then, with whatever forces were on hand, the Allies would have to invade the continent in 1942 (SLEDGEHAMMER)—and no later than September, before bad weather closed in over the channel. The Allies would follow the same course in the unlikely event that Germany itself showed signs of serious weakness in 1942.

In London, Mr. Hopkins and General Marshall found the British delighted that the United States was ready to commit itself to a major offensive against Germany in 1943. The British readily agreed that preparations should begin immediately for an invasion the following spring, and they undertook to provide more than half the shipping needed to move about a million American troops and immense quantities of materiel to the United Kingdom. They warned, however, that their first concern at present was to maintain their position in the Middle East, where late in January Rommel's revitalized *Africa*

Corps had inflicted a serious reverse on the Eighth Army. Both sides were now feverishly building up for a new offensive. The British also expressed deep misgivings over the proposed emergency cross-channel operation in the fall. Nevertheless, the British approved the American plan, essentially the War Department's plan, "in principle"—a phrase that was to give much trouble in the coalition war. The immediate relief General Marshall's staff felt in Washington was reflected by General Eisenhower, then Chief, Operations Division, War Department General Staff, who noted: "At long last, and after months of struggle … we are all definitely committed to one concept of fighting. If we can agree on major purposes and objectives, our efforts will begin to fall in line and we won't just be thrashing around in the dark."

But there were also strong reservations on the American side. Admiral King did not contest in principle the Germany-first strategy. But he was determined not to allow preparations for the cross-channel invasion to jeopardize "vital needs" in the Pacific, by which, as he candidly stated early in May, he meant the ability of U.S. forces "to hold what we have against any attack that the Japanese are capable of launching." Only the President's peremptory order on May 6 that the invasion buildup in Britain must not be adversely affected (indeed, it had scarcely begun) prevented a large-scale diversion of forces and shipping to the Pacific to counter the Japanese offensive that culminated in the great naval battles of the Coral Sea and Midway. The President himself made it clear, on the other hand, that aid to the Soviet Union would have to continue on a mounting scale, whatever the cost to BOLERO (the American buildup in the United Kingdom) in materiel and shipping. And even Army leaders were unwilling to assign shipping for the movement until the scheduled buildup of garrisons in the western hemisphere and various other overseas stations had been completed, which, it was estimated, would not be until August at the earliest. Until then British shipping would have to carry the main burden.

Not until June 1942, therefore, did the first shipload of American troops under the new plan set sail for England in the great British luxury liner *Queen Elizabeth*. Almost simultaneously a new crisis erupted in the Middle East. At the end of May, after a four-month lull, Rommel seized the initiative and swept around the southern flank of the British Eighth Army, which held strong positions in eastern Libya from El Gazala on the coast, south to Bir Hacheim. After two weeks of hard fighting in which the British seemed to be holding their own, Rommel succeeded in taking Bir Hacheim, the southern anchor of the British line. During the next few days British armor, committed piecemeal in an effort to cover a withdrawal to the northeast, was virtually wiped out by skillfully concealed German 88-mm. guns. The Eighth Army once again retreated across the Egyptian frontier; on June 21 Tobruk, which the British had expected to hold out behind Axis lines as in 1941, was captured with its garrison and large stores of trucks, gasoline, and other supplies.

News of this disaster reached Prime Minister Churchill in Washington, where he had gone early in the month to tell the President that the British were unwilling to go through with an emergency cross-channel landing late in 1942. General Marshall immediately offered to send an armored division to help the hard-pressed British in Egypt, but it was decided for the present to limit American aid to emergency shipments of tanks,

> "At long last, and after months of struggle … we are all definitely committed to one concept of fighting. If we can agree on major purposes and objectives, our efforts will begin to fall in line and we won't just be thrashing around in the dark."

101

artillery, and the ground components of three combat air groups. This move required the diversion for many weeks of a substantial amount of U.K. shipping from the North Atlantic on the long voyage around the Cape of Good Hope. But the heaviest impact on the invasion buildup in the United Kingdom resulted from the diversion of British shipping to the Middle East and the retention there of shipping the British had earmarked for the buildup. For the time being, British participation in the BOLERO program virtually ceased.

By the end of August, with only seven months to go before the invasion was to be launched, only about 170,000 American troops were in or on their way to the British Isles. The shipment of equipment and supplies, particularly for the development of cantonments, airfields, and base facilities, was hopelessly behind schedule. There seemed little likelihood that enough shipping would be available to complete the movement across the Atlantic of a million troops, with the 10–15 million tons of cargo that must accompany them, by April 1943 as scheduled. And even if the shipping could have been found, Britain's ports and inland transportation system would have been swamped before the influx reached its peak. Thus, by the late summer of 1942, a spring 1943 invasion of the continent seemed a logistical impossibility.

TORCH Replaces SLEDGEHAMMER/ROUNDUP

By this time, in fact, American military leaders had become discouraged about a cross-channel invasion in the spring of 1943, though not primarily because of the lag in the buildup program. In June the British had decided that SLEDGEHAMMER, for which they had never had any enthusiasm, could not be undertaken except in a situation that offered good prospects of success—that is, if the Germans should seem about to collapse. At the moment, with the German summer offensive just starting to roll toward the Caucasus and the lower Don, such a situation did not appear to be an imminent possibility. The British decision was influenced in part by the alarming lag in deliveries of American landing craft, of which less than two-thirds of the promised quota for the operation was expected to materialize. The British also argued that the confusion and losses attendant upon executing SLEDGEHAMMER— and the cost of supporting the beachhead once it was established— were likely to disrupt preparations for the main invasion the following spring. Since SLEDGEHAMMER, if carried out, would have been in the main a British undertaking, the British veto was decisive. The operation was canceled.

As a substitute, the British proposed a less risky venture—landings in French North Africa—that they were confident could be accomplished in stride, without jeopardizing ROUNDUP. To Stimson, Marshall, King, and Arnold this proposal was unacceptable. Failure would be a costly, perhaps fatal rebuff to Allied prestige. Success might be even more dangerous, the Americans feared, for it might lead the Allies step-by-step into a protracted series of operations around the southern periphery of Europe. Such operations could not be decisive and would only postpone the final test of strength with Germany. At the very least, an invasion of North Africa would, the Americans were convinced, rule out a spring 1943 invasion of the continent. The Army planners preferred the safer alternative of simply reinforcing the British in Egypt.

The British proposal was nevertheless politically shrewd, for it was no secret that President Roosevelt had long before expressed a predilection for this very undertaking. He was determined, besides, to send American ground forces into action somewhere in the European area before the end of 1942. Already half persuaded, he hardly needed Churchill's enthusiastic rhetoric to win him over to the new project. When General Marshall and his colleagues in the Joints Chiefs of Staff suggested as an alternative that the United States should immediately go on the defensive in Europe and turn its main attention against Japan, Roosevelt brusquely rejected the idea.

In mid-July Hopkins, Marshall, and King went to London under orders from the President to reach agreement with the British on some operation in 1942. After a vain effort to persuade the British to reconsider an invasion of the continent in 1942, the Americans reluctantly agreed on July 24 to the North Africa operation, now christened TORCH, to be launched before the end of October. The President, overruling Marshall's suggestion that a final decision be postponed until mid-September to permit a reappraisal of the Soviet situation, cabled Hopkins that he was "delighted" and that the orders were now "full speed ahead." Into the final agreement, however, Marshall and King wrote their own conviction that the decision on TORCH "in all probability" ruled out an invasion of the continent in 1943 and meant further that the Allies had accepted "a defensive, encircling line of action" in the European-Mediterranean war.

End of the Defensive Stage

With the decision for TORCH, the first stage in the search for a strategic plan against Germany came to an end. In retrospect, 1941–1942 had been a period in which scarcity and the need for defense had shaped the Allies' strategy. The British and American approaches to war had their first conflict, and the British had won the first round. That British notions of strategy tended to prevail was not surprising. British forces had been mobilized earlier and were in the theaters in far greater numbers than American forces. The United States was still mobilizing its manpower and resources. It had taken the better part of the year after Pearl Harbor for U.S. forces to have an appreciable effect in the theaters. Strategic planning in 1942 had been largely opportunistic, hand-to-mouth, and limited by critical shortages in shipping and munitions. Troops had been parceled out piecemeal to meet immediate threats and crises. Despite the Germany-first decision, the total U.S. Army forces deployed in the war against Japan by the end of the year actually exceeded the total U.S. Army forces deployed in the war against Germany. The one scheme to put Allied planning on an orderly, long-range basis and to achieve the concepts of mass and concentration in which General Marshall and his staff had put their faith had failed. By the close of the critical first year after Pearl Harbor, an effective formula for halting the dissipation of forces and materiel in ventures regarded as secondary still eluded the Army high command.

> Strategic planning in 1942 had been largely opportunistic, hand-to-mouth, and limited by critical shortages in shipping and munitions.

DISCUSSION QUESTIONS

1. Why was the United States caught so unprepared by the Japanese attacks against Hawaii and the Philippines? What were the similarities and differences between the two garrisons and the defense each put up?

2. The surrender of U.S. forces at Bataan and Corregidor was the worst disaster in the history of the U.S. Army. Could it have been avoided? How?

3. Why did the United States see Germany as the greatest threat in late 1941? Was this policy correct? Why or why not?

4. When Churchill heard the news about Pearl Harbor, he reportedly said that he immediately thanked God that victory was now sure for Britain. Why did he have such confidence?

5. How did the United States and Great Britain coordinate their forces during World War II? How did the methods differ from those the Allies had adopted in World War I?

6. Under what circumstances could the Allies have launched an invasion of the European continent in 1942? What could the United States have contributed to such an operation? Why did the diversion of resources to the Mediterranean affect the timetable for an invasion of the continent in 1943?

RECOMMENDED READINGS

Greenfield, Kent Roberts, ed. *Command Decisions*. Washington, D.C.: U.S. Army Center of Military History, 2002, chs. 5–7.

Kirkpatrick, Charles E. *An Unknown Future and a Doubtful Present: Writing the Victory Plan of 1941*. Washington, D.C.: U.S. Army Center of Military History, 1992.

Leighton, Richard M., and Robert W. Coakley. *Global Logistics and Strategy, 1940–1943*. U.S. Army in World War II. Washington, D.C.: U.S. Army Center of Military History, 1995, chs. 6–7, 14–15.

Matloff, Maurice, and Edwin M. Snell. *Strategic Planning for Coalition Warfare, 1941–1942*. U.S. Army in World War II. Washington, D.C.: U.S. Army Center of Military History, 1995, chs. 8, 12, 16–17.

Prange, Gordon. *At Dawn We Slept: The Untold Story of Pearl Harbor*. New York: Penguin Books, 2001.

Whitman, John W. *Bataan Our Last Ditch: The Bataan Campaign, 1942*. New York: Hippocrene Books, 1990.

Other Readings

Churchill, Winston S. *The Second World War,* 6 vols. Boston: Houghton Mifflin, 1950, vols. 3, 4.

Cline, Ray S. *Washington Command Post: The Operations Division*. U.S. Army in World War II. Washington, D.C.: U.S. Army Center of Military History, 1990, chs. 5–7.

Conn, Stetson, Rose C. Engelman, and Byron Fairchild. *Guarding the United States and Its Outposts*. U.S. Army in World War II. Washington, D.C.: U.S. Army Center of Military History, 2000.

Craven, Wesley F., and James L. Cate, eds. *The Army Air Forces in World War II*, 7 vols. Washington, D.C.: Office of Air Force History, 1983, vol. 1.

Green, Constance M., Harry C. Thomson, and Peter C. Roots. *The Ordnance Department: Planning Munitions for War.* U.S. Army in World War II. Washington, D.C.: U.S. Army Center of Military History, 1990.

Gwyer, J. M. A., and J. R. M. Butler. *History of the Second World War*, 6 vols., ed. J. R. M. Butler. London: Her Majesty's Stationery Office, 1964, vol. 3.

Millett, John D. *The Organization and Role of the Army Service Forces.* U.S. Army in World War II. Washington, D.C.: U.S. Army Center of Military History, 1989, ch. 2.

Morison, Samuel E. *History of U.S. Naval Operations in World War II,* 15 vols. Urbana: University of Illinois Press, 2001–2002, vols. 1, 3, 4.

Morton, Louis. *The Fall of the Philippines.* U.S. Army in World War II. Washington, D.C.: U.S. Army Center of Military History, 1989.

Pogue, Forrest C. *George C. Marshall: Ordeal and Hope, 1939–1942.* New York: Viking, 1966.

Watson, Mark S. *Chief of Staff: Prewar Plans and Preparations.* U.S. Army in World War II. Washington, D.C.: U.S. Army Center of Military History, 1991, ch. 15.

4

GRAND STRATEGY AND THE
WASHINGTON HIGH COMMAND

In 1943 the debate within the Grand Alliance over strategy against the Axis powers entered a new stage. The midwar period (roughly to the establishment of a foothold in Normandy in the summer of 1944) was the time of increasing plenty. The power to call the tune on strategy and to choose the time and place to do battle passed to the Allies. U.S. troops and supplies flowed out in ever-increasing numbers and quantity, and the full impact of American mobilization and production was felt not only in the theaters but also in Allied councils. But the transition to the strategic initiative introduced many new and complex problems for the high command in Washington. Active and passive fronts were now established all over the world. The TORCH decision had thrown all Allied planning into a state of uncertainty. For Army Chief of Staff General George C. Marshall and the Army planners in the Washington command post, the basic strategic question was how to limit operations in subsidiary theaters and decisively carry the war to the Axis powers. They had to start over and seek new and firmer long-range bases upon which to plan for victory in the multifront coalition war.

Strategic Planning for Offensive Warfare: Midwar

The decision for TORCH continued to affect the great debate on European strategy between the Americans and the British that endured down to the summer of 1944. The issues that emerged were disputed in and out of the big international conferences of midwar, from Casablanca in January 1943 to Second Quebec in September 1944. In that debate Prime Minister Winston Churchill eloquently urged ever onward in the Mediterranean: Sicily, landing in Italy, Rome, the Pisa-Rimini line; then "north and northeast." President Franklin D. Roosevelt, himself fascinated by the possibilities in the Mediterranean, to a considerable extent seconded these moves, despite the reluctance of the American chiefs. Pleading his case skillfully, the British leader stressed the need to continue the momentum, the immediate advantages, the "great prizes" to be picked up in the Mediterranean and the need to continue the softening-up process while the Allies awaited a favorable opportunity to invade the continent across the English Channel. That sizable Allied forces were present in the Mediterranean and that there was an immediate chance to weaken the enemy in that area were telling arguments.

At the same time the Americans, with General Marshall as the foremost military spokesman, gradually made progress toward limiting the Mediterranean advance, toward directing it to the west rather than to the east, toward linking it directly with a definite major cross-channel operation, and thereby winning their way back to the idea of waging a war of mass on the continent. Part of the task of military planners was to reconcile the strategic concepts of Roosevelt, Churchill, and Soviet Premier Joseph V. Stalin—a nearly impossible task. The series of decisions reached at the 1943 conferences—Casablanca in January, Washington (TRIDENT) in May, First Quebec (QUADRANT) in August, and Cairo-Tehran (SEXTANT-EUREKA) in November and December—reflect the compromises of the Americans and the British between opportunism and long-range commitments, between a war of attrition and a war of concentration. They also mirrored the constant pressure of Marshall Stalin for a second front on the continent of Europe to aid him in his desperate struggle with the Nazis.

Each of these conferences marked a milestone in coalition strategy and in the maturation of American strategic planning. At Casablanca, General Marshall made a last vigorous but vain stand for a cross-channel operation in 1943. The conferees did approve the round-the-clock Combined Bomber Offensive against Germany that both the Americans and the British viewed as a prerequisite to a future cross-channel operation. The conferees' establishment of the COSSAC (Chief of Staff to the Supreme Allied Commander) to begin planning such an operation was another major accomplishment. They also assigned first priority to the U-boat war, both because of the criticality of the British food supply and the importance of control of the seas to any cross-channel operations. But no real long-range plan for the defeat of the Axis powers emerged. Casablanca merely recognized that the Anglo-Americans would retain the initiative in the Mediterranean and defined the short-range objective in terms of a prospective operation against Sicily.

THE ARMY AND THE OSS

The success of special operations early in World War II led William J. Donovan to persuade President Roosevelt to form the Office of Strategic Services (OSS). Although the OSS lay outside the armed services, it came under Joint Chiefs of Staff supervision in wartime and included several military personnel. In Western Europe, the Mediterranean, China, and Southeast Asia, the OSS engaged in intelligence collection, propaganda, guerrilla warfare, sabotage, and subversion—in short, almost anything that appealed to Donovan's innovative mind. At war's end, President Harry S. Truman inactivated the OSS, but its activities later inspired the formation of the Central Intelligence Agency.

Unlike the small, disunited American delegation, the well-prepared British operated as a cohesive team and presented a united front. President Roosevelt, still attracted to the Mediterranean, had not yet made the notion of a decisive cross-channel attack his own. A striking illustration of the want of understanding between the White House and the military staffs came in connection with the unconditional-surrender formula to which Roosevelt and Churchill publicly committed themselves at Casablanca. The President had simply informed the Joint Chiefs of Staff (JCS) of his intention to support that concept as the basic Allied aim in the war at a meeting at the White House shortly before the conference. But neither the Army nor the Joint Staff made any study of the meaning of this formula for the conduct of the war before or during the conference, nor did the President encourage his military advisers to do so.

To the American military staff it appeared at the time that the long experience of the British in international negotiations had carried the day. Keenly disappointed, Brig. Gen. Albert C. Wedemeyer, General Marshall's principal adviser at Casablanca, wrote: "we lost our shirts and … are now committed to a subterranean umbilicus operation in midsummer…. we came, we listened, and we were conquered." General Wedemeyer admired the way the British had presented their case:

They swarmed down upon us like locusts with a plentiful supply of planners and various other assistants with prepared plans…. As an American I wish that we might be more glib and better organized to cope with these super negotiators. From a worm's eye viewpoint it was apparent that we were confronted by generations and generations of experience in committee work and in rationalizing points of view. They had us on the defensive practically all the time.

The members of the American military staff took the lessons of Casablanca to heart. If they did not become glibber, they at least organized themselves better. To meet the British on more equal terms, they overhauled their joint planning system and resolved to reach closer understandings with the President in advance of future meetings. As a by-product of the debate and negotiation over grand strategy in midwar, the planning techniques and methods of the Americans became more nearly like those of their British ally, even if their strategic ideas still differed. They became more skilled in the art of military diplomacy, of quid pro quo, or what might be termed the tactics of strategic planning. At the same time their strategic thinking became more sophisticated. The Casablanca Conference represented the last fling for the "either-or" school of thought in the American military staff. Henceforth, staff members began to think not in terms of this or that operation, but in terms of this *and* that—or what one planner fittingly called "permutations and combinations." The outstanding strategic questions for them were no longer to be phrased in terms of either a Mediterranean or a cross-channel operation, but in terms of defining the precise relations between them and how they related to the Combined Bomber Offensive, as well as the war against Japan.

In the debate, the American Joint Chiefs of Staff countered British demands for more emphasis upon the Mediterranean, particularly the eastern Mediterranean, by supporting further development of Pacific offensives. Holding open the "Pacific alternative" carried with it the threat of no cross-channel operation at all. The war in the Pacific thereby offered the U.S. staff a significant lever for keeping the Mediterranean issue under control. At the same time General Marshall recognized that the Mediterranean offensive could not be stopped completely with North Africa or Sicily and that definite advantages would accrue from knocking out Italy, further opening up the Mediterranean for Allied shipping, and widening the air offensive against Germany.

Beginning with the compromise agreements at TRIDENT in the spring of 1943, the American representatives could point to definite steps toward fixing European strategy in terms of a major cross-channel undertaking for 1944. At that conference they assented to a plan for eliminating Italy from the war, which the British urged as the "great prize" after Sicily. But the forces, the Americans insisted, were to be limited as much as possible to those already in the Mediterranean. At the same time they won British agreement to the transfer of four American and three British divisions from the Mediterranean to the United Kingdom. Both sides agreed to continue the Combined Bomber Offensive from the United Kingdom in four phases to be completed by April 1944 and leading up to an invasion across the channel shortly thereafter. Most encouraging was the President's unequivocal announcement in favor of a cross-channel undertaking for the spring of 1944. The British agreed that planning should start for mounting such an operation with a target date of May 1944 on the basis of twenty-nine divisions built up in the United Kingdom (Operation ROUNDHAMMER, later called OVERLORD). The bare outlines of a new pattern of European strategy began to take shape.

That pattern took clearer shape at QUADRANT. There, the American chiefs urged a firm commitment to OVERLORD, the plan developed by a British-American planning staff in London. The British agreed but refused to give it the "overriding priority" over all operations in the Mediterranean area that the Americans desired. Plans were to proceed for eliminating Italy from the war, establishing bases as far north as Rome, seizing Sardinia and Corsica, and landing in southern France. Forces for these operations would be limited to those allotted at TRIDENT. With a definite limitation on the Mediterranean offensive and authorization for a definite allocation of forces for the approved cross-channel operation and for an extended Combined Bomber Offensive in support of it, the strategic pattern against Germany was taking on more final form.

After QUADRANT came new danger signals for the Washington high command. The British were making overtures for active operations in the Aegean, which the Americans interpreted, wrongly or rightly, as a prelude to a move on the Balkans (Churchill's "soft-underbelly" of Europe fixation) and a consequent threat to the cross-channel strategy. At the Moscow Conference in October 1943 came other warning signs from another and more unexpected source. At that meeting of the foreign ministers, a prelude to the full-dress conference at Tehran to follow, the representatives of the Anglo-American staffs met for the first time with the Russian staff. In a surprise maneuver, the Russians, who from the beginning had been pleading for the second front in Europe, intimated that they might be willing to accept an active campaign in

Italy as the second front. The Russian delegation would never have generated such an idea without the personal approval of Stalin.

With these portents in mind, the uneasy American Joint Chiefs of Staff accompanied President Roosevelt on board the USS *Iowa* en route to the Cairo Conference in November 1943. During the rehearsals on that voyage for the meetings ahead, the President afforded his military advisers a rare glimpse into his reflections on the political problems that were bound up with the war and its outcome. His concern lest the United States be drawn into a permanent or lengthy occupation of Europe came out sharply in the discussion with the JCS on the zones of occupation in postwar Germany. He told the JCS, "We should not get roped into accepting any European sphere of influence." Nor did he wish the United States to become involved in a prolonged task of reconstituting France, Italy, and the Balkans. "France," he declared, "is a British baby." Significantly, the President added: "There would definitely be a race for Berlin. We may have to put the United States Divisions into Berlin as soon as possible." With a pencil he quickly sketched on a simple map of Europe the zonal boundaries he envisaged, putting Berlin and Leipzig in a big American zone in northern Germany—one of the most unusual records of the entire war and later brought back to Washington by Army officers in the American delegation.

Tehran proved to be the decisive conference in determining the strategy for the war in Europe. There, for the first time in the war, President Roosevelt, Prime Minister Churchill, and their staffs met with Marshal Stalin, the Soviet dictator, and his staff. Churchill made eloquent appeals for operations in Italy, the Aegean, and the east Mediterranean, even at the expense of a delay in OVERLORD. For reasons of its own, the USSR put its weight behind the American concept of strategy. Confident of its capabilities, demonstrated in its great comeback since the critical days of Stalingrad, the Soviet Union asserted its full power as an equal member of the Allied coalition. Stalin came out vigorously in favor of OVERLORD and limiting further operations in the Mediterranean to one operation directly assisting OVERLORD, an invasion of southern France. In turn, the Russians promised to launch an all-out offensive on their front to accompany the Allied moves and to enter the war against Japan as soon as Germany was defeated. Stalin's strong stand put the capstone on the Western strategy against Germany. The Anglo-American chiefs agreed to launch OVERLORD during May 1944 in conjunction with a southern France operation and to consider these the supreme operations for that year.

The final blueprint for Allied victory in Europe had taken shape. Germany was to be crushed between

Stalin, Roosevelt, and Churchill at the Tehran Conference

the jaws of a gigantic vise applied from the west and the east. How much reliance President Roosevelt had come to place in General Marshall was reflected in his decision not to release Marshall for the command of the cross-channel attack. He told General Marshall, "I … could not sleep at night with you out of the country." While it must have been a major disappointment to Marshall, he put the long-hoped-for command behind him and focused on the job at hand. President Roosevelt gave the nod to General Dwight D. Eisenhower, who had built a solid reputation as the successful leader of coalition forces in the Mediterranean. Preparations for the big cross-channel attack began in earnest.

The last lingering issue in the long-drawn-out debate was not settled until the summer of 1944. In the months following the Tehran Conference, the southern France operation came perilously close to being abandoned in favor of the British desire for further exploitation in Italy and possibly even across the Julian Alps into the Hungarian plain. Complicating the picture was a shortage of landing craft to carry off both OVERLORD and the southern France attack simultaneously. But General Marshall and the Washington military authorities, backed by President Roosevelt, remained adamant on the southern attack. The British and the Americans did not reach final agreement on a southern France operation until August—two months after the OVERLORD landings—just a few days before the operation was actually launched, when Churchill reluctantly yielded. This concluding phase of the debate represented the last gasp of the peripheral strategy with a new and sharper political twist. Churchill was now warily watching the changing European scene with one eye on the retreating Germans and the other on the advancing Russians.

A number of misconceptions would arise during the postwar period about this Anglo-American debate over strategy. What was at stake in the midwar debate was not whether to launch a cross-channel operation. Rather, the question was: Should that operation be the full-bodied drive with a definite target date that the Americans desired or the final blow to an enemy critically weakened in a war of opportunity that the British desired? It is a mistake to assume that the British did not from the first want a cross-channel operation. The difference lay essentially in the precise timing of that attack and in the extent and direction of preparatory operations. Once agreed on the major blow, the British stoutly held out for a strong initial assault that would ensure success in the operation. It is also a mistake to assume that the Americans remained opposed to all Mediterranean operations. Indeed, much of their effort in 1943–1944 was spent in reconciling those operations with a prospective cross-channel operation.

What about the question of a Balkan alternative that has aroused so much controversy? Would it not have been wiser to have invaded the continent through the Balkans, thereby forestalling Soviet domination? We must emphasize the fact that this is a postwar debate. The Balkan invasion was never proposed by any responsible leader in Allied strategy councils as an alternative to OVERLORD, nor did any Allied debate or combined planning take place in those terms. After the war Churchill steadfastly denied that he wanted a Balkan invasion. The British contended that the Americans had been frightened by the specter rather than by the substance of the British proposals. Indeed, the American staff had been frightened by the implications of Churchillian proposals for raids, assistance to native populations, throwing in a few armored divisions, and the like—for the eastern Mediterranean and Balkan regions. For the American staff, Mediterranean operations had offered a striking demonstration of how great the costs of a war of attrition could be. The so-called soft underbelly of Italy, to which the Prime Minister had glowingly referred, turned out to be a hard-shelled back demanding more and more increments of American and Allied men and means. The mere thought of being sucked step by step, by design or by circumstance, into a similar undertaking in the Balkans, an area of poor terrain and communications—even if it were an unrealistic fear on the part of the American staff—was enough to send shivers up the spines of American planners. Certainly, neither the President nor the American staff wanted to get involved in the thorny politics of the Balkan area, and both were determined to stay out. The Allies never argued out the Balkan question in frank military or political terms during World War II.

Frustrated by the loss of what he regarded as glittering opportunities in the Mediterranean, Churchill struck out after the war at the American wartime "logical, large-scale mass-production thinking." But Gordon Harrison, the author of *Cross-Channel Attack*, argued: "To accuse Americans of mass-production thinking is only to accuse them of having a mass-production economy and of recognizing the military advantage of such an economy. The Americans were power-minded." From the beginning they thought in terms of taking on the main German armies and beating them. Behind the Americans' fear of a policy of attritional and peripheral warfare against Germany in midwar lay a continued anxiety over its ultimate costs in men, resources, and time. This anxiety was increased by their concern with getting on with the war against Japan. Basic in their thinking was a growing realization of the ultimate limits of American manpower and a growing anxiety about the effects of a long, continuous period of maximum mobilization on the home front. All these factors combined to confirm their faith in the doctrine of military concentration. It was an exercise in the principle of mass on a large scale.

As it turned out, the final strategy against Germany was a compromise of American and British views—of British peripheral strategy and the American principle of mass. To the extent that the cross-channel operation was delayed a year later than the Americans wished in order to take advantage of Mediterranean opportunities and to continue the softening-up process, the British prevailed. Perhaps still haunted by the ghosts of Passchendaele and Dunkerque, the British were particularly sensitive to the requisite conditions for OVERLORD, for example, how many enemy troops could be expected to oppose it. But, as the Americans had hoped from the beginning, the cross-channel attack turned out to be a conclusive operation with a fixed target date; it was given the highest priority and the maximum force to drive directly at the heart of German power.

Thus, by the summer of 1944 the final blueprinting of the Allied strategy for defeating Germany was complete. Despite the compromises with opportunism, American staff notions of fighting a concentrated, decisive war had been clearly written into the final pattern.

Those notions had been reinforced by the addition, from Casablanca onward, of the unconditional-surrender aim. The peripheral trend had been brought under control, and General Marshall had managed to conserve American military power for the big cross-channel blow. The Americans had learned to deal with the British on more equal terms. The military chiefs had drawn closer to the President, and the U.S. side was able to present a united front vis-à-vis the British.

During the midwar Anglo-American debate, significant changes had taken place in the alignment of power within the Grand Alliance. These shifts had implications as important for war strategy as for future relations among the wartime partners. By the close of 1943 the mighty American industrial and military machine was in high gear. The growing flow of American military strength and supplies to the European Theater assured the acceptance of the American strategic concept. The Soviet Union, steadily gathering strength and confidence in 1943, made its weight felt at a critical point in the strategic debate. Britain had virtually completed its mobilization by the end of 1943, and stresses and strains had begun to appear in its economy. Relative to the Soviet Union and the United States, Britain was becoming weaker. In midwar the Americans drew up with and threatened to pass the British in deployed strength in the European Theater. Within the coalition,

INDUSTRIAL MOBILIZATION

The reverse of Axis fortunes in World War II roughly coincided with the entry of the "arsenal of democracy" into the conflict. In 1944 the United States produced more than 40 percent of global munitions output and greatly exceeded the combined output of either all the Axis or all the Allied countries.

Left: *Women workers install fixtures and assemblies to a tail fuselage section of a B–17 bomber.* Above: *Production Aids for the Grumman Aircraft Engineering Corporation.*

Britain's military power and notions of fighting the war were being overtaken. Tehran, which fixed the final European strategy, marked a subtle but important change in the foundations of the Alliance. For the strategists of the Pentagon and of the Kremlin the doctrine of concentration had provided a common bond.

Completing the Strategic Patterns

From the standpoint of the Washington high command, the main story of military strategy in World War II, except for the important and still unanswered question of how to defeat Japan, came to an end in the summer of 1944. The last stage, culminating in the surrender of Germany and of Japan, was the period of the payoff, of the unfolding of strategy in the field. In this final phase, the problems of winning the war began to run up against the problems of winning the peace.

Once the Allied forces became firmly lodged on the European continent and took up the pursuit of the German forces, the war became for General Marshall and his staff essentially a matter of tactics and logistics with the Supreme Allied Commander, General Eisenhower, assuming the responsibility for making decisions as military circumstances in the field dictated. But to Churchill, disturbed by the swift Soviet advance into Poland and the Balkans, the war seemed more than ever a contest for great political stakes. In the last year of the European conflict, therefore, the two approaches often became a question of military tactics versus political considerations.

By the summer of 1944 the shape of things to come was already apparent. Once on the continent, General Eisenhower was given more and more responsibility for political decisions or fell heir to them by default. Lacking political guidance from Washington, the commander in the field made decisions on the basis of military considerations. He fell back on the U.S. staff notions of defeating the enemy and ending the war quickly and decisively with the fewest casualties. This trend became even more marked in 1945 in the commander's decision to stop at the Elbe and not to attempt to take Berlin or Prague ahead of the Russians.

As usual, General Marshall and the U.S. staff backed the decisions of the commander in the field. Typical of Marshall's approach were two statements he made in April 1945: one in response to a British proposal to capture Berlin, the other concerning the liberation of Prague. With reference to Berlin, Marshall joined with his colleagues in the JCS in emphasizing to the British Chiefs of Staff "that the destruction of the German armed forces is more important than any political or psychological advantages which might be derived from possible capture of the German capital ahead of the Russians.... Only Eisenhower is in a position to make a decision concerning his battle and the best way to exploit successes to the full." With respect to Prague, Marshall wrote to Eisenhower, "Personally and aside from all logistic, tactical or strategic implications, I would be loath to hazard American lives for purely political purposes."

Such views of the Army Chief of Staff took on added significance, for during Roosevelt's final and his successor's early days in office the burden of dealing with important issues fell heavily on the senior military advisers in the Washington high command. Marshall's stand on these issues was entirely consistent with earlier Army strategic planning. Whatever the ultimate political outcome, from the standpoint of a decisive military conclusion of the war against Germany it made little difference whether the forces of the United States or those of the Soviet Union took Berlin and Prague. At the same time, in purely military dealings with the Russians in the closing months of the European conflict, and as Soviet and American troops drew closer, the American staff began to stiffen its stand and a firmer note crept into its negotiations for coordination of Allied efforts. Early in 1945 Marshall advised Eisenhower to forget diplomatic niceties in dealing with the Russians and urged him to adopt a direct approach "in simple Main Street Abilene style."

Churchill's inability to reverse the course of the last year of the war underscored the changed relationships between U.S. and British national military weight and the shifting bases of the Grand Alliance. With British manpower already mobilized to the hilt, after the middle of 1944 British production became increasingly unbalanced; the British fought the remainder of the war with a contracting economy. The Americans did not hit the peak of their military manpower mobilization until May 1945—the month Germany surrendered. Reaching their war production peak at the end of 1943, they were able to sustain it at high levels to the end of the war. The greater capacity of the American economy and population to support a sustained, large-scale Allied offensive effort showed up clearly in the last year of the European war. Once entrenched on the continent, American divisions began to outnumber the British more and more. Through the huge stockpiles of American materiel already built up and through control of the growing U.S. military manpower on the continent, General Eisenhower ensured the primacy of U.S. staff thinking on how to win the war. Whatever his political predilections, Churchill had to yield. As the war against Germany lengthened beyond the hoped-for end in 1944, British influence in high Allied councils went into further decline. The last year of the war saw the United States and the Soviet Union emerging as the two strongest military powers in Europe, the one as intent on leaving Europe soon as the other was on pushing its strategic frontiers westward. On the Western side, the struggle was to be concluded the way the American military chiefs had wished to wage it from the beginning—as a conventional war of concentration.

Meanwhile, as the war with Germany was drawing to a close, the strategy for defeating Japan had gradually been taking shape. Despite the Germany-first principle, the so-called secondary war simply would not stand still. From the beginning, in the defensive as well as in the offensive stage, the Pacific exerted a strong pull on American forces and resources. Though final plans had to await the defeat of Germany, American public opinion would not tolerate a strictly defensive, limited war against Japan in the meantime. The pace of advance in the Pacific became so fast that it almost caught up with the European conflict. In the Pacific, as in the Mediterranean, American strategists learned that forces in being had a way of creating their own strategy.

While the European war strategy was fashioned on the international level, the war against Japan from the beginning was almost exclusively

The greater capacity of the American economy and population to support a sustained, large-scale Allied offensive effort showed up clearly in the last year of the European war.

an American affair, its strategy essentially an interservice concern. The American plans and decisions in the Pacific war were presented to the international conferences, where they usually received Allied approval with little debate. Disputes and arguments were on the service level for the most part, with General Marshall and Admiral Ernest J. King (Chief of Naval Operations) working out compromises between themselves. In the process General Marshall often acted as mediator between the Navy and General Douglas MacArthur, the Commander of the Southwest Pacific Area.

The traditional naval concern with the Pacific and the necessarily heavy reliance in the theater upon shipping, especially assault shipping, put the main burden of developing offensive strategy upon the Navy. But Navy plans for a central Pacific offensive had to be reconciled with General MacArthur's concept of approaching Japan via the New Guinea–Philippines axis. Thus a twofold approach, "a one-two punch," replaced the original single-axis strategy. This double-axis advance produced a strategy of opportunity similar to what the British had urged for the war in Europe and took the Allies to the threshold of Japan by the time the European war ended. Long debated was the critical question of whether Japan could be defeated by bombardment and blockade alone or if an invasion would be necessary. In Washington, during the late spring of 1945, the Army's argument that plans and preparations should be made for an invasion was accepted as the safe course to follow.

The rapid pace of the Pacific advance outran the American plans for the China-Burma-India Theater, and that theater declined in strategic importance in the war against Japan. Disillusioned by Chinas' inability to play an active role in the final defeat of Japan, American military leaders sought to substitute the USSR. To save American lives in a Pacific OVERLORD, those leaders in general became eager to have the USSR enter the war against Japan and pin down Japanese forces on the Asiatic mainland. Before final plans for a Pacific OVERLORD could be put into effect, however, the Japanese surrendered. The dramatic dropping of atomic bombs on August 6 and 9 on Hiroshima and Nagasaki, respectively, came as a complete surprise to the American public and to the Army strategic planners, with the exception of a handful of top officers in the Washington command post who were in on the secret. In a sense the supersession of strategic plans by a revolutionary development of weapons was a fitting climax to a war that had throughout shown a strong tendency to go its own way.

The last year of the war witnessed, along with the finishing touches on grand strategy, the changeover from the predominantly military to the politico-military phase. As victory loomed, stresses and strains within the coalition became more apparent. With the Second Quebec Conference in September 1944, agreement among the Allies on military plans and war strategy became less urgent than the need to arrive at acceptable politico-military terms on which the winning powers could continue to collaborate. That need became even more marked at Yalta in February 1945 and at the Potsdam Conference in July 1945. To handle these new challenges after building up a staff mechanism geared to the predominantly military business of fighting a global and coalition war necessitated considerable adjustment of Army staff processes and planning. In midwar, Army planning had been geared to achieve the decisive blow on the continent that had been a cardinal element in the planners' strategic faith. Scarcely were the Western Allies ensconced on the continent, however, when the challenges of victory and peace were upon the Army planners. They entered the last year of the war with the coalition disintegrating, the President failing in health, and a well-organized politico-military machine lacking. Besides the frictions generating on the foreign fronts, the Army still had to cope with the immense problem of what to do with the beaten foe—with terms of surrender, occupation, and postwar bases. The military inherited by default problems no longer easily divided into military and political.

Expansion and Distribution of the Wartime Army

To the Washington high command, strategic plans were one vital ingredient in the formula for victory. Manpower was another. Indeed, at stake in the midwar debate was the fresh and flexible military power of the United States. That power was also General Marshall's trump card in negotiations with the coalition partners. To put a brake on diversionary deployments to secondary theaters and ventures and to conserve American military manpower for the big cross-channel blow became the major preoccupation of the Chief of Staff and his advisers in midwar. Behind their concern for effective presentation of the American strategic case at the midwar international conferences lay the growing uneasiness of General Marshall and his staff over the American manpower problem. To continue what appeared to them to be essentially a policy of drift in

HOMELAND SECURITY DURING WORLD WAR II

Prior to World War II, U.S. national strategy had centered on defending the United States and its possessions against invasion and other foreign military threats. With the outbreak of war in Europe, U.S. strategic planning shifted to embrace participation in a coalition war against Germany, Italy, and Japan. Despite prosecuting a global war, however, the Army retained significant responsibilities for homeland security. That mission entailed theater air defense, maintaining coastal fortifications near major harbors, guarding major defense plants and railroads, and supporting the Office of Civilian Defense that coordinated the efforts of some 5 million volunteers nationwide. The War Department feared with good reason that the last two functions could impair the Army's meeting its strategic commitments overseas. The lack of any realized threat to the United States allowed the Army to gradually deemphasize its homeland security mission and reduce troops assigned to this mission to fewer than 65,000 in mid-1944, with troops being replaced by auxiliary military police and state guard forces.

Homefront Fires Are Enemy Victories, *Jes W. Schlaikjer, 1944*

Allied strategy raised grave issues about mobilizing and deploying U.S. forces. To support a war of attrition and peripheral action, in place of concentrated effort, raised serious problems about the size and kind of Army the United States should and could maintain.

To establish a proper manpower balance for the United States in wartime was as difficult as it was important. In light of the estimated 15–16 million men physically fit for active military service, on the surface it seemed hard to understand why there should be any U.S. manpower problem at all. The problem as well as the answer stemmed basically from the fact that the Allies had from the beginning accepted the proposition that the single greatest tangible asset the United States brought to the coalition in World War II was the productive capacity of its industry. From the very beginning, U.S. manpower calculations had to be closely correlated with the needs of war industry.

The Army therefore had to compete for manpower not only with the needs of the other services but also with the claims of its own industry. By 1943 the arsenal of democracy was just beginning to hit its full productive stride. To cut too deeply into the industrial manpower of the country in order to furnish men for the Army and Navy might interfere seriously with arming U.S. and Allied troops. Furthermore, the United States was fighting a global conflict. To service its lines of communications extending around the world required large numbers of men, and great numbers of troops were constantly in transit to and from the theaters. To carry the fight across the oceans demanded a powerful Navy and a large merchant fleet that also had to be given a high priority for manpower. Each industry as well as each theater commander was continually calling for more men. The problem for the Army was not only how much it should receive for its share of the manpower pool but also how it should divide that share most effectively to meet the diverse demands made upon it.

By 1943 the Army Staff increasingly realized that the U.S. manpower barrel did have a bottom. Even before the end of 1942 the bottom was becoming visible. Also evident was the fact that, while the United States would remain the major arsenal of democracy, it could no longer be regarded as a limitless source of munitions. The pool of unemployed that had cushioned the shock of mobilization for three years had been almost drained. Industrial expansion had slowed; labor had become tight in many areas; and in November 1942 the President had placed a ceiling of 8.2 million officers and men upon the Army's expansion during 1943, intimating at the same time that this limit would probably hold for the duration of the war. General Marshall and his colleagues in the JCS were still determined that the United States make a major contribution in fighting forces to the defeat of the Axis powers. But postponement of the invasion of northwestern Europe, together with the indicated limitations on American manpower and resources, made it necessary to reconsider the nature of that contribution. To match strategy, manpower, and production for the offensive phase of the war became a basic task of the Washington high command during the remainder of the war.

Supply programs for 1943 reflected prospective changes in the American role in the war. Cuts fell most heavily on the ground munitions program, which was reduced by more than one-fifth, and on Lend-Lease

Americans Will Always Fight for Liberty, *Bernard Perlin, 1943*

to nations other than the Soviet Union. Some reductions were also made in naval ship construction, but the program for building escort vessels was left intact and the merchant shipbuilding program was actually enlarged. The emphasis was on producing first all the tools needed to defeat the U-boats and secure the sea lanes for the deployment of American forces overseas and at the same time to ensure that ample shipping would be available for this purpose. Soviet armies had to be assured a continuous flow of munitions to stave off the Germans. Meanwhile, airpower—heavy bombers to batter the German homeland, carrier-borne aircraft to restore mobility and striking power to the forces in the Pacific—had to be built up and brought to bear as rapidly as possible, while the slower mobilization and deployment of ground forces was under way. The ground army, finally, had to be shaped to operate, at least during the coming year and a half, in relatively small packages at the end of long lines of communications in a great variety of terrain. Its units had to be compact, versatile, and easily transportable, but also mobile and able to hit hard. Every ton of shipping, as Lt. Gen. Lesley J. McNair, head of the Army Ground Forces, declared, had to deliver the maximum of fighting power.

The changing requirements and circumstances of coalition warfare in the offensive phase greatly affected plans and programs for expanding the U.S. Army—in total growth and internal distribution of strength as well as in overseas deployment. Manpower squeezes, together with strategic, logistical, and operational considerations, helped to change the shape as well as the size of the Army. By the end of 1942 the U.S. Army had grown to a strength of 5.4 million officers and men. Although this was still well under the ceiling of 8.2 million the President set in November, the mobilization of ground combat elements was already nearing completion. Seventy-three divisions were then in being, and no more than 100 were expected to be activated. In June 1943 the goal was reduced to ninety divisions, with an overall strength ceiling of 7.7 million men—far under the heavily mechanized force of 215 divisions that the framers of the Victory Program in 1941 had considered none too large to take on the German Army. Actually, the U.S. Army in 1945 reached a peak strength of 8.3 million and eighty-nine divisions. The last division was activated in August 1943.

The strength of ground combat units in the Army increased hardly at all after 1942, even though sixteen divisions and some 350 separate artillery and engineer battalions were added after that date. These additional units had to be formed by means of redistribution and economies within existing personnel allotments in the same categories. Since the Army as a whole increased by almost 3 million men after 1942, its ground combat elements, even including replacements, declined from over half the Army's total strength at the beginning of 1942 to about a third in the spring of 1945. It was no mean achievement to maintain the Army's combat units at full strength during the heavy fighting of 1944 and 1945. Neither the Germans nor the Japanese were able to do as much.

Mindful of the untrained divisions sent overseas in World War I, General Marshall from the first set as his goal thorough and realistic training of large units in the United States culminating in large-scale maneuvers by corps and armies. Since all divisions had been activated by August 1943 and the mass deployment of the Army overseas did not begin until late in that year, most divisions were thoroughly trained. The major threat to an orderly training program came in 1944, when many trained divisions had to be skeletonized to meet the demand for trained replacements. Equipment shortages were a serious obstacle to effective training in early 1943, as in 1942, as was the shortage of trained commissioned and noncommissioned officers to provide cadres.

In 1943 the Army's ground combat forces continued to undergo the drastic reorganization and streamlining begun in 1942. Changes in the types of units required reduced the planned number of armored divisions from twenty to sixteen, eliminated all motorized divisions, and cut back tank-destroyer and antiaircraft units. The armored corps disappeared. Armored and infantry divisions were reduced in personnel and equipment. Tanks taken from armored divisions were organized into separate tank battalions, to be attached to divisions as needed; motor transport was pooled under corps or army headquarters for greater flexibility.

The division remained the basic fighting team of arms and services combined in proportions designed for continuous offensive action under normal battle conditions. It retained a triangular organization. The infantry division contained 3 regiments and included, besides 4 artillery battalions (3 armed with 105-mm. howitzers, 1 with 155-mm. howitzers), a reconnaissance troop (scout cars and light tanks), and engineer, ordnance, signal, quartermaster, medical, and military police units. Each regiment could readily be teamed with an artillery battalion. Reinforced with other elements of the division or with elements assigned by corps or army headquarters, it formed the regimental combat team. The total strength of the infantry division was reduced from its prewar strength of 15,245 to 14,253.

The armored division as organized in 1942 had consisted of 2 tank regiments and 1 armored infantry regiment plus 3 battalions of armored artillery and an armored reconnaissance battalion. This arrangement was calculated to produce 2 combat commands with varying proportions of tanks and infantry in division reserve. The armored division also included supporting elements corresponding to those in the infantry divisions but motorized to increase mobility. In the armored division as reorganized in 1943, battalions replaced regiments. The new model contained 3 medium tank battalions, 3 armored infantry battalions, and 3 armored artillery battalions. These, with supporting elements, could be combined readily into 3 combat commands (A, B, and Reserve). The total strength of the armored division was reduced from 14,620 to 10,937. Two armored divisions remained "heavy" divisions, with the old organization, until the end of the war.

The only other special type of division of real importance retained in 1943 was the airborne division. Including parachute and glider-borne regiments, it was designed as a miniature infantry division, with lighter, more easily transportable artillery and the minimum of vehicles and service elements needed to keep it fighting after an airdrop until it could be reinforced. Its strength was only 8,500 until early 1945, when it was raised to 12,979. By the beginning of 1945 other experimental and special-type divisions (mountain, motorized, light, jungle, and cavalry) had either disappeared or largely lost their special characteristics.

Underlying all this change were the basic aims of making ground forces mobile, flexible, and easily transportable by increasing the proportion of standardized and interchangeable units in less rigid tactical combinations. Nor did this streamlining involve any sacrifice of effective power. Army leaders were convinced, and experience on the whole proved, that these units could not only move faster and farther, but they could also strike even harder than the units they replaced.

Premobilization planning had contemplated that African Americans would be included in the ranks of a wartime Army proportionately to their number in the whole population and proportionately also in each of the arms and services. The Army achieved neither goal; but the number of African-American troops reached a peak strength of over 700,000, and more than 500,000 of them served overseas. Contemporary attitudes and practices in American society kept African Americans in segregated units throughout the war. Most African-American soldiers overseas were in supply and construction units. In truck units such as the famous Red Ball Express in Northern France in 1944, African-American manpower proved a critical asset in winning the supply battle so crucial to victory at the front. Many others who served in the two African-American combat divisions (the 92d and 93d Infantry Divisions), in separate combat support battalions, and in a fighter group directly engaged the enemy on the ground and in the air.

In 1944 the manpower shortage became nationwide. The Army, under the double pressures of accelerated deployment schedules and heavy demands for infantry replacements for battle casualties in the two-front full-scale war, was driven to stringent measures. The Army Specialized Training Program, which had absorbed 150,000 soldiers in college study, was dissolved; the aviation cadet training program was drastically curtailed. To release soldiers for battle, the Army drew heavily on limited-service personnel and women for noncombat duties. The induction of female volunteers had begun in mid-1942; and in the following year, for the first time in the Army's history, women had been given a full legal military status in the Women's Army Corps (WAC). Growing in strength, the WAC reached a peak of 100,000 by the spring of 1945.

As the Army moved overseas, many posts were consolidated or closed, releasing large numbers of overhead personnel. Overstrength tactical units were reduced in size and the excess manpower transferred to other units or the individual replacement pool. Coast artillery units were converted to heavy artillery, hundreds of antiaircraft units were dissolved, and nondivisional infantry regiments became a source of infantry replacements. To meet the threat of the German counteroffensive in the Ardennes in December 1944, the handful of divisions remaining in the United States, most of them earmarked for the Pacific, were rushed to Europe; the United States was left without a strategic reserve. In May 1945 the overall ground army numbered 68 infantry, 16 armored, and 5 airborne divisions.

The extent to which the Army depended on its air arm to confer striking power and mobility is suggested by the enormous growth of the Army Air Forces (AAF): from about 400,000 men at the beginning of 1942 to a peak of over 2.4 million early in 1944. At the end of the war in Europe, it had 243 organized groups in being and a numerical strength of 2.3 million men. More than 1.5 million of the worldwide AAF strength in March 1945 consisted of service troops, troops in training, and overhead.

After 1942 the growth of the ground army also occurred for the most part in services and administrative elements. By March 1945 these comprised 2.1 million (not counting hospital patients and casuals en route) of the ground army's 5.9 million personnel. This growth reflected both the global character of the war, with its long lines of communications, and the immense numbers of noncombatant specialists needed to operate and service the equipment of a modern mechanized army. They were also a manifestation of the American people's insistence on providing the American citizen-soldier with something like his accustomed standard of living. Less tangible and more difficult to control was the demand for large administrative and coordinating staffs, which was self-generating since administrators themselves had to be administered and coordinators coordinated. One of the most conspicuous phenomena of global war was the big headquarters. In the European Theater in 1944, overhead personnel, largely in higher headquarters, numbered some 114,000 men. On the eve of V-E Day, with overseas deployment for the two-front war complete, almost 1.3 million of the 2.8 million men who remained in the United States were in War Department, Army Ground Forces, Army Service Forces, and Army Air Forces overhead agencies to operate the Zone of the Interior establishment.

The assignment to the Army of various administrative tasks swelled the demand for noncombatant personnel. One such task was the administration of military Lend-Lease. Another was the development of the atomic bomb, the super-secret, $2 billion Manhattan Project assigned to the Corps of Engineers. Two of the Army's overseas commands (the China-Burma-India Theater and the Persian Gulf Command) had missions largely logistical in character. From the first the Pacific theaters generated the heaviest demands for service troops to build, operate, and service the manifold facilities a modern army needed in regions where these had been virtually nonexistent. To a lesser degree these needs were also present in the Mediterranean, and operations against the Germans everywhere involved the task of repairing the ruin the enemy had wrought. Big construction projects like the Alcan Highway (from western Canada to Alaska) and the Ledo Road in Burma added to the burden. To carry out the Army's vast procurement program (to compute requirements, negotiate contracts, and expedite production) called for a multitude of highly trained administrators, mostly civilian businessmen whom the Army put into uniform.

Thus, for every three fighting men in the ground army there were two technicians or administrators somewhere behind, engaged in functions other than killing the enemy. Behind the fighting front stretched the pipeline filled with what General McNair once called "the invisible horde of people going here and there but seemingly never arriving." In March 1945 casuals en route or in process of assignment numbered 300,000. Far more numerous were the replacements, who at this time totaled 800,000 in the ground army; AAF replacements numbered 300,000. The Army had made almost no provision for replacements in the early plans for creating units. The necessity of providing spaces for them as well as for larger numbers of service and AAF troops in the Army's total allotment of manpower went far to account for the difference between the 215 divisions in the original Victory Program and the 89 actually organized.

Replacements kept the effective strength of the Army from declining. The number of soldiers in hospitals in World War II seldom fell below 200,000 and at the beginning of 1945 reached a peak of almost 500,000. Throughout the war the Army suffered a total of 936,000 battle casualties, including 235,000 dead; to the latter must be added 83,400 nonbattle deaths. The Army's dead represented about 3 percent of the 10.4 million men who served in its ranks during World War II.

Despite the acknowledged primacy of the European war, only gradually did the flow of American troops overseas take the direction the Army planners desired. Not until OVERLORD was given top priority at the Tehran Conference at the end of 1943 could the two-front war finally begin to assume the focus and flow into the channels the War Department had planned for in the early stages of the coalition war. During 1943 the Army sent overseas close to 1.5 million men, including 13 divisions. Over two-thirds of these totals, including more than 1 million troops and 9 divisions, were deployed against Germany. In these terms the balance was finally being redressed in favor of the war against Germany. The cumulative totals at the end of 1943 showed 1.4 million men, including 17 divisions, deployed against Germany, as opposed to 913,000 troops, including 13 divisions, lined up against Japan—a sharp contrast to the picture at the end of 1942, when in manpower and number of divisions the war against Japan had maintained an edge over the war in Europe.

On the other hand, the failure of the Allies to agree on a specific plan for the cross-channel attack until Tehran permitted deployment in the war against Japan to develop at a much quicker pace than the planners had expected. It was not until October 1943 that the divisions in Europe exceeded those in the Pacific. And when the efforts of the Navy and Marine Corps, especially in the Pacific, are added to Army deployment overseas, a different picture emerges. Actually, after two years of war, the balance of U.S. forces—and resources—between the European and Japanese arenas was fairly even. Indeed, of the total of 3.7 million men (Army, Navy, and Marines) overseas during 1943, slightly more than half were arrayed against Japan. By the close of that year Army planners fully comprehended the growing costs of fighting a multifront war on an opportunistic basis and the difficulty of keeping a secondary war secondary in the absence of a firm long-range plan for the primary war.

By the end of the midwar period, in September 1944, General Marshall and his staff could survey the state of Army deployment with considerable satisfaction. Channeling U.S. military power to the United Kingdom for a concentrated attack against Germany had been a long struggle. More divisions were sent overseas in the first nine months of 1944, with the bulk of them going to the European Theater, than had been shipped overseas during the previous two years. To support OVERLORD and its follow-up operations, the Army funneled forces into the European Theater and later into continental Europe in ever-increasing numbers during the first three quarters of 1944. Slightly over 2 million men, including 34 divisions and 103 air groups, were in the European Theater at the end of September 1944—over 45 percent of the total number of troops overseas in all theaters. By then, the overall breakdown of Army troops overseas gave the war against Germany a 2:1 advantage over the Japanese conflict, and this was matched by the Army divisional distribution. Forty divisions were located in Europe and the Mediterranean, with 4 more en route, compared with 21 in the Pacific. In the air, the preponderance lay even more heavily in favor of Europe. With the bulk of the Army's combat strength overseas deployed against the Third Reich and with most of the divisions still in the United States slated to go to the European Theater, General Marshall and his planners could consider their original concept well on the way to accomplishment. Though there were still over 3.5 million men left in the Continental United States at the end of September, there were only 24 combat divisions remaining. The Army planners had hoped to maintain some of the divisions as a strategic reserve to cope with emergencies.

When the crisis caused by the Ardennes breakthrough of December 1944 denuded the United States of all the remaining divisions, the possibility of having raised too few divisions caused War Department leaders from Secretary of War Henry L. Stimson on down some anxious moments. Fortunately, this was the last unpleasant surprise; another such crisis would have found the divisional cupboard bare. Indeed, the decision for ninety divisions—the Army's "cutting edge"—was one of the greatest gambles the Washington high command took during World War II.

Thus, in the long run, Marshall and his staff were not only able to reverse the trend toward the Pacific that had lasted well into 1943 but had gone to the other extreme during 1944. Because of unexpected developments in the European war, not one division was sent to the Pacific after August 1944; and planned deployment totals for the Pacific

THE 90-DIVISION DECISION

One of the most under-appreciated strategic risks that U.S. Army leaders, particularly Chief of Staff Marshall, accepted during World War II was the midwar decision to limit to ninety the number of U.S. Army combat divisions created. This decision, finally reached in May 1944 after more than two years of debate and analysis, above all reflected Marshall's astute judgment and ability to see the full spectrum of issues from broad national needs down to American combat capabilities. Crediting the fighting ability of U.S. soldiers and units, Marshall recognized that every additional division absorbed men required more elsewhere. With only a finite number of trained officers, and relying upon the steady flow of individual replacements to keep those ninety divisions up to strength, the United States was able to ensure that it provided steady, decisive combat power. Although tested by the emergency of the Battle of the Bulge in late 1944, Marshall's calculated risk proved correct.

for 1944 were never attained. European deployment, on the other hand, mounted steadily and substantially exceeded the planners' estimates. At the end of April 1945, when the Army reached its peak strength of 5.4 million overseas, over 3 million were in the European Theater and 1.2 million in the Pacific. Regardless of the type of war fought in World War II—concentration and invasion in Europe or blockade, bombardment, and island-hopping in the Pacific—each required a tremendous outlay of American military strength and resources.

Balancing Means and Ends

Throughout the conflict the matching of means with ends, of logistics with strategy, continued to be a complex process, for World War II was the greatest coalition effort and the first really global war in which the United States had participated. The wherewithal had to be produced and delivered to a multitude of allies and far-flung fronts over long sea lines of communications and all somehow harnessed to some kind of strategic design to defeat the enemies. As the war progressed, the Army strategic planners learned to appreciate more and more the limits of logistics in the multifront war. From the standpoint of the Americans, the basic strategic decisions they had supported from the beginning (the Germany-first decision and the primacy of the cross-channel attack) were in large measure justified by logistics. Each would capitalize on the advantages of concentrating forces and material resources on a single major line of communications and link the major arsenal represented by the United States with the strategically located logistical base offered by Great Britain. The realities of logistics had in part defeated their original BOLERO strategy, and forces and resources in being in other theaters had generated their own offensive strategy.

In the midwar era, while Allied plans remained unsettled, the competing claims of the Pacific and Mediterranean for a strategy of opportunism, the continuing needs of other far-flung fronts, added to the accumulated "fixed charges" (e.g., aid to China, Britain, and the Soviet Union and the rearming of the French) took a heavy toll on American resources. The full-blown war economy was matched by the full-blown war on the global scale. In and out of the international conferences of midwar in the era of relative plenty, the adjustment of means and ends went on and logistics remained a limiting, if not always the final determining, factor in the strategic debate. The scope, timing, landing places, and even the choice of specific operations were to a large extent influenced by the availability of the wherewithal, by the quantities that could be produced and delivered to the fighting fronts.

To logisticians in World War II, the balance among supplies and equipment, trained troops, and the shipping to transport them—the only means then feasible for mass movement overseas—was of continuing concern. In planning for that balance the factor of lead time was particularly important. For example, for the invasion of Normandy in June 1944 planning for the production of materiel had to start two years in advance, the buildup in England at least a year in advance, and the actual planning of detailed logistical support six months before the landings. Usually the shorter the lead time for logistical preparations, the narrower the range of strategic choices tended to be.

To the end the Army was of course one cog in the mighty American war machine, and it had to compete for resources with its sister services and with Allies. The home front also had to be supported. While the war cut deeply into the life of the American people, it was fought based on a "guns and butter" policy without any real sacrifice in the American standard of living. The Army was not anxious to cut into that standard of living. Nor did it have final say over the allocation and employment of key resources. To balance the allocation of forces, supplies, and shipping among the many fronts and nations, within the framework of the close partnership with the British, required a degree of central logistical control and direction at both combined and national levels unknown in earlier wars. A complex network of Anglo-American and national civilian and military agencies for logistical planning emerged. In the melding of resources and plans that continued in and out of the international conferences, planners took their cue from the basic decisions of the Combined Chiefs of Staff (CCS)—in this sense, the top logistical as well as strategic planning organization.

An imposing structure of federal agencies and committees grew up in Washington to control the nation's economic mobilization. Its keystone was the influential War Production Board (WPB) that controlled the allocation and use of raw materials, machine tools, and facilities with powers similar to those of the War Industries Board in World War I. In the military sphere the War Department, like the Navy Department, had a large degree of autonomy in controlling requirements planning, production, and distribution of materiel for its forces. The actual procurement (purchasing and contracting of munitions and other war materials) was carried out directly by the Army's technical services and the Navy's bureaus. Within the Joint Chiefs of Staff organization many logistical problems at issue between the services were settled by negotiation. The War Shipping Administration (WSA) operated and allocated the critical U.S. merchant shipping. Close cooperation between WSA and the British Ministry of War Transport resulted in the pooling of the two merchant fleets comprising the bulk of the world's mercantile tonnage. Other civilian agencies dealt with such critical commodities as food, petroleum products, and rubber. In the spring of 1943 most of the mobilization agencies were subordinated to a new coordinating unit, the Office of War Mobilization headed by former Justice James F. Byrnes.

Theoretically, U.S. munitions production along with that of the British Empire was placed in a common pool and distributed according to strategic need. Two Munitions Assignments Boards, each representing both countries and responsible to the CCS, made allocations. One board, sitting in Washington, allocated U.S. production, while a second in London allocated British production. Using the principles of Lend-Lease and reciprocal aid, these two boards made allocations to other Western Allied countries as well as to the United States and Britain. Supplies for the Soviet Union were governed by separate diplomatic protocols, and the boards seldom attempted to alter their provisions in making assignments. The common-pool theory, however, proved somewhat too idealistic for complete application. From the start it really applied almost entirely to American production, for the British had little surplus to distribute. Their contributions to the American effort, though substantial, normally took the form of services and soft goods rather than military hardware. In these circumstances the Americans almost inevitably came to question the application of the common-pool theory and to make assignments on the premise that each partner had first call on its own resources. British participation in the allocation of American production became only nominal in the later war years.

However imperfect the application of the common-pool concept, Lend-Lease, with its counterpart, reciprocal aid, proved an admirable instrument in coalition warfare. Lend-Lease did what President Roosevelt had initially intended it should. It removed the dollar sign from Allied supply transactions and gave the Allies an unprecedented flexibility in distributing materiel without generating complicated financial transactions or postwar problems such as the war debts World War I had created. Under the Lend-Lease Act of March 1941, the War Department turned over to Allied countries approximately $25 billion worth of war materials. About 58 percent went to Britain, 23 percent to Russia, 8 percent to France, 7 percent to China, and the remainder to other countries. Included in these supplies were some 37,000 light and medium tanks, nearly 800,000 trucks, and 3,400 locomotives. The Army Service Forces was the Army's operating agency for administering this program; and from 1942 on, military Lend-Lease requirements were included with U.S. Army requirements in the Army supply program. This American largess was distributed almost exclusively to achieve complete military victory in the war, not to contribute to the postwar political purposes of any ally.

Even with American production in high gear during 1943–1945, critical shortages or bottlenecks developed to hamper operations at various stages. In early 1943, as in 1942, the most stringent limiting factor was the production of ships to transport troops and supplies. Indeed, in the spring of 1943, when President Roosevelt decided to divert scarce shipping to support the faltering British economy, he had to overrule the JCS, deeply concerned over American military requirements. After mid-1943, amid the changing requirements of the war in full bloom, the logistical bottlenecks tended to be specialized rather than general. From late 1943 until June 1944, the most serious critical shortage became the supply of assault shipping to land troops and supplies in amphibious operations. In the case of landing craft, the shortage was most severe in one specific category, the Landing Ship, Tank (LST). In April 1944 Winston Churchill became exasperated enough to wonder whether history would ever understand why "the plans of two great empires like Britain and the United States should be so much hamstrung and limited" by an "absurd shortage of the L.S.T.'s." In the last stage, after troops were ashore and fighting on the European continent, the principal bottleneck shifted to port and inland clearance capacity in that area and in the Pacific.

The basic problem of allocating resources between the war against Germany and the war against Japan remained almost to the end. Although the basic Germany-first decision held throughout the conflict, one of the most persistent questions concerned the proportion by which available resources should be divided between the two wars. This question reflected some divergence of political, military, geographical, and psychological

LST Discharging Cargo over a Pontoon Causeway

factors in the Anglo-American strategy of the war. For Britain, the war against Japan tended to be a sideshow; its leaders tended to emphasize the effort in Europe and the Mediterranean at the expense of the Pacific. The United States more than met its commitments in Europe but insisted from the beginning on a margin of safety in the war against Japan, for which it early had taken major responsibility. Furthermore, the pull to the Pacific in midwar that the U.S. Navy and General MacArthur, both now on the offensive, particularly welcomed became for the Washington high command a lever against overcommitment in the Mediterranean. At the midwar conferences the Anglo-American debate focused on the division of resources among the theaters where the two nations combined their efforts: the Mediterranean, northwest Europe, and Southeast Asia. For the Pacific, American military leaders simply presented their decisions, logistical as well as strategic, to the conferences for the stamp of approval. In effect, American military leaders in midwar went far toward asserting unilateral control over the division of American resources between the two wars.

In the final analysis, the multifront nature of the war developed as a product of changing circumstances rather than of a predetermined grand design. Coalition strategy evolved as a result of a complex, continuing process—a constant struggle to adjust ends and means, to reconcile diverse pressures, pulls, and shifting conditions in the global war, and to effect compromises among nations with diverse national interests. That strategy, frequently dictated by necessity, often emerged from events rather than having determined them.

The Washington high command was to end the war as it began it, without a fully developed theory on how to match strategic plans, manpower, and resources for a coalition, global war. But throughout its search for the formula for victory it had consistently pursued its goal of winning the war decisively, of complete military victory. This was the overriding goal; all secondary issues, such as postwar political aims, while not ignored, were clearly of lesser importance. This does not mean that the joint chiefs were naïve to the dangers, especially after it was clear in 1944 that the war would be won, of postwar Soviet power and its domination of Eastern Europe. There were voices within the highest levels of government that clearly saw the dangers of any single power dominating Europe. There is evidence that the attitude of total cooperation with the Soviets began to break down in the middle of 1945, when it became clearer that U.S. national security interests might not be well served by blindness to the obvious dangers of a dominant or expansionist Soviet Union. Nevertheless, the focus of the military strategists remained on completing the military defeat of Germany and then turning all the power of the "United Nations" against Japan. For that, cooperation with the Soviet Union remained vital; no other agenda could upset that goal. Whatever general political objectives the President had—he was a supremely political animal—he was committed to the strategic doctrine of complete victory first. The military planners, while not ignoring the future any more than the President did, maintained a similar focus.

Institutionally, World War II became for American strategists and logisticians an organization war, a war of large planning staffs in the capitals and the theater headquarters. Strategy and logistics became big business, established industries in the huge American wartime military establishment. World War II contributed significantly to the education of American Army planners in these arts. General Marshall, for example, once succinctly observed that his military experience in World War I had been based on roads, rivers, and railroads; for World War II he had to learn all over again and to acquire "an education based on oceans."

Throughout, Americans evinced their national habit in war: a penchant for quick, direct, and total solutions. The strategic principles they stressed were entirely in harmony with their own traditions and capacities. They proved particularly adept in adapting their mass-production economy to war purposes and in applying power on a massive scale. How far they had come in the quarter-century since World War I was evidenced by a comparison of their strategic experience in the two coalition world wars of the twentieth century. In World War I the United States, a junior partner, conformed to the strategy set by the Allies; in World War II the United States came to hold its own in Allied war councils and played an influential role in molding Allied strategy, virtually dictating the strategy of the Pacific war. By the end of the war America was the senior partner in the coalition with Britain and potentially the only direct rival to the growth of Soviet power. In meeting the problems of global coalition warfare, in the greatest conflict in which the United States had been involved, American strategists and logisticians came of age.

The multifront war of mass, technology, and mobility that taxed the strategists and logisticians in Washington also challenged the overseas commands and the tacticians in the field. As the war had progressed, the role of the theater commands in strategy, logistics, and tactics had become increasingly significant. It is appropriate, therefore, at this point to turn from the Washington high command to the Army overseas and to trace the actual course of operations in the double war.

DISCUSSION QUESTIONS

1. Why did the Americans invade North Africa? If you were planning the American strategy for 1942–1943, what would you do?

2. Discuss the comparative roles of Britain, the Soviet Union, and the United States in the fight against Germany. To what degree was the invasion of North Africa and then Italy a second front against Germany? How would Marshall Stalin have viewed this issue?

3. To what degree was Churchill motivated by his view of what postwar Europe would look like? Roosevelt? Stalin?

4. Why did the proposal to invade southern France in 1944 cause such a major disagreement between the Americans and the British?

5. Why was it so important to obtain the Soviet Union's involvement in the war against Japan? What was the strategic situation in the war against Japan at the time of the Yalta Conference in February 1945? At Potsdam in July 1945?

6. Discuss the background of the Army's decision to activate only ninety divisions. What impact would more divisions have had?

RECOMMENDED READINGS

Cline, Ray S. *Washington Command Post: The Operations Division*. U.S. Army in World War II. Washington, D.C.: U.S. Army Center of Military History, 2003.

Coakley, Robert W., and Richard M. Leighton. *Global Logistics and Strategy, 1943–1945*. U.S. Army in World War II. Washington, D.C.: U.S. Army Center of Military History, 1989.

Greenfield, Kent R., ed. *Command Decisions*. Washington, D.C.: U.S. Army Center of Military History, 2002.

Hayes, Grace P. *The History of the Joint Chiefs of Staff in World War II: The War against Japan*. Annapolis: Naval Institute Press, 1982.

Leighton, Richard M., and Robert W. Coakley. *Global Logistics and Strategy, 1940–1943*. U.S. Army in World War II. Washington, D.C.: U.S. Army Center of Military History, 1995.

Matloff, Maurice. Strategic Planning for Coalition Warfare, 1943–1944. U.S. Army in World War II. Washington, D.C.: U.S. Army Center of Military History, 2003.

Overy, Richard. Why the Allies Won. New York: W. W. Norton, 1996.

Paret, Peter, ed. Makers of Modern Strategy: From Machiavelli to the Nuclear Age. Princeton, N.J.: Princeton University Press, 1986.

Pogue, Forrest C. George C. *Marshall: Organizer of Victory, 1943–1945*. New York: Viking, 1973.

Reynolds, David, Warren F. Kimball, and A. O. Chubarian, eds. *Allies at War: The Soviet, American, and British Experience, 1939–1945*. New York: St. Martin's Press, 1994.

Ross, Steven T. American War Plans, 1941–1945: The Test of Battle. London: Frank Cass, 1997.

Stoler, Mark A. Allies and Adversaries: The Joint Chiefs of Staff, the Grand Alliance, and U.S. *Strategy in World War II*. Chapel Hill: University of North Carolina Press, 2000.

Other Readings

Brown, John S. *Draftee Division: The 88th Infantry Division in World War II.* Lexington: University Press of Kentucky, 1986.

Churchill, Winston S. The Second World War, 6 vols. Boston: Houghton Mifflin, 1948–1953, esp. vols. 4, 5, 6.

Edmonds, Robin. The Big Three: Churchill, Roosevelt, and Stalin in Peace & War. New York: W. W. Norton, 1991.

Feis, Herbert. Churchill, Roosevelt, Stalin: The War They Waged and the Peace They Sought. Princeton, N.J.: Princeton University Press, 1957.

Greenfield, Kent R. American Strategy in World War II: A Reconsideration. Malabar, Fla.: Krieger Pub. Co., 1982.

Hinsley, F. H. *British Intelligence in the Second World War*, 5 vols. New York: Cambridge University Press, 1979–1990.

———, Robert P. Palmer, and Bell I. Wiley. *The Organization of Ground Combat Troops.* U.S. Army in World War II. Washington, D.C.: U.S. Army Center of Military History, 1988.

Laqueuer, Walter, ed. The Second World War: Essays in Military and Political History. London: Sage Publications, 1982.

Lee, Ulysses. The Employment of Negro Troops. U.S. Army in World War II. Washington, D.C.: U.S. Army Center of Military History, 2000.

Love, Robert William, Jr. "Fighting a Global War, 1941–45." In *In Peace and War: Interpretations of American Naval History, 1775–1984*, 2d ed., ed. Kenneth J. Hagan. Westport, Conn.: Greenwood Press, 1984.

McJimsey, George T. The Presidency of Franklin Delano Roosevelt. Lawrence: University Press of Kansas, 2000.

Morison, Elting E. Turmoil and Tradition: A Study of the Life and Times of Henry L. *Stimson.* Boston: Houghton Mifflin, 1960.

Pogue, Forrest C., et al., "The Wartime Chiefs of Staff and the President." In *Soldiers and Statesmen: Proceedings of the 4th Military History Symposium*, ed. Monte D. Wright and Lawrence J. Paszek. Washington, D.C.: Office of Air Force History, 1989.

Stimson, Henry L., and McGeorge Bundy. *On Active Service in Peace and War.* New York: Octagon Books, 1971.

5

WORLD WAR II THE WAR AGAINST GERMANY AND ITALY

With the invasion of North Africa (Operation TORCH), the U.S. Army in late 1942 began a European ground offensive that it would sustain almost without pause until Italy collapsed and Germany was finally defeated. For the next two-and-one-half years, more than a million Americans would fight in lands bordering the Mediterranean Sea and close to 4 million on the European continent, exclusive of Italy, in the largest commitment to battle the U.S. Army had ever made. Alongside these Americans marched British, Canadian, French, and other Allied troops in history's greatest demonstration of coalition warfare; on another front, massed Soviet armies contributed enormously to the victory. In company with these allies, after a shaky start in North Africa, the U.S. Army came of age. Taking advantage of its strengths in mobility, artillery firepower, and close air support and forcing its way back onto a continent from which the Axis had driven the Allies four years before, American ground forces did their part to defeat the most vaunted military machine in the world at the time.

North Africa, November 1942–May 1943

Although the Allies made the decision to launch Operation TORCH largely because they could not mount a more direct attack against the European Axis early in the war, they also had more specific and attractive objectives: to gain French-controlled Morocco, Algeria, and Tunisia as a base for enlisting the French empire in the war; to assist the British in the Libyan Desert in destroying Axis forces in North Africa; to open the Mediterranean to Allied shipping; and to provide a steppingstone for subsequent operations.

Insignia of the 1st Armored Division, the First American Armored Division To See Combat

The Germans and their Italian allies controlled a narrow but strategic strip of the North African littoral between Tunisia and Egypt with impassable desert bounding the strip on the south. (*See Map 4.*) Numbering some 100,000 men under a battle-tested German leader, Field Marshal Erwin Rommel, the German-Italian army in Libya posed a constant threat to Egypt, the Near East, and French North Africa and by controlling the northern shores of the Mediterranean denied the Mediterranean to Allied shipping. Only a few convoys seeking to supply British forces on the island of Malta ever ventured into the Mediterranean, and these frequently took heavy losses.

Moving against French Africa posed for the Allies special problems rooted in the nature of the Armistice that had followed French defeat in 1940. Under the terms of that Armistice, the Germans had left the French empire nominally intact, along with much of the southern half of Metropolitan France; in return the French government was pledged to drop out of the war. Although an underground resistance movement had already begun in France and the Allies were equipping a "Free French" force, that part of the regular French Army and Navy left intact by the Armistice had sworn allegiance to the Vichy government. This pledge had led already to the anomaly of Frenchman fighting Frenchman and of the British incurring French enmity by destroying part of the fleet of their former ally.

If bloodshed was to be averted in the Allied invasion, French sympathies had to be enlisted in advance, but to reveal the plan was to risk French rejection of it and German occupation of French Africa. Although clandestine negotiations were conducted with a few trusted French leaders, these produced no guarantee that the French in North Africa would cooperate.

General Alexander

An air transport plane flies urgently needed supplies over the pyramids of Egypt en route to the battle zone.

Partly because of this intricate situation, the Allies designated an American, Lt. Gen. Dwight D. Eisenhower, to command the invasion to capitalize on the relative absence of rancor between French and Americans by giving the invasion an American rather than a British complexion. American troops were to make up the bulk of the assault force, and the Royal Navy was to keep its contribution as inconspicuous as possible.

The operation would coincide with an Allied counteroffensive in western Egypt, where the British Commander in Chief, Middle East, General Sir Harold R. L. G. Alexander, was to attack with the veteran British Eighth Army under Lt. Gen. Bernard L. Montgomery against Rommel's German-Italian army. Coming ashore in French Africa, General Eisenhower's combined U.S.-British force was to launch a converging attack against Rommel's rear.

In selecting beaches for the invasion, U.S. planners insisted upon a assault on the Atlantic coast of Morocco lest the Germans seal the Strait of Gibraltar and cut off support to landings inside the Mediterranean. Because both troops and shipping were limited, a landing on the Atlantic coast restricted the number and size of potential assaults inside the Mediterranean. Although a landing as far east as Tunisia was desirable because of vast overland distances (from the Atlantic coast to Tunis is more than 1,000 miles), the proximity of Axis aircraft on Sicily and Sardinia made that course too perilous.

Making the decision on the side of security, the Allies planned simultaneous landings at three points: one in Morocco near the Atlantic port of Casablanca and two in Algeria near the ports of Oran and Algiers. Once the success of these landings was assured, a convoy was to put ashore small contingents of British troops to seize ports in eastern Algeria while a ground column headed for Tunisia in a race to get there before the Germans could move in.

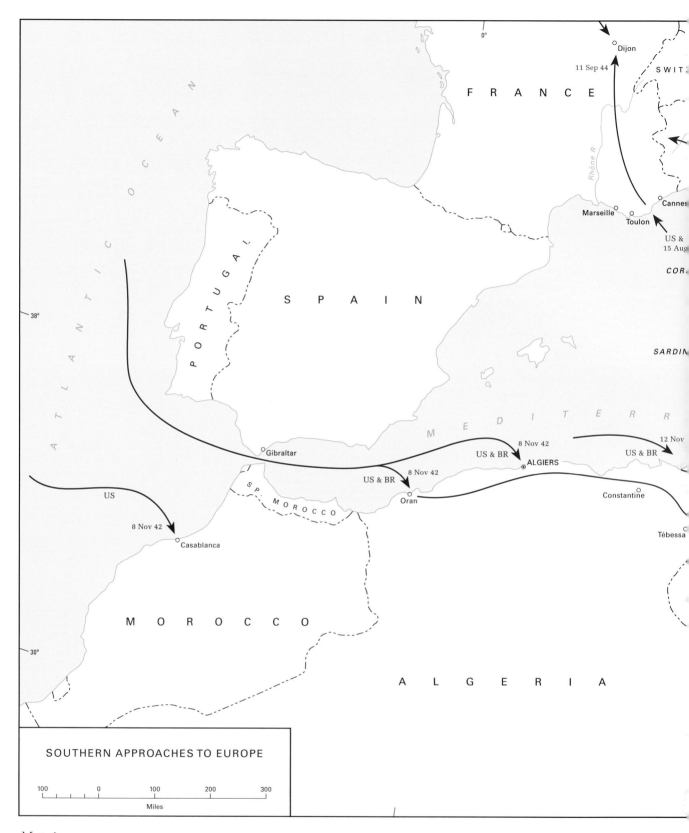

SOUTHERN APPROACHES TO EUROPE

100   0   100   200   300
Miles

Map 4

AUSTRIA

HUNGARY

RUMANIA

BLACK
SEA

YUGOSLAVIA

BULGARIA

Gothic Line
Jan–Apr 45

ITALY

TURKEY

ADRIATIC SEA

ALBANIA

Winter Line
Oct 43–May 44

ROME

Cassino

Foggia

GREECE

Anzio

US & BR
22 Jan 44

Naples
Salerno

Taranto

US
9 Sep 43

BR
9 Sep 43

38°

Palermo

Messina

SICILY

CRETE

BR
3 Sep 43

rte

C. Bon

US
10 Jul 43

TUNIS

May 43

BR
10 Jul 43

A N   S E A

S I A

areth

Feb 43

TRIPOLI

Tobruk

El Alamein

Jan 43
BR

Nov 42

30°

EGYPT

L I B Y A

20°

Troop Quarters in the Hold of a Transport

Having been given the assignment to invade North Africa only at the end of July 1942, the U.S. Army faced enormous difficulties in meeting a target date in November. Troops had received little training in amphibious warfare, landing craft were few and obsolete, and much equipment was inferior to that of the Axis forces. So few U.S. troops were available in England that troops for the landing near Casablanca had to be shipped directly from the United States in one of history's longest sea voyages preceding an amphibious assault.

After soundly defeating an Axis attack, Montgomery's Eighth Army on October 23 auspiciously opened an offensive at El Alamein, scoring a victory that was to be a turning point in British fortunes. A little over two weeks later, before daylight on November 8, the U.S. Navy put U.S. Army forces ashore near Casablanca, while the Royal Navy landed other U.S. troops and contingents of British troops near Oran and Algiers. The entire invasion force consisted of over 400 warships, 1,000 planes, and some 107,000 men, including a battalion of paratroopers jumping in the U.S. Army's first airborne attack.

Although the invasion achieved strategic surprise, the opposing French in every case but one fought back at the beaches. Dissidence among various French factions limited the effectiveness of some of the opposition, but any resistance at all raised the specter of delay that might enable the Germans to beat the Allies into Tunisia. Three days passed before the French agreed to cease fire and take up arms on the Allied side.

French support at last assured, the Royal Navy put British troops ashore close to the Tunisian border while an Allied column began the long overland trek. The British troops were too few to do more than secure two small Algerian ports, the ground column too late. Over the narrow body of water between Sicily and North Africa the Germans poured planes, men, and tanks. They met no French resistance. Except for barren mountains in the interior, Tunisia was for the moment out of Allied reach.

The Tunisia Campaign, November 1942–May 1943

Rommel, recoiling from the defeat at El Alamein and aware of the allied landings to his rear in November, withdrew his German-Italian army by January 1943 to the Mareth Line, old French fortifications near the southern border of Tunisia. There, he confronted Montgomery's Eighth Army while more than 100,000 enemy troops under General Juergen von Arnim faced westward against General Eisenhower's Allied force. Although the Italian high command in Italy exercised loose control, the Axis nations failed to establish a unified command over these two forces.

The Allied plan to defeat Rommel by converging attacks having been foiled, General Eisenhower had no choice but to dig in to defend in the Tunisian mountains until he could accumulate enough strength to attack in conjunction with a renewed strike by Montgomery against the Mareth Line. Before this could be accomplished, Rommel on February 14 sent strong armored forces through the passes in central Tunisia against the U.S. II Corps, commanded by Maj. Gen. Lloyd R. Fredendall. Rommel planned to push through the Kasserine Pass, then turn northwestward by way of an Allied supply base at Tébessa to reach the coast and trap the Allied units.

In a series of sharp armored actions, Rommel quickly penetrated thinly held American positions and broke through the Kasserine Pass. Although success appeared within his grasp, the lack of unified command interfered. Planning an attack of his own, General von Arnim refused to release an armored division needed to continue Rommel's thrust. Concerned that Rommel lacked the strength for a deep envelopment by way of Tébessa, the Italian high command directed a northward turn, a much shallower envelopment.

SIDI BOU ZID AND KASSERINE PASS

Artillery Firing at Night, *Gary Sheadan, n.d.*

On February 14, 1943, two German panzer divisions attacked elements of the 1st Armored Division, defending the village of Sidi Bou Zid at the western end of the strategically important Faid Pass in central Tunisia. Two battalions of the 168th Infantry were cut off and later forced to surrender. The attacking Germans continued to advance eastward until they encountered the main body of the 1st Armored Division at Sbeitla. Although delayed by a day's hard fighting, the Germans overcame the American defense and continued to press on toward the main Allied supply depot at Tebessa. The 19th Engineers, reinforced by a battalion each from the 26th, 39th, and 6th Armored Infantries, conducted an uncoordinated but stubborn defense of Kasserine Pass against the *Africa Corps* for two days until forced to retreat. Facing increasingly superior Allied forces, the Germans retreated from Kasserine on February 23. General Fredendall's slow counterattack three days later cost him his command; he was replaced by General Patton.

The turn played into Allied hands, for the British already had established a blocking position astride the only road leading north. At the height of a clash between Rommel's tanks and the British, four battalions of American artillery arrived after a forced march from Oran. On February 22 these guns and a small band of British tanks brought the Germans to a halt. Warned by intelligence reports that the British Eighth Army was about to attack the Mareth Line, Rommel hurriedly pulled back to his starting point.

The Axis offensive defeated, the U.S. II Corps, commanded now by Maj. Gen. George S. Patton, Jr., after the relief of General Fredendall, launched a diversionary attack on March 17 toward the rear of the Mareth Line. A few days later Montgomery's Eighth Army struck the line in force. By the end of the first week of April, the two forces had joined.

With all their forces now linked under the tactical command of General Alexander, the Allies opened a broad offensive that within a month captured the ports of Bizerte and Tunis and compressed all Axis troops into a small bridgehead covering the Cape Bon peninsula at the northeastern tip of Tunisia. The last of some 275,000 Germans and Italians surrendered on May 13.

Although the original Allied strategy had been upset by the delay imposed by French resistance and the swift German buildup in Tunisia—resulting in postponement of the launching of the "Second Front" in northwest Europe from 1943 to 1944—Allied troops achieved victory in six months, impressive in view of their limited numbers and long lines of communications. A few days later the first unopposed British convoy since 1940 reached beleaguered Malta.

American troops in their first test against German arms had made many mistakes. Training, equipment, and leadership had failed in many

Hill 609—Tunisia, *George Biddle, 1943*

instances to meet the requirements of the battlefield; but the lessons were clear and pointed to nothing that time might not correct. More important was the experience gained, both in battle and in logistical support. Important too was the fact that the Allied campaign had brought a French army back into the war. Most important of all, the Allies at last had gained the initiative.

The Sicily Campaign, July–August 1943

The next step after North Africa had already been decided in January 1943 at the Casablanca Conference. That step, Operation HUSKY, the invasion of Sicily, followed from the recognition that the Allies still were unready for a direct thrust across the English Channel. Utilizing troops already available in North Africa, they could make the Mediterranean safer for Allied shipping by occupying Sicily, perhaps going on to invade Italy and knocking that junior Axis partner out of the war.

As planning proceeded for the new operation, General Eisenhower (promoted now to four stars) remained as supreme commander; General Alexander, heading the 15th Army Group, served as ground commander. Alexander controlled Montgomery's Eighth Army and a newly created Seventh U.S. Army under Patton (now a lieutenant general).

How to invade the Vermont-size, three-cornered island posed a special problem. The goal was Messina, the gateway to the narrow body of water between Sicily and Italy, the enemy's escape route to the Italian mainland. Yet the Strait of Messina was so narrow and well fortified that Allied commanders believed the only solution was to land

GEORGE S. PATTON, JR. (1885–1945)

A descendant of Revolutionary and Civil War heroes, Patton became the Allies' foremost practitioner of armored warfare in World War II. In North Africa, Sicily, and Northwest Europe, he won fame for his speed, intuitive sense of the mobile battlefield, and sheer audacity. His volatile personality—devoutness, profanity, sensitivity, loudness, interest in history, belief in reincarnation, compassion, and shameless self-promotion—has fascinated generations of scholars and enthusiasts. But the opening scene of the 1970 movie "Patton" (featuring George C. Scott in gleaming helmet, stars, and riding boots in front of a huge American flag) completed his transformation from legend to folk hero.

Patton Inspecting the Troops in Sicily

elsewhere and march on Messina by way of shallow coastal shelves on either side of towering Mount Etna.

Applying the principle of mass, Alexander directed that all landings be made in the southeastern corner of the island, with the British on the east coast and the Americans on the southwest. A brigade of glider troops was to capture a critical bridge behind British beaches, while a regiment of U.S. paratroopers took high ground behind the American beaches. After seizing minor ports and close-in airfields, Patton's Seventh Army was to block to the northwest against Axis reserves while Montgomery mounted a main effort up the east coast.

Because Sicily was an obvious objective after North Africa, complete strategic surprise was hardly possible, but bad weather helped the Allies achieve tactical surprise. As a huge armada bearing some 160,000 men steamed across the Mediterranean, a mistral (a form of unpredictable gale common to the Mediterranean) sprang up, so churning the sea that General Eisenhower was for a time tempted to order a delay. While the heavy surf swamped some landing craft and made all landings difficult, it also put the beach defenders off their guard. Before daylight on July 10, both British and Americans were ashore in sizable numbers.

As presaged in North Africa, poor performance by Italian units left to German reserves the task of repelling the invasion. Although a preattack bombardment by Allied planes and confusion caused by a scattered jump of U.S. paratroopers delayed the German reaction, a panzer division mounted a sharp counterattack against American beaches before the first day was out. It came dangerously close to pushing some American units into the sea before naval gunfire and a few U.S. tanks and artillery pieces that had landed drove off the German tanks.

To speed reinforcement, the Allies on two successive nights flew in American and British paratroopers. In both instances, antiaircraft gunners on ships standing offshore and others on land mistook the planes for enemy aircraft and opened fire. Losses were so severe that for a time some Allied commanders questioned the wisdom of employing this new method of warfare.

When the Germans formed a solid block in front of the British along the east coast, the latter took over one of the main routes assigned to the Seventh Army, prompting General Patton to expand his army's role. Cutting the island in two with a drive by the II Corps, commanded now by Maj. Gen. Omar N. Bradley, Patton also sent a provisional corps pushing rapidly through faltering Italian opposition to the port of

FRATRICIDE AT SICILY

On the night of July 11, 1943, scores of Americans died in one of the worst combat accidents of the war. Hard-pressed by Axis counterattacks, General Patton decided to reinforce the beachhead with a nighttime parachute drop. Despite efforts to make sure that everyone was informed of the impending operation, when the planes arrived someone opened fire. Within minutes virtually every Allied antiaircraft gun ashore and afloat was blazing away at the hapless aircraft. Twenty-three of the 144 transport planes were shot down and another thirty-seven damaged. The paratroopers suffered 229 casualties.

Palermo and the northwestern tip of the island. Having accomplished this within fourteen days of coming ashore, Patton turned to aid the British by attacking toward Messina along a narrow northern coastal shelf.

As both Allied armies in early August readied a final assault to gain Messina, the enemy began to withdraw to the mainland. Despite the Allied command of sea and air, the Germans managed to evacuate all their forces, some 40,000 troops. When on August 17, thirty days after the invasion, U.S. patrols pushed into Messina, the Germans had incurred some 10,000 casualties, the Italians probably more than 100,000 (mostly prisoners of war). The Allies lost about 20,000.

The American force that fought in Sicily was far more sophisticated than that which had gone into battle in North Africa. New landing craft, some capable of bearing tanks, had made getting ashore much quicker and surer, and new amphibious trucks called DUKWs eased the problem of supply over the beaches. Gone was the Grant tank with its side-mounted gun, lacking a wide traverse; in its place was the Sherman with a 360-degree power-operated traverse for a turret-mounted 75-mm. piece. It was reliable and effective armored weapon. Commanders were alert to avoid a mistake often made in North Africa of parceling out divisions in small increments, and the men were sure of their weapons and their own ability. Some problems of coordination with tactical air remained, but these soon would be worked out.

The Surrender of Italy

Even as the Allies had been preparing to invade Sicily, the Italian people and their government had become increasingly disenchanted with the war. Under the impact of the loss of North Africa, the invasion of Sicily, and a first bombing of Rome, the Italian king forced Mussolini to resign as head of the government.

Anxious to find a way out of the war, a new Italian government made contact with the Allies through diplomatic channels, which led to direct talks with General Eisenhower's representatives. The Italians, it soon developed, were in a quandary: they wanted to pull out of the war, yet they were virtual prisoners of German forces in Italy that Hitler, sensing the potential for Italian defection, had strongly reinforced. Although the Allies had drawn plans for airborne landings to secure Rome coincident with an announcement of Italian surrender, the plans were canceled in the face of the Italian vacillation and inability to guarantee strong assistance in fighting the Germans. The Italian government nevertheless agreed to surrender, a fact General Eisenhower announced on the eve of the principal Allied landing at Salerno.

The Italian Campaign, September 1943–May 1945

Since the Allied governments had decided to pursue after Sicily whatever course offered the best chance of knocking Italy from the war, an invasion of the mainland logically followed. This plan also presented an opportunity to tie down German forces and prevent their employment either on the Russian Front or against the eventual Allied attack across the English Channel. Occupying Italy would also provide airfields close to Germany and the Balkans and might even induce Turkey to join the Allied cause.

How far up the peninsula of Italy the Allies were to land depended almost entirely on the range of fighter aircraft based on Sicily, for all Allied aircraft carriers were committed to the war in the Pacific, operations in the Indian Ocean, and the battle of the Atlantic. Another consideration was a desire to control the Strait of Messina to shorten sea supply lines. On September 3 a British force under Montgomery crossed the Strait of Messina and landed on the toe of the Italian boot against almost no opposition. Following Eisenhower's announcement of Italian surrender, a British fleet steamed brazenly into the harbor of Taranto in the arch of the Italian boot to put a British division ashore on the docks, while the Fifth U.S. Army under Lt. Gen. Mark W. Clark staged an assault landing on beaches near Salerno, twenty-five miles southeast of Naples.

Reacting in strength against the Salerno invasion, the Germans mounted a vigorous counterattack that threatened to split the beachhead and force the Allies to abandon part of it. For four days, the issue was in doubt. Quick reinforcement of the ground troops (including a regiment of paratroopers jumping into the beachhead), gallant fighting, liberal air support, and unstinting naval gunfire at last repulsed the German attack. On September 17 the Germans began to withdraw, and within two days patrols of the British Eighth Army arrived from the south to link the two Allied forces. Two weeks later American troops took Naples, thereby gaining an excellent port, while the British seized valuable airfields around Foggia on the other side of the peninsula.

Although the Germans seriously considered abandoning southern Italy to pull back to a line in the Northern Apennines (a fact the Allies learned from ULTRA, the interception and decryption of high-level German radio transmissions by British intelligence), the local commander, Field Marshal Albert Kesselring, insisted that he could hold for a considerable time on successive lines south of Rome. He was right. The Allied advance was destined to proceed slowly, partly because of the difficulty of offensive warfare in rugged, mountainous terrain and partly because the Allies limited their commitment to the campaign, not only in troops but also in shipping and the landing craft necessary if the enemy's strong defensive positions were to be broken by other than frontal attack.

ULTRA

Until the publication in 1974 of F. W. Winterbotham's *The ULTRA Secret*, even most historians were unaware of the degree of success of British efforts to read German messages sent via ENIGMA machines. The British Government Code and Cipher School at Bletchley Park decoded more than 80,000 German messages per month from late 1943 until May 1945. Britain, viewing ULTRA as its most secret weapon of the war, temporarily ceased providing President Roosevelt decoded messages after an ULTRA message was carelessly tossed into an office trash can in the White House. ULTRA provided the Allies an unparalleled view into some of the innermost secrets of the German war-fighting machine.

Because the buildup for a cross-channel attack—the main effort against Germany—was beginning in earnest, the Allies could spare few additional troops or ships to pursue the war in Italy. Through the fall and winter of 1943–1944, the armies would have to do the job in Italy with what was at hand, a total of eighteen Allied divisions.

A renewed offensive in October 1943 broke a strong German delaying position at the Volturno River, twenty miles north of Naples, and carried as far as the so-called Winter Line, an imposing position anchored on towering peaks around the town of Cassino. Casting about for a way to break this line, General Eisenhower obtained permission to temporarily retain from the buildup in Britain enough shipping and landing craft to make an amphibious end run. General Clark was to use a corps of his Fifth U.S. Army to land on beaches near Anzio, some thirty miles south of Rome and sixty miles behind the Winter Line. By threatening or cutting German lines of communications to the Winter Line, the troops at Anzio were to facilitate the Allied advance through the line and up the valley of the Liri River, the most obvious route to Rome.

Provided support by a French corps equipped with American arms, General Clark pulled out the U.S. VI Corps under Maj. Gen. John P. Lucas to make the envelopment. While the VI Corps (which included a British division) sailed toward Anzio, the Fifth Army launched a massive attack aimed at gaining access to the Liri valley. Although the VI Corps landed unopposed at Anzio on January 22, 1944, the attack on the Winter Line gained little. As General Lucas waited on the beachhead to build up more supplies before striking inland, the Germans reacted.

Rushing reserves to Anzio, Field Marshal Kesselring quickly erected a firm perimeter about the Allied beachhead and successfully resisted every attempt at breakout. Through February Kesselring launched determined attacks to eliminate the beachhead. Only a magnificent defense by U.S. and British infantry supported by artillery, tanks, planes, and naval gunfire at last repulsed these attacks. However, the attempt to break the stalemate had failed.

Through the rest of the winter and early spring, the Fifth and Eighth Armies regrouped and built their combined strength to twenty-five divisions, mainly with the addition of troops from France, Great Britain, New Zealand, and the British Empire (India). General Eisenhower, meanwhile, had relinquished command in the Mediterranean early in January to go to Britain to prepare for the coming invasion of France. He was succeeded by British Field Marshal Sir Henry M. Wilson.

On May 11 the Fifth and Eighth Armies launched a new, carefully synchronized attack to break the Winter Line. Passing through almost trackless mountains, French troops under General Clark's command scored a penetration that unhinged the German position. As the

Soldiers enter the town of Caiazzo after crossing the Volturno River.

145

Germans began to fall back, the VI Corps attacked from the Anzio beachhead but at Clark's direction turned north toward Rome, away from the enemy's routes of withdrawal. On June 4 U.S. troops entered the "Eternal City."

With D-Day in Normandy only two days off, the focus of the Allied war against Germany shifted to France; with the shift came a gradual diminution of Allied strength in Italy. Allied forces nevertheless continued to pursue the principle of the offensive. Reaching a new German position in the Northern Apennines, the Gothic Line, they started in August a four-month campaign that achieved penetrations; but they were unable to break out of the mountains. This period also saw a change in command as General Clark became commander of the Allied army group and Lt. Gen. Lucian K. Truscott assumed command of the Fifth Army.

In the spring of 1945 the Fifth and Eighth Armies penetrated a final German defensive line to enter the fertile plains of the Po River valley. On May 2 the Germans in Italy surrendered. Less generally acclaimed than other phases of World War II, the campaign in Italy nevertheless had a vital part in the overall conduct of the war. At the crucial time during the Normandy landings, Allied troops in Italy were tying down perhaps as many as twenty-six German divisions that well might have upset the balance in France. As a result of this campaign, the Allies obtained airfields useful for strategic bombardment of Germany and the Balkans; the conquest of the peninsula further guaranteed the safety of Allied shipping in the Mediterranean.

Cross-Channel Attack

Even as the Allied ground campaign was proceeding on the shores of the Mediterranean, three other campaigns were under way from the British Isles: the campaign of the U.S. and the Royal Navies to defeat the German submarine; a U.S.-British strategic bombing offensive against Germany; and, intricately tied in with the other two, a logistical marathon to assemble the men and tools necessary for a direct assault.

Most critical of all was the antisubmarine campaign, for without success in that the two others could progress only feebly at best. The turning point in that campaign came in the spring of 1943, when the full effect of all the various devices used against the U-boat began to appear. Despite the subsequent German introduction of an acoustical torpedo that homed on the noise of an escort's propellers and later of the *schnorkel*, a steel tube extending above water by means of which the U-boat could charge its

African-American troops cross the Arno during the drive to the Gothic Line.

batteries without surfacing, Allied shipping losses continued to decline. In the last two years of the war the submarines would sink only one-seventh of the shipping they had in the earlier years.

In the second campaign, the Combined Bomber Offensive the U.S. and British chiefs directed at Casablanca, the demands of the war in the Pacific and the Mediterranean slowed American participation. Not until the summer of 1943 were sufficient U.S. bombers available in Britain to make a substantial contribution, and not until February 1944 were U.S. airmen at last able to match the thousand-plane raids of the British.

While the Royal Air Force struck by night, bombers of the U.S. Army Air Forces hit by day; both directed much of their attention to the German aircraft industry in an effort to cripple the German air arm before the invasion. Although the raids imposed some delays on German production, the most telling effect was the loss of German fighter aircraft and trained pilots to oppose the Allied bombers. As time for the invasion approached, the German air arm had ceased to represent a real threat to Allied ground operations, and Allied bombers could shift their attention to transportation facilities in France in an effort to restrict the enemy's ability to move reserves against the invasion.

The logistical buildup in the British Isles, meanwhile, had been progressing at an ever-increasing pace, one of the greatest logistical undertakings of all time. The program entailed transporting more than 1.6 million men across the submarine-infested Atlantic before D-Day and providing for their shelter, hospitalization, supply, training, and general welfare. Mountains of weapons and equipment, ranging from locomotives and big bombers to dental fillings, also had to be shipped.

Planning for the invasion had begun long before as the British, standing alone, looked to the day when they might return to the continent. Detailed planning began in 1943, when the Combined Chiefs of Staff appointed British Lt. Gen. Frederick E. Morgan as Chief of Staff to a Supreme Commander yet to be named. Under Morgan's direction,

As time for the invasion approached, the German air arm had ceased to represent a real threat to Allied ground operations.

Eisenhower gives the order of the day, "Full Victory—nothing else."

British and American officers drew up plans for several contingencies, one of which, Operation OVERLORD, anticipated a large-scale assault against a still-powerful German Army. This plan served as the basis for a final plan developed early in 1944 after General Eisenhower, designated as the Supreme Commander, arrived in Britain and established his command, Supreme Headquarters, Allied Expeditionary Force, or SHAEF.

The overall ground commander for the invasion was the former head of the British Eighth Army, General Montgomery, who also commanded the 21st Army Group, the controlling headquarters for the two Allied armies scheduled to make the invasion. The British Second Army under Lt. Gen. Sir Miles C. Dempsey was to assault on the left, the First U.S. Army under Bradley (promoted now to lieutenant general) on the right.

The choice of invasion beaches was sharply limited by numerous requirements. They had to be within easy range of fighter aircraft based in Britain and close to at least one major port and usable airfields. The state of German defenses and the need to fool the enemy into thinking that the main invasion was yet to come in another location further narrowed the selection, leaving only one logical site: the base of the Cotentin peninsula in Normandy, southeast of Cherbourg. To facilitate supply until Cherbourg or some other port could be opened, two artificial harbors were to be towed from Britain and emplaced off the invasion beaches.

Despite a weather forecast of high winds and a rough sea, General Eisenhower made a fateful decision to go ahead with the invasion on

OMAHA BEACH

The landing on OMAHA Beach of the U.S. 1st and 29th Infantry Divisions and U.S. Army Rangers was the most difficult of the Normandy invasion. Seven thousand yards long and backed by bluffs that stood up to 170 feet in height, the beach ranged from 18 feet in width at high tide to 900 at low. Putting those advantages to good use, the Germans had laid a tangle of underwater obstructions just offshore to sink incoming landing craft and had dug positions into the cliffs to place any troops who landed under deadly cross-fires. Unknown to the Americans, the enemy's highly disciplined 352d Infantry Division manned many of those defenses. The defenses were so effective that

American soldiers land on the coast of France under heavy fire from the Germans, June 6, 1944.

for a time General Bradley contemplated withdrawing. Even so, brave young Americans slowly fought their way across the sand and through the cliffs. By nightfall, first in a trickle and then in a stream, some 34,000 soldiers had made their way ashore.

June 6. During the night over 5,000 ships moved to assigned positions; at two o'clock on the morning of the sixth the Allies began the operation for which the world had long and anxiously waited. One British and two U.S. airborne divisions (the 82d and 101st) dropped behind the beaches to secure routes of egress for the seaborne forces. Following preliminary aerial and naval bombardment, the first waves of infantry and tanks began to touch down at 6:30, just after sunrise. A heavy surf made the landings difficult but, as in Sicily, put the defenders off their guard.

U.S. Troops Moving Ashore at OMAHA *Beach on D-Day*

The assault went well on the British beaches, where one Canadian and two British divisions landed, and also at UTAH, westernmost of the U.S. beaches, where the 4th Infantry Division came ashore. (*See Map 5.*) The story was different at OMAHA Beach. Although ULTRA had pinpointed most of the German divisions manning the coastal defenses, it had missed a powerful enemy division that occupied the high bluffs laced with pillboxes overlooking the landing beach. When Allied intelligence detected the *352d Division*'s presence, it was too late to alter the landing plan. Only through improvisation, personal courage, and accurate naval gunfire support were the men of two regiments of the 1st Division and one of the 29th at last able to work their way up the bluffs to move slowly inland. Some 50,000 U.S. troops made their way ashore on the two beaches before the day was out. American casualties were approximately 6,500, British and Canadian 3,000—in both cases lighter than expected.

The German command was slow to react to the invasion, having been misled not only by the weather but also by an Allied deception plan that continued to lead the enemy to believe that this was only a diversionary assault and that the main landings were to come later on the Pas de Calais. Only in one instance, against the British who were solidly ashore, did the Germans mount a sizable counterattack on D-Day.

Buildup and Breakout

While ULTRA monitored the success of the Allied deception plan and Allied aircraft and French resistance fighters impeded the movement of those German reserves that did move to Normandy, the Allies quickly built up their strength and linked the beachheads. U.S. troops then moved against Cherbourg, taking the port after bitter fighting, three weeks following the invasion. Other Allied forces had in the meantime deepened the beachhead between Caen and the road center of St. Lô, so that by the end of June the most forward positions were twenty miles from the sea. The Germans still had been able to mount no major counterattack.

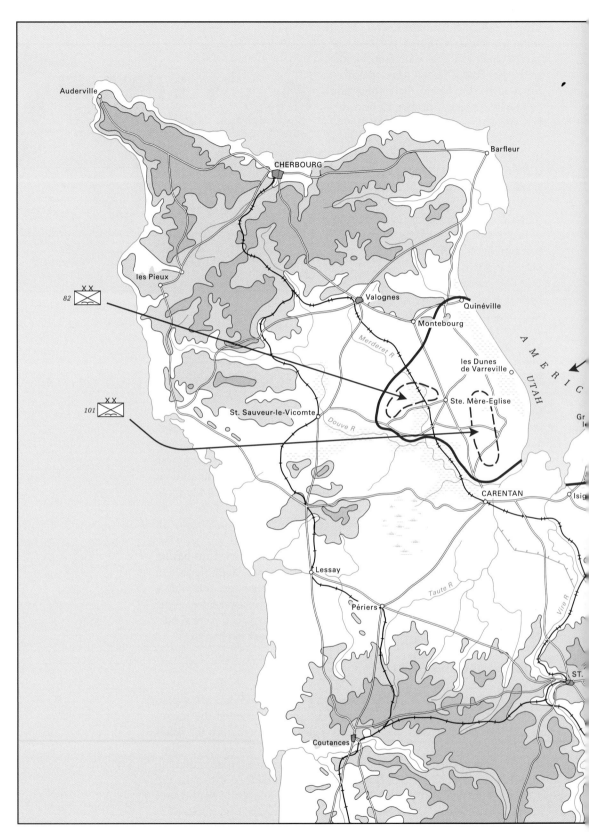

Map 5

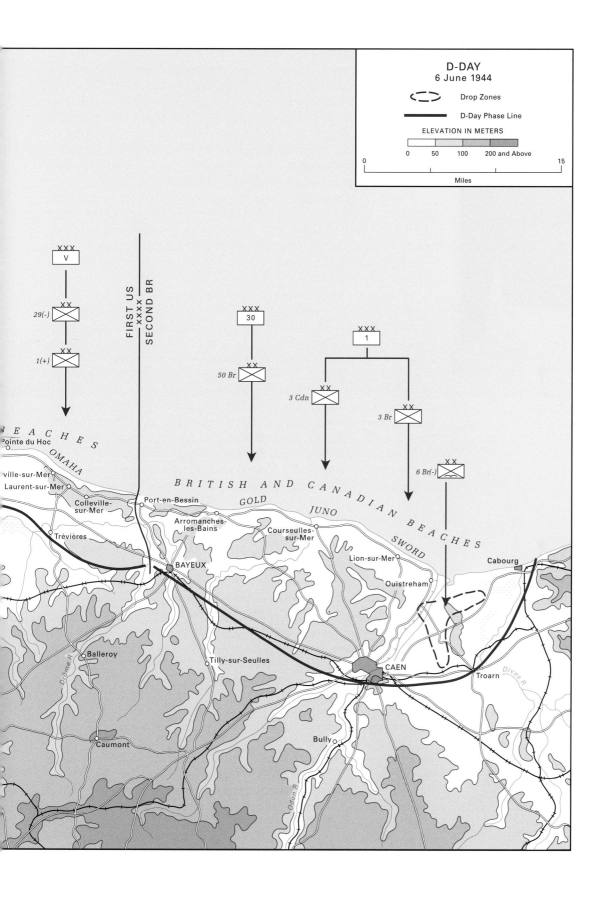

D-DAY
6 June 1944

Drop Zones

D-Day Phase Line

ELEVATION IN METERS

0   50   100   200 and Above

0   15
Miles

XXX
V

29(-)

1(+)

FIRST US
xxxx
SECOND BR

XXX
30

50 Br

XXX
1

3 Cdn

3 Br

6 Br(-)

B E A C H E S
Pointe du Hoc
OMAHA
-ville-sur-Mer
Laurent-sur-Mer
Colleville-sur-Mer
Trévières
Port-en-Bessin
Arromanches-les-Bains
GOLD
Courseulles-sur-Mer
JUNO
Lion-sur-Mer
SWORD
Ouistreham
Cabourg

B R I T I S H   A N D   C A N A D I A N   B E A C H E S

BAYEUX

Balleroy
Dîome R.
Tilly-sur-Seulles
CAEN
Troarn
Dives R.

Caumont
Bully
Odon R.

Olive Drab Field Jacket of the 104th Infantry Division, 1945

Commanded by Field Marshal Gerd von Rundstedt, the enemy nevertheless defended tenaciously in terrain ideally suited to the defense. This was hedgerow country, where through the centuries French farmers had erected high banks of earth around every small field to fence in livestock and protect crops from coastal winds. These banks were thick with the roots of shrubs and trees; and in many places, sunken roads screened by a canopy of tree branches ran between two hedgerows. Tunneling into the hedgerows and using the sunken roads for lines of communication, the Germans had turned each field into a small fortress.

For all the slow advance and lack of ports (a gale on June 19 demolished one of the artificial harbors and damaged the other), the Allied buildup was swift. By the end of June close to a million men had come ashore, along with some 586,000 tons of supplies and 177,000 vehicles. General Bradley's First Army included four corps with two armored and eleven infantry divisions. British strength was about the same.

Seeking to end the battle of the hedgerows, the British attempted to break into more-open country near Caen, only to be thwarted by concentrations of German armor. General Bradley then tried a breakout on the right near St. Lô. Behind an intensive aerial bombardment that utilized both tactical aircraft and heavy bombers, the First Army attacked on July 25. By the second day American troops had opened a big breach in German positions, whereupon armored divisions drove rapidly southward twenty-five miles to Avranches at the base of the Cotentin peninsula. While the First Army turned southeastward, the Third U.S. Army under General Patton entered the line to swing through Avranches into Brittany in quest of ports.

The arrival of the Third Army signaled a major change in command. General Bradley moved up to command the 12th Army Group, composed of the First and Third Armies; his former deputy, Lt. Gen. Courtney H. Hodges, assumed command of the First Army. Montgomery's 21st Army Group consisted of the British Second Army and a newcomer to the front, the First Canadian Army under Lt. Gen. Henry D. G. Crerar. General Montgomery continued to function as overall ground commander, an arrangement that was to prevail for another five weeks until General Eisenhower moved his headquarters to the continent and assumed direct command of the armies in the field.

In terms of the preinvasion plan, General Eisenhower intended to establish a solid lodgment area in France extending as far east as the Seine River to provide room for air and supply bases. Having built up strength in this area, he planned then to advance into Germany on a broad front. Under the 21st Army Group he would concentrate his greatest resources north of the Ardennes region of Belgium along the most direct route to the Ruhr industrial region, Germany's largest complex of mines and industry. Bradley's 12th Army Group, meanwhile, was to make a subsidiary thrust south of the Ardennes to seize the Saar industrial region along the Franco-German frontier. A third force invading southern France in August was to provide protection on Bradley's right.

The First Army's breakout from the hedgerows changed that plan, for it opened the German armies in France to crushing defeat. When the Germans counterattacked toward Avranches to try to cut off leading columns of the First and Third Armies, other men of the First Army stood firm, setting up an opportunity for exploiting the principle of maneuver to the fullest. While the First Canadian Army attacked toward Falaise, General Bradley directed mobile columns of both the First and Third Armies on a wide encircling maneuver in the direction of Argentan, not far from Falaise. This caught the enemy's counterattacking force in a giant pocket. Although the Allies closed the fifteen-mile gap between Falaise and Argentan only after many of the Germans escaped, more than 60,000 were killed or captured in the pocket. Great masses of German guns, tanks, and equipment fell into Allied hands.

While the First Army finished the business at Argentan, Patton's Third Army dashed off again toward the Seine River with two objects: eliminating the Seine as a likely new line of German defense and making a second, wider envelopment to trap those German troops that had escaped from the first pocket. Patton largely accomplished both objectives. In the two pockets, the enemy lost large segments of two field armies.

Invasion of Southern France

Even as General Eisenhower's armies were scoring a great victory in Normandy, on August 15 the Allies staged another invasion, this one in southern France. Operation DRAGOON, originally code-named ANVIL, sought to establish a supplementary line of communications through the French Mediterranean ports and to prevent the Germans in the south from moving against the main Allied armies in the north. It also provided an opportunity for the Allies to bring to bear in France the troops from the Mediterranean Theater, including the sizable Free French forces in North Africa and Italy. Lack of landing craft had precluded launching this invasion at the same time as OVERLORD.

Under control of the Seventh U.S. Army, commanded now by Lt. Gen. Alexander M. Patch, three U.S. divisions, plus an airborne task force and French commandos, began landing just after dawn. The defending Germans were spread too thin to provide much more than token resistance, and by the end of the first day the Seventh Army had 86,000 men and 12,000 vehicles ashore. The next day French troops staged a second landing and moved swiftly to seize the ports of Toulon and Marseille.

Faced with entrapment by the spectacular Allied advances in the north, the Germans in southern France began to withdraw on August 17. U.S. and French columns followed closely and on September 11 established contact with Patton's Third Army. Under the 6th Army Group, commanded by Lt. Gen. Jacob L. Devers, the Seventh Army and French forces organized as the 1st French Army passed to General Eisenhower's command.

Pursuit to the Frontier

As Allied columns were breaking loose all over France, men and women of the French resistance movement began to battle the Germans in the streets of the capital. Although General Eisenhower had intended to bypass Paris, hoping to avoid heavy fighting in the city and to postpone the necessity of feeding the civilian population, he felt

Men of the First Army stood firm, setting up an opportunity for exploiting the principle of maneuver to the fullest.

compelled to send help lest the uprising be defeated. On August 25 a column including U.S. and French troops entered the city.

With surviving enemy forces falling back in defeat toward the German frontier, General Eisenhower abandoned the original plan of holding at the Seine while he opened the Brittany ports and established a sound logistical base. Determined to take advantage of the enemy's defeat, he reinforced Montgomery's 21st Army Group by sending the First U.S. Army close alongside the British, thus providing enough strength in the northern thrust to assure quick capture of ports along the English Channel, particularly the great Belgian port of Antwerp. Because the front was fast moving away from Brittany, the channel ports were essential.

Ports posed a special problem: with the stormy weather of fall and winter approaching, the Allies could not much longer depend upon supply over the invasion beaches; Cherbourg had only a limited capacity. Even though Brittany now was far behind the advancing front, General Eisenhower still felt a need for the port of Brest. (*See Map 6.*) He put those troops of the Third Army that had driven into the peninsula under a new headquarters, the Ninth U.S. Army commanded by Lt. Gen. William H. Simpson, and set them to the task. When Brest fell two weeks later, the port was a shambles. The port problem nevertheless appeared to be solved when on September 4 British troops took Antwerp, its wharves and docks intact; but the success proved illusory. Antwerp is on an estuary sixty miles from the sea, and German troops clung to the banks, denying access to Allied shipping.

The port situation was symptomatic of multitudinous problems that had begun to beset the entire Allied logistical apparatus (organized much like Pershing's Services of Supply but called the Communications Zone). The armies were going so far and so fast that the supply services

RED BALL EXPRESS

With supply deliveries to the Allied armies slowing to a trickle beyond the Seine, and the military desperate for a solution, Red Ball's trucks began rolling on August 25, 1944. Four days later the Red Ball Express had 132 truck companies, the majority being African-American units, operating 5,958 vehicles. Working almost around the clock and ignoring blackout rules at night, they moved over 12,000 tons of critical materiel—especially fuel and ammunition—from St. Lô to Chartres. This was the peak of the operation. When the Red Ball Express finally suspended activity in mid-November, it had averaged 7,000 tons of supplies every day and, contrary to initial expectations, was operating east of the Seine in support of the advance.

An MP waves on a convoy of the Red Ball Express near Alençon, France.

were unable to keep pace. Although enough supplies were available in Normandy, the problem was to get them to forward positions sometimes more than 500 miles beyond the depots. Despite extraordinary measures such as establishing a one-way truck route called the Red Ball Express, supplies of such essential commodities as gasoline and ammunition began to run short. This was the penalty the Allied armies would have to pay for the decision to not to pause at the Seine.

The logistical crisis sparked a difference over strategy between Generals Eisenhower and Montgomery. In view of the logistical difficulties, Montgomery insisted that General Patton's Third Army should halt to allow all transportation resources to concentrate behind his troops and the First Army. This allocation, he believed, would enable him to make a quick strike deep into Germany and impel a German surrender.

Acting on the advice of logistical experts on his staff, Eisenhower refused Montgomery's request. Such a drive could succeed, his staff advised, only if all Allied armies had closed up to the Rhine River and if Antwerp were open to Allied shipping. The only choice, General Eisenhower believed, was to keep pushing all along the line while supplies held out, ideally to go so far as to gain bridgeheads over the Rhine.

Obstacles other than supply stood in the way of that goal. Some were natural, like the Moselle and Meuse Rivers, the Vosges Mountains in Alsace, the wooded hills of the Ardennes, and a dense Huertgen Forest facing the First Army near Aachen. Other obstacles were manmade: old French forts around Metz and the French Maginot Line in northeastern France, as well as dense fortifications all along the German border (the Siegfried Line, or, as the Germans called it, the West Wall). By mid-September the First Army had penetrated the West Wall at several points but lacked the means to exploit the breaks. Meanwhile, Patton's Third Army was encountering tough resistance in its attempts to establish bridgeheads over the Moselle near Metz and Nancy.

Although General Eisenhower assigned first priority to clearing the seaward approaches to Antwerp, he sanctioned a Montgomery proposal to use Allied airborne troops in a last bold stroke to capitalize on German disorganization before logistics should force a halt. While the British Second Army launched an attack called Operation GARDEN, airborne troops of the recently organized First Allied Airborne Army (Lt. Gen. Lewis H. Brereton) were to land in Operation MARKET astride three major water obstacles in the Netherlands: the Maas, Waal, and Lower Rhine Rivers. Crossing these rivers on bridges to be secured by the airborne troops, the Second Army was to drive all the way to the Ijssel Meer (Zuider Zee), cutting off Germans farther west and putting the British in a position to outflank the West Wall and drive into Germany along a relatively open north German plain.

Employing one British and two U.S. airborne divisions, the Allies began the airborne attack on September 17. On the first day alone approximately 20,000 paratroopers and glider troops landed in the largest airborne attack of the war. Although the drops were spectacularly successful and achieved complete surprise, the presence near the drop zones of two panzer divisions—which ULTRA spotted but Allied planners discounted—enabled the Germans to react swiftly. Resistance to the ground attack also was greater than expected, delaying a quick linkup with the airheads. The combined operation gained a salient

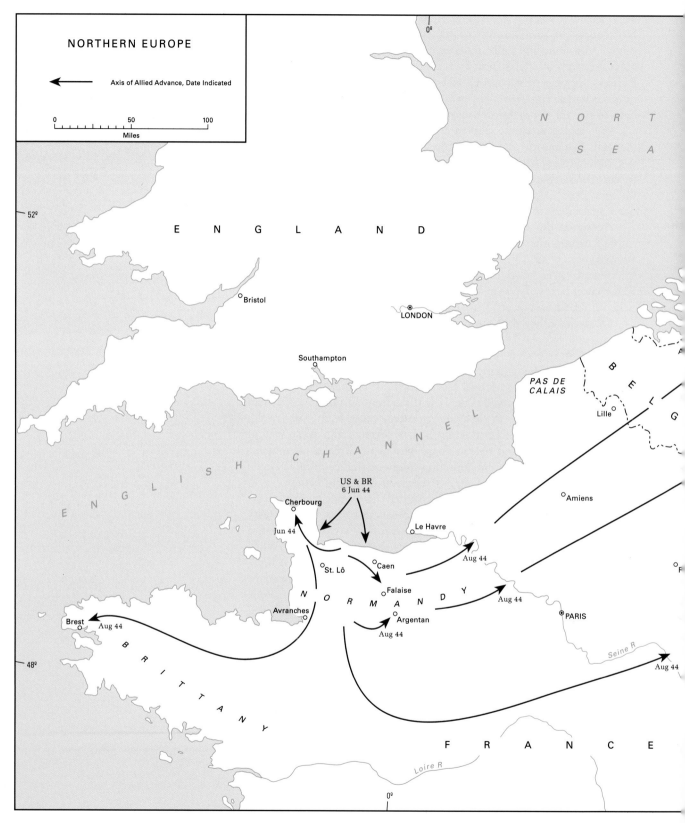

NORTHERN EUROPE

Axis of Allied Advance, Date Indicated

0   50   100
Miles

52º

E N G L A N D

N O R T

S E A

Bristol

LONDON

Southampton

PAS DE
CALAIS

B
E
L
G

Lille

E N G L I S H   C H A N N E L

Amiens

US & BR
6 Jun 44

Cherbourg

Jun 44

Le Havre

Aug 44

St. Lô

Caen

N

Falaise

O R M A N D Y

Aug 44

PARIS

Avranches

Argentan

Aug 44

Brest

Aug 44

B
R
I
T
T
A
N
Y

Aug 44

Seine R

48º

Aug 44

F R A N C E

Loire R

0º

Map 6

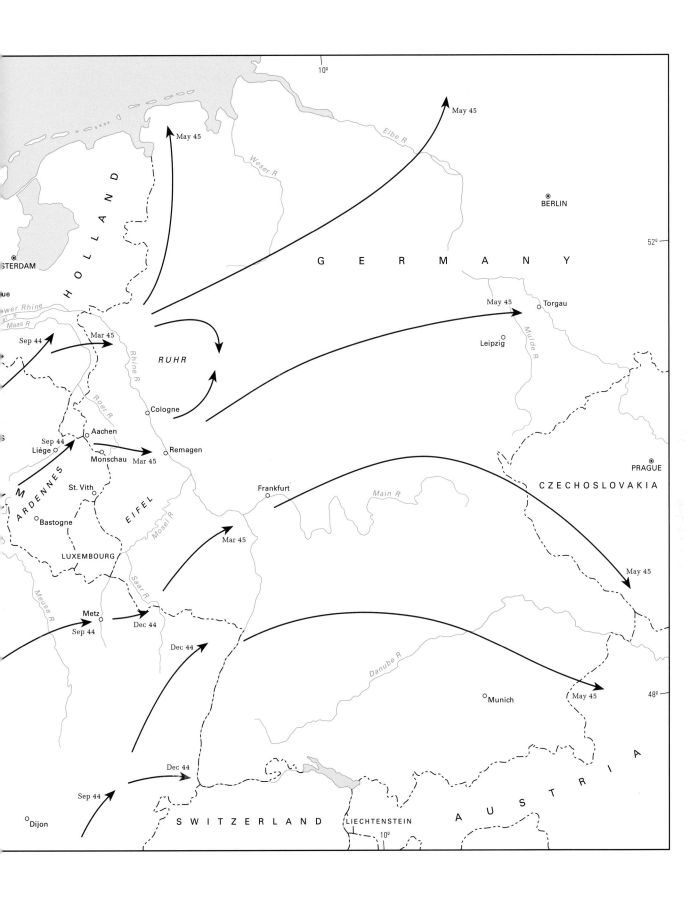

some fifty miles deep into German-held territory but fell short of the ambitious objectives, including a bridgehead across the Lower Rhine.

At this point, Montgomery (promoted now to field marshal) concentrated on opening Antwerp to Allied shipping, but so determined was German resistance and so difficult the conditions of mud and flood in the low-lying countryside that it was well into November before the job was finished. The first Allied ship dropped anchor in Antwerp only on November 28.

As a result of a cutback in offensive operations and the extraordinary efforts of the supply services, aided by the availability of the Mediterranean ports, the logistical situation had been gradually improving. In early November resources were sufficient to enable the U.S. armies to launch a big offensive aimed at reaching the Rhine; but, despite the largest air attack in direct support of ground troops during the war (Operation QUEEN), it turned out to be a slow, arduous fight through the natural and artificial obstacles along the frontier. Heavy rain and severe cold added to the difficulties. By mid-December the First and Ninth Armies had reached the Roer River east of Aachen, twenty-three miles inside Germany, and the Third Army had come up to the West Wall along the Saar River northeast of Metz; but only the Seventh Army and the 1st French Army in Alsace had touched any part of the Rhine.

Having taken advantage of the pause imposed by Allied logistical problems to create new divisions and rush replacements to the front, the Germans in the west had made a remarkable recovery from the debacle in France. Just how remarkable was soon to be forcefully demonstrated in what had heretofore been a quiet sector held by the First Army's right wing.

> It turned out to be a slow, arduous fight through the natural and artificial obstacles along the frontier.

Dismal Weather at Metz, *Gary Sheadan, n.d.*

The Ardennes Counteroffensive

As early as the preceding August, Adolf Hitler had been contemplating a counteroffensive to regain the initiative in the west. Over the protests of his generals, who thought the plan too ambitious, he ordered an attack by twenty-five divisions, carefully conserved and secretly assembled, to hit thinly manned U.S. positions in the Ardennes region of Belgium and Luxembourg, cross the Meuse River, then push on northwestward to Antwerp. In taking Antwerp, Hitler expected to cut off and destroy the British 21st Army Group and the First and Ninth U.S. Armies and thereby turn around the whole course of the war.

Under cover of inclement winter weather, Hitler concentrated his forces in the forests of the Eifel region, opposite the Ardennes. Although in hindsight ULTRA and other Allied sources of intelligence gave some clues of the coming attack, the indicators did not stand out enough from other data to allow Allied

American Infantrymen of the 290th Regiment Fighting in Belgium in January 1945

intelligence agencies to forecast the coming offensive. Before daylight on December 16, the Germans attacked along a sixty-mile front, taking the VIII Corps and the south wing of the V Corps by surprise (*See Map 7.*) In most places, German gains were rapid; the American divisions were either inexperienced or seriously depleted from earlier fighting, and all were stretched thin. In one instance, two inexperienced regiments of the 106th Infantry Division were forced to surrender in the largest mass surrender of U.S. troops during the course of the war in Europe.

German Planes Strafe Road in Belgium, *Gary Sheadan, n.d.*

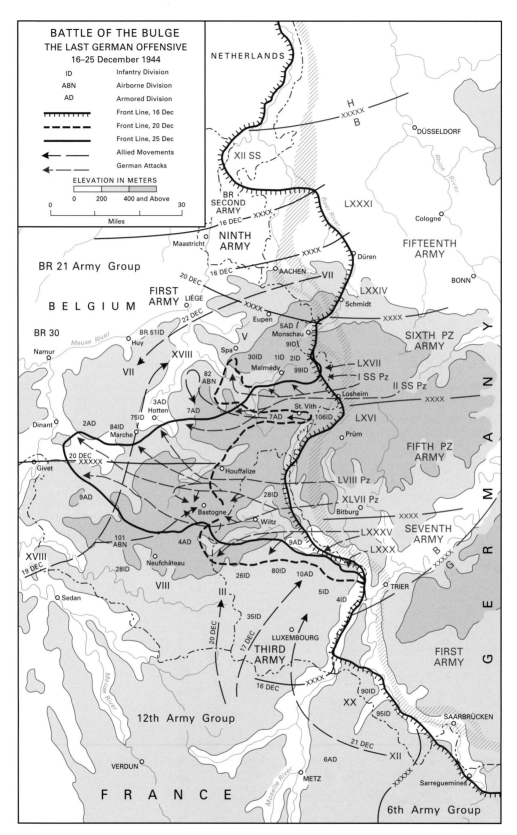

BATTLE OF THE BULGE
THE LAST GERMAN OFFENSIVE
16–25 December 1944

ID	Infantry Division
ABN	Airborne Division
AD	Armored Division

Front Line, 16 Dec
Front Line, 20 Dec
Front Line, 25 Dec
Allied Movements
German Attacks

ELEVATION IN METERS

0   200   400 and Above

0   30
Miles

NETHERLANDS

DÜSSELDORF

H
XXXXX
B

XII SS

Rhine River

BR
SECOND
ARMY

LXXXI

Roer River

FIFTEENTH
ARMY

16 DEC

NINTH
ARMY

XXXX

Düren

Cologne

Maastricht

BR 21 Army Group

20 DEC

16 DEC

AACHEN

VII

BONN

FIRST
ARMY

LIÈGE

LXXIV

Schmidt

BELGIUM

XXXX

Eupen

22 DEC

BR 30

Meuse River

BR 51ID

Huy

V

Monschau

5AD

9ID

SIXTH PZ
ARMY

Spa

30ID 1ID 2ID

XXXX

XVIII

Namur

VII

30ID

Malmédy

99ID

LXVII

I SS Pz

82
ABN

II SS Pz

3AD
Hotten

Losheim

XXXX

75ID

7AD

St. Vith

7AD 106ID

LXVI

Dinant

2AD

84ID
Marche

Prüm

FIFTH PZ
ARMY

9AD

20 DEC
XXXXX

Houffalize

LVIII Pz

Givet

28ID

XLVII Pz

Bitburg

XXXX

Bastogne

Wiltz

LXXXV

SEVENTH
ARMY

101
ABN

4AD

9AD

LXXX

B
G

XVIII

28ID

Neufchâteau

VIII

26ID

80ID

10AD

TRIER

19 DEC

5ID 4ID

Sedan

III

35ID

LUXEMBOURG

FIRST
ARMY

G
E
R
M
A
N
Y

20 DEC

17 DEC

THIRD
ARMY

16 DEC

XXXX

90ID

XX

95ID

SAARBRÜCKEN

12th Army Group

Meuse River

21 DEC

XII

VERDUN

6AD

Moselle River

METZ

Sarreguemines

F R A N C E

6th Army Group

Map 7

The Germans nevertheless encountered difficulties from the first. Cut off and surrounded, many small U.S. units continued to fight. At the northern shoulder of the penetration, divisions of the V Corps refused to budge from the vicinity of Monschau, thereby denying critical roads to the enemy and limiting the width of the penetration. At St. Vith, American troops held out for six days to block a vital road center. To Bastogne in the southwest, where an armored detachment served as a blocking force, General Eisenhower rushed an airborne division that never relinquished that communications center even though surrounded. Here, Brig. Gen. Anthony C. McAuliffe delivered a terse reply to a German demand for surrender: "Nuts!"

Denied important roads and hampered by air attacks as the weather cleared, the Germans fell a few miles short of even their first objective, the Meuse River. The result after more than a month of hard fighting that cost the Americans 75,000 casualties and the Germans close to 100,000 was nothing but a big bulge in the lines from which the battle drew its popular name.

Faced with a shortage of infantry replacements during the enemy's counteroffensive, General Eisenhower offered African-American soldiers in service units an opportunity to volunteer for duty with the infantry. More than 4,500 responded, many taking reductions in grade in order to meet specified requirements. The 6th Army Group formed these men into provisional companies, while the 12th Army Group employed them as an additional platoon in existing rifle companies. The excellent record established by these volunteers, particularly those serving as platoons, presaged major postwar changes in the traditional approach to employing African-American troops.

Although the counteroffensive had given the Allied command some anxious moments, the gallant stands by isolated units had

Pamphlet for Bastogne, Olin Dows, 1945

BASTOGNE

General Eisenhower's strategy of pursuing offensive operations on a broad front left him with scant reserves when the Germans launched their Ardennes offensive on December 16, 1944. Eisenhower ordered one of his two reserve divisions, the 101st Airborne Division, to the Belgian crossroads town of Bastogne. Its mission was to block the German advance, winning time for Eisenhower to mass forces for a counterattack on the German flanks. They held out against four German divisions and inflicted a fatal delay on the enemy. The siege ended on December 26, when the U.S. 4th Armored Division broke through the encirclement.

American servicemen celebrate news of the German surrender with civilians at Piccadilly Circus, London, May 7, 1945.

As the month of April opened, Allied armies fanned out from the Rhine all along the line with massive columns of armor and motorized infantry. Encircling the Ruhr, the First and Ninth Armies took 325,000 prisoners, totally destroying an entire German army group. Although the Germans managed to rally determined resistance at isolated points, a cohesive defensive line ceased to exist.

Since the Russians were within forty miles of Berlin and apparently would reach the German capital first—which in any case lay within their already arranged postwar zone of occupation—General Eisenhower decided against sending his troops to join a costly battle for the city. Instead he put the main weight of his offensive behind the U.S. armies moving through central Germany to eliminate a remaining pocket of German industry and to link with the Russians. The 21st Army Group meanwhile sealed off the Netherlands and headed toward the base of the Jutland peninsula, while the 6th Army Group turned southeastward to obviate any effort by the Nazis to make a last-ditch stand in the Alps of southern Germany and Austria.

By mid-April Allied armies in the north and center were building up along the Elbe and Mulde Rivers, an agreed line of contact with the Red Army approaching from the east. First contact came on April 25 near the town of Torgau, followed by wholesale German surrenders all along the front and in Italy.

With Berlin in Soviet hands, Hitler a suicide, and almost every corner of Germany overrun, emissaries of the German government surrendered on May 7, 1945, at General Eisenhower's headquarters in Reims, France. The next day, May 8, was V-E Day, the official date of the end of the war in Europe.

The Situation on V-E Day

As V-E Day came, Allied forces in Western Europe consisted of 4.5 million men, including 9 armies (5 of them American—1 of which, the Fifteenth, saw action only at the last), 23 corps, 91 divisions (61 of them American), 6 tactical air commands (4 American), and 2 strategic air forces (1 American). The Allies had 28,000 combat aircraft, of which 14,845 were American; and they had brought into Western Europe more than 970,000 vehicles and 18 million tons of supplies. At the same time they were achieving final victory in Italy with 18 divisions (7 of them American).

The German armed forces and the nation were prostrate, beaten to a degree never before seen in modern times. Hardly any organized units of the German Army remained except in Norway, Denmark, Czechoslovakia, and the Balkans; these would soon capitulate. What remained of the air arm was too demoralized even for a final suicidal effort, and the residue of the German Navy lay helpless in captured northern ports. Through five years of war, the German armed forces had lost over 3 million men killed, 263,000 of them in the west, since D-Day. The United States lost 135,576 dead in Western Europe; while Britain, Canada, France, and other Allies combined incurred after D-Day approximately 60,000 military deaths.

Unlike in World War I, when the United States had come late on the scene and provided only those forces to swing the balance of power to the Allied side, the American contribution to the reconquest of Western Europe had been predominant, not just in manpower but as a true arsenal of democracy. American factories produced for the British almost three times more Lend-Lease materials than for the Russians, including 185,000 vehicles, 12,000 tanks, and enough planes to equip four tactical air forces and for the French all weapons and equipment for 8 divisions and 1 tactical air force plus partial equipment for 3 more divisions.

Although strategic air power had failed to prove the decisive instrument many had expected, it was a major factor in the Allied victory, as was the role of Allied navies; for without control of the sea lanes, there could have been no buildup in Britain and no amphibious assaults. It was nonetheless true that the application of the power of ground armies finally broke the German ability and will to resist.

While the Germans had developed a flying bomb and later a supersonic missile, the weapons with which both sides fought the war were in the main much improved versions of those that had been present in World War I: the motor vehicle, the airplane, the machine gun, indirect-fire artillery, the tank. The difference lay in such accoutrements as improved radio communications and in a new sophistication in terms of mobility and coordination that provided the means for rapid exploitation that both sides in World War I had lacked.

From North Africa to the Elbe, U.S. Army generalship proved remarkably effective. Such field commanders as Bradley, Devers, Clark, Hodges, Patton, Simpson, Patch, and numerous corps and division commanders could stand beside the best that had ever served the nation. Having helped develop Army doctrine during the years between the two great wars, these same men put the theories to battlefield test with enormous success. Some indication of the magnitude of the responsibilities they carried is apparent from the fact that late in the war General Bradley as commander of the 12th Army Group had under his command 4 field armies, 12 corps, and 48 divisions, more than 1.3 million men, the largest exclusively American field command in U.S. history.

These commanders consistently displayed a steady devotion to the principles of war. Despite sometimes seemingly insurmountable

Having helped develop Army doctrine during the years between the two great wars, these same men put the theories to battlefield test with enormous success.

obstacles of weather, terrain, and enemy concentration, they were generally able to achieve the mass, mobility, and firepower to avoid a stalemate, maintaining the principles of the objective and the offensive and exploiting the principle of maneuver to the fullest. On many occasions they achieved surprise, most notably in the amphibious assaults and at the Rhine. They were themselves taken by surprise twice, in central Tunisia and in the Ardennes; yet in both cases they recovered quickly. Economy of force was particularly evident in Italy, and simplicity was nowhere better demonstrated than in the Normandy landings, despite a complexity inherent in the size and diversity of the invasion forces. From the first, unity of command abided in every campaign, not just at the tactical level but also in the combined staff system that afforded the U.S. and Britain a unity of command and purpose never approached on the Axis side.

Discussion Questions

1. What mistakes did an inexperienced U.S. Army make in North Africa? Should it have played a more subsidiary role to the British until it acquired more experience?

2. Did the campaigns in the Mediterranean justify the investment in resources?

3. Why did the Allies invade in Normandy rather than another part of France or Europe? How did they achieve their breakout in July and August 1944?

4. Which was the proper strategy for the Allies in the late summer and fall of 1944: Montgomery's single thrust or Eisenhower's broad front? Defend your answer in light of both MARKET-GARDEN and the Battle of the Bulge.

5. Why did the Allies encounter logistical problems in the fall of 1944? Should General Eisenhower have done more to consolidate his logistics prior to continuing his pursuit of the Germans toward the frontier?

6. What factors contributed to the success of American arms in the war against Germany and Italy during World War II? In your opinion, which ally contributed most to the eventual victory? Which branch of the armed services? Explain.

Recommended Readings

Ambrose, Stephen E. *Band of Brothers: E Company, 506th Regiment, 101st Airborne from Normandy to Eagle's Nest.* New York: Simon and Schuster, 2001.

Atkinson, Rick. An Army at Dawn: The War in North Africa, 1942–1943. New York: Henry Holt & Co., 2002.

D'Este, Carlo. *Fatal Decision: Anzio and the Battle for Rome.* New York: HarperCollins, 1991.

———. Patton: *A Genius for War.* New York: HarperCollins, 1995.

Heller, Charles E., and William A. Stofft, eds. *America's First Battles, 1776–1965*. Lawrence: University Press of Kansas, 1986.

MacDonald, Charles B. *Company Commander*. Short Hills, N.J.: Burford Books, 1999.

————. *The Mighty Endeavor: American Armed Forces in the European Theater during World War II*. New York: Oxford University Press, 1969.

————. *A Time for Trumpets: The Untold Story of the Battle of the Bulge*. New York: William Morrow, 1985.

Murray, Williamson, and Allan R. Millett. *A War To Be Won: Fighting the Second World War*. Cambridge, Mass.: Belknap Press of Harvard University Press, 2000.

Ryan, Cornelius. *The Longest Day: June 6, 1944*. New York: Simon and Schuster, 1994.

Other Readings

Bennett, Ralph. *ULTRA and Mediterranean Strategy*. New York: Morrow, 1989.

————. *ULTRA in the West: The Normandy Campaign, 1944–45*. New York: Scribner, 1979.

Blumenson, Martin. *Breakout and Pursuit*. U.S. Army in World War II. Washington, D.C.: U.S. Army Center of Military History, 1990.

————. *Salerno to Cassino*. U.S. Army in World War II. Washington, D.C.: U.S. Army Center of Military History, 2002.

Clarke, Jeffrey J., and Robert R. Smith. *Riviera to the Rhine*. U.S. Army in World War II. Washington, D.C.: U.S. Army Center of Military History, 1993.

Cole, Hugh M. *The Ardennes: Battle of the Bulge*. U.S. Army in World War II. Washington, D.C.: U.S. Army Center of Military History, 1994.

————. *The Lorraine Campaign*. U.S. Army in World War II. Washington, D.C.: U.S. Army Center of Military History, 1997.

Fisher, Ernest F., Jr. *Cassino to the Alps*. U.S. Army in World War II. Washington, D.C.: U.S. Army Center of Military History, 2002.

Garland, Albert N., and Howard M. Smyth. *Sicily and the Surrender of Italy*. U.S. Army in World War II. Washington, D.C.: U.S. Army Center of Military History, 2002.

Harrison, Gordon. *Cross-Channel Attack*. U.S. Army in World War II. Washington, D.C.: U.S. Army Center of Military History, 2002.

Howe, George G. *Northwest Africa: Seizing the Initiative in the West*. U.S. Army in World War II. Washington, D.C.: U.S. Army Center of Military History, 2002.

Huston, James A. *The Sinews of War: Army Logistics, 1775–1953*. Washington, D.C.: U.S. Army Center of Military History, 1997, ch. 30.

MacDonald, Charles B. *The Last Offensive*. U.S. Army in World War II. Washington, D.C.: U.S. Army Center of Military History, 1990.

————. *The Siegfried Line Campaign*. U.S. Army in World War II. Washington, D.C.: U.S. Army Center of Military History, 2001.

and ultimately losing substantial air and naval resources in the effort to hold Guadalcanal. The Americans had to reinforce heavily, deploying naval power, planes, soldiers, and marines in the battle at the expense of other theaters. Before the island was secured in November, another Marine division (the 2d), two Army divisions (the 25th and Americal), and one separate regiment, to mention only the major ground combat elements, had been thrown into the battle. The last act came in February 1943, when the 43d Division moved into the Russell Islands, thirty-five miles northwest of Guadalcanal. On Guadalcanal and in the Russells, American forces then began to construct major air and logistical bases for further advances.

A Japanese overland drive toward Port Moresby in New Guinea had meanwhile forced General MacArthur to begin an offensive of his own—the Papua Campaign. During the late summer the Japanese had pushed across the towering Owen Stanley Mountains toward Port Moresby from the Buna-Gona area on New Guinea's northeastern coast and by mid-September were only twenty miles from their objective. Australian ground forces drove the Japanese back to the north coast, where they strongly entrenched themselves around Buna and Gona. It took two Australian divisions, a U.S. Army division (the 32d), and another U.S. Army regiment almost four months of bitter fighting to dislodge the Japanese. Casualties were high and disease rampant; but as at Guadalcanal, the Allied forces learned much about jungle fighting, the importance of air power, and the need for thorough logistical preparation. They also discovered that the Japanese soldier, though a skillful, stubborn, and fanatic foe, could be defeated. The myth of Japanese invincibility was forever laid to rest in the jungles of Guadalcanal and Papua.

After Papua and Guadalcanal the tempo of operations in the South and Southwest Pacific Areas slowed while General MacArthur and Admiral Halsey gathered resources and prepared bases for the next phase. The Japanese in turn undertook to reinforce their main bases in New Guinea and the northern Solomons. In March 1943 they attempted to send a large convoy to Lae in New Guinea. Forewarned by signals intelligence, U.S. Army Air Force and Australian land-based aircraft repeatedly struck the slow-moving convoy. The four-day running air-sea fight became known as the Battle of the Bismarck Sea and cost the Japanese some 3,500 soldiers and sailors and much valuable shipping. During the following months Rabaul-based planes, reinforced by carrier planes flown in from the Carolines, sought unsuccessfully to knock out American air power in the southern Solomons.

BUNA-GONA

Japan's lodgment on the northeastern shore of New Guinea centered on its control of the outposts at Buna and Gona. To eliminate this threat, the Americans and Australians had to attack the Japanese frontally across the Owen Stanley Mountains and along the coast. Short of artillery ammunition and food, poorly trained and led, and suffering heavily from jungle diseases, the soldiers faltered; and the U.S. offensive soon sputtered to a halt. Only through dynamic leadership and persistent small-unit actions did the Allies take the two Japanese outposts, at a heavy cost. MacArthur determined there would be "No more Bunas!"

Search for a Strategy

Meanwhile, in the spring and summer of 1943, a strategy for the defeat of Japan began to take shape within Allied councils. The major Allied objective was control of the South China Sea and a foothold on the coast of China to sever Japanese lines of communications southward and to establish bases from which to subject Japan first to an intensive aerial bombardment and naval blockade and then, if necessary, an invasion. The first plans for this objective envisioned Allied drives from several different directions: by American forces across the Pacific (from the south and southwest toward the Philippines and from Hawaii across the Central Pacific) and by British and Chinese forces along a land line through Burma and China and a sea line from India via the Netherlands Indies, Singapore, and the Strait of Malacca into the South China Sea. Within the framework of this tentative long-range plan, the U.S. Joint Chiefs fitted their existing plans for completion of the campaign against Rabaul and a subsequent advance to the Philippines and developed a plan for the second drive across the Central Pacific. In 1942 and 1943 they also pressed the Chinese and British to get a drive under way in Burma to reopen the supply line to China in phase with their Pacific advances, offering extensive air and logistical support.

The North Pacific line running from Alaska through the Kuriles to the northernmost Japanese island of Hokkaido also beckoned in early 1943 as a possible additional avenue of approach to Japan. The Joint Chiefs decided, however, that although the Japanese perimeter

Kiska Raid, *Edward Laning, 1943*

Armor in Alaska, *Edward Laning, 1943*

should be pushed back in this region, the foggy, cold North Pacific with its rock-bound and craggy islands was not a profitable area in which to undertake a major offensive. In May 1943 the U.S. 7th Division went ashore on Attu and, after three weeks of costly fighting through icy muck and over windswept ridges in a cold, almost constant fog, destroyed the 3,000-man Japanese garrison. In August a combined American-Canadian expedition landed on Kiska, some distance away, only to find that the Japanese had evacuated the island three weeks earlier. With the Japanese perimeter pushed back to the Kuriles, the Allied advance stopped; further operations were limited to nuisance air raids against these Japanese-held islands. Ground forces used in the attacks on Attu and Kiska were redeployed to the Central Pacific, and some of the defensive forces deployed in Alaska were also freed for employment elsewhere.

Prospects of an advance through China to the coast faded rapidly in 1943. At the Casablanca Conference in January, the Combined Chiefs agreed on an ambitious operation, called ANAKIM, to be launched in the fall to retake Burma and reopen the supply line to China. ANAKIM was to include a British amphibious assault on Rangoon and an offensive into central Burma, plus an American-sponsored Chinese offensive in the north involving convergence of forces operating from China and India. ANAKIM proved too ambitious; even limited offensives in Southeast Asia were postponed time and again for lack of adequate resources.

By late 1943 the Americans had concluded that their Pacific forces would reach the China coast before either British or Chinese forces could come in through the back door. At the SEXTANT Conference in late November and early December 1943, the Combined Chiefs agreed that the main effort against Japan should be concentrated in the Pacific along two lines of advance, with operations in the North Pacific, China, and Southeast Asia to be assigned subsidiary roles.

In this strategy the two lines of advance in the Pacific—one across the Central Pacific via the Gilberts, Marshalls, Marianas, Carolines, and Palaus toward the Philippines or Formosa (Taiwan) and the other in the Southwest Pacific via the north coast of New Guinea to the Vogelkop and then to the southern Philippines—were viewed as mutually supporting. Although the Joint Chiefs several times indicated a measure of preference for the Central Pacific as the area of main effort, they never established any real priority between the two lines, seeking instead to retain a flexibility that would permit striking blows along either line as opportunity offered. (*See Map 8.*) The Central Pacific route promised to force a naval showdown with the Japanese and, once the Marianas were secured, to provide bases from which the U.S. Army Air Forces' new B–29 bombers could strike the Japanese home islands. The Southwest Pacific route was shorter, if existing bases were taken into consideration, and offered more opportunity to employ land-based air power to full advantage. The target area for both drives, in the strategy approved at SEXTANT, was to be the Luzon–Formosa–China coast area. Within this triangular area, the natural goal of the Southwest Pacific drive was the Philippines; but the goal of the Central Pacific drive could be either the Philippines or Formosa. As the drives along the two lines got under way in earnest in 1944, the choice between the two became the central strategic issue.

CARTWHEEL: The Encirclement of Rabaul

In June 1943 MacArthur and Halsey resumed their offensive to reduce the Japanese stronghold at Rabaul—a prerequisite to further advances along the Southwest Pacific axis toward the Philippines. The plan for the campaign provided for a carefully phased series of operations in each theater, each designed to secure a strategic position where air cover could be provided for further advances. The first of the series started in late June, when MacArthur landed American troops on the Woodlark and Kiriwina Islands off eastern New Guinea and at Nassau Bay on

At an Advanced South Pacific Base, *Howard Brodie, 1943*

the New Guinea coast and Halsey's forces made their first landings on the New Georgia group in the central Solomons. From these beginnings, the operations proceeded up the ladder of the Solomons, along the coast of New Guinea, and across the straits to New Britain Island generally as scheduled, despite strong Japanese reaction.

In the Solomons, by early August Army forces under Halsey had secured New Georgia with its important Munda airfield; but the campaign was not completed until October, when U.S. and New Zealand troops occupied Vella Lavella, between New Georgia and Bougainville. At the end of October New Zealanders and U.S. marines landed on Treasury and Choiseul Islands to secure bases for the assault on Bougainville. That assault got under way on November 1, when the marines landed, soon followed by the Army's 37th Division. During each phase of the Solomons campaign, the Japanese sought unsuccessfully to contest Allied air and naval supremacy, to land reinforcements, and to launch strong counterattacks against Allied beachheads, losing in the effort both planes and combat ships they could ill afford to spare. Air and naval losses in the Solomons crippled the Japanese Fleet for months to come and diverted forces otherwise available to contest the successful Central Pacific drive that got under way in November. With the repulse of the Japanese counterattack on Bougainville, by the end of November security of the American beachhead on that island was assured, permitting the development of a major American air base. With the taking of Bougainville, the main part of the South Pacific Area's task in Operation CARTWHEEL was completed.

MacArthur's forces meanwhile continued their offensives, with Australian troops carrying most of the burden in New Guinea. In early September the U.S. Army's 503d Parachute Regiment, in the first airborne operation of the Pacific war, seized an airfield at Nadzab, inland from Lae and Salamaua. Amphibious assaults by Australian troops cleared Lae and Salamaua by mid-September. Elements of the U.S. 32d Division landed at the western end of the Huon peninsula in January 1944 in an attempt to trap a large Japanese force; but by the time Australian and American units had sealed the western exits to the peninsula, most of the Japanese had escaped northwest to Hansa Bay and Wewak.

In the meantime, MacArthur and Halsey had assembled the forces to launch a final offensive

SKETCHED THIS PIX OF PVT. MERLIN MURRAY AS HE SAT ON RIDGE GUARDING THE NATIVE SUPPLY BEARERS FROM JAP SNIPERS —

HOWARD BRODIE

Howard Brodie for Yank Magazine, *1943*

Soldiers use flamethrowers to smoke out the enemy on Kwajalein Island.

toward Rabaul; but the Joint Chiefs decided that the actual seizure of that objective would be too costly in terms of men, equipment, and time. They preferred to encircle Rabaul, neutralize it by air bombardment, and push on to seize an offensive base farther west, in the Admiralty Islands. A new series of operations toward these ends started in MacArthur's theater on December 15, 1943, when U.S. Army units landed on the south coast of western New Britain; on the twenty-sixth the 1st Marine Division landed on the north coast. In mid-February 1944 New Zealand troops of the South Pacific Area secured an air base site on Green Island, north of Rabaul. On the last day of the month MacArthur began landing the 1st Cavalry Division (an infantry unit retaining its former designation) on the Admiralties, closing the western and northwestern approaches to Rabaul. Marines under Halsey seized a final air base site on Emirau, north of Rabaul, on March 20; Marine and Army units under MacArthur secured additional positions in western and central New Britain from March to May 1944. The major Japanese base at Rabaul, with its 100,000-man garrison, was as effectively out of the war as if it had been destroyed. In the process of encircling Rabaul, the Allies had also left to wither on the vine another important Japanese base at Kavieng on New Ireland, north of Rabaul.

In the last phase of the campaign against Rabaul, a pattern developed that came to characterize much of the war in the Southwest and Central Pacific. The Allies, taking full advantage of intelligence gleaned from deciphering Japanese military and naval radio communications, would mount no frontal attacks against strongly entrenched Japanese forces if they could avoid it; they would not advance island by island across a vast ocean studded with myriad atolls and island groups. Rather, they would advance in great bounds, limited only by the range of land-based air cover or the availability of carrier-based air support. The Allies would deceive, surprise, and outflank the Japanese; they would bypass major strong points and leave them reduced to strategic and tactical impotence. The Japanese would be given no chance to recover from one strike before they would face another one from a different, often unexpected, direction.

JAPANESE IN THE MILITARY INTELLIGENCE SERVICE (MIS)

Despite the poor treatment of Japanese Americans after the attack on Pearl Harbor, many volunteered to serve their country in combat. Thousands also volunteered for potentially more dangerous duty. They enlisted as interpreters and translators in the MIS to serve in the Pacific interrogating Japanese prisoners of war and translating captured documents and intercepted transmissions. Had they been captured, there was little doubt of their fate. They volunteered nonetheless and served in the forward areas throughout the Pacific war and later in the occupation of Japan.

The Central Pacific Drive Begins

In the South and Southwest Pacific, the necessity for relying primarily on support of land-based aircraft curtailed the length of the jumps to the operational radius of fighter planes. The Navy's limited supply of aircraft carriers could not be employed to best advantage in the restricted waters around New Guinea and the Solomons. By mid-1943, however, new larger and faster carriers of the *Essex* class (27,000 tons) and lighter carriers of the *Independence* class (11,000 tons) were joining the Pacific Fleet. Around these new carriers Admiral Nimitz built naval task forces tailored to each particular operation. The task forces consisted of a mix of carriers, destroyers, cruisers, battleships, submarines, minesweepers, and support craft. In the broad expanses of the Central Pacific, these air-carrier task forces could provide both air and naval support for far longer leaps forward, while the entire Pacific Fleet stood ready to confront the main Japanese Fleet at any time the Japanese chose to give battle.

The Central Pacific drive got under way on November 20, when Nimitz sent Army and Marine forces to the Gilbert Islands to seize bases from which to support subsequent jumps into the Marshalls. Troops and supplies for the Gilberts loaded at Hawaii on newly developed assault shipping and sailed more than 2,000 miles to be set ashore by specially designed landing craft and amphibian vehicles. Makin, the Army objective, fell to the 27th Division after four days of hard fighting. Tarawa, where the 2d Marine Division went ashore, proved a bloody affair that provided a stiff test for American amphibious doctrine, techniques, and equipment. Naval gunfire vessels and carrier-based aircraft provided support during and after the assault.

The advance to the Gilberts disclosed that U.S. forces had not entirely mastered certain aspects of amphibious warfare, especially naval gunfire support, coordination of air support, and ship-to-shore communications. But the Americans learned valuable lessons that, added to the earlier experiences of the South and Southwest Pacific Areas, established a pattern of island warfare that represented one of the major tactical developments of the war. First, air and naval forces isolated an objective, softened its defenses, and isolated it from outside reinforcement; simultaneously, joint forces would attack or feint toward other islands to deceive the Japanese. The approach of convoys carrying the ground assault forces to the main objective signaled the opening of final, intensive air and naval bombardment of the landing beaches. Whenever practicable, small forces occupied neighboring islands as sites for land-based artillery. Under cover of all these supporting fires, the landing forces moved from ship to shore in echelons, or waves, rocket-firing landing craft in the lead and amphibian tanks and tractors following to carry the assault troops directly onto the beaches and inland. Finally came landing craft with more infantry and with tanks, artillery, and supporting troops. Supplies followed rapidly as the assault forces secured and expanded the beachhead. Amphibious techniques were refined and modified to some extent after the Gilberts, but the lessons learned there made it unnecessary to effect any radical changes in amphibious doctrine throughout the rest of the war.

Preoccupied with the Solomons and New Guinea, the Japanese did not react strongly to the loss of the Gilberts; at the end of January 1944 Nimitz' Army and Marine forces moved into the eastern and central Marshalls to seize Majuro and Kwajalein. The strength employed in this operation proved so preponderant and Japanese defenses so weak that Nimitz was able to accelerate his next advance by two-and-a-half months and on February 17 landed Marine and Army units on Eniwetok Atoll in the western Marshalls. Concurrently, he conducted a long-awaited carrier strike against Truk in the central Carolines, considered Japan's key naval bastion in the Central Pacific. The raid revealed that the Japanese had virtually abandoned Truk as a naval base, obviating its capture. Nimitz then drew up plans to invade the Marianas in mid-June and move on to the western Carolines and Palaus in mid-September, again accelerating the pace of the advance.

Cautiously Moving in on a Japanese Machine-Gun Position

Acceleration of the Pacific Drive

General MacArthur had also pushed the Southwest Pacific Area's timetable forward. Having landed in the Admiralties a month ahead of his original schedule, he proposed to cancel operations against Hansa Bay and Wewak on the northeast coast of New Guinea in favor of a jump to Hollandia and Aitape on the north-central coast in April, two months earlier than previously planned. His operations took full advantage of a windfall of deciphered Japanese Army communications that revealed not only the enemy's dispositions along the New Guinea coast but his intentions as well. Armed with this awareness, MacArthur would then continue northwestward along the coast in a campaign to seize successive air base sites until he reached the Vogelkop at the eastern end of New Guinea. (*See Map 9.*) He would then proceed to Mindanao, southernmost of the Philippine Islands.

The Joint Chiefs, quickly seizing the fruits of their strategy of opportunism, on March 12 rearranged the schedule of major Pacific operations. They provided for the assault by MacArthur's forces on Hollandia and Aitape in April with the support of a carrier task force from the Pacific Fleet, to be followed by Nimitz' move into the Marianas in June and into the Palaus in September. While Nimitz was employing the major units of the Pacific Fleet in these ventures, MacArthur was to continue his advance along the New Guinea coast with the forces at his disposal. In November he was again to have the support of main units of the Pacific Fleet in an assault on Mindanao. Refusing still to make a positive choice of what was to follow, the Joint Chiefs directed MacArthur to plan for the invasion of Luzon and Nimitz to plan for the invasion of Formosa early in 1945.

The March 12 directive served as a blueprint for an accelerated drive in the Pacific in the spring and summer of 1944. On April 22 Army forces under MacArthur landed at weakly held Hollandia and Aitape far behind the main Japanese ground forces. At neither place was the issue ever in doubt, although during July the Japanese who had been bypassed at Wewak launched an abortive counterattack against the Aitape perimeter. Protected by land-based aircraft staging from Hollandia, MacArthur's Army units next jumped 125 miles northwest on May 17 to seize another lightly defended air base site at Wakde Island, landing first on the New Guinea mainland opposite the chief objective. A ground campaign of about a month and a half ensued against a Japanese division on the mainland; but, without waiting for the outcome of the fight, on May 27 other Army troops carried the advance northwestward another 180 miles to Biak Island.

At this point the wisdom of conducting twin drives across the Pacific became apparent. The Japanese Navy was preparing for a show-down battle it expected to develop off the Marianas in June. MacArthur's move to Biak put land-based planes in position to keep under surveillance and harass the Japanese Fleet, which was assembling in Philippine waters before moving into the Central Pacific. Reckoning an American-controlled Biak an unacceptable threat to their flank, the Japanese risked major elements of their fleet to send strong reinforcements in an attempt to drive MacArthur's exposed forces from the island. They also deployed to bases within range of Biak about half their land-based air strength from the Marianas, Carolines, and Palaus—planes upon which their fleet would depend for support during the forthcoming battle off the Marianas.

Again alerted by signals intelligence, the U.S. Seventh Fleet parried two unsuccessful attempts to reinforce Biak, but the Japanese assembled for a third try enough naval strength to overwhelm local American naval units. Just as the formidable force was moving toward Biak, the Japanese learned that the U.S. Pacific Fleet was off the Marianas. They scrapped the Biak operation, hastily assembled their naval forces, and sailed northwestward for the engagement known as the Battle of the Philippine Sea. Having lost the chance to surprise the U.S. Navy, handicapped by belated deployment, and deprived of anticipated land-based air support, the Japanese suffered another shattering naval defeat. This defeat, which assured the success of the invasions of both Biak and the Marianas, illustrates well the interdependence of operations in the two Pacific areas. It also demonstrated again that the U.S. Pacific Fleet's carrier task forces were the decisive element in the Pacific war.

Army and Marine divisions under Nimitz landed on Saipan in the Marianas on June 15, 1944, to begin a bloody three-week battle for control of the island. Next, on July 21, Army and Marine units invaded Guam, 100 miles south of Saipan; three days later marines moved on to Tinian Island. An important turning point of the Pacific war, the American seizure of the Marianas brought the Japanese home islands within reach of the U.S. Army Air Forces' new B–29 long-range bombers, which in late November began to fly missions against the Japanese homeland.

At Biak, Japanese resistance delayed the capture of the best airfield sites until late June. On July 2 MacArthur's Army forces moved on to Noemfoor Island, ninety miles to the west, in a combined parachute-amphibious operation designed to broaden the base of the Southwest Pacific's air deployment. On July 30 the 6th Division continued on to the northwestern tip of New Guinea to secure another air base; and on September 15 MacArthur landed the reinforced 31st Division on Morotai Island, between New Guinea and Mindanao in the Philippines. On the same day Nimitz sent the 1st Marine Division ashore on Peleliu in the southern Palaus. On the seventeenth the 81st Division from Nimitz' command landed on Angaur, just south of Peleliu. A regimental combat team of the 81st Division secured Ulithi Atoll, midway between Peleliu and the Marianas, without opposition on September 23.

With these landings the approach to the Philippines was virtually completed. The occupation of Morotai proved easy, and the island provided airfields for the support of advances into the Philippines and Indies. The Pacific Fleet employed Ulithi as a forward anchorage. Hard fighting dragged on in the Palaus through November; but as the result of another acceleration in the pace of Pacific operations, these islands never played the role originally planned for them.

In twin drives, illustrating the principles of maneuver, objective, economy of force, surprise, and mass, the Allied forces of the Pacific had arrived in mid-September 1944 at the threshold of their strategic objective, the Luzon–Formosa–China coast triangle. In seven months MacArthur's forces had leapfrogged forward nearly 1,500 miles from

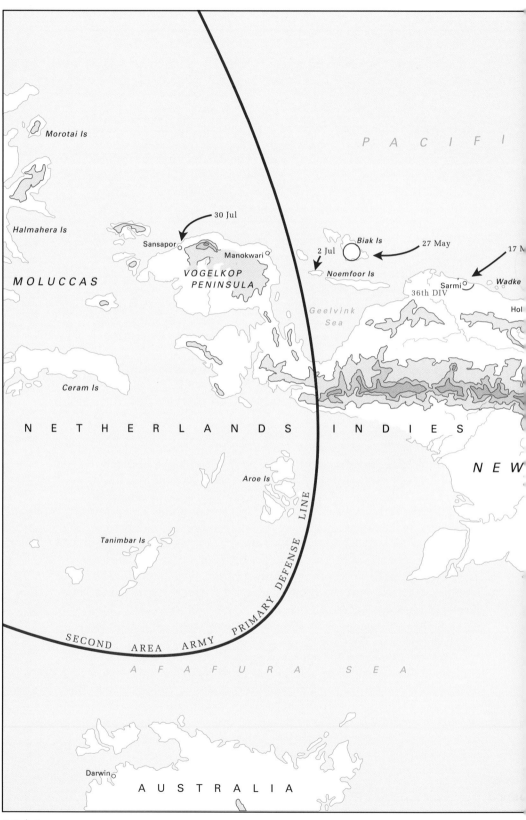

Map 9

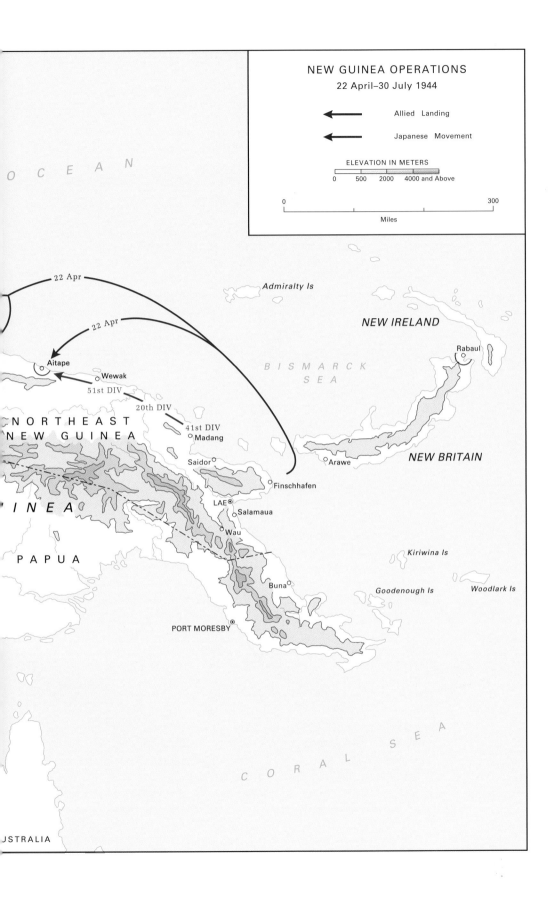

NEW GUINEA OPERATIONS
22 April–30 July 1944

→ Allied Landing

→ Japanese Movement

ELEVATION IN METERS
0 500 2000 4000 and Above

0   300
Miles

O C E A N

Admiralty Is

NEW IRELAND

BISMARCK
SEA

Rabaul

22 Apr

22 Apr

Aitape

Wewak

51st DIV

20th DIV

41st DIV

NORTHEAST
NEW GUINEA

Madang

Saidor

Arawe

NEW BRITAIN

Finschhafen

INEA

LAE

Salamaua

Wau

PAPUA

Kiriwina Is

Buna

Goodenough Is

Woodlark Is

PORT MORESBY

C O R A L   S E A

USTRALIA

the Admiralties to Morotai; in ten months Nimitz' forces had advanced over 4,500 miles from Hawaii to the Palaus. The time had now come to make a final choice of the main objective in the target area.

The Decision To Invade Luzon

During the summer of 1944, as the battles raged along both lines of advance, the strategic debate over the choice of Luzon versus Formosa also waxed hot. General MacArthur argued fervently that the proper course was to move through the Philippines to Luzon, cutting the Japanese lines of communications southward, establishing a base for bombardment and invasion of Japan, and fulfilling a solemn national obligation to liberate the Philippine people. Admiral Ernest J. King, Chief of Naval Operations, just as adamantly insisted that the war could be shortened by directing the Pacific advance from the Marianas and Palaus toward Formosa, the China coast, and Japan proper, seizing only the essential positions in the southern and central Philippines necessary to render air support for these advances.

The arguments for Formosa were cogent enough. Its strategic position made it a better island stepping stone to the China coast or the Japanese home islands, a position from which Japanese communications to the south could be cut more effectively than from Luzon, and a closer-in position from which to conduct strategic bombardment. But it also could prove a more difficult position to take, and Nimitz did not have in his theater sufficient Army supporting and service troops to sustain a land campaign on the island without reinforcement. It might be difficult, too, to mount an invasion of Formosa as long as Japanese air and surface forces could, from strong positions on Luzon, interfere with the Allied line of communications.

Another strategic consideration involved the real value of a foothold on the China coast. By the early fall of 1944, air base sites in east China from which the Allies had hoped to support Pacific operations and bomb Japan appeared irretrievably lost to the Japanese *Ichi-go* offensive. Technology also undercut the argument for air bases in China because the extended range of the giant B–29 bombers enabled them to attack Tokyo from newly constructed bases in the Marianas. The need to seize and develop a port on the China coast for logistics support of air operations thus lost much of its urgency, and the argument that Formosa was the best stepping stone to China became less compelling. Then, too, a successful invasion of either Luzon or Formosa required some concentration of forces from the two theaters. It was far easier to shift highly mobile naval resources in Nimitz' theater to the Philippines than it was to redeploy Army troops from the Southwest Pacific to support Nimitz' invasion of Formosa and the jump to the China coast with which he hoped to follow it.

At the time of the Morotai and Palaus landings, MacArthur's plans for invasion of the Philippines called for a preliminary assault in southern Mindanao on November 15, 1944, to secure air bases for the support of a larger attack at Leyte, in the east-central Philippines, on December 20. He would follow this with a large-scale assault on Lingayen Gulf in February 1945. Nimitz meanwhile planned to mount an invasion of Yap in the Carolines in October 1944 and then would prepare to launch his attack on Formosa as soon as the elements of the Pacific Fleet required for operations in the southern and central Philippines could return. Obviously, the Joint Chiefs had to choose between Luzon and Formosa, for the Pacific Fleet would need to support either operation.

The course of events went far to dictate the final choice. In mid-September Admiral Halsey's carrier task forces providing strategic support for the Morotai and Palaus operations struck the central and southern Philippines. Halsey found Japanese air strength unexpectedly weak and uncovered few signs of significant ground or naval activity. Although signals intelligence revealed strong Japanese forces in the Philippines, on the basis of Halsey's reports MacArthur and Nimitz proposed to the Joint Chiefs a move directly to Leyte in October, bypassing Mindanao. Nimitz agreed to divert to the Leyte invasion the three-division corps then mounting out of Hawaii for the assault against Yap. The Joint Chiefs quickly approved the new plan, and the decision to invade Leyte two months ahead of schedule gave MacArthur's arguments to move on to Luzon almost irresistible force. MacArthur now reported that he could undertake the invasion of Luzon in December 1944, whereas all the planners' estimates indicated that resources for an invasion of Formosa—particularly service troops and shipping—could not be readied before February 1945. Nimitz proposed to shift the Central Pacific attack northward against Iwo Jima in the Bonins in January and then against Okinawa and other islands in the Ryukyus early in March. On October 3 Admiral King, bowing to the inevitable, accepted the new plans. The Joint Chiefs issued directives to MacArthur for the invasion of Luzon on December 20 and to Nimitz for the invasion of Iwo Jima and Okinawa early in 1945.

Pacific strategy had been cast into a nearly final mold. In the end, the China coast objective disappeared entirely from planning boards. Final plans for the defeat of Japan envisaged a gradual tightening of the ring by blockade and bombardment from the Marianas, Philippines, and Ryukyus with an invasion of the home islands to be mounted from these bases.

The Philippines Campaign

The main assault at Leyte took place on October 20, 1944, as four Army divisions landed abreast in the largest amphibious operation yet conducted in the Pacific. (*See Map 10.*) Vice Adm. Thomas C. Kinkaid, MacArthur's naval subordinate, controlled the amphibious phases, including naval gunfire support and close air support by planes based on escort carriers. Ground forces were under Lt. Gen. Walter Krueger, commanding the U.S. Sixth Army; land-based air forces of the Southwest Pacific Area in general support were commanded by Lt. Gen. George C. Kenney. MacArthur himself exercised unified command over the air, ground, and naval commanders. The fast carrier task forces of the Pacific Fleet, providing strategic support, operated under the control of Admiral Halsey, who reported to Nimitz, not MacArthur. There was no provision for unified naval command, and Halsey's orders were such that he could make his principal mission the destruction of the

Japanese Fleet rather than the support of MacArthur's entry into the Philippines.

The Japanese had originally planned to make their stand in the Philippines on Luzon, but the invasion of Leyte moved them to reconsider. The *Fourteenth Area Army Headquarters* wanted to fight on Luzon, but the *Southern Army* decided that the entire Philippine archipelago would be strategically lost if the U.S. Army secured a foothold in the central islands. The *Southern Army* therefore ordered the *Fourteenth Army* to send ground reinforcements to Leyte. Concurrently the *Imperial General Headquarters* in Tokyo launched the *SHO* (Victory) operation as it increased land-based air strength in the Philippines in the hope of destroying Allied shipping in Leyte Gulf and maintaining local air superiority and dispatched Japan's remaining naval strength to Leyte Gulf to destroy Kinkaid's invasion fleet and to block Allied access to the Philippines. The ensuing air-naval Battle of Leyte Gulf was the most critical moment of the campaign and proved one of the most decisive actions of the Pacific war.

Admiral Halsey, without consulting MacArthur or Kinkaid, pulled the bulk of his carrier forces northward to intercept some Japanese aircraft carriers, a decoy fleet stripped of its aircraft to draw U.S. naval power from the fragile beachhead and leave Leyte Gulf open to other converging Japanese Fleet units. Kinkaid's old battleships annihilated one Japanese fleet approaching Leyte from the south, but only gallant, desperate action by American destroyers and escort carriers turned back the Japanese battleships steaming undetected into the gulf from the north. The small, lightly armed U.S. ships suffered heavy losses to ensure the safety of the landing forces. It had been a close call, clearly demonstrating the dangers of divided command. In the end, however, the combined operations of Kinkaid's and Halsey's forces virtually eliminated the Japanese Navy as a factor in the Pacific war.

With the Leyte beaches secure, U.S. Army units proceeded to destroy the Japanese ground forces. Miserable weather on Leyte's east coast bogged down the pace of operations, made supply difficult, delayed airfield construction, curtailed air support, and permitted the Japanese to continue to ship reinforcements to the western port of the island. The reinforcement program came to a sudden halt early in December, when the 77th Division executed an amphibious envelopment on Leyte's west coast; by late December the Sixth Army had secured the most important sections of the island, those required for air and logistical bases. Japanese troops in the mountains of northwestern Leyte continued organized resistance well into the spring of 1945, occupying the energies of large portions of Lt. Gen. Robert L. Eichelberger's newly formed Eighth Army.

While the fight on Leyte continued, MacArthur's forces moved on to Luzon only slightly behind schedule. The first step of the Luzon Campaign was the seizure of an air base in southwestern Mindoro, 150 miles south of Manila, on December 15; two Army regiments accomplished the task with ease. The invasion of Luzon itself started on January 9, 1945, when four Army divisions landed along the shores of the Lingayen Gulf. Command arrangements were similar to those at Leyte, and again fast carrier task forces under Halsey operated in general support and not under MacArthur's control. Within three days,

The combined operations of Kinkaid's and Halsey's forces virtually eliminated the Japanese Navy as a factor in the Pacific war.

THE LIBERATION OF MANILA

The month-long fight for Manila was one of few battles waged in a major city in the Pacific Theater. The Japanese naval garrison organized a defense of the city in direct defiance of the Japanese Army commander's orders to evacuate. Because the Americans were eager to preserve the city's water and power supplies, they avoided air strikes and artillery fires, except against known enemy positions. Mounting casualties and intense fighting eventually resulted in these restrictions' being lifted. By February 24 the 37th Infantry Division entered the ancient fortress of Intramuros, triggering the breakdown of the entire Japanese defensive effort. On March 3 the Commanding General of the XIV Corps reported that all resistance had ceased. Most of Manila had been left in ruins.

five Army divisions, a separate regimental combat team, two artillery groups, an armored group, and supporting service units were ashore and had begun a drive down the Central Plains of Luzon toward Manila. The Japanese were incapable of naval intervention at Lingayen Gulf, and their most significant reaction was to throw a new weapon, kamikaze (suicide planes) against Kinkaid's naval forces for four days.

General Tomoyuki Yamashita, commanding Japanese forces in the Philippines, did not intend to defend the Central Plains–Manila Bay region, the strategic prize of Luzon. Knowing he would receive no reinforcements and believing the issue in the Philippines had been decided at Leyte, he sought only to pin down major elements of MacArthur's forces in the hope of delaying Allied progress toward Japan. For this purpose he moved the bulk of his troops into mountain strongholds, where they could conduct a protracted, bloody defensive campaign. But Japanese naval forces on Luzon, only nominally under Yamashita,

MacArthur wades ashore during initial landings at Leyte, October 1944.

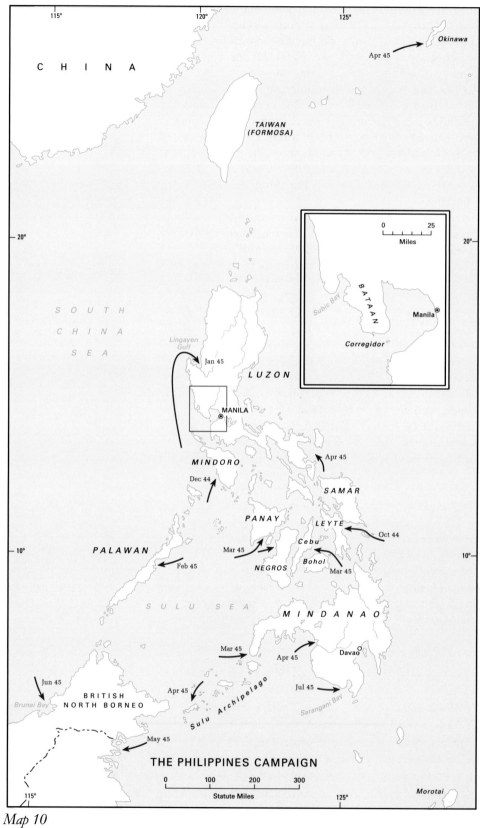

THE PHILIPPINES CAMPAIGN

Map 10

decided to ignore this concept in favor of defending Manila and Manila Bay to the death. Thus, when U.S. Army units reached Manila on February 3, it took them a month of bitter building-to-building fighting to root out the Japanese at the cost of over 1,000 U.S. and over 16,000 Japanese dead and 100,000 civilian casualties. Meanwhile, operations to clear Manila Bay had begun with a minor amphibious landing at the southern tip of Bataan on February 15. The next day a combined parachute-amphibious assault, involving two Army regiments, initiated a battle to seize Corregidor Island. Other forces cleared additional islands in Manila Bay and secured the south shore. By mid-March the bay was open for Allied shipping, but the Allies would have to do an immense salvage and repair job before they could fully exploit Manila's excellent port facilities.

The reinforced 38th Division had landed meanwhile near Subic Bay and had cut across the base of the Bataan peninsula to prevent the Japanese from holing up on Bataan as had MacArthur's forces three years earlier. The 11th Airborne Division undertook both amphibious and parachute landings in southern Luzon to start clearing that region, and the 158th Regimental Combat Team made an amphibious assault in southeastern Luzon to secure the Bicol peninsula. Turning against Yamashita's mountain strongholds, MacArthur continued to pour reinforcements onto Luzon, and the land campaign there ultimately evolved into the largest of the Pacific war. Altogether MacArthur committed to Luzon 10 divisions, 2 regiments of another division, and 3 separate regimental combat teams. Filipino guerrillas, many of whom had been formed under defiant U.S. officers and men escaping surrender in 1942, also played a large role. One guerrilla unit came to substitute for a regularly constituted division, and other guerrilla forces of battalion and regiment size supplemented the efforts of the U.S. Army units. Moreover, the loyal and willing Filipino population immeasurably eased the problems of supply, construction, and civil administration. In one instance, the surprise raid to liberate the American POW camp at Cabanatuan by U.S. Army Rangers and Alamo Scouts, the support of Filipino guerrillas was critical to achieving victory and saving hundreds of American lives.

Except for a strong pocket in the mountains of north central Luzon, organized Japanese resistance ended by late June 1945. The rugged terrain in the north, along with rainy weather, prevented Krueger's Sixth Army from applying its full strength to the reduction

"WE REMAINED"

In March 1942, under presidential order, General MacArthur escaped from the besieged Philippines to Australia, where he vowed, "I shall return." Two months later U.S. conventional resistance ended in surrender. But some Filipinos and Americans disobeyed orders, fled into the jungle, and, aided by friendly natives, formed guerrilla bands. From Australia, the Allies sent in supplies and agents by submarine. Thus, when MacArthur returned to the Philippines in late 1944 he found a movement able to help with intelligence, elimination of bypassed units, and even conventional attacks. In northern Luzon, guerrilla patches bore their motto, "We Remained."

of this pocket. Eichelberger's Eighth Army took over responsibility for operations on Luzon at the end of June and continued the pressure against Yamashita's force in the last-stand redoubt, but the Japanese held out there until the end of the war.

While the Sixth Army was destroying Japanese forces on Luzon, Eighth Army ultimately employed five divisions, portions of a sixth division, a separate regimental combat team, and strong guerrilla units in its campaign to reconquer the southern Philippines. This effort began when a regimental combat team of the 41st Division landed on Palawan Island on February 28, 1945. Here, engineers built an air base from which to help cut Japan's line of communications to the south and to support later advances in the southern Philippines and the Indies. On March 10 another regimental combat team of the 41st, later reinforced, landed near Zamboanga in southwestern Mindanao; and soon thereafter Army units began moving southwest toward Borneo along the Sulu Archipelago. In rapid succession Eighth Army units then landed on Panay, Cebu, northwestern Negros, Bohol, central Mindanao, southeastern Negros, northern Mindanao, and finally at Sarangani Bay in southern Mindanao, once intended as the first point of reentry into the Philippines. At some locales, bitter fighting raged for a time; but the issue was never in doubt and organized Japanese resistance in the southern Philippines had largely collapsed by the end of May. Mopping up continued to the end of the war, with reorganized and reequipped guerrilla forces bearing much of the burden.

The last offensives in the Southwest Pacific Area started on May 1, when an Australian brigade went ashore on Tarakan Island, Borneo. Carried to the beaches by landing craft manned by U.S. Army engineers, the Australians had air support from fields on Morotai and in the southern Philippines. On June 10 an Australian division landed at Brunei Bay, Borneo. Another Australian division went ashore at Balikpapan on July 1 in the final amphibious assault of the war.

Iwo Jima and Okinawa

Slow base development at Leyte had forced MacArthur to delay the Luzon invasion from December to January. Nimitz in turn had to postpone his target dates for the Iwo Jima and Okinawa operations, primarily because the bulk of the naval resources in the Pacific—fast carrier task forces, escort carrier groups, assault shipping, naval gunfire support vessels, and amphibious assault craft—had to shift between the two theaters for major operations. The alteration of schedules again illustrated the interdependence of the Southwest and Central Pacific Areas.

The Iwo Jima assault finally took place on February 19, 1945, with the 4th and 5th Marine Divisions supported by minor Army elements making the landings. The 3d Marine Division reinforced the assault, and an Army regiment ultimately took over as island garrison. The marines had to overcome fanatic resistance from firmly entrenched Japanese who held what was probably the strongest defensive system the American forces encountered during the Pacific war, and it took a month of bloody fighting to secure the island. In early March a few crippled B–29s made emergency landings on Iwo; by the end of the month an airfield

LT. GEN. SIMON BOLIVAR BUCKNER, JR. (1886–1945)

Son of a famous Confederate general, Buckner was commissioned in the Infantry when he graduated from West Point in 1908. In May–June 1943 Buckner oversaw the recapture of the Aleutian Islands of Kiska and Attu from the Japanese. In 1945 General Buckner was given command of the Tenth U.S. Army and with it the mission of securing the strategic island of Okinawa. Leading from the front, Buckner repeatedly exposed himself to danger as he toured the front lines to gain a firsthand assessment of the tactical situation. While visiting a forward observation post four days before the campaign concluded, Buckner was mortally wounded by direct fire from a Japanese 47-mm. antitank gun. He was the most senior American officer to lose his life in the Pacific Theater of Operations.

was fully operational for fighter planes. Later, engineers constructed a heavy bomber field and another fighter base on the island.

The invasion of the Ryukyus began on March 26, when the 77th Division landed on the Kerama Islands, fifteen miles west of Okinawa, to secure a forward naval base, a task traditionally assigned to marines. On April 1 the 7th and 86th Divisions and the 2d and 6th Marine Divisions executed the assault on the main objective, Okinawa. (*See Map 11.*) Two more Army divisions and a Marine infantry regiment later reinforced it. Another amphibious assault took place on April 16, when the 77th Division seized Ie Shima, four miles west of Okinawa; the final landing in the Ryukyus came on June 26, when a small force of marines went ashore on Kume Island, fifty miles west of Okinawa. Ground forces at Okinawa were first under the U.S. Tenth Army, Lt. Gen. Simon B. Buckner commanding. When General Buckner was killed in action on June 18, Marine Lt. Gen. Roy S. Geiger took over until General Joseph W. Stilwell, formerly U.S. commander in China and Burma, assumed command on the twenty-third.

The Japanese made no attempt to defend the Okinawa beaches but instead fell back to prepared cave and tunnel defenses on inland hills. Bitterly defending every inch of ground, the Japanese continued organized resistance until late June. Meanwhile, Japanese suicide planes had inflicted extensive damage on Nimitz' naval forces, sinking 34 ships and damaging another 268 in an unsuccessful attempt to drive Allied naval power from the western Pacific. Skillful small-unit tactics, combined with great concentrations of naval, air, and artillery bombardment, turned the tide of the ground battle on Okinawa itself. Especially noteworthy was the close gunfire support the Navy provided the ground forces and the close air support Army, Navy, and Marine aircraft furnished.

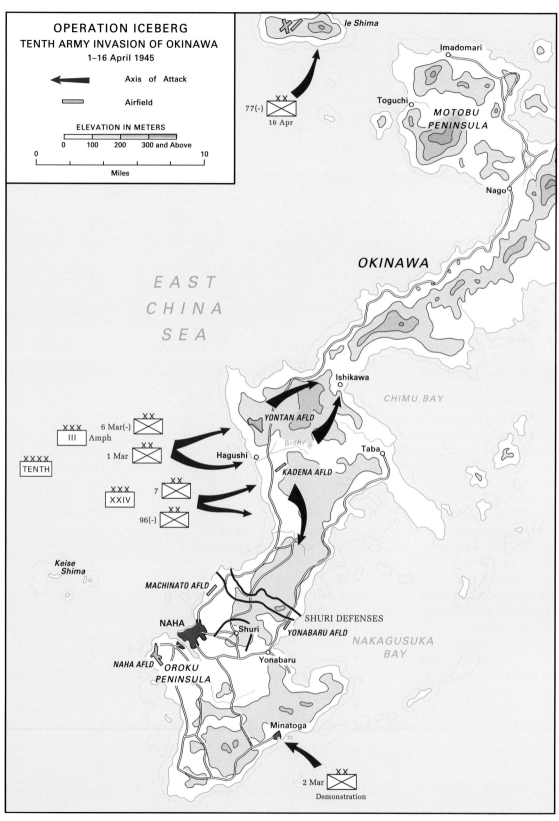

Map 11

The capture of Okinawa and other positions in the Ryukyus gave the Allies both air and naval bases within easy striking distance of Japan. By early May fighter planes from Okinawa had begun flights over Japan; as rapidly as fields became available, bombers, including units from the Southwest Pacific Area, came forward to mount attacks to prepare for the invasion of the home islands. The forward anchorages in the Ryukyus permitted the Pacific Fleet to stay in almost continuous action against Japanese targets. The Ryukyus campaign had brought Allied forces in the Pacific to Japan's doorstep.

The American Effort in China, Burma, and India

While American forces in the Pacific under the unified direction of the U.S. Joint Chiefs of Staff made spectacular advances, the Allied effort in Southeast Asia bogged down in a mire of conflicting national purposes. The hopes Americans held in the early stages of the war that Chinese manpower and bases would play a vitally important role in the defeat of Japan were doomed to disappointment. Americans sought to achieve great aims on the Asiatic mainland at small cost, looking to the British in India and the Chinese, with their vast reservoirs of manpower, to carry the main burden of ground conflict. Neither proved capable of exerting the effort the Americans expected of them.

Early in 1942 the United States had sent General Stilwell to the Far East to command American forces in China, Burma, and India and to serve as Chief of Staff and principal adviser to Chiang Kai-shek, the leader of Nationalist China and Allied commander of the China Theater. Stilwell's stated mission was "to assist in improving the efficiency of the Chinese Army." The Japanese conquest of Burma, cutting the last overland supply route to China, frustrated Stilwell's designs, for it left a long and difficult airlift from Assam to Kunming over the high peaks of the Himalayas as the only remaining avenue for the flow of supplies. The Americans assumed responsibility for the airlift, but its development was slow, hampered by a scarcity of transport planes, airfields, and trained pilots. Not until late in 1943 did it reach a monthly capacity of 10,000 tons, and in the intervening months few supplies reached China. The economy of the country continually tottered on the brink of collapse; and the Chinese Army, although it was a massive force on paper, remained ill organized, ill equipped, poorly led, and generally incapable of offensive action.

STILWELL IN CHINA

Having served for thirteen years in China between the World Wars as a language officer and military attaché, Joseph W. Stilwell (1883–1946) seemed a natural as the American Chief of Staff to Generalissimo Chiang Kai-shek. But his caustic demeanor eventually led to his recall from China at Chiang's request. His 140-mile trek by train, truck, jeep, and on foot away from Japanese forces and into India was typical of his leadership style—he led from the front. His acerbic wit, candor, and identification with the common infantryman led to his well-deserved nickname, Vinegar Joe.

Stilwell thought that the only solution was to retake Burma and reopen the land supply line to China, and this became the position of the U.S. Joint Chiefs of Staff. To achieve the goal, Stilwell undertook the training and equipping of a Chinese force in India that eventually consisted of three divisions and sought to concentrate a much larger force in Yunnan Province in China and to give it offensive capability. With these two Chinese forces he hoped to form a junction in north Burma, thus reestablishing land communications between China and India. Stilwell's scheme became part of the larger plan, ANAKIM, which the Combined Chiefs of Staff had approved at the Casablanca Conference. Neither the British nor the Chinese, however, had any real enthusiasm for ANAKIM, and in retrospect it seems clear that its execution in 1943 was beyond the capabilities of forces in the theater. Moreover, Chiang was quite dilatory in concentrating a force in Yunnan, and the British were more interested in southern Burma. Maj. Gen. Claire L. Chennault, commanding the small American air force in China, urged that the supplies flowing by air over the Himalayas (the "Hump") should be used to support an air effort in China, rather than to supply Chinese ground forces. Chennault promised amazing results at small cost, and his proposals attracted President Franklin D. Roosevelt as well as the British and the Chinese. As an upshot, at the TRIDENT Conference in May 1943, the amphibious operation against Rangoon was canceled and a new plan for operations emerged that stressed Chennault's air operations and provided for a lesser ground offensive in central and northern Burma. Under this concept a new road would be built from Ledo in Assam Province, India, to join with the trace of the old Burma Road inside China. The Americans assumed responsibility for building the Ledo Road in the rear of Chinese forces advancing from India into Burma.

Logistical difficulties in India again delayed the opening of any land offensive and kept the airlift well below target figures. Until the supply line north from Calcutta to the British and Chinese fronts could be improved—this took well over a year—both air and ground operations against the Japanese in Burma were handicapped. In October

THE BURMA ROAD

In early 1942 the Japanese closed the Burma Road, 700 miles of dirt highway representing China's last overland link to the outside world. While transports flew supplies through the Himalayas to China and forces under General Stilwell cleared northern Burma, American engineers built a new route from India through rugged jungle terrain to connect with the old road. In February 1945 the first convoy passed the linkup on the renamed Stilwell Road, covering 928 miles from Ledo to Kunming, China.

General Stilwell (seated, left) *confers with Maj. Gen. Liao Yau Siang, who commanded one of the divisions pushing back the Japanese in northern Burma.*

1943 Chinese troops under Stilwell did start to clear northern Burma, and in the spring of 1944 a U.S. Army unit of regiment size, nicknamed Merrill's Marauders, spearheaded new offensives to secure the trace for the overland road. But Myitkyina, the key point in the Japanese defenses in north Burma, did not fall until August 2; by that time the effort in Burma had been relegated to a subsidiary role.

After the SEXTANT Conference in late 1943, in fact, the American staff no longer regarded as probable that the overland route to China could be opened in time to permit Chinese forces to drive to the coast by the time American forces advancing across the Pacific arrived. While the Americans insisted on continuing the effort to open the Ledo Road, they now gave first priority to an air effort in China in support of the Pacific campaigns. The Army Air Forces in May 1944 started to deploy the first of its B–29 groups to airfields in eastern China to commence bombing of strategic targets in Korea, Manchuria, and Japan. At the same time Chennault's Fourteenth Air Force was directed to stockpile supplies for missions in support of Pacific forces as they neared the China coast. Again these projects proved to be more than could be supported over the Hump, particularly since transports also had to supply the ground effort of both British and Chinese forces. Then the Japanese reacted strongly to the increased air effort and launched a ground offensive that overran most of the existing fields and proposed air base sites in eastern China. Both air and ground resources inside China had to be diverted to oppose the Japanese advance. The B–29s were removed to India in January 1945 and two months later were sent to Saipan, where the major strategic bombing offensive against Japan was by that time being mounted. The air effort in China without the protection of an efficient Chinese Army fulfilled few of the goals proclaimed for it.

To meet the crisis in China, President Roosevelt urged Chiang to place his U.S.-supported armies under the command of General Stilwell; Chiang eventually refused and asked for Stilwell's recall, which the President honored. In September 1944 Maj. Gen. Albert C. Wedemeyer replaced Stilwell as Chief of Staff to Chiang and commander of American forces in the China Theater; a separate theater in India and Burma was created with Lt. Gen. Dan I. Sultan as its commanding general. The command issue was dropped, and the American strategy in China became simply trying to realize at least something from previous investments without additional commitments.

Ironically enough, it was in this phase, after the Pacific advances had outrun those in Southeast Asia, that objects of the 1942 strategy were realized, in large part because the Japanese, having failed in their 1944 offensive against India and hard pressed everywhere, could no longer adequately support their forces in Burma and China. British and Chinese forces advanced rapidly into Burma in the fall of 1944; and, on January 27, 1945, the junction between Chinese forces advancing from India and Yunnan finally took place, securing the trace of the Ledo Road. To the south, the British completed the conquest of central Burma and entered Rangoon overland from the north early in May. The land route to China was thus finally secured on all sides, but the Americans had already decided that they would develop the Ledo Road only as a one-way highway, though they did expand the airlift to the point where in July 1945 it carried 74,000 tons of supplies into China.

With increased American supply support, Wedemeyer was able to make more progress in equipping and training the Chinese Army. Under his tutelage the Chinese were able to halt the Japanese advance at Chihchiang in April 1945. As the Japanese began to withdraw to prepare a citadel defense of their home islands, Wedemeyer and the Chinese laid plans to seize a port on the Chinese coast. The war came to an end before this operation even started and before the training and equipping of a Chinese Army was anywhere near complete. Chiang's forces commenced the reoccupation of their homeland still, for the most part, ill equipped, ill organized, and poorly led.

The Japanese Surrender

Allied prisoners of war at a camp near Yokohama cheer for their rescuers.

During the summer of 1945 Allied forces in the Pacific had stepped up the pace of their air and naval attacks against Japan. In June and July carrier-based planes of the U.S. Pacific Fleet and U.S. Army Air Forces planes from the Marianas, Iwo Jima, and Okinawa struck the Japanese home islands continuously. During July Pacific Fleet surface units bombarded Japan's east coast, and in the same month a British carrier task force joined the attack. Planes from the Philippines hit Japanese shipping in the South China Sea and extended their strikes as far as Formosa and other targets along the South China coast. American submarines redoubled their efforts to sweep Japanese shipping from the sea and sever the shipping lanes from Japan to the Indies and Southeast Asia. Throughout the war, in fact, submarines had preyed on Japanese merchant and combat vessels, playing a major role in isolating Japan from its conquests and thereby drastically reducing Japan's ability to wage war.

After Germany's surrender in May the United States embarked upon a huge logistical effort to redeploy to the Pacific more than a million troops from Europe, the United States, and other inactive theaters. The aim was to complete the redeployment in time to launch an invasion of Japan on November 1, and the task had to be undertaken in the face of competing shipping demands for demobilization of long-service troops, British redeployment, and civil relief in Europe. By the time the war ended, some 150,000 men had moved from Europe directly to the

Pacific; but a larger transfer from the United States across the Pacific had scarcely begun. In the Pacific, MacArthur and Nimitz had been sparing no effort to expand ports and ready bases to receive the expected influx and to mount invasion forces. The two commanders were also completing plans for the invasion of Japan. In the last stage of the war, as all forces converged on Japan, the area unified commands gave way to an arrangement that made MacArthur commander of all Army forces in the Pacific and Nimitz commander of all Navy forces.

By midsummer of 1945 most responsible leaders in Japan realized that the end was near. In June those favoring a negotiated settlement had come out in the open, and Japan had already dispatched peace feelers through the Soviet Union, a country it feared might also be about to enter the war in spite of a nonaggression treaty between the two nations. As early as the Tehran Conference in late 1943 Stalin had promised to enter the war against Japan, and all agreed at Yalta in February 1945 that the USSR would do so three months after the defeat of Germany. At the Potsdam Conference in July, the Soviet Union reaffirmed its agreement to declare war on Japan. The United States and Britain with China issued the famed Potsdam Declaration calling upon Japan to surrender promptly; about the same time President Harry S. Truman decided to employ the newly tested atomic bomb against Japan in the event of continued Japanese resistance.

Despite the changing climate of opinion in Japan, the still-powerful Japanese military blocked negotiations by insisting on fighting a decisive battle of defense of the empire's home shores. Thus the Japanese government announced its intention to ignore the terms of the Potsdam Declaration. Accordingly, on August 6 a lone American B–29 from the Marianas dropped an atomic bomb on Hiroshima. On the ninth the Soviet Union came into the war and attacked Japanese forces in Manchuria and another B–29 dropped an atomic bomb on Nagasaki. The next day Japan sued for peace. With the signing of surrender terms aboard the USS *Missouri* in Tokyo Bay on September 2, the bitter global war came to an end.

Retrospect

In winning the Pacific war the Allies had found it unnecessary to press home their attacks and destroy the Japanese military forces except for the Japanese Fleet. By the end of the war Japan's Navy had virtually ceased to exist, Japanese industry had been so hammered by air bombardment that Japan's ability to wage war was seriously reduced, and U.S. submarine and air actions had cut off sources of raw material. At the time of the surrender Japan still had 2 million men under arms in the homeland and was capable of conducting a tenacious ground defense; about 5,000 Japanese aircraft were also operational. Nevertheless, the Japanese could not have continued the war into the spring of 1946. The Japanese Army had concentrated its forces along the designated U.S. invasion beaches expecting to bloody the invaders in hopes of securing better terms. The fact that an invasion was not necessary doubtless spared many American and Japanese lives.

The great arbiter of the Pacific war had been the American industrial power that had produced a mighty war machine. Out of this production had come the Pacific Fleet, a potent force that could overcome the vast reaches of the Pacific upon which the Japanese had depended so heavily as a defensive advantage. The decisive combat element of the fleet was the fast carrier task force, which carried the war deep into Japanese territory and supported advances far beyond the range of land-based aircraft. Land-based air power also played a decisive part. When carriers were not available to support offensives, land-based aviation measured the distance of each forward move. Land-based aviation proved important as well in providing close support for ground operations, while aerial supply operations and troop movements contributed greatly to the success of the Allied campaigns.

Both naval and air forces depended on shore installations, and the war in the Pacific demonstrated that even in a predominantly naval/air theater, ground combat forces are an essential part of the offensive team. The Japanese had also depended on far-flung bases, so that much of the Allied effort during the war had gone into the seizure or neutralization of Japan's air and naval strongholds. Thus, the Pacific war was in large measure a struggle for bases. However, the U.S. Pacific Fleet, in one of the greatest logistical developments of the war, went far in the direction of carrying its own bases with it by organizing fleet trains

MacArthur Reviews Battle, *Gary Sheadan, 1944*

of support vessels that could maintain the fleet at sea over extended periods, minimizing some of its basing requirements.

Another important facet of the Pacific war, the development and employment of amphibious assault techniques, repeatedly demonstrated the need for unified command. Air, ground, and naval teamwork, supremely important in the struggle against Japan, occasionally broke down; but the success of the Allied campaigns illustrates that all three elements achieved that cooperation to a large degree. Strategic air bombardment in the Pacific, designed to cripple Japan's industrial capacity, did not get under way until much of 1945 had passed. The damage inflicted on Japanese cities, especially by incendiary aerial bombardment, was enormous. The effect, as in the case of the bomber offensive against Germany, remains contentious; though the bombardment began to bring home to the Japanese people that the war was lost. The atomic bombings were the capstone of that effort. The submarine played a vital role in reducing Japan's capabilities by taking a huge toll of Japanese shipping and by helping to cut Japan off from the resources of Southeast Asia.

In the final analysis Japan lost because the country did not have the means to fight a total war against the combination of industrial, air, naval, and human resources represented by the United States and its Allies. Admiral Isoroku Yamamoto, commander of the Japanese Fleet at the outbreak of the war, put his finger on the fatal weakness of the Japanese concept of the war: "It is not enough that we should take Guam and the Philippines, or even Hawaii and San Francisco. We should have to march into Washington and sign the treaty in the White House." This the Japanese could never do; because they could not, they had to lose the war.

Discussion Questions

1. Why did Japan go to war? How did she plan to win?

2. How successful was Army and Navy cooperation in the Pacific? In the Central Pacific? In the Southwest Pacific?

3. Why was the United States so deeply involved in operations in Burma? Was this the best use of resources?

4. Would it have made more strategic sense to bypass the Philippines and strike Formosa directly before moving against Okinawa? Why or why not?

5. Was the Allied dual-thrust strategy the best one to use in the Pacific war? Why or why not?

6. Should the United States have resorted to using the atomic bomb to force Japan's surrender? What about the second atomic bomb? Justify your answers.

Recommended Readings

Clayton, James D. *The Years of MacArthur,* 3 vols. Boston: Houghton Mifflin, 1970–1985.

Drea, Edward J. *MacArthur's Ultra: Codebreaking and the War against Japan, 1942–1945.* Lawrence: University Press of Kansas, 1992.

Frank, Richard B. DOWNFALL: *The End of the Imperial Japanese Empire.* New York: Random House, 1999.

Griffith, Thomas E. *MacArthur's Airman: General George C. Kenney and the War in the Southwest Pacific.* Lawrence: University Press of Kansas, 1998.

Heller, Charles E., and William A. Stofft, eds. *America's First Battles, 1776–1965.* Lawrence: University Press of Kansas, 1986.

Leary, William M., ed. *We Shall Return! MacArthur's Commanders and the Defeat of Japan, 1942–1945.* Lexington: University Press of Kentucky, 1988.

Pogue, Forrest C. *George C. Marshall: Organizer of Victory, 1943–1945.* New York: Viking, 1973.

Prange, Gordon W., et al. *At Dawn We Slept: The Untold Story of Pearl Harbor.* New York: Viking, 1991.

Spector, Ronald H. *Eagle against the Sun: The American War with Japan.* Norwalk, Conn.: Easton Press, 1989.

Tuchman, Barbara W. *Stilwell and the American Experience in China, 1911–1945.* New York: Grove Press, 2001.

Other Readings

Crowl, Philip A. *Campaign in the Marianas.* U.S. Army in World War II. Washington, D.C.: U.S. Army Center of Military History, 1995.

Falk, Stanley L. *Decision at Leyte.* Norwalk, Conn.: Easton Press, 1989.

Miller, John, Jr. *Guadalcanal: The First Offensive.* U.S. Army in World War II. Washington, D.C.: U.S. Army Center of Military History, 1995.

Morison, Samuel E. *History of United States Naval Operations in World War II,* 15 vols. Urbana: University of Illinois Press, 2001–2002, vol. 7.

Perret, Geoffrey. *Old Soldiers Never Die: The Life of Douglas MacArthur.* New York: Random House, 1996.

Romanus, Charles F., and Riley Sunderland. *Stilwell's Command Problems.* U.S. Army in World War II. Washington, D.C.: U.S. Army Center of Military History, 1987.

Smith, Robert R. *Triumph in the Philippines.* U.S. Army in World War II. Washington, D.C.: U.S. Army Center of Military History, 1991.

Taaffe, Stephen R. *MacArthur's Jungle War: The 1944 New Guinea Campaign.* Lawrence: University Press of Kansas, 1998.

Toland, John. The Rising Sun: *The Decline and Fall of the Japanese Empire, 1936–1945.* New York: Modern Library, 2003.

7

PEACE BECOMES COLD WAR
1945–1950

The United States did not return to its prewar isolationism after World War II. The balance of power in Europe and Asia and the safety of ocean distances east and west that made isolation possible had vanished: the war upset the balance, and advances in air transportation and weaponry surpassed the protection of the oceans. There was now little inclination to dispute the essential rightness of the position Woodrow Wilson espoused after World War I that the nations of the world were interdependent, the peace indivisible. Indeed, in the years immediately following World War II, full participation in world events became a governing dynamic of American life.

With the end of the war, American hopes for a peaceful future focused on the United Nations (UN) formed at San Francisco in 1945. The fifty countries signing the UN Charter agreed to employ "effective collective measures for the prevention and removal of threats to the peace and for the suppression of acts of aggression," including the use of armed force if necessary. The organization included a bicameral legislature: the General Assembly, in which all member nations had representation and a smaller Security Council. The latter had authority to determine when the peace was threatened, to decide what action to take, and to call on member states to furnish military formations. Five founding members of the United Nations (the United States, the Union of Soviet Socialist Republics, the United Kingdom, China, and France) had permanent representation on the Security Council and the power of veto over any council action. Since the United Nations' effectiveness depended largely on the full cooperation of these countries, the primary objective of American foreign policy as the postwar era opened was to continue and strengthen the solidarity those nations had displayed during the war.

U.S. membership in the United Nations implied a responsibility to maintain sufficient military power to permit an effective contribution to any UN force that might be necessary. Other than this, it was

U.S. veterans of the China-Burma-India campaigns arrive in New York on September 27, 1945.

difficult in the immediate aftermath of war to foresee national security requirements in the changed world and consequently to know the proper shape of a military establishment to meet them. The immediate task was to demobilize a great war machine and at the same time maintain occupation troops in conquered and liberated territories. Beyond this lay the problems of deciding the size and composition of the postwar armed forces and of establishing the machinery that would formulate national security policy and govern the military establishment.

Demobilization

The U.S. Army and Navy had separately determined during the war their reasonable postwar strengths and had produced plans for an orderly demobilization. The Navy developed a program for 600,000 men, 370 combat and 5,000 other ships, and 8,000 aircraft. The Army Air Forces was equally specific, setting its sights on becoming a separate service with 400,000 members, 70 combat groups, and a complete organization of supporting units. The Army initially established as an overall postwar goal a regular and reserve structure capable of mobilizing 4 million men within a year of any future outbreak of war; later it set the strength of the active ground and air forces at 1.5 million. Demobilization plans called for the release of troops on an individual basis with each soldier receiving point credit for length of service, combat participation and awards, time spent overseas, and parenthood. The General Staff considered the shipping available to bring overseas troops home and the capacity to process discharges in setting the number of points required for release. The whole scheme aimed at producing a systematic transition to a peacetime military structure.

WAR CRIMES TRIALS (JAPAN)

The International Military Tribunal for the Far East, held in Tokyo after World War II, prosecuted suspected Japanese war criminals. Only 28 of the 80 Class A war suspects appeared before the court. Of these individuals, 4 had been prime ministers and 19 had been military officers. Twenty-five of the 28 were found guilty, 2 others died during trial, and 1 was found mentally incompetent. Seven were sentenced to death by hanging, 16 to life in prison, and 2 to shorter terms. The emperor was not indicted.

War Crimes Trials (Germany)

In the 1943 Moscow Declaration, Allied leaders announced that German war criminals would be tried where they committed their crimes, but that the Allies would prosecute the leadership of the Nazi regime together. The famous International Military Tribunal trials at Nuremberg lasted from October 20, 1945, until October 1, 1946. Twenty-two defendants, including Hermann Göring, Commander in Chief of the *Luftwaffe* (Air Force), and Rudolf Hess, Deputy *Führer*, stood trial for crimes against peace, war crimes, crimes against

Defendants in the Nuremberg Trials. On the front row are Hermann Goering, Rudolf Hess, Joachim von Ribbentrop, and Wilhelm Keitel.

humanity, and conspiracy to commit such crimes. The trials resulted in twelve death sentences, three acquittals, and prison terms ranging from a few years to life imprisonment.

Pressure for faster demobilization from the public, Congress, and the troops upset War and Navy Department plans for an orderly process. The Army felt the greatest pressure and responded by easing the eligibility requirement and releasing half of its 8 million troops by the end of 1945. Early in 1946 the Army slowed the return of troops from abroad in order to meet its overseas responsibilities. A crescendo of protest greeted the decision, including troop demonstrations in the Philippines, China, England, France, Germany, Hawaii, and even California. The public outcry diminished only after the Army more than halved its remaining strength during the first six months of 1946.

President Harry S. Truman, determined to balance the national budget, also affected the Army's manpower. He developed and through fiscal year 1950 employed a "remainder method" of calculating military budgets. He subtracted all other expenditures from revenues before recommending a military appropriation. The dollar ceiling for fiscal year 1947 dictated a new maximum Army strength of just over 1 million. To reduce to that level, the Army stopped draft calls and released all postwar draftees along with any troops eligible for demobilization. By June 30, 1947, the Army was a volunteer body of 684,000 ground troops and 306,000 airmen. It was still large for a peacetime Army, but losses of capable maintenance specialists resulted in a widespread deterioration of equipment. Active Army units, understrength and infused with barely trained replacements, represented only shadows of the efficient organizations they had been at the end of the war.

General Marshall

General Dwight D. Eisenhower
G. Ryan, 1945

Unification

While demobilization proceeded, civil and military officials wrestled with reorganizing the national security system to cope with a changed world. Army reformers, led by General of the Army George C. Marshall, Jr., and his successor as Chief of Staff, General of the Army Dwight D. Eisenhower, argued for strong centralized control at the national and theater levels, using as their model the European Theater of Operations. They wanted to preserve the basic World War II command arrangements but also to go substantially beyond them. Navy Secretary James V. Forrestal advocated a looser, more decentralized system that would essentially continue World War II practices. The largest group of reformers, including President Truman and most members of Congress, desired efficiency and its supposed corollary, economy, above all else. Forrestal and the Navy prevailed in the three-year debate that culminated in the passage of the National Security Act of 1947.

The act created a National Security Council (NSC) and a loosely federated National Military Establishment. The latter was not an executive department of the federal government, though a civilian Secretary of Defense with cabinet rank headed the organization. Only a minimal number of civilians assisted him in coordinating the armed services. The Air Force became a separate service equal to the Army and Navy; the law designated all three as executive departments. They were led by civilian secretaries who lacked cabinet rank but enjoyed direct access to the President.

Members of the National Security Council included the Secretary of State, the Secretary of Defense, the three service secretaries, and heads of other governmental agencies as appointed by the President. One of the appointees was the Chairman of the National Security Resources Board, an agency established by the act to handle the problems of industrial, manpower, and raw material mobilization in support of an overall national strategy. In theory, the National Security Council was to develop coordinated diplomatic, military, and industrial plans; recommend integrated national security policies to the President; and guide the execution of those policies the President approved. In practice, because of the inherent complexity of the responsibility, the council would produce something less than precise policy determinations.

The National Military Establishment included the Departments of the Army, Navy, and Air Force and the Office of the Secretary of Defense. The Secretary of Defense exercised general direction over the three departments. The Joint Chiefs of Staff, composed of the military chiefs of the three services, became a statutory body in the Office of the Secretary of Defense. The chiefs functioned as the principal military advisers to the President, the National Security Council, and the Secretary of Defense. They also formulated joint military plans, established unified (multiservice) commands in various areas of the world as well as single service (subsequently called specified) commands, and gave strategic direction to those commands. By mid-1950 the chiefs had established unified commands in the Far East, the Pacific, Alaska, the Caribbean, and Europe and a few specified commands, the most important of which was the Air Force's Strategic Air Command

(SAC), then the nation's only atomic strike force. Within each unified command, at least theoretically, Army, Navy, and Air Force personnel served under commanders of their respective services but came under the overall supervision of the Commander in Chief (CINC), whom the Joint Chiefs designated from one of the services. In fact, each component commander looked to his own service chief for guidance and only secondarily to his unified commander. The unified commander exercised true command authority only over the component commander of his own service. All else was subject to negotiation and the impacts of prestige and personalities.

Under the National Security Act, each military service retained much of its former autonomy because it was administered within a separate department. In 1948 Forrestal, ironically as the first Secretary of Defense, negotiated an interservice accord on roles and missions that hardened the separation. The Army received primary responsibility for conducting operations on land, for supplying antiaircraft units to defend the United States against air attack, and for providing occupation and security garrisons overseas. The Navy, besides remaining responsible for surface and submarine operations, retained control of its sea-based aviation and of the Marine Corps with its organic aviation. The new Air Force received jurisdiction over strategic air warfare, air transport, and combat air support of the Army.

The signal weakness of the act was not that it left the armed forces more federated than unified but that the Secretary of Defense, empowered to exercise only general supervision, could do little more than encourage cooperation among the departments. Furthermore, giving the three service secretaries direct access to the President tended to confuse lines of authority. Forrestal's suicide shortly after stepping down as Secretary vividly highlighted these faults, which prompted an amendment to the act in 1949 that partially corrected the deficiencies. It converted the National Military Establishment into an executive department, renamed the Department of Defense.

The legislation reduced the Departments of the Army, Navy, and Air Force to military departments within the Department of Defense and added a chairman to preside over the Joint Chiefs without any further substantive powers. General of the Army Omar N. Bradley became the first chairman. The Secretary of Defense received at least some of the appropriate responsibility and authority to make him truly the central figure in coordinating the activities of the three services. The latter, although reduced in strength, remained formidable. The three service secretaries retained authority to administer affairs within their respective departments; and the departments remained the principal agencies for administering, training, and supporting their respective forces. The service chiefs in their capacity as members of the Joint Chiefs of Staff retained primary responsibility for military operations.

Unification also touched officer education, though each service continued to maintain schools to meet its own specialized needs. Wartime experiences led the Joint Chiefs of Staff to open three schools designed to educate officers of all the services and selected civilians: the Armed Forces Staff College to train officers in planning and conducting joint military operations; the Industrial College of the Armed Forces to instruct logisticians in mobilizing the nation's

General Bradley

resources for war; and the National War College to develop officers and civilians for duties connected with the execution of national policy at the highest levels.

In May 1950 Congress enacted a new Uniform Code of Military Justice applying to all the armed forces. This code, besides prescribing uniformity, reduced the severities of military discipline in the interest of improving the lot of the individual serviceman. In another troop matter, part of a larger effort for civil rights, President Truman directed the armed forces to eliminate all segregation of troops by race. The Navy and the Air Force abolished their all–African American units by June 1950. The Army, with more African-American members than its sister services, took some four years longer to desegregate. There was also high-level opposition: Secretary of the Army Kenneth C. Royall resigned rather than implement President Truman's order.

Occupation

Throughout the demobilization, about half the Army's diminishing strength remained overseas, the bulk of that involved in the occupation of Germany and Japan. The Army also maintained a significant force in the southern portion of the former Japanese colony of Korea and smaller forces in Austria and the Italian province of Trieste.

Under a common occupation policy developed principally in conferences at Yalta and Potsdam in 1945, the Allied Powers assumed joint authority over Germany. American, British, Soviet, and French forces occupied separate zones; national matters came before an Allied Control Council composed of the commanders of the four occupation armies. The Allies similarly divided and governed the German capital, Berlin, which lay deep in the Soviet zone.

In the American zone, Army occupation troops proceeded rapidly with disarmament, demilitarization, and the eradication of Nazi influence from German life. American officials participated as members of the International Military Tribunal that tried 22 major leaders of the Nazi party and sentenced 12 to death, imprisoned 7, and acquitted 3. The Office of Military Government supervised German civil affairs within the American zone, working increasingly through German local, state, and zonal agencies, which military government officials staffed with politically reliable men. A special U.S. Constabulary, which the

THE OCCUPATION OF BERLIN

In September 1944 American, British, and Soviet representatives in London agreed to divide Berlin into national sectors of occupation (France joined later) and to govern the city jointly. Berlin's garrison surrendered to the Soviets on May 2, 1945. On July 4 soldiers of the 2d Armored Division entered the American sector. The four powers cooperated reasonably well until the summer of 1946, when ideological warfare between German political parties, coupled with East-West disagreements, transformed Berlin into the "Front City" of the Cold War. The sheer example of West Berlin's freedom and prosperity constantly subverted Communist authority in East Germany.

THE U.S. CONSTABULARY

To accomplish its occupational mission in postwar Germany, the Army established a mobile police force, the Constabulary, which went into operation in July 1946. In view of small numbers (its strength never exceeded 35,000), the Constabulary adopted a tactic of preventing disorder by maintaining visibility through frequent patrols. Constabulary soldiers wore a distinctive uniform with a shoulder-strap belt and ascot; their training included courses on German government and law. In 1947, in step with improvements in the German police, Constabulary units began training as combat reserves, completing this transformation by 1950. The Constabulary was inactivated at the end of that year.

Army organized as demobilization cut away the strength of units in Germany, operated as a mobile police force.

Each of the other occupying powers organized its zone along similar lines, but the Allied Control Council could act only by unanimous agreement. It failed to achieve unanimity on such nationwide matters as central economic administrative agencies, political parties, labor organizations, foreign and internal trade, currency, and land reform. Soviet demands and dissents accounted for most of the failures. Each zone inevitably became a self-contained administrative and economic unit; two years after the German surrender, the wartime Allies had made very little progress toward restoring German national life. In January 1947 the British and the Americans began coordinating their zonal economic policies. The eventual result, first taking shape in September 1949, was a Germany divided between the Federal Republic of Germany in the area of the American, British, and French zones and a Communist government in the Soviet zone in the east.

The occupation of Japan proceeded along different lines as a result of President Truman's insistence that all of Japan come under American control. Largely because the war in the Pacific had been primarily an American war, the President secured Allied approval to appoint General of the Army Douglas MacArthur as Supreme Commander, Allied Powers, for the occupation of Japan. A Far East Advisory Commission representing the eleven nations that had fought against Japan resided in Washington. A branch of that body, with representatives from the United States, Great Britain, China, and the USSR, was located in Tokyo. These provided forums for Allied viewpoints on occupation policies, but the real power rested with General MacArthur.

Unlike Germany, Japan retained its government, which, under the supervision of General MacArthur's occupation troops, disarmed the nation rapidly and without incident. An International Military Tribunal similar to the one in Germany tried twenty-five high military and political officials, sentencing seven to death. MacArthur encouraged reforms to alter the old order of government in which the emperor claimed power by divine right and ruled through an oligarchy of military, bureaucratic, and economic cliques. By mid-1947 the free election of a new Diet (legislature) and a thorough revision of the nation's constitution began the transformation of Japan into a democracy with the emperor's role

The Occupation of Korea, September 1945–August 1948

The United States in 1945 decided to occupy the southern half of Korea to prevent the Soviet Union, which had attacked Japanese forces in northern Korea, from dominating the peninsula and thus threatening American access and influence in Northeast Asia. The American occupation had two objectives: remove the Japanese colonial government and repatriate Japanese military personnel and civilians to Japan and establish a democratic and Capitalist regime controlling the entire peninsula that could survive with minimal American economic and military assistance. The United States quickly achieved its first objective, but growing Cold War tensions left each superpower unwilling to allow its rival to dominate the peninsula. Each settled for a client regime controlling half of the peninsula. When the American occupation of southern Korea ended in August 1948, the peninsula was divided into competing regimes, each dedicated to destroying the other.

limited to that of a constitutional monarch. The way was thus open for the ultimate restoration of Japan's sovereignty.

West of the Japanese islands, on the peninsula of Korea, the course of occupation resembled that in Germany. Soviet forces, following their brief campaign against the Japanese in Manchuria, moved into Korea from the north in August 1945. U.S. Army forces, departing from Okinawa, entered from the south a month later. The 38th Parallel of north latitude that crossed the peninsula at its waist became the boundary between the forces. The Americans accepted the Japanese surrender south of the line and the Soviets above it, releasing Korea from forty years of Japanese rule.

According to wartime agreements, the Allies would give Korea full independence following a period of military occupation during which native leadership was to be regenerated and the country's economy rehabilitated. Lack of agreement among the occupying powers very quickly blighted these expectations. While the Americans regarded the 38th Parallel as only a temporary boundary between the occupation forces, the Soviets considered it a permanent delineation between spheres of influence. This interpretation, as in Germany, ruptured the administrative and economic unity of the country.

The Truman administration hoped to remove this obstacle during a meeting of foreign ministers at Moscow in December 1945. The ministers agreed that a joint U.S.-USSR commission would develop a provisional Korean government. A four-power trusteeship composed of the United States, the Soviet Union, the United Kingdom, and China would guide the provisional government for a maximum of five years. But when the commission met, the Soviet members proved willing to reunite Korea only if the Communists dominated the provisional government. The Americans refused. The resulting impasse finally prompted the United States to lay the whole Korean question before the General Assembly of the United Nations in September 1947.

The Rise of a New Opponent

Soviet intransigence, as demonstrated in Germany, in Korea, and in other areas, dashed American hopes for Great Power unity. The USSR, former British Prime Minister Winston S. Churchill warned early in 1946, had lowered an "Iron Curtain" across the European continent. The Soviets quickly drew eastern Germany, Poland, Hungary, Rumania, Bulgaria, Yugoslavia, and Albania behind that curtain. In Greece, where political and economic disorder led to civil war, the rebels received support from Albania, Bulgaria, and Yugoslavia. In the Near East, the Soviets kept a grip on Iran by leaving troops there beyond the time specified in the wartime arrangement. They also tried to intimidate Turkey into giving them special privileges in connection with the strategic Dardanelles. In Asia, besides insisting on full control in northern Korea, the USSR had turned Manchuria over to the Chinese Communists under Mao Zedong and was encouraging him in a renewed effort to wrest power from Chiang Kai-shek and the Kuomintang government.

Whatever the impulse behind the Soviet drive—a search for national security or a desire to promote Communist world revolution— the Soviet strategy appeared to be expansion. The Truman administration could see no inherent limits to the outward push. Each Communist gain, it seemed, would serve as a springboard from which to try another. With a large part of the world still suffering from the ravages of war, the possibilities appeared limitless. President Truman responded by blocking any extension of Communist influence until popular pressures for a better life forced a liberalization of the regime—a policy known as containment. But, viewing the industrialized European continent as the decisive area, the administration at first limited its containment policy to Western Europe, the Mediterranean, and the Middle East and attempted other solutions in East Asia.

China in any case presented a dilemma. On the one hand, American military observers doubted that Chiang Kai-shek could defeat the Communists with aid short of direct American participation in the civil war. President Truman considered such an open-ended commitment unacceptable. On the other hand, an attempt by the President's special envoy, General Marshall, following his Army retirement, to negotiate an end to the war on terms that would allow Communist participation in a Kuomintang-dominated government proved futile. The Truman administration consequently adopted the attitude of "letting the dust settle." Part of the basis for this view was a prevalent American belief that the Chinese Communist revolt was more Chinese than Communist, that its motivation was nationalistic, not imperialistic. Though the dust

THE GREEK CIVIL WAR

In January 1945 British troops suppressed a Greek Communist coup in Athens. The Communists renewed guerrilla war in March 1946. Severe financial difficulties forced the British government to terminate its responsibilities in the spring of 1947. The United States intervened with economic and military aid. Lt. Gen. James Van Fleet commanded an advisory mission of 250 officers who took operational control of Greek forces. Reinvigorated Greek troops went to the offensive in 1948. The war ended in the summer of 1949, when Yugoslav Marshal Josip B. Tito split with Stalin and closed Yugoslavia's borders to the pro-Moscow Greek Communists, forcing many to retreat into Albanian exile.

American Truce Team with Chinese Communists
Wayne DeWitt Larabee, 1946

appeared to be settling in favor of the Chinese Communists by the end of 1948, the administration had some hope that an American-Chinese friendship could still be restored.

Next door in Korea, the United Nations, acting in response to the request of the Truman administration, sent a commission to supervise free elections throughout the peninsula. But Soviet authorities declared the UN project illegal and refused the commission entry above the 38th Parallel. The United Nations then sponsored an elected government in the southern half of the peninsula, which in August 1948 became the Republic of Korea (South Korea). The following month the Soviets countered by establishing a Communist government, the Democratic People's Republic of Korea (North Korea), above the parallel. Three months later they announced the withdrawal of their occupation forces. The United States followed suit in mid-1949, leaving only an advisory group to help train the South Korean armed forces.

In the main arena in Western Europe, the Mediterranean, and the Middle East, blunt diplomatic exchanges finally produced a withdrawal of Soviet forces from Iran. But it was around America's economic strength that the United States constructed its containment strategy, an approach based on the judgment that the American monopoly on atomic weapons would deter the USSR from direct military aggression in favor of exploiting civil strife in countries prostrated by the war. The American strategy focused on providing economic assistance to friends and former enemies alike to alleviate the social conditions conducive to Communist expansion.

To ease the situations in Turkey and Greece, President Truman in 1947 obtained $400 million from Congress with which to assist those two countries. "I believe," the President declared, "that it must be the policy of the United States to support free peoples who are resisting attempted subjugation by armed minorities or by outside pressures … that we must assist free peoples to work out their own destinies in their own way … that our help should be primarily through economic and financial aid which is essential to economic stability and orderly political processes." This policy, subsequently labeled the Truman Doctrine, had only limited application at the time; but the President's appeal to universal principles to justify the program in effect placed the United States in the position of opposing Communist expansion in any part of the world.

A broader program of economic aid followed. General Marshall, who became Secretary of State in January 1947, proposed that the United States pursue the economic recovery in Europe as a single task, not nation by nation, and that a single program combine the resources of European countries with American aid. This Marshall Plan drew an immediate response. Sixteen nations, who also considered the needs and resources of West Germany, devised a four-year European Recovery Program incorporating their resources and requiring some $16 billion from the United States. In a last effort to promote Great Power unity, the Truman administration invited the USSR to participate. The Soviet Union refused and discouraged the initial interest of some countries within its sphere of influence. In October the Soviet Union organized the Cominform, a committee for coordinating Communist parties in Europe to fight the Marshall Plan as "an instrument of American imperialism." More effective opposition came from isolationists in Congress, who balked when President Truman first requested approval of the program. Only after the Soviets engineered a coup d'etat that placed a Communist government in power in Czechoslovakia did Congress appropriate funds in April 1948.

Meanwhile, to protect the western hemisphere against Communist intrusion, the Truman administration in September 1947 helped devise the Inter-American Treaty of Reciprocal Assistance (Rio Treaty), the first regional arrangement for collective defense under provisions of the UN Charter. Eventually signed by all twenty-one American republics, the treaty considered armed aggression against one signatory as an attack upon all. Responses, by independent choice of each signatory, could range from severance of diplomatic relations to economic sanctions to military counteraction.

In March 1948 a second regional arrangement, the Brussels Treaty, drew five nations of Western Europe (Great Britain, France, Belgium, the Netherlands, and Luxembourg) into a long-term economic and military alliance. The signatories received encouragement from President Truman, who declared before Congress his confidence "that the determination of the free countries of Europe to protect themselves will be matched by an equal determination on our part to help them." Republican Senator Arthur H. Vandenberg of Michigan, in a notable display of bipartisan cooperation, followed with a resolution, which the Senate passed in June, authorizing the commitment of American military strength to regional alliances such as the Brussels Treaty.

Out of all of this activity grew the real basis of postwar international relations: West versus East, anti-Communists against Communists, and those nations aligned with the United States confronting those

The President's appeal to universal principles to justify the program in effect placed the United States in the position of opposing Communist expansion in any part of the world.

assembled under the leadership of the Soviet Union, a Cold War between power blocs. Leadership of the Western bloc fell to the United States, because it was the only Western power with sufficient resources to take the lead in containing Soviet expansion.

The Trends of Military Policy

Although pursued as a program of economic assistance, the American policy of containment needed military underpinning. Containment first of all was a defensive measure: The USSR had not completely demobilized. On the contrary, it was maintaining over 4 million men under arms, keeping armament industries in high gear, and rearming some of its satellites. Containment needed the support of a military policy of deterrence, a strategy and force structure possessing sufficient strength and balance to discourage any Soviet or Soviet-supported military aggression.

Postwar military policy, however, did not develop as a full response to the needs of containment. The traditional and current trend of American military thinking focused on mobilization in the event of war, not the maintenance of ready forces to prevent war. Army plans for manpower mobilization concentrated on instituting Universal Military Training (UMT). Technological advances, argued advocates such as Brig. Gen. (Ret.) John M. Palmer, had eliminated the grace of time and distance that had in the past permitted the nation the opportunity to mobilize its untrained citizenry. Modern warfare needed a huge reservoir of trained men. Late in 1945 President Truman asked the Congress for legislation requiring male citizens to undergo a year of military training (not *service*) upon reaching the age of eighteen or after completing high school. Universal Military Training quickly became the subject of wide debate. Objections ranged from mild criticism that it was "a system in which the American mind finds no pleasure" to its denunciation as a "Nazi program." Regardless of the President's urgings, studies that produced further justification, and various attempts to make the program more palatable, Congress with broad public support refused to act on the controversial issue for the next five years.

Lacking Universal Military Training, the Army would depend almost entirely on the reserve components for reinforcements of trained personnel during mobilization. Limited funds also affected the strength of the reserve components. Enrollment in the National Guard and Reserves of all three services at mid-1950 totaled over 2.5 million. Owing largely to restricted budgets, members in active training numbered fewer than 1 million. The bulk of this active strength rested in the Army National Guard and Organized Reserve Corps. The National Guard, with 325,000 members, included 27 understrength divisions. The active strength of the Organized Reserve Corps, some 186,000, primarily manned a multitude of small combat support and service units, also generally understrength. The Reserve Officers' Training Corps provided a final source of trained strength. In early 1950 it contained about 219,000 high school and college students.

The fear of another depression constituted the single most important inhibitor to increased military spending by the Truman administration. Moreover, the advent of the atomic bomb appeared to provide

Olive Drab Field Jacket with Double Brass, Used 1947–1949

an economic alternative to large standing armies and navies. President Truman in particular considered the American nuclear monopoly as the primary deterrent to direct Soviet military action. Determining the size of the force meant balancing what the President perceived as a low risk of Soviet invasion of Western Europe against the real possibility that an unbalanced federal budget required to maintain large conventional forces would lead to economic downturn and would fatally undermine containment.

The size of the budget thus limited the size of the armed forces. The total strength of active forces gradually decreased from the figure reached at the end of demobilization. The Army, Navy, and Marine Corps declined in strength, while the Air Force actually grew slightly larger. About a third of the Air Force constituted the SAC, the main deterrent to Soviet military aggression. Louis A. Johnson, who became Secretary of Defense in March 1949, gave full support to a defense based primarily on strategic air power, largely because of his dedication to economy. Intent on ridding the Department of Defense of what he considered "costly war-born spending habits," Johnson reduced defense expenditures below even the restrictive ceilings in President Truman's recommendations. As a result, by mid-1950 the Air Force, with 411,000 members, maintained only 48 combat groups. The Navy, with 377,000 sailors, had 670 ships in its active fleet and 4,300 operational aircraft. The Marine Corps, 75,000 strong, mustered 2 skeleton divisions and 2 air wings. The Army, down to 591,000 members, fielded 10 weak divisions and 5 regimental combat teams with the constabulary in Germany equal to another division.

Everyone recognized that war with the Soviet Union posed immense dangers. The joint war plans of the period postulated the possibility of a Soviet sweep deep into Western Europe. Initial iterations of these plans envisioned that the Western occupation forces would simply withdraw from the continent as quickly as possible. Subsequent versions postulated a fighting retreat and possible maintenance of an enclave from which to launch a counteroffensive once the United States had mobilized. Only with the advent of the North Atlantic Treaty Organization (NATO) did joint planners seriously consider the defense of Western Europe in depth. Toward the midpoint of these efforts, the planners added an air-atomic offensive from the Middle East and North Africa against the Soviet industrial infrastructure. It would weaken the Soviet military capacity for a long war, but it would not provide a close defense of Western Europe.

The strength reductions, mobilization strategy, and heavy reliance on the atomic bomb and strategic air power indicated that the idea of deterring aggression through balanced ready forces played only a limited role in postwar military policy. As of early June 1950 this calculated risk still appeared adequate to the situation.

President Truman

The Army of 1950

As the Army underwent its drastic postwar reduction, from 8 million men and 89 divisions in 1945 to 591,000 men and 10 divisions in 1950, it also underwent numerous structural changes. At the department level, General Eisenhower in 1946 had approved a reorganization that restored the General Staff to its prewar position. The principal adjustment involved the elimination of the very powerful Operations Division (OPD) from which General Marshall had controlled wartime operations. Eisenhower brought back the prewar structure of the General Staff with five coequal divisions under new names: Personnel and Administration; Intelligence; Organization and Training; Service, Supply, and Procurement; and Plans and Operations. He also abolished the Headquarters, Army Service Forces, in 1946. The administrative and technical services formerly under that headquarters regained their prewar status as departmental agencies. In 1948 Eisenhower's successor, General Bradley, redesignated the Army Ground Forces as the Army Field Forces and restricted its responsibilities to education, training, doctrine, and the service test of new equipment.

These and other organizational changes became a matter of statute with the passage of the Army Reorganization Act in 1950. The act confirmed the power of the Secretary of the Army to administer departmental affairs and relieved the Army Chief of Staff from command of the field forces. Under the Secretary, the Army Chief of Staff was responsible for the Army's readiness and operational plans and for worldwide implementation of the approved plans and policies of the department. He had the assistance of general and special staffs whose size and composition could be adjusted as requirements changed. Below the Chief of Staff, the Chief of Army Field Forces was directly responsible for developing tactical doctrine, for controlling the Army school system, and for supervising the field training of Army units. He exercised these responsibilities through the headquarters of the six Continental Army Areas into which the United States was divided.

> The Army Chief of Staff was responsible for the Army's readiness and operational plans and for worldwide implementation of the approved plans and policies of the department.

Under the new act, the Secretary of the Army received the authority to determine the number and strength of the Army's combat arms and services. Three combat arms—Infantry, Armor, and Artillery—received statutory recognition. Armor became a continuation of another older arm, now eliminated, the Cavalry. Artillery represented a merger of the old Field Artillery, Coast Artillery, and Antiaircraft Artillery. The services numbered fourteen and included The Adjutant General's Corps, Army Medical Service, Chaplain's Corps, Chemical Corps, Corps of Engineers, Finance Corps, Inspector General's Corps, Judge Advocate General's Corps, Military Police Corps, Ordnance Corps, Quartermaster Corps, Signal Corps, Transportation Corps, and Women's Army Corps. Army Aviation, designated neither arm nor service, existed as a quasi-arm equipped with small fixed-wing craft and a very few primitive helicopters.

The Army's best body of troops at mid-1950 consisted largely of World War II veterans, a sizable but diminishing group. The need to obtain replacements quickly during demobilization, the distractions and relaxed atmosphere of occupation duty, and a postwar training program less demanding than that of the war years impeded the combat readiness of newer Army members. Some veterans claimed that the new Uniform Code of Military Justice, because it softened military discipline, had blunted the Army's combat ability even more.

Half the Army's major combat units were deployed overseas. Of the 10 divisions, the Far Eastern Command controlled 4 infantry divisions on occupation duty in Japan. The European Command had another infantry division in Germany. The remaining 5 (2 airborne, 2 infantry, and 1 armored divisions) in the United States constituted a general reserve to meet emergencies. All 10 divisions had undergone organizational changes, most of them prompted by the war experience. Under new tables of organization and equipment, the firepower and mobility of the infantry division received a boost through the addition of a tank battalion and an antiaircraft battalion and through a rise in the number of pieces in each artillery battery from 4 to 6. At the regimental level, the World War II cannon and antitank companies had disappeared; the new tables added a tank company and a 4.2-inch mortar company, as well as 57-mm. and 75-mm. recoilless rifles. The postwar economies, however, had forced the Army to skeletonize its combat units. Nine of the 10 divisions were far under their authorized strength. Their infantry regiments had only 2 of the normal 3 battalions, and most artillery battalions had only 2 of the normal 3 firing batteries. Most lacked organic armor. No unit had its wartime complement of weapons, and those weapons on hand as well as other equipment were largely worn-out leftovers from World War II. None of the combat units, as a result, came anywhere near to possessing the punch conceived under the new organizational design.

The Cold War Intensifies

The deterioration in military readiness through mid-1950 proceeded in the face of a worsening trend in international events, especially from mid-1948 forward. In Germany, in further protest against Western attempts to establish a national government and in particular against efforts to institute currency reforms in Berlin, the USSR in June 1948 moved to force the Americans, British, and French out of the capital by blockading the road and rail lines through the Soviet occupation zone over which troops and supplies from the West reached the Allied sectors of the city. Although General Lucius D. Clay, the American military governor, preferred to test Soviet resolve with an armed convoy, at the

THE ARMY AND THE BERLIN AIRLIFT

Russian forces blocked the routes of supply by road, rail, and canal from the West to the American and British occupation sectors in Berlin. General Clay's attempt to gain approval for a plan to run armored columns down the roads and crash through these barricades failed because the British and Americans feared it would help precipitate a war. Clay came up with the "impossible" idea of supplying Berlin by air. Following the first modest food deliveries in June 1948, the airlift steadily gained proficiency. When the blockade ended in May 1949, the U.S.-U.K. Air Forces had flown in 1.218 million net metric tons of supplies, chiefly coal and food, to Berlin.

Berliners watch a C–54 land at Tempelhof, Berlin, 1948.

suggestion of his British counterpart, General Sir Brian Robertson, he countered with an airlift. The U.S. Army and U.S. Air Force, with some help from the British and U.S. Navies, loaded, flew in, and distributed food, fuel, and other necessities to keep the Allied sectors of Berlin supplied. The success of the airlift and a telling counterblockade, which shut off shipments of goods to the Soviet sector from West Germany, finally moved the Soviets to lift the blockade in May 1949.

Meanwhile, in April 1949, the United States joined NATO, the military alliance growing out of the Brussels Treaty. The United States and Canada combined with ten Western European nations so that "an armed attack against one or more of them" would "be considered an attack against them all," a provision aimed at discouraging a Soviet march on Europe. The signatories agreed to earmark forces for service under NATO direction. For the United States' part, the budgetary restrictions, mobilization strategy, and continuing emphasis on air power and the bomb handicapped its military commitment to the alliance. The basic budget ceiling and Secretary of Defense Johnson's ardent economy drive defeated an effort by some officials to increase the nation's conventional forces. Nevertheless, by joining NATO, the United States pledged that it would fight to protect common Allied interests in Europe and thus explicitly enlarged containment beyond the economic realm.

Concurrently with negotiations leading to the NATO alliance, the National Security Council reviewed all postwar military aid programs, some of which stemmed from World War II obligations. By 1949 the United States was providing military equipment and training assistance to Greece, Turkey, Iran, China, Korea, the Philippines, and the Latin American republics. Based on this examination, President Truman proposed combining all existing programs and extending eligibility to any anti-Communist government. This became the administration's primary means of containing communism outside of Europe. The result was the Mutual Defense Assistance Program of October 1949. The Department of the Army, executive agent for the program, sent each recipient country a military assistance advisory group. Composed of Army, Navy, and Air Force sections, each advisory group assisted its host government in determining the amount and type of aid needed and helped train the armed forces of each country in the use and tactical employment of materiel received from the United States.

A new and surprising turn came in the late summer of 1949, when, two to three years ahead of Western intelligence estimates, an explosion over Siberia announced the Soviets had an atomic weapon. On the heels of the USSR's achievement, the civil war in China ended in favor of the Chinese Communists. Chiang Kai-shek withdrew to the island of Taiwan in December 1949. Two months later Communist China and the USSR negotiated a treaty of mutual assistance, an ominous event in terms of future U.S.-China relations.

The United States' loss of the atomic monopoly prompted its broad review of the entire political and strategic position at top staff levels in the National Security Council, Department of State, and Department of Defense. A special National Security Council committee at the same time considered the specific problem posed by the Soviet achievement. Out of the committee came a decision to intensify research on the hydrogen bomb to assure the United States the lead in the field

Communist China and the USSR negotiated a treaty of mutual assistance, an ominous event in terms of future U.S.-China relations.

of nuclear weapons. Out of the broader review, completed in April 1950, came recommendations known as NSC 68 (the file number of the paper) for a large expansion of American military, diplomatic, and economic efforts to meet the changed world situation. The planning staffs in the Department of Defense began at once to translate the military recommendations into force levels and budgets. There remained the question of whether the plans when completed would persuade President Truman to lift the ceiling on military appropriations. Events in Korea soon resolved the issue.

After the Communist victory in China, the United States applied its policy of containment in Asia. In January 1950 Secretary of State Dean G. Acheson publicly defined the U.S. "defense line" in Asia as running south from the Aleutian Islands to Japan, to the Ryukyu Islands, and then to the Philippines. This delineation raised a question about Taiwan and Korea, which lay outside the line. Secretary Acheson stated that if they were attacked, "the initial reliance must be on the people attacked to resist it and then upon the commitments of the entire world under the Charter of the United Nations." A question remained whether the Communist bloc would construe his statement as a definite American commitment to defend Taiwan and Korea if they came under attack.

The United States had responded to the emergence of a bipolar world with a policy of containing the political ambitions of the Communist bloc while at the same time deterring general war. In the view of senior Army leaders, by mid-1950 the United States had not yet backed that policy with a matching military establishment.

DISCUSSION QUESTIONS

1. Why did the United States demobilize so quickly after World War II? What were the consequences? Have there been parallels since?

2. What did unification entail? What are some reasons for greater unification of the services, and what are some against?

3. What were the areas of friction between the United States and the Soviet Union after World War II? How did they affect the U.S. Army?

4. What were the major components of the U.S. policy of containment in Europe? How successful was the effort? Could the new United Nations have filled this role?

5. Why were Berlin and Germany so important to the United States?

6. Discuss the pros and cons of Universal Military Training. Why did the attempt to pass UMT legislation fail?

RECOMMENDED READINGS

Backer, John H. *Winds of History: The German Years of Lucius DuBignon Clay.* New York: Van Nostrand Reinhold, 1983.

Bradley, Omar, and Clay Blair. *A General's Life: An Autobiography.* New York: Simon & Schuster, 1983.

Friedman, Norman. *The Fifty Year War: Conflict and Strategy in the Cold War*. Annapolis: Naval Institute Press, 2000.

Gaddis, John L. *Strategies of Containment: A Critical Appraisal of Postwar American National Security Policy*. New York: Oxford University Press, 1982.

James, D. Clayton. *The Years of MacArthur*, 3 vols. Boston: Houghton Mifflin, 1985, vol. 3.

MacGregor, Morris J., Jr. *The Integration of the Armed Forces, 1940–1965*. Washington, D.C.: U.S. Army Center of Military History, 2001.

Perry, John C. *Beneath the Eagle's Wings: Americans in Occupied Japan*. New York: Dodd, Mead, 1980.

Pogue, Forrest C. George C. *Marshall: Statesman, 1945–1959*. New York: Penguin Books, 1989.

Other Readings

Carafano, James J. *Waltzing into the Cold War: The Struggle for Occupied Austria*. College Station: Texas A&M University Press, 2002.

Clay, Lucius D. *Decision in Germany*. Westport, Conn.: Greenwood Press, 1970.

Condit, Kenneth W. *History of the Joint Chiefs of Staff: The Joint Chiefs of Staff and National Policy, 1947–1949*, 7 vols. Washington, D.C.: Office of Joint History, 1996, vol. 2.

Gimbel, John. *The American Occupation of Germany: Politics and the Military, 1945–1949*. Stanford: Stanford University Press, 1968.

Leffler, Melvyn P. *A Preponderance of Power: National Security, the Truman Administration, and the Cold War*. Stanford, Calif.: Stanford University Press, 1992.

Miller, Roger G. *To Save a City: The Berlin Airlift, 1948–1949*. College Station: Texas A&M University Press, 2000.

Nelson, Daniel J. *A History of U.S. Military Forces in Germany*. Boulder, Colo.: Westview Press, 1987, ch. 1.

Rearden, Steven L. *The Formative Years, 1947–1950: History of the Office of the Secretary of Defense*. Washington, D.C.: Historical Office, Office of the Secretary of Defense, 1984.

Reid, Escott. *Time of Fear and Hope: The Making of the North Atlantic Treaty, 1947–1949*. Toronto: McClelland and Stewart, 1977.

Ross, Steven T. *American War Plans, 1945–1950*. Portland, Ore.: Frank Cass, 1996.

Schaller, Michael. *The American Occupation of Japan: The Origins of the Cold War in Asia*. New York: Oxford University Press, 1985.

Schnabel, James F. *History of the Joint Chiefs of Staff: The Joint Chiefs of Staff and National Policy, 1945–1947*, 7 vols. Washington, D.C.: Office Joint History, 1996, vol. 1.

Ziemke, Earl F. *The U.S. Army in the Occupation of Germany, 1944–1946*. Washington, D.C.: U.S. Army Center of Military History, 2003, chs. 17–24.

8

THE KOREAN WAR 1950–1953

T he North Korean invasion of South Korea on June 25, 1950, in a narrow sense was only an escalation of a continuing civil war among Koreans that began with Japan's defeat in 1945. In a larger sense, the invasion marked the eruption of the Cold War between the United States and the USSR into open hostilities because each of the Great Powers backed one of the competing Korean governments. The war that followed would devastate Korea, lead to a large expansion of the U.S. armed forces and America's military presence around the world, and frustrate many on both sides by ending in an armistice that left the peninsula still divided.

The Great Powers' connection to Korea dated back to the decision in August 1945 by the United States and the USSR to dismantle the Japanese colonial system there by dividing the peninsula into two occupation zones. In December 1945 the United States and the USSR agreed to form a joint commission from among American and Soviet personnel in Korea that would recommend, after consultation with various Korean groups, the form of a government for Korea. Almost all Koreans in 1945 desired an independent Korea, but there were many competing visions of how to organize a new government. Between September 1945 and August 1948, the United States became entangled in this complex and violent Korean struggle that occurred in the context of increasing tensions between the United States and the USSR. Many Korean political groups in 1945 had Socialist or Leftist orientations or were openly Communist. Americans, both in the occupation force and in Washington, feared that these groups would create a Korea unfriendly to American interests, a fear intensified by reports coming out of the northern occupation zone that the Soviets were sponsoring a Communist revolution there led by Kim Il Sung.

By the summer of 1947 Kim Il Sung had crushed opposition to his rule in the north. In the south, violence had destroyed the political center and driven the Leftists and Communists underground or into

Kim Il Sung

the hills to begin preparations for a guerrilla war against the Rightist groups that the U.S. military government had favored. Soviet intransigence in negotiations over Korea's future and the political violence in the South, which had erupted into rebellion against the Syngman Rhee regime in April 1948, led the United States to propose a United Nations Temporary Commission on Korea and an end to the American occupation of South Korea. The United Nations accepted the proposal to supervise efforts to create a unified Korea through a national election; but Kim Il Sung refused to cooperate, and thus the elections for a new Korean legislature in May 1948 took place only in the U.S. zone. Dominated by Rightist parties, the new legislature elected Rhee president of the republic in July 1948; on August 15 he was inaugurated, bringing an end to the U.S. occupation in southern Korea but not to the guerrilla war in the south. In the north, the Soviets had withdrawn all but advisers and the Democratic People's Republic of Korea (DPRK), headed by Kim, was established in September 1948.

The Decision for War

The Western bloc was surprised by North Korea's decision to invade South Korea. American intelligence reports had documented the DPRK's military buildup, and by June 1950 the CIA had concluded that the DPRK could invade South Korea. Analysis of these reports by American civilian and military intelligence agencies was colored by the greater attention given to other areas of the world, previous false alarms of impending invasion, North Korean security measures, and the judgment that the DPRK was a firmly controlled satellite of the Soviet Union. This interpretation held that the DPRK could not destroy the Republic of Korea (ROK) government without Soviet assistance and that the Soviets would not provide such assistance, fearing it would spark a general war with the United States. Instead, American intelligence judged that the DPRK would continue its efforts to destabilize

General of the Army Douglas MacArthur and Dr. Syngman Rhee at a Ceremony, 1948

the ROK, a conclusion reinforced by the National Assembly elections in May 1950 that highlighted widespread dissatisfaction with the Rhee government in South Korea.

The DPRK, while dependent on Soviet military and economic aid, was not a client state completely controlled by the Soviet Union; the initiative for the invasion came from Kim Il Sung, who was committed to unifying the country under his rule. Kim petitioned Stalin several times in 1949 for permission to invade South Korea. In late January 1950 Stalin finally gave his assent and dispatched large amounts of military aid and Soviet advisers to prepare the invasion. Stalin finally approved Kim's request because the United States had withdrawn its last ground combat unit from South Korea in June 1949 and Kim promised that the *Korean People's Army (KPA)* could conquer the South before the United States could intervene decisively. Another consideration was that the United States had indicated that Korea was not needed for "strategic purposes," a euphemism for bases from which to fight the Soviet Union in World War III. The chances of a direct confrontation with the United States thus appeared small.

Kim in June 1950 had good reason to be confident of a quick victory. A force of 135,000, about half of whom were veterans of the Soviet Army or the *Chinese People's Liberation Army*, the *KPA* had 8 full divisions, each including a regiment of artillery; 2 divisions at half strength; 2 separate regiments; an armored brigade with 120 Soviet T–34/85 medium tanks; and 5 border constabulary brigades. In support of the *KPA* were 180 Soviet aircraft, mostly fighters and attack bombers, and a few naval patrol craft. Soviet advisers prepared an invasion plan that called for tank-led combined-arms forces to advance 15–20 kilometers per day, occupying Seoul within three days and completing the operation in 22–27 days. Stalin, however, would not permit the Soviet advisers to accompany the *KPA* once it crossed into South Korea.

The ROK Army of 95,000 men was far less fit for war. Raised as a constabulary during the American occupation and assisted by the U.S. Military Advisory Group to the Republic of Korea (KMAG), the ROK Army had since April 1948 been fighting a bitter war against guerrillas who received support from the DPRK. In 1948 and 1949 the ROK Army also fought battles in up to regimental strength with North Korean border constabulary units, with each side making incursions into the other's territory. These operations had interfered with effective training for conventional operations, and in June 1950 three of the eight ROK divisions were dispersed for counterguerrilla duties or small-unit training. The ROK Army was a light infantry force: its artillery totaled eighty-nine light 105-mm. howitzers outranged by *KPA* artillery, and it had neither tanks nor any antitank weapons effective against the T–34/85s. The ROK Navy matched its North Korean counterpart, but the ROK Air Force had only a few trainers and liaison aircraft. U.S. equipment, war-worn when furnished to South Korean forces, had deteriorated further, and supplies on hand could sustain combat operations no longer than fifteen days.

The North Korean main attack was on the western side of the peninsula; the *KPA* quickly crushed South Korean defenses at the 38th Parallel and entered Seoul on June 28. (*See Map 12.*) A secondary attack down the peninsula's center encountered stiff resistance in rugged terrain; the *KPA* had more success on the east coast in keeping pace with the main drive. ROK units in the Seoul area withdrew in disorder and abandoned most of their equipment because the bridges over the Han River at the south edge of the city were prematurely demolished. North Korean units in the west halted briefly after capturing Seoul to bring tanks and artillery across the Han River.

In Washington, a fourteen-hour time difference made it June 24 when the North Koreans crossed the parallel, and the first report of the invasion arrived that night. The next day, at a meeting the United States requested, the UN Security Council adopted a resolution demanding an immediate cessation of hostilities and a withdrawal of North Korean forces to the 38th Parallel. The USSR did not exercise its veto power against the resolution because the Soviet delegate had been boycotting the council since January 1950 in protest of the United Nation's decision not to recognize the People's Republic of China (PRC), recently victorious in the Chinese Civil War, as China's legitimate government.

On the night of the twenty-fifth, after meetings between officials of the State and Defense Departments and then between President Harry S. Truman and his key advisers, the President directed General of the Army Douglas MacArthur, Commander in Chief of Far East Command (FEC), to supply ROK forces with ammunition and equipment, evacuate American dependents from Korea, and survey conditions on the peninsula to determine how best to further assist the republic. The President also ordered the U.S. Seventh Fleet from its current location in Philippine and Ryukyu waters to Japan. On the twenty-sixth, in a broad interpretation of a UN Security Council request for "every assistance" in supporting the June 25 resolution, President Truman authorized General MacArthur to use air and naval strength against North Korean targets below the 38th Parallel. The President also redirected the bulk of the Seventh Fleet to Taiwan; by standing between the Chinese Communists on the mainland and the Nationalists on the island it could discourage either one from attacking the other and thus prevent a widening of hostilities.

When it became clear in Washington on June 27 that North Korea would ignore the UN demands, the Security Council, again at the urging of the United States, asked member states to furnish military assistance to help South Korea repel the invasion. President Truman immediately broadened the range of U.S. air and naval operations to include North Korea and authorized the use of U.S. Army troops to protect Pusan, Korea's major port at the southeastern tip of the peninsula. MacArthur meanwhile had flown to Korea and, after witnessing failing ROK Army efforts in defenses south of the Han River, recommended to Washington that a U.S. Army regimental combat team (RCT) be committed immediately to support the ROK Army in the area south of Seoul. He also proposed building up the American presence in Korea to a two-division force for a counteroffensive. President Truman on June 30 approved MacArthur's request to dispatch an RCT and then later that same day directed him to use all forces available to him.

Thus the United Nations for the first time since its founding reacted to aggression with a decision to use armed force. The United States would accept the largest share of the obligation in Korea but, still deeply tired of war, would do so reluctantly. President Truman later described his decision to enter the war as the hardest of his days

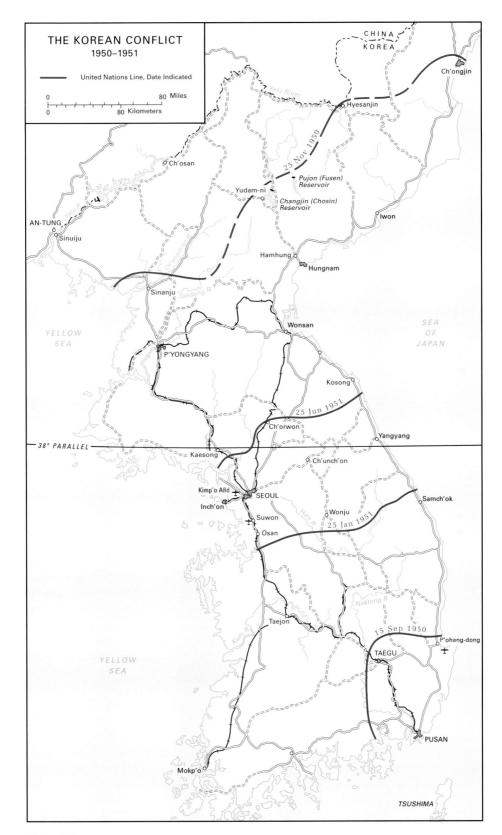

THE KOREAN CONFLICT
1950–1951

───── United Nations Line, Date Indicated

0	80 Miles
0	80 Kilometers

CHINA
KOREA

Ch'ongjin

Yalu River

Hyesanjin

25 Nov 1950

Ch'osan

Pujon (Fusen)
Reservoir

Yudam-ni

Changjin (Chosin)
Reservoir

Iwon

AN-TUNG

Sinuiju

Hamhung

Hungnam

Sinanju

Taedong R.

YELLOW
SEA

Wonsan

P'YONGYANG

SEA
OF
JAPAN

Kosong

25 Jun 1951

Ch'orwon

Yangyang

38° PARALLEL

Kaesong

Ch'unch'on

Kimp'o Afld

SEOUL

Inch'on

Suwon

Wonju

Han R.

Samch'ok

25 Jan 1951

Osan

Taejon

Kum R.

Naktong R.

15 Sep 1950

P'ohang-dong

TAEGU

YELLOW
SEA

PUSAN

Mokp'o

TSUSHIMA

Map 12

in office. A Communist Korea would pose a major threat to Japan and thus the U.S. position in Asia. Also, American leaders believed that the Soviets had ordered the DPRK to attack to test the Western bloc's resolve. They feared that if South Korea fell, the USSR would be encouraged to attack other countries in this manner and other countries would doubt America's commitment to defend them from Communist aggression. The American people, conditioned by World War II to battle on a grand scale to complete victory, would experience a deepening frustration over the Korean conflict, brought on in the beginning by embarrassing reversals on the battlefield.

South to the Naktong

Ground forces available to MacArthur included the 1st Cavalry Division and the 7th, 24th, and 25th Infantry Divisions, all under the Eighth U.S. Army in Japan, and the 29th Regimental Combat Team on Okinawa. While MacArthur in 1949 had relieved Eighth Army of most occupation duties in order to concentrate on combat training, the postwar economies had left its units inadequately prepared for battle. The divisions' maneuverability and firepower were sharply reduced by a shortage of organic units, by a general understrength among existing units, and by the worn condition of weapons and equipment. Some weapons and ammunition, medium tanks and antitank ammunition in particular, could scarcely be found in the Far East. MacArthur's air arm, the Far East Air Forces (FEAF), was organized principally for air defense; much of its strength consisted of short-range jet interceptors that had to fly from bases in Japan. Propeller-driven F–51s stored in Japan and more of these World War II planes rushed from the United States would prove crucial in meeting close air support needs during the war's early months, because they could fly many sorties each day from Korean airfields. Naval Forces Far East, MacArthur's sea arm, controlled only five combat ships and a skeleton amphibious force, although reinforcement was near in the Seventh Fleet.

When MacArthur received permission to commit ground units, the main North Korean force already had crossed the Han River. By July 3 a westward enemy attack had captured a major airfield at Kimpo and the West Sea port of Inch'on. Troops attacking south moved into the town of Suwon, twenty-five miles below Seoul, on the fourth.

During July MacArthur and Lt. Gen. Walton H. Walker, Eighth Army's commander, disregarded the principle of mass and committed units piecemeal to trade space for time as the speed of the North Korean drive threatened to outpace the Far East Command's ability to deploy American units from Japan.

Infantrymen Observing Enemy Positions along the Naktong River

WILLIAM F. DEAN (1899–1981)

Commander of an infantry division in World War II, Dean served as the last military governor of South Korea in 1947–1948 and took command of the 24th Infantry Division in 1949. On July 20, when a much larger North Korean tank-infantry force overran elements of the division at Taejon, Dean took to the streets to hunt tanks and then led a group of soldiers out of the town. Becoming separated from the group, he evaded capture until August 25. Dean successfully resisted all attempts to force him to make statements that supported the enemy and was released in September 1953. For his actions in Taejon, Dean received the Medal of Honor.

General Dean studies the map of Korea.

Where to open a delaying action was clear, for there were few good roads in the profusion of mountains making up the Korean peninsula. The best of these below Seoul, running on a gentle diagonal line through Suwon, Osan, Taejon, and Taegu to the port of Pusan in the southeast, was the obvious main axis of North Korean advance. Which unit to use was also clear: the 24th Infantry Division was stationed nearest the ports in southern Japan. On July 1 General Walker directed Maj. Gen. William F. Dean, the 24th's commander, to move immediately by air two rifle companies, reinforced with heavy mortars and recoilless rifles, to Korea, with the remainder of his division to follow as fast as available air and sea transport could move it. The two reinforced companies, joined by a field artillery battery that had moved by sea, moved into positions astride the main road near Osan, ten miles below Suwon, by dawn on July 5. Some Americans believed that the arrival of this 540-man force on the battlefield—designated Task Force SMITH for its commander, Lt. Col. Charles B. Smith—from the Army that had defeated far stronger opponents five years earlier would so awe the *KPA* that it would withdraw.

Around 8:00 A.M. on a rainy July 5, a North Korean division supported by tanks attacked the Americans. Task Force SMITH lacked antitank mines, the fire of its recoilless rifles and 2.36-inch rocket launchers failed to penetrate the T–34 armor, and the artillery battery quickly fired its six antitank rounds. The North Korean tanks did not stop to support an infantry assault; the task force inflicted numerous casualties on the *KPA* infantry, but it was too small to prevent a North Korean double envelopment. After Colonel Smith ordered a withdrawal, discipline broke down and the task force fell back in disarray with over 180 casualties and the loss of all equipment save small arms. Another casualty was American morale as word of the defeat reached other units of the 24th Infantry Division then moving into delaying positions below Osan.

The next three delaying actions by the 24th Infantry Division had similar results. In each case a North Korean force used armor and infantry assaults against the front of the American position, accompanied by an infantry double envelopment that established roadblocks

75-mm. Recoilless Rifle in Action

behind the American position. This tactic often resulted in American units' withdrawing in disarray, with the loss of weapons and equipment, to the next delaying position. The heavy losses and relative ease with which the *KPA* broke through American positions, together with the physical strain of delay operations in the Korean summer and the poor performance of a number of unit commanders, sapped American morale. By July 15 the 24th Infantry Division had been forced back sixty miles to Taejon, where it initially took position along the Kum River above the town. South Korean units, some just remnants and others still in good order, also fell back on either flank of the 24th.

Fifty-three UN members meanwhile signified support of the Security Council's June 27 action, and twenty-nine of these made specific offers of assistance. Ground, air, and naval forces eventually sent to assist South Korea would represent twenty UN members and one nonmember nation. The United States, Great Britain, Australia, New Zealand, Canada, Turkey, Greece, France, Belgium, Luxembourg, the Netherlands, Thailand, the Philippines, Colombia, and Ethiopia would furnish ground combat troops. India, Sweden, Norway, Denmark, and Italy (the non–United Nations country) would furnish medical units. Air forces would arrive from the United States, Australia, and the Union of South Africa; naval forces would come from the United States, Great Britain, Australia, Canada, and New Zealand.

The wide response to the council's call pointed out the need for a unified command. Acknowledging the United States as the major contributor, the UN Security Council on July 7 asked it to form a command into which all forces would be integrated and to appoint a commander. In the evolving command structure, President Truman became executive agent for the UN Security Council. The National Security Council, Department of State, and Joint Chiefs of Staff participated in developing the grand concepts of operations in Korea. In the strictly military channel, the Joint Chiefs issued instructions through the Army member to the unified command in the field, designated the United Nations Command (UNC) under the command of General MacArthur.

MacArthur superimposed the headquarters of his new command over that of his existing Far East Command. Air and naval units from other countries joined the Far East Air Forces and Naval Forces Far East, respectively. MacArthur assigned command of ground troops in Korea to the Eighth Army, and General Walker established his headquarters at Taegu on July 15, assuming command of all American ground troops on the peninsula and, at the request of President Rhee, of the ROK Army. When ground forces from other nations reached Korea, they too were assigned to Eighth Army.

Between July 14 and 18, MacArthur moved the 25th Infantry and 1st Cavalry Divisions to Korea after cannibalizing the 7th Infantry Division to strengthen them. By then the battle for Taejon had opened. New 3.5-inch rocket launchers hurriedly airlifted from the United States proved effective against T–34 tanks, but three worn-out infantry battalions and the remnants of the 24th Infantry Division's 105-mm. howitzer battalions could not delay for long after two *KPA* divisions established bridgeheads over the Kum River and encircled the town. The 24th withdrew from Taejon and was relieved by the 1st Cavalry Division. In eighteen days the 24th had disrupted the timetable of the KPA's main attack but at the cost of over 30 percent of its men and most of its equipment.

After taking Taejon, the main North Korean force split, one division moving south to the coast then turning east along the lower coastline. The remainder of the force continued southeast beyond Taejon toward Taegu. Southward advances by the secondary attack forces in the central and eastern sectors matched the main thrust, all clearly aimed to converge on Pusan. North Korean supply lines grew long in the advance and less and less tenable under heavy UNC air attacks, as FEAF quickly achieved air superiority and UNC warships wiped out North Korean naval opposition and clamped a tight blockade on the Korean coast. These achievements and the arrival of two battalions of the 29th RCT from Okinawa notwithstanding, American and South Korean troops steadily gave way. American casualties now passed 6,000, and South Korean losses had reached 70,000.

Having run out of space to trade for time, Walker at the end of July ordered a stand along a 140-mile line arching from the Korean Strait to the Sea of Japan west and north of Pusan. His three understrength U.S. divisions occupied the western arc, basing their position on the Naktong River. South Korean forces, which KMAG advisers had reorganized into five divisions, defended the northern segment. A long line and few troops kept positions thin in this Pusan Perimeter. But replacements and additional units now entering or on the way to Korea would help relieve the problem, and fair interior lines of communications radiating from Pusan allowed Walker to move troops and supplies with facility.

A motorized combined-arms force, the *KPA* had followed the few good roads south from the 38th Parallel; the delaying actions that ROK and American units fought along these roads during July, while dispiriting for the defenders in their immediate results, had robbed Kim Il Sung of his expected quick victory. These actions had also cost the *KPA* some 58,000 trained men and many tanks. Raising brigades to division

U.S. Military Advisory Group to the Republic of Korea (KMAG)

U.S. Army advisers had worked with the ROK Army since its organization in 1946 as the Korean National Constabulary. With the withdrawal of U.S. forces from Korea in 1949, KMAG was activated to continue this work. KMAG used the counterpart system, pairing American officers with Korean commanders down to the battalion level and with key staff officers. During the war, much of KMAG's effort necessarily went into providing advisers for units in

Instructing ROK Trainees on the Browning Automatic Rifle

combat; but it also supervised the training of the many new units the ROK Army organized. From its activation, KMAG's authorized strength never kept pace with the size of the ROK Army, forcing it to leave some positions empty and after July 1951 to use U.S. units to help train new ROK units.

status and conscripting large numbers of recruits (many from overrun regions of South Korea), the *KPA* over the next month and a half committed thirteen infantry divisions and an armored division against Walker's perimeter. But the additional strength failed to compensate for the loss of trained men and tanks suffered in the advance to the Naktong.

While air strikes against *KPA* supply lines significantly reduced the combat power it could mass against the UN perimeter, Eighth Army's defense hinged on a shuttling of scarce reserves to block a gap, reinforce a position, or counterattack wherever the threat appeared greatest at a given moment. The North Koreans shifted their main attack to various points of the perimeter, seeking a decisive breakthrough, but General Walker made effective use of intelligence provided by intercepts of *KPA* communications to prevent serious enemy penetrations and inflict telling losses that steadily drew off North Korean offensive power. His own strength, meanwhile, was on the rise. By mid-September he had over 500 medium tanks. Replacements, many of them recalled Army reservists, arrived. Additional units came in: the 5th Regimental Combat Team from Hawaii, the 2d Infantry Division and 1st Provisional Marine Brigade from the United States, and a two-battalion British infantry brigade from Hong Kong. For the 1st Cavalry and 24th and 25th Infantry Divisions, infantry battalions and artillery batteries hastily assembled in the United States arrived to bring these divisions to their full complement of subordinate units. Bomber and fighter squadrons also arrived to strengthen the FEAF.

Thus, as the *KPA* lost irreplaceable men and equipment, UNC forces acquired an offensive capability.

North to the Parallel

General MacArthur at the entry of U.S. forces into Korea had perceived that the deeper the North Koreans drove, the more vulnerable they would become to a turning movement delivered by an amphibious assault. He began work on plans for such a blow almost at the start of hostilities, favoring Inch'on, the West Sea port halfway up the west coast, as the landing site. Just twenty-five miles east lay Seoul, where Korea's main roads and rail lines converged. A force landing at Inch'on would have to move inland only a short distance to cut North Korean supply routes, and the recapture of the capital city could also have a helpful psychological impact. Combined with a general northward advance by the Eighth Army, a landing at Inch'on could produce decisive results. Enemy troops retiring before the Eighth Army would be cut off by the amphibious force behind them or be forced to make a slow and difficult withdrawal through the mountains farther east.

Though pressed to meet Eighth Army troop requirements, MacArthur was able to shape a two-division landing force. He formed the headquarters of the X Corps from members of his own staff, naming his chief of staff, Maj. Gen. Edward M. Almond, as corps commander. He rebuilt the 7th Infantry Division by giving it high priority on replacements from the United States and by assigning it 8,600 South Korean recruits, most of them poorly trained. The latter measure was part of a larger program, the Korean Augmentation to the United States Army (KATUSA). The KATUSA program began when the U.S. Army could not supply Eighth Army with all the replacements it required. KATUSAs, usually newly conscripted South Koreans, were assigned mostly to American infantry units. At the same time Almond acquired from the United States the greater part of the 1st Marine Division, which he planned to fill out with the Marine brigade currently in the Pusan Perimeter. The X Corps, with these two divisions, the ROK 17th Infantry, and two ROK Marine Corps battalions, was to make its landing as a separate force, not as part of the Eighth Army.

Many judged the Inch'on plan dangerous. Naval officers considered the extreme Yellow Sea tides and narrow channel approaches to Inch'on, easily blocked by mines, as big risks to shipping. Marine officers saw danger in landing in the middle of a built-up area and in having to scale high sea walls to get ashore. The Joint Chiefs of Staff (JCS) anticipated serious consequences if the Inch'on plan failed, since MacArthur would be committing his last major units. The General Reserve in the United States was nearly exhausted by September 1: the 187th Airborne RCT and the 3d Infantry Division would arrive in Japan in mid-September, but the 3d would need time to recover after being stripped to provide men for Eighth Army, leaving the 82d Airborne Division the only uncommitted major unit. The Army had begun a substantial expansion, activating new Regular units and mobilizing National Guard and Organized Reserve Corps units; but this increase would not yield combat ready units until 1951. In light of the uncertainties, MacArthur's decision was a remarkable gamble; but if

General Almond

The Inch'on Landing

results are what count, his action was one of exemplary boldness. The 1st Marine Division swept into Inch'on on September 15 against light resistance. Although opposition stiffened, X Corps steadily pushed inland over the next two weeks. One arm struck south and seized Suwon, while the remainder of the corps cleared Kimpo Airfield, crossed the Han, and fought through Seoul. MacArthur, with dramatic ceremony, returned the capital city to President Rhee on September 29.

General Walker meanwhile attacked out of the Pusan Perimeter on September 16. His forces gained ground slowly at first; but on September 23, after the portent of Almond's envelopment and Walker's frontal attack became clear, the North Korean forces broke. The Eighth Army, by then organized as 4 corps, 2 U.S. and 2 ROK, rolled forward in pursuit, linking with the X Corps on September 26. About 30,000 North Korean troops escaped above the 38th Parallel through the eastern mountains. Several thousand more bypassed in the pursuit hid in the mountains of South Korea to fight as guerrillas. But by the end of September the Korean People's Army ceased to exist as an organized force anywhere in the Southern republic.

North to the Yalu

In 1950 President Truman frequently described the American-led effort in Korea as a police action, a euphemism for the war that produced both criticism and amusement. But the President's term was an honest reach for perspective. Determined to halt the aggression, he was equally determined to limit hostilities to the peninsula and to avoid taking steps that would prompt Soviet or Chinese participation. By Western estimates, Europe with its highly developed industrial resources, not Asia, held the high place on the Communist schedule of expansion; hence, the North Atlantic Treaty Organization (NATO) alliance needed the deterrent strength that otherwise would be drawn off by a heavier involvement in the Far East. Indeed, Truman and many of his advisers, believing that Kim Il Sung was Stalin's puppet, suspected that Stalin had ordered the DPRK to attack in order to weaken the West's defenses elsewhere. To counter that possibility and to reassure America's allies, Truman in July had ordered a massive expansion of the U.S. armed forces, an enormous increase in nuclear weapons production, and a great increase in military aid to other nations. To reinforce NATO, the President in September announced a major buildup of American forces in Europe. For the Army, this meant dispatching four divisions and other units to Germany during 1951, where they joined the 1st Infantry Division to form the Seventh Army.

On this and other bases, a case could be made for halting MacArthur's forces at the 38th Parallel. In reestablishing the old border, the UNC had met the UN call for assistance in repelling the attack on South Korea. In an early statement, Secretary of State Dean Acheson had said the United Nations was intervening "solely for the purpose of restoring the Republic of Korea to its status prior to the invasion from the north." A halt, furthermore, would be consistent with the U.S. policy of containment.

There were, on the other hand, substantial military reasons to carry the war into North Korea. Failure to destroy the 30,000 North Korean troops who had escaped above the parallel and an estimated 30,000 more in northern training camps could leave South Korea in little better position than before the start of hostilities. Complete military

The 38th Parallel in the Kaesong Area

victory, by all appearances within easy grasp, also would achieve the longstanding U.S. and UN objective of reunifying Korea. Against these incentives had to be balanced muted warnings against a UNC entry into North Korea from both Communist China and the USSR in August and September. But these were counted as attempts to discourage the UNC, not as genuine threats to enter the war. President Truman decided to order the Eighth Army into North Korea.

On September 27, the JCS sent MacArthur instructions for future operations. The directive authorized him to cross the 38th Parallel in pursuit of his military objective, the destruction of the North Korean armed forces. Once he had achieved that objective, he was to occupy North Korea and await action by the United Nations on the unification of Korea. To avoid escalation of the conflict, MacArthur could not enter North Korea if major Chinese or Soviet forces entered North Korea before his forces did or if the USSR or the PRC announced it intended to enter. As a further safeguard, MacArthur was to use only Korean forces in the extreme northern territory abutting the Yalu River boundary with Manchuria and that in the far northeast along the Tumen River boundary with the USSR. Ten days later the UN General Assembly voted for the restoration of peace and security throughout Korea, thereby approving the UNC's entry into North Korea.

There were two options for the invasion of North Korea. General MacArthur considered the best option keeping the X Corps separate from the Eighth Army and withdrawing it through Inch'on and Pusan to conduct an amphibious assault at Wonsan, North Korea's major seaport on the east coast, while the Eighth Army advanced on P'yongyang, the DPRK's capital. Both forces would then move to the Yalu. This option reflected MacArthur's conclusion that an amphibious attack on Wonsan would allow the X Corps to operate without burdening the Eighth Army's logistical system and would trap thousands of retreating *KPA* troops and that he could coordinate both forces from Japan.

Another factor was that MacArthur had been favorably impressed by General Almond's performance.

General Walker, who did not have as close a relationship with MacArthur as did General Almond, considered the best option the assignment of the X Corps to the Eighth Army. The X Corps already was in position to continue the attack toward P'yongyang, and other divisions could drive east across the peninsula to Wonsan, linking up with the ROK I Corps moving up the east coast. The Eighth Army would then advance north to the Yalu. This option, Eighth Army planners concluded, made the best use of the limited UNC logistical capabilities and maintained the momentum of the UNC's advance, since the Eighth Army's I Corps would have to pause before advancing on P'yongang. Walker, however, never formally presented this option to MacArthur, and the October 2 UNC order to advance used MacArthur's concept.

President Rhee, impatient to unify his country, had already directed the ROK I Corps on the east coast to advance; it crossed the parallel on October 1 and captured Wonsan on the tenth. The ROK II Corps at nearly the same time opened an advance through central North Korea. On October 7 the I Corps moved north, and on October 19 it entered P'yongyang. Five days later the corps had advanced to the Ch'ongch'on River within fifty miles of the Manchurian border. The ROK II Corps veered northwest to come alongside. To the east, past the unoccupied spine of the axial Taebaek Mountains, the ROK I Corps by October 24 moved above Wonsan, entering Iwon on the coast and approaching the huge Changjin Reservoir. Meanwhile, the X Corps had boarded ships at Pusan and Inch'on, in the process greatly impeding the flow of supplies to Eighth Army, and sailed for Wonsan. Although the ROK I Corps had captured the port earlier, the X Corps had to wait until October 26 to begin landing in order to allow UNC naval forces to clear the heavily mined coastal waters.

Despite this setback, the outlook for the UNC in the last week of October was distinctly optimistic. The *KPA* had collapsed as an effective military force. Despite further warnings emanating from Communist China, American civilian and military leaders concluded that Chinese intervention was very unlikely, and that if the PRC did dispatch units of the People's Liberation Army to Korea, UNC air power would destroy them. After meeting with MacArthur at Wake Island on October 15, President Truman revised his instructions to MacArthur only to the extent that if Chinese forces should appear in Korea, MacArthur should continue his advance if he believed his forces had a reasonable chance of success.

In hopes of ending operations before the onset of winter, MacArthur on October 24 ordered his ground commanders to advance to the northern border as rapidly as possible and with all forces available. In the west, the Eighth Army sent several columns toward the Yalu, each free to advance as fast and/or as far as possible without regard for the progress of the others. General Almond, adding the ROK I Corps to his command upon landing, proceeded to clear northeastern Korea. The ROK I Corps advanced up the coast, closing to within sixty-five miles of the Soviet border by November 21, while the 1st Marine and the 7th Infantry Divisions moved through the mountains toward the Yalu and the Changjin Reservoir. In the United States, a leading newspaper expressed the prevailing optimism with the editorial comment that "Except for unexpected developments … we can now be easy in our minds as to the military outcome."

Unexpected developments soon occurred. Mao Zedong had decided to intervene and dispatched an expeditionary force, called the *Chinese People's Volunteer Force* (*CPVF*), across the Yalu. Highly skilled in camouflage, hundreds of Chinese units had moved into North Korea without detection. In the Eighth Army zone, the first Chinese soldier was discovered among captives taken on October 25 by the I Corps' 1st ROK Division and units of the ROK II Corps. The Chinese attacked both of Eighth Army's corps, inflicting especially heavy losses on ROK units and on a regiment of the 1st Cavalry Division when it came forward at Unsan to cover the withdrawal of the 1st ROK Division. General Walker ordered the I Corps and the ROK II Corps to fall back on the Ch'ongch'on River to regroup and ordered the IX Corps forward to the Ch'ongch'on. Once that corps had arrived, Walker planned to resume the advance in accordance with MacArthur's orders. The Chinese forces continued to attack until November 6, when they abruptly broke contact. In the X Corps zone, the Chinese stopped a ROK column on the mountain road leading to the Changjin Reservoir. American marines relieved the South Koreans and by November 6 pushed through the resistance to within a few miles of the reservoir, whereupon the Chinese also broke contact.

At first it appeared that individual Chinese soldiers, possibly volunteers, had reinforced the North Koreans. The estimate rose higher by November 24, but interrogation of captives did not convince Far East Command that there had been a large Chinese commitment. Aerial observation of the Yalu and the ground below the river did not detect signs of such a commitment, and the voluntary withdrawal from contact on November 6 seemed no logical part of a full Chinese effort. (In fact, the Chinese withdrew because they had achieved their first objectives, forcing the UNC advance to pause and evaluating UNC units' performance.) Some commanders, notably Generals Walker, Almond, and Paik Sun Yup, the 1st ROK Division commander, did believe that the Chinese had intervened in strength. General MacArthur, however, concluded that the PRC would not mount a full-scale offensive. Confident that UNC air power and American artillery would destroy any Chinese expeditionary force, he ordered the advance to the Yalu resumed.

In northeastern Korea, the X Corps, now strengthened by the arrival of the 3d Infantry Division, resumed its advance on November 11. In the west, General Walker requested a delay until November 24; Eighth Army's supply lines were still inadequate, and he wanted the IX Corps to complete its move. The Chinese were waiting to catch Eighth Army as it left its defensive positions along the Ch'ongch'on; on the night of November 25, one day after the Eighth Army resumed its advance, the Chinese launched a massive offensive to eject UNC forces from North Korea. Strong *CPVF* attacks hit the Eighth Army's IX and ROK II Corps, collapsing the ROK II Corps on the army's right flank. On the twenty-seventh the attacks engulfed the leftmost forces of the X Corps at the Changjin Reservoir, and by the next day the UNC position in North Korea began to crumble.

"Except for unexpected developments … we can now be easy in our minds as to the military outcome."

235

TASK FORCE MACLEAN/FAITH

On November 25, 1950, General Almond ordered the 7th Infantry Division to move one RCT to the east side of the Changjin Reservoir to cover the advance of the 1st Marine Division to the Yalu. Consisting of little more than two weak infantry battalions and an artillery battalion, this force was initially known as Task Force MACLEAN after its commander, Col. Allan D. MacLean. When the Chinese attacked the X Corps on the night of November 27–28, the task force held on the east side of the reservoir for four days. On December 1 Lt. Col. Don C. Faith, Jr., who had taken command after the capture of Colonel MacLean, ordered a breakout to the south. Low on ammunition, worn down by extreme cold and bitter fighting, and burdened with many wounded, the task force was stopped at a Chinese roadblock and destroyed. About 1,000 of the soldiers were killed, taken prisoner, or declared missing, including Colonel Faith, who received a posthumous Medal of Honor. Their ordeal was not in vain, and their sacrifice helped save the 1st Marine Division.

"We face an entirely new war," MacArthur notified Washington on November 28. On the following day he instructed General Walker to make whatever withdrawals were necessary to escape being enveloped by Chinese pushing hard and deep through the hole left by ROK II Corps' collapse and ordered the X Corps to pull into a beachhead around the east coast port of Hungnam, north of Wonsan.

The entirely new war also featured Soviet Mig–15 jet interceptors flown by Soviet pilots from bases in Manchuria protected by Soviet anti-aircraft units. To counter this new threat, the U.S. Air Force hurriedly dispatched its premier jet fighter, the F–86, to Korea. Stalin, fearing that the evidence provided by the body of a Soviet pilot would force the U.S. government to strike directly at the USSR, limited his air units to operations over Communist-controlled territory. The Soviets trained Chinese and Korean units in the Mig–15, but FEAF defeated attempts later in the war to stage these units in North Korea by bombing their airfields. Although the UNC had abundant evidence of Soviet participation in air operations, the U.S. government refused throughout the war to make it public out of the same fear of provoking pressure from the American public to escalate the war. Both sides, fearing escalation would lead to World War III, did not launch air attacks on logistical bases in Manchuria and Japan.

The New War

Eighth Army's withdrawal from the Ch'ongch'on led to one of the greatest ordeals ever suffered by a U.S. division. Chinese forces established a strong roadblock below the town of

Convoy from Wonsan to Hamhung, *Robert Weldy Baer, 1950*

Kunu-ri and took positions on the hills along the road on which the 2d Infantry Division was moving. Already weakened by several days of combat in bitter cold weather, on November 30 most of the division literally had to run a gauntlet of fire that tore units apart. Emerging from the gauntlet with about one-third of its men dead, wounded, or missing and most of its equipment lost, the division staggered back into South Korea to refit.

General Walker initially believed that he could hold a line based on P'yongyang, but he quickly concluded that the Chinese would be able to outflank such a line and pin down the Eighth Army. This conclusion, as well as his concern that his still inadequate supply lines would negate Eighth Army's firepower advantage, led him to abandon P'yongyang and withdraw to positions north of Seoul. There, he hoped, shorter supply lines, better defensive terrain, and the arrival of the X Corps from northeastern Korea would allow Eighth Army to repeat against the Chinese the strategy that had defeated the *KPA*. The light infantry Chinese force could not keep up with the motorized Eighth Army, and the latter withdrew into South Korea without opposition.

In the X Corps' withdrawal to Hungnam, the center and right-most units experienced little difficulty. But the 1st Marine Division and the remnants of the 7th Infantry Division task force at the Changjin Reservoir encountered Chinese positions overlooking the mountain road leading to the sea. Marine Maj. Gen. O. P. Smith skillfully led a withdrawal that reached the coast on December 11. General MacArthur briefly visualized the X Corps beachhead at Hungnam as a "geographic threat" that could deter Chinese to the west from deepening their advance. Later, with prompting from the Joint Chiefs, he ordered the X Corps to withdraw by sea and proceed to Pusan, where it would join Eighth Army, ending its independent status. Almond started the evacuation on the eleventh, contracting the Hungnam perimeter as he loaded troops and materiel aboard ships in the harbor. With little interference from enemy forces, which had suffered heavy casualties from American firepower and the extreme cold, he completed the evacuation and set sail for Pusan on Christmas Eve.

WALTON H. WALKER (1880–1950)

A highly regarded corps commander in World War II, Walker took command of Eighth Army in 1948 and supervised its shift from an occupation force to one focused on readiness. He skillfully used Eighth Army's slender reserves to counter breakthroughs on the Pusan Perimeter, frequently flying at low altitude to reconnoiter the front line. The defeat in North Korea and the withdrawal into South Korea gravely damaged Eighth Army's morale, but Walker had little opportunity to reverse this damage before he died in a vehicle accident on December 23, 1950. He was promoted posthumously to the rank of four-star general.

The day before General Walker was killed in a motor vehicle accident while traveling north from Seoul toward the front. Lt. Gen. Matthew B. Ridgway flew from Washington to assume command of the Eighth Army. After conferring in Tokyo with MacArthur, who instructed Ridgway to hold a position as far north as possible but in any case to maintain the Eighth Army intact, the new army commander reached Korea on the twenty-sixth.

Ridgway himself wanted at least to hold the Eighth Army in its positions north of Seoul and to attack if possible. But his initial inspection of the front raised serious doubts. Deeply unsatisfied with the caliber of Eighth Army's senior leadership, he began arrangements to remove those officers who failed to meet his standards. The sudden reversal of fortune in combat, the long retreat without significant enemy contact, and the bitter winter weather for which most troops did not have the proper clothing and equipment had so worn down Eighth Army's morale that Ridgway judged it temporarily incapable of mounting effective large-scale offensive actions. He also discovered much of the defense line to be thin and weak. The Chinese had finally caught up with Eighth Army and appeared to be massing in the west for a push on Seoul, and twelve reconstituted North Korean divisions seemed to be concentrating for an attack in the central region. From all available evidence, New Year's Day seemed a logical date for the enemy's opening assault.

Withdrawal from Kot'o-ri, 1950, *Henrietta Snowden, 2000*

To strengthen the line, Ridgway committed the 2d Infantry Division to the central sector where positions were weakest, even though that unit had not fully recovered from losses in the Kunu-ri gauntlet, and pressed General Almond to quicken the preparation of the X Corps whose forces needed refitting before moving to the front. Realizing that time probably was against him, he also ordered his western units to organize a bridgehead above Seoul, one deep enough to protect the Han River bridges, from which to cover a withdrawal below the city should an enemy offensive compel a general retirement.

Enemy forces opened attacks on New Year's Eve, directing their major effort toward Seoul. When the offensive gained momentum, Ridgway ordered his western forces back to the Seoul bridgehead and pulled the rest

MATTHEW B. RIDGWAY (1895–1993)

A well-respected commander of an airborne division and a corps during World War II, General Ridgway in 1950 was the Army's Deputy Chief of Staff for Administration and played a key role in mobilizing the service for war. His success in reviving the Eighth Army in 1951 led to his selection to replace MacArthur as Commander in Chief of the Far East Command. Promoted to four-star general in May 1951, Ridgway in 1952 succeeded Eisenhower as the Supreme Allied Commander in Europe. Eisenhower selected Ridgway in 1953 to be the Army's Chief of Staff, but the general strenuously argued against the President's New Look strategy. Because of this disagreement, Eisenhower did not reappoint him to a second term as Chief of Staff and Ridgway retired in 1955.

of the Eighth Army to positions roughly on line to the east. After strong Chinese units assaulted the bridgehead, he withdrew to a line forty miles below Seoul. In the west, the last troops pulled out of Seoul on January 4, 1951, demolishing the Han bridges on the way out as the Chinese entered the city from the north.

Only light Chinese forces pushed south of the city, and enemy attacks in the west diminished. In central and eastern Korea, North Korean forces pushed forward; but the 1st Marine Division cut off and then destroyed them. This pause highlighted a major Communist operational weakness: the enemy's logistical system, short of mechanical transport and with lengthening supply lines under FEAF attack, permitted him to undertake offensive operations for no more than a week or two before he had to pause for replacements and supplies.

Ridgway used this pause to continue his rehabilitation of Eighth Army's aggressive spirit and to introduce a new operational concept. Gaining territory would be incidental to inflicting maximum casualties on the enemy at minimum cost to UNC units. On the attack or on the defense, Ridgway insisted that his units always maintain contact with the enemy and use every available source of firepower—infantry, armor, artillery, and air—against them. Ridgway expected that the tremendous losses these "meat grinder" tactics would inflict on Communist units would at least greatly assist the advance of the Eighth Army to the 38th Parallel and at best convince the enemy to end the war. In mid-January the Eighth Army began RCT-size probes forward of UNC lines to gather intelligence and inflict losses on the enemy with meat grinder tactics. These probes, carefully planned to ensure success, had a further objective: to restore the Eighth Army's confidence and aggressiveness. These operations met all their goals, and Ridgway grew confident that the Eighth Army would hold. On January 25 the I and IX Corps began a slow advance forward by phase lines to prevent units from being cut off, and on January 30 Ridgway ordered the rest of Eighth Army to advance in a similar manner.

Where Ridgway grew more confident, MacArthur was far less optimistic. Earlier, in acknowledging the Chinese intervention, he had notified Washington that the Chinese could drive the UNC out of Korea unless he received major reinforcement. At the time, however, there were no major reinforcements available; the Army was still rebuilding the General Reserve and had ordered more National Guard and Reserve units mobilized, but these efforts could not produce ready units until mid-1951. The massive military buildup begun earlier in 1950, in any case, had not been ordered with commitment in Korea in mind. The main concern in Washington was the possibility that the Chinese entry into Korea was only one part of a USSR move toward global war, a concern great enough to lead President Truman to declare a state of national emergency on December 16. Washington officials in any event considered Korea no place to become involved in a major war. For all these reasons, the Joint Chiefs of Staff notified MacArthur that a major buildup of UNC forces was out of the question. MacArthur was to stay in Korea if he could; but should the Chinese drive UNC forces back on Pusan, the Joint Chiefs would order a withdrawal to Japan.

Contrary to the reasoning in Washington, MacArthur meanwhile proposed four retaliatory measures against the Chinese: blockade the China coast, destroy China's war industries through naval and air attacks, reinforce the troops in Korea with Chinese Nationalist forces, and allow diversionary operations by Nationalist troops against the China mainland. These proposals for escalation received serious study in Washington but were eventually discarded in favor of sustaining the policy that confined the fighting to Korea.

Interchanges between Washington and Tokyo next centered on the timing of a withdrawal from Korea. MacArthur believed that Washington should establish all the criteria of an evacuation, whereas Washington wanted MacArthur first to provide the military guidelines on timing. The whole issue was finally settled after General J. Lawton Collins, Army Chief of Staff, visited Korea, saw that the Eighth Army was improving under Ridgway's leadership, and became as confident as Ridgway that the Chinese would be unable to drive the Eighth Army off the peninsula.

The Eighth Army continued its cautious northward advance in early February and retook Inch'on; but there were growing indications of Chinese preparations for another offensive in the center of the peninsula. That offensive began on the night of February 11–12, and Chinese attacks quickly crushed the X Corps' ROK 8th Division and badly damaged two other ROK divisions in the corps. Because ROK divisions had little artillery, X Corps had attached, via cumbersome command and control arrangements, U.S. artillery support forces to these divisions. The unwieldy arrangements prevented the 8th ROK Division support force's receiving timely permission to withdraw; most of this artillery force, taken from the 2d Infantry Division, was destroyed. The X Corps fell back on the key road junction of Wonju. There, American and South Korean units applied Ridgway's new operational concept, shredding repeated Chinese attacks on the town. On the X Corps western flank, the 2d Infantry Division's 23d RCT, with an

Taking a Village at Night, *Robert Weldy Baer, 1951*

attached French battalion, had dug in at Chip'yong-ni, another key road junction. Cut off from the rest of Eighth Army, the force defeated attacks by six *CPVF* regiments.

For Ridgway, the defeat of the Communists' February offensive showed that his operational concept was a success and, more importantly, that his army had recovered its spirit. He ordered the Eighth Army to continue the advance. The Communists offered only light resistance as they withdrew, and on March 14 the I Corps liberated Seoul. Between March 27 and 31, the Eighth Army closed in on the 38th Parallel. From there, it advanced, again with little resistance to a line, designated KANSAS, which followed the Imjin River in the west and the east to the coast near Yangyang. Most of the Eighth Army began digging in on Line KANSAS in preparation for the Chinese offensive expected sometime later in the spring. Ridgway sent elements of the I and IX Corps toward the Iron Triangle in central Korea. This area, 20–30 miles above the 38th Parallel and bounded by P'yongyang in the north and Ch'orwon and Kumwha in the south, was in the gap between northern and southern ranges of the Taebaek Mountains and connected the eastern and western halves of the Communist front. Key road and rail links ran through this area, and it had become a vital logistical area for the *CPVF* and the *KPA*.

In Washington, President Truman and his military and civilian advisers had been considering the possibility that, with the Eighth Army's northward advance and the heavy casualties it had inflicted on the enemy, the Communists might be willing to open negotiations. The United Nations' call to eject the invaders from South Korea had again been achieved; and both in Washington and in other capitals, there was growing sentiment that this achievement was sufficient and that unification of Korea should be negotiated after the war. On March 20 the Joint Chiefs notified MacArthur that a presidential announcement was being drafted that would indicate a willingness to negotiate with the Chinese and the North Koreans to make "satisfactory arrangements for concluding the fighting." They asked for MacArthur's recommendations on what latitude he required for operating north of the 38th Parallel.

Before the President could make his announcement, MacArthur on March 24 issued his own offer to enemy commanders to discuss an end to the fighting, but it was an offer that placed the UNC in the role of victor and indeed sounded like an ultimatum. "The enemy ... must by now be painfully aware," MacArthur said in part, "that a decision of the United Nations to depart from its tolerant effort to contain the war to the area of Korea, through an expansion of our military operations to its coastal areas and interior bases, would doom Red China to the risk of imminent military collapse." President Truman considered the statement at cross-purposes with the one he would have issued and so canceled his own, hoping the enemy might sue for an armistice if kept under pressure.

While President Truman after this episode considered relieving Mac-Arthur, he had yet to make a final decision when the next incident occurred. On April 5 Joseph W. Martin, Republican leader in the House of Representatives, rose and read MacArthur's response to a request for comment on an address Martin had made suggesting the use of Nationalist Chinese forces to open a second front. In that response, MacArthur said he believed in "meeting force with maximum counter-force" and that the use of Nationalist Chinese forces fitted that belief. Convinced, also, that "if we lose this war to Communism in Asia the fall of Europe is inevitable, win it and Europe most probably would avoid war." He added that there could be "no substitute for victory" in Korea.

MacArthur returned to the United States to receive the acclaim of a nation shocked by the relief of one of its greatest military heroes.

President Truman could not accept MacArthur's open disagreement with and effort to change national policy. Concluding that MacArthur was "unable to give his wholehearted support to the policies of the United States government and of the United Nations in matters pertaining to his official duties," President Truman recalled MacArthur on April 11 and named General Ridgway his successor. MacArthur returned to the United States to receive the acclaim of a nation shocked by the relief of one of its greatest military heroes. Before the Congress and the public, he defended his own views against those of the Truman administration. The controversy was to endure for many months, but in the end the nation accepted the fact that whatever the merit of MacArthur's arguments the President as Commander in Chief had cause to relieve him.

Lt. Gen. James A. Van Fleet, commander of the Second Army in the United States, was selected to succeed Ridgway as commander of the Eighth Army. On April 14 General Ridgway turned over the Eighth Army to General Van Fleet and left for Tokyo to take up his new duties. The drive toward the Iron Triangle had continued during this time; however, there were increasing indications that the Communists were nearly ready to launch another offensive. On April 22 twenty-one Chinese and nine North Korean divisions launched strong attacks in western and central Korea and lighter attacks in the east, with the major effort aimed against the I Corps defending the approaches to Seoul. The ROK 6th Division, on the IX Corps left flank, immediately collapsed, which threatened the I Corps with envelopment. This threat and the sheer weight of the Chinese forces targeting Seoul forced the I and IX Corps to withdraw, in good order and inflicting severe casualties on the Chinese as they moved, through successive delaying positions to previously established defenses a few miles north of Seoul. There, the UNC's terrific firepower advantage and the weaknesses of the Chinese logistical system halted the enemy advance. When enemy forces withdrew to reorganize, Van Fleet laid plans for a return to Line KANSAS but then postponed the counter-move when his intelligence sources indicated he had stopped only the first effort of the enemy offensive. Instead, he directed his senior commanders to fortify positions and prepare to fire artillery at up to five times the standard U.S. Army daily rate of fire, a measure that came to be called the Van Fleet Day of Fire.

The Communists renewed their offensive after darkness on May 15. Van Fleet had expected the major assault again to be directed against Seoul, but enemy forces this time drove hardest in the east

JAMES A. VAN FLEET (1892–1992)

One of the outstanding combat leaders of World War II, General Van Fleet in 1948–1950 headed the American advisory effort in Greece, transforming the Greek Army into an effective force that won the civil war there. Following Eighth Army's victories in the spring of 1951, he several times proposed a major offensive into North Korea to bring the war to an end. Promoted to four-star general in July 1951, Van Fleet established a close relationship with the ROK Army and was instrumental in improving its performance. After the apparent death of his son, an Air Force pilot declared missing in action over North Korea, Van Fleet relinquished command of Eighth Army in February 1953. After retiring the next month, Van Fleet sharply criticized the decision not to seek a decisive military victory.

central region against the X Corps and the ROK III Corps. Two of the X Corps' ROK divisions quickly gave way under Chinese assaults, and *KPA* and *CPVF* attacks to the east of the X Corps shattered the ROK III Corps by May 18. While Van Fleet shifted units from the west, the X Corps' 2d Infantry Division bent its line back and denied the Chinese a decisive breakthrough. Applications of the Van Fleet Day of Fire destroyed entire *CPVF* and *KPA* units, and by May 20 the Eighth Army had defeated the offensive. Determined to destroy the enemy's remaining major units, Van Fleet immediately ordered a counterattack. These units, however, had already begun withdrawing; this head start, monsoon rains, and mountainous terrain prevented the Eighth Army from catching them. By May 31 the Eighth Army was just short of Line KANSAS. The next day Van Fleet sent part of his force toward Line WYOMING, whose seizure would give him control of the lower portion of the Iron Triangle. The Eighth Army occupied both Line KANSAS and the WYOMING bulge by mid-June.

Since the KANSAS-WYOMING Line followed ground suitable for a strong defense, the Joint Chiefs directed that the Eighth Army hold that line and wait for a bid for armistice negotiations from the Chinese and North Koreans, who should have realized by this time that their committed forces lacked the ability to conquer South Korea. In line with this decision, Van Fleet began to fortify his positions. Enemy forces meanwhile used the respite from attack to recoup heavy losses and to develop defenses opposite the Eighth Army. The fighting lapsed into patrolling and small local clashes.

The Static War

After back-channel coordination through George W. Kennan, a prominent American diplomat on leave from the State Department, Jacob Malik, the Soviet delegate to the United Nations, on June 23, 1951, announced in New York during a broadcast of a UN radio program that the USSR believed the war in Korea could be settled by negotiations. "Discussions," he said, "should be started between the belligerents for a cease-fire and an armistice." When the PRC endorsed Malik's proposal over Beijing radio, President Truman authorized General Ridgway to arrange armistice talks with his enemy counterpart.

PORK CHOP HILL

A company-size position established in 1952 as part of the UN outpost line, this outpost's nickname came from its shape on the map. Pork Chop became emblematic of the combat actions fought during the war's final eighteen months. The Chinese launched three major attacks in 1953 to take the outpost; and the third attack, starting on July 6, was the heaviest. The 7th Infantry Division rotated five infantry battalions in five days through the position to hold it with the assistance of tremendous amounts of artillery fire. With the Chinese apparently determined to take the outpost at whatever cost and an armistice imminent, General Taylor ordered Pork Chop Hill abandoned. Through a clever ruse, the 7th Infantry Division removed its troops during the day on July 11 without any casualties.

Through an exchange of radio messages, both sides agreed to open negotiations on July 10 at the town of Kaesong, in territory the Communists controlled.

At the first armistice conference the two delegations agreed that hostilities would continue until an armistice agreement was signed. By July 26 the two delegations fixed the points to be settled in order to achieve an armistice. But China, while having forced the United States to negotiate, remained both very conscious of its relative military weakness and contemptuous of Western resolve. Seeking to sustain its newly won image as a major power, it feared that concessions at the negotiations would undermine that image. On the night of August 22–23 the Communists claimed that a UNC plane had attacked the conference site, impeded any investigation of the alleged attack, and then broke off negotiations.

Meanwhile, in late July General Van Fleet had decided to mount a series of attacks to seize positions three to seven miles above the KANSAS-WYOMING Line. These attacks had three objectives: keep the Communists off balance, probe Communist positions, and maintain an aggressive spirit in Eighth Army. From August to September the X Corps and ROK I Corps in east central Korea fought bloody battles against tenacious *KPA* defenders to take objectives such as the Punchbowl, Bloody Ridge, and Heartbreak Ridge. In west central Korea, the I and IX Corps attacked in October to seize new positions and had to defeat a tenacious *CPVF* defense to take their objectives. Van Fleet proposed a follow-on offensive, but the heavy casualties UNC units had taken in the recent limited attacks dissuaded Ridgway; he first postponed and then canceled the operation.

Armistice negotiations resumed on October 25, this time at Panmunjom, a tiny village southeast of Kaesong. Hope for an early armistice grew on November 27: the two delegations agreed that a line of demarcation for an armistice would be the existing line of contact, provided the belligerents reached an armistice within thirty days. Hence, while both sides awaited the outcome of negotiations, fighting during the remainder of 1951 tapered off to patrol clashes, raids, and small battles for possession of outposts in No Man's Land. On November 12 Ridgway had directed Van Fleet to assume an "active defense"; the Eighth Army was to establish an outpost line forward of its current main line of resistance, fortify both lines, patrol aggressively, and use its firepower to inflict maximum casualties on the enemy. Van Fleet could counterattack to retake lost positions but could not mount any further multi-division operations without Ridgway's permission.

Discord over several issues, including the exchange of prisoners of war, prevented an armistice within the stipulated thirty days. The prisoner

During the Panmunjom cease-fire talks, Col. James Murray, Jr., USMC, and Col. Chang Chun San, KPA, initial maps showing the north and south boundaries of the demarcation zone.

of war quarrel heightened in January 1952, after UNC delegates proposed to give captives a choice in repatriation after the armistice. Thousands of Korean prisoners held by the UNC were actually South Koreans impressed into the *KPA* in 1950, and thousands of Chinese prisoners were former Nationalist soldiers impressed into the People's Liberation Army after the Chinese Civil War. Most of these men had no desire to return to the DPRK or the PRC, and their refusal to do so would be a dramatic propaganda victory for the Western bloc. American leaders, recalling Stalin's brutal treatment of Soviet soldiers taken prisoner by the Germans and returned to the USSR by the United States after World War II, also believed that voluntary repatriation was the moral course. The Communist delegates protested vigorously that this was a violation of the Geneva Conventions of 1949. The resulting impasse deadlocked the negotiations until 1953.

The Communists opened another front on the prisoner issue on May 7, 1952. Communists held in the UNC prison camp on Koje-do, on orders smuggled to them from North Korea, lured the U.S. camp commander to a compound gate and dragged him inside. The strategy, which became clear in subsequent prisoner demands, was to trade the officer's life and release for UNC admissions of inhumane treatment of captives, including alleged cruelties during previous screenings of prisoners in which a large number of prisoners refused repatriation. The obvious objective was to discredit the voluntary repatriation stand the UNC delegation had taken at Panmunjom. Although a new camp commander secured his predecessor's release, in the process he signed a damaging statement including an admission that "there have been instances of bloodshed where many prisoners of war have been killed and wounded by U.N. Forces." (There had been numerous violent incidents in the poorly designed and poorly run camp, and the Communists exploited the statement widely at Panmunjom and elsewhere for its propaganda value.)

Amid the Koje-do trouble, General Ridgway left Tokyo to replace General of the Army Dwight D. Eisenhower as the NATO Supreme Commander. Ridgway's replacement was General Mark W. Clark, Chief, Army Field Forces. Clark became the new commander in the Far East, with one less responsibility than MacArthur and Ridgway had carried. On April 28, 1952, a peace treaty with Japan had gone into effect, restoring Japan's sovereignty and thus ending the occupation.

KOJE-DO

In January 1951 the Eighth Army established a prison camp on Koje-do, an island off the southern coast of Korea. By May 1952 the camp held approximately 170,000 prisoners of war and civilian internees in poorly designed facilities, and it had been assigned a disproportionately high percentage of low-quality U.S. and ROK personnel. Eighth Army paid little attention to the camp even after a number of riots between Communist and anti-Communist prisoners and clashes between Communist prisoners and guards. After General Boatner reestablished control over the camp in June 1952, General Clark relieved the Eighth Army of responsibility for prisoners of war and most of those held on Koje-do were moved to new, better-designed camps.

Faced immediately with the Koje-do affair, General Clark repudiated the prison camp commander's statement and placed Brig. Gen. Haydon L. Boatner, one of the U.S. Army's old China hands, in charge of the camp. Clark ordered Boatner to move the prisoners into smaller, more manageable compounds and to institute other measures that would eliminate the likelihood of another uprising. General Boatner, in a carefully planned series of actions using tanks and infantry, crushed Communist resistance at the camp and completed the task in June.

In the United States, the growing unpopularity of the war made limiting casualties a key objective for Eighth Army. General Van Fleet successfully argued for a major expansion of the ROK Army, and he devoted much attention to strengthening the ROK Army's greatest weaknesses during the war's first year: inadequate training and poor leadership. While the number of U.S. divisions in Korea did not drop until after the war, the growing number of ROK divisions, and their higher quality, allowed the Eighth Army to gradually turn over more of its front to ROK units and keep U.S. divisions in reserve for longer periods. Because even limited attacks had produced high casualties in relation to the ground gained, the Eighth Army restricted subordinate commanders' freedom to attack. Since it could not pressure the enemy with ground attacks, the UNC turned to an "air pressure" campaign, striking at targets across North Korea.

General Clark

The Far East Air Forces also mounted a renewed interdiction campaign against Communist supply lines, but the effort failed to prevent the *CPVF* and the *KPA* from receiving large amounts of artillery from the USSR. At the start of 1952 the Communist forces had 71 artillery battalions with an estimated 852 guns at the front and an additional 361 battalions and 3,500 guns just to their rear to defend against UN breakthroughs. By October 1952 they had something around 131 artillery battalions with 1,300 guns at the front and another 383 battalions and 4,000 guns just behind. The Communists used these weapons and their willingness to suffer, according to Western standards, exorbitant casualties to exert tremendous pressure on the UNC. From July to December 1952 *CPVF* and *KPA* units assaulted UNC outposts using their own version of meat grinder tactics. The resulting battles, at hills UNC troops gave nicknames such as Old Baldy, the Hook, White Horse, and Reno, were small in scale compared to the war's first year. The intensity of the combat for soldiers, however, rivaled that of World War I, with terrific artillery bombardments and hand-to-hand fighting in trenches. Between these assaults, both sides harassed each other with artillery fire and sent out patrols to contest the area between the opposing lines.

As this war of posts continued, the U.S. Army in 1952 was an institution in crisis. The opening of negotiations had erased the crisis atmosphere of 1950 and early 1951, and traditional fears about the dangers to the American economy from high military spending reasserted themselves. President Truman and the Congress cut military spending and allocated a greater share of the defense budget to the Air Force to expand the nuclear deterrent force. These cuts, along with the decisions to institute an individual rotation policy in Korea and not to hold draftees and mobilized guardsmen and reservists for the duration of the war, left the Army unable to support all its commitments. The service gave first priority in personnel to supporting the Eighth Army

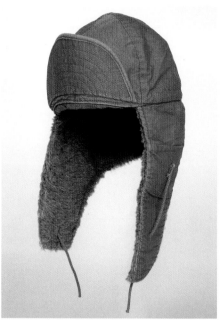

Model 1951 Pile Cap

and second priority to supporting the Seventh Army in Germany, but commanders in both armies complained of serious declines in their units' proficiency. In the Continental United States, the manpower crisis crippled the Army's contribution to building an air defense system, nearly destroyed the service's training system, and by the end of 1952 had once again ruined the General Reserve (of its seven divisions, only the 82d Airborne was ready for use).

While the manpower crisis had negative effects on units, it did force the Army finally to comply with President Truman's 1948 order to end racial segregation. With only a partial mobilization for war and high casualties in Korea, racial segregation began to break down in the Eighth Army during 1950 as some commanders accepted any replacements they could obtain. In 1951 the Army began a racial integration program for units in Korea and extended it to the rest of the service later in the war.

In November the American people elected Dwight D. Eisenhower as the next President. A major issue in the campaign had been the war in Korea; and in a pledge to "go to Korea," Eisenhower implied that if elected he would attempt to end the war quickly. Consequently, when

A foot-weary soldier demonstrates the versatility of the standard
U.S. Army helmet.

the President-elect in early December fulfilled his promise to visit Korea, there was indeed some expectation of a dramatic change in the conduct of the war. In October General Clark had proposed a plan to obtain a military victory; it required extensive reinforcements for the UNC, a ground offensive supported by amphibious and airborne operations, air and naval attacks on targets in China, and possible use of nuclear weapons. But it quickly became clear that Eisenhower, like President Truman, considered the costs of such an operation unacceptable and that he also preferred to seek an honorable armistice.

A UNC proposal in February 1953 that the two sides exchange sick and wounded prisoners initially brought no Communist response, but on March 5 Stalin died. The Soviet Politburo wanted an end to the high costs of supplying the Chinese and North Koreans; and without Soviet supplies and air power, the *CPVF* and the *KPA* would become vulnerable to a UNC offensive. On March 28 the Communists favorably replied to the February proposal and also suggested that this exchange perhaps could "lead to the smooth settlement of the entire question of prisoners of war." With that, the armistice conference resumed in April. An exchange of sick and wounded prisoners was carried out that same month, and on June 4 the Communist negotiators conceded on the issue of voluntary repatriation of prisoners.

During the spring of 1953 the Eighth Army fought some of the bloodiest battles of the outpost war as the *CPVF* and the *KPA* launched attacks to maintain pressure on the UNC and to take attention away from the concessions made at Panmunjom. UNC units grimly defended some positions, but Lt. Gen. Maxwell D. Taylor, who had succeeded Van Fleet as the Eighth Army's commander in February, ordered others abandoned when it appeared that the enemy was willing to pay any price to take them. Concerned over the steep increase in American casualties and aware that an armistice was imminent, Taylor decided that the costs of holding such outposts outweighed any tactical benefits. The enemy paid particular attention to ROK units, and on June 10 the *CPVF* attacked the five ROK divisions in the Kumsong salient in east central Korea. Outnumbered, the ROK forces were pushed back an average of three kilometers across the salient before the *CPVF* broke off the attack, but their performance demonstrated a great improvement over that of ROK units under comparable conditions in the spring of 1951.

The UNC also sought to pressure its opponent, by bombing irrigation dams in North Korea but found ROK President Rhee as great a problem when on June 18 he ordered the release of over 25,000 Korean prisoners, many of them Southerners impressed into the *KPA*, who had refused repatriation. Rhee had long opposed any armistice that left the peninsula divided and had made threats to remove ROK forces from UNC control. He also feared that with an armistice the ROK would lose the support and protection of the United States, especially if the United States withdrew all its ground forces. In the end Rhee backed down when the U.S. government suggested that it would sign a mutual defense treaty with the ROK and provide it with significant economic and military assistance.

Furious over the release of the prisoners, the Communists decided to teach Rhee a lesson before concluding the armistice negotiations.

On July 13 the *CPVF* attacked the Kumsong salient in greater strength than in June. Shattering one division, the attack forced the ROK units to withdraw south of the Kumsong River. Again the ROK units' performance showed that this army had greatly improved since 1951. General Taylor on July 16 ordered the ROK II Corps, with U.S. air and artillery support, to counterattack; but he halted the operation on July 20 short of the original line since by that date the armistice delegations had come to a new accord and needed only to work out a few small details. Taylor's order to halt ended the last major battle of the war.

After a week of dealing with administrative matters, each chief delegate signed the military armistice at Panmunjom at 10:00 A.M. on July 27; later that day General Clark and the enemy commanders affixed their signatures to the agreement. As stipulated in the agreement, all fighting stopped twelve hours after the first signing, at 10:00 P.M., July 27, 1953. Thirty-seven months of fighting had exacted a high toll. South Korea had lost over 187,000 soldiers dead, an estimated 30,000 missing, and about 429,000 wounded. South Korea's civilians also had suffered greatly: estimates of the dead and missing range from 500,000 to 1 million. Up to 1.5 million North Korean soldiers and civilians died in the war. Estimates for Chinese dead and missing range from 600,000 to 800,000. Non-American members of the UNC forces lost a total of 3,063 dead and missing and a further 11,817 wounded. American losses from hostile action totaled 137,025: 33,741 killed and 103,284 wounded. Another 2,835 died from nonhostile causes. Of the dead, the remains of over 8,000 have yet to be recovered. The U.S. Army bore the brunt of American losses: 27,731 killed; 2,125 dead from nonhostile causes; and 77,596 wounded. Of the Army's dead, the remains of over 6,000 have yet to be recovered.

The Aftermath

By the terms of the armistice, the line of demarcation between North and South Korea closely approximated the front line as it existed at the final hour and represented a relatively small adjustment of the prewar division. (*Map 13*) Within three days of the signing of the armistice, each opposing force withdrew two kilometers from this line to establish a demilitarized zone. The armistice provisions forbade either force to bring additional troops or new weapons into Korea, although replacement one for one and in kind was permissible. To oversee the enforcement of all armistice terms and to negotiate resolution of any violations, the armistice established a Military Armistice Commission composed of an equal number of officers from the UN Command, China, South Korea, and North Korea. This body was assisted by the Neutral Nations Supervisory Commission whose members came from Sweden, Switzerland, Czechoslovakia, and Poland. Representatives of those same countries, with India furnishing an umpire and custodial forces, formed the Neutral Nations Repatriation Commission to handle the disposition of prisoners refusing repatriation. Finally, a provision of the armistice recommended that the belligerent governments convene a political conference to negotiate a final political settlement of the whole Korean question.

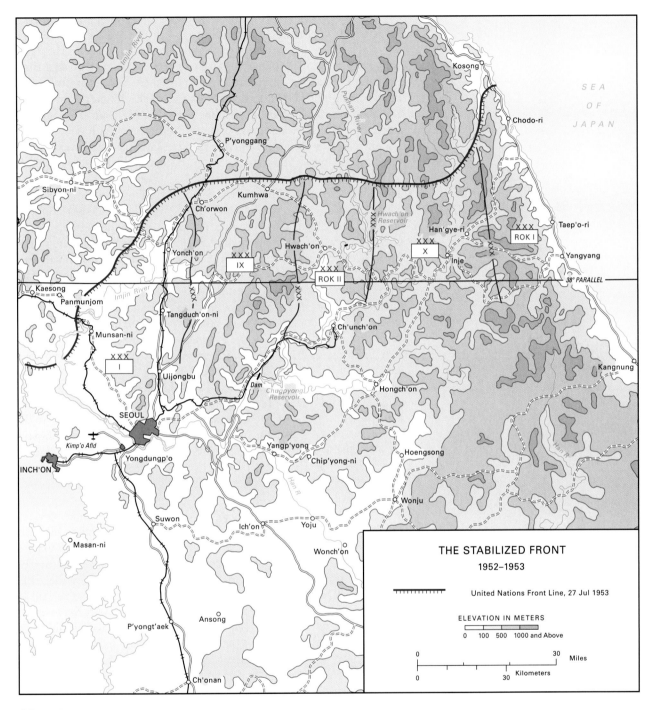

Map 13

By September 6 all prisoners wishing to be repatriated had been exchanged. From the UNC returnees came full details of brutally harsh treatment—murder, torture, and starvation—in enemy prison camps and of an extensive Communist political indoctrination program designed to produce prisoner collaboration. Several hundred U.S.

returnees were investigated on charges of collaborating with the enemy, but few were convicted.

The transfer of nonrepatriates to the Neutral Nations Repatriation Commission came next. In the drawn-out procedure that followed, few of the prisoners changed their minds as officials from both sides attempted to convince former members of their respective commands that they should return home. Of twenty-three Americans who at first refused repatriation, two decided to return. On February 1, 1954, the Neutral Nations Repatriation Commission dissolved itself after releasing the last of the nonrepatriates as civilians free to choose their own destinations.

The main scene then shifted to Geneva, Switzerland, where the political conference recommended in the armistice agreement convened on April 26. There was a complete impasse from the beginning: the representatives of UNC member nations wanted to reunify Korea through UN-supervised elections; the Communist delegation refused to recognize the United Nations' authority to deal with the matter. The conference on Korea closed June 15. Leaving Korea divided essentially along the prewar line, the Geneva impasse merely reestablished the prewar confrontation between the two Korean governments. However, the ROK now had a military vastly increased in size and ability and the United States had promised the ROK huge amounts of economic and military aid. Later in 1954 the United States would sign a mutual defense treaty with the ROK; and the Eighth Army, although reduced to two U.S. divisions, would remain in Korea.

The war's impact reached far beyond Korea. Despite criticism of the armistice by those who agreed with General MacArthur that there was no substitute for victory, the UNC had upheld the principle of suppressing armed aggression. True, the Security Council had been able to enlist forces under the UN banner in June 1950 only in the absence of the USSR veto. Nevertheless, the UNC success strengthened the possibility of keeping or restoring peace through the UN machinery, at the General Assembly.

For China, the war brought several benefits. It had maintained in the DPRK a buffer state on its sensitive northern border. Soviet assistance, especially in improving the Chinese army and air force, gave China a more powerful military posture at war's end than when it had intervened. Its performance in Korea, despite vast losses, won China respect as a nation to be reckoned with, not only in Asian but also in world affairs.

For the United States, the war brought a major change in its containment strategy against the USSR. Instead of relying principally on economic and political tools backed by a small nuclear deterrent force, containment's emphasis shifted during the war to military means. While Eisenhower did reduce military spending after the war, the U.S. armed forces remained much larger than they had been in 1950, possessed many more and increasingly powerful nuclear weapons, and were ensured a steady supply of manpower through the retention of conscription. The American military, after the humiliating and bloody defeats of the war's first six months, shifted its focus from preparing for a World War II–type mobilization to maintaining forces ready for immediate use. This larger military, eager to put the frustrations

The U.S. armed forces remained much larger than they had been in 1950, possessed many more and increasingly powerful nuclear weapons, and were ensured a steady supply of manpower through the retention of conscription.

of the Korean War behind it, now was widely dispersed around the world, including Indochina, where American advisers assisted the new Republic of Vietnam.

DISCUSSION QUESTIONS

1. To what degree was the Korean War a civil war? How did the United States and Russia view it?

2. How did the relationships between the two Korean governments and their allies affect the origins and course of the war?

3. How did American war aims change in 1950 and 1951, and what were the effects of these changes?

4. Should President Truman have decided to seek a decisive military victory in mid-1951 by again invading North Korea, and should President Eisenhower have approved General Clark's plan for a major offensive in 1953? What are the good and bad points about waging limited war?

5. How did the use of intelligence affect the course of the war?

6. Why was there no armistice in 1951? Why did it take two more years of fighting to end the war?

RECOMMENDED READINGS

Appleman, Roy E. *East of Chosin: Entrapment and Breakout in Korea, 1950.* College Station: Texas A&M University Press, 1987.

Blair, Clay. *The Forgotten War: America in Korea, 1950–1953.* Annapolis: Naval Institute Press, 2003.

Fehrenbach, T. R. *This Kind of War: A Study in Unpreparedness.* New York: Macmillan, 1963.

Marshall, S. L. A. *Pork Chop Hill: The American Fighting Man in Action, Korea, Spring 1953.* New York: Berkley Books, 2000.

Stueck, William W. *The Korean War: An International History.* Princeton: Princeton University Press, 1995.

Other Readings

Appleman, Roy E. *Disaster in Korea: The Chinese Confront MacArthur.* College Station: Texas A&M University Press, 1989.

———. *Ridgway Duels for Korea.* College Station: Texas A&M University Press, 1990.

———. *South to the Naktong, North to the Yalu.* U.S. Army in the Korean War. Washington, D.C.: U.S. Army Center of Military History, 2000.

Bowers, William T., William M. Hammond, and George L. MacGarrigle. *Black Soldier, White Army: The 24th Infantry Regiment in Korea.* U.S. Army in the Korean War. Washington, D.C.: U.S. Army Center of Military History, 1996.

Crane, Conrad C. *American Airpower Strategy in Korea,1950–1953.* Lawrence: University Press of Kansas, 2000.

Evanhoe, Ed. *Darkmoon: Eighth Army Special Operations in the Korean War.* Annapolis: Naval Institute Press, 1995.

Flint, Roy K., "Task Force Smith and the 24th Division: Delay and Withdrawal, 5–19 July 1950," in *America's First Battles, 1776–1965,* ed. Charles E. Heller and William A. Stofft. Lawrence: University Press of Kansas, 1986.

Gugeler, Russell A. *Combat Actions in Korea.* Washington, D.C.: U.S. Army Center of Military History, 1987.

Hamburger, Kenneth E. *Leadership in the Crucible: The Korean War Battles of Twin Tunnels and Chipyong-ni.* College Station: Texas A&M University Press, 2003.

Hermes, Walter G. *Truce Tent and Fighting Front.* U.S. Army in the Korean War. Washington, D.C.: U.S. Army Center of Military History, 2000.

James, D. Clayton. *Refighting the Last War: Command and Crisis in Korea, 1950–1953.* New York: Free Press, 1993.

Mahoney, Kevin. *Formidable Enemies: The North Korean and Chinese Soldier in the Korean War.* Novato, Calif.: Presidio Press, 2001.

Marshall, S. L. A. *The River and the Gauntlet: Defeat of the Eighth Army by the Chinese Communist Forces, November, 1950, in the Battle of the Chongchon River, Korea.* Alexandria, Va.: Time-Life Books, 1982.

Robertson, William G. *Counterattack on the Naktong, 1950.* Fort Leavenworth, Kans.: Combat Studies Institute, U.S. Army Command and General Staff College, 1985.

Schnabel, James F. *Policy and Direction: The First Year.* U.S. Army in the Korean War. Washington, D.C.: U.S. Army Center of Military History, 1990.

Tucker, Spencer, ed. *Encyclopedia of the Korean War: A Political, Social, and Military History.* New York: Checkmark Books, 2002.

Westover, John G. *Combat Support in Korea: The United States Army in the Korean Conflict.* Washington, D.C.: Combat Forces Press, 1955.

9

THE ARMY OF THE COLD WAR FROM THE "NEW LOOK" TO FLEXIBLE RESPONSE

Although the Korean War ended in stalemate, it had shown clearly that the United States was the only nation strong enough to offer determined resistance to Communist expansion. In the past the nation had turned to its military only when threatened. From 1953 onward, however, it would have little choice but to use its armed forces as an open and indispensable element in its conduct of foreign affairs. Confronting opponents who regarded war as a logical and necessary extension of politics, the United States would turn their own tactics against them by backing its diplomats with the threat of force. The American people accepted the new approach with remarkable composure. In so doing, they revealed a willingness to shoulder not only the huge costs but also the heavy moral obligations that leadership of the free world necessarily entailed.

Massive Retaliation and the New Look

With the end of hostilities, the Eisenhower administration had to provide for the nation's defense by determining a strategy for the future and by configuring military forces to carry it out. Torn between pressures from worldwide commitments and a desire to cut back on defense spending, the administration devised a policy that laid major emphasis upon air power and America's nuclear superiority. "The basic decision," Secretary of State John Foster Dulles observed, "was to depend primarily upon a great capacity to retaliate, instantly, by means and at places of our choosing." This would allow the Department of Defense to mold the armed forces into a shape that best suited official policy without having to prepare for every threat the Communists might pose.

With the new emphasis on massive retaliation, the armed forces took on a New Look as the 1950s progressed. The Air Force increased the size of its strategic bombing forces, spending huge sums on new bombers and missiles. The Navy concentrated on developing a new submarine-launched nuclear missile known as the Polaris, and the Army sought to perfect tactical nuclear weapons to support the soldier on the battlefield. Since the military budget divided along service rather than functional lines, the annual allocation of funds almost inevitably provoked bitter infighting.

Over time, the Air Force's share of the budget became so large that it diminished the capacity of the United States to wage a conventional war. As it did, opposition to massive retaliation mounted. The Army's Chief of Staff, General Matthew B. Ridgway, was particularly pointed in his criticism. As Soviet nuclear capabilities grew, he noted in June 1955, nuclear parity between the two sides would ensure that neither had an advantage. When that parity occurred, the Soviets could gain the edge by provoking confrontations so limited in size that they could never justly resort to nuclear weapons. Armed with "leftovers" from the budget process, America's conventional forces would lack the means to respond. A balanced force was necessary, Ridgway implied, one that could cope with either a general or a limited war.

Ridgway's successor, General Maxwell D. Taylor, supported his plea, as did many prominent academics. Change, however, came only at the end of the decade, when the Soviet Union's parity with the United States was no longer in dispute. At that point, supporters of the nuclear option had little choice but to concede that a general war would result in mutual self-destruction and that massive retaliation should be only a *last* resort.

The NATO Buildup

While the word battles raged, a major American buildup had taken place in Europe. Concerned that the Soviet Union might yet launch an offensive on the continent, the United States had increased its forces there from one to five divisions and had strengthened NATO's ground, air, and naval forces. In response, the alliance had adopted a "forward defense" strategy that contemplated a defense of West Germany as far east of the Rhine as possible.

The conclusion of the Korean War, the death of Stalin, and the launch of a Soviet peace initiative a short while later led to a release of international tensions and a slowing of the NATO buildup. This allowed the United States and its allies to shift their attention to their need for improved communications and to the construction of roads, airfields, and logistical depots. As those efforts proceeded, the United States began to press for German rearmament. Despite strong opposition from the Communist bloc, the Western allies agreed to the idea in 1954, approving the formation of a twelve-division German army.

The United States also moved to remedy a growing imbalance between Communist and NATO ground forces by fitting tactical nuclear warheads to artillery shells and missiles. As the weapons came on line, the alliance based its planning on an assumption that they would form the foundation of its response to a Soviet attack. Cracks appeared in

NATO's common front, however, when the United States declined to share its exclusive control of the devices through consultation with its allies. In the end, the French and British decided to lessen their dependence upon their ally by developing nuclear weapons of their own.

Continental Defense

The Soviet Union was hardly idle. Responding to NATO's efforts, it strengthened its defenses by arming its ground forces with tactical nuclear weapons, developing hydrogen bombs and an intercontinental jet bomber to deliver them, and pushing ahead with production of long-range missiles. By 1955, as a result, the race between the two sides had produced such huge nuclear arsenals that both became concerned. Meeting at a conference in Geneva, American and Soviet representatives agreed that a full-scale nuclear war could lead only to mutual suicide. From then on, an understanding between the sides grew that neither would use nuclear weapons unless its own survival was at stake.

If tensions eased on the strategic level, competition continued unabated on every other. Russian Premier Nikita Khrushchev set the mood. Avowing in early 1956 that the East and West could coexist as competitors, he insisted nonetheless that peaceful coexistence hardly meant acquiescence. The Soviet Union would continue its struggle with Capitalist imperialism through "wars of national liberation" and by other means less destructive than full-scale war.

Under the circumstances, the United States took no chances. Cooperating with the Canadian government, it began construction in 1957 of a distant early warning (DEW) radar network. Designed to provide advance word of a Soviet air or missile attack from the north, the system consisted of a line of radar stations that ran across Alaska and northern Canada. Radar outposts in the Aleutian Islands supplemented it, along with stations in central and southern Canada, radar towers and picket boats in the Atlantic, and circling early warning aircraft.

Answering to the Air Force, which served as executive agent for the Secretary of Defense, the Continental Air Defense Command had responsibility for America's overall air defenses. The Army contributed ground antiaircraft defenses in support of the command's interceptor aircraft and developed the nation's first antiaircraft missile, the Ajax.

HOMELAND DEFENSE DURING THE COLD WAR

By the end of the Korean War, the Army was deeply involved in activities intended to defend the United States against direct Soviet attack or Soviet-directed subversion. The Army built gun positions around major U.S. cities that were soon replaced by Nike Ajax and then Nike Hercules surface-to-air missiles that would intercept Soviet bombers. At the height of the Cold War in the late 1950s, the Army had deployed 145 Nike Hercules batteries. A second Army homeland defense function was to support the U.S. civil defense efforts as it had during World War II. The Army laid plans for assuming martial law to maintain order in the wake of a nuclear attack. Also, the Army Corps of Engineers participated in the National Fallout Shelter Survey for the Office of Civil Defense that identified shelter space for the entire population.

Later, it fitted more sophisticated members of the Nike family with nuclear warheads and developed the Hawk missile to defend against low-flying aircraft. By the 1960s, the service had also situated antiaircraft missile sites on the outskirts of many American cities to protect vital defense areas.

The Missile Era

Throughout the period, the United States had keyed its efforts to the strategic bomber; but to be on the safe side, it had also pushed development of offensive missiles. To that end the Army produced the Jupiter and the Air Force the Thor, both intermediate-range ballistic missiles that could strike targets at a distance of 1,500 miles. The Air Force was also working on Atlas and Titan, intercontinental ballistic missiles (ICBMs) with a reach of 5,000 miles. A jurisdictional dispute between the Army and the Air Force prompted by the roles and missions agreement led the Secretary of Defense in 1957 to give the Air Force charge of all land-based ballistic missiles. Although the Army retained control over development and testing of the Jupiter missile, tensions with the Soviet Union soon eased, lessening the sense of urgency that had propelled the program to that point.

The lull lasted only until October 1957, when the Russians launched Sputnik, the first earth satellite. The feat came as a shock to the United States, which lacked the sort of high-thrust rocket the Russians had used. To sustain public morale, the United States boosted several small American satellites into orbit with existing ballistic missile motors. Considerable time would elapse, however, before the nation would produce a rocket engine equal to that of the Russians.

Since every new weapon evoked a counterweapon, the Army took responsibility for developing an anti-ICBM system. A running debate quickly broke out, however, over whether any missile could protect the United States from a saturation attack by ICBMs. More talk centered on whether the United States needed to maintain airfields and missile sites overseas within striking range of the Soviet Union and Communist

WERNHER VON BRAUN (1912–1977)

With the defeat of Germany imminent, von Braun and his rocket research team decided to surrender rather than stay in hiding and wait for capture. A close relative rode his bike down an unpaved road and led the U.S. Army's spy catchers (the Counter Intelligence Corps) to the German rocket team. Dr. Braun's work under Army auspices was instrumental in creating the Redstone, Jupiter, and Pershing missile systems. America's first satellite, the Explorer I, and America's first man in space, Navy Commander Alan B. Shepard, Jr., were launched into space on modified Redstone missiles. Von Braun ended his Army affiliation in 1960, when he went to work for the newly created National Aeronautics and Space Administration.

China. The costs of maintaining these facilities and the troops to man them seemed questionable since long-range missiles launched from the Continental United States or from submarines promised to fill that role. In the end, the debate led nowhere. Although the new alternatives had potential, they would take years to test and put into operation.

Challenges and Responses

The nuclear threat overshadowed developments in other areas during the fifties. Although the United States sought to avoid involvement in limited war, for example, challenges arose continually that required it to supply military or economic aid or to dispatch combat forces. American commitments ßto provide advisory groups and military missions around the world thus multiplied throughout the period, despite drives in Congress and the Executive Branch to cut costs.

The nation did, nevertheless, have its limits. It had little choice but to maintain two Army divisions south of the demilitarized zone in Korea and to provide substantial military assistance to South Korea's armed forces. It drew the line, however, when France sought American support for its effort to reclaim its empire in Indochina. Confronted by French threats of noncooperation with NATO, the United States compromised by providing military supplies, equipment, and economic

Pershing Missile in Winter, *Wayne Duncan, 1960*

aid. Lacking support from its other allies, however, it declined to commit American troops or bombers.

Although the United States was clearly reluctant to become embroiled in Asia so soon after the Korean War, it could hardly fail to recognize that the region was under threat. Following the Geneva Conference of 1954, which set up two Vietnams, the nation attempted to take up the slack by sponsoring the Southeast Asia Treaty Organization (SEATO), a collective defense arrangement. The pact called for mutual help and consultation to resist overt aggression or other threats to internal security. Australia, France, New Zealand, Pakistan, the Philippines, Thailand, the United Kingdom, and the United States were its initial signatories.

AMERICAN MILITARY HISTORY

Troubles nonetheless proliferated in both Asia and Southeast Asia as the 1950s lengthened. A prime point of contention stood in the Strait of Taiwan, where Chinese Communist forces were bombarding Nationalist Chinese positions on two tiny offshore islands, Quemoy and Matsu. Since loss of the two might have opened the way for an invasion of Taiwan, Congress issued a joint resolution in 1955 empowering the President to act immediately if the Communists moved to seize either. The shelling tapered off after that; but it picked up again in the summer of 1958, when the Communists again began to shell the islands. In response, the United States provided warships to convoy supply vessels and armed Nationalist Chinese aircraft with missiles. A U.S. composite Air Strike Force also took up station on Taiwan to strengthen Nationalist defenses against a Communist invasion. The Communists ended the crisis by reducing their fire shortly thereafter, but Quemoy and Matsu would remain a bone of contention between the United States and China for years to come.

Meanwhile, in Southeast Asia, pressure from the Communists eased but hardly ceased. Instead, attention shifted to the small state of Laos to the west of Vietnam, where a Communist movement, the Pathet Lao, had taken control of several provinces bordering North Vietnam and China. The nation's non-Communist government had signed a peaceful coexistence agreement with the group in 1956, but open warfare broke out again in 1959. Neither side gained the upper hand in the fighting that followed, despite U.S. assistance to the government's 25,000-man army and substantial military aid to the Pathet Lao from the Communist bloc. With concern growing that the struggle might lead to a direct East-West confrontation, suggestions arose that the Great Powers should convene a conference to neutralize the country. By then, however, the Eisenhower administration was giving way to a new government headed by President-Elect John F. Kennedy. The likelihood of an agreement seemed remote until Kennedy could settle in.

If the tensions in the Far East were the products of Cold War competition, others arising in the Middle East were attributable to nationalism and Arab hostility to the Jewish state of Israel. Although the United States took a standoff approach to the region's intermittent crises, President Dwight D. Eisenhower understood that America had deep interests in the area. As a result, in January 1957 he requested and obtained a joint resolution from Congress that pledged American military assistance to Middle Eastern nations subject to Communist aggression. Empowering the President to use the armed forces if necessary, the legislation became known as the Eisenhower Doctrine.

President Eisenhower meets with Secretary of State Dulles.

American action came in 1958, when factions favoring Egyptian leader Gamal Abdel Nasser became active in Lebanon, Jordan, and Iraq. When rebellion followed in Lebanon and killers assassinated the King of Iraq to establish a republic under pro-Nasser leadership, the President of Lebanon and the King of Jordan requested U.S. assistance. Within twenty-four hours, naval units from the U.S. Sixth Fleet took up station off Lebanon and a battalion of marines landed near the nation's capital, Beirut. Additional marines arrived two days later, and the Army began to move airborne, tank, and combat engineer troops into the country to stabilize the situation. By early August U.S. forces in Lebanon totaled more than 5,800 marines and 8,500 soldiers. A U.S. composite Air Strike Force had moved into Turkey to back them, and a British airborne contingent had positioned itself in Jordan. Those efforts had the desired effect. By October tensions had subsided enough for the United States to withdraw its forces. In their place, it gave Lebanon and Jordan special assistance to build up their defenses and to prevent additional outbreaks. Shortly after that, it concluded separate defense treaties with Turkey, Iran, and Pakistan. When those three countries and Great Britain formed the Central Treaty Organization (CENTO) along NATO lines the following year, the United States declined membership. However, it participated in the association's economic, military, and antisubversion committees and sent representatives to its meetings.

Closer to home, the United States chose not to intervene in a revolution on the island of Cuba in 1958, but it kept careful tabs on the movement's leader, Fidel Castro, and his followers. When they succeeded in overthrowing the government of President Fulgencio Batista, the United States initially recognized their new regime, but Cuban-American relations deteriorated quickly when Castro aligned his nation with the Communist camp. American military and economic assistance to Cuba ceased in 1960, but Castro replaced it with arms and other aid from the Soviet Union and Communist China. The United States responded by cutting off diplomatic relations with Cuba in January 1961.

> Cuban-American relations deteriorated quickly when Castro aligned his nation with the Communist camp.

The Military Budget

With U.S. forces and assistance either on call or committed around the world, it appeared that the United States was more likely to become involved in local wars than in a general conflagration. American military budgets, however, had emphasized deterrence of nuclear conflict over preparations for lower-level contingencies and limited conventional wars.

It was hardly surprising that President Eisenhower would seek to cut defense spending following the high cost of the Korean War. His decision to rely more heavily upon strategic air power than on ground units, however, created imbalances both in the military budget and in the distribution of forces. In 1953, for example, the Army had more than 1.5 million men: 20 combat divisions (8 in the Far East, 5 in Europe, and 7 in the United States). The service's budget came to nearly $13 billion, 38 percent of the total allocated to the military for the 1954 fiscal year. Over the next four years the Joint Chiefs of Staff trimmed more than 600,000 men from the armed services. Although the Air Force and Navy experienced reductions, most of the cuts came from the ground forces. By 1958, as a result, the Army had shrunk to 15 divisions and fewer than 900,000 men. Two reduced-strength divisions remained in Korea, one in Hawaii. The totals for Europe and the United States remained the same, but several stateside divisions were operating at reduced strength. Funds obligated to the Army for fiscal year 1959 had fallen to about $9 billion, some 22 percent of the total military budget. Despite these economies, the defense budget climbed from $34 billion in 1954 to more than $41 billion in 1959. Much of the expense was attributable to the high-tech air and missile systems necessary to deter and defend against nuclear attack. Not only were these weapons costly to obtain, they sometimes became obsolescent overnight as newer, better models came on line. In addition, the personnel necessary to maintain them not only came at high cost, they also required expensive, on-the-job training to keep abreast of trends.

Defense Reorganization

Perennial disputes between the services over strategy, force levels, and funds fostered neither the unity nor the flexibility that the United States required of its armed services during the period. Seeking a remedy, President Eisenhower decided to lessen the autonomy of the military departments, to strengthen the authority of the Secretary of Defense, and to provide a more direct chain of command from the Commander in Chief downward. Congress approved the reorganization in August 1958.

Sweeping changes followed. The new arrangement abolished the system that made the military departments executive agents for operations in the field. Instead, most of the nation's active combat forces came under unified commands that answered to the President and the Secretary of Defense through the Joint Chiefs of Staff. As part of his enlarged role, the Secretary of Defense received greater freedom to transfer functions within the services. In doing so, he was to have the assistance of a new Directorate of Research and Development that would oversee all military research and development programs.

The Joint Chiefs of Staff meanwhile received leave to shift many of their routine duties to subordinates by delegating more authority to their vice chiefs. The Joint Staff that answered to them grew in size as a result. Because of service sensitivities, however, it received specific instructions to avoid organizing or operating as an overall general staff.

The military services, for their part, had already reorganized internally to improve efficiency and to adjust to the changes required by the threat of nuclear war. By 1955, for example, in an attempt to reduce the number of commands reporting directly to the Chief of Staff, the Army had replaced its Army Field Forces Command with a new Continental Army Command (CONARC). The new organization took responsibility for the six U.S. armies and the Military District of Washington along with certain other units, activities, and installations. It had charge of training the Active Army and Reserves, preparing the future Army and its equipment, and planning and conducting the ground defenses of the United States.

Those functions continued under the new system. The Army and the other military services kept their roles in training, equipping, and organizing combat forces. The difference was that the units transferred to unified commands when war threatened. Answering to the Secretary of Defense, the services also developed the weapons and equipment the troops would need. If the unified commands had control of the units assigned to them, moreover, the services retained command of everyone else and provided logistical support to all their personnel whether attached to unified commands or not.

A Dual-Capability Army

The need to adjust to the nuclear threat had a deep impact on the Army. Old ways of organizing for combat seemed inadequate to meet a nuclear attack, yet historical precedents were lacking when it came to devising new ones. The vast destructive power of nuclear weapons argued that armies could no longer mass to launch offensives or to hold along a solid front. An enemy could sweep aside all opposition with atomic bombs.

One recourse was to establish a checkerboard pattern with mobile, well-armed units occupying alternate squares. Those forces could concentrate quickly to carry out their missions and just as rapidly disperse when a nuclear counterattack threatened. The key to success would lie in well-trained troops armed with high-power weapons and equipped with fast, reliable ground and air transport. Sharpening the edge, commanders would have at their disposal first-class communications, dependable intelligence on enemy dispositions and intentions, and an efficient logistical system.

Following that pattern, the Army replaced its old triangular infantry and airborne divisions with units composed of five self-contained battle groups capable of independent action. Manned by 13,500 men rather than the usual 17,000, these "pentomic" divisions would have the support of artillery and missile units armed with both conventional and nuclear warheads. Longer-range missiles in the hands of the missile commands would also be available. The seven divisions stationed in the United States would back these forces as a strategic reserve. In 1957

THE PENTOMIC DIVISION

After Korea the Army faced declining manpower levels and intense competition for limited funds, combined with the twin threats of brushfire conflicts in remote theaters and general war on a nuclear battlefield. These challenges led to a new divisional design. The pentomic division replaced the triangular division with five "battle groups," intermediate in size between regiments and battalions, which theoretically increased survivability and responsiveness while reducing overhead. The new division also integrated new technology, particularly tactical nuclear weapons, for greater combat power and strategic mobility. These features turned out to be problematic: the battle group organization made the pentomic division difficult to control and supply, and many of the technological innovations turned out to be immature. As a result, the pentomic division itself was soon superseded.

four of these reserve units (two airborne and two infantry) became the Strategic Army Corps (STRAC), which stood in high readiness for quick deployment in case of an emergency. The other three served both as reinforcements and as a training base for an Army expansion should a prolonged crisis or a full-scale war develop. The Army's regular divisions completed the changeover by 1958. National Guard and Reserve units took until 1960.

Scientists, engineers, and designers combined to produce a steady stream of new weapons and equipment for the nuclear Army. From improved rifles and mortars at the company level to powerful rockets and artillery in the support commands, the firepower of America's combat forces grew. New families of surface-to-surface and surface-to-air missiles also emerged, as did larger and heavier weapons designed to be air transportable.

A program to improve air and ground transportation led to the development of the M113 armored personnel carrier. Equipped with light but sturdy aluminum armor, the vehicle could both protect the troops and move them rapidly to the scene of action. Dual-capability amphibious vehicles that could travel on rough terrain and swim across rivers and swamps also came into being. They freed fighting units from total dependence on roads. The diesel-powered M60 battle tank became operational in 1960. Mounting a 105-mm. main gun, it weighed more than fifty-two tons and had a cruising range of 300 miles.

Perhaps the most dramatic efforts to increase the Army's mobility occurred in the field of aviation. To secure both firepower and maneuverability, the service pushed development of helicopters and low-speed fixed-wing aircraft. The helicopter had already proved itself in Korea by moving troops and supplies and evacuating casualties. Some of the new fixed-wing planes were designed for short takeoffs and landings that would increase the Army's ability to deliver heavy payloads to forward areas. Experiments also began on vertical takeoff and landing aircraft that would combine the helicopter's small footprint with the speed of fixed-wing planes.

As the Army's mobility and firepower increased, so did the need for good communications. With rapidly moving pentomic units operating independently over large areas, light but reliable radio equipment was essential. Dramatic technological breakthroughs in the miniaturization of component parts spurred by the space program provided the solutions the service needed. With tiny transistors replacing bulky tubes, radio equipment became lighter, smaller, and more reliable. Easily transportable by individual soldiers, in small vehicles, or in light aircraft, it eased command and control problems that had always accompanied quick-developing military maneuvers.

The improvement of tactical communications was only one benefit of the technological revolution. Ponderous early computers began to give way to smaller versions that could process, store, and recall more information more swiftly than ever before. From the coordination of weapons fire to the storage and retrieval of personnel and logistical information, these computers assumed many functions at all levels of the Army.

They became particularly valuable where the storage and retrieval of intelligence were concerned. Indeed, the need to secure the data necessary to feed the machines required the development of new families of surveillance equipment. More sophisticated radar and sonar sets emerged. So did infrared, acoustic, and seismic devices to aid ground and air surveillance; highly accurate cameras; and side-looking radar that could detect enemy concentrations by day and night under all weather conditions.

Once operations had gotten under way, the Army would have to supply the troops on the battlefield. Since nuclear wars would probably be short, its planners expected to rely upon stockpiled munitions rather than wait for American industry to gear up. This meant that they would have to establish depots both at home and abroad. The effort to move supplies from those facilities to the troops would pose problems, but modern technology seemed to hold the answers. Processing requisitions in computers, logisticians would use fast naval vessels, air transport, and cross-country vehicles to deliver at least the minimum essential requirements to the points where they were needed most.

As with the logisticians, the Army's personnel specialists soon decided that forces in being would have to fight future conflicts. In earlier wars, the service had used the draft to mobilize and train civilians for up to two years before committing them to war. This would no longer be possible. The war would be over before anyone would arrive to fight it. Well-trained forces on hand or in ready reserve would have to do the fighting.

Given the Army's growing inventory of complex weapons and equipment, recruiters had to try to retain the most capable of its officers and enlisted men. Administrators with scientific or engineering backgrounds and well-schooled technicians had to be on hand to operate and maintain the sophisticated systems the service was developing. And if it were going to allocate funds for long and expensive training courses, it needed to ensure that the graduates would remain in uniform long enough to pay off the investment. Since those individuals would be qualified to fill well-paid positions in private industry, it would have to compete with attractive civilian offers to maintain its technological edge.

Fortunately for the Army, the advantages of a military career were many. The twenty-year retirement option was a strong inducement for soldiers who had already served ten years or more learning their specialty. Free family medical care, post exchange and commissary privileges, and the Army's extensive recreational and educational facilities also figured in. It also mattered that military service had gained prestige because of the many civilians who had served in World War II and Korea. The Army was no longer as isolated from American society it had been.

> Military service had gained prestige because of the many civilians who had served in World War II and Korea.

In one respect, however, a military career had become less inviting. Military pay had failed to keep pace with civilian salaries. In response, Congress in 1958 voted to increase service members' salaries, to improve retirement benefits, and to authorize proficiency pay for highly skilled personnel.

The Reserve Forces

Although the Army made significant gains in retaining key personnel, it could not depend upon voluntary enlistments to fill its need for manpower. In an emergency it could fall back upon its Ready and Standby Reserves, but neither force was available on a day-to-day basis. The Ready Reserve became available only when the President declared an emergency and only in numbers authorized by Congress. The Standby Reserve became liable for service only in a war or emergency declared by Congress itself. For all other needs, the Army had to rely on the draft, which Congress had enacted during the Korean War. It obligated all physically and mentally qualified males between the ages of eighteen and twenty-six to eight years of combined active and reserve military service.

There were several ways an eligible male could fulfill his obligation. By spending five of his eight years on active duty or in a combination of active duty and membership in the Ready Reserve, he could transfer to the Standby Reserve for his final three years. As an alternative, he might join the National Guard at the age of eighteen. By rendering satisfactory service for ten years, he would avoid active duty unless the President or Congress called his unit into federal service. A college student could meanwhile enroll in a Reserve Officer Training Corps (ROTC) course. This would allow him to spend two or three years on active duty and the remainder of his eight years as a reserve officer.

The system had many weaknesses. No one had to serve in the Army except those who were drafted, and Selective Service quotas dwindled rapidly after the end of the Korean War. Similarly, the armed services found it impossible to accommodate all ROTC graduates for their required active duty. The obligation of those individuals to remain in the Reserve, moreover, carried no requirement for them to enlist in a reserve unit or to participate in continued training. Complicating matters, since the National Guard required no prior preparation for enlistees, Guard units had to spend most of their time drilling recruits. Although the Reserve seemed strong enough on paper, most of its units were unprepared for rapid mobilization in an emergency.

Seeking remedies, Congress passed new legislation in 1955 that reduced the term of obligatory service for reserve enlistees to six years and imposed a requirement for active participation in reserve training on those with an unexpired obligation. It also authorized voluntary enlistment in the Reserve of up to 250,000 young men. These youths would serve six months on active duty followed by seven years in the Reserve. Under the new law, the President could call up to a million ready reservists to active duty in an emergency he alone proclaimed. He could also recall selected members of the Standby Reserve in case of a Congress-declared national emergency.

Whatever the efforts of Congress, in a period of restricted funding and irregular enlistments, many reserve units fell below authorized strength. Responding, the Army concentrated on filling out units it planned to mobilize in the early stages of a conflict. The cure, however, may have been as bad as the ailment. To find enough troops, the service often had no choice but to assign men to units without regard to military specialty. This created imbalances that bore heavily on the ability of some units to deploy. That members of the Ready Reserve Mobilization Reinforcement Pool, which contained individuals never assigned to organized units, failed to keep their parent organizations informed of changes in address or reserve status only made matters worse.

Under the new law, the President could call up to a million ready reservists to active duty in an emergency he alone proclaimed.

Although budget cuts forced the Active Army to lower its manpower ceiling, the Army continued its efforts to strengthen the Reserve. To that end, the Reserve Forces Act of 1955 provided for a total Ready Reserve of 2.9 million by 1970. The Army's share came to about 1.5 million men in 1957—more than 1 million in the Army Reserve and more than 440,000 in the National Guard. Paid drill strengths came to 305,000 and 422,000 men, respectively. The number of Army Reserve divisions fell from 25 to 10 in the reorganization, but manning levels for those forces increased substantially to give the units a higher readiness capability. The number of National Guard divisions rose from 26 to 27. Those changes aside, since the Reserve could never support 37 divisions on a paid drill strength of only 727,000, the ability of those forces to attain combat readiness remained open to serious question.

Convinced that the United States was spending about $80 million a year to sustain reserve units that were of little or no military value, President Eisenhower tried to cut paid drill strength during the late 1950s. With reserve units scattered in congressional districts across the country, however, Congress was loath to do anything of the sort. Instead, it voted a mandatory 700,000 figure in 1959 to force the administration to seek congressional approval before introducing further reductions.

The Changing Face of the Cold War

When President Kennedy assumed office in the opening days of 1961, the prospects for peace were hardly encouraging. The leader of the Soviet Union, Chairman Nikita Khrushchev, had been cool to the United States since the spring of 1960, when a Soviet missile had shot down an American U–2 intelligence-gathering aircraft in Russian airspace. Although the possibility of a general nuclear war had receded by the time Kennedy took office, Soviet support for wars of national liberation had increased.

Kennedy was willing to renew the quest for peace, but he was well aware that the effort might be long and success elusive. In that light, he was determined to give the American armed forces the sort of flexibility that would back the nation's diplomacy with a credible military threat. "Any potential aggressor contemplating an attack on any part of the free world with any kind of weapons, conventional or nuclear," he informed Congress, "must know that our response will be suitable, selective, swift, and effective."

Kennedy's deemphasis of massive retaliation and his stress on the need for ready, nonnuclear forces as a deterrent to limited war came none too soon. By 1961 the tight bipolar system that had developed between the United States and the Soviet Union following World War II was breaking down. Russia's ally in the east, Communist China, had become impatient with Soviet conservatism and strongly opposed to peaceful coexistence. To the west, Fidel Castro was pursuing his own program of intrigue and subversion in Latin America. Complicating matters further, groups favoring the Soviet, the Chinese, or the Cuban brand of communism were emerging in many countries.

Disunion was also mounting within the Western alliance. With the success of the Marshall Plan and the return of economic prosperity

After World War II, Marshall Plan aid to a devastated West Germany enabled that country to surpass its prewar industrial production.

to Western Europe during the fifties, France, West Germany, and other nations had become creditor countries less and less dependent on the United States. The efforts of French President Charles de Gaulle to rekindle his nation's former glory by playing an increasingly independent role in international affairs had meanwhile produced growing discord within NATO.

Outside of Soviet and American circles, the presence of a third force in the world had also become apparent. Most of Europe's former colonial possessions in the Middle East, Asia, and Africa had received their independence during the fifteen years following World War II. Since these new nations contained about one-third of the world's population and a large portion of its raw materials, particularly oil, both sides courted them. Many suffered, however, from basic political and economic failings that made them apt candidates for Communist subversion and wars of national liberation. The great battleground of the sixties would be in "the lands of the rising peoples," Kennedy avowed, and it would involve a conflict "for minds and souls as well as lives and territory." As revolts to end injustice, tyranny, and exploitation broke out, he said, the Communists would inevitably supply arms, agitators, and technicians to capture the rebel movements. The United States could hardly stand by passively and allow them free rein.

With half the world still in the balance; insurgent movements blooming in areas as diverse as Laos, Vietnam, the Congo, and Algeria; and the threat of revolutionary outbreaks hanging over other countries in South America, Africa, and Asia, it was perhaps ironic that President Kennedy's first brush with the Communists would result from American support for an insurgent group.

Cuba and Berlin

The United States had severed diplomatic relations with Cuba during the closing days of the Eisenhower administration, but the presence of a Communist satellite so close to the American mainland remained a constant source of irritation. In April 1961 a band of U.S.-sponsored Cuban exiles moved to remedy that problem by launching an invasion of the island at the Bay of Pigs. When the Cuban people failed to rally in support of the attack, the operation collapsed, damaging American prestige and emboldening the Russians. Khrushchev seized the moment to drop dark hints that he was ready to employ Russian missiles in support of his Communist ally if that became necessary.

The timing of the fiasco was particularly unfortunate. President Kennedy was scheduled to meet with Premier Khrushchev in Vienna during June to discuss Berlin, where the growing prosperity of the Western zone contrasted sharply with the poverty and drabness of the Soviet sector. In that sense West Berlin had become as great an irritation to the Communists as Cuba was to the United States. In 1958 Khrushchev had threatened to conclude a separate treaty with East Germany unless Western forces withdrew from the city within six months. This would have given the Germans sovereignty over the transportation corridors into the area and would have allowed the Soviets to abandon the obligation they had assumed in 1945 to guarantee Western access to the city. Though Khrushchev later backed off from this threat and even showed signs of a conciliatory attitude, he returned to the issue at the Vienna meeting. Unless the West accepted the Soviet position, he informed Kennedy, he would move on his own to resolve the Berlin impasse.

Khrushchev and Kennedy meet in June 1961.

If Khrushchev hoped to intimidate the new President in the wake of the Cuban setback, his threat had the opposite effect. Rather than concede another victory to the Communists, Kennedy requested and received additional defense funds from Congress and authority to call as many as 250,000 members of the Ready Reserve to active duty. The President refrained at that time from declaring a national emergency, but he was determined to strengthen America's conventional forces in case Soviet pressure on Berlin required some sort of armed response.

Tensions mounted during August, when thousands of refugees crossed from East to West Berlin and the Communists responded by constructing a high wall around their sector to block further departures. With pressure rising, Kennedy decided in September to increase the size of the American force by adding ground, air, and naval units. He also called a number of reservists and reserve units to active duty to strengthen continental U.S. forces. By October, as a result, the Army's regular troop strength had grown by more than 80,000 and almost 120,000 troops, including two National Guard divisions, had returned to active duty.

YOU ARE LEAVING THE AMERICAN SECTOR

SIE VERLASSEN DEN AMERIKANISCHEN SEKTOR

US ARMY

Checkpoint Charlie Warning Sign

East Berlin policemen make repairs after an East German citizen rammed the wall with an armored car to escape to West Germany.

When the Soviets realized that the United States might call their bluff, they pulled back. The wall remained, but threats and other pressures diminished. In the same way, Kennedy's Reserve callup had ended by mid-1962 but the increase in the regular force remained.

The Soviets' next move was less direct but more dangerous than the Berlin threat. After the Bay of Pigs invasion, Khrushchev had dispatched military advisers and equipment to Cuba to bolster the Castro government and to repel future attacks. In the summer of 1962 rumors began to rise in the United States that the Soviets were installing offensive weapons: not only medium-range bombers but also medium-range ballistic missiles.

It took until mid-October to obtain photographic evidence of the missiles' presence in Cuba, but then Kennedy took quick steps to have the weapons removed. Warning Khrushchev that the United States would mount a nuclear response if Cuban missiles struck American soil, he put the Strategic Air Command's heavy bombers on fifteen-minute alert. Fighter squadrons and antiaircraft missile batteries meanwhile deployed to Florida and other states near Cuba. Submarines armed with Polaris missiles also took up station at sea within range of the Soviet Union.

On October 22 Kennedy announced that he would seek the endorsement of the Organization of American States (OAS) for quarantine on all offensive military equipment in transit to Cuba. He added that he would tighten surveillance of the island and reinforce the U.S. naval base at Guantanamo on the island's western tip. With OAS approval, the quarantine went into effect two days later. Meanwhile, the armed forces removed all dependents from Guantanamo and marines

THE CUBAN MISSILE CRISIS

In response to the discovery of Russian medium-range ballistic missiles (MRBMs) in Cuba on October 15, 1962, the 82d and 101st Airborne Divisions were alerted for immediate movement to southern Florida. The 1st Armored Division from Fort Hood, Texas, augmented by the 2/69th Armor from Fort Benning, Georgia, deployed to Camp Stewart, Georgia, in preparation for movement by ship. Third Army also established staging areas at five Air Force bases. Three Hawk/Nike Hercules Air Defense (AD) Missile Battalions and one Automatic Weapons AD Battalion were sent to protect the staging bases; while twelve support units, ranging in size from detachment to battalion, also deployed to Florida to provide logistical support. After the end of the crisis in late October, all U.S. Army forces deployed to Florida and Georgia were ordered to return to their home stations.

arrived by air and sea to defend the base. As those steps continued, the Army began to move some 30,000 troops, including the 1st Armored Division, and more than 100,000 tons of supplies and equipment into the southeastern states to meet the emergency. The Navy's Second Fleet started to enforce the quarantine on October 25. Hundreds of Air Force and Navy planes also spread out over the Atlantic and Caribbean to locate and track ships that might be carrying offensive weapons to Cuba. With activity continuing at the Russians' missile construction sites in Cuba, the world seemed on the brink of nuclear war.

As the crisis mounted, negotiations proceeded between Kennedy and Khrushchev. On October 28, after quietly negotiating an "understanding" that the United States would soon remove some obsolete Jupiter missiles from Turkey, the Soviet Union agreed to remove its offensive weapons from Cuba. Over the next three weeks it gradually did so, dismantling the missile sites and loading both missile systems and technicians on ships. Negotiations for the removal of the Russian bombers ended in November. They shipped out for home in early December. In turn, the United States ended the quarantine on November 20. The troops the Army deployed had all returned to base by Christmas, but many U.S. air units remained behind to ensure that the missile sites remained inactive.

Detente in Europe

The aftermath of the crises in Berlin and Cuba produced several unexpected developments. Apparently convinced that further confrontations might be unwise, the Soviet Union adopted a more conciliatory attitude in its propaganda and suggested that at long last it might be willing to conclude a nuclear test ban treaty. Under the provisions of the accord that followed in the fall of 1963, the Soviet Union, the United Kingdom, and the United States agreed to refrain from conducting nuclear test explosions underwater, in the atmosphere, or in space. Only underground explosions would be permissible, but no radioactive material from such tests was ever to reach the surface. Although France weakened the treaty by declining to either ratify or adhere to it, the pact still marked a major breakthrough in what had been a long history of fruitless negotiation over nuclear weapons.

One possible explanation for the Soviet willingness to cooperate with the West in the sixties may have been the growing independence of Communist China. The Chinese had never embraced the idea of peaceful coexistence with Capitalist countries and had criticized Moscow as too soft on the West. As the Sino-Soviet rift had widened, the Soviet Union seemed to adopt a less threatening stance in Europe, although no direct correlation could be proven.

The shift had far-reaching effects on the system of alliances the United States had designed to guard Western Europe against Soviet aggression. The North Atlantic Treaty Organization had centered its defenses on the American strategic deterrent. With the growth of the Soviet Union's ability to devastate the United States with nuclear weapons, the credibility of America's determination to defend Western Europe came into serious question. The reinforcement of U.S. conventional forces in Europe at the time of the Berlin crisis served to demonstrate American good faith.

With the growth of the Soviet Union's ability to devastate the United States with nuclear weapons, the credibility of America's determination to defend Western Europe came into serious question.

271

In 1963 the United States assigned three Polaris submarines to the U.S. European Command and suggested that NATO consider the launch of a multilateral naval force. The idea stood until 1965, when it became clear that President de Gaulle intended to disengage France militarily from NATO. The French cut their ties gradually, participating less and less in the alliance's military exercises while increasing the size of their own nuclear strike force. De Gaulle served notice in 1966 that although France had no intention of abandoning the alliance, French forces would withdraw from NATO command during the year and all NATO troops would have to depart French territory. Conditions had changed in Europe since 1949, he explained. The threat to the West from the Soviet Union had diminished.

De Gaulle's decision marked a major setback for NATO in that the alliance's main headquarters was in Paris and many elaborate lines of communication supporting its forces ran through France. When representations to the French proved fruitless, the exodus of NATO troops got under way. By early 1967 the Supreme Headquarters, Allied Powers Europe (SHAPE), had moved to Belgium; the U.S. European Command had shifted its headquarters to Germany; and the Allied Command Central Europe had transferred to the Netherlands. Supplies and equipment went to bases in the United Kingdom, Belgium, Germany, and the Netherlands.

Changes within the alliance had been slow. Although the idea of massive retaliation no longer held sway except as a last resort, it was not until 1967 that the United States officially adopted a strategy of flexible response. In late 1969 the United States and the Soviet Union opened Strategic Arms Limitation Talks to explore ways to stop the nuclear arms race and to begin the task of disarmament. Progress was slow because of many technical points that had to be settled, but it was a start.

Meanwhile, despite considerable congressional and public opposition, the United States proceeded with plans to deploy a ballistic missile defense system. Known as Safeguard, the program envisioned a phased installation of missiles, radars, and computers at key sites across the country by the mid-1970s. Although the proposed system provided at best a thin line of defense, the United States declined to halt construction until the Strategic Arms Limitation talks had produced an agreement.

A Growing Commitment to Underdeveloped Areas

The American policy of containment met its most serious challenge in Southeast Asia, where Communist efforts to take control of Laos and South Vietnam had gained momentum. Using to advantage the political instability of those countries, the Communists had gradually brought large segments of both under control. Efforts by local governments to regain control through military operations had proven unsuccessful despite the presence of both American advisers and arms. Indeed, the United States soon discovered that the effort to keep Laos and South Vietnam from falling into the Communist camp was even more complicated than it seemed. By the early 1960s, following decades of French rule, many Indochinese leaders were willing to accept American assistance but were plainly unenthusiastic

Although the idea of massive retaliation no longer held sway except as a last resort, it was not until 1967 that the United States officially adopted a strategy of flexible response.

about launching political and economic reforms that might diminish their own power.

Laos was a case in point. Until 1961 the United States had supported the nation's pro-West military leaders with aid and advice; but all efforts to unify the country by force had failed, and three different factions controlled segments of the country. With conditions growing worse, President Kennedy sought to avoid a Communist takeover by pushing for a neutralized Laos. In July 1962 fourteen nations signed a declaration confirming the independence and neutrality of the country, which was to be ruled by a coalition government. Laos in turn pledged to refrain from military alliances and to clear all foreign troops from its territory. By the end of 1962, as a result, more than 600 American advisers and technicians officially had left the country, although covert advisers remained.

By that time, with Communist troops maneuvering in Laos near the Thai border, the United States was also becoming concerned about Thailand, which was part of the Southeast Asia Treaty Organization. To deter Communist expansion into the country, it set up a joint task force at the request of the Thai government, dispatched a reinforced battalion of marines to Thailand, and followed up with a battle group from the 25th Infantry Division. Army signal, engineer, transportation, and service troops provided support for those forces and training and advice to the Thais. The quick response so strengthened the Thai government's position that the Communist threat abated, enabling first the Marine and then the Army troops to withdraw. The service support forces stayed on, however, in order to maintain training and support programs. As the war in Vietnam intensified, the roads, airfields, depots, and communications they built became extremely important to the evolving American effort in that country.

Trouble in the Caribbean

Although Europe and Asia remained critical to America's pursuit of its containment policy, U.S. interest in the Caribbean increased sharply after Cuba embraced communism. As a result, in April 1965, when a military counterrevolution followed a military revolt to oust a civilian junta in the Dominican Republic, the United States kept close tabs on the situation.

When the country's capital city, Santo Domingo, became a bloody battleground and diplomacy failed to restore peace, Kennedy's successor, President Lyndon B. Johnson, decided to send in first the marines and then portions of the Army's 82d Airborne Division. He justified the operation as an effort to restore order while protecting the lives of American nationals, but he also wanted to ensure that Communists would have no chance to gain another foothold in the region. By the end of the first week in May all nine battalions of the airborne division and four battalions of marines were in country, with Army Special Forces units spread throughout the countryside. Including supporting forces, the total number of Americans soon reached 23,000.

The 82d landed to the east of Santo Domingo while the marines consolidated a hold on the western portion of the city. Since the rebel forces held the southern part of town, the American commander, Lt. Gen. Bruce Palmer, Jr., decided to drive a wedge between the warring factions by linking up the two parts of his command. In the operation that followed, using the night as cover, the 82d's troops established a secure corridor across the city with remarkable ease and speed. Joining up with the marines, they rendered further heavy fighting impossible by creating a buffer between the two sides. With combat out of the question, the belligerents began a series of negotiations that lasted until September.

The intervention became the subject of spirited discussion around the world. Despite unfavorable public reactions in some Latin American countries, the Organization of American States asked its members to send troops to the Dominican Republic to help restore order. Brazil, Costa Rica, El Salvador, Honduras, Nicaragua, and Paraguay did so, joining the United States in forming the first inter-American peace-keeping force ever established in the western hemisphere. To emphasize the international nature of the effort, Palmer ceded all command of the operation to Lt. Gen. Hugo Panasco Alvim of Brazil, stepping aside to become Alvim's deputy even though American troops constituted the largest contingent of the force. U.S. troop withdrawals began almost immediately after the Latin American units arrived.

The adoption of a provisional government by both sides in early September relieved much of the problem in the Dominican Republic. By the end of 1965, as a result, all but three battalions of the 82d had returned to the United States. Tensions eased further in mid-1966, when free elections occurred. The last elements of the peacekeeping force departed shortly thereafter in September. In all, the intervention had lasted sixteen months.

Civil Rights and Civil Disturbances

Within the United States itself, meanwhile, tensions growing out of the efforts of African Americans to achieve equal rights had forced the federal government to intervene in civil disturbances on a scale not seen since the nineteenth century. The first and most dramatic instance came in September 1957. Responding to rioting in Little Rock, Arkansas, that had followed a court order admitting nine African American students to the city's Central High School, President Eisenhower federalized the Arkansas National Guard and called in a battle group from the 101st Airborne. The troops dispersed a mob that gathered at the school, stabilizing the situation. It was one of the few times in American history that a Chief Executive had used either Regular Army or National Guard forces despite the opposition of a state's governor.

Other instances of the sort followed during the Kennedy and Johnson administrations. In September 1962, for example, the governor of Mississippi attempted to block the court-ordered registration of an African American, James H. Meredith, at the University of Mississippi in Oxford. President Kennedy sought at first to enforce the law by calling in federal marshals, but when they proved incapable of restoring order, he deployed troops: eventually some 20,000 regulars and 10,000 federalized Mississippi National Guardsmen. Most stood in reserve, but 12,000 took up station near the university. With the military in firm

Soldiers from the 101st Airborne Division escort students to class at Central High School in Little Rock, Arkansas, in 1957.

DOMESTIC DISORDERS

Beginning in the 1950s with civil rights disturbances due to desegregation in the schools and with antiwar riots in the 1960s, the Army gradually increased its efforts in monitoring and controlling domestic disturbances. Troops were involved in desegregation struggles and the preservation of domestic disorder in Little Rock, Arkansas; Oxford, Mississippi; Chicago, Illinois; and other locations throughout the fifties and sixties. When the National Guard, the Federal Bureau of Investigation, and local law enforcement proved unable to provide the necessary security, the Army established a command post in the Pentagon and an elaborate communications system and employed numerous intelligence officers to provide information to President Johnson and his national security team. Accused of spying on civilians, the Army ended its domestic intelligence collection efforts in the mid-1970s.

control, the tension eased. Most of the troops went home within a short while, but federal forces nevertheless maintained a presence in the area throughout the remainder of the school year.

The year that followed provided little respite. Bombings and other racially motivated incidents in Birmingham, Alabama, forced President Kennedy to send regular troops into the city during May. Later in 1963 integration crises in the public schools of several Alabama cities and at the University of Alabama led him to federalize the Alabama National Guard.

Racial disturbances continued to occur throughout the country over the next several years. Particularly serious outbreaks occurred in Rochester, New York, during 1964 and in the Watts area of Los Angeles during 1965. Also that year President Johnson employed both regulars and guardsmen to protect civil rights advocates attempting to march from

Selma to Montgomery, Alabama. Other disturbances followed in 1966 in Cleveland, Ohio; San Francisco, California; and Chicago and Cicero, Illinois. As if that were not enough, the violence increased sharply in 1967, with more than fifty cities reporting disorders during the first nine months of the year. These ranged from minor disturbances to extremely serious outbreaks in Newark, New Jersey, and Detroit, Michigan. The outbreak in Detroit was so destructive that the governor of Michigan not only used the National Guard, he also requested and obtained federal troops. In the end, the task force commander at Detroit had more than 10,000 guardsmen and 5,000 regulars at his call. He deployed nearly 10,000 of them before the crisis ended.

Since disorders were occurring with greater frequency, President Johnson appointed a National Advisory Commission on Civil Disorders on July 28, 1967, to determine the problem's causes and to seek possible cures. Governor Otto Kerner of Illinois chaired it. The Kerner Commission, as it became known, concluded early in 1968 that "our Nation is moving toward two societies, one black and one white— separate and unequal." Concluding in that light that more riots were inevitable and that the National Guard was itself racially imbalanced, the Army strengthened its troop-training programs and began advance planning to control possible future disturbances.

The planning proved all to the good in April 1968, when the assassination of Dr. Martin Luther King, Jr., in Memphis, Tennessee, produced waves of rioting, looting, and arson in cities across the country. The states were able to use their National Guard units to subdue the rioters in most places. The federal government, however, deployed some 40,000 federalized guardsmen and regular troops in Washington, Baltimore, and Chicago.

In the wake of the riots, on April 22 the Army established the Directorate for Civil Disturbance Planning and Operations in the Office of the Chief of Staff. This unit provided command facilities for the service when it operated as agent for the Department of Defense in civil disturbances. It became the Directorate of Military Support in September 1970.

Although the years immediately following 1968 produced no great racial outpourings, they did see a number of antiwar demonstrations that required the callup of both federal and National Guard troops. Massive antiwar protests had begun even before 1968. In October 1967, for example, a large demonstration took place at the Pentagon. In preparation, the government assembled a force that included 236 federal marshals and some 10,000 troops. Massive antiwar protests likewise occurred in Washington, D.C., in November 1969 and May 1970, but these were generally peaceful. Although federal troops stood by in the national capital region, none deployed. Student protests against a U.S. incursion into Cambodia in 1970, however, led to tragedy at Kent State University in Ohio. Panicked National Guardsmen fired on antiwar demonstrators, killing four bystanders and wounding a dozen others.

An extended series of antiwar rallies in the nation's capital during April and May 1971 proved to be of particular significance. On May 1, following a peaceful demonstration by Vietnam veterans, youthful protesters attempted to keep federal workers from reaching their jobs by snarling Washington's traffic. Anticipating the move, the government deployed some 3,000 marines and 8,600 troops of the Regular Army along with 2,000 National Guardsmen who had been sworn in as special policemen. The force kept traffic moving.

Secretary McNamara and the New Management System

The role of the armed forces in civil disturbances received much attention during the Kennedy and early Johnson administrations. Important changes, however, were also occurring in much less publicized areas of military affairs. The period put an end, for example, to the primacy of the manned bomber as the nation's main nuclear deterrent. Following trends already begun during the Eisenhower administration, President Kennedy and his Secretary of Defense, Robert S. McNamara, replaced some of the big aircraft with nuclear missiles. As for the Army, the growth of the Vietnam War brought a reaffirmation that in conventional and limited conflicts ground forces remained supreme. By 1961, as a result, the decline of the Army that had begun during the Eisenhower years ceased. The force began to grow in size, as did its share of the defense budget.

Secretary McNamara

Within the Department of Defense itself, Secretary McNamara began to make heavy use of the extensive authority the holders of his office had received under the reorganization act of 1958. The guidelines he received from President Kennedy were simple: Operating the nation's armed forces at the lowest possible cost, he was to develop the force structure necessary to meet American military requirements without regard to arbitrary or predetermined budget ceilings.

In accord with McNamara's idea of centralized planning, the Joint Chiefs of Staff, assisted by the services, continued to draw up the military plans and force requirements they deemed necessary to support U.S. national security interests. The forces were now separated according to function—strategic retaliation, general purpose, reserves, etc.—with each going into what planners called a program package. When McNamara received these packages, he weighed each against the goal it sought to achieve, correlated the costs and effectiveness of the weapon systems involved, and inserted the approved packages in the annual budget that he sent to the President and Congress. To improve long-range planning, he also drew up and annually reviewed a five-year projection of all forces, weapon systems, and activities that fell within the scope of his authority.

Initially, the Kennedy administration had three basic defense goals: to strengthen strategic forces, to build up conventional forces so they could respond flexibly to lesser challenges, and to improve the overall effectiveness and efficiency of the nation's defenses. To attain the first objective, McNamara supported a nuclear triad that included strategic bombers, intercontinental ballistic missiles in steel-reinforced concrete silos, and Polaris nuclear submarines. If one of the three went down in a Soviet attack, the other two could retaliate.

The second goal gained quick impetus from the Berlin Crisis of 1961, when the Army's strength alone rose from 860,000 troops to more than 1.06 million. Navy and Air Force conventional units also made modest gains. The government released the National Guard units it had called up for the crisis in mid-1962, but it authorized the

Army to reactivate two regular divisions, bringing the total to sixteen. The service also received leave to maintain a permanent strength of 970,000 men. The presence of the new troops allowed many units to fill out their ranks. The Army's budget also rose from $10.1 billion to $12.4 billion in fiscal years 1961 and 1962. Almost half of that increase went for the purchase of such new weapons and equipment as vehicles, aircraft, and missiles.

Seeking greater efficiency at reduced cost, McNamara instituted changes in organization and procedure that made use of the latest management techniques and computer systems. In that way, he directed that the Defense Department's intelligence operations should be centralized and coordinated through one office, which would prepare his intelligence estimates. Following that plan, the Defense Intelligence Agency came into being in 1961.

McNamara also gradually centralized many activities each service formerly administered separately. Since a great number of supply items were in common use, for example, he established the Defense Supply Agency in 1961 to centralize their procurement and distribution. The organization took charge of the Defense Traffic Management Service, some five commodity management systems, and a number of functions involving cataloging and inventory control. The broad range of activities that fell under its supervision included the wholesale purchase and distribution of food, medical supplies, petroleum products, automotive parts, and construction materials.

Tied in closely with the new agency came the launch of a five-year cost reduction program. Designed to cut overhead and procurement expenses, it had three main goals: to buy only what was needed with no frills, to purchase at the lowest sound price after competitive bidding when at all possible, and to decrease operating costs. Centralized purchasing at competitive prices soon became the norm. With it came the consolidation of formerly redundant supply installations, tighter inventory controls through the use of computers, and the elimination of duplication through the standardization of items.

The effects of the 1958 reorganization were most noticeable in the decision-making process. By maintaining close watch over budgets and finances, manpower, logistics, research, and engineering, McNamara tightened civilian control over the services and carried unification much farther than had any of his predecessors. His creation of the U.S. Strike Command in 1961 was a case in point. By combining the Army's Strategic Army Corps with the Air Force's Tactical Air Command, the new organization had combat-ready air and ground forces available that could deploy quickly to meet contingencies. The Army and Air Force components of the new command remained under their own services until an emergency arose. Then they passed to the operational control of the command itself.

Army Reorganization

In view of the changes occurring in the Defense Department, it was hardly surprising in 1961 that Secretary McNamara would also direct a thorough review of the Army's makeup and procedures. A broad reorganization plan resulted. Approved by the President in early 1962, it

By maintaining close watch over budgets and finances, manpower, logistics, research, and engineering, McNamara tightened civilian control over the services and carried unification much farther than had any of his predecessors.

called for major shifts in the tasks performed by the Army Staff and the agency's technical services. The Army Staff became primarily responsible for planning and policy, while the execution of decisions fell squarely upon field commands. In an effort to centralize personnel, training, and research and development while integrating supply operations, the new system abolished most of the technical services. The offices of the Chief Chemical Officer, the Chief of Ordnance, and the Quartermaster General disappeared completely. The Chief Signal Officer and the Chief of Transportation continued to perform their duties, but as special staff officers rather than as chiefs of services. Chief Signal Officer later regained a place on the General Staff when he became Assistant Chief of Staff for Communications-Electronics in 1967. The Chief of Transportation's activities, however, were absorbed in 1964 by the Deputy Chief of Staff for Logistics. For a time, the Chief of Engineers retained his special status only with respect to civil functions. His military functions came under the general supervision of the Deputy Chief of Staff for Logistics. That changed in 1969, when the office again achieved independent status. Among the technical services, only the Office of the Surgeon General emerged unscathed from the reorganization.

As for the administrative services, the Adjutant General and the Chief of Finance also lost their independent status and became special staff officers. Later, in 1967, the functions of the Office of the Chief of Finance transferred to the Office of the Comptroller of the Army. Meanwhile, a new Office of Personnel Operations came into being on the special staff level to provide central control for assignments and the career development of all Army personnel. Although many of the most important Quartermaster functions went to the Defense Supply Agency, a new Chief of Support Services assumed control of graves registration and burials, commissaries, clothing and laundry facilities, and other operations of the sort.

Most of the operating functions released by the Army Staff and the technical services went to the U.S. Continental Army Command and to two new commands: the U.S. Army Materiel Command and the U.S. Army Combat Developments Command. The Continental Army Command became responsible for almost all the Army's schools and for the training of all individuals and units in the United States. It relinquished control over the development, testing, production, procurement, storage, maintenance, and distribution of supplies and equipment to the Army Materiel Command, which set up subordinate commands to handle those functions. The Combat Developments Command meanwhile assumed responsibility for answering questions on the Army's organization and equipment and how it was to fight in the field. It developed organizational and operational doctrine, produced materiel objectives and qualitative requirements, conducted war games and field experiments, and did cost effectiveness studies.

The new commands became operational in the summer of 1962. Over the next year other major changes affecting staff responsibilities followed. In January 1963 an Office of Reserve Components came into being to exercise general supervision over all plans, policies, and programs concerning National Guard and Reserve forces. The responsibility of the Chief, National Guard Bureau, to advise the Chief of Staff on National Guard affairs and to serve as the link between the

Army and the state adjutants general did not change. The Chief of the Army Reserve, however, lost control over the ROTC program. It transferred to the Office of Reserve Components in February and to the Deputy Chief of Staff for Personnel in 1966.

Since the Deputy Chief of Staff for Military Operations (DCSOPS) was heavily involved in planning for joint operations, the Army created in 1963 an Assistant Chief of Staff for Force Development to ensure that its own concerns received adequate attention. The Deputy Chief of Staff for Military Operations continued its role in the joint arena and retained responsibility for strategic planning and the employment of combat-ready Army troops. Under its guidance, however, and within the limits set by manpower and budget considerations, the new office assumed responsibility for preparing the Army's force plans and structures.

Neither the new Assistant Chief of Staff for Force Development nor the Army Comptroller had sufficient authority either to manage the Army's resources or to integrate the service's proliferating automatic data processing systems. Gradually, responsibility for coordinating these functions fell to the General Staff's secretariat, which became almost a "super staff." To remedy the problem, the Army established the Office of the Assistant Vice Chief of Staff in February 1967. Headed by a lieutenant general, the new agency provided centralized control for resource management programs, management information systems, force planning, and weapon system analysis.

Tactical Readjustment for Flexible Response

A major overhaul of the Army's tactical organization accompanied the reorganization of the service's staff. Experience had demonstrated that the pentomic division lacked staying power and that it needed more troops to conduct sustained combat operations. The Army addressed those issues in 1961 by revising its divisional structure to ensure greater flexibility and a better balance between mobility and firepower.

Under the Reorganization Objective Army Division (ROAD) concept it developed, the Army formed four types of divisions: infantry, armor, airborne, and mechanized. Each contained a base and three brigade headquarters. The base contained a headquarters company, a military police company, a reconnaissance squadron, division artillery, and a battalion each of supply and transportation, engineer, signal, medical, and maintenance troops. The size and composition of the remainder of the force could vary with the mission it received. Although a standard ROAD division would normally contain eight infantry and two mechanized battalions, if the need arose and the terrain permitted, it could shuffle the composition of its brigades to reduce its infantry component and to add armored and mechanized units. When operating in swamps, jungles, or other hostile environments, however, it could just as easily replace its mechanized units with infantry battalions.

The Army tested the idea in 1962 by reactivating its 1st Armored and 5th Infantry (Mechanized) Divisions. When the idea worked, beginning in 1963, it set to work to convert its remaining fourteen divisions and to reorganize the National Guard and Army Reserve. It completed the process in mid-1964.

Experience had demonstrated that the pentomic division lacked staying power and that it needed more troops to conduct sustained combat operations.

THE HOWZE BOARD

In 1962 the U.S. Army Tactical Mobility Requirements Board, better known by the name of its president, Lt. Gen. Hamilton Howze, proposed forming an air assault division. Capitalizing on the unique mobility conferred by the new generation of turbine-powered helicopters, the new division would contain enough helicopters to lift one of its three brigades at one time. The 11th Air Assault Division successfully tested the concept at Fort Benning in 1963 and 1964. Redesignated as the 1st Cavalry Division (Airmobile), it proved itself in combat in Vietnam during the Ia Drang Valley campaign of November 1965.

By then, it was hard at work on another tactical innovation. Seeking to improve mobility, an Army board in 1962 had compared the cost and efficiency of air and ground vehicles. Concluding that air transportation had much to commend it, the group recommended that the service consider forming new air combat and transport units. The idea that an air assault division employing air-transportable weapons and aircraft-mounted rockets might replace artillery raised delicate questions about the Air Force and Army missions, but Secretary McNamara decided to give it a thorough test.

Organized in February 1963, the 11th Air Assault Division went through two years of testing. By the spring of 1965, the Army deemed it ready for a test in combat and decided to send it to Vietnam, where the war was heating up. To that end, the service inactivated the 11th and transferred its personnel and equipment to the 1st Cavalry Division, which relinquished its mission in Korea to the 2d Infantry Division and moved to Fort Benning, Georgia. Renamed the 1st Cavalry Division (Airmobile), the reorganized unit had an authorized strength of 15,787 men, 428 helicopters, and 1,600 road vehicles (half the number of an infantry division). Though the total of rifles and automatic weapons in the unit remained the same as in an infantry division, the force's direct-support artillery moved by helicopter rather than truck or armored vehicle. In the same way, it employed an aerial rocket artillery battalion rather than the normal tube artillery. In all, the division's total weight came to just 10,000 tons, less than a third of what a normal infantry division deployed.

The development of the air assault division was part of a long-term effort by the Army to improve its aviation capabilities. Although Army–Air Force agreements and decisions at the Defense Department level during the 1950s had restricted the size and weight of Army aircraft and had limited the areas in which they could operate, the service possessed more than 5,500 aircraft in its inventory by 1960. Close to half of them were helicopters. The versatility of the rotary-wing aircraft made them ideal for observation and reconnaissance, medical evacuation, and command and control missions. Under the Army's agreements with the Air Force, all these activities were permissible on the battlefield. When the service moved to provide itself with armed helicopters as it had with the 1st Cavalry Division, however, it inevitably raised questions with the Air Force, which considered the provision of airborne fire support its own function.

The two services reassessed and reapportioned their role and mission assignments in 1966. The Army ceded its larger transport aircraft to the Air Force but kept control of its helicopters because of their demonstrated value to ground combat operations. Although its inventory of fixed-wing aircraft declined slightly over the years that followed, because of the war the number of its helicopters soared from about 2,700 in 1966 to over 9,500 in mid-1971.

The war also accelerated the development of many new and improved Army aircraft models. Among them were the Huey Cobra, a gunship that could carry various combinations of rockets, machine guns, and 7.62-mm. miniguns; the Cayuse, an observation helicopter; and the Cheyenne, the first helicopter specifically designed to provide fire support to ground troops. Advances also occurred in support systems, equipment design, communications, command and control, and intelligence gathering. Drawing everything together was a rapidly expanding complex of computer networks that improved coordination of everything the Army did, from personnel management to the operation of elaborate logistical systems in the field.

Though the soldier's professional skills required continual resharpening, battlefield proficiency was only part of the Army's task. Military victories might gain real estate; but as the war in Vietnam showed, they were of little consequence in counterinsurgency environments unless the victors won the support of local populations. The main goal in conflicts such as the one in Vietnam was less to destroy the enemy than to convince the target area's common people that their government had their best interests in mind. With that goal in hand, victory would be permanent. Without it, nothing was sure because the enemy retained his base within the population.

Civic action and counterinsurgency operations were nothing new to the U.S. Army. They had figured large in the opening of the American West and in the pacification of the Philippines following the Spanish-American War. During the occupations of Germany and Japan after World War II, indeed, economic assistance and political and educational reorientation programs had simplified the problem of reconstituting civil authority. In underdeveloped countries, however, the task was usually much more difficult because communications were poor and the bonds between central authorities and rural groups were seldom strong. The Army needed specially trained military units capable of operating independently and working with indigenous people at the lowest level of their society.

Though the Army had trained small units in psychological warfare and counterinsurgency operations during the fifties, President Kennedy's interest in the program gave the effort a significant boost. The U.S. Army Special Forces expanded sharply after he became President: from 1,500 to 9,000 men in 1961 alone. Even more important, new emphasis in Army schools and camps provided all soldiers with basic instruction in counterinsurgency techniques.

The Special Forces helped train local forces to fight guerrillas, teaching them skills that would help strengthen their nations internally. Each Special Forces Group was oriented toward a specific geographic area and received language training to facilitate its operations in the field. The groups were augmented with whatever aviation, engineer,

Drawing everything together was a rapidly expanding complex of computer networks that improved coordination of everything the Army did, from personnel management to the operation of elaborate logistical systems in the field.

medical, civil affairs, intelligence, communications, psychological warfare, military police, or other elements they needed to complete particular assignments. If necessary, individual members of the teams also received training in other skills to increase their versatility. Overall, by working on a person-to-person basis, the Special Forces strove to improve the good image of a government's armed forces to foster cooperative attitudes among that nation's rural people.

Reserve forces also received special warfare training so they could remain current with counterinsurgency doctrine and the most up-to-date means for neutralizing internal aggression and subversion. One phase of this training—crowd and riot control tactics—became of particular importance during the period because of a growing threat of civil disturbance within the United States itself.

The Reserve Forces and the Draft

Concerned over the expenditure of defense funds for Reserves that were long on numbers but short on readiness, in 1962 Secretary McNamara announced a plan to reorganize the Army National Guard and to lower the paid drill strength of the Army Reserve. Opposition from Congress and many state officials led him to delay the move until the following year. When he finally acted, however, he not only realigned reserve forces, he also eliminated four National Guard divisions, four Army Reserve divisions, and hundreds of smaller units.

At the end of 1964 McNamara proposed a far more drastic reorganization to bring the Reserves into balance with the nation's contingency war planning. Contending that the National Guard–Army Reserve management system was redundant, he suggested that the Army could trim paid drill strength from 700,000 to 550,000 by consolidating units. He proposed to eliminate fifteen National Guard and six Army Reserve divisions for which there was no military requirement. All remaining units would come under the National Guard. The Army Reserve would carry only individuals.

A storm of protest rose from Congress, the states, and reserve associations. With the debate continuing, McNamara sought to carry out at least part of his reorganization by inactivating Army Reserve units that had no role in contingency war plans. Despite strong congressional opposition, he managed by the end of 1965 to eliminate all six Army Reserve combat divisions and a total of 751 company- and detachment-size units. In the end, during the fall of 1967, Congress and the Department of Defense agreed on a compromise plan that achieved McNamara's basic objectives. Under the new structure, the Army Reserve retained all its training and support units but only three combat brigades. Its paid drill strength fell from 300,000 to 260,000. Army National Guard strength continued at 400,000 men. While the number of its separate brigades rose from 7 to 18, however, the total of its divisions fell from 23 to 8. All the units in the Guard and Reserve were to run at 93 percent or better of their wartime strength, and each was to have a full supply of whatever equipment, spare parts, and technical support it needed.

To obtain the troops necessary to fill out the Reserve, Congress revised the Reserve Forces Act of 1955 in September 1963. The new law provided for direct enlistment—an optional feature of the 1955 act—and reduced the term of obligated service from eight to six years. The length of the initial tour ranged from four to seven months, depending upon the particular military specialty a recruit was entering and how much training it required.

As McNamara's reorganization continued, the Army revised the ROTC program to improve the flow of qualified officers into both the Active Army and the Army Reserve. Beginning in 1964, it strengthened the four-year program at colleges and universities by providing for scholarships. It also added a two-year program for students who had been unable to complete the first two years of ROTC but who had undergone the six weeks of field training necessary for entrance into the advanced course, which covered the final two years of college. Beginning in 1966, Congress also authorized the military departments to establish junior ROTC programs at qualified public and private secondary schools.

Although most newly commissioned National Guard officers were products of state-run officer candidate schools, the ROTC was the primary source of new officers for both the Regular Army and the Army Reserve between 1965 and 1970. Cutbacks in Active Army officer requirements from 1971 on led to the release of most ROTC graduates from their agreement to perform a two-year stint on active duty. Instead, following three to six months' training, they were released to the Army National Guard or the Army Reserve.

The Army buildup for the war in Vietnam created pressure for a reserve callup to fill in for the regular troops and draftees going overseas. President Johnson declined to make the move, however, preferring to avoid the discussion of the war and its goals that would have accompanied the callup. Instead, the Army established a Selected Reserve Force in August 1965 to provide for the quick response to emergencies that the Regular Army had always supplied. It contained over 150,000 men—about 119,000 National Guardsmen and 31,000 Army Reservists—and consisted of three divisions and six separate brigades with combat and service support elements. All were to maintain 100 percent strength, received extra training, and had priority in equipment allocation. The Army abolished the force in September 1969, when the United States began to draw down in Vietnam.

By mid-April 1968 a budding democratic revolution in Soviet-dominated Czechoslovakia, Communist provocations in Korea, and the Tet offensive in Vietnam had increased world tensions to such a level that President Johnson finally decided to mobilize a portion of the Army's Ready Reserve. He specified, however, that the deployment was to last for no more than twenty-four months, and he kept as small as possible the number of men involved: some 19,874. Of the 76 Army National Guard and Army Reserve units mobilized, 43 went to Vietnam and 33 to the Strategic Army Forces. As with earlier mobilizations, peacetime failures to attain training objectives and shortages of equipment prevented many of the units from meeting readiness objectives upon activation. Even so, the effort succeeded where it mattered most, in providing temporary augmentation for the strategic reserve and deploying troops to Vietnam much sooner than would have been possible with new recruits. The callup ended in December 1969, when the last of the units involved returned to reserve status.

Only a three-month lull intervened, however, before President Johnson's successor, President Richard M. Nixon, decided he had no choice but to call upon the Reserves and National Guard again. On March 18, 1970, New York City mail carriers began an unauthorized work stoppage that threatened to halt essential postal services. Nixon declared a national emergency on the twenty-third, paving the way for a partial mobilization the next day. This time, more than 18,000 National Guard and Army Reserve members saw service, working with other regular and reserve forces to get the mail through. The postal workers soon returned to work, and by April 3 the last of the reservists had returned to civilian status.

The phase-down of U.S. military operations in Vietnam and accompanying cutbacks in active-force levels caused the nation to place renewed reliance on its reserve forces. As early as November 1968 Congress had passed the reserve forces "Bill of Rights." The act gave the service secretaries responsibility for developing reserve forces capable of attaining peacetime training goals and of meeting mobilization readiness objectives. The act also established positions for Assistant Secretaries for Manpower and Reserve Affairs within each of the military departments and gave statutory status to the position of Chief of the Army Reserve.

By mid-1971 the Defense Department was planning for yet another reorganization of the Reserves to bring them into line with organizational concepts developed during the Vietnam War. Since the President had declined to call up the reserve forces in the early stages of the conflict, the main burden of meeting the Army's need for manpower in Vietnam had fallen upon the Selective Service. The increased draft calls and voluntary enlistments that followed had swelled the Army from 970,000 troops in mid-1965 to over 1.5 million in 1968.

The approach might not have mattered in a popular war. As the conflict in Vietnam lengthened, however, and opposition to it grew, reliance upon the Selective Service to meet the Army's requirements for manpower drew criticism from both Congress and the public. That the Army could never have absorbed all the men available for service at the time figured little in the debate. The nub of the matter was that the system seemed unfair because it selected some for service while exempting others. Playing to the trend, Nixon promised to end the draft during his campaign for President in 1968. True to his word, in late 1969 he introduced a lottery system that eliminated most deferments but limited the period of eligibility to one year. It was a poor but necessary compromise. Elimination of the draft in favor of an all-volunteer Army in the midst of an ongoing war seemed impossible.

Problems and Prospects

Since the Army was drawn from the American people and reflected their society, it had to deal with the same social problems that confronted the nation as the war lengthened. The polarization of opinion over the war in Vietnam, increasing drug abuse by America's young, and mounting racial tensions within the United States all took their toll.

The widespread opposition to the war in Vietnam that swept college campuses in the late sixties made its way into the Army, where

> Since the President had declined to call up the reserve forces in the early stages of the conflict, the main burden of meeting the Army's need for manpower in Vietnam had fallen upon the Selective Service.

some soldiers participated in demonstrations, formed protest groups, or circulated antiwar literature. While soldier dissent was hardly new to the American military, the dissidence generated by the Vietnam War was more explicit than ever before. Even so—if instances of indiscipline proliferated in Vietnam and a scattering of highly publicized combat refusals occurred—the vast majority of the troops did their duty commendably and without demur.

Increasing drug abuse by young people in the United States also caused problems for the Army, particularly since many recruits had already been exposed to drugs before entering the service. The low cost and easy availability of narcotics in Vietnam complicated matters, as did the loose enforcement procedures of local Vietnamese authorities, who often were themselves involved in the drug trade. The situation became so bad by the end of American involvement in the war that medics were evacuating more soldiers for drug problems than for wounds. The Army conducted massive drug information campaigns to warn potential abusers of the dangers. In an attempt to identify and treat heavy abusers before they returned home, it also initiated a program of urine testing in 1971 for all soldiers leaving South Vietnam. Those who failed became subject to immediate detoxification then received followup treatment on arrival in the United States. Those efforts notwithstanding, the problem continued for years, receding only gradually as those prone to drug abuse left the Army and a new force of carefully screened volunteers took their place.

Racial discrimination was another pressing problem that plagued the nation and the Army as the conflict in Vietnam lengthened. The service had desegregated during the Korean War, insisting that all soldiers receive equal treatment regardless of their race. Over the years that followed, despite the bitter civil rights struggle of the sixties, it opened up recreational facilities to all soldiers and made considerable progress in securing adequate off-post housing for its African Americans. Commanders took pride in that record. By the time of the Vietnam War, most felt confident that they had at least their portion of the problem under control.

The war proved them mistaken. Many of the soldiers who joined the Army during the period came from racially prejudiced backgrounds and maintained their beliefs. Racial divisions tended to disappear in combat because of the common danger and the need to work together for survival. In the rear, however, race relations were sometimes just as uneasy and disjointed as they were in many American cities. One African-American chaplain commented that the troops would "go out on missions and the racism would drop.... and they'd come back to the compound and kill each other. I didn't understand it." It took some time for Army commanders to recognize that they had a problem; but once they did, they worked hard to build the confidence of African Americans in the fairness of the service's promotion and judicial systems and to foster better communication between the groups. In the end, however, as with drugs, the Army had a race problem because America had a race problem. Long-term solutions depended upon the success of national efforts to achieve racial equality.

The Army faced many challenges in the fifties and sixties, not the least of which was the search for a mission that would garner sufficient

It took some time for Army commanders to recognize that they had a problem; but once they did, they worked hard to build the confidence of African Americans in the fairness of the service's promotion and judicial systems and to foster better communication.

resources to maintain a core of well-trained ground forces ready for a variety of missions. The Army found it difficult to compete with the new glamour of the Air Force and the Navy with their strategic deterrence missions. At the close of the Korean War, the American urge to avoid all future ground combat and rely, again, upon "cost-effective" strategic forces with their alluring prospects of "push button" war, had been too seductive a picture for a succession of budget-conscious administrations. "More bang for the buck" and the overarching strategic deterrence mission drove the budget and the outlook of much of the political and military establishments and had led them down numerous blind alleys of poorly conceived reorganizations and abortive technologies. Yet the greatest threat to maintaining the credibility of U.S. deterrence in the 1960s was to come not from the arms race or from competing strategic forces, but in the jungles of Southeast Asia, in the small country of South Vietnam.

Discussion Questions

1. What was the New Look? How new do you think it really was?

2. How much defense spending do you think was justified during the Cold War? Which programs were cost-effective?

3. Why did the Army adopt the pentomic organization? Why did it later drop the approach? What had changed?

4. What were the similarities and differences between the Cold War in the late 1940s and the one that prevailed during the late 1950s? Compare and contrast how the United States responded to the challenges that arose during the two periods.

5. What was flexible response? What practical consequences did the strategy have for the Army? How did this differ from massive retaliation? How did the flexible response help or hinder deterrence?

6. What roles did the Kennedy and Johnson administrations envision for the reserve components? How did Johnson's approach to the Vietnam War affect them?

Recommended Readings

Cole, Alice C., et al., eds. *Documents on Establishment and Organization, 1944–1978.* Washington, D.C.: Office of the Secretary of Defense, Historical Office, 1978.

Gavin, James M. *War and Peace in the Space Age.* New York: Harper, 1958.

Hewes, James E., Jr. *From Root to McNamara: Army Organization and Administration, 1900–1963.* Washington, D.C.: U.S. Army Center of Military History, 1983, chs. 8–10.

Kinnard, Douglas. *The Certain Trumpet, Maxwell Taylor & the American Experience in Vietnam.* New York: Brassey's, 1991, Preface, chs. 1–4.

Kissinger, Henry A. *Nuclear Weapons and Foreign Policy.* Boulder, Colo.: Westview Press, 1984, chs. 2, 12.

McNamara, Robert S. *In Retrospect: The Tragedy and Lessons of Vietnam.* New York: Times Books, 1995, chs. 1–4.

Osgood, Robert E. Limited War: *The Challenge to American Strategy.* Chicago: University of Chicago Press, 1957, chs. 1, 9, 10.

Palmer, Bruce, Jr. *Intervention in the Caribbean: The Dominican Crisis of 1965.* Lexington: University Press of Kentucky, 1989.

Ridgway, Matthew B. *Soldier: The Memoirs of Matthew B. Ridgway.* Westport, Conn.: Greenwood Press, 1974, chs. 30–38.

Spector, Ronald H. *Advice and Support, The Early Years, 1941–1960.* U.S. Army in Vietnam. Washington, D.C.: U.S. Army Center of Military History, 1985.

Taylor, Maxwell D. *The Uncertain Trumpet.* Westport, Conn.: Greenwood Press, 1974, chs. 3, 4, 8.

Wilson, John. *Maneuver and Firepower: The Evolution of Divisions and Separate Brigades.* Army Lineage Series. Washington, D.C.: U.S. Army Center of Military History, 1998, chs. 9–11.

Yates, Lawrence A. *Power Pack: U.S. Intervention in the Dominican Republic, 1965–1966.* Fort Leavenworth, Kans.: U.S. Army Command and General Staff College, Combat Studies Institute, 1988.

Other Readings

Acheson, Dean. *Power and Diplomacy.* Cambridge: Harvard University Press, 1958.

Dallek, Robert. *An Unfinished Life, John F. Kennedy, 1917–1963.* New York: Little Brown and Co., 2003.

Doubler, Michael D. *Civilian in Peace, Soldier in War: The Army National Guard, 1636–2000.* Lawrence: University Press of Kansas, 2003.

Gaddis, John L. *Strategies of Containment: a Critical Appraisal of Postwar American National Security Policy.* New York: Oxford University Press, 1982.

———. *We Now Know: Rethinking Cold War History.* New York: Oxford University Press, 1997.

Howze, Hamilton. *A Cavalryman's Story: Memoirs of a Twentieth-Century Army General.* Washington, D.C.: Smithsonian Institution Press, 1996.

Kahn, Herman. *On Thermonuclear War.* Westport, Conn.: Greenwood Press, 1978.

Kaplan, Lawrence. *The Long Entanglement: NATO's First Fifty Years.* Westport, Conn.: Praeger, 1999.

Kinnard, Douglas. *President Eisenhower and Strategy Management, A Study in Defense Politics.* New York: Pergamom-Brassey's, 1989.

Millis, Walter. *Arms and Men: A Study in American Military History.* New Brunswick, N.J.: Rutgers University Press, 1981, ch. 7.

Shapley, Deborah. *Promise and Power: The Life and Times of Robert McNamara.* New York: Little, Brown, 1993.

10

THE U.S. ARMY IN VIETNAM BACKGROUND, BUILDUP, AND OPERATIONS, 1950–1967

The Vietnam War was complex in its origins and followed France's failure to suppress nationalist forces in Indochina as it struggled to restore its colonial dominion after World War II. Led by Ho Chi Minh, a Communist-dominated revolutionary movement, the Viet Minh, waged a political and military struggle for Vietnamese independence that frustrated the efforts of the French and resulted ultimately in their ouster from the region.

The U.S. Army's first encounters with Ho Chi Minh were brief and generally sympathetic. During World War II, Ho's anti-Japanese resistance fighters helped to rescue downed American pilots and furnished information on Japanese forces in Indochina. U.S. Army officers stood at Ho's side in August 1945 as he basked in the short-lived satisfaction of declaring Vietnam's independence. Five years later, however, in an international climate tense with ideological and military confrontation between Communist and non-Communist powers, Army advisers of the newly formed U.S. Military Assistance Advisory Group (MAAG), Indochina, were aiding France against the Viet Minh. With combat raging in Korea and mainland China having recently fallen to the Communists, the war in Indochina now appeared to Americans as one more pressure point to be contained on a wide arc of Communist expansion in Asia. By underwriting French military efforts in Southeast Asia, the United States enabled France to sustain its economic recovery and to contribute, through the North Atlantic Treaty Organization (NATO), to the collective defense of Western Europe.

Provided with aircraft, artillery, tanks, vehicles, weapons, and other equipment and supplies, a small portion of which they distributed to an anti-Communist Vietnamese army they had organized, the French did not fail for want of equipment. Instead, they put American aid at the service of a flawed strategy that sought to defeat the elusive Viet Minh in set-piece battles but neglected to cultivate the loyalty and support of the Vietnamese people. Too few in number to provide more than a veneer of security in most rural areas, the French were unable to suppress the guerrillas or to prevent the underground Communist shadow government from reappearing whenever French forces left one area to fight elsewhere.

The French fought the last and most famous of the set-piece battles in Indochina at Dien Bien Phu. Located near the Laotian border in a rugged valley in remote northwestern Vietnam, Dien Bien Phu was far from the coast and depended almost entirely on air resupply. The French, expecting the Viet Minh to invade Laos, occupied Dien Bien Phu in November 1953 to force a battle. They established their positions in a valley surrounded by high ground that the Viet Minh quickly fortified. While bombarding the besieged garrison with artillery and mortars, the attackers tunneled closer to the French positions. Supply aircraft that successfully ran the gauntlet of intense antiaircraft fire risked destruction on the ground from Viet Minh artillery. Eventually, supplies and ammunition could be delivered to the defenders only by parachute drop. As the situation became critical, France asked the United States to intervene. Believing that the French position was untenable and that even massive American air attacks using small nuclear bombs would be futile, General Matthew B. Ridgway, the Army Chief of Staff, helped to convince President Dwight D. Eisenhower not to aid them. Ridgway also opposed the use of U.S. ground forces, arguing that such an effort would severely strain the Army and possibly lead to a wider war in Asia.

Dien Bien Phu surrendered on May 7, 1954, just as peace negotiations were about to start in Geneva. On July 20 France and the Viet Minh agreed to end hostilities and to divide Vietnam temporarily into two zones at the 17th Parallel. (*Map 14*) In the North, the Viet Minh established a Communist government with its capital at Hanoi. French forces withdrew to the South; hundreds of thousands of civilians, most of whom were Roman Catholics, accompanied them. The question of unification was left to be decided by an election scheduled for 1956.

The Emergence of South Vietnam

As the Viet Minh consolidated control in the North, Ngo Dinh Diem, a Roman Catholic of mandarin background, sought to assert his authority over the chaotic conditions in South Vietnam in hopes of establishing an anti-Communist state. A one-time minister in the French colonial administration, Diem enjoyed a reputation for honesty. He had resigned his office in 1933 and had taken no part in the tumultuous events that swept over Vietnam after World War II. Diem returned to Saigon in the summer of 1954 as premier with no political following except his family and a few Americans. His authority was challenged, first by the independent Hoa Hao and Cao Dai religious sects and then by the Binh Xuyen, an organization of gangsters that controlled Saigon's gambling dens and brothels and had strong influence with the police. Rallying an army, Diem defeated the sects and gained their grudging allegiance. Remnants of their forces fled to

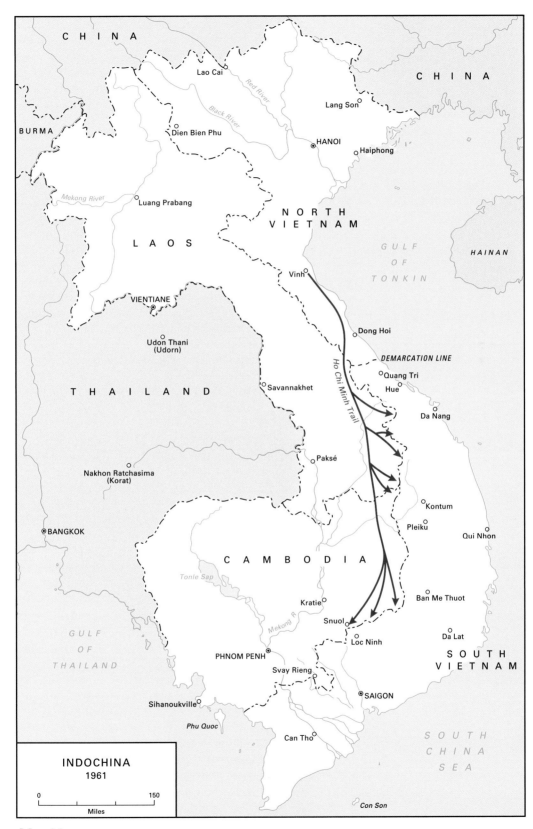

CHINA

Lao Cai

Red River

Black River

CHINA

Lang Son

BURMA

Dien Bien Phu

HANOI

Haiphong

Mekong River

Luang Prabang

NORTH
VIETNAM

GULF
OF
TONKIN

HAINAN

LAOS

Vinh

VIENTIANE

Dong Hoi

DEMARCATION LINE

Udon Thani
(Udorn)

Savannakhet

Quang Tri

Hue

Ho Chi Minh Trail

Da Nang

THAILAND

Paksé

Kontum

Nakhon Ratchasima
(Korat)

Pleiku

Qui Nhon

BANGKOK

CAMBODIA

Tonle Sap

Ban Me Thuot

Kratie

Mekong R.

Snuol

Da Lat

GULF
OF
THAILAND

Loc Ninh

SOUTH
VIETNAM

PHNOM PENH

Svay Rieng

SAIGON

Sihanoukville

SOUTH

Phu Quoc

Can Tho

CHINA

SEA

Con Son

INDOCHINA
1961

0   150

Miles

Map 14

NGO DINH DIEM (1901–1963)

Diem, a Catholic from the imperial city of Hue in central Vietnam, knew when he became leader of South Vietnam in 1954 that his base of support was thin in that mostly Buddhist country. He therefore entrusted close family members, most notably his shrewd and secretive brother Ngo Dinh Nhu and Nhu's beautiful and outspoken wife Madame Nhu, to run the most important parts of the government while he used a combination of political favors and strong-arm tactics to keep his rivals weak and divided. For Diem, the Viet Cong were but one of many dangers to his regime.

President Diem meets with village elders.

the jungle to continue their resistance; some at a later date became the nucleus of Communist guerrilla units.

Diem was also challenged by members of his own army, where French influence persisted among the highest-ranking officers. But he weathered the threat of an army coup, dispelling American doubts about his ability to survive in the jungle of Vietnamese politics. For the next few years, the American commitment to defend South Vietnam's independence was synonymous with support for Diem. Americans now provided advice and support to the Army of the Republic of Vietnam; at Diem's request, they replaced French advisers throughout his nation's military establishment.

As the American role in South Vietnam was growing, U.S. defense policy was undergoing review. Officials in the Eisenhower administration believed that wars like those in Korea and Vietnam were too costly and ought to be avoided in the future. "Never again" was the rallying cry of those who opposed sending U.S. ground forces to fight a conventional war in Asia. Instead, the Eisenhower administration relied on the threat or use of massive nuclear retaliation to deter or, if necessary, to defeat the armies of the Soviet Union or Communist China. Ground forces were relegated to a minor role, and mobilization was regarded as an unnecessary luxury. In consequence, the Army's share of the defense budget declined, the modernization of its forces was delayed, and its strength was reduced by 40 percent: from 1,404,598 in 1954 to 861,964 in 1956.

General Ridgway and his successor, General Maxwell D. Taylor, opposed the Eisenhower administration's new strategy. Both advocated balanced forces to enable the United States to cope realistically with a variety of military contingencies. The events of the late 1950s appeared to support their demand for flexibility. The United States intervened in Lebanon in 1958 to restore political stability there. That same year an American military show of force in the Straits of Taiwan helped to dampen tensions between Communist China and the Nationalist Chinese government on Taiwan. Both contingencies underlined the importance of avoiding any fixed concept of war.

Advocates of the flexible-response doctrine foresaw a meaningful role for the Army as part of a more credible deterrent and as a means of intervening, when necessary, in limited and small wars. They wished to strengthen both conventional and unconventional forces, to improve strategic and tactical mobility, and to maintain troops and equipment at forward bases close to likely areas of conflict. They placed a premium on highly responsive command and control to allow a close meshing of military actions with political goals. The same reformers were deeply interested in the conduct of brushfire wars, especially among the underdeveloped nations. In the so-called Third World, competing Cold War ideologies and festering nationalistic, religious, and social conflicts interacted with the disruptive forces of modernization to create the preconditions for open hostilities. Southeast Asia was one of several such areas the Army identified. Here, the United States' central concern was the threat of North Vietnamese and perhaps Chinese aggression against South Vietnam and other non-Communist states.

The United States took the lead in forming a regional defense pact, the Southeast Asia Treaty Organization, signaling its commitment to contain Communist encroachment in the region. Meanwhile, the 342 American advisers of MAAG, Vietnam (which replaced MAAG, Indochina, in 1955), trained and organized Diem's fledgling army to resist an invasion from the North. Three MAAG chiefs—Lt. Gens. John W. O'Daniel, Samuel T. Williams, and Lionel C. McGarr—reorganized South Vietnam's light mobile infantry groups into infantry divisions compatible in design and mission with U.S. defense plans. The South Vietnamese Army, with a strength of about 150,000, was equipped with standard U.S. Army equipment and given the mission of delaying the advance of any invasion force until the arrival of American reinforcements. The residual influence of the army's earlier French training, however, lingered in both leadership and tactics. The South Vietnamese had little or no practical experience in administration and the higher staff functions from which the French had excluded them.

The MAAG's training and reorganization work was often interrupted by Diem's using his army to conduct pacification campaigns to root out stay-behind Viet Minh cadre. Hence responsibility for most internal security was transferred to poorly trained and ill-equipped paramilitary forces, the Civil Guard and Self-Defense Corps, which numbered about 75,000. For the most part, the Viet Minh in the South avoided armed action and subscribed to a political action program in anticipation of Vietnam-wide elections in 1956, as stipulated by the Geneva Accords. But Diem, supported by the United States, refused to hold elections, claiming that undemocratic conditions in the North precluded a fair contest. (Some observers thought Ho Chi Minh sufficiently popular in the South to defeat Diem.) Buoyed by his own election as President in 1955 and by the adulation of his American supporters, Diem's political strength rose to its apex. While making some political and economic reforms, he pressed hard his attacks on political opponents and former Viet Minh, many of whom were not Communists at all but patriots who had joined the movement to fight for Vietnamese independence.

HO CHI MINH
(1890–1969)

All his adult life Nguyen Tat Thanh, who used the pseudonym Ho Chi Minh, was a devoted Nationalist. Settling in Paris following World War I, Ho gained renown as the author of a petition to the Allies gathered at Versailles demanding independence for all countries under colonial rule. (The petition was ignored.) Over the next decade Ho's ideology evolved through travels in China and the USSR, and in 1930 he helped form the Indochina Communist Party. Following World War II, Ho became the first president of a provisional Communist government in Vietnam and fought to expel the French. He succeeded in 1954, only to have international politics divide Vietnam in two.

By 1957 Diem's harsh measures had so weakened the Viet Minh that Communist leaders in the South feared for the movement's survival there. The Southerners urged their colleagues in the North to sanction a new armed struggle in South Vietnam. For self-protection, some Viet Minh had fled to secret bases to hide and form small units. Others joined renegade elements of the former sect armies. From bases in the mangrove swamps of the Mekong Delta, in the Plain of Reeds near the Cambodian border, and in the jungle of War Zones C and D north of Saigon, the Communists began to rebuild their armed forces, to reestablish an underground political network, and to carry out propaganda, harassment, and terrorist activities to advance their goals and undermine the people's faith in their government's ability to protect them. As reforms faltered and Diem became more dictatorial, the ranks of the rebels swelled with the politically disaffected.

The Rise of the Viet Cong

The insurgents, now called the Viet Cong, had by 1959 organized several companies and a few battalions, the majority in the Mekong Delta and the provinces around Saigon. As Viet Cong military strength increased, attacks against the paramilitary forces, and occasionally against the South Vietnamese Army, became more frequent. The guerrillas conducted many to seize equipment, arms, and ammunition but flaunted all their successes as evidence of the government's inability to protect its citizens. Political agitation and military activity also quickened in the Central Highlands, where Viet Cong agents recruited among the Montagnard tribes. In 1959, after assessing conditions in the South, the leaders in Hanoi agreed to resume the armed struggle, giving it equal weight with political efforts to undermine Diem and reunify Vietnam. To attract the growing number of anti-Communists opposed to Diem, as well as to provide a democratic facade for administering the party's policies in areas controlled by the Viet Cong, North Vietnam in December 1960 created the National Liberation Front of South Vietnam. The revival of guerrilla warfare in the South found the advisory group, the South Vietnamese Army, and Diem's government ill prepared to wage an effective campaign. In their efforts to train and strengthen Diem's army, U.S. advisers had concentrated on meeting the threat of a conventional North Vietnamese invasion. The South Vietnamese Army's earlier antiguerrilla campaigns, while seemingly successful, had confronted only a weak and dormant insurgency. The Civil Guard and Self-Defense Corps, which bore the brunt of the Viet Cong's attacks, were not under the MAAG's purview and proved unable to cope with the audacious Viet Cong. Diem's regime, while stressing military activities, neglected political, social, and economic reforms. American officials disagreed over the seriousness of the guerrilla threat, the priority to be accorded political or military measures, and the need for special counterguerrilla training for the South Vietnamese Army. Only a handful of the MAAG's advisers had personal experience in counterinsurgency warfare.

Yet the U.S. Army was no stranger to such conflict. Americans had fought insurgents in the Philippines at the turn of the century, conducted a guerrilla campaign in Burma during World War II, helped the Greek and Philippine governments to subdue Communist insurgencies after the war, and studied the French failure in Indochina and the British success in Malaya. However, the Army did not yet have a comprehensive doctrine for dealing with insurgency. For the most part, insurgent warfare was still equated with the World War II–type of guerrilla or partisan struggles behind enemy lines in support of conventional operations. Only beginning to emerge was an appreciation of the political and social dimensions of insurgency and its role in the larger framework of revolutionary war. Insurgency meant above all a contest for political legitimacy and power—a struggle between contending political cultures over the organization of society. Most Army advisers and Special Forces went to South Vietnam in the early 1960s poorly prepared to wage such a struggle. A victory for counterinsurgency in South Vietnam would require Diem's government not only to outfight the guerrillas but also to compete successfully with their efforts to organize the population in support of the government's cause.

The Viet Cong thrived on their access to and control of the people, who formed the most important part of their support base. The population provided both economic and manpower resources to sustain and expand the insurgency; the people of the villages served the guerrillas as their first line of resistance against government intrusion into their "liberated zones" and bases. By comparison with their political effort,

VO NGUYEN GIAP (1912–)

Known for his organizational skills and a mercurial temper, Giap trained a Communist guerrilla army for Ho Chi Minh during World War II and went on to become General and Commander of the *People's Army of Vietnam* (1946–1972) and the Minister of National Defense (1946–1980). Chief military architect of the Viet Minh victory over the French in the First Indochina War (1946–1954), Giap gained lasting notoriety for capturing the French garrison at Dien Bien Phu in May 1954. During the war against the United States, Giap advocated guerrilla tactics, putting him at odds with Politburo members who pushed for a more conventional struggle.

the strictly military aims of the Viet Cong were secondary. The insurgents' goal was not necessarily to destroy government forces—although they did so when they could isolate and defeat weaker elements—but to extend their influence over the population. By mobilizing the population, the Viet Cong compensated for their numerical and material disadvantages. A rule of thumb that ten soldiers were needed to defeat one guerrilla reflected the insurgents' political support rather than their military superiority. For the Saigon government, the task of isolating the Viet Cong from the population was difficult under any circumstances and impossible to achieve by force alone.

Viet Cong military forces ran the gamut from hamlet and village guerrillas, farmers by day and fighters by night, to full-time professional soldiers. Organized into squads and platoons, part-time guerrillas had several military functions. They gathered intelligence, passing it on to district or provincial authorities. They proselytized, propagandized, recruited, and provided security for local cadres. They reconnoitered the battlefield, served as porters and guides, created diversions, evacuated wounded, and retrieved weapons. Their very presence and watchfulness in a hamlet or village inhibited the population from aiding the government.

By contrast, the local and main-force Viet Cong units consisted of full-time soldiers, most often recruited from the area where the unit operated. Forming companies and battalions, local forces were attached to a village, district, or provincial headquarters. Often they formed the protective shield behind which a Communist Party cadre established its political infrastructure and organized new guerrilla elements at the hamlet and village levels. As the link between guerrilla and main-force units, a local force served as a reaction force for the former and as a pool of replacements and reinforcements for the latter. Having limited offensive capability, local forces usually attacked poorly defended, isolated outposts or weaker paramilitary forces, often at night and by ambush. Main-force units were organized as battalions, regiments, and, as the insurgency matured, divisions. Subordinate to provincial, regional, and higher commands, such units were the strongest, most mobile, and most offensive minded of the Viet Cong forces; their mission often was to attack and defeat a specific South Vietnamese unit.

Guerrillas Sorting Grain

Missions were assigned and approved by a political officer who in most cases was superior to the unit's military commander. Party cells in every unit inculcated and reinforced policy, military discipline, and unit cohesion. Among the insurgents, war was always the servant of policy.

As the Viet Cong's control over the population increased, their military forces grew in number and size. Squads and platoons became companies, companies formed battalions, and battalions were organized into regiments. This process of creating and enlarging units continued as long as the Viet Cong had a base of support among the population. After 1959, however, infiltrators from the North also became important. Hanoi activated a special military transportation unit to control overland infiltration along a complex of roads and trails from North Vietnam through Laos and Cambodia. This infiltration network was to be called the Ho Chi Minh Trail. A special naval unit conducted sea infiltration. At first, the infiltrators were Southern-born Viet Minh soldiers who had regrouped in the North after the French Indochina War. Each year until 1964, thousands returned south to join or to form Viet Cong units, usually in the areas where they had originated. Such men served as experienced military or political cadres, as technicians, or as rank-and-file combatants wherever local recruitment was difficult.

When the pool of about 80,000 so-called regroupees ran dry, Hanoi began sending native North Vietnamese soldiers as individual replacements and reinforcements. In 1964 the Communists started to introduce entire North Vietnamese Army units into the South. Among the infiltrators were senior cadres, who manned the expanding Viet Cong command system—regional headquarters, interprovincial commands, and the *Central Office for South Vietnam (COSVN)*, the supreme military and political headquarters. As the Southern branch of the Vietnamese Communist Party, *COSVN* was directly subordinate to the Central Committee in Hanoi. Its senior commanders were high-ranking officers of North Vietnam's Army. To equip the growing number of Viet Cong forces in the South, the insurgents continued to rely heavily on arms and supplies captured from South Vietnamese forces. But, increasingly, large numbers of weapons, ammunition, and other equipment arrived from the North, nearly all supplied by the Sino-Soviet bloc.

From a strength of approximately 5,000 at the start of 1959, the Viet Cong's ranks grew to about 100,000 at the end of 1964. The number of infiltrators alone during that period was estimated at 41,000. The growth of the insurgency reflected not only North Vietnam's skill in infiltrating men and weapons but also South Vietnam's inability to control its porous borders, Diem's failure to develop a credible pacification program to reduce Viet Cong influence in the countryside, and the South Vietnamese Army's difficulties in reducing long-standing Viet Cong bases and secret zones. Such areas facilitated infiltration and served as staging areas for operations: they contained training camps, hospitals, depots, workshops, and command centers. Many bases were in remote areas the South Vietnamese Army seldom visited, such as the U Minh Forest or the Plain of Reeds. But others existed in the heart of populated areas, in the liberated zones. There, Viet Cong forces, dispersed among hamlets and villages, drew support from the local economy. From such centers the Viet Cong expanded their influence into adjacent areas that were nominally under the South Vietnamese government's control.

A New American President Takes Charge

Soon after John F. Kennedy became President in 1961, he sharply increased military and economic aid to South Vietnam to help Diem defeat the growing insurgency. For Kennedy, insurgencies (or "wars of national liberation" in the parlance of Communist leaders) challenged

> To equip the growing number of Viet Cong forces in the South, the insurgents continued to rely heavily on arms and supplies captured from South Vietnamese forces.

international security every bit as seriously as nuclear war. The administration's approach to both extremes of conflict rested on the precepts of the flexible response. Regarded as a form of "sub-limited," or small war, insurgency was treated largely as a military problem—conventional war writ small—and hence susceptible to resolution by timely and appropriate military action. Kennedy's success in applying calculated military pressures to compel the Soviet Union to remove its offensive missiles from Cuba in 1962 reinforced the administration's disposition to deal with other international crises, including the conflict in Vietnam, in a similar manner.

Kennedy's policy, though commendable in its degree of flexibility, also had limitations. Long-term strategic planning typically yielded to short-term crisis management. Planners tended to assume that all belligerents were rational and that the foe subscribed as they did to the seductive logic of the flexible response. Hoping to give the South Vietnamese a margin for success, Kennedy periodically authorized additional military aid and support between 1961 and November 1963, when he was assassinated. But the absence of a coherent operational strategy for the conduct of counterinsurgency and chronic military and political shortcomings on the part of the South Vietnamese nullified potential benefits.

The U.S. Army played a major role in Kennedy's "beef up" of the American advisory and support efforts in South Vietnam. In turn, that role was made possible in large measure by Kennedy's determination to increase the strength and capabilities of Army forces for both conventional and unconventional operations. Between 1961 and 1964, the Army's strength rose from about 850,000 to nearly 1 million men and the number of combat divisions grew from eleven to sixteen. These increases were backed up by an ambitious program to modernize Army equipment and, by stockpiling supplies and equipment at forward bases, to increase the deployability and readiness of Army combat forces. The buildup, however, did not prevent the callup of 120,000 reservists to active duty in the summer of 1961, a few months after Kennedy assumed office. Facing renewed Soviet threats to force the Western Powers out of Berlin, Kennedy mobilized the Army to reinforce NATO, if need be. But the mobilization revealed serious shortcomings in Reserve readiness and produced a swell of criticism and complaints from Congress and reservists alike. Although Kennedy sought to remedy the exposed deficiencies and set in motion plans to reorganize the Reserves, the unhappy experience of the Berlin Crisis was fresh in the minds of national leaders when they faced the prospect of war in Vietnam a few years later.

Facing trouble spots in Latin America, Africa, and Southeast Asia, Kennedy took a keen interest in the U.S. Army Special Forces, formed in 1952 to prepare to lead guerrilla wars against the Soviet Union in Eastern Europe. He believed their skills in unconventional warfare also made them well suited to countering insurgency. During his first year in office, he increased the strength of the Special Forces from about 1,500 to 9,000 and authorized them to wear distinctive headgear: the green beret. In the same year he greatly enlarged their role in South Vietnam. First under the auspices of the Central Intelligence Agency and then under a military commander, the Special Forces organized the highland tribes into the Civilian Irregular Defense Group (CIDG) and in time

> Planners tended to assume that all belligerents were rational and that the foe subscribed as they did to the seductive logic of the flexible response.

Special Forces troops lead a Montagnard commando team on a mission in I Corps.

sought to recruit other ethnic groups and sects in the South as well. To this scheme, underwritten almost entirely by the United States, Diem gave only tepid support. Indeed, the civilian irregulars drew strength from groups traditionally hostile to the South Vietnamese government. Treated with disdain by the lowland Vietnamese, the Montagnards developed close, trusting relations with their Army advisers. Special Forces detachment commanders frequently were the real leaders of CIDG units. This strong, mutual bond of loyalty between adviser and highlander benefited operations, but some tribal leaders sought to exploit the special relationship to advance Montagnard political autonomy. On occasion, Special Forces advisers found themselves in the awkward position of mediating between militant Montagnards and South Vietnamese officials who were suspicious and wary of the Americans' sympathy for the highlanders.

Through a village self-defense and development program, the Special Forces aimed initially to create a military and political buffer to the growing Viet Cong influence in the Central Highlands. Within a few years, approximately 60,000 highlanders had enlisted in the CIDG program. As their participation increased, so too did the range of Special Forces activities. In addition to village defense programs, the Green Berets sponsored offensive guerrilla activities and border surveillance and control measures. To detect and impede the Viet Cong, the Special Forces established camps astride infiltration corridors and near enemy base areas, especially along the Cambodian and Laotian borders. But the camps themselves were vulnerable to enemy attack and, despite their presence, infiltration continued. At times, border control diverted tribal units from village defense, the original heart of the CIDG program.

Valor in Vietnam, *John Witt, 1965*

By 1965, as the military situation in the highlands worsened, many CIDG units had changed their character and begun to engage in quasi-conventional military operations. In some instances, irregulars under the leadership of Army Special Forces stood up to crack enemy regiments, offering much of the military resistance to enemy efforts to dominate the highlands. Yet the Special Forces—despite their efforts in South Vietnam and in Laos, where their teams helped to train and advise anti-Communist Laotian forces in the early 1960s—did not provide an antidote to the virulent insurgency in Vietnam. Longstanding animosities between Montagnard and Vietnamese prevented close, continuing, cooperation between the South Vietnamese Army and the irregulars. Long on promises but short on action to improve the lot of the Montagnards, successive South Vietnamese regimes failed to win the loyalty of the tribesmen. And the Special Forces usually operated in areas remote from the main Viet Cong threat to the heavily populated and economically important Mekong Delta and coastal regions of the country.

Besides the Special Forces, the Army's most important contribution to the fight was the helicopter. Neither President Kennedy nor the Army anticipated the rapid growth of aviation in South Vietnam when the first helicopter transportation companies arrived in December 1961. Within three years, however, each of South Vietnam's divisions and corps was supported by Army helicopters, with the faster, more reliable, and versatile UH–1 Iroquois, or Huey, replacing the older H–21 Shawnee. In addition to transporting men and supplies, helicopters were used to reconnoiter, to evacuate wounded, and to provide command and control. The Vietnam conflict became the crucible in which Army airmobile and air-assault tactics evolved. As armament was added first machine gun–wielding door-gunners, and later rockets and miniguns, armed helicopters began to protect troop carriers against antiaircraft fire, to suppress enemy fire around landing zones during air assaults, and to deliver fire support to troops on the ground.

Army fixed-wing aircraft also flourished. Equipped with a variety of detection devices, the OV–1 Mohawk conducted day and night surveillance of Viet Cong bases and trails. The CV–2 Caribou, which the Air Force later called the C–7, with its sturdy frame and ability to land and take off on short, unimproved airfields, proved ideal to supply remote camps.

An H–21 helicopter lifts South Vietnamese troops into battle near Saigon.

Army aviation revived old disagreements with the Air Force over the roles and missions of the two services and the adequacy of Air Force close air support. The expansion of the Army's own "air force" nevertheless continued, abetted by the Kennedy administration's interest in extending airmobility to all types of land warfare, from counterinsurgency to the nuclear battlefield. Secretary of Defense Robert S. McNamara himself encouraged the Army to test an experimental air-assault division. During 1963 and 1964, the Army demonstrated that helicopters could successfully replace ground vehicles for mobility and provide fire support in lieu of ground artillery. The result was the creation in 1965 of the 1st Cavalry Division (Airmobile), the first such unit in the Army. In South Vietnam, the helicopter's effect on organization and operations was as sweeping as the influence of mechanized forces in World War II. Many of the operational concepts of airmobility, rooted in cavalry doctrine and operations, were pioneered by helicopter units between 1961 and 1964 and later adopted by the new airmobile division and by all Army combat units that fought in South Vietnam.

In addition to Army Special Forces and helicopters, Kennedy greatly expanded the entire American advisory effort. Advisers were placed at the sector (provincial) level and were permanently assigned to infantry battalions and certain lower-echelon combat units; additional intelligence advisers went to South Vietnam. The Army made wide use of temporary training teams in psychological warfare, civic action, engineering, and a variety of logistical functions. With the expansion of the advisory and support efforts came demands for better communications, intelligence, and medical, logistical, and administrative support, all of which the Army provided from its active forces, drawing upon skilled men and units from U.S.-based forces. The result was a slow, steady erosion of its capacity to meet worldwide contingency obligations. But if Vietnam depleted the Army, it also provided certain advantages. The war was a laboratory in which to test and evaluate new equipment and techniques applicable to counterinsurgency—among others, the use of chemical defoliants and herbicides, both to remove the jungle canopy that gave cover to the guerrillas and to destroy their crops. As the activities of all the services expanded, U.S. military strength in South Vietnam increased from under 700 at the start of 1960 to almost 24,000 by the end of 1964. Of these, 15,000 were Army, including a little over 2,000 Army advisers.

Changes in American command arrangements attested to the growing commitment. In February 1962 the Joint Chiefs of Staff established the U.S. Military Assistance Command, Vietnam (MACV), in Saigon as the senior American military headquarters in South Vietnam and appointed General Paul D. Harkins as commander (COMUSMACV). Harkins reported to

U.S. Adviser Planning Operations with South Vietnamese Troops

the Commander in Chief, Pacific, in Hawaii but because of high-level interest in South Vietnam enjoyed special access to military and civilian leaders in Washington as well. Soon MACV moved into the advisory effort hitherto directed by the Military Assistance Advisory Group. To simplify the advisory chain of command, the latter was disestablished in May 1964 and MACV took direct control. As the senior Army commander in South Vietnam, the MACV commander also commanded Army support units; for day-to-day operations, however, control of such units was vested in the corps and division senior advisers. For administrative and logistical support Army units looked to the U.S. Army Support Group, Vietnam (later the U.S. Army Support Command, Vietnam), established in mid-1962.

Though command arrangements worked tolerably well, complaints were heard in and out of the Army. Some officials pressed for a separate Army component commander with responsibility both for operations and for logistical support—an arrangement the other services enjoyed in South Vietnam. Airmen tended to believe that an Army command already existed, disguised as MACV. They believed that General Harkins, though a joint commander, favored the Army in the bitter interservice rivalry over the roles and missions of aviation in South Vietnam. Some critics thought his span of control excessive, for Harkins' responsibility extended to Thailand, where Army combat units had deployed in 1962, aiming to overawe Communist forces in neighboring Laos. The Army undertook several logistical projects in Thailand, and Army engineers, signalmen, and other support forces remained there after combat forces withdrew in the fall of 1962.

While the Americans strengthened their position in South Vietnam and Thailand, the Communists tightened their grip in Laos. Agreements signed in Geneva in 1962 required all foreign military forces to leave that small, land-locked nation. American advisers, including hundreds of Special Forces, departed. But North Vietnam did not honor the agreements. Its army, together with Laotian Communist forces, consolidated its hold on areas adjacent to both North and South Vietnam through which passed the network of jungle roads called the Ho Chi Minh Trail. As a result, it became easier to move supplies south to support the Viet Cong in the face of the new dangers embodied in U.S. advisers, weapons, and tactics.

Counterinsurgency Falters

At first the enhanced mobility and firepower afforded the South Vietnamese Army by helicopters, armored personnel carriers, and close air support surprised and overwhelmed the Viet Cong. The South Vietnamese government's forces reacted more quickly to insurgent attacks and penetrated many Viet Cong areas. Even more threatening to the insurgents was Diem's strategic hamlet program launched in late 1961. Diem and his brother Ngo Dinh Nhu, an ardent sponsor of the program, hoped to create thousands of new, fortified villages, often by moving peasants from their existing homes. Hamlet construction and defense were the responsibility of the new residents, with para-military and South Vietnamese Army forces providing initial security while the peasants were recruited and organized. As security improved,

STRATEGIC HAMLETS

The program of fortifying villages to separate the peasants from the insurgents emulated a model the British used successfully in Malaya in the 1950s. In addition to impairing the Viet Cong's control of the countryside, Diem saw the hamlets as a way to solicit more American aid and to control his own population, which outside of the Catholic minority had little enthusiasm for his regime. The program affected nearly one-third of South Vietnam's 14,000 hamlets; but when the government abandoned it in early 1964, only a small percentage of the hamlets remained in friendly hands. Diem's over-ambitious program created too many such hamlets, widely scattered and often indefensible, thus dooming the initiative to failure.

Diem and Nhu hoped to enact social, economic, and political reforms that when fully carried out would constitute the central government's revolutionary response to Viet Cong promises of social and economic betterment. If successful, the program might destroy the insurgency by separating and protecting the rural population from the Viet Cong, threatening the rebellion's base of support.

By early 1963, however, the Viet Cong had learned to cope with the South Vietnamese Army's new weapons and more aggressive tactics and had begun a campaign to eliminate the strategic hamlets. The insurgents became adept at countering helicopters and slow-flying aircraft and learned the vulnerabilities of armored personnel carriers. In addition, their excellent intelligence, combined with the predictability of the South Vietnamese Army's tactics and pattern of operations, enabled the Viet Cong to evade or ambush government forces. The new weapons the United States had provided the South Vietnamese did not compensate for the stifling influence of poor leadership, dubious tactics, and inexperience. The much publicized defeat of government forces at the Mekong Delta village of Ap Bac in January 1963 demonstrated both the Viet Cong's skill in countering the South Vietnamese Army's new capabilities and the latter's inherent weaknesses. Faulty intelligence, poorly planned and executed fire support, and overcautious leadership contributed to the outcome. But Ap Bac's significance transcended a single battle. The defeat was a portent of things to come. Now able to challenge regular army units of equal strength in quasi-conventional battles, the Viet Cong were moving into a more intense stage of revolutionary war.

As the Viet Cong became stronger and bolder, the South Vietnamese Army became more cautious and less offensive minded. Government forces became reluctant to respond to Viet Cong depredations in the countryside, avoided night operations, and resorted to ponderous sweeps against vague military objectives, rarely making contact with their enemies. Meanwhile, the Viet Cong concentrated on destroying strategic hamlets, showing that they considered the settlements, rather than the South Vietnamese Army, the greater danger to the insurgency. Poorly defended hamlets and outposts were overrun or subverted by enemy agents who infiltrated with peasants arriving from the countryside.

The Viet Cong's campaign profited from the government's failures. The government built too many hamlets to defend and scattered them around the countryside, often outside of range for mutual support. Hamlet militia varied from those who were poorly trained and armed to those who were not trained or armed at all. Fearing that weapons given to the militia would fall to the Viet Cong, local officials often withheld arms. Forced relocation, use of forced peasant labor to construct hamlets, and tardy payment of compensation for relocation were but a few reasons why peasants turned against the program. Few meaningful reforms took place. Accurate information on the program's true condition and on the decline in rural security was hidden from Diem by officials eager to please him with reports of progress. False statistics and reports misled U.S. officials, too, about the progress of the counterinsurgency effort.

If the decline in rural security was not always apparent to Americans, the lack of enlightened political leadership on the part of Diem was all too obvious. Diem habitually interfered in military matters: bypassing the chain of command to order operations, forbidding commanders to take casualties, and appointing military leaders on the basis of political loyalty rather than competence. Many military and civilian appointees, especially province and district chiefs, were dishonest and put career and fortune above the national interest. When Buddhist opposition to certain policies erupted into violent antigovernment demonstrations in 1963, Diem's uncompromising stance and use of military force to suppress the demonstrators caused some generals to decide that the President was a liability in the fight against the Viet Cong. On November 1, with American encouragement, a group of reform-minded generals ousted Diem, who was subsequently murdered along with his brother.

Political turmoil followed the coup. Emboldened, the insurgents stepped up operations and increased their control over many rural areas. North Vietnam's leaders decided to intensify the armed struggle, aiming to demoralize the South Vietnamese Army and further undermine political authority in the South. As Viet Cong military activity quickened, regular North Vietnamese Army units began to train for possible intervention in the war. Men and equipment continued to flow down the Ho Chi Minh Trail, with North Vietnamese conscripts replacing the dwindling pool of Southerners who had belonged to the Viet Minh.

Setting the Stage for Confrontation

The critical state of rural security that came to light after Diem's death again prompted the United States to expand its military aid to Saigon. General Harkins and his successor, General William C. Westmoreland, urgently strove to revitalize pacification and counterinsurgency. Army advisers helped their Vietnamese counterparts to revise national and provincial pacification plans. They retained the concept of fortified hamlets as the heart of a new national counterinsurgency program but corrected the old abuses, at least in theory. To help implement the program, Army advisers were assigned to the subsector (district) level for the first time, becoming more intimately involved in local pacification efforts and in paramilitary operations. Additional advisers were assigned to units and training centers, especially those of the Regional and Popular Forces (formerly called the Civil Guard and Self-Defense Corps). All Army activities, from aviation support

WILLIAM C. WESTMORELAND (1914–2005)

General William Westmoreland, a West Point graduate and highly experienced officer who had served in World War II and Korea, was forced to fight the war in Vietnam under severe limitations. Without the authority to attack North Vietnam, or even the enemy base areas in Laos and Cambodia, he relied instead on attrition to wear the enemy down. Confronted by two interrelated threats—Communist main-force units and guerrillas—Westmoreland chose to emphasize the main-force war, which he considered the more immediate threat. He believed that mobility and firepower could prevent a war of attrition from turning into a stalemate and that by 1967 the North Vietnamese would reach a "crossover point," after which they would be unable to reinforce the war in the South. After Vietnam, General Westmoreland served as Chief of Staff of the U.S. Army from 1968 to 1972.

General Westmoreland (center) *answers questions from the media. Ambassador Maxwell Taylor is on the left.*

to Special Forces, were strengthened in a concerted effort to undo the effects of years of Diem's mismanagement.

At the same time, American officials in Washington, Hawaii, and Saigon began to explore ways to increase military pressure against North Vietnam. In 1964 the South Vietnamese launched covert raids under MACV's auspices. Some military leaders, however, believed that only direct air strikes against North Vietnam would induce a change in Hanoi's policies by demonstrating American determination to defend South Vietnam's independence. Air strike plans ranged from immediate massive bombardment of military and industrial targets to gradually intensifying attacks spanning several months.

The interest in using air power reflected lingering sentiment in the United States against once again involving American ground forces in a land war on the Asian continent. Many of President Lyndon B. Johnson's advisers—among them General Maxwell D. Taylor, who was appointed Ambassador to South Vietnam in mid-1964—believed that a carefully calibrated air campaign would be the most effective means of exerting pressure against the North and, at the same time, the method least likely to provoke China's intervention. Taylor deemed conventional U.S. Army ground forces ill suited to engage in day-to-day counterinsurgency operations against the Viet Cong in hamlets and villages. Ground forces might, however, be used to protect vital air bases in the South and to repel any North Vietnamese attack across the demilitarized zone that separated North from South Vietnam. Together, a more vigorous counterinsurgency effort in the South and military pressure against the North might buy time for the South Vietnamese government to put

President Johnson

its political house in order, boost flagging military and civilian morale, and strengthen its military position in the event of a negotiated peace. Taylor and Westmoreland, the senior U.S. officials in South Vietnam, agreed that North Vietnam was unlikely to change its course unless convinced that it could not succeed in the South. Both recognized that air strikes were neither a panacea nor a substitute for military efforts in the South.

As each side undertook more provocative military actions, the likelihood of a direct military confrontation between North Vietnam and the United States increased. The crisis came in early August 1964 in the international waters of the Gulf of Tonkin. North Vietnamese patrol boats attacked U.S. naval vessels surveying North Vietnam's coastal defenses. The Americans promptly launched retaliatory air strikes. At the request of President Johnson, Congress overwhelmingly passed the Southeast Asia Resolution, the so-called Gulf of Tonkin Resolution, authorizing all actions necessary to protect American forces and to provide for the defense of the nation's allies in Southeast Asia. Considered by some in the administration as the equivalent of a declaration of war, this broad grant of authority encouraged Johnson to expand American military efforts within South Vietnam, against North Vietnam, and in Southeast Asia at large.

By late 1964 each side was poised to increase its stake in the war. Regular North Vietnamese Army units had begun moving south and stood at the Laotian frontier, on the threshold of crossing into South Vietnam's Central Highlands. U.S. air and naval forces stood ready to renew their attacks. On February 7, 1965, Communist forces attacked an American compound in Pleiku in the Central Highlands and a few days later bombed American quarters in Qui Nhon. The United States promptly bombed military targets in the North. A few weeks later, President Johnson approved Operation ROLLING THUNDER, a campaign of sustained, direct air strikes of progressively increasing strength against military and industrial targets in North Vietnam. Signs of intensifying conflict appeared in South Vietnam as well. Strengthening forces at all echelons, from village guerrillas to main-force regiments, the Viet Cong quickened military activity in late 1964 and in the first half of 1965. At Binh Gia, a village forty miles east of Saigon in Phuoc Tuy Province, a multiregimental Viet Cong force fought and defeated several South Vietnamese battalions.

By the summer of 1965 the Viet Cong, strengthened by several recently infiltrated North Vietnamese Army regiments, had gained the upper hand over government forces in some areas of South Vietnam. With U.S. close air support and the aid of Army helicopter gunships, South Vietnamese forces repelled many enemy attacks but suffered heavy casualties. Elsewhere, highland camps and border outposts had to be abandoned. South Vietnamese Army losses from battle deaths and desertions amounted to nearly a battalion a week. The government in Saigon was hard pressed to find men to replenish these heavy losses and completely unable to match the growth of Communist forces from local recruitment and infiltration. Some American officials doubted whether the South Vietnamese could hold out until ROLLING THUNDER created pressures sufficiently strong to convince North Vietnam's leaders to reduce the level of combat in the South. General

Westmoreland and others believed that U.S. ground forces were needed to stave off an irrevocable shift of the military and political balance in favor of the enemy.

For a variety of diplomatic, political, and military reasons, President Johnson approached with great caution any commitment of large ground combat forces to South Vietnam. Yet preparations had been under way for some time. In early March 1965, a few days after ROLLING THUNDER began, American marines went ashore in South Vietnam to protect the large airfield at Da Nang—a defensive security mission. Even as they landed, General Harold K. Johnson, Chief of Staff of the Army, was in South Vietnam to assess the situation. Upon returning to Washington, he recommended a substantial increase in American military assistance, including several combat divisions. He wanted U.S. forces either to interdict the Laotian panhandle to stop infiltration or to counter a growing enemy threat in the central and northern provinces.

But President Johnson sanctioned only the dispatch of additional marines to increase security at Da Nang and to secure other coastal enclaves. He also authorized the Army to begin deploying nearly 20,000 logistical troops, the main body of the 1st Logistical Command, to Southeast Asia. (Westmoreland had requested such a command in late 1964.) At the same time, the President modified the marines' mission to allow them to conduct offensive operations close to their bases. A few weeks later, to protect American bases in the vicinity of Saigon, President Johnson approved sending the first Army combat unit, the 173d Airborne Brigade (Separate), to South Vietnam. Arriving from Okinawa in early May, the brigade moved quickly to secure the air base at Bien Hoa, just northeast of Saigon. With its arrival, U.S. military strength in South Vietnam passed 50,000. Despite added numbers and expanded missions, American ground forces had yet to engage the enemy in full-scale combat.

Indeed, the question of how best to use large numbers of American ground forces was still unresolved on the eve of their deployment. Focusing on population security and pacification, some planners saw U.S. combat forces concentrating their efforts in coastal enclaves and around key urban centers and bases. Under this plan, such forces would provide a security shield behind which the Vietnamese could expand the pacification zone; when required, American combat units would venture beyond their enclaves as mobile reaction forces.

This concept, largely defensive in nature, reflected the pattern the first Army combat units to enter South Vietnam had established. But the mobility and offensive firepower of U.S. ground units suggested their use in remote, sparsely populated regions to seek out and engage main-force enemy units as they infiltrated into South Vietnam or emerged from their secret bases. While secure coastal logistical enclaves and base camps still would be required, the weight of the military effort would be focused on the destruction of enemy military units. Yet even in this alternative, American units would serve indirectly as a shield for pacification activities in the more heavily populated lowlands and Mekong Delta. A third proposal had particular appeal to General Johnson. He wished to employ U.S. and allied ground forces across the Laotian panhandle to interdict enemy infiltration into South Vietnam. Here was a more direct and effective way to stop infiltration than the use of air power. Encumbered by military and political problems, the idea was periodically revived but always rejected. The pattern of deployment that actually developed in South Vietnam was a compromise between the first two concepts.

For any type of operations, secure logistical enclaves at deepwater ports (Cam Ranh Bay, Nha Trang, and Qui Nhon, for example) were a military necessity. In such areas, combat units arrived and bases developed for regional logistical complexes to support the troops. As the administration neared a decision on combat deployment, the Army began to identify and ready units for movement overseas and to prepare mobilization plans for Selected Reserve forces. The dispatch of Army units to the Dominican Republic in May 1965 to forestall a Leftist takeover necessitated only minor adjustments to the buildup plans. The episode nevertheless showed how unexpected demands elsewhere in the world could deplete the strategic reserve, and it underscored the importance of mobilization if the Army was to meet worldwide contingencies and supply trained combat units to Westmoreland as well.

The prospect of deploying American ground forces also revived discussions of allied command arrangements. For a time Westmoreland considered placing South Vietnamese and American forces under a single commander, an arrangement similar to that of U.S. and South Korean forces during the Korean War. In the face of South Vietnamese opposition, however, Westmoreland dropped the idea. Arrangements with other allies varied. Americans in South Vietnam were joined by combat units from Australia, New Zealand, South Korea, and Thailand and by noncombat elements from several other nations. Westmoreland entered into separate agreements with each commander in turn; the compacts ensured close cooperation with MACV but fell short of giving Westmoreland command over the allied forces.

While diversity marked these arrangements, Westmoreland strove for unity within the American buildup. As forces began to deploy to South Vietnam, the Army sought to elevate the newly established U.S. Army, Vietnam (USARV), to a full-fledged Army component command with responsibility for combat operations. But Westmoreland successfully warded off the challenge to his dual role as unified commander of MACV and its Army component. For the remainder of the war, USARV performed solely in a logistical and administrative capacity; unlike MACV's air and naval component commands, the Army component did not exercise operational control over combat forces, Special Forces, or field advisers. However, through its logistical, engineer, signal, medical, military police, and aviation commands established in the course of the buildup, USARV commanded and managed a support base of unprecedented size and scope.

Despite this victory, unity of command over the ground war in South Vietnam eluded Westmoreland, as did overall control of U.S. military operations in support of the war. Most air and naval operations outside of South Vietnam, including ROLLING THUNDER, were carried out by the Commander in Chief, Pacific, and his air and naval commanders from his headquarters thousands of miles away in Hawaii. This patchwork of command arrangements contributed to the lack of a unified strategy, the fragmentation of operations, and the pursuit of parochial service interests to the detriment of the war effort. No

Americans in South Vietnam were joined by combat units from Australia, New Zealand, South Korea, and Thailand and by noncombat elements from several other nations.

single American commander had complete authority or responsibility to fashion an overall strategy or to coordinate all military aspects of the war in Southeast Asia. Furthermore, Westmoreland labored under a variety of political and operational constraints on the use of the combat forces he did command. Like the Korean War, the struggle in South Vietnam was complicated by enemy sanctuaries and by geographical and political restrictions on allied operations. Ground forces were barred from operating across South Vietnam's borders in Cambodia, Laos, or North Vietnam, although the border areas of those countries were vital to the enemy's war effort. These factors narrowed Westmoreland's freedom of action and detracted from his efforts to make effective use of American military power.

Groundwork for Combat: Buildup and Strategy

On July 28, 1965, President Johnson announced plans to deploy additional combat units and to increase American military strength in South Vietnam to 175,000 by year's end. The Army already was preparing hundreds of units for duty in Southeast Asia, among them the newly activated 1st Cavalry Division. Other combat units (the 1st Brigade, 101st Airborne Division, and all three brigades of the 1st Infantry Division) were either ready to go or already on their way to Vietnam. Together with hundreds of support and logistical units, these combat units constituted the first phase of the buildup during the summer and fall of 1965.

At the same time Johnson decided not to mobilize any reserve units. The President's decision profoundly affected the manner in which the Army supported and sustained the buildup. To meet the call for additional combat forces, to obtain manpower to enlarge its training base, and to maintain a pool for rotation and replacement of soldiers in South Vietnam, the Army had to increase its active strength over the next three years by nearly 1.5 million men. Necessarily, it relied on larger draft calls and voluntary enlistments, supplementing them with heavy drawdowns of experienced soldiers from units in Europe and South Korea and extensions of some tours of duty to retain specialists, technicians, and cadres who could train recruits or round out deploying units. Combat units assigned to the strategic reserve were used to meet a large portion of MACV's force requirements, and reservists were not available to replace them. Mobilization could have eased the additional burden of providing officers and noncommissioned officers to man the Army's growing training bases. As matters stood, requirements for experienced cadres competed with the demands for seasoned leaders in units deploying to South Vietnam.

The personnel turbulence caused by competing demands for the Army's limited manpower was intensified by a one-year tour of duty in South Vietnam. Large numbers of men were needed to sustain the rotational base, often necessitating the quick return to Vietnam of men with critical skills. The heightening demand for leaders led to accelerated training programs and the lowering of standards for NCOs and junior officers. Moreover, the one-year tour deprived units in South Vietnam of experienced leadership. In time, the infusion of less-seasoned NCOs and officers contributed to a host of morale problems that afflicted some Army units. At a deeper level, the administration's decision against calling the reserves to active duty sent the wrong signal to friends and enemies alike, implying that the nation lacked the resolution to support an effort of the magnitude needed to achieve American objectives in South Vietnam.

Hence the Army began to organize additional combat units. Three light infantry brigades were activated, and the 9th Infantry Division was reactivated. In the meantime the 4th and 25th Infantry Divisions were alerted for deployment to South Vietnam. With the exception of a brigade of the 25th, all the combat units activated and alerted during the second half of 1965 deployed to South Vietnam during 1966 and 1967. By the end of 1965, U.S. military strength in South Vietnam had reached 184,000; a year later it stood at 385,000; and by the end of 1967 it approached 490,000. Army personnel accounted for nearly two-thirds of the total. Of the Army's eighteen divisions, by the end of 1967 seven were serving in South Vietnam.

Facing a deteriorating military situation, in the summer of 1965 Westmoreland planned to use his combat units to blunt the enemy's spring-summer offensive. As units arrived in the country, he moved them into a defensive arc around Saigon and secured bridgeheads for the arrival of subsequent units. His initial aim was defensive: to stop losing the war and to build a structure that could support a later transition to an offensive campaign. As additional troops poured in, Westmoreland planned to seek out and defeat major enemy forces. Throughout both phases the South Vietnamese, relieved of major combat tasks, were to refurbish their forces and conduct an aggressive pacification program behind the American shield. In a third and final stage, as enemy main-force units were driven into their secret zones and bases, Westmoreland hoped to achieve victory by destroying those sanctuaries and shifting the weight of the military effort to pacification, thereby at last subduing the Viet Cong throughout rural South Vietnam.

The fulfillment of this concept rested not only on the success of American efforts to find and defeat enemy forces, but also on the success of the South Vietnamese government's pacification program. In June 1965 the last in a series of coups that followed Diem's overthrow brought in a military junta headed by Lt. Gen. Nguyen Van Thieu as Chief of State and Air Vice Marshal Nguyen Cao Ky as Prime Minister. The new government provided the political stability requisite for successful pacification. Success hinged also on the ability of the U.S. air campaign against the North to reduce the infiltration of men and materiel, dampening the intensity of combat in the South and inducing Communist leaders in Hanoi to alter their long-term strategic goals. Should any strand of this threefold strategy—the campaign against Communist forces in the South, the South Vietnamese government's pacification program, and the air war in the North— falter, Westmoreland's prospects would become poorer. Yet he was directly responsible for only one element, the U.S. military effort in the South. To a lesser degree, through American advice and assistance to the South Vietnamese forces, he also influenced the South Vietnamese government's efforts to suppress the Viet Cong and to carry out pacification.

Success hinged also on the ability of the U.S. air campaign against the North to reduce the infiltration of men and materiel, dampening the intensity of combat in the South and inducing Communist leaders in Hanoi to alter their long-term strategic goals.

The Highlands, 1965

Spearheaded by at least three North Vietnamese Army regiments, Communist forces mounted a strong offensive in South Vietnam's Central Highlands during the summer of 1965. Overrunning border camps and besieging some district towns, the enemy seemed poised to cut the nation in two. To meet the danger, Westmoreland proposed to introduce the newly organized Army airmobile division, the 1st Cavalry Division, with its large contingent of helicopters, directly into the highlands. Some of his superiors in Hawaii and Washington opposed this plan, preferring to secure coastal bases. Though Westmoreland contended that enclave security made poor use of U.S. mobility and offensive firepower, he was hard pressed to overcome the fear of an American Dien Bien Phu if a unit in the highlands should be isolated and cut off from the sea.

Despite a sparse population and limited economic resources, the highlands were strategically important. Around the key highland towns (Kontum, Pleiku, Ban Me Thuot, and Da Lat), the South Vietnamese and their advisers had created enclaves. Allied forces protected the few roads that traversed the highlands, screened the border, and reinforced outposts and Montagnard settlements from which the irregulars and Army Special Forces sought to detect enemy cross-border movements and to strengthen tribal resistance to

Dropping in on Charlie, *Michael R. Crook, 1967*

the Communists. Such border posts and tribal camps, rather than major towns, most often were the object of enemy attacks. Combined with road interdiction, such attacks enabled the Communists to disperse the limited number of defenders and to discourage the maintenance of outposts.

Such actions served a larger strategic objective. The enemy planned to develop the highlands into a major base area from which to mount or support operations in other areas. The Communist-dominated highlands would be a strategic fulcrum, enabling the enemy to shift the weight of his operations to any part of South Vietnam. The highlands were also a potential killing zone where Communist forces could mass. American units arriving there were going to be confronted immediately.

Commanded by Maj. Gen. Harry W. O. Kinnard, the 1st Cavalry Division (Airmobile) moved with its more than 450 helicopters into this hornet's nest in September 1965. It established its main base at An Khe, a government stronghold on Highway 19, halfway between the coastal port of Qui Nhon and the highland city of Pleiku. The location was strategic: at An Khe, the division could help to keep open the vital east-west road from the coast to the highlands and could pivot between the highlands and the coastal districts, where the Viet Cong had made deep inroads.

One month later the division received its baptism of fire. The North Vietnamese Army attacked a Special Forces camp at Plei Me; when it was repulsed, Westmoreland directed the division to launch an offensive to locate and destroy enemy regiments that had been identified in the vicinity of the camp. The result was the Battle of the Ia Drang, named for a small river that flowed through the valley, the area of operations. (*Map 15*) For thirty-five days the division pursued and fought the North Vietnamese *32d, 33d*, and *66th People's Army of Vietnam (PAVN) Regiments*, until the enemy, suffering heavy casualties, returned to his bases in Cambodia.

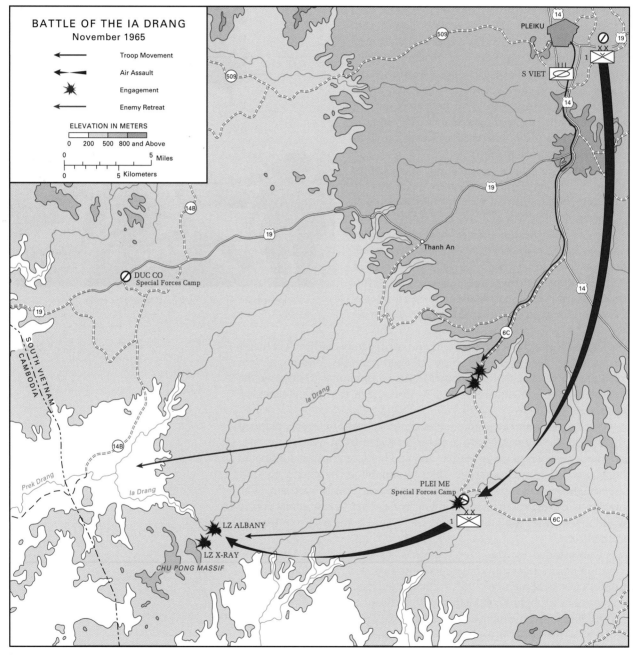

Map 15

With scout platoons of its air cavalry squadron covering front and flanks, each battalion of the division's 1st Brigade established company bases from which patrols searched for enemy forces. For several days neither ground patrols nor aeroscouts found any trace, but on November 4 the scouts spotted a regimental aid station several miles west of Plei Me. Quick-reacting aerorifle platoons converged on the site. Hovering above, the airborne scouts detected an enemy battalion nearby and attacked from UH–1B Huey gunships with aerial rockets and machine guns. Operating beyond the range of their ground artillery, Army units engaged the enemy in an intense firefight, killing ninety-nine, capturing the aid station, and seizing many documents.

The search for the main body of the enemy continued for the next few days, with Army units concentrating their efforts in the vicinity of the Chu Pong Massif, a mountain range and likely enemy base near the Cambodian border. Communist forces were given little rest, as patrols harried and ambushed them.

The heaviest fighting was yet to come. As the division began the second stage of its campaign, enemy forces began to move out of the Chu Pong base. Units of the U.S. 1st Cavalry Division's 3d Brigade, which took over from the 1st Brigade, advanced to establish artillery bases and landing zones at the base of the mountain. Landing Zone X-Ray was one of several U.S. positions vulnerable to attack by the enemy forces that occupied the surrounding high ground. Here on November 14 began fighting that pitted three battalions against elements of two North Vietnamese regiments. Withstanding repeated mortar attacks and infantry assaults, the Americans used every means of firepower available to them—the division's own gunships, massive artillery bombardment, hundreds of strafing and bombing attacks by tactical aircraft, earth-shaking bombs dropped by B–52 bombers from Guam, and, perhaps most important, the individual soldier's M16 rifle—to turn back a determined enemy. The Communists lost more than 600 dead, the Americans 79.

Although badly hurt, the enemy did not leave the Ia Drang Valley. Elements of the *33d* and *66th PAVN Regiments*, moving east toward Plei Me, encountered the U.S. 2d Battalion, 7th Cavalry, a few miles north of X-Ray at Landing Zone Albany, on November 17. The fight that resulted was a bloody reminder of the North Vietnamese mastery of the ambush, as the Communists quickly snared four U.S. companies in their net. As the trapped units struggled for survival, nearly all semblance of organized combat disappeared in the confusion and mayhem. Neither reinforcements nor effective firepower could be brought in. At times combat was reduced to valiant efforts by individuals and small units to avert annihilation. When the fighting ended that night, almost 70 percent of the Americans were casualties and almost one of every three soldiers in the battalion had been killed.

Despite the horrific casualties from the ambush near Landing Zone Albany, the Battle of the Ia Drang was lauded as the first major American triumph of the Vietnam War. The airmobile division, committed to combat less than a month after it arrived in country, relentlessly pursued the enemy over difficult terrain and defeated crack North Vietnamese Army units. In part, its achievements underlined the flexibility that Army divisions had gained in the early 1960s under the heliborne assaults and accustomed itself to the rigors of jungle operations. It also established a pattern of operations that was to grow all too familiar. Airmobile assaults, often in the wake of B–52 air strikes, were followed by extensive patrolling, episodic contact with the Viet Cong, and withdrawal after a few days' stay in the enemy's territory. In early November the airborne soldiers uncovered evidence of the enemy's recent and hasty departure: abandoned camps, recently vacated tunnels, and caches of food and supplies. However, the Viet Cong, by observing the brigade, began to formulate plans for dealing with the Americans.

On November 8, moving deeper into War Zone D, the brigade encountered significant resistance. A Viet Cong battalion attacked and forced the Americans into a tight defensive perimeter. Close-quarters combat ensued as the enemy tried to "hug," or stay close to, American units to prevent the delivery of supporting air and artillery fire. Unable to prepare a landing zone to receive reinforcements or to evacuate casualties, the beleaguered Americans withstood repeated enemy assaults. During the afternoon the Viet Cong ceased their attack and withdrew. Next morning, when reinforcements arrived, the brigade pursued the enemy, finding evidence that he had suffered heavy casualties. Such operations inflicted losses but failed either to destroy the enemy's base or to prevent him from returning to it later on.

Like the airborne brigade, the 1st Infantry Division initially divided its efforts. In addition to securing its base camps north of Saigon, the division helped South Vietnamese forces clear an area west of the capital in the vicinity of Cu Chi in Hau Nghia Province. Reacting to reports of enemy troop concentrations, units of the division launched a series of operations in the fall of 1965 and early 1966 that entailed quick forays into the Ho Bo and Boi Loi woods, the Michelin Rubber Plantation, the Rung Sat swamp, and War Zones C and D.

An Air Force B–52 bombards an enemy base in III Corps.

But the defense of Saigon was the first duty of the 1st Infantry Division ("Big Red One") as well as of the 25th Infantry Division, which arrived in the winter of 1966. The 1st Infantry Division took up a position protecting the northern approaches, blocking Highway 13 from the Cambodian border. The 25th guarded the western approaches, chiefly Highway 1 and the Saigon River. The two brigades of the 25th Division served also as a buffer between Saigon and the enemy's base areas in Tay Ninh Province. Westmoreland hoped, however, that the 25th Division would loosen the insurgents' tenacious hold on Hau Nghia as well. Here, American soldiers found to their amazement that the division's camp at Cu Chi had been constructed atop an extensive Viet Cong tunnel complex. Extending over an area of several miles, this subterranean network, one of several in the region, contained hospitals, command centers, and storage sites. The complex, though partially destroyed by Army "tunnel rats," was never completely eliminated and remained usable by the enemy for the duration of the war. The 25th Infantry Division worked closely with South Vietnamese Army and para-military forces throughout 1966 and 1967 to foster pacification in Hau Nghia and to secure its own base. But suppressing insurgency in Hau Nghia proved as difficult as eradicating the tunnels at Cu Chi.

Troops of the 1st Infantry Division flush the Viet Cong from a tunnel near Saigon.

As the number of Army combat units in Vietnam grew larger, Westmoreland established two corps-size commands, I Field Force in the II Corps area and II Field Force in the III Corps area. Reporting directly to the MACV commander, the field force commander was the senior Army tactical commander in his area and the senior U.S. adviser to South Vietnamese Army forces there. Working closely with his South Vietnamese counterpart, he coor-dinated South Vietnamese and American operations by establishing territorial priorities for combat and pacification efforts. Through his deputy senior adviser, a position established in 1967, the field force commander kept abreast both of the activities of U.S. sector (prov-ince) and subsector (district) advisers and of the progress of the South Vietnamese government's pacification efforts. The I Corps had a similar arrangement, where the commander of the III Marine Amphibious Force was the equivalent of a field force commander. Only in IV Corps, in the Mekong Delta where few American combat units served, did Westmoreland choose not to establish a corps-size command. There, the senior U.S. adviser served as COMUSMACV's representative; he commanded Army advisory and support units but no combat units.

Although Army commanders in III Corps were eager to seek out and engage enemy main-force units in their strongholds along the Cambodian border, operations at first were devoted to base and area security and to clearing and rehabilitating roads. The 1st Infantry Division's first major encounter with the Viet Cong occurred in November 1965, as division elements carried out a routine road security operation along Highway 13 in the vicinity of the village of Bau Bang. Trapping convoys along Highway 13 had long been a profitable Viet Cong tactic. On this occasion, ambushed by a large, well-entrenched enemy force, division troops reacted aggressively and mounted a fire support boats called monitors. Howitzers and mortars mounted on barges provided artillery support. The 2d Brigade, 9th Infantry Division, began operations against the Cam Son Secret Zone, approximately ten miles west of Dong Tam, in May 1967.

Meanwhile, the war of main-force units along the borders waxed and waned in relation to seasonal weather cycles, which affected the enemy's pattern of logistical activity, his ability to infiltrate men and supplies from North Vietnam, and his penchant for meticulous preparation of the battlefield. By the fall of 1967 enemy activity had increased again in the base areas, and sizable forces began appearing along South Vietnam's border from the demilitarized zone to III Corps. By year's end, American forces had returned to War Zone C to screen the Cambodian border to prevent Communist forces from reentering South Vietnam. Units of the 25th Infantry Division that had been conducting operations in the vicinity of Saigon moved to the border. Elements of the 1st Infantry Division had resumed road-clearing operations along Highway 13, but the division soon faced another major enemy effort to capture Loc Ninh. On October 29 Viet Cong units assaulted the CIDG camp and the district command post, breaching the defense perimeter. Intense air and artillery fire prevented its complete loss. Within a few hours, South Vietnamese and U.S. reinforcements reached Loc Ninh, their arrival made possible by the enemy's failure to capture the local airstrip.

When the buildup at Loc Ninh ended, four Army battalions were positioned within the town and between the town and the Cambodian border. During the next two days allied units warded off repeated enemy attacks as Communist forces desperately tried to score a victory. Tactical air support and artillery fire prevented the enemy from massing, though he outnumbered allied forces by about ten to one. At the end of a ten-day battle, over 800 enemy were left on the battlefield, while allied deaths numbered 50. Some 452 close air support sorties, 8 B–52 bomber strikes, and 30,125 rounds of artillery had been directed at the enemy.

II Corps Battles, 1966–1967

Despite the relative calm that followed the Ia Drang fighting in late 1965, the North Vietnamese left no doubt of their intent to continue infiltration and to challenge American forces in II Corps. In March 1966 enemy forces overran the Special Forces camp at A Shau on the remote western border of I Corps. (*Map 18*) The loss of the camp had long-term consequences, enabling the enemy to make the A Shau Valley a major logistical base and staging area for forces infiltrating into the piedmont and coastal areas. The loss also highlighted certain differences between operational concepts of the Army and the marines. Concentrating their efforts in the coastal districts of I Corps and lacking the more extensive helicopter support Army units enjoyed, the marines avoided operations in the highlands. On the other hand, Army commanders in II Corps sought to engage the enemy as close to the border as possible and were quick to respond to threats to Special Forces camps in the highlands. Operations near the border were essential to Westmoreland's efforts to keep main-force enemy units as far as possible from the population and to wear them down.

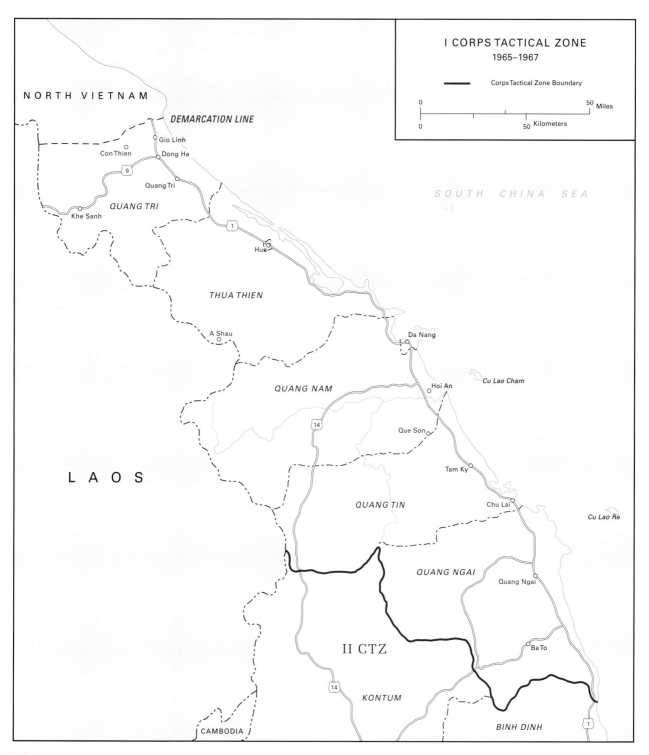

Map 18

For Hanoi's strategists, however, a reciprocal relation existed between highlands and coastal regions. Here, as in the south, the enemy directed his efforts to preserving his own influence among the population near the coast, from which he derived considerable support. At the same time he maintained a constant military threat in the highlands to divert allied forces from pacification efforts. In its broad outlines, Hanoi's strategy to cope with U.S. forces was the same employed by the Viet Minh against the French and by Communist forces in 1964 and 1965 against the South Vietnamese Army. Whether it would be equally successful remained to be seen.

The airmobile division spent the better part of the next two years fighting Viet Cong and North Vietnamese units in the coastal plain and piedmont valleys of Binh Dinh Province. (*Map 19*) Here the enemy had deep roots, especially in the piedmont's craggy hills and jungle-covered uplands, where local and main-force Viet Cong units had long flourished by exacting food, taxes, and recruits from the lowland population through a well-entrenched shadow government. Pacification efforts were almost dead. Starting in early 1966, the 1st Cavalry Division, now under the command of Maj. Gen. John Norton, embarked on a series of operations against the *2d PLAF*, *12th PAVN*, and *22d PAVN Regiments* of the *3d PAVN Division*. For the most part the 1st Cavalry Division operated in the Bong Son plain and the adjacent hills, from which enemy units reinforced the hamlet and the village guerrillas who gathered taxes, food, and recruits. As in the highlands, the division exploited its airmobility, using helicopters to establish positions in the upper reaches of the valleys. The division sought to flush the enemy from his hiding places and drive him toward the coast, where American, South Vietnamese, and South Korean forces held blocking positions. When trapped, the enemy was attacked by ground, naval, and air fire. The scheme was a new version of an old tactical concept, the "hammer and anvil," with the coastal plain and the natural barrier formed by the South China Sea forming the anvil, or killing zone. Collectively the operations became known as the Binh Dinh Pacification Campaign.

For forty-two days elements of the airmobile division scoured the An Lao and Kim Son Valleys, pursuing enemy units that had been surprised and routed from the Bong Son plain. Meanwhile, Marine forces in neighboring Quang Ngai Province in southern I Corps sought to bar the enemy's escape routes to the north. The enemy took heavy casualties, and

UH–1 Hueys pick up soldiers of the 1st Cavalry Division during operations on the Bong Son Plain in 1966.

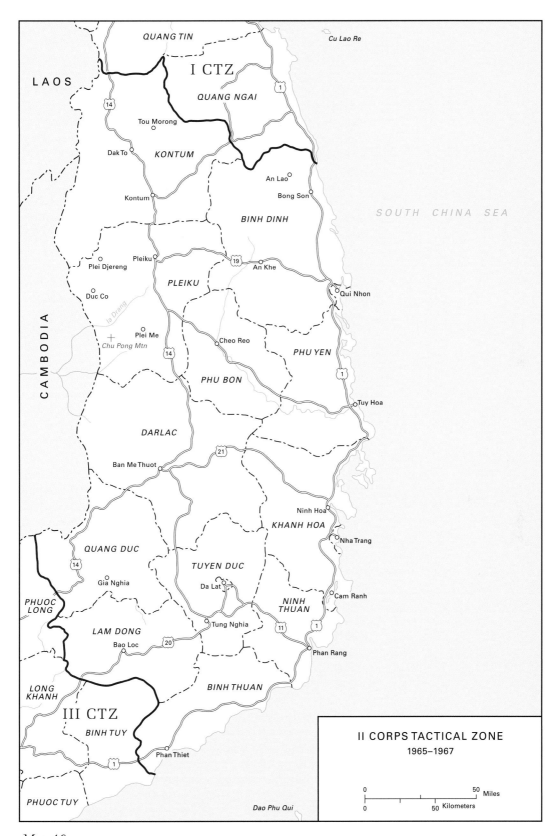

QUANG TIN

Cu Lao Re

LAOS

I CTZ

QUANG NGAI

14

Tou Morong ○

Dak To ○

KONTUM

An Lao ○

Kontum ○

Bong Son ○

BINH DINH

SOUTH CHINA SEA

C A M B O D I A

Plei Djereng ○

Pleiku ○

19

An Khe ○

PLEIKU

Duc Co ○

Qui Nhon ○

Ia Drang

Plei Me ○

+
Chu Pong Mtn

Cheo Reo ○

14

PHU YEN

PHU BON

1

Tuy Hoa ○

DARLAC

21

Ban Me Thuot ○

Ninh Hoa ○

KHANH HOA

Nha Trang ○

QUANG DUC

14

TUYEN DUC

Gia Nghia ○

Da Lat ○

PHUOC
LONG

Cam Ranh ○

NINH
THUAN

LAM DONG

20

Tung Nghia ○

11

1

Bao Loc ○

Phan Rang ○

LONG
KHANH

BINH THUAN

III CTZ

BINH TUY

1

Phan Thiet ○

PHUOC TUY

Dao Phu Qui

II CORPS TACTICAL ZONE
1965–1967

0   50 Miles

0   50 Kilometers

Map 19

thousands of civilians fled from the Viet Cong–dominated valleys to government-controlled areas. Although the influx of refugees taxed the government's already strained relief services, the exodus of peasants weakened the Viet Cong's infrastructure and aimed a psychological blow at the enemy's prestige. The Communists had failed either to confront the Americans or to protect the population over which they had gained control.

After the An Lao Valley operations, units of the airmobile division assaulted another enemy base area, a group of valleys and ridges southwest of the Bong Son plain known as the Crow's Foot or the Eagle's Claw. Here some Army units sought to dislodge the enemy from his upland bases while others established blocking positions at the "toe" of each valley (where it found outlet to the plain). In six weeks over 1,300 enemy soldiers were killed. Enemy forces in northern Binh Dinh Province were temporarily thrown off balance. Beyond this, the long-term effects of the operation were unclear. The 1st Cavalry Division did not stay in one area long enough to exploit its success. Whether the South Vietnamese government could marshal its forces effectively to provide local security and to reassert its political control remained to be seen.

After a brief interlude in the highlands, the division returned to Binh Dinh Province in September 1966. Conditions in the Bong Son area differed little from those the division had first encountered. For the most part, the Viet Cong rather than the South Vietnamese government had been successful in reasserting their authority; pacification was at a standstill. The division devoted most of its resources for the remainder of 1966 and throughout 1967 to supporting renewed pacification efforts. In the fall of 1966, for the first time in a year, all three of the division's brigades were reunited and operating in Binh Dinh Province. Although elements of the division were occasionally transferred to the highlands as the threat there waxed and waned, the general movement of forces was toward the north. Army units increasingly were sent to southern I Corps during 1967, replacing Marine units in operations similar to those in Binh Dinh Province.

Operations on the coast continued through 1967 and into early 1968. In addition to offensive operations against enemy main forces, Army units in Binh Dinh worked in close coordination with South Vietnamese police, Regional and Popular Forces, and the South Vietnamese Army to help the central government gain a foothold in villages and hamlets that the Communists dominated or contested. The 1st Cavalry Division adopted a number of techniques in support of pacification. Army units frequently participated in cordon and search operations: airmobile forces seized positions around a hamlet or village at dawn to prevent the escape of local forces or cadres, while South Vietnamese authorities undertook a methodical house-to-house search. The Vietnamese checked the legal status of inhabitants, took a census, and interrogated suspected Viet Cong to obtain more information about the enemy's local political and military apparatus. At the same time allied forces engaged in a variety of civic action and psychological operations, and specially trained pacification cadres established the rudiments of local government and provided various social and economic services. At other times, the division participated in "checkpoint and snatch" operations establishing surprise roadblocks and inspecting traffic on roads frequented by the insurgents.

In many respects, the Binh Dinh campaign was a microcosm of Westmoreland's overall campaign strategy. It showed clearly the intimate relation between the war against enemy main-force units and the fight for pacification waged by the South Vietnamese, and it demonstrated the effectiveness of the airmobile concept. After two years of persistent pursuit of the *3d PAVN Division*, the 1st Cavalry Division had reduced the combat effectiveness of each of its three regiments. By the end of 1967 the threat to Binh Dinh Province posed by enemy main-force units had been markedly reduced. The airmobile division's operations against the North Vietnamese *3d Division*, as well as its frequent role in operations directly in support of pacification, had weakened local guerrilla forces and created an environment favorable to pacification.

The campaign in Binh Dinh also exposed the vulnerabilities of Westmoreland's campaign strategy. Despite repeated defeats at the hands of the Americans, the three enemy regiments still existed. They contrived to find respite and a measure of rehabilitation, building their strength anew with recruits filtering down from the North, with others found in country, and with Viet Cong units consolidated into their ranks. Although much weakened, Communist forces persistently returned to areas the 1st Cavalry Division had cleared. Even more threatening to the allied cause, the central government's pacification efforts languished as South Vietnamese forces failed in many instances to provide security to the villages and effective police action to root out local Viet Cong cadres. And the government, dealing with an already-skeptical population, failed to grant the political, social, and economic benefits it had promised.

Progress or Stalemate?

The allies could not concentrate their efforts everywhere as they had in strategic Binh Dinh. The expanse of the highlands compelled Army operations there to proceed with economy of force. During 1966 and 1967, the Americans engaged in a constant search for tactical concepts and techniques to maximize their advantages of firepower and mobility and to compensate for the constraints of time, distance, difficult terrain, and an inviolable border. Here the war was fought primarily to prevent the incursion of North Vietnamese units into South Vietnam and to erode their combat strength. In the highlands, each side pursued a strategy of military confrontation, seeking to weaken the fighting forces and will of its opponent through attrition. Each sought military victories to convince opposing leaders of the futility of continuing the contest.

For Americans the most difficult problem was locating the enemy. Yet Communist strategists sometimes created threats to draw U.S. troops into ambushes. Recurrent menaces to Special Forces camps reflected the enemy's seasonal cycle of operations, his desire to harass and eliminate such camps, and his hope of luring allied forces into situations where he held the military advantages. Thus Army operations in the highlands during 1966 and 1967 were characterized by wide-ranging, often futile searches punctuated by sporadic but intense battles fought usually at the enemy's initiative.

> The Americans engaged in a constant search for tactical concepts and techniques to maximize their advantages of firepower and mobility and to compensate for the constraints of time, distance, difficult terrain, and an inviolable border.

For the first few months of 1966, the Communists lay low. In May, however, a significant concentration of North Vietnamese forces appeared in Pleiku and Kontum Provinces. The 1st Brigade, 101st Airborne Division, the reserve of I Field Force, was summoned to Pleiku and subsequently moved elements to Dak To, a CIDG camp in central Kontum Province, to assist a besieged South Vietnamese force at the nearby government post at Tou Morong. Although the *24th PAVN Regiment* had surrounded Tou Morong, allied forces secured the road to the beleaguered base and evacuated the government troops, leaving one battalion of the 101st Division at the abandoned camp and reinforcing with two companies to the north. On June 9, during a sweep of the battlefield, one of the companies ran into the North Vietnamese, who threatened to overrun it. Facing disaster, the commander called in air strikes just forward of his position to stop the enemy's human-wave attacks. Relief arrived the next morning, as helicopters carried additional elements of the brigade to the battlefield to pursue and trap the North Vietnamese. Fighting to close off the enemy's escape routes, the Americans called in renewed air strikes, including B–52s. By June 20 enemy resistance had ended and the North Vietnamese regiment that had begun the fighting had left behind its dead in its haste to escape to the safety of its Laotian base.

Although the enemy's push in Kontum Province was blunted, the siege of Tou Morong was only one aspect of his summer offensive in the highlands. Suspecting that the North Vietnamese meant to return to the Ia Drang Valley, Westmoreland sent the 3d Brigade, 25th Infantry Division, back into the valley in May. Dividing the area like a checkerboard, the brigade methodically searched each square. Small patrols set out ambushes and operated for several days without resupply to avoid having helicopters reveal their location. After several days in one square, the patrols leapfrogged by helicopter to another. Though the Americans made only light, sporadic contacts, the cumulative toll of enemy killed was equal to many short, violent battles. The Americans made one significant contact in late May near the Chu Pong Massif; running battles ensued, as the enemy again sought safety in Cambodia. Westmoreland now appealed to Washington for permission to maneuver Army units behind the enemy, possibly into Cambodian territory. But officials refused, fearing international repercussions; the North Vietnamese sanctuary remained inviolate.

Border battles continued, some very sharp. When enemy forces appeared in strength around a Special Forces camp at Plei Djereng in October, elements of the 4th Infantry and 1st Cavalry Divisions rapidly reinforced the camp, clashing with the enemy in firefights during October and November. As

Infantry Patrol in a Clearing, *Roger Blum, 1966*

North Vietnamese forces began to withdraw through the Plei Trap Valley, the 1st Brigade, 101st Airborne Division, flew from Phu Yen to northern Kontum to try to block their escape but failed to trap them before they reached the border. The 4th Infantry Division continued operations in the highlands. In addition to screening the border to detect infiltration, the division constructed a new road between Pleiku and the highland outpost at Plei Djereng and helped the South Vietnamese government resettle thousands of Montagnards in secure camps. Contact with the enemy generally was light, the heaviest occurring in mid-February 1967 in an area west of the Nam Sathay River near the Cambodian border, when Communist forces unsuccessfully tried to overrun several American firebases. Despite infrequent contacts, however, 4th Division troops killed 700 of the enemy over a period of three months.

In I Corps as well, the enemy seemed intent on fighting the Americans on the borders. Heightened activity along the demilitarized zone drew marines from southern I Corps. Into the area the marines had vacated Army units were transferred from III and II Corps, among them the 196th Light Infantry Brigade, which pulled out of Operation Junction City, and the 3d Brigade, 25th Infantry Division, heretofore operating in the II Corps Zone. Together with the 1st Brigade, 101st Airborne Division, these units formed Task Force Oregon, activated at Chu Lai on April 12, 1967, and placed under the operational control of the III Marine Amphibious Force. Army infantry units were now operating in all four of South Vietnam's corps areas.

Once at Chu Lai, the Army forces supported an extensive South Vietnamese pacification effort in Quang Tin and Quang Ngai Provinces. To the north, along the demilitarized zone, Army heavy artillery engaged in almost daily duels with North Vietnamese guns to the north. In Quang Tri Province, the marines fought a hard, twelve-day battle to prevent North Vietnamese forces from dominating the hills surrounding Khe Sanh. The enemy's heightened military activity along the demilitarized zone, which included frontal attacks across it, prompted American officials to begin construction of a barrier consisting of highly sophisticated electronic and acoustical sensors and strong-point defenses manned by allied forces. Known as the McNamara Line, after Secretary of Defense McNamara, who had vigorously promoted the concept, the barrier was to extend across South Vietnam and eventually into Laos. Westmoreland was not enthusiastic about the project. He hesitated to commit large numbers of troops to man the necessary strong points, doubting that the barrier was capable of preventing the enemy from breaching the demilitarized zone. Hence the McNamara Line was never completed and only a limited success in detecting infiltration into the South.

Throughout the summer of 1967, Marine forces endured some of the most intense enemy artillery barrages of the war and fought several battles with North Vietnamese Army units that infiltrated across the 17th Parallel. Their stubborn defense, supported by massive counterbattery fire, naval gunfire, and air attacks, ended the enemy's offensive in northern I Corps, but not before Westmoreland had to divert additional Army units as reinforcements. A brigade of the 1st Cavalry Division and South Korean units were deployed to southern I Corps to replace additional marines who had shifted farther north. The depth of the Army's

The enemy's heightened military activity along the demilitarized zone, which included frontal attacks across it, prompted American officials to begin construction of a barrier consisting of highly sophisticated electronic and acoustical sensors and strong-point defenses manned by allied forces.

commitment in I Corps was shown by Task Force OREGON's reorganization as the 23d Infantry Division (Americal). The only Army division to be formed in South Vietnam, its name echoed a famous World War II division that had also been organized in the Pacific.

Even as Westmoreland shifted allied forces from II Corps to I Corps, fighting intensified in the highlands. After Army units made several contacts with enemy forces during May and June, Westmoreland moved the 173d Airborne Brigade from III Corps to II Corps to serve as the I Field Force's strategic reserve. Within a few days, however, the brigade was committed to an effort to forestall enemy attacks against the Special Forces camps of Dak To, Dak Seang, and Dak Pek in Kontum Province. Under the control of the 4th Infantry Division, the operation continued throughout the summer until the enemy threat abated. A few months later, however, reconnaissance patrols in the vicinity of Dak To detected a rapid and substantial buildup of enemy forces in regimental strength. Believing an attack to be imminent, 4th Infantry Division forces reinforced the garrison. In turn the 173d Airborne Brigade returned to the highlands, arriving on November 2. From November 3–15, an estimated 12,000 enemy probed, harassed, and attacked American and South Vietnamese positions along the ridges and hills surrounding the camp. As the attacks grew stronger, more U.S. and South Vietnamese reinforcements were sent, including two battalions from the airmobile division and six South Vietnamese Army battalions. By mid-November allied strength approached 8,000.

Despite daily air and artillery bombardments, the North Vietnamese launched two attacks against Dak To on November 15, destroying two C–130 aircraft and causing severe damage to the camp's ammunition dump. Allied forces strove to dislodge the enemy from the surrounding hills, but the North Vietnamese held fast in fortified positions. The center of enemy resistance was Hill 875. Here, two battalions of Brig. Gen. Leo H. Schweiter's 173d Airborne Brigade made a slow and painful ascent against determined resistance and under grueling physical conditions, fighting for every foot of ground. Enemy fire was so intense and accurate that at times the Americans were unable to bring in reinforcements by helicopter or to provide fire support. In fighting that resembled the hill battles of the final stage of the Korean War, the confusion at Dak To pitted soldier against soldier in classic infantry battle. In desperation, beleaguered U.S. commanders on Hill 875 called in artillery and even B–52 air strikes perilously close to their own positions. On November 23 American forces at last gained control of Hill 875.

The Battle of Dak To was the longest and most violent in the highlands since the Battle of the Ia Drang

Men of the 173d Airborne Brigade prepare for airlift into the Central Highlands in 1967.

two years before. Enemy casualties numbered in the thousands, with an estimated 1,600 killed. Americans had suffered too. Approximately one-sixth of the 173d Airborne Brigade had become casualties, with 191 killed, 642 wounded, and 15 missing in action. If the Battle of the Ia Drang exemplified airmobility in all its versatility, the battle of Dak To, with the arduous ascent of Hill 875, epitomized infantry combat at its most basic, as well as the crushing effect of supporting air power.

Dak To was only one of several border battles in the waning months of 1967. At Song Be and Loc Ninh in III Corps and all along the northern border of I Corps, the enemy exposed his positions in order to confront U.S. forces in heavy fighting. By the end of 1967 a reinforced brigade of the 1st Infantry Division had again drifted north toward Cambodia and a brigade of the 25th Infantry Division had returned to War Zone C. The enemy's threat in I Corps caused Westmoreland to disperse more Army units. In the vacuum left by their departure, local Viet Cong sought to reconstitute their forces and to reassert their control over the rural population. In turn, Viet Cong revival often was a prelude to the resurgence of Communist military activity at the district and village levels. Hard-pressed to find additional Army units to shift from III Corps and II Corps to I Corps, Westmoreland asked the Army to accelerate deployment of two remaining brigades of the 101st Airborne Division from the United States. Arriving in December 1967, the brigades were added to the growing number of Army units operating in the northern provinces.

While allied forces were under pressure, the border battles of 1967 also led to a reassessment of strategy in Hanoi. Unwavering in their long-term aim of unification, the leaders of North Vietnam recognized that their strategy of military confrontation had failed to stop the American military buildup in the South or to reduce U.S. military pressure on the North. Regular and main-force units had failed to inflict a salient military defeat on American forces. Although the North Vietnamese Army maintained the tactical initiative, Westmoreland had kept its units at bay and in some areas, like Binh Dinh Province, diminished their influence on the contest for control of the rural population. Many Communist military leaders perceived the war to be a stalemate and believed that continuing on their present course would bring diminishing returns, especially if their local forces were drastically weakened.

On the other side, Westmoreland could rightly point to some modest progress in improving South Vietnam's security and to punishing defeats inflicted on several North Vietnamese regiments and divisions. Yet none of his successes were sufficient to turn the tide of the war. The Communists had matched the buildup of American combat forces: the number of enemy divisions in the South increased from one in early 1965 to nine at the start of 1968. Against 363 allied combat battalions, the North Vietnamese and Viet Cong could marshal 209. Despite heavy air attacks against enemy lines of infiltration, the flow of men from the North had continued unabated, even increasing toward the end of 1967.

Although the Military Assistance Command had succeeded in warding off defeat in 1965 and had gained valuable time for the South Vietnamese to concentrate their political and military resources on pacification, security in many areas of South Vietnam had improved little.

More and more, success in the South seemed to depend not only on Westmoreland's ability to hold off and weaken enemy main-force units, but also on the equally important efforts of the South Vietnamese Army, the Regional Forces (RF), the Popular Forces (PF), and a variety of paramilitary and police forces to pacify the countryside. Writing to President Johnson in the spring of 1967, outgoing Ambassador Henry Cabot Lodge warned that if the South Vietnamese "dribble along and do not take advantage of the success which MACV has achieved against the main force and the Army of North Viet-Nam, we must expect that the enemy will lick his wounds, pull himself together and make another attack in '68." Westmoreland's achievements, he added, would be "judged not so much on the brilliant performance of the U.S. troops as on the success in getting [the South Vietnamese Army], RF and PF quickly to function as a first-class … counter-guerrilla force." Meanwhile, the war appeared to be in a state of equilibrium. Only an extraordinary effort by one side or the other could bring a decision.

DISCUSSION QUESTIONS

1. In Vietnam, the helicopter provided allied forces with unprecedented mobility. Describe the helicopter's role in ground combat. What were its drawbacks?

2. During the war, certain officers and civilian analysts said that General Westmoreland paid too much attention to the enemy's main forces and not enough to pacification. How do you think the general would have responded?

3. President Johnson declined to mobilize the reserves when he committed ground troops to Vietnam in 1965. What was the impact of this decision on the U.S. Army for the duration of the war?

4. Until 1970 the enemy's cross-border sanctuaries were off-limits to U.S. ground forces. How did this affect the American conduct of the war?

5. Among the earliest U.S. forces introduced into Vietnam were U.S. Army Special Forces. To what extent were they the ideal force for counterinsurgency? What were their weaknesses?

RECOMMENDED READINGS

Bergerud, Eric M. *The Dynamics of Defeat: The Vietnam War in Hau Nghia Province.* Boulder, Colo.: Westview Press, 1991.

Carland, John M. *Combat Operations: Stemming the Tide, May 1965 to October 1966.* U.S. Army in Vietnam. Washington D.C.: U.S. Army Center of Military History, 2000.

Davidson, Phillip B. *Vietnam at War: The History, 1946–1975.* Novato, Calif.: Presidio Press, 1988.

Hammond, William M. *Public Affairs: The Military and the Media, 1962–1968.* U.S. Army in Vietnam. Washington, D.C.: U.S. Army Center of Military History, 1996.

Herring, George C. *America's Longest War: The United States and Vietnam, 1950–1975.* Boston: McGraw-Hill, 2002.

MacGarrigle, George L. *Combat Operations: Taking the Offensive, October 1966 to October 1967*. U.S. Army in Vietnam. Washington, D.C.: U.S. Army Center of Military History, 1998.

Palmer, Dave R. *Summons of the Trumpet: U.S.-Vietnam in Perspective*. San Rafael, Calif.: Presidio Press, 1978.

Race, Jeffrey. *War Comes to Long An: Revolutionary Conflict in a Vietnamese Province*. Berkeley: University of California Press, 1972.

Spector, Ronald H. *Advice and Support: The Early Years, 1941–1960*. U.S. Army in Vietnam. Washington, D.C.: U.S. Army Center of Military History, 1985.

Westmoreland, William C. *A Soldier Reports*. New York: Da Capo Press, 1989.

Other Readings

Berman, Larry. *Lyndon Johnson's War: The Road to Stalemate in Vietnam*. New York: W. W. Norton & Co., 1989.

Blaufarb, Douglas S. *The Counterinsurgency Era: U.S. Doctrine and Performance, 1950 to the Present*. New York: Free Press, 1977.

Bowers, Ray L. *Tactical Airlift*. The United States Air Force in Southeast Asia. Washington, D.C.: Office of Air Force History, 1983.

Cash, John A., John N. Albright, and Allan W. Sandstrum. *Seven Firefights in Vietnam*. Washington, D.C.: U.S. Army Center of Military History, 1989.

Duiker, William J. *The Communist Road to Power in Vietnam*, 2d ed. Boulder, Colo.: Westview Press, 1996.

Gelb, Leslie H., with Richard K. Betts. *The Irony of Vietnam: The System Worked*. Washington, D.C.: Brookings Institution, 1979.

Kaiser, David E. *American Tragedy: Kennedy, Johnson, and the Origins of the Vietnam War*. Cambridge: Belknap Press of Harvard University Press, 2000.

Krepinevich, Andrew F. *The Army and Vietnam*. Baltimore: Johns Hopkins University Press, 1986.

Meyerson, Joel D. *Images of a Lengthy War*. U.S. Army in Vietnam. Washington, D.C.: U.S. Army Center of Military History, 1989.

The Military History Institute of Vietnam. *Victory in Vietnam: The Official History of the People's Army of Vietnam, 1954–1975,* trans. Merle L. Pribbenow. Lawrence: University Press of Kansas, 2002.

Moore, Harold G., and Joseph L. Galloway. *We Were Soldiers Once … and Young: Ia Drang, the Battle That Changed the War in Vietnam*. New York: Harper Perennial, 1992.

Palmer, Bruce, Jr. *The 25-Year War: America's Military Role in Vietnam*. New York: Da Capo Press, 1990.

The Pentagon Papers: The Defense Department History of United States Decisionmaking on Vietnam. Senator Gravel edition, 5 vols. Boston: Beacon Press, 1971.

Pike, Douglas E. *Viet Cong: The Organization and Techniques of the National Liberation Front of South Vietnam*. Cambridge: M.I.T. Press, 1966.

11

The U.S. Army in Vietnam from Tet to the Final Withdrawal, 1968–1975

By the beginning of 1968 the United States had been involved in military operations in Vietnam for over seven years and in major ground combat for two-and-a-half years. In-country U.S. military strength had risen to 485,000, and General William C. Westmoreland had been using his troops aggressively in all parts of South Vietnam to pursue the enemy's main forces and to help shield the population from enemy attack. U.S. and allied forces had conducted hundreds of operations both large and small, and some forty of that number had each achieved a verified body count of 500 or more enemy soldiers. According to MACV estimates, 81,000 Communist soldiers had been killed in 1967, giving substance to Westmoreland's belief that the allies were slowly winning the war in Vietnam.

Other trends seemed to confirm his optimism. While the American public appeared to be growing weary of recitations of statistics, the Johnson administration continued to put faith in them as one way to make sense of a war that was so difficult to measure. The pacification trends were especially heartening. By 1967 some two-thirds of the hamlets in South Vietnam were judged secure and under the control of the central government. (In early 1965 the government was being chased from the countryside and on the verge of collapse.) Meanwhile, enemy troop strength in the South had dropped by a quarter to 220,000, the result both of attrition on the battlefield and declines in infiltration from the North and recruitment in the South. In 1965 and 1966 some 9,000 North Vietnamese a month were coming down the Ho Chi Minh Trail to fight in the South, whereas in 1967 the figure was 6,000 a month. (*See Chart 1 for yearly infiltration rates.*) Viet Cong recruitment in the villages had fallen to half its previous monthly average of 7,000. All this gave precious breathing space to the South Vietnamese as they

Chart 1—*PAVN* Infiltration of the South: 1965–1975 (in thousands)

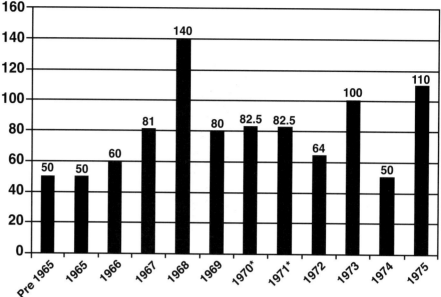

*Figures are estimates only, averaging the *PAVN*-stated total of 165,000 for 1970 and 1971 combined.

expanded their security programs in the countryside and prepared to assume from the United States more of the burden of responsibility for the main-force war. Westmoreland reported that if all went well he could begin a phased withdrawal of U.S. forces in 1970.

The Johnson administration worked hard to put these projections before a restive Congress and the American people in order to bolster support for the war. It was critical, the President's advisers told him, to show progress and an eventual end of the fighting if the American people were to continue to back the administration. This was especially so as the number of U.S. casualties climbed. By the end of 1967 some 16,000 Americans had been killed in action in Vietnam, and the recent weekly average had exceeded 150. McGeorge Bundy, the former National Security Adviser, told President Lyndon B. Johnson: "I think people are getting fed up with the endlessness of the fighting. What really hurts, then, is not the arguments of the doves, but the cost of the war in lives and money, coupled with the lack of light at the end of the tunnel."

Westmoreland agreed: in November 1967, during a visit to Washington for consultations, he put a positive face on the fighting, stating to the press and Congress that he believed that the war had entered a new phase "when the end begins to come into view." Similar expressions of confidence followed from other officials in the administration as the campaign for opinion spilled over into the new year. Not even suspicious signs of enemy movement and consolidations and an upsurge of terrorism in the cities dampened the optimism issuing from Saigon and Washington. The American public was still taking those assurances at face value and appeared to be momentarily mollified when the enemy launched his Tet offensive at the end of January, thus changing the course of the war.

The Tet Offensive

The Tet offensive marked a unique stage in the evolution of North Vietnam's "People's War." Hanoi's solution to the stalemate in the South was the product of several factors. North Vietnam's large-unit war was unequal to the task of defeating American combat units. South Vietnam became politically and militarily stronger, while the Viet Cong's grip over the rural population eroded. Hanoi's leaders suspected that the United States, frustrated by the slow progress, might intensify its military opera-

A Viet Cong ambush in Saigon took a toll of U.S. Army MPs.

tions against the North. (Indeed, Westmoreland had broached plans for an invasion of the North when he appealed for additional forces in 1967.) The Tet offensive was Hanoi's brilliant stroke of strategy designed to change the arena of war from the battlefield to the negotiating table.

Communist plans called for violent, widespread, simultaneous military actions in rural and urban areas throughout the South—a general offensive. But as always, military action was subordinate to the larger political goal. By focusing attacks on South Vietnamese units and facilities, Hanoi sought to undermine the morale and will of South Vietnam's forces. Through a collapse of military resistance, the North Vietnamese hoped to subvert public confidence in the government's ability to provide security, triggering a crescendo of popular protest to halt the fighting and force a political accommodation. In short, they aimed at a general uprising.

Hanoi's generals, however, were not completely confident that the general offensive would succeed. Viet Cong forces, hastily reinforced with new recruits and part-time guerrillas, bore the brunt. Except in the northern provinces, the North Vietnamese Army stayed on the sidelines, poised to exploit success. While hoping to spur negotiations, Communist leaders probably had the more modest goals of reasserting Viet Cong influence and undermining the central government's authority so as to cast doubt on its credibility as the United States' ally. In this respect, the offensive was directed toward the United States and sought to weaken American confidence in the South Vietnamese government, discredit Westmoreland's claims of progress, and strengthen American antiwar sentiment. Here again, the larger purpose was to bring the United States to the negotiating table and hasten American disengagement from Vietnam.

The enemy offensive began in mid-January 1968 in the remote northwest corner of South Vietnam. Elements of three North Vietnamese divisions had massed near the Marine base at Khe Sanh. At first the ominous proportions of the buildup led the Military Assistance

THE TIMING OF THE TET OFFENSIVE

On January 29, only a day before the offensive was to begin, officials in Hanoi instructed their front headquarters in South Vietnam to postpone the attack for twenty-four hours. They had realized that their lunar calendar was one day out of sync with the calendar used in the South. Some of the Communist units in southern I Corps and in II Corps either did not receive the new instructions in time or decided to go ahead with their assault because their troops were already in exposed forward positions. The premature attacks alerted the allies that a larger blow was imminent. Nevertheless, the degree of surprise and the scope of the attacks startled the American people and undercut support for the war.

Command to expect a major offensive in the northern provinces. To some observers the situation at Khe Sanh resembled that at Dien Bien Phu, the isolated garrison where the Viet Minh had defeated French forces in 1954.

While pressure around Khe Sanh increased, 84,000 Communist troops prepared for the Tet offensive. Since the fall of 1967, the enemy had been infiltrating arms, ammunition, and men, including entire units, into Saigon and other cities and towns. Most of these meticulous preparations went undetected, although MACV received warnings of a major enemy action to take place in early 1968. Growing edgy, Westmoreland did pull thirteen battalions closer to Saigon before the attack, nearly doubling U.S. strength around the capital. However, concern over the critical situation at Khe Sanh and preparations for the Tet holiday festivities preoccupied most Americans and South Vietnamese. Even when Communist forces prematurely attacked Kontum City, Qui Nhon, Da Nang, and other towns in the central and northern provinces on January 30, the Americans were unprepared for what followed.

On January 31 combat erupted throughout the entire country. Thirty-six of 44 provincial capitals and 64 of 242 district towns were attacked, as well as 5 of South Vietnam's 6 autonomous cities, among them Hue and Saigon. (*Map 20*) Once the shock and confusion wore off, most attacks were crushed in a few days. During those few days, however, the fighting was some of the most violent ever seen in the South or experienced by many South Vietnamese Army units. And though the South Vietnamese were the main target, American units were swept into the turmoil.

All U.S. Army units in the vicinity of Saigon helped to repel Viet Cong attacks there and at the nearby bases of Long Binh and Bien Hoa. Cooks, radiomen, and clerks in some American compounds took up arms in their own defense. Elements of the 716th Military Police Battalion helped to root out enemy soldiers from downtown Saigon, and Army helicopter gunships were in the air almost continuously, assisting allied forces. Racing through the night to Tan Son Nhut Airport, armored cavalry from the 25th Infantry Division helped to defeat an enemy regiment threatening to overrun the giant installation.

Elsewhere the battle was just as furious. South of Saigon, the riverine troops of the 2d Brigade, 9th Infantry Division, fought successively at My Tho, Cai Lay, and Vinh Long and by the second

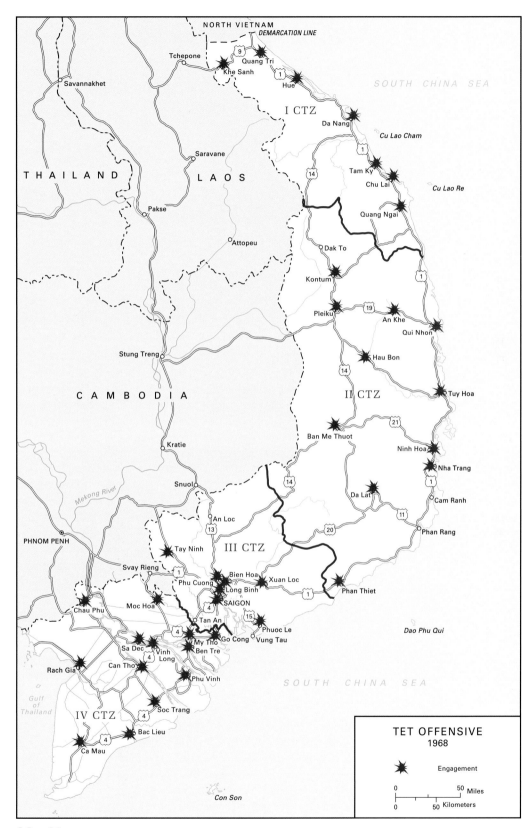

NORTH VIETNAM
DEMARCATION LINE

Tchepone
Savannakhet

THAILAND
LAOS

Saravane

Pakse

Attopeu

Stung Treng

CAMBODIA

Kratie

Snuol

PHNOM PENH

Svay Rieng

Chau Phu

Moc Hoa

Rach Gia

Gulf of
Thailand

IV CTZ

Ca Mau

Bac Lieu

Soc Trang

Can Tho

Sa Dec

Vinh
Long

Phu Vinh

Ben Tre

My Tho

Tan An

Go Cong

SAIGON

Long Binh

Phu Cuong

Bien Hoa

Tay Ninh

An Loc

III CTZ

Xuan Loc

Phuoc Le

Vung Tau

Phan Thiet

Da Lat

Phan Rang

Cam Ranh

Nha Trang

Ninh Hoa

II CTZ

Ban Me Thuot

Tuy Hoa

Hau Bon

Qui Nhon

An Khe

Pleiku

Kontum

Dak To

Quang Ngai

Chu Lai

Tam Ky

Da Nang

I CTZ

Hue

Khe Sanh

Quang Tri

SOUTH CHINA SEA

Cu Lao Cham

Cu Lao Re

Dao Phu Qui

SOUTH CHINA SEA

Con Son

Mekong River

TET OFFENSIVE
1968

Engagement

0   50 Miles

0   50 Kilometers

Map 20

Aftermath of Heavy Fighting in Downtown Saigon

week of February had crippled the offensive in the upper Mekong Delta. In the western highlands town of Pleiku, American tankers, cavalrymen, artillerymen, and engineers joined South Vietnamese cavalry and infantry to hold off Viet Cong assaults for nearly a week. The situation was particularly grave in northern I Corps. There, the Viet Cong and North Vietnamese struck at roads, waterways, and bridges and threatened to sever the allies' logistical lifeline. Writing on February 9 to the Chairman of the Joint Chiefs of Staff, General Earle G. Wheeler, Westmoreland observed that logistics would be the key to winning the fight in the northern provinces. Tactical airlift for a time was the major source of supplies for the 1st Cavalry Division just moved to I Corps. While the fight for Quang Tri City was essentially over after two days, the critical stretch of Highway 1 from Da Nang northward to Phu Bai and Hue had to wait until marines, paratroopers, and their engineers linked up in the flatlands to the north of the Hai Van Pass. Although the highway finally became passable to U.S. convoys on March 1, the flow of supplies remained unsatisfactory for several weeks, necessitating the opening just east of Quang Tri City of a large shore operation at Wunder Beach (Than My Thuy). Marines, Navy Seabees, and Army lighterage and port units, chiefly the 159th Transportation Battalion, were all involved.

The most tenacious combat occurred in Hue, the ancient capital of Vietnam. There, the 1st Cavalry and 101st Airborne Divisions, together with marines and South Vietnamese forces, including the South Vietnamese 1st Infantry Division, participated in the only extended urban combat of the war. Hue had a tradition of Buddhist activism with overtones of neutralism, separatism, and anti-Americanism; North Vietnamese strategists thought that here if anywhere the general offensive/general uprising might gain a political foothold. Hence they threw most of seven North Vietnamese regiments into the battle, bringing several units down from Khe Sanh, an indication that the stakes at Hue were higher than elsewhere in the South. House-to-house and street-to-street fighting caused enormous destruction, necessitating massive reconstruction and community assistance programs after the battle. The allies took more than three weeks to recapture the city and could not shut down the enemy's supply conduit into Hue until February 24.

Throughout the country, the South Vietnamese forces acquitted themselves well, despite high casualties and many desertions. Stunned by the attacks, civilian support for the government of President Nguyen Van Thieu coalesced instead of weakening. Many Vietnamese for whom the war had been a mere annoyance were outraged, not the least by confirmation that the Communists had executed almost 3,000 civilians at Hue. Capitalizing on the new feeling, South Vietnam's leaders for the first time enacted a general mobilization. The change from grudging toleration of the Viet Cong to active resistance provided an opportunity to create new local defense organizations and to attack the Communist infrastructure. Spurred by American advisers, the Vietnamese began to revitalize pacification. Most important, the Viet Cong suffered a major military defeat, losing thousands of experienced combatants and seasoned political cadres, seriously weakening the insurgent base in the South.

Americans at home saw a different picture. Dramatic images of the Viet Cong storming the grounds of the American Embassy in the heart of Saigon and of the North Vietnamese Army clinging tenaciously to Hue obscured Westmoreland's assertion that the enemy had been defeated. Claims of progress in the war, already greeted with skepticism, lost more credibility in both public and official circles. The psychological jolt to President Johnson's Vietnam policy was redoubled when the military requested an additional 206,000 troops. Most were intended to reconstitute the strategic reserve in the United States exhausted by Westmoreland's appeals for combat units between 1965 and 1967. But the magnitude of the new request, at a time when almost a half-million U.S. troops were already in Vietnam, cast doubts on the conduct of the war and prompted a reassessment of American policy and strategy.

Without mobilization the United States was overcommitted. The Army could send few additional combat units to Vietnam without making deep inroads on forces destined for NATO or South Korea. The dwindling strategic reserve left Johnson with fewer options in the spring of 1968 than in the summer of 1965. His problems were underscored by heightened international tensions when North Korea captured an American naval vessel, the USS *Pueblo*, a week before the Tet offensive; by Soviet armed intervention in Czechoslovakia in the summer of 1968; and by chronic crises in the Mideast. In addition, Army units in the United States were needed often between 1965 and 1968 to enforce federal civil rights legislation and to restore public order in the wake of civil disturbances.

Again, as in 1967, Johnson refused to sanction a major troop levy, but he did give Westmoreland some modest reinforcements to bolster the northern provinces. Again tapping the strategic reserve, the Army sent him the 3d Brigade, 82d Airborne Division, and the 1st Brigade, 5th Infantry Division (Mechanized)—the last Army combat units to

General Westmoreland's Tropical Combat Coat, 1965

deploy to South Vietnam. In addition, the President called to active duty a small number of reserve units, totaling some 40,000 men, for duty in Southeast Asia and South Korea, the only use of reserves during the Vietnam War. For Westmoreland, Johnson's decision meant that future operations would have to make the best possible use of American forces and that the South Vietnamese Army would have to shoulder a larger share of the war effort. To spur negotiations, the President also curtailed air strikes against North Vietnam. Finally, on March 31 Johnson announced his decision not to seek reelection in order to give his full attention to resolving the conflict. North Vietnam had suffered a military defeat but had won a political and diplomatic victory by shifting American policy toward disengagement.

For the Army the new policy meant a difficult time. In South Vietnam, as in the United States, its forces were stretched thin. The Tet offensive had concentrated a large portion of its combat forces in I Corps, once a Marine preserve. A new command, XXIV Corps, had to be activated for the northern provinces; Army logistical support, previously confined to the three southern corps zones and southern I Corps, now extended to the demilitarized zone as well. While Army units reinforced Hue and the demilitarized zone, the marines at Khe Sanh held fast. Enemy pressure on the besieged base increased daily, but the North Vietnamese refrained from an all-out attack. Recognizing that he could ill afford Khe Sanh's defense or its loss, Westmoreland decided to subject the enemy to the heaviest air and artillery bombardment of the war. His tactical gamble succeeded. The enemy withdrew, and the Communist offensive slackened.

The enemy nevertheless persisted in his effort to weaken the South Vietnamese government, launching nationwide "mini-Tet" offensives in May and August. Pockets of stiff fighting occurred throughout the South, and enemy forces again infiltrated into Saigon, leading to heavy destruction in several neighborhoods. But these were the last gasps of the general offensive/ general uprising. Thereafter the Viet Cong and North Vietnamese generally dispersed and avoided contact with Americans. In turn the allies withdrew from Khe Sanh in the summer of 1968. Its abandonment signaled the demise of the McNamara Line and further postponement of MACV's hopes for large-scale American cross-border operations. For the remainder of 1968, Army units in I Corps were content to help restore security around Hue and other coastal areas, working closely with the marines and the South Vietnamese in support of pacification. North Vietnamese and Viet Cong forces,

Marines patrol a street in Hue after the Tet offensive.

having suffered heavy losses, generally avoided offensive operations. As armistice negotiations began in Paris, both sides prepared to enter a new phase of the war.

Vietnamization

The last phase of American involvement in South Vietnam was carried out under a broad policy called Vietnamization. Its main goal was to create strong, largely self-reliant South Vietnamese military forces, an objective consistent with that espoused by U.S. advisers as early as the 1950s. But Vietnamization also meant the withdrawal of a half-million American soldiers. Past efforts to strengthen and modernize South Vietnam's Army had proceeded at a measured pace, without the pressure of diminishing American support, large-scale combat, or the presence of formidable North Vietnamese forces in the South. Vietnamization entailed three overlapping phases: redeployment of American forces and the assumption of their combat role by the South Vietnamese; improvement of the South Vietnamese Army's combat and support capabilities, especially firepower and mobility; and replacement of the Military Assistance Command by an American advisory group. Vietnamization had the added dimension of fostering political, social, and economic reforms to create a vibrant South Vietnamese state based on popular participation in national political life. Such reforms, however, depended on progress in the pacification program, which never had a clearly fixed timetable.

The task of carrying out the military aspects of Vietnamization fell to General Creighton W. Abrams, who succeeded General Westmoreland as MACV commander in mid-1968, when the latter returned to the United States to become Chief of Staff of the Army. Although Abrams had the aura of a blunt, hard-talking, World War II tank commander, he had spent a year as Westmoreland's deputy, working closely with South Vietnamese commanders. Like Westmoreland before him, Abrams viewed the military situation after Tet as an opportunity to make gains in pacifying rural areas and to reduce the strength of Communist forces in the South. Until the weakened Viet Cong forces could be rebuilt or replaced with North Vietnamese, both guerrilla and regular Communist forces had adopted a defensive posture. Nevertheless, 90,000 North Vietnamese Army troops were in the South or in border sanctuaries waiting to resume the offensive at a propitious time.

VIETNAM ADVISERS

At the height of the war in December 1968, there were nearly 11,000 advisers working at all levels of the South Vietnamese Army and the irregular forces assigned to pacification duty. Because advisers had no formal authority over the South Vietnamese, they had to develop a bond of trust in order to be effective. This required them to overcome vast language and cultural differences and to untangle the intricate web of politics that suffused the South Vietnamese officer corps. Generally, an adviser spent much of his tour developing an effective working relationship with his counterpart.

Abrams still had strong American forces, which reached their peak at 543,000 in March 1969. But he was also under pressure from Washington to minimize casualties, to conduct operations with an eye toward leaving the South Vietnamese in the strongest possible military position when U.S. forces withdrew, and to convince the American people with progress on the battlefield that the tide had turned in the allies' favor. With these considerations in mind, Abrams pressed the attack, especially against enemy bases near the border to prevent their use as staging areas for offensive operations. At the same time, to enhance the South Vietnamese government's pacification efforts and improve local security, he called on his commanders to intensify small-unit operations with extensive patrolling and ambushes, aiming to reduce the enemy's base of support among the rural population.

General Abrams with General Wheeler (left) *and Secretary of Defense Melvin R. Laird*

To the greatest extent possible, Abrams planned to improve the South Vietnamese Army's performance by enhancing training and conducting combined operations with American combat units. As the South Vietnamese Army assumed the lion's share of combat, it was expected to shift operations toward the border and to assume a role similar to that of U.S. forces between 1965 and 1969. The Regional and Popular Forces in turn were to take over the South Vietnamese Army's role in area security and pacification support, while the newly organized People's Self-Defense Force took on the task of village and hamlet defense. Stressing the close connection between combat and pacification operations, the need for cooperation between American and South Vietnamese forces, and the importance of coordinating all echelons of Saigon's armed forces, Abrams spoke of a "one war" concept.

Yet even in his emphasis on combined operations, his targeting of enemy base areas, and American support of pacification, Abrams' strategy had strong elements of continuity with Westmoreland's. For the first and second, operations in War Zones C and D and in the Binh Dinh piedmont in 1966 and 1967 were ample precedents. Westmoreland had also laid the foundation for a more extensive U.S. role in pacification in 1967 by establishing Civil Operations and Rural (later changed to Revolutionary) Development Support (CORDS). Under CORDS, the Military Assistance Command took charge of all American activities, military and civilian, in support of pacification.

Abrams' contribution was to enlarge the Army's role. Under him, the U.S. advisory effort at provincial and district levels grew as the territorial forces gained importance. During 1967, for example, there were 108 American advisers attached to the Regional Forces and Popular

Forces; one year later the number was 2,243. Another important step pushed by CORDS was establishment of the PHOENIX program, a concerted effort to eliminate the Communist political apparatus by capturing or killing enemy leaders in the villages and provinces. This crucial aspect of the counterinsurgency campaign had been run by the Central Intelligence Agency in the early 1960s but lacked the manpower to take on the importance it deserved. Under CORDS, PHOENIX expanded into virtually every district in South Vietnam, using a combination of conventional forces, militia, police, and psychological and intelligence operations not previously possible on such a large scale.

South Vietnamese soldiers train in the use of artillery as part of the Vietnamization program.

Despite all efforts, many Americans doubted whether South Vietnam's armed forces could successfully play their enlarged role under Vietnamization. On paper, the armed forces were formidable and improving. Thanks to the Thieu government's mobilization law and American aid and assistance, South Vietnam's forces had become among the largest and most heavily equipped in the world. The regular and territorial troop level, some 850,000 in late 1968, would rise to over a million in less than two years. The newest weapons in the American arsenal were being turned over to the South Vietnamese, from M16 rifles and M60 machine guns to helicopter gunships, jeeps, and jet fighters. Combat effectiveness was also apparently on the rise. Of the ten South Vietnamese infantry divisions, two of them—the 1st in I Corps and the 21st in IV Corps—were considered to be uniformly

CORDS
(CIVIL OPERATIONS AND REVOLUTIONARY DEVELOPMENT SUPPORT)

From the beginning of American involvement in Vietnam, the allies agreed that pacification—"winning the hearts and minds" of the Vietnamese people—was a primary objective of the war effort. However, there was no consensus on how to accomplish it, which resulted in inefficiency and bureaucratic infighting. Before pacification was consolidated under the military with the CORDS program in 1967, it was considered a political problem best handled by civilians. The U.S. embassy in Saigon ran a "country team" of representatives from the civilian agencies, but the team lacked both the political power and the budget to establish an effective pacification effort. Under MACV, however, CORDS established an effective civic-action program throughout the countryside.

reliable; three others—the 2d in I Corps, the 23d in the highlands, and the 9th in the Delta—received good ratings when strong commanders were in charge. In reserve were the airborne division and the Marine division, the elite of the entire group, and they had been fighting well since before Tet. Nonetheless, earlier counterinsurgency efforts had languished under less demanding circumstances, and the government's forces continued to be plagued with a high desertion rate, spotty morale, and shortages of high-quality leaders. Like the French before them, U.S. advisers had assumed a major role in providing and coordinating logistical and firepower support, leaving the Vietnamese inexperienced in the conduct of large combined-arms operations. Despite the Viet Cong's weakened condition, South Vietnamese forces also continued to incur high casualties.

Similarly, pacification registered gains in rural security and other measures of progress, but such improvements often obscured its failure to establish deep roots. On the one hand were the pacification statistics. Although complicated and often misleading, they clearly indicated that the government with U.S. assistance was making headway in the countryside. By early 1970, 93 percent of the South Vietnamese lived in "relatively secure" towns and villages, an increase of almost 20 percent from the middle of 1968, a year marred by the Tet offensive. Ironically, because the statistics themselves became a point of controversy, they may have obscured the reality behind the numbers, the fact that the enemy's losses truly were significant. The difficulty, however, was that the enemy underground had not been eliminated and still constituted a potent threat to the government. The PHOENIX program, despite its success in seizing low- and middle-level cadres, rarely caught hard-core, high-level party officials, many of whom survived, as they had in the mid-1950s, by taking more stringent security measures. Furthermore, some South Vietnamese officials abused the program, using it as a vehicle for personal vendettas. In some cases, district PHOENIX officials accepted bribes from the Viet Cong for the release of certain suspects. Some districts released as many as 60 percent of the suspected members of the enemy underground.

Even land reform, the South Vietnamese government's most successful program for building political strength in the countryside, rested on an uncertain foundation. Enacted in 1970, the land-to-the-tiller program was one of the most advanced undertaken anywhere in the developing world. President Thieu gave it unwavering support and placed strong leaders in charge. Land tenancy dropped from 60 to 10 percent between 1970 and 1973.

A PHOENIX program paramilitary team enters a village in Tay Ninh Province.

Computers sped up the process of registering ownership and issuing land titles, bypassing the sclerotic South Vietnamese bureaucracy. Even so, the social and economic benefits for the peasantry were understood to be only as durable as American aid and the conventional-force security shield. In that sense, despite the progress made, the entire South Vietnamese enterprise remained in doubt.

Influencing all parts of this struggle to hold the South was a new defense policy enunciated by Richard M. Nixon, who became President in January 1969. The Nixon Doctrine hearkened back to the precepts of the New Look, placing greater reliance on nuclear retaliation, encouraging allies to accept a larger share of their own defense burden, and barring the use of U.S. ground forces in limited wars in Asia, unless vital national interests were at stake. Under this policy, American ground forces in South Vietnam, once withdrawn, were unlikely to return. For President Thieu in Saigon, the future was inauspicious. For the time being, large numbers of American forces were still present to bolster his country's war effort; what would happen when they departed, no one knew.

Military Operations, 1968–1969

The U.S. troop withdrawals began in the summer of 1969, when two brigades of the 9th Infantry Division pulled out of III and IV Corps and a regiment of the 3d Marine Division departed from northern I Corps. These units were selected because they were considered first-rate and would consequently make the reduction in forces credible to all concerned—not just to the governments in Hanoi and Saigon but also to the American public. The 9th Division was chosen, according to General Abrams, because the war south of Saigon had been a South Vietnamese affair for years and was apparently going well. The marines would be leaving their area of operations to the best South Vietnamese division, the 1st Infantry Division, and to the remainder of their parent Marine unit, now reinforced along the demilitarized zone by the heavy brigade of the U.S. Army's 5th Division. The northernmost provinces, by all accounts, were thus also secure. The one area of the country where Abrams refused to thin out his forces was the territory north and west of Saigon, the arc protecting the capital. Saigon was the ultimate war prize, and everything depended on its security, from holding fast to public support in the United States and building a negotiating advantage to giving the South Vietnamese time to grow strong in their own defense. Abrams was not prepared to gamble Saigon's security on a military experiment, at least not yet.

Consequently, when a new threat emerged in III Corps—seven North Vietnamese regiments, including the entire *1st People's Army of Vietnam (PAVN) Division*, arrived from the highlands to reinforce the *Central Office for South Vietnam (COSVN)*—Abrams went on the offensive. Starting in late 1968 and for the next year and a half, U.S. forces, including the 1st Cavalry Division operating in III Corps for the first time in the war, engaged in a corps-wide counterattack to locate and destroy enemy units. The Americans combined large- and small-unit operations, frequent sweeps through enemy bases, and persistent screening of the Cambodian border to prevent the main forces from returning. Commanded by Maj. Gens. George I. Forsythe and Elvy B. Roberts, the 1st Cavalry Division waged the border battle. Straddling the enemy's jungle trails through Tay Ninh, Binh Long, and Phuoc Long Provinces and making full use of its helicopter mobility, it fought the enemy's units as they crossed from Cambodia.

The link between the division's mobility and its ability to carry on the fight as light infantry was the firebase. Although the firebase had evolved over the course of the war into a familiar component of American operations, the 1st Cavalry Division raised its use to a tactical art. Most Army firebases in South Vietnam contained an artillery battery or two and the command post of an infantry battalion and were built for temporary occupation. The 1st Cavalry Division's firebases tended to be smaller and more fleeting still. In its first month in III Corps, November 1968, the division built a line of fifteen bases right up to the border. When Firebase Dot, one of four bases west of Quan Loi, was nearly overrun, commanders established a new screen across the middle of War Zone C, far enough from Cambodia to give them warning of any attack. Throughout 1969 the division expanded its interdiction both east and west, leapfrogging from firebase to firebase and chewing up enemy troop concentrations as they tried to sideslip south. This made it easier for allied units closer to Saigon to keep the enemy remnants away from the population.

Nearer the capital, the 1st and 25th Infantry Divisions continued the fight in their traditional haunts to the north and west, but in somewhat reduced operating territory since border coverage was no longer required. Intensifying their operations behind the border screen of the airmobile division, they zeroed in on pockets of enemy resistance that still threatened the city. For the 1st Division, few of the battles were dramatic, except for the soldiers who fought them, but were typically small sweeps and night ambushes in the rolling hills along Highway 13, punctuated by clear-and-hold missions with South Vietnamese regulars,

Long Range Patrol, *James R. Drake, 1969*

Regional Forces, and the police. The more dramatic encounters took place in the tactical arena of the 25th Division. Here lay the Tay Ninh corridor, one of the traditional enemy funnels from the Cambodian sanctuary to the outskirts of Saigon. When the division erected fire-base defenses squarely in the enemy's path, a contest of wills was inevitable. One of those fortresses, near Tay Ninh City, was Firebase CROOK. Small, unprepossessing, and seemingly vulnerable, defended by a battery of light artillery and a company of infantry, CROOK was in fact a formidable redoubt with major tactical advantages: deeply dug with reinforced bunkers, equipped with remote sensors and radar, and well within range of medium and heavy artillery and, like all bases, supported by air power. In June 1969 the *9th People's Liberation Armed Forces (PLAF) Division* determined to overrun it and spent three days and over 400 dead in the vain attempt (one American soldier died). Further attacks followed on Tay Ninh City and other bases, all beaten back with heavy enemy casualties. By late 1969 the corridor had quieted; the 25th Division turned to pacification, running scores of medical aid missions and hundreds of joint operations with South Vietnamese forces and gathering in large numbers of defectors from local guerrilla units, prob-ably the best indication available of pacification's success. Whatever the situation elsewhere in Vietnam, III Corps was the one place where U.S. commanders had enough troops to deal with the threat.

As III Corps stabilized behind the allied shield, an uneasy sense of hope took hold in Saigon. The city was not impregnable. During the Tet celebration in 1969 heavy fighting broke out near Bien Hoa and Long Binh; into the early summer, enemy troops could still penetrate close enough to launch the occasional rocket attack or set off a bomb. Such incidents terrorized civilians, caused military casualties, and raised questions about the central government's ability to protect its citizens. The rocket attacks were especially troublesome. An economy-of-force measure, they brought little risk to the enemy and compelled allied forces to suspend other operations while they cleared the "rocket belt" around the urban center. By the autumn, however, the attacks had virtu-ally ceased. Saigon seemed to fall back into a period of tranquility and prosperity in which the main concern seemed to be not the fighting off in the distance but a wartime inflation eating into the purchasing power of the urban population. The trauma visited upon the city during Tet 1968 had become a bad memory on the wane.

In the Central Highlands, the war of attrition continued. Until its redeployment in 1970, the 4th Infantry Division protected major high-land population centers and kept important interior roads clear. Special Forces worked with the tribal highlanders to detect infiltration and harass enemy secret zones. As in the past, highland camps and outposts were a magnet for enemy attacks, meant to lure reaction forces into an ambush or to divert the allies from operations elsewhere. Ben Het in Kontum Province was besieged from March to July of 1969. Other bases—Tien Phuoc and Thuong Duc in I Corps; Bu Prang, Dak Seang, and Dak Pek in II Corps; and Katum, Bu Dop, and Tong Le Chon in III Corps—were attacked because of their proximity to Communist strongholds and infiltration routes. In some cases camps had to be abandoned; but in most, the attackers were repulsed. By the time the 5th Special Forces Group left South Vietnam in March 1971, all CIDG

> Such incidents terrorized civilians, caused military casualties, and raised questions about the central government's ability to protect its citizens.

units had been converted to Regional Forces or absorbed by the South Vietnamese rangers. The departure of the Green Berets brought an end to any significant Army role in the highlands.

Following the withdrawal of the 4th and 9th Divisions, Army units concentrated in the northern provinces as well as around Saigon. Operating in Quang Ngai, Quang Tin, and Quang Nam Provinces, the 23d Infantry Division (American) conducted a series of operations in 1968 and 1969 to secure and pacify the heavily populated coastal plain of southern I Corps. Along the demilitarized zone, the 1st Brigade, 5th Division, helped marines and South Vietnamese forces to screen the zone and secure the northern coastal region, including the stretch of Highway 1 that the enemy had cut during the 1968 Tet offensive. The 101st Airborne Division (converted to the Army's second airmobile division in 1969) divided its attention between the defense of Hue and forays into the enemy's base in the A Shau Valley.

Since the 1968 Tet offensive, the Communists had restocked the A Shau Valley with ammunition, rice, and equipment. The logistical buildup pointed to a possible North Vietnamese offensive in early 1969. In quick succession, Army operations were launched in the familiar pattern: air assaults, establishment of firebases, and exploration of the lowlands and surrounding hills to locate enemy forces and supplies. As the Army always had in the A Shau Valley, it once again met stiff resistance, especially from antiaircraft guns. The North Vietnamese had expected the American forces and now planned to hold their ground.

On May 11, 1969, a battalion of the 101st Airborne Division climbing Hill 937 found elements of the *29th PAVN Regiment* waiting for it. The struggle for Hamburger Hill raged for ten days and became one of the war's fiercest and most controversial battles. Entrenched in tiers of fortified bunkers with well-prepared fields of fire, the enemy forces withstood repeated attempts to dislodge them. Supported by intense artillery and air strikes, Americans made a slow, tortuous climb, fighting at close quarters. By the time the allies took Hill 937, three U.S. Army battalions and a South Vietnamese battalion from the 1st Division had been committed to the battle. Victory, however, was ambiguous as well as costly: the hill itself had no strategic or tactical importance and was abandoned soon after its capture. Critics charged that the battle wasted American lives and exemplified the irrelevance of large-unit tactics in Vietnam. Defending the operation, the commander of the 101st, Maj. Gen. Melvin Zais, acknowledged that the hill's only significance was that the enemy occupied it. "My mission," he said, "was to destroy enemy forces and installations. We found the enemy on Hill 937, and that is where we fought them."

About one month later the 101st Airborne Division left the A Shau Valley, and the North Vietnamese were free to use it again. American plans to return in the summer of 1970 came to nothing when enemy pressure forced the abandonment of two firebases needed for operations there. The loss of Firebase O'REILLY, only eleven miles from Hue, was an ominous sign that enemy forces had reoccupied the A Shau and were seeking to dominate the valleys leading to the coastal plain. Until redeployed in 1971, the 101st Airborne Division, with the marines and South Vietnamese forces, now devoted most of its efforts to protecting Hue. While the operations in western I Corps had inflicted casualties on the enemy and bought the allies some time, it remained to be seen whether the South Vietnamese Army could hold the area once American forces departed.

Operations on the coastal plain brought uncertain outcomes as well. Here, the Americal Division fought in an area where the population had long been sympathetic to the Viet Cong. As in other areas, pacification in southern I Corps seemed to improve after the 1968 Tet offensive, though enemy units still dominated the piedmont and continued to challenge American and South Vietnamese forces on the coast. Operations against them proved to be slow, frustrating exercises in warding off North Vietnamese and Viet Cong main-force units while enduring harassment from local guerrillas and the hostile population. Except during spasms of intense combat, as in the summer of 1969 when the Americal Division confronted the *1st PAVN Regiment*, most U.S. casualties were from snipers, mines, and booby traps. Villages populated by old men, women, and children were as dangerous as the elusive enemy main-force units. Operating in such conditions day after day induced a climate of fear and hatred among the Americans. The already thin line between civilian and combatant was easily blurred and violated. In the hamlet of My Lai, elements of the Americal Division killed about two hundred civilians in March 1968. Although only one member of the division was tried and found guilty of war crimes, the atrocity reverberated throughout the Army. However rare, such acts undid the benefit of countless hours of civic action by Army units and individual soldiers and raised unsettling questions about the conduct of the war.

War crimes such as at My Lai were born of a sense of frustration that also contributed to a host of morale and discipline problems among enlisted men and officers alike. As American forces were withdrawn by a government eager to escape the war, the lack of a clear military objective contributed to a weakened sense of mission and a slackening of discipline. The short-timer syndrome, the reluctance to take risks in combat toward the end of a soldier's one-year tour, was compounded by the last-casualty syndrome. Knowing that all U.S. troops would soon leave Vietnam, no soldier wanted to be the last to die. Meanwhile, in the United States, harsh criticism of the war, the military, and traditional military values had become widespread. Heightened individualism, growing permissiveness, and a weakening of traditional bonds of authority pervaded American society and affected the Army's rank and

FRAGGING

One of the more disturbing aspects of the unpopular war in Vietnam was the practice known as fragging. Disenchanted soldiers in Vietnam sometimes used fragmentation grenades, popularly known as frags, or other explosives to threaten or kill officers and NCOs they disliked. The full extent of the problem will never be known; but it increased sharply in 1969, 1970, and 1971, when the morale of the troops declined in step with the American role in the fighting. A total of 730 well-documented cases involving 83 deaths have come to light. There were doubtless others and probably some instances of fragging that were privately motivated acts of anger that had nothing to do with the war. Nonetheless, fragging was symptomatic of an Army in turmoil.

file. The Army grappled with problems of drug abuse, racial tensions, weakened discipline, and lapses of leadership. While outright refusals to fight were few in number, incidents of "fragging" (murderous attacks on officers and noncoms) occurred frequently enough to compel commands to institute a host of new security measures within their cantonments. All these problems were symptoms of larger social and political forces and underlined a growing disenchantment with the war among soldiers in the field.

As the Army prepared to leave Vietnam, lassitude and war-weariness at times resulted in tragedy, as at Firebase Mary Ann in 1971. There, soldiers of the Americal Division, soon to go home, relaxed their security and were overrun by a North Vietnamese force. Such incidents reflected a decline in the quality of leadership among both commissioned and noncommissioned officers. Lowered standards, abbreviated training, and accelerated promotions to meet the high demand for noncommissioned and junior officers often resulted in the assignment of squad, platoon, and company leaders with less combat experience than the troops they led. Careerism and ticket-punching in officer assignments, false reporting and inflated body counts, and revelations of scandal and corruption all raised disquieting questions about the professional ethics of Army leadership. Critics indicted the tactics and techniques the Army used in Vietnam, noting that airmobility, for example, tended to distance troops from the population they were sent to protect and that commanders aloft in their command and control helicopters were at a psychological and physical distance from the soldiers they were supposed to lead.

Cross-Border Operations

With most U.S. combat units slated to leave South Vietnam during 1970 and 1971, time was a critical factor for the success of Vietnamization and pacification. Neither program could thrive if South Vietnam's forces were distracted by enemy offensives launched from bases in Cambodia or Laos. While Abrams' operations temporarily reduced the level of enemy activity in the South, bases outside South Vietnam had been strictly off limits to allied ground forces. This rankled U.S. commanders, who regarded the restriction as a potentially fatal mistake. By harboring enemy forces, command facilities, and logistical depots, the Cambodian and Laotian bases threatened all the progress the allies had made in the South since Tet 1968. To the Nixon administration, Abrams' desire to attack the Communist sanctuaries had the special appeal of gaining more time for Vietnamization and of compensating for the bombing halt over North Vietnam.

Because of the proximity of the Cambodian bases to Saigon, they received first priority. Planning for the cross-border attack occurred at a critical time in Cambodia. In early 1970 Cambodia's neutralist leader, Prince Norodom Sihanouk, was overthrown by his pro-Western Defense Minister, General Lon Nol. Nol closed the port of Sihanoukville to supplies destined for Communist forces in the border bases and in South Vietnam. He also demanded that Communist forces leave Cambodia and accepted the South Vietnamese government's offer to apply pressure against those located near the border. (A year earlier American B–52 bombers had begun in secret to bomb enemy bases in Cambodia.) By mid-April 1970 South Vietnamese armored cavalry and ranger units, with no U.S. advisers accompanying them, were mounting large-scale operations across the border from III Corps and uncovering large caches of enemy supplies and equipment.

The main assault began on the twenty-ninth. That morning three South Vietnamese task forces, this time with a full complement of U.S. advisers, and preceded by heavy air and artillery attacks, launched Operation TOAN THANG 42, knifing into Cambodia's Svay Rieng Province and pushing through enemy resistance. Two days later, on May 1, units of the 1st Cavalry Division; 25th Infantry Division; 3d Brigade, 9th Infantry Division; 11th Armored Cavalry Regiment (ACR); and South Vietnamese 3d Airborne Brigade, under the command of Brig. Gen. Robert L. Shoemaker, followed from slightly to the north. The 4th Infantry Division attacked from II Corps four days later.

While this 9th Division soldier fought in Cambodia, students back home protested the expanded war.

Cambodia became a new battlefield of the Vietnam War. By May 2 South Vietnamese forces had cut off the Parrot's Beak, an area that jutted into South Vietnam near the III Corps–IV Corps border, and U.S. and South Vietnamese troops had linked up near Memot in the so-called Fishhook, meeting little opposition from enemy security forces. (*See Map 21.*) Snuol, a large enemy logistical hub, fell to the tanks of the 11th ACR three days later. In the weeks that followed the allies cut a broad swath through the enemy's sanctuary and uncovered storage sites, training camps, and hospitals far larger and more complex than anyone had anticipated. One site in the Fishhook, dubbed "the city" in deference to its size, covered three square kilometers and contained mess halls, a livestock farm, supply issuing and receiving stations, and over two hundred caches of weapons and other materiel, most of it new. By one estimate, the allies in Cambodia seized enough weapons and ammunition to arm fifty-five battalions of main-force infantry. Main-force offensives against South Vietnam's III and IV Corps were derailed for at least a year.

However, the allies did not find large enemy forces or the *COSVN* headquarters. Only relatively small delaying forces offered resistance, while main-force units retreated deeper into Cambodia. Meanwhile, the expansion of the war produced violent demonstrations in the United States. In response to the public outcry Nixon imposed geographical

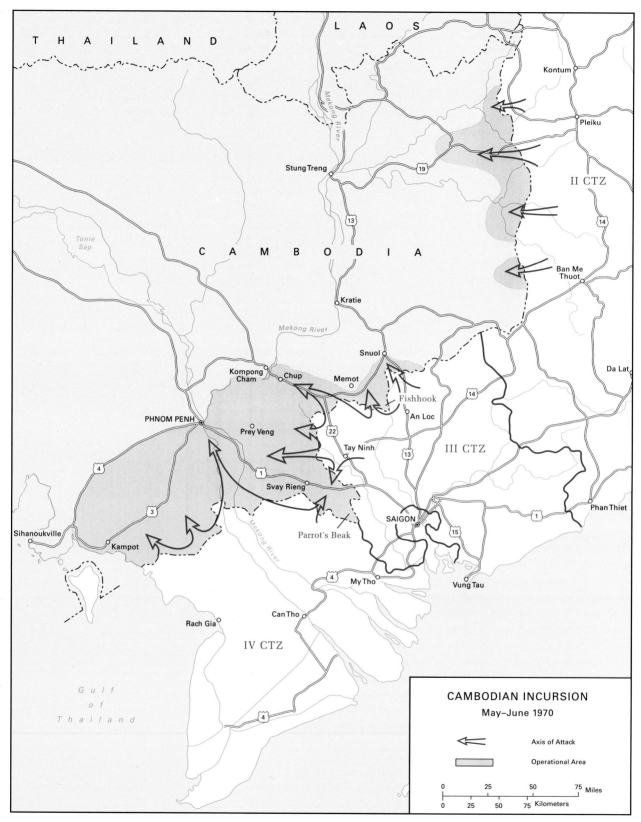

THAILAND

LAOS

Kontum

Pleiku

Stung Treng

19

II CTZ

14

C A M B O D I A

Tonle
Sap

13

Kratie

Ban Me
Thuot

Mekong River

Da Lat

Snuol

Kompong
Cham

Chup

Memot

Fishhook

PHNOM PENH

Prey Veng

22

An Loc

14

III CTZ

Tay Ninh

13

4

1

Svay Rieng

3

SAIGON

Sihanoukville

Kampot

Parrot's Beak

15

1

Phan Thiet

4

My Tho

Vung Tau

Gulf

of

Thailand

Rach Gia

Can Tho

IV CTZ

4

CAMBODIAN INCURSION
May–June 1970

Axis of Attack

Operational Area

0   25   50   75 Miles

0   25   50   75 Kilometers

Map 21

and time limits on operations in Cambodia, which enabled the enemy to stay beyond reach. At the end of June, one day short of the sixty days allotted to the operation, all advisers accompanying the South Vietnamese and all U.S. Army units had left Cambodia.

Political and military events in Cambodia triggered changes in the war as profound as those the Tet offensive had engendered. From a quiescent sideshow of the war, Cambodia became an arena for the major belligerents. Military activity increased in northern Cambodia and southern Laos as North Vietnam established new infiltration routes and bases to replace those lost during the incursion. North Vietnam made clear that it regarded all Indochina as a single theater of operations. Cambodia itself was engulfed in a civil war.

As U.S. Army units withdrew, the South Vietnamese Army found itself in a race against Communist forces to secure the Cambodian capital of Phnom Penh. Americans provided South Vietnam's over-extended forces air and logistical support to enable them to stabilize the situation there. The time to strengthen Vietnamization gained by the incursion now had to be weighed in the balance against the South Vietnamese Army's new commitment in Cambodia. To the extent that South Vietnam's forces bolstered Lon Nol's regime, they were unable to contribute to pacification and rural security in their own country. Moreover, the South Vietnamese performance in Cambodia was mixed. When working closely with American advisers, the army acquitted itself well; though there were flaws in planning and the use of air and artillery support. The South Vietnamese logistical system, with a few exceptions, proved adequate. The difficulty was that the North Vietnamese Army largely chose not to fight, so the South Vietnamese Army was never really tested. Furthermore, the South Vietnamese command had relied on rangers, armored cavalry, and airborne troops—elite units— bypassing the mediocre infantry divisions hampered by their politics. If the elite units performed credibly, the shortcomings in the regular army remained intact, starting with poor leadership and lack of discipline.

Despite equivocal results in Cambodia, less than a year later the Americans pressed the South Vietnamese to launch a second cross-border operation, this time into Laos. Although the United States would provide air, artillery, and logistical support, Army advisers would not accompany South Vietnamese forces. The Americans' enthusiasm for the operation exceeded that of their allies. Anticipating high casualties, South Vietnam's leaders were reluctant to involve their army once more in extended operations outside their country. But American intelligence had detected a North Vietnamese buildup in the vicinity of Tchepone, Laos, a logistical center on the Ho Chi Minh Trail approximately twenty-five miles west of the South Vietnamese border. The Military Assistance Command regarded the buildup as a prelude to a North Vietnamese spring offensive in the northern provinces. Like the Cambodian incursion, the Laotian invasion was justified as benefiting Vietnamization, but with the added bonuses of spoiling a prospective offensive and cutting off the Ho Chi Minh Trail.

This would be the last chance for the South Vietnamese to cut the Ho Chi Minh Trail while American forces were available to provide support. A decade earlier military analysts had developed plans to use corps-size American and allied forces to block the infiltration routes

HO CHI MINH TRAIL

The lifeline of the Communist war effort in South Vietnam, the Ho Chi Minh Trail grew from a network of footpaths in 1959 into an all-weather roadway by 1972. Beginning in southern North Vietnam, the trail wound through Laos and northern Cambodia, with spurs branching into each of almost two-dozen base areas along the border. During the war the United States bombed the trail in an unsuccessful attempt to stanch the flow of enemy troops and materiel. According to Communist accounts, between 1959 and 1975, over 915,000 men and almost 1 million tons of supplies arrived in South Vietnam via the Ho Chi Minh Trail. Keeping the trail open was one of the key elements of North Vietnamese victory.

in Laos permanently as part of the overall defense of Southeast Asia. While the political climate in Washington had militated against widening the ground war, officials had viewed the sanctuaries in Laos as a strategic threat to the South sufficient to justify taking some form of punitive action against them. A bombing campaign, accordingly, started early, at the end of 1964, initially complementing the air raids against the North and the air war in South Vietnam but intensifying after the bombing halt over the North in 1968.

The other campaign against the Ho Chi Minh Trail was covert action. The agency responsible for covert operations in Laos was the euphemistically named Studies and Observations Group (SOG). Formed in 1964 under a special office in the Pentagon, SOG was initially expected to take over the clandestine agent program that the Central Intelligence Agency had been running for several years against North Vietnam. When the ground war in the South heated up in 1965, however, officials decided that the group could be helpful in Laos. In September the Johnson administration authorized Operation SHINING BRASS (later renamed PRAIRIE FIRE), allowing teams of Special Forces and South Vietnamese to cross the border in secret to conduct reconnaissance and bomb-damage assessment in order to improve the accuracy of the air campaign against the trail. In 1967 SOG's mission expanded to include sabotage. All operations were limited to a strip along the border extending no more than twenty kilometers into Laos. Later operations expanding into Cambodia were code-named DANIEL BOONE, later SALEM HOUSE. Between 1965 and late 1970, SHINING BRASS/PRAIRIE FIRE/SALEM HOUSE/DANIEL BOONE launched more than 1,600 missions into the enemy base and trail complex, providing a useful supplement to aerial and electronic intelligence but not tying down several North Vietnamese divisions as advocates of the program maintained. SOG was still running operations in Laos when the allies launched their cross-border offensive in 1971.

Planning for the offensive began in great secrecy in January and involved staff from Lt. Gen. James W. Sutherland's XXIV Corps and Lt.

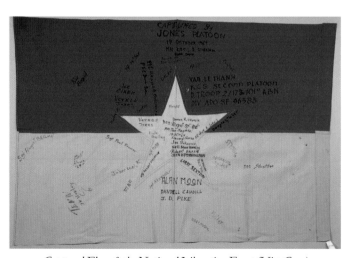

Captured Flag of the National Liberation Front (Viet Cong)

LAM SON 719

Planning for the invasion of Laos in a belated attempt to restrict the flow of supplies down the Ho Chi Minh Trail began in extreme secrecy. In December 1970 the Joint Chiefs of Staff authorized MACV to prepare for an invasion of the enemy base areas opposite I Corps; but, fearing leaks from the South Vietnamese, General Abrams told only his immediate staff, South Vietnamese President Thieu, and the top South Vietnamese general, Cao Van Vien. In the end, secrecy accomplished little: there were only a few possible places for an invasion of Laos. The North Vietnamese expected some sort of an attack; when LAM SON 719 was launched in February 1971, they quickly defeated it.

Gen. Hoang Xuan Lam's I Corps. So tightly held was information on the impending operation that logistical and signal preparations that required long lead time were put in jeopardy and a combined tactical command post was not established until well into the offensive. In preparation for the attack, Army helicopters, artillery, and supplies were moved at the last minute to the vicinity of the abandoned base at Khe Sanh. The 101st Airborne Division conducted a feint toward the A Shau Valley to conceal the true objective. On February 8, 1971, spearheaded by M41 tanks and with units from the 1st Infantry, 1st Airborne, and Marine Divisions leapfrogging into Laos to establish firebases on the flanks of the attack, a South Vietnamese column from the 1st Armored Brigade advanced down Highway 9 toward Tchepone. (*See Map 22.*) Operation LAM SON 719 had begun.

Because of security leaks, the North Vietnamese were not deceived. Within a week South Vietnamese forces numbering about 17,000 became bogged down by heavy enemy resistance, bad weather, and poor attack management. Conflicting orders from I Corps headquarters and the airborne division delayed the reinforcement of a critical landing zone north of the highway, and the position was lost. The drive into Laos stalled. Before long the South Vietnamese were facing elements of five North Vietnamese divisions, as well as a tank regiment, two artillery regiments, and numerous antiaircraft battalions. Departing from the evasive tactics they had used a year earlier in Cambodia, the North Vietnamese had decided to stand and fight for their sanctuaries. Nonetheless, aided by heavy U.S. air strikes, including B–52s, and plenty of artillery and helicopter gunship support, the South Vietnamese inched forward and after a bloody, month-long delay, air-assaulted on March 6 into the heavily bombed town of Tchepone. This was the last bit of good news from the front.

By that time the North Vietnamese had counterattacked with Soviet-built tanks, heavy artillery, and infantry. They struck the rear of the South Vietnamese forces strung out on Highway 9, blocking their main avenue of withdrawal. Enemy forces also overwhelmed several South Vietnamese firebases, depriving South Vietnamese units of desperately needed flank protection. The South Vietnamese also lacked enough antitank weapons to counter the North Vietnamese armor that appeared on the Laotian jungle trails and were inexperienced in the use of those they had. U.S. Army helicopter pilots flying gunship and resupply

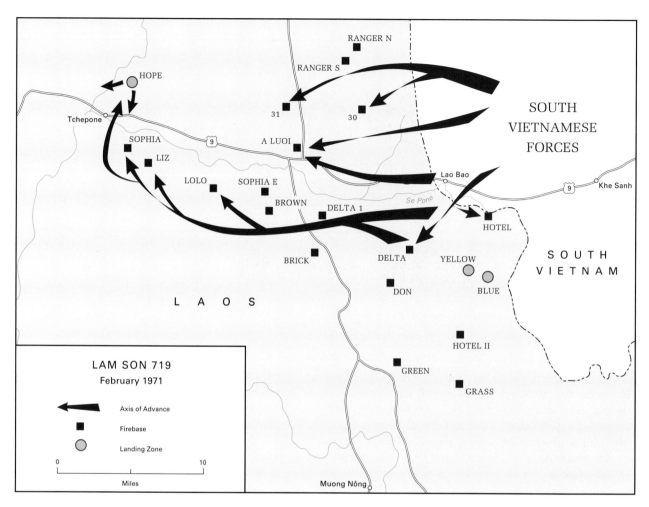

Map 22

missions and trying to rescue South Vietnamese soldiers from their besieged hilltop firebases encountered intense antiaircraft fire. One pilot lamented that enemy gunners were "getting better because of all the practice we've given them." Planners initially thought that the 101st Airborne Division and its attached units could provide all the helicopters the operation needed; but as enemy resistance stiffened, Abrams had to shift more and more helicopters to northern I Corps, some from the Americal Division in southern I Corps, others from aviation units in II Corps, even from a 1st Cavalry Division element in III Corps that was about to leave Vietnam. When the availability rate of the UH–1C Huey gunship during LAM SON slipped to 40 percent, the USARV commander, Lt. Gen. William J. McCaffrey, put in an urgent call to the Department of the Army. He asked that all available AH–1G Cobra helicopters, the latest gunship in the Army's arsenal, be airlifted to South Vietnam.

On March 16, ten days after Tchepone was taken, President Thieu issued the order to pull out, turning aside General Abrams' plea for an expansion of the offensive to do serious damage to the trail. Command

AH–1G Cobras made thousands of high-speed runs across the border against targets in Laos.

and control problems that had surfaced during the attack were magnified in the withdrawal, despite warnings from General Sutherland that the maneuver had to be carefully planned and closely coordinated. General Lam was in a hurry and soon lost control of the operation. While many units maintained their cohesiveness and fought well, for others all semblance of order vanished. The 1st Armored Brigade, its infantry protection on the flanks prematurely removed, ran into a series of ambushes in which it lost 60 percent of its tanks and half its armored personnel carriers. The infantry, airborne, and marine divisions, under continuous harassing fire, did succeed in extricating themselves, but they left behind many casualties and much equipment, including ninety-six artillery pieces. Eventually, South Vietnamese forces punched their way out of Laos but only after paying a heavy price.

That the South Vietnamese Army had reached its objective of Tchepone was of little consequence. Its stay there was brief and the supply caches it discovered disappointing, since most were in the mountains to the east and west. South Vietnam's forces had failed to sever the Ho Chi Minh Trail; infiltration reportedly increased during LAM SON 719, as the North Vietnamese shifted traffic to roads and trails farther to the west in Laos. In addition to equipment

Chopper Pick-up, *Brian H. Clark, 1968*

Point Crossing, *Konrad F. Hack, 2003*

losses, the South Vietnamese lost nearly 1,600 men. The U.S. Army's lost 215 men killed, 1,149 wounded, and 38 missing. The Army also lost 108 helicopters, the highest number in any one operation of the war. Supporters of helicopter warfare pointed to heavy enemy casualties and argued that equipment losses were reasonable, given the large number of helicopters and helicopter sorties (more than 160,000) that supported LAM SON 719. The battle nevertheless raised disturbing questions among Army officials about the vulnerability of helicopters in mid- or high-intensity conflict to any significant antiaircraft capability.

LAM SON 719 was a test of Vietnamization less ambiguous than the Cambodian incursion. The South Vietnamese Army did not perform well in Laos. Reflecting on the operation, Lt. Gen. Ngo Quang Truong, a former commander of the 1st Division who took command of I Corps in 1972, noted the South Vietnamese Army's chronic weakness in planning for and coordinating combat support. He also observed that from the battalion to the division level the army had become dependent on U.S. advisers. At the highest levels of command, he added, "the need for advisers was more acutely felt in two specific areas: planning and leadership. The basic weakness of [South Vietnamese] units at regimental and sometimes division level in those areas," he continued, "seriously affected the performance of subordinate units." LAM SON 719 scored one success, forestalling a Communist spring offensive in the northern provinces; in other respects it failed and was an ill omen for the future.

Withdrawal: The Final Battles

As the Americans withdrew, South Vietnam's combat capability declined. The United States furnished its allies heavier M48A3 tanks to match the North Vietnamese Army's T–54 tanks and heavier artillery to counter North Vietnamese 130-mm. guns, though past experience suggested that additional arms and equipment could not compensate for poor skills and mediocre leadership. In fact, the weapons and equipment were insufficient to offset the reduction in U.S. combat strength. In mid-1968, for example, some forty-five allied infantry battalions were present in South Vietnam's two northern provinces; in 1972, with U.S. infantry gone, only twenty-one battalions were in the same area. Artillery strength in the northern region suffered a similar decline, and ammunition supply rates fell as well. Similar reductions took place throughout South Vietnam, causing declines in mobility, firepower, intelligence support, and air support. American specialties (B–52 strikes, photo reconnaissance, and the use of sensors and other means of target acquisition) were drastically curtailed.

Such losses were all the more serious because operations in Cambodia and Laos had illustrated how deeply ingrained in the South Vietnamese Army the American style of warfare had become. Nearly two decades of U.S. military involvement were exacting an unexpected price. A South Vietnamese division commander commented, "Trained as they were through combined action with US units, the [South Vietnamese] unit commander was used to the employment of massive firepower." That habit, he added, "was hard to relinquish."

By November 1971, when the 101st Airborne Division withdrew from South Vietnam, North Vietnam was preparing for its 1972 spring offensive. With the South's combat capacity diminished and nearly all U.S. combat troops gone, the North sensed an opportunity to demonstrate the failure of Vietnamization, hasten the South Vietnamese Army's collapse, and revive the stalled peace talks. In its broad outlines and goals, the 1972 offensive resembled Tet 1968, except that the North Vietnamese Army, instead of the Viet Cong, bore the major burden of combat.

The allies had plenty of warning of an impending attack. In December U.S. intelligence had started detecting enemy concentrations of armor and artillery farther south along the Ho Chi Minh Trail than ever before encountered, and analysts had also noted a dramatic increase in the number of North Vietnamese soldiers infiltrating into the South. By mid-January Abrams was so certain of his information that he was predicting a major conventional attack in which massed enemy formations and enemy armor and artillery operating in the open would play the decisive role. This gave confidence to those officials who believed in the efficacy of U.S. air power. In fact, as the winter wore on, air power advocates felt that a succession of "protective reaction" air strikes President Nixon had authorized in December had actually forestalled the expected offensive. While this point was controversial, all did agree that U.S. ground forces in Vietnam were no longer in a position to exercise influence over the battlefield. By March 1972 total military strength in the South had fallen to about 100,000, with one brigade, the 196th Light Infantry, at Da Nang, another, the 3d Brigade, 1st Cavalry Division, at Bien Hoa. The task of countering any offensive on the ground would fall almost exclusively to the South Vietnamese.

EASTER OFFENSIVE

By January 1972 U.S. intelligence knew full well that North Vietnam was planning a major offensive. Infiltration of enemy troops had increased sharply, and overhead surveillance spotted new supply caches along the Ho Chi Minh Trail. MACV also knew that the enemy would for the first time be employing armor and heavy artillery in large numbers. All this was coming at a time when the United States was withdrawing; on the eve of the offensive in March 1972, U.S. military strength in South Vietnam was down to 103,824, the lowest figure since mid-1965.

The Nguyen Hue, or Easter, offensive began on March 30, 1972. Attacking on three fronts, the North Vietnamese poured across the demilitarized zone and out of Laos into northern I Corps, pushed eastward into the Central Highlands, and drove down Highway 13 toward Loc Ninh and An Loc, one of the traditional invasion routes to Saigon. Surprised by the ferocity of the attacks, the South Vietnamese fell back everywhere. The most devastating assaults took place in Quang Tri Province. (*Map 23*) While enemy artillery struck every firebase in the northern defense sector, infantry and armor quickly routed the 3d Infantry Division, formed just months before, and slashed their way toward Dong Ha. Momentarily held up by the 20th Tank Regiment, by May 1 North Vietnamese forces had taken Quang Tri City and the rest of Quang Tri Province and were threatening to move on Hue. In one month of battle, the South Vietnamese in northern I Corps had lost almost all their artillery and all but one of their M48s. The marines and rangers had also lost heavily, and several U.S. advisers had died. As refugees streamed south toward the dubious safety of Hue, South Vietnamese forces established a defense line at the My Chanh River on the Quang Tri–Thua Thien provincial border and President Thieu replaced the I Corps commander, General Lam.

Elsewhere, South Vietnamese losses were nearly as serious. Though the enemy attack in II Corps developed more slowly, by April 24 North Vietnamese forces had destroyed the 22d Division at Tan Canh and Dak To, seized control of northern Kontum Province, and were knocking on the door of Kontum City. President Thieu removed another corps commander, leaving the senior adviser, John Paul Vann, a civilian, in command of II Corps and Kontum City braced for all-out assault. The III Corps area also was sorely threatened. Realizing too late that the main attack was developing in Binh Long, not Tay Ninh, Province, the South Vietnamese and their advisers were slow to reinforce the corridor down Highway 13. Loc Ninh fell to the *5th PLAF Division* in a week, and a few days later enemy infantry and armor invaded An Loc's northern neighborhoods and could not be ejected. The U.S. adviser with the South Vietnamese 5th Division thought defeat was near.

This was the grim situation, enemy pressure unrelenting everywhere and the contest in doubt, when, sometime during May, the battlefield on all three fronts began to stabilize. The change was barely perceptible at first, but slowly the enemy offensive ran out of steam. Much of the enemy's difficulty turned out to be logistical. For the first time in the war huge amounts of fuel and ammunition were required to sustain the enemy's fighting forces in South Vietnam. Those supply lines became targets of a renewed aerial offensive in both North and South Vietnam that isolated the Southern battlefield as never before. Every front felt the impact of U.S. air power. At Kontum City, with supplies and artillery running low, the North Vietnamese Army spent its infantry in city fighting until it was too weak to withstand a counterattack by the 23d Division. Harried by U.S. helicopters and tactical air strikes, enemy forces were soon in retreat toward Cambodia. An Loc was touch-and-go a little longer; but by mid-June, buttressed by air drops from U.S. Air Force C–130s, and massive B–52 bombing runs, the South Vietnamese made their stand at the city center, decimating the attacking formations. After several more desperate assaults, the enemy survivors

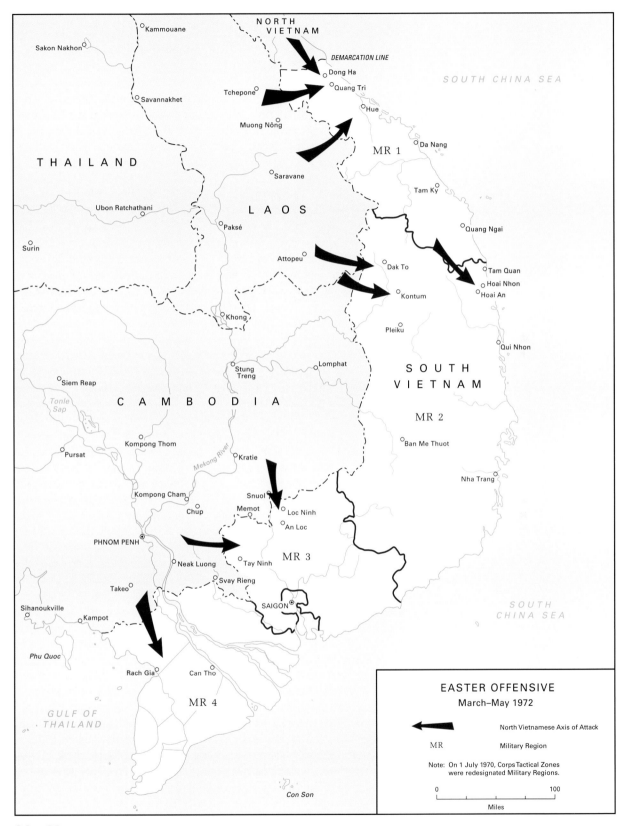

NORTH VIETNAM

DEMARCATION LINE

SOUTH CHINA SEA

Kammouane

Sakon Nakhon

Savannakhet

Tchepone

Dong Ha

Quang Tri

Hue

Muong Nông

MR 1

Da Nang

THAILAND

Saravane

Tam Ky

LAOS

Ubon Ratchathani

Paksé

Quang Ngai

Surin

Attopeu

Dak To

Tam Quan

Hoai Nhon

Kontum

Hoai An

Khong

Pleiku

Qui Nhon

Stung
Treng

Lomphat

SOUTH
VIETNAM

Siem Reap

Tonle
Sap

CAMBODIA

MR 2

Ban Me Thuot

Kompong Thom

Pursat

Kratie

Nha Trang

Mekong River

Kompong Cham

Snuol

Chup

Memot

Loc Ninh

An Loc

PHNOM PENH

MR 3

Neak Luong

Tay Ninh

Takeo

Svay Rieng

Sihanoukville

Kampot

SAIGON

SOUTH
CHINA SEA

Phu Quoc

GULF
OF
THAILAND

Rach Gia

Can Tho

MR 4

Con Son

EASTER OFFENSIVE
March–May 1972

North Vietnamese Axis of Attack

MR   Military Region

Note: On 1 July 1970, Corps Tactical Zones
were redesignated Military Regions.

0   100

Miles

Map 23

In August the South Vietnamese took Quang Tri City and this Russian-built T–54 tank.

slipped away into the forests to the west. The toughest fight took place in Quang Tri Province, where for the next four months North and South Vietnamese forces waged a slow, grinding attrition struggle that had all the bloody hallmarks of World War I. By the time South Vietnamese marines took Quang Tri City in September, tens of thousands of North Vietnamese soldiers had perished and the Marine Division had bled as well. But the Easter offensive had finally run its course.

In the aftermath the governments in Saigon and Hanoi both claimed victory, but the balance had not been significantly altered. On one side of the ledger were the declines in rural security wherever North Vietnamese divisions had forced their way into South Vietnam. By the end of the offensive substantial parts of Quang Tri and Binh Long Provinces remained in enemy hands, while northwest Tay Ninh Province had also become safe enough for the Communists to reestablish *COSVN* headquarters there. In addition, there were new and disturbing signs of North Vietnamese penetration of the Mekong Delta to compensate for Viet Cong losses there to pacification. A rise in attacks on government outposts in the delta pointed to the fragility of pacification in this crucial arena. Looking at the country as the whole, on the other hand, CORDS officials insisted that the offensive had not undone the gains since 1968, at least not permanently. Although the measurements of hamlet security remained controversial and subject to interpretation, the trends seemed to suggest that government programs for security and rural development were well on the way to recovery by the end of 1972.

What had changed in 1972 were the tactics of the war, bringing new levels of destructiveness to the battlefield. Communist forces had made extensive use of armor and artillery. Among the new weapons in the enemy's arsenal was the Soviet SA–7 handheld antiaircraft missile, which posed a threat to slow-flying tactical aircraft and helicopters and inflicted losses at Quang Tri City. The Soviet AT–3 Sagger antitank missile destroyed allied armor and bunkers in northern I Corps and at Tan Canh in II Corps. On the other hand, Army helicopter gunships, some of them newly outfitted with TOW (Tube-launched, Optically tracked, Wire-guided) antitank missiles, proved effective against North Vietnamese armor at standoff range. In their antitank role, Army attack helicopters were crucial to the South Vietnamese Army's successes at An Loc and Kontum City, suggesting a larger role for helicopters in the future as part of a combined-arms team in conventional combat.

The other major development in 1972 was the decisive application of air power and the encouragement this offered to South Vietnamese leaders facing a future without American ground forces. President Nixon's resumption of the bombing of North Vietnam during the Easter offensive and, for the first time, his mining of North Vietnamese ports, gave confidence to the belief that the South Vietnamese could count on U.S. air support in the years ahead. So did the intense B–52 bombing of Hanoi and Haiphong, the LINEBACKER II raids, in December 1972. But such pressure was intended at least in part to force North Vietnam to sign an armistice. If President Thieu was encouraged by the display of U.S. military muscle, the course of negotiations in Paris could only have been a source of discouragement. The long deadlock was broken in August, when North Vietnam, in the wake of its failed Easter offensive and under pressure from the Soviet Union to find a solution, dropped an earlier demand for Thieu's removal. At the same time the United States gave up its insistence on North Vietnam's withdrawal from South Vietnam. With that agreement, the talks hastened to a conclusion. In early 1973 the United States, North and South Vietnam, and the Viet Cong signed an armistice that promised a cease-fire and national reconciliation. In fact, fighting continued; but MACV was dissolved, remaining U.S. forces withdrawn, and American military action in South Vietnam terminated. Perhaps most important of all, American advisers—still in many respects the backbone of the South Vietnamese Army's command structure—were withdrawn.

Between 1973 and 1975, South Vietnam's military security declined through a combination of old and new factors. Plagued by poor maintenance and shortages of spare parts, much of the advanced equipment provided South Vietnam's forces under Vietnamization became inoperable. A rise in fuel prices stemming from a worldwide oil crisis further restricted the South Vietnamese military's use of vehicles and aircraft. Government forces in many areas of the country were on the defensive, confined to protecting key towns and installations. Seeking to preserve its diminishing assets, the South Vietnamese Army became garrison bound and either reluctant or unable to react to a growing number of guerrilla attacks that eroded rural security. Congressionally mandated reductions in U.S. aid further reduced the delivery of spare parts, fuel, and ammunition. American military activities in Cambodia and Laos, which had continued after the cease-fire in South Vietnam went into effect, ended in 1973 when Congress cut off funds. Complaining of this austerity, President Thieu noted that he had to fight a "poor man's war." Vietnamization's legacy was that South Vietnam had to do more with less.

In 1975 North Vietnam's leaders began planning for a new offensive, still uncertain whether the United States would resume bombing or once again intervene in the South. When their forces overran Phuoc Long Province, north of Saigon, without any American military reaction, they decided to proceed with a major offensive in the Central Highlands. Neither President Nixon, weakened by the Watergate scandal and forced to resign, nor his successor, Gerald R. Ford, was prepared to challenge Congress by resuming U.S. military activity in Southeast Asia. The will of Congress seemed to reflect the mood of an American public weary of the long and inconclusive war.

What had started as a limited offensive in the highlands now became an all-out effort to conquer South Vietnam. Thieu, desiring

> Seeking to preserve its diminishing assets, the South Vietnamese Army became garrison bound and either reluctant or unable to react to a growing number of guerrilla attacks that eroded rural security.

to husband his military resources, decided to retreat rather than to reinforce the Central Highlands. The result was panic among his troops and a mass exodus toward the coast. As North Vietnamese forces spilled out of the Central Highlands, they cut off South Vietnamese defenders in the northern provinces from the rest of the country. (*Map 24*) Other North Vietnamese units now crossed the demilitarized zone, quickly overrunning Hue and Da Nang and signaling the collapse of South Vietnamese resistance in the north. Hurriedly established defense lines around Saigon held back the enemy offensive against the capital for a while, but not for long. As South Vietnamese leaders waited in vain for American assistance, Saigon fell to the Communists on April 30, 1975.

The time South Vietnamese forces bought near Saigon allowed the United States to complete a final evacuation from the capital. All day long on the twenty-ninth of April, Air Force and Marine Corps helicopters shuttled nearly 7,000 people, including the American ambassador, to U.S. Navy ships waiting off shore. Among the 5,600 non-American evacuees were South Vietnamese who were related to Americans or who faced a doubtful future because of the work they had done in Vietnam for U.S. agencies. Two U.S. marines were killed when North Vietnamese shells struck the compound of the former MACV headquarters that was serving as an evacuation site. Two pilots died when their helicopter went down at sea. These were the final U.S. casualties in Vietnam while the war still raged. When the last helicopter lifted off from the American embassy the next morning, taking with it a contingent of marine guards, the long American war for Vietnam came to a close.

An Assessment

Saigon's fall was a bitter end to the long American effort to sustain South Vietnam. Ranging from advice and support to direct participation in combat and involving nearly 3 million U.S. servicemen, the effort failed to stop Communist leaders from reaching their goal of unifying a divided nation. South Vietnam's military defeat tended to obscure the crucial inability of this massive military enterprise to compensate for South Vietnam's political shortcomings. Over a span of two decades, a series of regimes had failed to mobilize fully and effectively their nation's political, social, and economic resources to foster a popular base of support. North Vietnamese conventional units ended the war, but insurgency and disaffection among the people of the South made that outcome possible.

The U.S. Army paid a high price for its long involvement in South Vietnam. American military deaths exceeded 58,000; of those, about two-thirds were soldiers. The majority of the dead were low-ranking enlisted men (E–2 to E–4), young men twenty-three years old or younger, of whom approximately 13 percent were African American. Almost a third of the deaths were caused by small-arms fire; but a significant portion, a little over a quarter, stemmed from mines, booby traps, and grenades. Artillery, rockets, and bombs accounted for only a small portion of the total fatalities. The deadliest year was 1968, followed by 1969 and 1967.

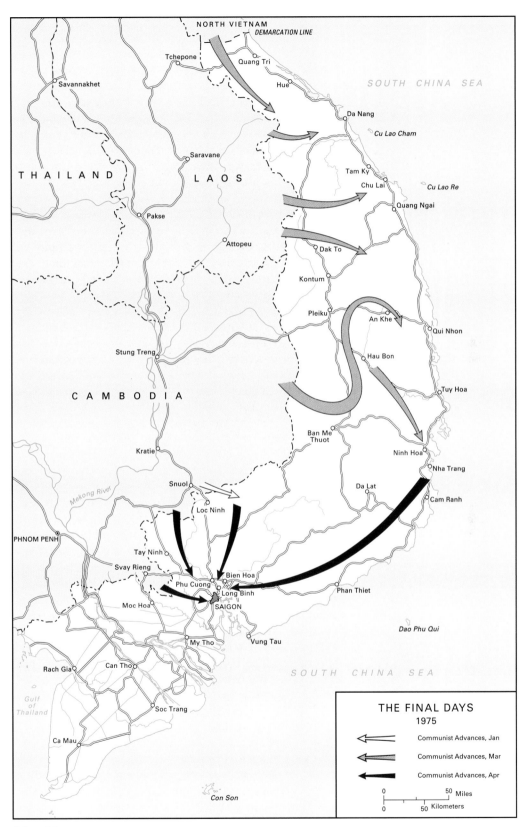

THE FINAL DAYS
1975

← Communist Advances, Jan

← Communist Advances, Mar

← Communist Advances, Apr

0   50 Miles
0   50 Kilometers

Map 24

If not for the unprecedented medical care that the Army provided in South Vietnam, the death toll would have been higher still. Of the nearly 300,000 Americans wounded, half required hospitalization. The lives of many seriously injured men, who would have become fatalities in earlier wars, were saved by rapid helicopter evacuation direct to hospitals close to the combat zone. Here, relatively secure from air and ground attack, usually unencumbered by mass casualties, and with access to an uninterrupted supply of whole blood, Army doctors and nurses availed themselves of the latest medical technology to save thousands of lives. As one medical officer pointed out, the Army was able to adopt a "civilian philosophy of casualty triage" in the battle zone that directed the "major effort first to the most seriously injured." But some who served in South Vietnam suffered more insidious damage from the adverse psychological effects of combat or the long-term effects of exposure to chemical agents. Moreover, three decades after the end of the war, almost 1,900 American soldiers remain listed as missing in action.

The war-ravaged Vietnamese, North and South, suffered the greatest losses. South Vietnamese military deaths exceeded 200,000. War-related civilian deaths in the South approached a half-million, while the injured and maimed numbered many more. Accurate estimates of enemy casualties run afoul of the difficulty in distinguishing between civilians and combatants, imprecise body counts, and the difficulty of verifying casualties in enemy-controlled areas. Nevertheless, nearly a million Viet Cong and North Vietnamese soldiers are believed to have perished in combat through the spring of 1975.

For the U.S. Army the scars of the war ran even deeper than the grim statistics showed. Given its long association with South Vietnam's fortunes, the Army could not escape being tarnished by its ally's fall. The loss compounded already unsettling questions about the Army's role in Southeast Asia, about the soundness of its advice to the South Vietnamese, about its understanding of the nature of the war, about the appropriateness of its strategy and tactics, and about the adequacy of the counsel Army leaders provided to our nation's decision makers. Marked by ambiguous military objectives and defensive strategy, sometimes ponderous tactics, and untidy command arrangements, the struggle in Vietnam seemed to violate most of the time-honored principles of war. Many officers sought to erase Vietnam from the Army's corporate memory, feeling uncomfortable with failure or believing that the lessons and experience of the war were of little use to the post-Vietnam Army. Although a generation of officers, including many of the Army's future leaders, cut their combat teeth in Vietnam, many regretted that the Army's reputation, integrity, and professionalism had been tainted in the service of a flawed strategy and a dubious ally.

DISCUSSION QUESTIONS

1. The Tet offensive was a desperate gamble on the part of the North Vietnamese leadership and a sign of military weakness: true or false? Why?

2. What were the main elements of the pacification program in Vietnam, and how did the program change over time?

3. General Abrams' methodology of war has sometimes been contrasted with that of General Westmoreland. How did it differ? How was it similar?

4. Discuss the division of labor on the battlefield between the U.S. Army and the South Vietnamese Army. Could the United States have done this differently? How?

5. Toward the end of the war, some observers called the U.S. Army the ultimate people's army. To what were they referring? Were they right?

6. "You know you never defeated us on the battlefield," said the American colonel during a conversation in Hanoi in April 1975. The North Vietnamese colonel replied, "That may be so, but it is also irrelevant." What did the North Vietnamese colonel mean?

Recommended Readings

Andrade, Dale. *America's Last Vietnam Battle: Halting Hanoi's 1972 Easter Offensive*. Lawrence: University Press of Kansas, 2001.

Clarke, Jeffrey J. *Advice and Support: The Final Years, 1965–1973*. U.S. Army in Vietnam. Washington, D.C.: U.S. Army Center of Military History, 1988.

Hammond, William M. *Public Affairs: The Military and the Media, 1968–1973*. U.S. Army in Vietnam. Washington, D.C.: U.S. Army Center of Military History, 1996.

Hunt, Richard A. *Pacification: The American Struggle for Vietnam's Hearts and Minds*. Boulder, Colo.: Westview Press, 1995.

Lewy, Guenter. *America in Vietnam*. New York: Oxford University Press, 1978.

Oberdorfer, Don. *Tet!: The Turning Point in Vietnam*. Baltimore: Johns Hopkins University Press, 2001.

Spector, Ronald H. *After Tet: The Bloodiest Year in Vietnam*. New York: Vintage Books, 1994.

Other Readings

Andrade, Dale. *Ashes to Ashes: The Phoenix Program and the Vietnam War*. Lexington, Mass.: Lexington Books, 1990.

Kimball, Jeffrey P. *Nixon's Vietnam War*. Lawrence: University Press of Kansas, 1998.

LeGro, William E. *Vietnam from Cease-Fire to Capitulation*. Vietnam Studies. Washington, D.C.: U.S. Army Center of Military History, 2001.

Pearson, Willard. *The War in the Northern Provinces, 1966–1968*. Vietnam Studies. Washington, D.C.: U.S. Army Center of Military History, 1991.

Pisor, Robert. *The End of the Line: The Siege of Khe Sanh*. New York: W. W. Norton, 1982.

Shulimson, Jack, et al. *U.S. Marines in Vietnam: The Defining Year, 1968*. Washington, D.C.: U.S. Marine Corps, 1997.

Stanton, Shelby L. *The Rise and Fall of an American Army: U.S. Ground Forces in Vietnam, 1965–1973*. Novato, Calif.: Presidio Press, 1985.

Starry, Donn A. *Mounted Combat in Vietnam*. Vietnam Studies. Washington, D.C.: U.S. Army Center of Military History, 2002.

Summers, Harry G. *On Strategy: A Critical Analysis of the Vietnam War*. Novato, Calif.: Presidio Press, 1982.

Tolson, John J. *Airmobility, 1961–1971*. Vietnam Studies. Washington, D.C.: U.S. Army Center of Military History, 1989.

Vien, Cao Van. *The Final Collapse*. Indochina Monographs. Washington, D.C.: U.S. Army Center of Military History, 1984.

Wirtz, James J. *The Tet Offensive: Intelligence Failure in War*. Ithaca: Cornell University Press, 1991.

12

REBUILDING THE ARMY VIETNAM TO DESERT STORM

The end of American ground forces' direct participation in the Vietnam War in January 1973 left the U.S. Army a much weakened institution. Public trust in the Army was at a low point, with many blaming the military for the war as much as they blamed the civilian policymakers whose orders the military was carrying out. Many of the soldiers who returned from Vietnam faced a hostile or at best indifferent public reception. A number of soldiers had become drug addicts in Vietnam, where the supply of heroin was plentiful. Discipline, especially in the rear base camps, had begun breaking down in many units toward the end of the war as it became apparent that America was only interested in leaving Vietnam. A common saying of the time was that no one wanted to be the last man to die in Vietnam. Racial tension and even instances of "fragging" (tossing a fragmentation grenade into the sleeping quarters or office of a superior officer or noncommissioned officer [NCO] to injure or "warn") led to some unit-cohesion problems. The Army that left Vietnam and returned to America and its garrisons in Germany and Korea in the early 1970s was at low ebb of morale, discipline, and military effectiveness.

The problems did not go away immediately with the end of the war. For those career soldiers and officers who remained in the Army, drug problems, poor leadership (especially at the junior NCO and officer levels), and severe racial problems often split units into hostile camps. Race riots were not uncommon, especially in the understrength *kasserns* of Germany as the Army tried to rebuild its European units that had been drained to support the Vietnam War. With the expiration of Selective Service induction authority on June 30, 1973, the establishment of a new, all-volunteer Army was under way. Many wondered if the Army could recover sufficiently to recruit enough quality soldiers and, even if it did so, if the country would be able to pay the bill. The result was far from certain.

THE ARMY IN GERMANY

Throughout the seventies, funding shortages undermined the readiness and morale of American soldiers in Germany. United States Army, Europe (USAREUR), suffered from under investment and under maintenance. Bad housing, dilapidated facilities, worn equipment, and inadequate training were the rule. The situation changed in the eighties. Large increases in USAREUR's capital budget made up for years of parsimony, while stepped-up training improved U.S. combat capabilities. For the remainder of the 1980s, the U.S. Army in Germany was perhaps the most-desired training and operational assignment for Army personnel.

The All-Volunteer Force

Even while the Vietnam War was raging, the Army and the Department of Defense had begun tentative planning to transition to an all-volunteer force. For most planners, this was new ground. Except for a short period of time immediately after World War II, the Army had not had a volunteer force since just before the United States entered World War II. Commanders could rely upon the steady flow of young men of reasonable physical and mental quality, since they had the entire manpower of the country to draw upon. Recruiting was not a high priority: it was not seen as entirely necessary. Why struggle to meet a quota for recruits when the draft guaranteed enough men to fill the force? The reserve components, both the National Guard and Army Reserve, were at full strength and even overstrength, as young men flocked to those units to fulfill their service obligations with a minimal risk of going to Vietnam.

With the election of President Richard M. Nixon in 1968, the prospect of ending the draft became a real possibility. As a result, the Defense Department started a study project entitled Project Volunteer in November 1968 to determine the feasibility of recruiting an all-volunteer force while still maintaining military effectiveness. Quickly, many key issues began surfacing: how to get enough high-quality soldiers, how to keep them, how to pay for them, and what management and leadership practices would create an effective military force out of this voluntary manpower.

In January 1969 the process of ending the draft accelerated. The newly inaugurated President specifically requested that the Defense Department take action to eliminate the draft and create an all-volunteer force. He formed an advisory commission, called the Gates Commission, to develop a complete plan on how to implement the new force. The Army, the service most affected by manpower levels, began its own study on how it could implement such an idea. Project Volunteer in Defense of the Nation (PROVIDE) addressed such topics such as cost, standards of quality, personnel management, numbers needed to recruit, and even the possible socioeconomic impact of an all-volunteer force.

Perhaps the biggest single hurdle in creating an all-volunteer force was money. The draft brought in young men for a short period of service at artificially low wages, essentially "taxing" a segment of society. With the ending of that tax, the government would have to find enough money to provide monetary incentives—viable wages and even bonuses for some specialties—for new recruits. Without competitive pay, the Army could not enlist or retain the best soldiers. Money was also needed for advertising for the United States Army Recruiting Command (USAREC) if the Army was to become an attractive career choice and bring in enough quality American youths.

Some negative aspects of Army life also required additional funding to eliminate. With virtually unlimited manpower, the Army over the years had diverted more and more of its soldiers to nonmilitary, even menial, tasks. Army posts had soldiers cutting the grass, painting quarters, working as "kitchen police" (KP) in the mess halls, and functioning as clerks in various support and morale activities often unrelated to military skills. Many considered Army soldiers just a source of "cheap" manpower. With the ending of the draft, however, the Army could no longer afford to waste manpower or divert highly trained soldiers to menial tasks. As the time for the end of the draft grew closer, the Army began lobbying for more money to hire civilian workers to take over many of the tasks deemed unsuitable for soldiers. This improved morale and increased the training time available for soldiers to improve their individual and unit military skills. Soldiers were on their way to being treated as professionals again, not merely as cheap, unskilled manpower. Money by itself was not enough, but it went a long way toward redressing some of the young soldiers' worst grievances.

As the Nixon administration reiterated its commitment to ending the draft, the Army moved to implement the new concept. In October 1970 Chief of Staff of the Army General William C. Westmoreland created the position of Special Assistant for the Modern Volunteer Army (SAMVA) to head the Modern Volunteer Army (MVA) program and appointed Lt. Gen. George I. Forsythe. Forsythe faced a formidable challenge as he tried to lay out a blueprint for what would amount to a major cultural change while a war still raged in Southeast Asia.

The most obvious problem the new volunteer Army faced was the difficulty of attracting and keeping enough manpower. Without a sufficient number of recruits, the entire experiment would collapse. The Army faced problems with raw manpower needs and with the basic requirement of getting enough soldiers to join the critical combat arms of Infantry, Field Artillery, and Armor. Fewer than half the men entering the Army in 1970 were considered volunteers, and only 4 percent of them joined the combat arms. Yet the Army, still involved in combat in Vietnam, needed thousands of combat soldiers. To make the new volunteer force work, the Army estimated that it had to increase enlistments for the combat arms by about 300 percent by June 1973. To achieve this goal, in the midst of an increasingly unpopular war for which all the services were beginning to share the blame, was going to require innovative leadership and a willingness to experiment, in addition to much more money.

One of the more controversial experiments under the MVA program was Project VOLAR (Volunteer Army) conducted at selected Army posts (Forts Benning, Carson, and Ord, joined by Bragg in April 1971) from January 1, 1971, to June 30, 1972. This project experimented with ways to raise morale, increase retention rates, and decrease

With the ending of the draft, ... the Army could no longer afford to waste manpower or divert highly trained soldiers to menial tasks.

disciplinary problems (especially absent without leave, or AWOL, rates) to prove that with the right combination of leadership and incentives a volunteer force was possible. At each selected post, the leadership abolished harassing or "Mickey Mouse," details; civilianized the infamous KP duties; relaxed grooming standards; allowed for weekends without duty or inspections; established junior enlisted councils to provide another channel for grievances; and put forth a host of other initiatives. When implemented consistently by conscientious officers and NCOs, the initiatives often resulted in soldiers' being treated like mature adults and not like children, with a concomitant increase in pride, morale, and reenlistment rates.

However, some ill-thought-out VOLAR initiatives such as beer in the barracks or severe relaxation of grooming and discipline standards led to more problems than they solved and presented the impression of a loss of control. Some programs, if implemented by poor leaders not really interested in taking care of soldiers or not believing that the volunteer force would work, sometimes led to a collapse of discipline, exacerbated existing racial problems, and alienated officers and noncommissioned officers. This time of experimentation showed what the Army needed to do to restore morale and improve the quality of life for soldiers, but it also revealed what it needed to avoid in order rebuild the force after decades of relying on the draft. The initial media and Army focus on making the Army more permissive and attractive soon faded as commanders and soldiers realized that the more important initiatives revolved around more and better training, instilling in the soldiers a stronger sense of professionalism, and building greater individual and unit pride.

With the formal ending of direct U.S. involvement in the Vietnam War and the formal establishment of the all-volunteer Army in 1973, the need to make the Army an effective military force rested first and foremost on the need to recruit more soldiers. At first it seemed an impossible task. Month after month in 1973 the Army, like many of the other services, failed to meet its recruiting quotas. Recruiters were initially able to fill only 68.5 percent of their quota for enlisting first-term male soldiers. Attempts to hold the line for high-quality recruits, those with high school diplomas, seemed doomed to failure. Some, including members of Congress, began claiming that the Army was secretly intent on subverting the Modern Volunteer Army Program and returning to the "safe" days of the unlimited manpower of the draft. Even with the reduction of the authorized end strength of the Army to 781,000 in 1974, the Army ended fiscal year 1973, the last year of the draft, understrength by almost 14,000.

The pivotal year for the survival of the all-volunteer Army was fiscal year 1974 (July 1, 1973–June 30, 1974). For the first time, recruiting began to turn the corner; in November 1973 recruiting quotas were topped. Army recruiters enlisted 104 percent of their overall quota in that month. By June of the following year, they had attained 123 percent of their quota. Of those recruited, 84 percent were in the average or above average mental groups, proving that the Army was starting to turn the corner on quality enlistees.

There were a number of reasons for this turnaround in recruiting. First, the smaller size of the Army helped. The Army during Vietnam

> When implemented consistently by conscientious officers and NCOs, the initiatives often resulted in soldiers' being treated like mature adults and not like children, with a concomitant increase in pride, morale, and reenlistment rates.

had peaked at 1.57 million soldiers in 1968 and declined to an authorized end strength of 785,000 by the end of June 1974. This relaxed some of the pressure on the recruiters. Congress also helped when it authorized bonuses for thirty-two of the most critical skills, including the combat arms, the Army needed. Congress had also authorized additional incentive pay bonuses for recruiters. With more and better-paid recruiters on the street and better deals to offer, the Army reached more and more potential recruits. Finally, the Army leadership, in particular Secretary of the Army Howard H. "Bo" Callaway, began to show an unwavering commitment to making the all-volunteer force succeed. The Army realized that there was no going back to the draft. As recruiting slogans changed from "The Army wants to join you" to "Join the people who have joined the Army" and finally to the classic "Be all that you can be, in the Army," the number and quality of recruits continued to increase.

Another reason for the improvement in the recruitment rates for the Army had lasting consequences. The Army, at first out of necessity and later out of a realization that it needed the highest-quality recruits it could get, began actively to expand the number of women in the Army and increased the numbers of specialties they could perform. From about 1948, the number of women in the Army had been limited to no more than 2 percent of the end strength. They were excluded from most combat and combat support (CS) specialties and concentrated in the clerical and supply fields. Married women could not enlist, and women who became pregnant in the service faced mandatory discharge. To meet the new all-volunteer Army manpower quotas, all that would have to change.

The changes in the role of women in the Army proceeded slowly but inexorably as the talent, skill, and dedication women brought to their task made believers out of the somewhat conservative male Army leadership. The numbers of women recruited went from 10,900 a year to 25,130 a year in just five years. By 1978 there were 53,000 women in the Army, growing to around 80,000 by the end of fiscal year 1983. The Army could not have made its recruiting quotas without this dramatic expansion of the number of women who willingly joined the service.

Training for women dramatically improved; new skill areas, many previously all male, opened for females. Units increasingly were mixed gender, and women were no longer discharged for pregnancy. Women were soon training on the use of small arms, initially on a voluntary basis, beginning in Women's Army Corps basic training in July 1974. Then, in a major symbolic event, 119 women were admitted to the U.S. Military Academy at West Point for the first time in July 1976, graduating as members of the class of 1980. The integration of women into the Army was so complete and irreversible that in October

A Drill Instructor Training Recruits in Basic Rifle Marksmanship

Servicing the Engine of a CH–47 Chinook Helicopter

1978 the Women's Army Corps was disestablished and all women were assigned to branches for management purposes just as all other soldiers. During time of war, they went to the theater just as men did. When the Army deployed to the Persian Gulf in 1990, 8.6 percent of the total force deployed to Saudi Arabia, 26,000, were women.

The increase in the number of women in the Army did not occur without problems. Change never comes easy to a large and somewhat conservative organization. Women continued to be excluded from the combat arms despite strong lobbying by women's organizations that often had their own agendas. This was codified to a certain extent by a February 1988 "risk rule" approved by then Secretary of Defense Richard Cheney. This rule prevented women from serving in positions where there was risk of direct combat or exposure to hostile fire or capture. Although modified over the years, much of this exclusion policy remained in place to the dismay of many females who believed their careers were thereby restricted.

Even more serious problems arose with the increase of sexual harassment charges and fraternization problems in the Army. With more women in units, there were more instances reported of inappropriate language, gestures, or actions of a sexual nature directed at women. As a result, the Army established regulations and policies (tied closely to the equal opportunity program that continued to grapple with lingering racial prejudice in the Army) to cope with the inevitable problems as a predominately male military adjusted to the greater number of female soldiers. Fraternization between soldiers, especially between superiors and subordinates (generally, but by no means always, between male superior officers and NCOs and subordinate females) was also an increasing problem as the Army tried to regulate human behavior in the Army workplace. Neither of these challenges was completely solved; but as the Army grew more professional and women began "proving" themselves as soldiers, male and female soldiers and officers began treating each other with the respect due a professional. Like racism, however, problems with sexual harassment and inappropriate relationships between ranks did not vanish completely and programs continued in place to mitigate the problem as much as possible.

While Army enlistments, the integration of women, and disputes about the quality of the soldiers would fluctuate in the 1970s and 1980s, the all-volunteer Army slowly proved itself a tremendous success. Training became tougher, standards were raised higher, and all levels of the Army began rediscovering the pride that comes with doing a job well. Recruitment rates remained relatively healthy throughout the buildup of forces during the tenure of President Ronald W. Reagan. However, it was also increasingly important to spread these changes in training and improvements in pride throughout the entire Army, including the Army Reserves and National Guard. A smaller Army necessarily relied more heavily upon its reserve components.

Women's Utility Coat, Olive Drab–107, 1970

The Total Force Policy

The Army's reliance on its reserve components changed the very nature of its active and reserve force structure and mobilization plans. The resulting Total Force Policy grew out of the closing days of the Vietnam War. In 1969 President Nixon established a policy of Vietnamization, under which the burden of the war was increasingly transferred to the South Vietnamese Army. This action and the eventual U.S. withdrawal from Vietnam in 1973 meant, among other things, lower defense budgets. Secretary of Defense Melvin R. Laird announced in August 1970 a Total Force Concept: there would be reductions in all facets of the active forces and concomitantly increased reliance on the reserve components for both combat and combat support capabilities. In 1973 this concept was declared policy by Laird's successor as Secretary of Defense, James R. Schlesinger. Thus the major reason behind the enunciation of the Total Force Policy was more budgetary and circumstantial than philosophical.

There were also modernization imperatives behind why the Army so readily accepted and institutionalized the Total Force Policy. Because the buildup for the Vietnam War had been accomplished by adding to the active forces instead of mobilizing the reserve components, there was a redundancy between the active force and the reserve components in certain types of units. Removing support capabilities from the active force and placing them in the reserve components not only solved the problem of duplication, it also saved money for the modernization of the active force. Having postponed modernization to meet the exigencies of the war in Southeast Asia, the Army could now afford to begin the long, slow process of becoming a more capable force but at the cost of increasing dependence on the reserves.

The budgetary and modernization rationales for the Total Force Policy do not fully explain the degree of dependence on the reserve components that the Army developed in the 1970s, however. The budget reductions meant a much smaller Army. From its Vietnam War high strength of 1.57 million in fiscal year 1968, the Army declined to 785,000 in fiscal year 1974. Army Chief of Staff General Creighton W. Abrams, Jr., in 1973 set up a study group that postulated a future multipolar world in which thirteen active Army divisions would constitute a

CREIGHTON W. ABRAMS (1914–1974)

As an armor officer steeped in conventional tactics, General Abrams was perhaps an unlikely choice to command MACV; but his experience as Westmoreland's deputy and a creative mind served him well during his tenure in Vietnam from July 1968 to June 1972. Like his predecessor, Abrams sought to fight the war within the restrictions Washington placed on him. However, the rules changed somewhat when President Nixon took office in 1969. Abrams was allowed to launch two cross-border incursions against enemy base areas, one into Cambodia in May 1970 and the second into Laos in February 1971. General Abrams became the twenty-seventh Chief of Staff of the Army in 1972 and began the long process of rebuilding the Army after the Vietnam War. He died in office in 1974.

"high-risk" force. Could such a small Army fulfill all its obligations and still retain an adequate contingency force?

In response, General Abrams obtained the Secretary of Defense's approval to increase the Army's active divisions to sixteen without an increase in Army end strength. Abrams laid the basis for the sixteen divisions by shifting manpower from the Table of Distribution and Allowances (TDA) Army (headquarters and educational infrastructure) to Table of Organization and Equipment (TO&E) units, assigning reserve component "round-out" brigades as integral units in late-deploying active divisions, and moving combat support and combat service support (CSS) functions to the reserve components. By the end of fiscal year 1973, 66 percent of CS/CSS was in the reserve components.

General Abrams and much of the Army's senior leadership, following the lead of Secretaries of Defense Laird's and Schlesinger's commitment to the total force policy, believed that President Lyndon B. Johnson's failure to fully mobilize the reserve components was a major cause of the lack of popular support for the Vietnam War. By helping ensure that the Army could not be involved in a major war again without the reserve components, Abrams and his successors sought to prevent such insufficient support in the future. The Army leadership realized that one of the dangers of a volunteer Army was that an elite professional force might weaken the bonds between the American people and the service that the draft had engendered. Greater integration of the reserve components into the active force would strengthen the Army's ties with the states, the Congress, and the public. Such ties were seen as increasingly important: the collapse of the national will to continue the struggle, rather than outright military defeat, had essentially ended the Vietnam War.

As the Army implemented its new Total Force Policy, the National Guard and Army Reserve recovered from Vietnam and the immediate post–Vietnam War doldrums to gain new heights of readiness. Each component was reduced in size throughout the 1970s but rebounded by the end of the 1980s. The National Guard, at an authorized strength of 402,175 in 1971, was down to only 368,254 soldiers a decade later, only to increase to 456,960 by 1989. The Army Ready Reserve end strength was only at 263,299 in 1971 and fell with the end of the draft to 202,627 by 1980. However, it had recovered to the level of 312,825 soldiers by 1989. By the eve of Operation DESERT SHIELD/STORM in 1990, the Guard and the Army Reserve would be, like their active-duty counterparts, as strong and well trained as they ever had been in the nation's history.

New Doctrine

The new volunteer Total Army needed more than mere numbers. It needed a mission; it needed to focus on what type of war it might need to fight. As a result, the Army began developing a new doctrine to regain its perspective and focus on its new missions after Vietnam. A reassessment of how the Army would fight began in essence with President Nixon's 1969 Guam Doctrine, in which he stated that the United States would maintain a smaller defense establishment to fight a "1 1/2 war" contingency. This was generally interpreted to mean that the Army would prepare to engage in a general war, probably in the European or Northeast Asian theaters, and at the same time fight a minor conflict, presumably a Third World counterinsurgency.

Nixon's smaller Army vision faced growing challenges, however. American intelligence agencies in the early 1970s noted an increase of five Soviet armored divisions in Europe, the continued restationing of Soviet Army divisions farther to the west, and a major improvement in equipment, with T–62 and T–72 tanks replacing older models and with a corresponding modernization of other classes of weapons. If general war had come to Europe during the 1970s, the U.S. Army and its North Atlantic Treaty Organization (NATO) allies would have confronted Warsaw Pact armies that were both numerically and qualitatively superior. With the Army mired down in Vietnam and with modernization postponed, this was a very sobering prospect.

The Arab-Israeli War that began on October 6, 1973, further intensified concerns about the modernization and preparedness of the Army for intense ground combat. The deadliness of modern weapons as well as the Army's Vietnam-era concentration on infantry-airmobile warfare at the expense of other forces led many to believe that we could not fight this new type of war. American observers who toured the battlefields of Egypt and Syria began to create a new tactical vocabulary when they reported on the "new lethality" of a Middle Eastern battlefield where in one month of fighting the Israeli, Syrian, and Egyptian Armies lost more tanks and artillery than the entire U.S. Army, Europe, possessed. Improved technology in the form of antitank and antiaircraft guided missiles, much more sophisticated and accurate fire-control systems, and vastly improved tank cannons heralded a far more costly and lethal future for conventional war.

Technology likewise brought changes to battlefield tactics. Egyptian infantry armed with missiles enjoyed significant successes against

General DePuy

Israeli tank units, bolstering the importance of carefully coordinated combined-arms units. It seemed clear that in future wars American forces would fight powerful and well-equipped armies with soldiers proficient in the use of extremely deadly weapons. Such fighting would consume large numbers of men and quantities of materiel. It became imperative for the Army to devise a way to win any future war quickly.

A new operations field manual, the Army's specific response to new conditions that required new doctrine, was preeminently the work of General William E. DePuy, commander of the new U.S. Army Training and Doctrine Command (TRADOC). General DePuy, a combat-tested infantry officer in World War II and the commander of the 1st Infantry Division in Vietnam during some of its hardest fighting, brought a wealth of experience to his position. Surveying conditions of modern warfare that appeared to reconfirm the lessons he and his men had learned so painfully in World War II, DePuy in 1976 wrote much of a new edition of Field Manual (FM) 100–5, *Operations*, the Army's premier tactical doctrine manual of the time. DePuy's FM 100–5 initially touted a concept known as the Active Defense, which once more focused on "the primacy of the defense." The handbook evolved from its first publication to become the keystone of a family of Army manuals that completely replaced the doctrine practiced at the end of the Vietnam War.

From these modest beginnings the Army's new doctrine, AirLand Battle, slowly emerged. In its final form AirLand Battle doctrine was actually a clear articulation of fundamentals that American generals had understood and practiced as early as World War II, with an appropriate and explicit recognition of the role air power played in making decisive ground maneuver possible. The U.S. Army Command and General Staff College at Fort Leavenworth, Kansas, acknowledged AirLand Battle's basis in traditional concepts of maneuver warfare by teaching it and making frequent use of historical examples to explain its principles more fully.

In practical terms, the doctrine required commanders to simultaneously supervise three types of operations: close, deep, and rear. In close operations, large tactical formations such as corps and divisions fought

FM 100–5

After Vietnam, Army planning emphasized the Warsaw Pact threat to NATO, in particular the need for U.S. forces to defeat a technically sophisticated and numerically superior opponent. This problem required a new approach, presented in the 1976 edition of Field Manual 100–5, *Operations*, the Army's central doctrinal publication. This Active Defense concept emphasized the tank as the pivotal element of land forces, promoted the concentration of fires over the concentration of forces wherever practical, and advocated replacement of tactical reserves with the lateral movement of unengaged forward units behind a strong covering force. Such a radical departure from earlier doctrine proved both controversial and difficult to implement in the field, especially outside the NATO area. The next edition of FM 100–5, issued in 1982 and revised in 1986, was organized around the idea of AirLand Battle, a more generalized concept stressing aggressive operations in depth with an increased emphasis on the exploitation of tactical air power.

battles through maneuver, close combat, and indirect fire support. Deep operations helped to win the close battle by engaging enemy formations not by contact, but chiefly through deception, deep surveillance, and ground and air interdiction of enemy reserves. Objectives of deep operations were to isolate the battlefield and influence when, where, and against whom later battles would be fought. Rear operations proceeded simultaneously with close and deep operations and focused on assembling and moving reserves in the friendly rear areas, redeploying fire support, continuing logistical efforts to sustain the battle, and providing continuity of command and control. Security operations, traffic control, and communications maintenance were critical to rear operations.

After 1976 AirLand Battle generated an extended doctrinal and tactical discussion in the service journals that helped to clarify and occasionally to modify the manual. General Donn A. Starry, who succeeded DePuy in 1977 at the Training and Doctrine Command, directed a substantial revision that concentrated on the offensive and added weight to the importance of deep operations by stressing the role of deep ground and air attack in disrupting the enemy's follow-on echelons of forces. Changes mainly dealt with ways to exploit what noted historian Basil H. Liddell Hart described as the indirect approach in warfare by fighting the enemy along a line where he least expects it.

General Starry

In 1982 the Army modified FM 100–5 to stress that the Army had to "fight outnumbered and win" the first battle of the next war, an imperative that required a trained and ready peacetime force. The manual acknowledged the armored battle as the heart of warfare, with the tank as the single most important weapon in the Army's arsenal. Success, however, hinged on a deft manipulation of all the arms, especially Infantry, Engineers, Artillery, and Air Power, to give free rein to the maneuver forces. Using that mechanized force, the doctrine required commanders to seize the initiative from the enemy; act faster than the enemy could react; exploit depth through operations extending in space, time, and resources to keep the enemy off balance; and synchronize the combat power of ground and air forces at the decisive point of battle.

AirLand Battle doctrine had additional utility because it helped to define both the proper equipment for its execution and the appropriate organization of military units for battle. This, along with the widespread promulgation of common terms and concepts, was at the very roots of the need for doctrine. Thus the new AirLand Battle doctrine explicitly acknowledged the growth of technology both as a threat and as a requirement for new equipment to meet the threat. The U.S. Army and its NATO allies could not hope to match Soviet and Warsaw Pact forces either in masses of manpower or in floods of materiel. To that extent, AirLand Battle served as the basis for both an organizational strategy and a procurement rationale. To fight outnumbered and survive, the Army needed to better employ the nation's qualitative edge in technology.

New Equipment

Military theorists generally agree that a defending army can hope for success if the attacking enemy has no greater than a 3:1 advantage in combat power. The best intelligence estimates in the 1970s concluded that the Warsaw Pact armies enjoyed a much larger advantage. Continuing budget constrictions made unlikely the possibility of increasing the size of the American military to match Soviet growth. To solve the problem of how to fight an enemy that would almost certainly be larger, the United States relied in part on technologically superior hardware that could defeat an enemy with an advantage ratio higher than 1:3. To achieve that end, the Army in the early 1970s began work on the new "big five" equipment systems: a tank, an infantry combat vehicle, an attack helicopter, a transport helicopter, and an antiaircraft missile.

Several factors affected new equipment design. Among the most important was the flourishing technology encouraged by the pure and applied research associated with space programs. Although the big five equipment originated in the years before AirLand Battle was first enunciated, that doctrine quickly had its effect on design criteria. Other factors were speed, survivability, and good communications, essential to economize on small forces and give them the advantages they required to defeat larger, but presumably more ponderous, enemies. Target acquisition and fire control were equally important, since the success of a numerically inferior force depended heavily on the ability to score first-round hits.

Even such simply stated criteria were not easy to achieve, with compromises and trade-offs often necessary between weight, speed, and survivability. All of the weapon programs suffered through years of mounting costs and production delays. A debate that was at once philosophical and fiscal raged around the new equipment, with some critics preferring simpler and cheaper machines fielded in greater quantities. The Department of Defense persevered, however, in its preference for technologically superior systems and managed to retain funding for most of the proposed new weapons. Weapon systems were expensive, but defense analysts recognized that personnel costs were even higher and pointed out that the services could not afford the manpower to operate increased numbers of simpler weapons. Nevertheless, spectacular procurement failures, such as the Sergeant York Division Air Defense (DIVAD) weapon, kept the issue before the public; such cases kept program funding for other equally complex weapons on the debate agenda.

The first of the big five systems was the M1 tank, soon to be named after General Abrams, a noted World War II tank leader who had died in 1974 during his tenure as Chief of Staff. Despite some growing pains, the tank weathered considerable criticism that in fact had derived from the failure of a preceding tank program. The standard tanks in the Army inventory had been various models of the M48 and M60, both surpassed in some respects by new Soviet equipment. The XM803 succeeded the abortive joint American-German Main Battle Tank–70 project and was intended to modernize the armored force. Concerned about expense, Congress withdrew funding for the XM803 in December 1971, thereby canceling the program, but agreed to leave the remaining surplus of $20 million in Army hands to continue conceptual studies.

For a time, designers considered arming tanks with missiles for long-range engagements. This innovation worked only moderately well in the M60A2 main battle tank and the M551 Sheridan armored reconnaissance vehicle, both armed with the MGM51 Shillelagh gun-launcher system. In the late 1960s tank guns were rejuvenated by new technical developments that included a fin-stabilized, very-high-velocity projectile that used long-rod kinetic energy penetrators. Attention centered on 105-mm. and 120-mm. guns as the main armament of any new tank.

Armored protection was also an issue of tank modernization. The proliferation of antitank missiles that could be launched by infantry, antitank vehicles, or mounted on helicopters demonstrated the need for considerable improvement. At the same time, weight was an important consideration because the speed and agility of the tank would be important determinants of its tactical utility. No less important was crew survivability; even if the tank were damaged in battle, it was important that a trained tank crew have a reasonable chance of surviving to man a new vehicle.

The Army made the decision for a new tank series in 1972 and awarded developmental contracts in 1973. The first prototype of the M1, known as the XM1, reached the testing stage in 1976; the tank began to arrive in battalions in February 1980. The M1 enjoyed a low silhouette and a very high speed, thanks to an unfortunately voracious gas turbine engine. Chobham spaced armor (ceramic blocks set in resin between layers of conventional armor) resolved the problem of protection versus mobility. A sophisticated fire-control system provided main-gun stabilization for shooting on the move; and a precise laser range-finder, thermal-imaging night sights, and a digital ballistic computer solved the gunnery problem, thus maximizing the utility of the 105-mm. main gun. Assembly plants had manufactured more than 2,300 of the 62-ton M1 tank by January 1985, when the new version, the M1A1, was approved for full production. The M1A1 had improved armor and a 120-mm. main gun that had increased range and kill probability. By the summer of 1990 several variations of the M1 had replaced the M60 in the active force and in a number of Army Reserve and National Guard battalions. Tankers had trained with the Abrams long enough to have confidence in it. In fact, many believed it was the first American tank since World War II that was qualitatively superior to Soviet models.

Abrams Tank

Bradley Fighting Vehicle

The second of the big five systems was the companion vehicle to the Abrams tank: the M2 Bradley infantry fighting vehicle, also produced in a cavalry fighting version as the M3. Its predecessor, the M113 armored personnel carrier, dated back to the early 1960s and was really little more than a battle taxi. The 1973 Arab-Israeli War demonstrated that infantry should accompany tanks, but it was increasingly clear that the M113 could not perform that function because it was far slower than the M1 and much more poorly armored.

European practice also influenced American plans for a new vehicle. German infantry used the well-armored Marder, a vehicle that carried seven infantrymen in addition to its crew of three, was armed with a 20-mm. gun and coaxial 7.62-mm. machine gun in a turret, and allowed the infantrymen to fight from within the vehicle. The French Army fielded a similar infantry vehicle in the AMX–10P in 1973. The Soviets had their BMP family of armored vehicles, which had a 73-mm. smoothbore cannon and an antitank guided missile as early as the late 1960s. Variations of the BMP were generally considered the best infantry fighting vehicles in the world during the 1980s. The United States had fallen at least a decade behind in the development of infantry vehicles. General DePuy at TRADOC and General Starry at the U.S. Army Armor Center and School at Fort Knox, Kentucky, agreed the Army needed a new infantry vehicle and began studies in that direction.

In 1980, when Congress restored funding to the Infantry Fighting Vehicle Program, the Army let contracts for prototypes, receiving the first production models the next year. Like the Abrams, the Bradley was a compromise among competing demands for mobility, armor protection, firepower, and dismounted infantry strength. As produced, the vehicle was thirty tons but carried a 25-mm. cannon and 7.62-mm. coaxial machine gun to allow it to fight as a scout vehicle and a TOW (Tube-Launched, Optically tracked, Wire-guided) missile launcher that enhanced the infantry battalion's antiarmor capability. The vehicle's interior was too small for the standard rifle squad of nine: it carried six or seven riflemen, depending on the model. That limitation led to discussions about using the vehicle as the "base of fire" element and to consequent revisions of tactical doctrine for maneuver.

The Bradley, with its superior weapons and armor protection, could move close into the battle, unload its infantrymen for dismounted combat, and stay in position to assist the infantrymen by accurate and powerful machine-gun and antitank or antibunker fire. It was both an infantry "taxi" (the former role of the M113 armored personnel carrier) and a supporting weapons platform that could lay down a base of fire to suppress the enemy and support the infantry assault. Another critical aspect of its usefulness in the combined-arms team, however, was that the Bradley could keep up with the Abrams tank on the battlefield. If tanks and infantry fought together, they brought their own level of synergy to the battlefield. However, this could only happen if the infantry vehicle could sustain the pace and speed of the formidable M1 tank.

By 1990 forty-seven battalions and squadrons of the Regular Army and four Army National Guard battalions had M2 and M3 Bradleys. A continuing modernization program that began in 1987 gave the vehicles, redesignated M2A1 and M3A1, the improved TOW 2 missile. Various redesigns to increase survivability of the Bradley began production in May 1988, with these most recent models designated A2.

The third of the big five systems was the AH–64A Apache attack helicopter. The experience of Vietnam showed that the existing attack helicopter, the AH–1 Cobra, was vulnerable even to light antiaircraft fire and lacked the agility to fly close to the ground for long periods of time. The AH–56A Cheyenne, canceled in 1969, had been intended to correct those deficiencies. The new attack helicopter program announced in August 1972 drew from the combat experience of the Cobra and the developmental experience of the Cheyenne to specify an aircraft that could absorb battle damage and had the power for rapid movement and heavy loads. The helicopter would have to be able to fly nap of the earth and maneuver with great agility to succeed in a new antitank mission on a high-intensity battlefield.

The first prototypes flew in September 1975, and in December 1976 the Army selected the Hughes YAM–64 for production. Sophisticated night-vision and target-sensing devices allowed the pilot to fly nap of the earth even at night. The aircraft's main weapon was the heat-seeking Hellfire missile, sixteen of which could be carried in four launchers. In place of the antitank missile the Apache could carry seventy-six 70-mm. (2.75-inch) rockets. It could also mount a combination of eight Hellfire missiles and thirty-eight rockets. In the nose, the aircraft mounted a Hughes 30-mm. single-barrel chain gun.

Full-scale production of the Apache began in 1982, and the Army received the first aircraft in December 1983. By the end of 1990 the McDonnell-Douglas Helicopter Company (which purchased Hughes in 1984) had delivered 629 Apaches to equip 19 active attack-helicopter battalions. When production was completed, the Apaches were intended to equip 26 Regular Army, 2 Reserve, and 12 National Guard battalions, a total of 807 aircraft.

The fourth of the big five systems, the fleet of utility helicopters, had already been modernized with the fielding of the UH–60A

Black Hawk to replace the UH–1 Iroquois ("Huey") used during the Vietnam War. The Black Hawk could lift an entire infantry squad or a 105-mm. howitzer with its crew and some ammunition. The new utility helicopter was both faster and quieter than the UH–1 and proved a reliable and sturdy platform during combat operations in Grenada and Panama.

The last of the big five equipment was the Patriot air defense missile, conceived in 1965 as a replacement for the HAWK (Homing All the Way Killer) and the Nike-Hercules missiles, both based on 1950s technology. The Patriot benefited from lessons drawn from design of the antiballistic missile system, particularly the highly capable phased-array radar. The solid-fuel Patriot missile required virtually no maintenance and had the speed and agility to match known threats. At the same time its system design was more compact, more mobile, and demanded smaller crews than had previous air-defense missiles. Despite its many advantages, or perhaps because of the ambitious design that yielded those advantages, the development program of the missile, initially known as the SAM-D (Surface-to-Air Missile–Developmental), was extraordinarily long, spanning virtually the entire careers of officers commissioned at the end of the 1960s. The long gestation and escalating costs incident to the Patriot's technical sophistication made it a continuing target of both media and congressional critics. Despite controversy, the missile went into production in the early 1980s; the Army fielded the first fire units in 1984.

A single battalion with Patriot missiles had more firepower than several HAWK battalions, the mainstay of the 32d Army Air Defense Command in Germany. Initial fielding plans envisaged forty-two units, or batteries, in Europe and eighteen in the United States; but funding and various delays slowed the deployment. By 1991 only ten half-battalions, each with three batteries, were active.

Originally designed as an antiaircraft weapon guided by a computer and radar system that could cope with multiple targets, the Patriot also had the potential to defend against battlefield tactical missiles such as the Soviet FROG (Free Rocket Over Ground) and Scud. About the time the first units were fielded, the Army began to explore the possibility that the Patriot could also have an ATBM, or antitactical ballistic missile, mission. In 1988 testing authenticated the PAC–1 (Patriot Antitactical ballistic missile Capability, Phase 1) computer software, which was promptly installed in existing systems. The PAC–2 upgrade was still being tested in early 1991 as it prepared for action in Desert Storm.

The big five were by no means the only significant equipment modernization programs the Army pursued between 1970 and 1991. Other important Army purchases included the Multiple-Launch Rocket System (MLRS); a new generation of tube artillery to upgrade fire support; improved small arms; tactical wheeled vehicles, such as a new 5-ton truck and utility vehicle (the high-mobility multipurpose wheeled vehicle, or HMMWV) to replace the venerable World War II jeep; and a family of new command, control, communications, and intelligence hardware. By the summer of 1990 this equipment had been tested and delivered to Army divisions.

While most of those developments began before the Training and Doctrine Command's first publication of AirLand Battle doctrine, a close relationship between doctrine and equipment swiftly developed. Weapons modernization encouraged doctrinal thinkers to consider more ambitious concepts that would exploit the capabilities new systems offered. A successful melding of the two, however, depended on the creation of tactical organizations properly designed to use the weapons in accordance with the doctrine. While doctrinal development and equipment modernization were under way, force designers also reexamined the structure of the field army.

New Organizations

After Vietnam the Army underwent a number of organizational changes at the higher headquarters and tactical levels. At the highest level the Army determined to reorganize its command structure for the Continental United States (CONUS) and separate its essentially command and control headquarters from its training base.

Following World War II, the Army had organized its operational forces in CONUS under six U.S. armies, each with a geographic area of responsibility. The chiefs of the Army's technical services retained responsibility for depots and other specialized facilities and activities that reported directly to them. In 1955 the Army established the U.S. Continental Army Command (CONARC) to command and control the six armies in CONUS and their subordinate operational forces and in 1962 created the Army Materiel Command (AMC) and the Combat Developments Command (CDC) to manage force development and control the technical services. Over the years, CONARC's control expanded to most Army schools and the various branch boards involved with Army combat developments, the Reserve Officers' Training Corps (ROTC), the U.S. Army Reserve, and support for the Army National Guard. CONARC was a multifunctional Army major command (MACOM) responsible for active and reserve component force readiness, collective training, individual training, recruiting, and officer procurement.

During the Army's expansion for the Vietnam War, CONARC was deeply involved with training and deploying units and individuals to the theater. As the Army began the withdrawal of forces from Vietnam in 1969, General Westmoreland, the Chief of Staff, directed an extensive review of the Army's organizational structure to determine its responsiveness to current and foreseeable requirements. He commissioned several studies that examined the Army's institutional organization, including a special review panel headed by Maj. Gen. D. S. Parker of the Office of the Chief of Staff. The Parker Panel issued its report in 1970 with sixty-eight recommendations that augured a significant overhaul of the Army's existing major commands in CONUS. Except for reorganizing the Military District of Washington as an Army MACOM, Westmoreland deferred action on most of these recommendations pending additional study by CONARC and CDC. In February 1971 CONARC completed its own study, in competition with the Parker Panel, recommending several realignments within the command but not addressing the gap between the combat development process in CDC and the Army school systems controlled by CONARC.

Weapons modernization encouraged doctrinal thinkers to consider more ambitious concepts that would exploit the capabilities new systems offered.

At an impasse between the Parker Panel and CONARC recommendations, Westmoreland in September 1971 directed his Assistant Vice Chief of Staff, then Lt. Gen. William E. DePuy, to begin a separate Headquarters, Department of the Army (HQDA), study to examine ways to streamline CONARC's organization and resource management processes. DePuy concluded that CONARC was unwieldy, unresponsive to HQDA and the Office of the Secretary of Defense, and slow to adapt Army school curricula to incorporate doctrinal innovations coming from CDC. In February 1972 DePuy obtained the Secretary of Defense's approval to break up CONARC and CDC and reassign their functions. Arguing that the collective training and maintaining of the readiness of active and reserve component Army units in the United States was a full-time job for any commander, DePuy recommended transferring all these functions from CONARC to a forces command. He further recommended consolidating CONARC's schools with its combat developments functions from CDC into a doctrine and training command.

Armed with the Secretary's approval, DePuy drove his reorganization past protesting CONARC and CDC commanders. Westmoreland appointed Maj. Gen. James G. Kalergis as Project Manager for implementing the reorganization, Operation STEADFAST. The detailed plan transferred all Army schools except the Army War College, the U.S. Military Academy, and medical professional training schools to the new Army Training and Doctrine Command on July 1, 1973, along with the responsibility for ROTC that would come under TRADOC's new Cadet Command. TRADOC would occupy the old CONARC headquarters at Fort Monroe, Virginia. On the same day, the new Army Forces Command (FORSCOM) at Fort McPherson, Georgia, assumed command of all active and reserve Army forces in CONUS and consolidated existing armies into three Continental United States Armies (CONUSAs). Army CONUS medical facilities had transferred to the new U.S. Army Health Services Command on April 1. Under the STEADFAST reorganization, the Army transferred the U.S. Army Recruiting Command from CONARC to a field operating agency reporting to HQDA. It also established the Concepts Analysis Agency and Operational Test and Evaluation Agency as HQDA field operating agencies (FOAs), which assumed certain functions formerly executed by CDC.

STEADFAST

At the end of the Vietnam War, the Army's leadership sought to reorganize the nondeployable side of the Army (those units organized on a TDA basis). Led by Assistant Vice Chief of Staff General DePuy, an Army study group began examining ways to reduce layers of command between HQDA and the Army's major commands. The group concluded that the Army should replace its large, multifunctional major command, CONARC. The resulting reorganization, STEADFAST, divided CONARC into functional commands. FORSCOM assumed oversight of all U.S. operational units in CONUS and focused on readiness. TRADOC combined oversight of most Army schools with combat developments functions that the new command inherited from the Army's Combat Developments Command.

The STEADFAST reorganization accelerated the process of creating functional major commands out of multifunctional Army commands. During the same time that STEADFAST focused on CONARC and CDC, the Army also established the U.S. Army Criminal Investigation Command and the Military Traffic Management Command as MACOMs. In 1984 the U.S. Army Information Systems Command consolidated operations from two FOAs into a separate MACOM until, pursuant to the Force XXI Functional Area Analyses, the Army subordinated this command to FORSCOM in 1997.

As in the post–World War II era, conflicting influences complicated decisions about the correct size and organization of divisions and corps. The hazards of the nuclear and chemical battlefield deeply ingrained the notion that any concentration of large bodies of troops was dangerous. Improved weapons technology further strengthened the imperative for dispersion, a trend facilitated by steadily improving communications systems. Despite that, the classic need to exert overwhelming force at the decisive point and time remained the basic prescription for winning battles.

America's isolated strategic position posed additional problems, particularly in view of the growth of Soviet conventional power in Europe in the 1960s and 1970s and the belief that the Warsaw Pact intended to fight a quick ground war that would yield victory before NATO could mobilize and before the United States could send divisions across the Atlantic. Time and politics thus governed decisions that led to forward deployment of substantial ground forces in overseas theaters and the pre-positioning of military equipment in threatened areas. Issues of strategic force projection likewise influenced decisions about the types, numbers, and composition of divisions.

> Time and politics governed decisions that led to forward deployment of substantial ground forces in overseas theaters and the pre-positioning of military equipment in threatened areas.

Differing schools of thought within the Army tended to pull force designers in different directions. There were those, strongly influenced by the war in Vietnam, who believed that the future of warfare lay in similar wars, probably in the Third World. Accordingly, they emphasized counterinsurgency doctrine, low-intensity conflict, and light and airmobile infantry organization. Advocates of light divisions found justification for their ideas in the Soviet invasion of Afghanistan in 1979, when it appeared possible that the United States might have to confront Soviet forces outside the boundaries of Europe. That uncertainty encouraged ideas that called for the creation of light, quickly deployable infantry divisions.

Still, the emphasis within the Army throughout the decade of the 1970s remained on conventional war in Europe. Generals Abrams and DePuy and like-minded officers believed the greatest hazard, if not the greatest probability of war, existed there. They conceived of an intense armored battle, reminiscent of World War II, to be fought in the European Theater. If the Army could fight the most intense battle possible, some argued, it also had the ability to fight wars of lesser magnitude.

While contemplating the doctrinal issues that led to publication of Field Manual 100–5, General DePuy also questioned the appropriateness of existing tactical organizations to meet the Warsaw Pact threat. He believed that the Army should study the problem more closely. Thus, in May 1976 DePuy organized the Division Restructuring Study Group to consider how the Army divisions might best use existing weapons of the 1970s and the planned weapons of the 1980s. DePuy's force structure planners, like those concerned with phrasing the new doctrine, were also powerfully influenced by the 1973 Arab-Israeli War.

The Division Restructuring Study Group investigated the optimum size of armored and mechanized divisions and the best mix of battalions within divisions. Weapons capabilities influenced much of the work and had a powerful effect on force design. Planners noted a continuing trend toward an increasing number of technicians and combat support troops (the "tail") to keep a decreasing number of combat troops (the "teeth") in action. In general, the group concluded that the division should retain three brigades, each brigade having a mix of armored and mechanized infantry battalions and supported by the same artillery and combat-service units. To simplify the task of the combat company commander, the group recommended grouping the same type of weapons together in the same organization, rather than mixing them in units, and transferring the task of coordinating fire support from the company commander to the more experienced battalion commander. The group suggested creating a combat aviation battalion to consolidate the employment of helicopters and adjusting the numbers of weapons in various units.

General Starry, Commander of the Training and Doctrine Command, a noted cavalry leader in Vietnam, and a soldier-scholar, had reservations about various details of the Division Restructuring Study. He was especially concerned that an emphasis on the division and tactics was too limiting. In his view, the operational level of war above the division demanded the focus of Army attention. After reviewing an evaluation of the Division Restructuring Plan, Starry ordered his planners to build on that work in a study he called Division 86.

The Division 86 proposal examined existing and proposed doctrine in designing organizations that could both exploit modern firepower and foster the introduction of new weapons and equipment. In outlining an armored division with six tank and four mechanized infantry battalions and a mechanized division with five tank and five mechanized infantry battalions, it also concentrated on heavy divisions specifically designed for combat in Europe, rather than on the generic division. Anticipating a faster pace of battle, planners also tried to give the divisions flexibility by increasing the number of junior leaders in troop units, thereby decreasing the span of control.

The Army adopted Division 86 before approving and publishing the new AirLand Battle doctrine, yet General Starry's planners assumed that the new doctrine would be accepted and therefore used it to state the tasks the new divisions would be called on to accomplish. Similar efforts, collectively known as the Army 86 studies, pondered the correct structure for the infantry division, the corps, and larger organizations. Although Infantry Division 86 moved in the direction of a much lighter organization that would be easy to transport to other continents, such rapidly deployable contingency forces lacked the endurance and, frankly, the survivability, to fight alongside NATO divisions in open terrain. The search for a high-technology solution that would give light divisions such a capacity led to a wide range of inconclusive experiments with the motorized 9th Infantry Division at Fort Lewis, Washington, officially designated a high-technology test-bed unit.

Anticipating a faster pace of battle, planners also tried to give the divisions flexibility by increasing the number of junior leaders in troop units, thereby decreasing the span of control.

Chart 2—Total Army Structure, September 30, 1990

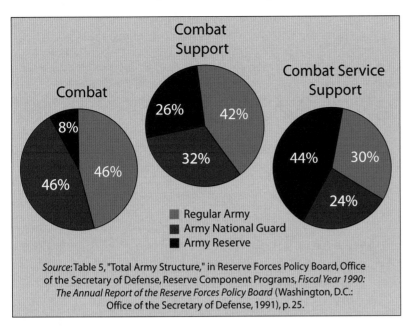

Combat Support

Combat

Combat Service Support

Combat: 8%, 46%, 46%

Combat Support: 26%, 42%, 32%

Combat Service Support: 44%, 30%, 24%

■ Regular Army
■ Army National Guard
■ Army Reserve

Source: Table 5, "Total Army Structure," in Reserve Forces Policy Board, Office of the Secretary of Defense, *Reserve Component Programs, Fiscal Year 1990: The Annual Report of the Reserve Forces Policy Board* (Washington, D.C.: Office of the Secretary of Defense, 1991), p. 25.

Under the Army of Excellence program, military leaders further investigated the Division 86 plans for a heavier mechanized and armored force but reconsidered the role of light divisions. In August 1983 Chief of Staff General John A. Wickham, Jr., directed the Training and Doctrine Command to restudy the entire question of organization. The resulting Army of Excellence force design acknowledged the need for smaller, easily transportable light infantry divisions for the express purpose of fighting limited wars. At the same time, the plan kept the heavy divisions of the Division 86 study with some modifications.

Thus the new force structure—five corps with a total of twenty-eight divisions—available to the U.S. Army (active and reserve) in the summer of 1990 was the product of almost twenty years of evolving design that had carefully evaluated the requirements of doctrine for battle and the capabilities of modern weapons. (*Chart 2*) Army leaders believed that they had found a satisfactory way to maximize the combat power of the division, enabling it to confidently fight a larger enemy force. The other vital task had been to devise a training system that imparted the necessary skills so properly organized and equipped soldiers could carry out their combat and support functions, effectively accomplishing the goals the new doctrine specified.

New Training

The Renaissance infantryman who trailed a pike and followed the flag, like his successor in later wars who shouldered a musket and stood in the line of battle, needed stamina and courage but required neither a particularly high order of intelligence nor sophisticated training. The modern infantryman, expected to master a wide range of skills and think for himself on an extended battlefield, faced a far more daunting challenge. To prepare such soldiers for contemporary battle, TRADOC planners in the 1970s and 1980s evolved a comprehensive and interconnected training program that systematically developed individual and unit proficiency and then tested that competence in tough, realistic exercises. To some in the Army it seemed as if they were on the verge of a revolution in training; to others it was a return to the basics of soldier training, focused on the simple concept "Be-Know-Do."

Individual training was the heart of the program, and the Training and Doctrine Command gradually developed a methodology for training that clearly defined the desired skills and then trained the soldier accordingly. This technique cut away much of the superfluous and was an exceptional approach to the repetitive tasks that made up much of soldier training. Once the soldier mastered the skills appropriate to his grade, skill qualification tests continued to measure his grasp of his profession through a series of written and performance tests.

The training of leaders for those soldiers became increasingly important through the 1970s and 1980s. By the summer of 1990 the Training and Doctrine Command had created a coherent series of schools to train officers in their principal duties at each major turning point in their careers. Lieutenants began with an officer basic course that introduced them to the duties of their branch of service. After a leavening of experience as senior lieutenants or junior captains, the officers returned for an officer advanced course that trained them for the requirements of company, battery, and troop command.

The new Combined Arms and Services Staff School at Fort Leavenworth instructed successful company commanders in the art of battalion staff duty. The premier officer school remained the Command and General Staff College, also at Fort Leavenworth, which junior majors attended before serving as executive and operations officers of battalions and brigades. Although all Army schools taught the concepts and language of AirLand Battle, it was at Leavenworth that the professional officer attained real fluency in that doctrine. For the select few, a second year at Fort Leavenworth in the School of Advanced Military Studies (SAMS) offered preparation as division and higher operations officers and Army strategists.

Finally, those lieutenant colonels with successful battalion commands behind them might be chosen to attend the services' prestigious senior schools: the Army War College, Carlisle Barracks, Pennsylvania; the Navy

SAMS

In 1983 the U.S. Army Command and General Staff College at Fort Leavenworth, Kansas, established the Advanced Military Studies Program (AMSP) as a one-year course taught at the School of Advanced Military Studies. The course supplemented the Army's Command and General Staff Officer Course or its equivalent. Intended to develop an advanced understanding of military science at the operational and tactical levels, the AMSP immersed officers in graduate-level education in operational art and advanced tactics. SAMS provided the Army with many of its top campaign planners for the late twentieth and early twenty-first centuries.

War College, Newport, Rhode Island; the Air War College, Maxwell Air Force Base, Alabama; and the National War College or Industrial College of the Armed Forces, Fort McNair, Washington, D.C. Beyond those major schools, officers might attend one or more short courses in subjects ranging from foreign language to mess management. The career officer thus expected to spend roughly one year of every four in some sort of school, either as student or as teacher.

The NCO corps also required a formal school structure, which ultimately paralleled that of the officer corps. Initially, the young specialist or sergeant attended the primary leadership development course at his local NCO academy, a school designed to prepare him for sergeant's duties. The basic noncommissioned officer course trained sergeants to serve as staff sergeants (squad leaders) in their arm or service. Local commanders selected the soldiers to attend that course.

Staff sergeants and sergeants, first class, selected by a Department of the Army board attended the advanced noncommissioned officer course, where the curriculum prepared them to serve as platoon sergeants and in equivalent duties elsewhere in the Army. At the apex of the structure stood the U.S. Army Sergeants Major Academy at Fort Bliss, Texas, where a 22-week course qualified senior sergeants for the top noncommissioned officer jobs in the Army.

Professional development, of course, went hand in hand with both individual- and unit-training programs. Progressively more sophisticated programs melded the individual's skills into those of the squad, platoon, company, and battalion. Just as the individual was tested, so were units, which underwent a regular cycle of evaluations, known at the lowest level as the Army Training and Evaluation Program (ARTEP). Periodically, both Regular Army and reserve component units in the Continental United States went to the National Training Center (NTC) at Fort Irwin, California, where brigade-size forces fought realistic, unscripted maneuver battles against an Army unit specially trained and equipped to emulate Warsaw Pact forces. Brigades assigned in Europe conducted similar exercises at the Combat Maneuver Training Center (CMTC) at Hohenfels, Germany, while light forces exercised at the Joint Readiness Training Center (JRTC) at Fort Chaffee, Arkansas, later moved to Fort Polk, Louisiana.

Army tactical units were subject to further tests and evaluations, the most important of which were exercises to reinforce units in Europe, generally known as REFORGER, or Return of Forces to Germany. Similarly, units went to the Middle East in BRIGHT STAR exercises, conducted in cooperation with the armed forces of the Republic of Egypt, and to Korea for TEAM SPIRIT exercises. Periodic readiness evaluations tested the divisions' capacity for quick deployment, especially the 82d Airborne Division, long the

During an exercise at Hohenfels, tanks and observation helicopters train to work together on the battlefield.

NATIONAL TRAINING CENTER

Consisting of 1,000 square miles in the Mojave Desert midway between Las Vegas and Los Angeles, the NTC was activated at Fort Irwin, California, in 1981 as the Army's premier facility for combined-arms training for heavy battalions. The NTC exemplified the Army's training revolution initiated in the post-Vietnam/volunteer-force era that required units to "train as they would fight" and to maintain high readiness levels. A permanent opposing force, exercise observer/controllers, sophisticated instrumentation, and a live-fire range with a simulated advancing force provided realistic battlefield training and a critical evaluation of unit performance.

Infantrymen prepare to fire a TOW missile system during a training exercise.

Army's quick-reaction force, and the new light divisions that had been designed for short-notice contingency operations.

The Army entered the summer of 1990 probably better trained than at any time in its history and certainly better trained than it had been on the eves of World War I, World War II, and the Korean War. Sound training practices produced confident soldiers. Realistic exercises acquainted soldiers with the stress of battle as thoroughly as possible in peacetime. Force-on-force maneuvers, such as those at the NTC, tested the abilities of battalion and brigade commanders to make the combined-arms doctrine work and confirmed commanders' confidence in their doctrine, their equipment, and their soldiers. But as thorough and professional as Army training was, the most important fact was that all training and exercises were specifically keyed to the doctrinal precepts laid down in Field Manual 100–5. Training brought the diverse strands of AirLand Battle together.

AirLand Battle would have been merely another academic exercise, however, had the Army not attended to the problems of morale, discipline, and professionalism that were obvious at the end of the Vietnam War. By directly confronting drug abuse, racism, and indiscipline, leaders gradually corrected the ills that had beset the Army in 1972. Schools and progressive military education played a part, as did strict qualitative management procedures that discharged the worst offenders. More important, officer and NCO education stressed the basics of leadership and responsibility to correct the problems that existed at the end of the Vietnam War. Over time, in one of its most striking accomplishments, the Army cured itself through higher standards of training and better leadership.

Military Operations for the Post-Vietnam Army

Improvements in personnel, doctrine, and weapons notwithstanding, the Army that went to Saudi Arabia in 1990 was largely untested in combat. The decades of the 1970s and 1980s were largely peaceful from the U.S. perspective, except for some low-intensity conflict operations in South and Central America. Initially, this peace was as much about concerns over American will power—the "Vietnam Syndrome"—as the lack of any threat. After the failure of the decades-long struggle to save South Vietnam from communism, American public opinion seemed allergic to the idea of using American power in other parts of the world. For a while it seemed the United States would retreat into isolation in "Fortress America" as it had so many times in the past. A series of direct threats to U.S. interests in South and Central America, however, sounded an unmistakable call for action in the 1980s and into the 1990s.

El Salvador

In 1979 a Communist-inspired takeover of Nicaragua led to Leftist insurrections in El Salvador and prompted U.S. concerns about the stability of a number of other countries in the region. Moving quickly to stem the tide, the United States focused on a combination of economic sanctions, political maneuvers, and military support to allies to cope with the threat from Communist insurgents. Various American intelligence agencies worked to undermine the Communist government of Nicaragua while the Army worked on providing open military support for the insurrection-wracked country of El Salvador. This small country was soon seen as a test case for American resolve in the use of the appropriate level of force for the emergency at hand, including advisers and limited direct military support. It was also an important test of how well we had learned our lessons from the defeat in Vietnam.

The political situation in El Salvador had been deteriorating since a military coup against the government in 1979. Successive military and civilian *juntas* had not been able to cope with the situation. In October 1980 the *FMLN* (*Farabundo Marti Liberacion Nacional*), a Communist front organization, was formed. Soon U.S. intelligence documented weapons deliveries from Vietnam through Nicaragua to the insurgents. In January 1981 the *FMLN* prematurely launched a "final offensive" to overthrow the government. The offensive was defeated, but the poorly trained El Salvadoran Army was not strong enough to destroy the guerrillas. Failure drove the insurgents back into the countryside and led to a series of attacks on military units, power lines, and other elements of the national infrastructure.

When the Salvadorans called for U.S. assistance, the U.S. Army focused on training El Salvadoran Army units using a variety of methods. The Americans trained a series of immediate reaction battalions (IRBs) in 1981 and 1982 to help stem the tide. Many of the trainers of these units included members of the newly revitalized Army Special Forces that had almost been eliminated after Vietnam. As the situation stabilized, the United States established the Regional Military Training Center in Honduras to train Salvadoran units without having to bring them to the United States and the following year organized the establishment of a similar facility inside El Salvador. As the Salvadorans became better trained in the basics of soldiering, they began to staff these facilities with their own officers and noncommissioned officers.

The U.S. Army in El Salvador

Limited American military assistance to El Salvador dates from the 1940s, but with the Reagan administration's policy of turning back communism in Central America, the U.S. Army became more deeply involved. Beginning in 1981, advisers trained the El Salvadoran Army in counterinsurgency; but Congress limited their number to 55 plus a handful of Special Forces soldiers. With American aid, the Salvadoran military grew from 20,000 men (17 maneuver battalions) in 1982 to 56,000 (41 maneuver battalions) in 1987, bolstered by an increase in security assistance during the same period from $42.2 million to $704.7 million. It was considered a highly successful counterinsurgency campaign.

In addition to training Salvadoran soldiers, noncommissioned officers, and officers, the U.S. Army sent advisers to each of the brigade headquarters in the six military zones of El Salvador. Regular teams of advisers (generally no more than two or three officers and NCOs) lived, worked, and trained with Salvadoran soldiers for six months to a year. It was not possible to send more to each location because a 1981 agreement between the government of El Salvador and the U.S. State Department limited the number of official advisers in country to fifty-five. Many sites would have only a single officer or NCO assigned, making close cooperation with Salvadoran counterparts a matter of life or death. However, U.S. advisers were strictly prohibited from engaging in offensive combat operations to avoid giving the impression that this was a U.S.-led war. The lesson learned from Vietnam was clear; the host nation had to fight its own war.

There were times, of course, when the strict adherence to the combat prohibition rule was not enough. The fight often came to the adviser. Given the nature of guerrilla war, an attack could occur at any El Salvador *cuartel* (fortified army camp) at any time. In the most publicized incident, which led to the death of a Special Forces NCO, the *FMLN* guerrillas attacked the headquarters of the 4th Infantry Brigade in El Paraiso, Chalatenango. The attack on March 31, 1987, included demolitions and mortars and was preceded by effective infiltration of the camp by well-trained assault squads. Sixty-four Salvadoran soldiers were killed and seventy-nine wounded. S. Sgt. Gregory A. Fronius of the 3d Battalion, 7th Special Forces Group (Airborne), was killed while attempting to organize the resistance to the attack.

In 1988 a similar attack on the 4th Brigade *cuartel* found the Salvadorans and their U.S. advisers more prepared. Despite some initial success in penetrating the wire, the El Salvadoran Army forces and U.S. advisers fought back and by dawn had recaptured the camp. At least 11 enemy guerrillas were killed at the cost of 17 friendly killed and 31 wounded.

Despite some continuing concerns about potential human rights abuses by Salvadorans, the U.S. advisory effort in El Salvador was remarkably successful. The professional training imparted to the Salvadoran military led to ultimate success on the battlefield against the guerrillas. Despite some military setbacks and the increase of international support to the enemy, the Salvadoran military fought back and beat the guerrillas to a standstill. When the final "final" offensive of the *FMLN* was launched in 1989, the Salvadoran military took some hard hits but rallied and decimated the rebels. Free elections, supported by the majority of the people, soon showed the world that the Communists had little public support. The *FMLN* was forced to seek victory through a political solution; a military victory was no longer an option.

Not only had U.S. advisers worked to make the El Salvadoran Army a more effective military force, they also helped ensure that its human rights record improved. Cases of human rights abuse by the military dropped dramatically over the decade as the El Salvadoran Army slowly recognized that such abuses only cost it popular support. Civic action projects, information programs, and a greater respect for the citizenry paid off for the El Salvadoran Army. Finally, on January 16, 1992, the *FMLN* signed peace accords with the government. In return for ending the armed struggle, the *FMLN* was recognized as a legitimate political party and would participate in the political life of the country. In addition, the government agreed to enact land- and judicial-reform measures, and to create a new, less politicized police force. As a side effect, the United States showed the world that it was capable of sustaining a long politico-military struggle in support of an ally when the stakes were high enough.

Between Vietnam and DESERT STORM, other than a limited military assistance role in the 1980s in the covert support to anti-Sandinista forces opposing the Leftist government in Nicaragua, there were only two other instances of limited combat actions. Neither was a full test of AirLand Battle doctrine, and neither gave very many soldiers experience under fire. Nevertheless, they infused the soldiers with increasing confidence and provided a useful testing ground for some new equipment and concepts.

Grenada

A bloody coup on the small Caribbean island of Grenada and the possible involvement of Cuba in those troubled waters prompted the United States to launch a hasty invasion, Operation URGENT FURY, in October 1983. (*See Map 25.*) This involved fewer than 8,000 Army soldiers, with actual Army combat limited to the 1st and 2d Battalions of the 75th Rangers, two brigades of the 82d Airborne Division, and some Special Forces elements. In fact, Army strength on the island during the period of combat probably did not exceed 2,500; the heaviest combat, occurring during the first hours of the landing on October 25, was borne by Company A, 1st Battalion, 75th Rangers. The operation, though successful, pointed out a number of problems with joint operations, especially communications and

Members of the 82d Airborne Division on Patrol during Operation URGENT FURY. Two of the soldiers on the road have M47 Dragon antitank weapons.

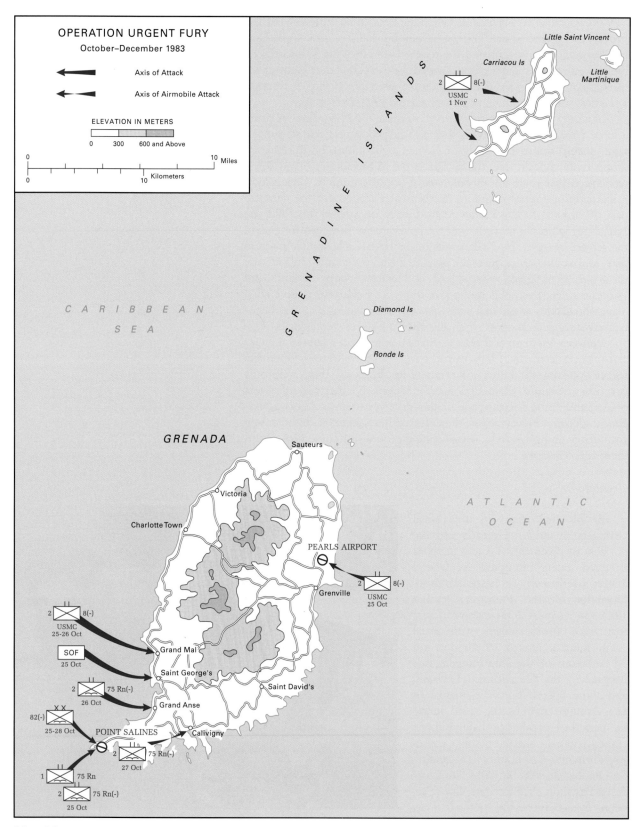

OPERATION URGENT FURY
October–December 1983

Axis of Attack

Axis of Airmobile Attack

ELEVATION IN METERS

0   300   600 and Above

0 _____ 10 Miles
0 _____ 10 Kilometers

GRENADINE ISLANDS

Little Saint Vincent

Carriacou Is

Little Martinique

2 ⊠ 8(-)
USMC
1 Nov

C A R I B B E A N

S E A

Diamond Is

Ronde Is

GRENADA

Sauteurs

Victoria

A T L A N T I C

O C E A N

Charlotte Town

PEARLS AIRPORT

Grenville

2 ⊠ 8(-)
USMC
25 Oct

2 ⊠ 8(-)
USMC
25-26 Oct

Grand Mal

SOF
25 Oct

Saint George's

2 ⊠ 75 Rn(-)
26 Oct

Grand Anse

Saint David's

82(-) ⊠⊠
25-28 Oct

POINT SALINES

Calivigny

2 ⊠ 75 Rn(-)
27 Oct

1 ⊠ 75 Rn

2 ⊠ 75 Rn(-)
25 Oct

Map 25

command and control. It highlighted the necessity of all the services to work and train together to achieve true synergy of operations, with the unique strength of each service working to complement the strengths of the others and cover for any weaknesses.

Soldiers with an M113 armored personnel carrier guard an entrance to Gorgas Army Community Hospital in Panama.

Invasion of Panama

The fighting during Operation JUST CAUSE in Panama in December 1989 was similarly limited. However, the highly successful nature of such a complex operation pointed out just how well the U.S. Army had learned the lessons of a decade of training and preparation.

The origins of the U.S. invasion of Panama are complex. Forty years of finely balanced confrontation with the Soviet Union had induced the United States to cooperate with many unsavory international leaders. Panama's General Manuel Antonio Noriega was among the worst. The last free election in Panama had been in 1968, when a military coup expelled the populist Arnulfo Arias from the Presidency he had won at the ballot box. Noriega, a capable intelligence officer at the time, ingratiated himself with the new military leadership of Panama by ruthlessly facilitating their consolidation of power. He subsequently gained a measure of favor with the United States by assisting the Central Intelligence Agency in covert operations against Nicaraguan and Salvadoran Leftists. Ultimately he himself attained absolute power, his rise assisted by blackmail, fraud, corruption, intimidation, drug dealing, and outright murder.

As the Cold War wound down, it became more difficult for the U.S. government to overlook Noriega's crimes. He was indicted in a Florida court for his direct involvement in the drug trade and was also suspected of colluding with Communist Cuba to help it avoid economic sanctions, as well as smuggling illicit arms to Colombian rebels. He sustained a brutal campaign of intimidation against critics and opponents and stood accused of spectacular, grisly political murders. When American leaders expressed concern with his outrageous behavior, Noriega turned his intimidation efforts against American soldiers and civilians in the Panama Canal Zone. His heavily armed Panama Defense Force (PDF) and paramilitary "dignity battalions" began a campaign of harassment that ebbed and flowed with Noriega's whims and with the current volume of criticism from Washington. Because of national preoccupations elsewhere, American military leaders in the Southern Command (SOUTHCOM) were ordered to handle the abuses quietly. Ultimately the PDF murdered an American marine, and the United States could turn the other cheek no longer.

Fortunately, the newly assigned SOUTHCOM commander, General Maxwell Thurman, was well along in planning an invasion

General Thurman

of Panama when the political decision to do so was made. Under the operational command of the XVIII Airborne Corps out of Fort Bragg, North Carolina, 13,000 soldiers from a half-dozen major posts across the United States airlifted into Panama to join the 13,000 soldiers and marines already there. H-hour was 1:00 A.M. on December 20, 1989. At that time the Americans simultaneously assaulted the two battalions, ten independent infantry companies, cavalry squadron, and special forces command of the PDF at over a dozen localities while fanning out to secure American lives and property in over a dozen more locations. (*See Map 26.*)

Typical of the fighting was the airfield takedown at Rio Hato, seventy-five miles west of Panama City. At H-hour two F–117A stealth fighter-bombers delivered two 2,000-lb. bombs in an attempt to stun the soldiers of two heavily armed infantry companies defending the airfield. Thirteen C–130 transport aircraft, having flown nonstop from the United States, parachuted in two battalions of rangers from the dangerously low altitude of 500 feet. Gathering quickly in the darkness, two companies of rangers fanned out to isolate the airfield, cut the Pan-American Highway running through it, and seize a nearby ammunition dump. Meanwhile, another company attacked a nearby NCO academy complex and yet another struck the two PDF companies deployed to defend the airfield.

The fighting turned into a ferocious exchange of fire, with the ground fire of the rangers heavily reinforced by fires from an AC–130 gunship and attack helicopters. Contested buildings fell in room-to-room fighting following a liberal use of grenades and automatic rifles at close ranges. Within five hours the rangers had secured Rio Hato, including Noriega's lavishly appointed beach house nearby. At Rio Hato, the Americans killed 34 Panamanians and captured 405 plus a huge inventory of weapons, themselves losing 4 killed, 18 wounded, and 26 injured in the jump. The fighting had been confusing and brutal but brief and decisive.

Air Assault, Tinajitas, Al Sprague, 1990

In many cases urban settings and the proximity of civilians—in particular American civilians—complicated the nature of the fighting. The PDF's La Comandancia Headquarters, for example, in the heart of Panama City, was seized only after a tough firefight. M113 armored personnel carriers found themselves peppered by fire from surrounding buildings as they pushed their way through obstacles en route. Operations assumed a third dimension when the Americans had to clear PDF snipers floor by floor from high-rise apartments. At Fort Amador, the firepower was less intense but the situation just as tricky; PDF objectives to be secured or neutralized were within a hundred meters of an American housing area, wherein dependents were still sleeping. At Omar Torrijos International Airport, some PDF soldiers attempted to escape by hiding among 300-plus passengers from a stranded Brazilian airliner and others attempted to escape by making hostages of American passengers. In some cases PDF soldiers and dignity battalion members fought in civilian clothes. As careful and disciplined as the American soldiers were, they could not altogether avoid civilian casualties in this confused and inter-mingled fighting. Somewhat more than 200 nonhostile Panamanian civilians were killed in the crossfire.

Within eight hours serious fighting ceased and the Panama Defense Force had been effectively subdued, thanks to a number

Final Glory (Father Ortiz), *Al Sprague, 1990*

of factors. Most of the fighting occurred in the dark; and the Americans had overwhelming advantages with respect to night combat, including more-effective night-vision devices. Such devices, in their infancy during Vietnam, were now sufficiently refined to provide near-daytime light quality or thermal imaging and were available to individual soldiers as well as to crew-served weapons. Even more important, American units had trained extensively in night fighting and were fully prepared to make the best use of their technical advantages. The Americans also enjoyed absolute air supremacy and had sufficient airlift to parachute or helicopter to dozens of targets at the same time—with overwhelming force at each such target. Air power meant radically enhanced firepower as well, particularly with respect to the formidable AC–130 Spectre gunships and deadly efficient munitions. A final and in some ways decisive advantage was that the Americans were long familiar with Panama and were not only exhaustively trained but also carefully rehearsed for their combat roles. Indeed, in many cases American soldiers had driven through, physically observed, or even exercised on their H-hour objectives during the weeks prior to the attack. The combat results were correspondingly lopsided; the Americans lost 26 killed and 325 wounded to the 314 killed and thousands of captured or wounded Panamanians.

Operations in Panama quickly shifted from combat to peacekeeping. The legitimately elected government was restored to power within days of the invasion. The American soldiers were welcomed as liberators virtually everywhere, which greatly eased such tasks as restoring law, order, public utilities, and civil government. Noriega had fled the fighting almost immediately, hidden in one refuge and then another, and ultimately sought asylum in the Papal Nunciature, which American troops quickly surrounded. He surrendered after a short siege. While frustrating for a number of days, Noriega's neutralization took the heart out of whatever sustained resistance the PDF or dignity battalions might have contemplated: open opposition collapsed. The American military presence in the Canal Zone soon dropped to precrisis levels, and U.S. attention turned to building a new Panamanian police force to replace the corrupt PDF. On December 14, 1999, true to earlier commitments, the American government surrendered its 100-year lease in Panama and shortly thereafter evacuated its military forces from the Canal Zone.

Neither URGENT FURY nor JUST CAUSE offered serious opposition of the kind the Army had been training for decades to meet. Far and away the most important aspects of both of these interventions were their utility in testing the effectiveness of U.S. joint forces command and control procedures, in which both operations, as well as subsequent joint deployments, revealed continuing problems. Joint doctrine and joint warfighting was so great a concern of Congress that it had created in 1986, after a major legislative struggle, the Goldwater-Nichols Defense Act that gave additional power to the Chairman of the Joint Chiefs of Staff, established the office of Deputy Chairman, and created seven warfighting Commanders in Chief to conduct joint military operations in their respective geographic regions or, in the case of the newly created U.S. Special Operations Command, anywhere in the world. (*See Map 27.*) The Army would have to fight all its future wars as part of a joint, if not combined, team.

GOLDWATER-NICHOLS

In 1986, after three years of testimony by retired military leaders and defense experts in favor of various reforms, Congress passed the Goldwater-Nichols Department of Defense Reorganization Act. As with past reorganizations, Goldwater-Nichols made provision for restructuring the Defense Department to address immediate needs rather than seeking to mandate a comprehensive overhaul. The act strengthened the authority of the Secretary of Defense and gave the Chairman of the Joint Chiefs of Staff and the combatant commanders an enhanced role in operational planning, officer assignments, and service program review. The Goldwater-Nichols Act overhauled headquarters functions within the three military departments, transferring oversight of such areas as financial management; information management; and research, development, and acquisition from the Army Staff to the Army Secretariat. Goldwater-Nichols has generally succeeded in its primary goal of forcing the services to become more tightly integrated within the Defense Department and more focused on joint warfare.

The Army at the End of the Cold War

Army accomplishments over the years between the end of the Vietnam War and the end of the 1980s were impressive. By 1990 the claim could be made reasonably that the service had arrived at a sound doctrine, the proper weapons, an appropriate organization, and a satisfactorily trained, high-quality force to fight the intense war for which Generals DePuy and Starry and their successors had planned. International developments in the first half of the year seemed, however, to have made the Army's modernization unnecessary. The apparent collapse of Soviet power and withdrawal of Soviet armies into the Soviet Union itself, the disintegration of the Warsaw Pact and even the dismemberment of the Soviet Union, and the pending unification of Germany removed almost all the justifications for maintaining a powerful presence in Europe. In view of all these developments, the immediate political question was whether the nation felt it needed to maintain such a large and expensive Army. In the interests of fiscal retrenchment, the Army projected budgets for the subsequent five years that would decrease the total size of the active service from approximately 780,000 in 1989 to approximately 535,000 soldiers in 1995. It seemed as if America, looking for a "peace dividend," would indulge in its normal belief that the end of one war meant that permanent peace was now the order of the day and we could dismantle our "bloated" military establishment.

A U.S. Soldier on Watch along the East/West German Border

Even after the Iraqi invasion of Kuwait and while Army units were in the midst of frantic preparations for movement to Saudi Arabia, Army organizations concerned with downsizing the service to meet the long-range strength ceilings continued to work. QUICKSILVER and VANGUARD task forces had deliberated on the size of the Army's field and base force structure, recommending inactivations that now directly affected the forces preparing to deploy to the Middle East. The Army 2000 study group at HQDA considered the implications of such decreases in size and pondered the ways a smaller Army could continue to carry out its major missions. Among the major actions that the group managed in July and August 1990 was a scheduled command post exercise named HOMEWARD BOUND, designed to test a possible removal of Army units from Europe. Army 2000 staff officers also weighed concerns voiced at the highest levels of the service that the drive to save defense dollars would not produce another "hollow" force and thus repeat the disaster of Task Force SMITH in July 1950 at the start of the Korean War.

Department of the Army planners in operations and logistics found themselves in the anomalous situation of pulling together the combat and support units scheduled for deployment to the Middle East at the same time their colleagues in personnel were proceeding with plans for a reduction in force. The Army temporarily suspended the latter plans when the deployment to Saudi Arabia was announced, and

13

BEYOND THE WALL
OPERATIONS IN A POST–COLD
WAR WORLD, 1990–2001

On November 9, 1989, crowds of elated Berliners surged back and forth through ever-enlarging holes in the wall that for so long had divided their city. Similar, albeit smaller, demonstrations also occurred all along the border separating the former East Germany from the West. American soldiers observing these festive affairs soon realized how much was changing in the strategic environment that had brought them to Germany in the first place. Within a few years, Soviet troops evacuated all of their former satellites in the Warsaw Pact countries, those satellites reconfigured themselves as independent and democratic states, the Soviet Union itself collapsed into fifteen different countries, and Germany reunited into a single nation. With little notice the Cold War ended and with it the American military's forty-year preoccupation with containing Communist expansion within an enormous arc that swept from the Norwegian border through Germany, around the southern rim of Eurasia, and across the Korean peninsula to the Bering Straits. (*See Map 28.*) In hot wars and in cold, two generations of American soldiers, sailors, airmen, and marines had secured the line separating the Free World from the Communist bloc; now this frontier suddenly disappeared everywhere except in Korea.

Soon the governments of the United States and its allies enthusiastically pursued a "peace dividend," slashing military budgets and manpower levels in order to reduce taxes or divert resources to other pursuits. By the late 1990s sobering international challenges had taken the bloom off, however; the enduring complexities of national security were apparent to many. Indeed, although the stakes were never as high as they had been during the potential life-or-death struggle with the Soviet Union, American armed forces found their operational tempo

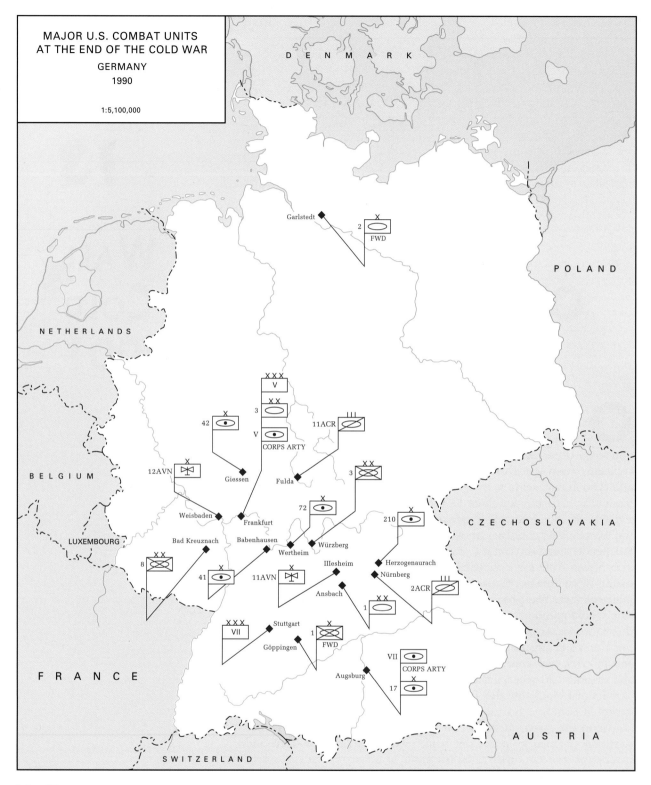

MAJOR U.S. COMBAT UNITS
AT THE END OF THE COLD WAR
GERMANY
1990

1:5,100,000

DENMARK

POLAND

NETHERLANDS

Garlstedt

2 FWD

BELGIUM

V

3

42

11ACR

V
CORPS ARTY

12AVN

Giessen

Fulda

3

LUXEMBOURG

Weisbaden

Frankfurt

72

CZECHOSLOVAKIA

Bad Kreuznach

Babenhausen

Würzberg

210

8

Wertheim

Illesheim

Herzogenaurach

41

11AVN

Ansbach

Nürnberg

2ACR

VII

Stuttgart

1

1
FWD

VII
CORPS ARTY

FRANCE

Göppingen

Augsburg

17

AUSTRIA

SWITZERLAND

Map 28

of deployment to distant theaters and into harm's way greater than it had been since the Vietnam War.

Several factors accounted for this proliferation of post–Cold War violence. First, the discipline the Soviets had exerted on satellites, clients, and occupied territories disappeared and long-suppressed national aspirations and ethnic quarrels bubbled up again. Some of these resolved themselves peacefully, but many did not. The disintegration of the totalitarian regime that Josip Broz "Tito" had constructed in Yugoslavia played itself out as a miniature version of the collapse of the Soviet Union. Second, huge inventories of weapons, many of them now surplus from Cold War needs and others manufactured by corporations competing for shrinking markets, were widely available for purchase. Indeed, by one count the adjusted military expenditure of developing countries soared from $20 billion in 1950 to $170 billion in 1999. An increasingly lethal array of weapons was now available to such nonstate actors as terrorists, criminal gangs, and drug lords. Third, through wide stretches of Africa, the Middle East, Southern Asia, and Latin America, population growth so outstripped economic growth that desperation and discontent remained widespread. This unrest provided fertile soil for insurgency, ethnic strife, sectarian violence, humanitarian crisis, and general lawlessness. Finally, precipitate military downsizing in both Russia and the West created an impression of vulnerability, thus opportunity, among those inclined to test such weakened military postures. Even if not seeking victory in the traditional sense, such opportunists could hope to present the United States and others with battlefield situations that would cost more in lives and money than they were willing to pay to reverse. The notion of asymmetrical warfare, focusing on narrow and specific vulnerabilities rather than competing across a broad spectrum of conflict, became topical among strategic thinkers. Many thought the American public would no longer accept significant casualties in international quarrels.

This change in America's strategic setting occurred at a time when technological advance suggested the possibility of what some called a revolution in military affairs. The primary driver of this technological advance was the microchip, whose ever-smaller size and ever-greater capacity proliferated the employment of computers through a wide range of uses. The most obvious such use was information technology, managing huge quantities of information and disseminating it discriminately at the speed of light. Wedded to advanced sensors, computers rendered the acquisition of targets evermore timely. Wedded to advanced ballistic controls or guidance systems, computers rendered the destruction of targets evermore precise. Precision-guided munitions, or PGMs, provided unprecedented lethality to those who used them effectively. The potential microchip revolution accompanied a sustained evolution in technologies of other types: plastics, light metals, stealth engineering, lasers, night-vision devices, battlefield surgery, and medicine—to name but a few.

As American military planners shifted their focus from the prospects of a titanic struggle with the Soviet Union, they faced risks perhaps less threatening but certainly more diverse. Flexible response, a concept born in the late 1950s to meet Communist aggression with means appropriate to the level at which it presented itself, was reborn their rear. Soon the attack would have driven into heavy and precisely surveyed artillery fires, then it would have encountered the deadly accuracy of M1A1 Abrams tanks and TOW (Tube-launched, Optically tracked, Wire-guided) missiles mounted on M2 and M3 Bradley fighting vehicles. American direct-fire weapons had double the effective range of their Iraqi counterparts; under pressure, American defenders would have had a sufficient range advantage to safely withdraw to subsequent firing positions. Iraqi losses would have been appalling well before they had the opportunity to engage in effective combat. This grim pattern would have repeated itself for the entire 200 kilometers the Iraqis would have had to attack through to reach a target of strategic significance.

Some idea of the probable results of an Iraqi attack can be gained from the abortive Iraqi probe into the town of Khafji on January 30–31, 1991. An Iraqi mechanized division lost 80 percent of its strength while attacking a town a mere seven miles inside the Saudi border. Weakened by the forward screen of security—including marines firing TOWs from light armored vehicles (LAVs)—and pummeled from the air, the Iraqis achieved little and lost much; the Saudis chased them back across the border in a day and a half.

In concert with coalition forces, the XVIII Airborne Corps was adequate to defend Saudi Arabia. By early November the objective had changed, however. Frustrated in efforts to achieve a diplomatic solution to the crisis, a worldwide coalition reinforced by UN mandates determined not to allow Saddam Hussein to enjoy the fruits of his aggression. President Bush committed the United States to the liberation of Kuwait as well as to the defense of Saudi Arabia. This objective would require offensive action, and forces deployed to Kuwait did not have sufficient mass to succeed in such an offensive with minimum losses. On November 9 President Bush announced his intent to deploy yet another corps, the VII Corps out of Europe, to Saudi Arabia and his determination that the Iraqi occupation of Kuwait would be reversed by force if necessary. Saddam Hussein had already developed elaborate defenses of his own and had opined he could make the cost of liberating Kuwait higher than the coalition would be willing to pay. His specific admonition to Americans was "Yours is a nation that cannot afford to take 10,000 casualties in a single day." The stage was set for DESERT SHIELD to become DESERT STORM.

By November 1990 the Iraqis occupying Kuwait had matured a layered defense of their own, with line infantry entrenched behind protective barriers along the border and reinforced by local mobile reserves of regular army tank and mechanized divisions. These local reserves were themselves backed up by the operational reserves of the heavily mechanized *Republican Guard*. Of these Iraqi forces, the line infantry

Like this Abrams tank, all vehicles used in Operation DESERT SHIELD/STORM were painted in desert camouflage.

was considered brittle, the regular army heavy divisions reliable, and the *Republican Guard* formidable. The most direct approach for the coalition would have been an attack into the teeth of Iraqi defenses along the Saudi Arabia–Kuwait border. The avenues available for such an attack included northward along the coastal road, from the "elbow" of the border northeast along the shortest route directly into Kuwait City, or along the Wadi al Batin in the far west of Kuwait. A more indirect approach would have been an envelopment through Iraq, either close in by punching through thinly held defenses immediately west of the Wadi al Batin or deeper by turning the Iraqi line altogether in its far west. Both the direct approach and the envelopment could be complemented by amphibious landings on the Kuwaiti coast and airborne or air-assault landings into the enemy's rear.

A factor complicating operational deliberations was the role allies were willing play. The United States, Great Britain, and France favored attacking Iraq directly. Their Arab allies believed the legitimate mission was to liberate Kuwait and were reluctant to commit their ground forces to a wider war. Over time a campaign plan emerged that accommodated allied preferences and borrowed heavily from each of the basic operational options available.

Fighting would begin with a multiphase air campaign to establish preconditions for ground assault. Coalition air forces would successively smash Iraqi air defenses, secure air supremacy, suppress Iraqi command and control, isolate the Kuwaiti Theater of Operations (KTO), and attrit enemy ground forces in the path of the proposed offensive. The ground assault would begin with a division-size feint up the Wadi al Batin and a supporting attack by the marines reinforced with an Army armored brigade through the elbow of Kuwait. Arab thrusts equivalent in size to that of the marines would go in to their left and right. A marine amphibious feint would tie Iraqi units into coastal defenses, while an air assault deep into Iraq would isolate the KTO from the Iraqi core around Baghdad. The main attack would be that of the VII Corps, consisting of five heavy divisions, four separate field artillery brigades, an armored cavalry regiment, and a separate aviation brigade. This mailed fist—as the Corps Commander, Lt. Gen. Frederick M. Franks, Jr., described it—would envelope the Iraqi line at its far west end, turning east to annihilate the *Republican Guard* before sweeping across the northern half of Kuwait. The four-division XVIII Airborne Corps, already commanding the air assault into Iraq, would ride the VII Corps' left flank and continue to isolate the Kuwaiti Theater from the west while assisting in closing the trap to the east.

Operation DESERT STORM, the liberation of Kuwait, began on January 17, 1991, with massive air strikes and missile bombardment throughout Iraq. Air supremacy was readily achieved and does in fact

Victory Division Soldier on Guard at Sunset, *Peter G. Varisano, 1990*

General Franks

419

seemed to be the future of warfare for the United States. However, the Army faced the daunting task of redesigning itself to meet such global challenges while reducing the active force from 772,000 in 1989 to 529,000 in 1994 with commensurate cuts in the National Guard and Army Reserve. Chief of Staff General Gordon R. Sullivan's "modern Louisiana Maneuvers" (LAM) Task Force (TF) replicated the spirit of operational adaptation and innovation embodied in the World War II LAM initiative while adapting the smaller force structure to the still-challenging requirements. This initiative resulted in an integrated array of battle labs, each capable of testing adjustments to organization, doctrine, and weaponry using the latest techniques for simulation and modeling.

In due course this intellectual fermentation diverted Army planners from feeling sorry about the force structure they had lost to feeling excited by the challenges for which they had to prepare—a major goal of General Sullivan. The 1993 version of Field Manual 100–5, *Operations*, greatly expanded the attention given to power projection and to operations other than war (peacekeeping, humanitarian relief, etc.). Initial efforts focused on expanding sealift, airlift, and the infrastructure that complemented them, soon followed by the establishment of stockpiles located in advance, called pre-positioning, close to likely trouble spots overseas. Over time these initiatives also included efforts to change the nature of the forces being moved. Improved strategic mobility would be the product of strategic lift, pre-positioning, and transformed forces.

As effective as the deployment for DESERT SHIELD had been, it retrospectively seemed frenzied and ad hoc to those who had participated in it. Convenient roll-on roll-off (RO-RO) shipping was not sufficiently available to accommodate the huge mass of vehicles. Break-bulk shipping, requiring cranes and heavy equipment to off-load, was more plentiful but required considerably more time in port. It took extraordinary efforts to keep track of supplies and equipment in international shipping containers, and maddening delays resulted when recordkeeping broke down. Units in Saudi Arabia too often found themselves piecing their hardware together first from one ship and then from another, rummaging through hundreds of containers to find items they had lost track of or pursuing supplies and equipment that had been unloaded from the ships but then wheeled past them to the "iron mountains" of supplies building up in the desert. The hasty preparations for war in a distant theater were a far cry from the methodical long-term preparations that characterized major Cold War plans.

An obvious first step was to procure more shipping, particularly RO-RO ships capable of accommodating entire battalions or brigades. Sealift in the Maritime Administration's Ready Reserve Fleet expanded from 17 RO-RO ships in 1990, through 29 in 1994, to 36 in 1996. Expanding sealift was accompanied by corresponding improvements in infrastructure and training. During DESERT SHIELD many divisions deployed through seaports not planned for that purpose, and others did so through facilities that were antiquated or in poor condition. By 1994 a massive $506 million deployment infrastructure refurbishment plan was under way, investing heavily in port facilities, railheads, and airfields to speed departing units on their way. The lion's share of this expenditure went to such high-profile troop establishments as Fort Bragg,

North Carolina, for airborne forces; Fort Campbell, Kentucky, for aviation; Fort Stewart, Georgia, and Fort Hood, Texas, for heavy forces; and Fort Bliss, Texas, for air defense. Training budgets adapted to ensure that units were proficient with respect to deployment processes. In 1994 alone, $26 million went to Sea Emergency Deployment Readiness Exercises wherein combat units raced to port, loaded themselves onto ships, and deployed into a training event featuring some combination of amphibious, over-the-shore, and through-port entry into a selected battlefield. National Training Center (NTC) scenarios, in which heavy battalions participated ostensibly on a rotating two-year basis, featured a speedy tactical draw of vehicles and equipment such as might be the case when uniting troops with hardware previously shipped or pre-positioned. By the mid-1990s, rotations to draw battalion sets of equipment into Kuwait and then to train in the Kuwaiti desert offered further expeditionary training.

The disposition of pre-positioned equipment for deploying U.S.-based units adjusted to the new realities. During the Cold War such equipment had been stockpiled in division sets in Germany and the Benelux countries. In annual REFORGER exercises, troops from the United States flew to Europe, drew and manned that equipment, and rolled out to training areas, thus demonstrating their capability to rapidly reinforce NATO. During the 1990s this capability dispersed more broadly, with a total of eight brigade sets spread throughout Europe, Korea, Kuwait, Qatar, and afloat. The set pre-positioned afloat in the Indian Ocean offered the most flexibility. It consisted of a brigade set of two armored and two mechanized infantry battalions with a thirty-day supply of food, fuel, and ammunition aboard sixteen ships, of which seven were roll-on, roll-off. Collectively considered, the sets in Kuwait, Qatar, and afloat could have positioned a heavy division into the Persian Gulf in days rather than the month plus of DESERT SHIELD. By the mid-1990s the expeditionary intent of the Army proposed a capability to deploy five-and-a-third divisions into a theater of war within seventy-five days.

Deployment on such a scale would rely on the reserve components as never before. The post-Vietnam force structure had allocated to the reserves and National Guard major fractions of the combat support and combat service support upon which the active component depended. During DESERT STORM (when active duty strength was 728,000, reserve strength was 335,000, and National Guard strength was 458,000), 39,000 reservists and 37,000 National Guardsmen were called up to support a total force of 297,000 deployed to Southwest Asia. As the active force shrank to 529,000 and continued to decline and the Army budget went from $77.7 billion in 1990 to $63.5 billion in 1994, early reliance upon the reserve components during major deployments became even more critical. The relative size, composition, balance, and roles of the active and reserve components would remain an important aspect of Army deliberations throughout the 1990s and beyond.

A major consideration with respect to strategic mobility was the logistical footprint of forces once deployed. American heavy divisions had gotten into the habit of accumulating huge iron mountains of spare parts and supplies of all types in their immediate rear in case they needed it. Without reliable means for precisely tracking and quickly delivering

The relative size, composition, balance, and roles of the active and reserve components would remain an important aspect of Army deliberations throughout the 1990s and beyond.

specific repair parts, they had no other options. During the 1990s information technology advanced to the point that it seemed possible to radically reduce the need for these stockpiles. Required materials might be delivered as they were needed rather than hoarded in advance. Emerging technologies offered to help solve this problem with bar coding, satellite communications, and global positioning systems (GPS) to provide visibility of supplies and repair parts as they moved through the supply and transportation network. Other technical advances, including embedded vehicle diagnostics, greater fuel efficiency, and on-board water generation systems held out hope of further reducing the amount of supplies needed on hand in the future. The expectation of rapid deployment would become a way of life for thousands of servicemen and women in the United States and overseas, and the material means to support that way of life became increasingly available as the decade progressed.

Northern Iraq: Operation PROVIDE COMFORT

America's first post–DESERT STORM experience with expeditionary operations came unexpectedly. The stunning Gulf War destruction of the Iraqi Army in Kuwait had seemed decisive, but Saddam Hussein had withheld or evacuated forces sufficient to secure his regime. Dissident Shi'ites in southern Iraq and Kurds in northern Iraq were emboldened by Hussein's defeat and revolted against his regime. Unfortunately for them, there was little external support for such revolt. The coalition had agreed to liberate Kuwait but not to a sustained intervention in Iraq. Americans were wary of Shi'ite fundamentalists in Iran and inclined to believe the Shi'ites in Iraq might prove as hostile to them as they were to Saddam Hussein. America's allies in the region, themselves by and large Sunni Muslims inclined toward secularism, advised against involvement. Moreover, NATO allies were sufficiently deferential to Turkish sensibilities to avoid any impression of supporting Kurdish autonomy. The Gulf War coalition restricted Iraqi use of some air assets but initially failed to ground Iraqi helicopter forces, thus allowing Hussein a vital edge to attack the rebels. Nervous about splintering Iraq, U.S. policymakers stood by as Hussein crushed first the Shi'ites in the south, then the Kurds in the north.

If the cause of the revolutionaries did not much excite world opinion, the plight of refugees did. Shi'ites tended to flee to coreligionists

PROVIDE COMFORT

After the end of Operation DESERT STORM, Saddam Hussein turned against his own people who were trying to throw off the shackles of tyranny. The Kurds in northern Iraq were particularly hard hit; and over 450,000 of them streamed north into the mountains of southern Turkey, where they faced disease, cold, and hunger. On April 7, 1991, U.S. and coalition forces moved into southern Turkey and helped set up refugee camps, deliver food and water, and provide rudimentary medical care. They quickly averted what could have been a humanitarian disaster. With a strong allied presence watching over them, the Kurds were induced to return in safety to their homes by the end of July with only minimal losses.

in Iran rather than westward, although a number did seek refuge in Saudi Arabia and Kuwait and were accommodated by coalition forces there. Many Kurds fled into Iran as well, but over a half-million fled into Turkey. Kurdish refugees in Turkey were in a desperate plight, dying by the hundreds. Iraqi control of the roads had forced them into the mountains; and in the mountains, they faced the bitter cold and drizzle of late winter without adequate food, water, clothing, or shelter. They quickly overwhelmed the capacity of relief agencies to support them in the border areas, yet the Turks were loath to move them out of those border areas because they already had significant problems with internal Kurdish insurgency and unrest. Rapid-fire discussions and negotiations crystallized into three sequential imperatives: stop the dying and suffering in the mountains, resettle the refugees in temporary camps, and return the refugees to their original homes.

American and NATO forces had long operated out of bases in eastern Turkey, and during DESERT STORM a composite U.S. air wing had flown 4,595 sorties out of them with over 140 aircraft while Special Operations Forces stood by to rescue downed pilots. This effort's Air Force commander, Maj. Gen. James L. Jamerson, and the Special Operations Command, Europe (SOCEUR), commander, Brig. Gen. Richard W. Potter, would later emerge as key players as the Kurdish crisis unfolded. Indeed, they had barely returned from Turkey to their home stations when calls over the night of April 5–6, 1991, notified them that they were going back. Units initially to deploy with them for the upcoming Operation PROVIDE COMFORT would include the 39th Special Operations Wing, the 10th Special Forces Group (Airborne), and the 7th Special Operations Support Command.

The quickest way to get relief to the Kurds was to airdrop supplies directly to them. This was also the least efficient, guaranteeing enormous losses and waste and unlikely to get supplies distributed to all who needed them. Heliborne delivery would be more efficient and routine truck delivery, when feasible, even more so. The urgent mission to stop the suffering and dying progressed through these increasingly efficient methods. At 11:00 A.M. on April 7, PROVIDE COMFORT began with two MC–130 aircraft dropping eight 2,000-lb. bundles of blankets and rations to the Kurds along the Turkish border. Numerous other airdrops followed, and within a week sufficient rotary-wing aircraft were on hand to begin heliborne deliveries of the tons of supplies accumulating at ports and airfields in Turkey. This shift to heliborne delivery was accompanied by frenzied construction efforts as Army and Air Force engineers refurbished airfields close enough to the refugees to facilitate the transition from cargo planes to helicopters. While this was going on, Army Special Forces teams pushed forward into the refugee encampments to organize the effort from that end. If encampments could be consolidated and camp life made routine, an orderly shift to ground transportation could begin.

Special Forces proved the Army's best choice to make contact with and assist in organizing the refugees. They were trained to deal with indigenous cultures, experienced in organizing such peoples, and contained a wide range of talents in a small, dozen-man team. Understandably, their medical proficiencies were most in demand initially. Their military bearing and prowess favorably impressed the martial Kurds. What was more, their communications and ability to reach back for transportation and logistics enabled a few soldiers on the spot to quickly get assistance forward where it was needed.

Special Forces organizational and reach-back capabilities also proved of great value in facilitating the integration of nongovernmental organizations (NGOs) and private volunteer organizations (PVOs) into the overall relief effort. These organizations, likely partners in the case of humanitarian relief, varied widely in structure and capabilities. Some, like the Red Cross and Red Crescent, featured substantial organization and means. Most, however, were smaller agencies with specialized skills and limited logistical assets. Many were deeply ambivalent about working alongside the military, but all appreciated what military communications, transportation, and logistics could do to enhance their contributions. Over time, useful working relationships developed among the Special Forces, the NGOs, PVOs, other allied soldiers in the encampments, and the Kurdish family and clan leadership. Tents were erected, food and water became routinely available, medical support matured, and the dying ceased.

As Kurdish camp life along the Turkish border stabilized into a survivable routine, allied leaders shifted their attention to returning the Kurds to their homes. This would require, in effect, yet another invasion of Iraq. The Kurds would not return to homes the Iraqi Army occupied, so coalition forces would have to provide a security envelope within Iraq into which the Kurds could resettle. American General John M. Shalikashvili was given overall responsibility for the operation, with Joint Task Force (JTF) ALPHA established under General Potter to sustain support to the encampments in Turkey and JTF BRAVO under Maj. Gen. Jay M. Garner to clear northern Iraq sufficiently to get the Kurds back into their homes. Soon American marines and soldiers accompanied by British marines and French soldiers entered northern Iraq. The allied forces met little opposition, with the Iraqis readily giving way before the intervening forces. Trusting their new benefactors to defend them, the Kurds swarmed out of the mountain camps and back to their ancestral homes. Civilian relief agency volunteers accompanied the return, and international efforts to replant, rebuild, and refurbish came on the heels of the returning tide of refugees. Within months, the local population seemed resettled and the United States and its allies sought to extricate themselves from the improved situation.

The Kurds were understandably nervous about being left in Iraq without American troops; initial attempts to withdraw were met by demonstrations, riots, and the threat of another refugee crisis. Ultimately, Americans persuaded the Kurds that the combination of international observers, air patrols over the no-fly zone, readily available American expeditionary forces, and Iraqi memories of the Gulf War would be enough to guarantee their future security. America and its allies sought to protect the Kurds so that their lives and property were reasonably secure, but not so that they became a politically autonomous entity. Within a few years factional fighting among the Kurds would enable the Iraqis to reassert a military presence within the region. However, in early 1991, faced with a huge and largely unanticipated refugee crisis, America and its allies had stopped the dying, resettled the refugees into sustainable camps, and returned them to their ancestral homes without unduly upsetting the delicate international political balance in that far-off region. It constituted a credible use of armed forces to resolve an unanticipated and unconventional international circumstance.

Somalia

Even as one humanitarian crisis subsided in northern Iraq, another emerged in Somalia, an arid, impoverished, and turbulent failed state on the horn of Africa. Americans had had some Cold War interest in Somalia, neighboring Ethiopia, and the strategically positioned horn of Africa; but the end of the Cold War and the dissolution of Somalia into sectarian and clan warfare demolished whatever attraction the region might have held for national policy considerations.

This disinterest reversed itself when a devastating drought precipitated famine, and internecine warfare rendered relief efforts ineffective. Combatant clans raided each other's food supplies, local warlords charged protection money to international relief agencies attempting to deliver supplies, and convoys delivering supplies were nevertheless looted to enhance the wherewithal and prestige of the warlords. Starvation became a weapon, and supplies did not make it into the hands of the hundreds of thousands who needed them most. Night after night international television broadcast images of starving, emaciated children covered with flies and dying in filth. A Pulitzer Prize went to a photographer who captured the agonies of a dying child with a painfully distended abdomen, crying as expectant vultures perched nearby. President Bush believed he could ignore this situation no longer.

On August 15, 1992, the United States launched Operation PROVIDE RELIEF, an effort to airlift supplies from nearby Kenya to airfields throughout the interior of Somalia. This would avoid the bottlenecks and uncertainty of clan politics in the congested port of Mogadishu while dispersing supplies throughout the country to get a head start in distribution. Local distribution was to remain in the hands of the international relief agencies already there, but the warring factions and armed gangs quickly adapted their operations to steal these relief supplies as well. They hoarded food, terrorized international agencies, killed those who did not pay protection money, and allowed tens of thousands to continue starving.

Embarrassed by this continuing confusion, the United States, supported by UN resolutions, launched Operation RESTORE HOPE on December 8. Heavily armed marines and soldiers of the 10th Mountain Division, supported by Special Forces elements, 13,000 all told, deployed by sea and air into Somalia to cow the warring factions with their

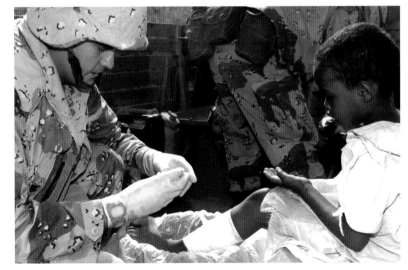

An Army medic renders aid to a Somali child.

Heavily armed desperadoes operating with autonomy and impunity in the wreckage of failed states required a more robust response to keep or, more properly, to impose a peace.

period while diplomats sought more permanent solutions. In the interests of impartiality, the United Nations preferred collections of small contingents of troops from all over the world, and most featured dual chains of command both to the United Nations and to their country of origin. This was not the kind of force for serious warfighting. The long, unhappy experience of the United Nations Interim Force in Lebanon (UNIFIL, 1978–1996) eroded the notion that former belligerents would behave as agreed or be able to control their own subordinates. Heavily armed desperadoes operating with autonomy and impunity in the wreckage of failed states required a more robust response to keep or, more properly, to impose a peace.

Fortunately for those who favored an energetic approach, the end of the Cold War removed an important brake on multinational activity. The remarkably broad-based coalition that fought the Gulf War featured a diverse mix of former allies and adversaries under an American lead with UN approval and Russian acquiescence. The UN Security Council found itself newly imbued with a spirit of consensus when cleaning up the debris of the Cold War. Angola, Cambodia, El Salvador, Mozambique, Namibia, and Nicaragua were Cold War battlegrounds whose internal quarrels were no longer of interest to the Great Powers. Strife in the former Yugoslavia, Tajikistan, and Georgia were viewed as threats to the general peace more so than as cracks in Russian hegemony. Each of these embattled war zones soon received substantial UN peacekeeping forces, generally numbering in the thousands and tens of thousands rather than in the hundreds of an earlier era. The impotence of UNIFIL in Lebanon was not to be repeated. This new team on the UN Security Council created an ambitious expectation on the council of what to expect from dispatched forces. Between 1945 and 1990, vetoes had paralyzed the Security Council 279 times; between 1990 and 1994, none did.

The United Nations' new-found energy had important implications for the U.S. Army. The distinguished world body had diminished the inviolability of the nation state when it endorsed intervention in destructive civil quarrels within failed states that could not control them. The simplicity of interposing lightly armed observers between the disciplined forces of two nation states was replaced by the complexity of controlling a highly lethal environment wherein factions could not ensure the compliance of their subordinates. Suddenly, peacekeepers might well need armored vehicles, attack helicopters, overwhelming firepower and an assertive attitude to make their mandates endure.

Only a few countries, like the United States, or alliances could provide the organizational and logistical framework within which such a force could be fielded. President Clinton had adopted a national strategy of "shape, prepare, respond," wherein shaping the international environment with a modest investment of forces and funds and preparing for worldwide contingencies became as important conceptually as responding to major crises after they had already occurred. Shaping and preparing argued for intense multinational activity during periods of peace or operations other than war and for developing capabilities useful worldwide at all levels of the combat spectrum rather than those focused narrowly on a specific threat. Chief of Staff General Dennis J. Reimer recognized the challenging human dimension of transitioning to a highly flexible capabilities-based force and set about revising the Officer Personnel Management System to, among other things, ensure appropriate career opportunities for officers not pursuing traditional combat-arms tracks. Indeed, he believed so strongly in putting a human face on the President's national strategy that he adopted the motto "Soldiers are our credentials."

The United States had taken the lead in northern Iraq and even went so far as to forcibly occupy the region to secure the resettlement of the Kurds. The United States also had taken the lead in Somalia, sending troops to the southern third of the country to guarantee the arrival of relief supplies until the worst of the food distribution crisis had been resolved, then turning over the operation to a UN force with a substantial American contingent. Similarly, intervention in Haiti had started as an American operation and then mutated into a UN one. Soon, as we shall see, the United States found itself heavily involved in multinational efforts to bring peace to Macedonia, Bosnia-Herzegovina, and Kosovo as well. In all cases operations were intensely multinational, and in most allied troops under UN auspices eventually outnumbered the Americans on the ground.

Recognizing that integrated multinational operations were increasingly likely, American soldiers gave considerable attention to preparing for them. In 1993 the North Atlantic Treaty Organization established the Partnership for Peace program, a concerted effort to draw neutrals, former Warsaw Pact nations, and former Soviet constituent republics into multinational military exercises. Training exercises emphasized search and rescue, humanitarian relief, and peacekeeping. Dozens of such exercises every year, involving dozens of nations at a time, became a standard feature of NATO training regimes. Similar exercises in Latin America and around the Pacific Rim followed suit, albeit with less consistency, diversity, and scale. Allied units were increasingly invited to participate in U.S. National Training Center, Joint Readiness Training Center (JRTC), and Combat Maneuver Training Center (CMTC) exercises on an evermore integrated basis. American soldiers had had ample experience working with allies but seldom in circumstances wherein the mix of nations was so great and the scale of combined operations so small. Individual patrols and even checkpoints often became multinational events during the conduct of peacekeeping. This contrasted with earlier operations in Europe, Korea, or Southwest Asia, where allies were present but American soldiers were largely independent in their own brigades and divisions.

The Breakup of Yugoslavia

During the early 1990s the former nation of Yugoslavia disintegrated into chaos. Yugoslavia had been a post–World War I construct that artificially conglomerated Serbs, Slovenes, Croats, Bosnian Muslims, Albanians, Macedonians, Montenegrans, Hungarians, and others into a single state. Historic ethnic rivalries had been exploited by German and Italian occupation authorities during World War II and then ruthlessly suppressed by Communist strongman Tito during his subsequent 35-year rule. After Tito's death in 1980, ethnic rivalries bubbled up again, achieving particular virulence with Serbian leader Slobodan Miloševic.

Fearing the worst from Milošević's ferocious Serbian nationalism, Slovenia and Croatia broke free from Yugoslavia in sharp, relatively brief wars of independence during 1991.

The Muslim plurality of Bosnia-Herzegovina was not so fortunate when it attempted to follow suit. At that time Bosnia was 44 percent Muslim, 33 percent Serb, and 17 percent Croat. When the European community recognized Bosnia-Herzegovina as an independent state on April 6, 1992, its constituent Serbs revolted from within it. The Serb-dominated Yugoslav National Army (JNA) heavily assisted the Bosnian Serbs; soon thousands on both sides were dead and over a million were refugees. The Serbs had the upper hand initially and forced Muslims and Croats out of one village after another. A gruesome campaign of murder, rape, and intimidation labeled "ethnic cleansing" forced dispossessed refugees from areas the Serbs wanted to control.

The United States had hoped to stay clear of this Balkan conflict, being preoccupied elsewhere and hopeful that European leaders or perhaps the United Nations would sort things out. The United Nations did embargo arms shipments to the former Yugoslavia in 1991 and deployed a United Nations Protection Force (UNPROFOR) in 1992 to enforce agreed-upon cease-fires and to facilitate humanitarian relief. Over time UNPROFOR became the largest and most expensive UN peacekeeping operation in history, featuring 38,000 troops from thirty-seven countries. It nevertheless proved no match for the heavily armed Serbs, who intermittently bullied or defied the peacekeepers. A particularly egregious demonstration of UNPROFOR's ineffectiveness occurred in July 1995, when Serbian forces overwhelmed the so-called UN Safe Area of Srebrenica in a calculated orgy of mass murder and forcible deportation.

NATO and the United States attempted to stiffen UNPROFOR with naval and air support. Over a two-year period an average of seventeen ships at a time enforced the arms embargo by challenging 31,400 ships, boarding 2,575, and diverting 643 into port for further inspection. A multinational humanitarian airlift labeled Operation PROVIDE PROMISE delivered more than 176,000 tons of humanitarian supplies over a three-year period while airdropping a further 19,800 tons into areas isolated by the Bosnian Serbs. NATO imposed and enforced a no-fly zone over Bosnia to deny combatants the option of inflicting mayhem from the air. The Serbs challenged this restriction once, and American F–16s shot down four of their Jastreb J–1s. NATO threats to engage Serbian ground targets worked less well, in part because of the difficulty of identifying them in the terrain and weather and in part because of

A Suburb of Sarajevo after a Clash between Serbs and Muslims

the fear that Serbs would retaliate by attacking UNPROFOR peace-keepers. Prior to August 1995 NATO aircraft struck or threatened to strike Serbian ground targets on only a few occasions, when UNPROFOR peacekeepers or their charges were at exceptional risk.

On one such occasion the Bosnian Serbs did in fact seize scores of UNPROFOR peacekeepers to use as shields against further attack. This embarrassment underscored the vulnerability of UNPROFOR and increased the inclination in frustrated NATO capitals for more resolute action. On August 28 Bosnian Serbs who had besieged the beautiful Bosnian capital of Sarajevo for three years were alleged to have fired a mortar round that dropped into a crowded market square, killing thirty-seven people. This was the last straw. UNPROFOR coiled into a defensive posture while NATO responded with a sustained air campaign against Serbian guns and heavy equipment surrounding Sarajevo. Over a three-week period NATO flew 3,515 sorties, of which 2,318 were American, before the Serbs agreed to break the siege and withdraw their big guns. In addition to air operations, the United States deployed an infantry battalion (Operation ABLE SENTRY) to newly independent Macedonia to ensure that the conflict did not widen.

The show of American and European resolve did much to bring Milošević into peace negotiations at Wright-Patterson Air Force Base in Dayton, Ohio, in the fall of 1995. The damage done by years of crippling international economic sanctions did even more. What perhaps accomplished the most was a dramatic reversal of Bosnian Serb fortunes in the ground fighting. Croatian strongman Franjo Tudjman had long resented the Serbian retention of some Croatian lands after his successful bid for independence. He had quietly built up his army into a capable offensive force, assisted somewhat by American advisers, many of them military retirees under contract. On August 4 he struck viciously and successfully to drive the Serbs out of Croatia. He then drove on to assist the now-allied Bosnian Muslims and Croats, who themselves were pressing successful attacks against the Serbs. In short order they rolled the Bosnian Serbs from controlling almost three-fourths of the country to controlling less than half. America and its allies were wary of too much Croatian success, however, fearing the direct intervention of the Yugoslav Army. They helped broker peace and brought Serbs, Croats, and Muslims to the table at Dayton.

The Bosnian Peace Agreement envisioned a robust UN-sanctioned, NATO-led Implementation Force (IFOR) responsible for ensuring: compliance with the cease-fire; separation of the forces; withdrawal of forces out of zones of separation into their respective territories; collection of heavy weapons into agreed cantonment sites; safe withdrawal of UN forces; and control of Bosnian air space. The IFOR would ultimately consist of 60,000 troops deployed into the area under the command of the Allied Rapid Reaction Corps (ARRC). In addition to NATO troops, IFOR included soldiers from Albania, Austria, the Czech Republic, Egypt, Estonia, Finland, Hungary, Jordan, Latvia, Lithuania, Malaysia, Morocco, Poland, Romania, Russia, Sweden, and the Ukraine. Russia's participation was particularly important because of her previous hostility to NATO and because of her special relationship with the Serbs. Most of the troops arriving as part of IFOR were well trained, well equipped, heavily armed, and prepared for combat should circumstances require—a posture very different from that of UNPROFOR.

In addition to leading the overall military effort from a head-quarters under the supervision of the United State Army, Europe (USAREUR), commander, the United States contributed to the IFOR 20,000 troops built around the Germany-based 1st Armored Division. About half as many international troops also worked under the 1st Armored Division's supervision, to include a Russian airborne brigade. Rather than competing with their allies for access through the damaged, diminutive, and restricted Adriatic ports, the Americans decided to deploy overland with an intermediate staging base in Taszar, Hungary, and an operational sector in northern Bosnia around Tuzla. The 3/325 Airborne Infantry Battalion Task Force from Vicenza, Italy, parachuted in to seize Tuzla and establish an early presence while the heavy division arrived by road and rail through Hungary. Severe winter weather, extensive flooding, and horrible mud forced the Americans into a monumental bridging exercise to get across the swollen Sava River. From December 20–31 the deployment had more to do with man against nature then it did with man against man. U.S. Army engineers persevered, installing a pontoon bridge, across which tanks, infantry fighting vehicles, trucks, and other vehicles rolled in a seemingly unending stream.

Once deployed, IFOR handled its military tasks fairly readily. The Serbs, Croats, and Muslims were weary of war and respectful of the NATO display of force. Occasional efforts to cheat with respect to hiding heavy weapons or avoiding inspection were abandoned in the face of further demonstrations of overwhelming military muscle. Fighting ceased. Landmines remained as a legacy of the earlier warfare, proving deadly to peacekeepers and civilians alike. De-mining operations fell behind schedule because of the sheer numbers involved, because of poor records kept when laying mines, and because of subsequent difficulty in finding them. De-mining progressed nevertheless.

American soldiers eventually settled into a routine of patrols, collateral training, and camp life. Civilian contractors built or deployed modular living and working facilities with electrical power, water, and waste disposal in the base camps. Original plans called for eight base camps with 3,000 soldiers each, but extremes of terrain compartmentalization forced the construction of twenty smaller camps. The soldiers needed expedient access to the secured population, who themselves benefited from employment in building or servicing the camps or in reconstructing roads and the infrastructure to support them. Within the camps, soldiers found

IFOR vehicles cross the Sava River on the hastily constructed bridge.

respite in post exchanges, long-distance telephones, Internet access, mess halls, and recreational facilities. Other than separation from loved ones, an air of normalcy emerged inside the wire surrounding the camps.

Outside the wire, things were not quite normal. Although the strictly military tasks of enforcing the cease-fire, separating former adversaries, and sustaining control of heavy weapons went generally as envisioned, issues for which civil resolution was anticipated went less well for a number of reasons. Crime was rampant. Apolitical incidence of theft, drugs, and prostitution were complicated by hate crimes involving arson, intimidation, and even murder. Efforts to resettle refugees in their original homes were clandestinely resisted by those who had forced them out, and freedom of movement became a hotly contested issue. Members of one ethnicity attempting to cross the territory of another to visit family, gravesites, or property were spat upon, bullied, or stoned. In the absence of a capable and reliable police force, allied soldiers soon found themselves deeply involved in law and order issues. In this difficult environment, economic recovery understandably lagged as well.

The mandate for the IFOR expired on December 20, 1996. Too many had assumed that in a year the difficulties of Bosnia could be resolved to a point at which the country no longer required outside assistance. Indeed, one American brigade commander created a media flap when he opined that Americans would be in Bosnia for years to come. Results bore him out. At the end of a year circumstances were still too fragile to hope that NATO could leave Bosnia without its reversion into chaos, and the allies were unwilling to continue the mission without U.S. participation. The parties involved agreed to continue the missions with a UN-sanctioned, NATO-led Stabilization Force (SFOR). (*See Map 32.*) Testimonial to the progress that had been made was the fact that 31,000 troops, about half the IFOR requirement, seemed sufficient for the SFOR.

NATO settled in for the long haul. For the American soldiers, one six-month rotation followed another as divisions took their turns in Bosnia. Slowly, progress was made. Houses were rebuilt, refugees resettled, freedom of movement restored, elections supervised and held, and economic enterprises undertaken. By 2003 SFOR 12, the twelfth American rotation into SFOR, included a U.S. contingent of only 1,450 troops. Their duties were a fairly routine round of presence patrols, security, and backup to local authorities. To that point, however, the Bosnian Serbs, Croats, and Muslims had become used to peaceably living apart more than they had learned to work together. Their effective governance and fledgling democratic processes were parallel rather than integrated, and there seemed to be no way to resolve disputes between them without the intervention of some UN or NATO leader or commander. A de facto partition of the country of Bosnia-Herzegovina emerged, with the predominately Muslim state of Bosnia-Herzegovina counterpoised by the predominately Christian Serb Republic. The creation of a truly viable, multiethnic Bosnian state may take generations, if it occurs at all. In the meantime, a peaceable, if divided, land policed by several thousand NATO-led soldiers is infinitely preferable to what happened before.

they could fight well against all else and offered a test bed for technology and doctrine intended for the future Objective Force. The Objective Force would be built around the FCS, when developed, and would embed all the technological advances possible. Interim Force brigades would be fielded at a pace of about one a year through 2006, and the Army would transition into the Objective Force in the dozen or so years following 2008.

To succeed, the Legacy Force, the Interim Force, and the Objective Force all required appropriate manning; and the prolonged downsizing of the 1990s had inhibited the incentive to recruit. When active-duty strength finally bottomed out at 480,000 in 1998, the Army had to replace each departing soldier with a new recruit—something it had not needed to do for some time. In 1999 the Army missed its recruiting goals by 6,000 in the active force and 10,000 in the Army Reserve. Within the next several years the Army revamped its emphasis on recruiting and introduced an initially controversial "Army of One" campaign. This campaign heavily emphasized the contributions of and skills acquired by individual soldiers and steered prospective recruits into Internet-based information to learn more about Army service. Indeed, one of the Internet's most popular role-playing games during the period was an action adventure based upon and sponsored by the U.S. Army. The Army met its recruiting goals while attracting a substantial number of computer-savvy young people interested in self-improvement who were an ideal match for its increasingly digital posture.

When fielded, the proposed Objective Force would embody a new way of war. Digital technology would provide it knowledge of its own forces, of the enemy, and of environmental circumstances so quickly that it could make decisions and act on them far more rapidly than could the enemy. That same digital technology, combined with a vast array of sensors and shooters, would rain PGMs onto a hapless enemy with devastating effects. Enabling information would course through a worldwide network drawing into the fight joint forces of all descriptions along with other government agencies and forces from other nations. This theoretical force of the future would take full advantage of the effectiveness of PGMs, more-fuel-efficient vehicles, and digital logistical-information networks to shrink the size of unit logistical footprints. Modular subordinate tactical elements would organize and reorganize at a rapid pace, enabled by the sureness of their battlefield knowledge to do so at the right time, each time. Gone would be the elaborate control measures and methodical coordination that had kept a less information-capable Army from shooting its own people. What need for unit boundaries, phase lines, and carefully maintained alignment when nimble units could speed through the battlefield in small, difficult-to-target swarms, each fully mindful of the presence of the others? The possibilities of this new force of the future, however dependent on the success of a number of technological breakthroughs, were dizzying.

To succeed, Army Transformation as envisioned would require a prolonged campaign of development, testing, and garnering of institutional, political, and financial support. Few had any illusions that it would reach fruition quickly, although successful lobbying in the

Enabling information would course through a worldwide network drawing into the fight joint forces of all descriptions along with other government agencies and forces from other nations.

halls of Congress provided transformation a measure of budgetary support and momentum. In 2000 the Army budget began to grow for several years, and important pieces did seem in place for long-term success. Skeptics to such a dramatic departure from the past did remain, especially among some in the Office of the Secretary of Defense, in civilian think tanks, and among retirees. These cautioned against committing to technology that had not yet matured, were concerned that emphasis on the FCS might evolve into too narrow a hardware solution, and believed that the huge reliance on communications technologies and bandwidth might make the Army unduly vulnerable to a sophisticated adversary who could compromise both. Transformation also seemed to further reinforce American supremacies that already existed in battlefield technology and logistics while not addressing weaknesses in peacekeeping, urban combat, etc., wherein the technical advances were not all that great an asset. Successful Army Transformation would require continued attention to doctrine, training, leadership development, and force structure addressing all levels of intensity on the combat spectrum.

Conclusion

The U.S. Army accomplished much in the years following the Cold War. It successfully fought a major war in Southwest Asia. It then downsized by a third while nevertheless sustaining high levels of overseas deployment. This requirement for overseas presence led it to improve upon its expeditionary capabilities while at the same time operating in such unfamiliar places as northern Iraq, Somalia, and Haiti. Tight budgets and international expectations suggested multinational operations, and the United States prepared for and proved the key player in successful operations in Bosnia and Kosovo. Even as it sustained a blistering operational tempo overseas, the Army undertook to transform itself. This transformation envisioned taking full advantage of technical leaps with respect to digitization and PGMs, as well as changes beyond technology.

Throughout the 1990s the Army's strategic focus remained broad and diffuse. No single adversary dominated its attention, and often it reacted to circumstances rather than adversaries. Paradigms developed, albeit slowly and deliberately, for a capabilities-based force, able to go almost anywhere and do almost anything, rather than for a threat-based force with a given adversary in mind. As busy as the Army was, it assumed its risks at some distance from the American people. Freedom's battles were being fought on Freedom's frontiers. The American people could go about their peaceable pursuits at home unmolested. How abruptly that would change.

DISCUSSION QUESTIONS

1. The end of the Cold War led to major reductions both in the size of the U.S. military structure and in the budgets available to the services. Discuss the benefits and dangers to America of this development.

2. Why did the United States deploy forces to Saudi Arabia so quickly in 1990 after the Iraqi occupation of Kuwait? Was this in the vital interest of the United States?

3. How did the Gulf War in 1991 highlight the changes made to the Army after Vietnam? How did the American people view these changes?

4. Why should the U.S. Army be used as a peacekeeping or nation building force? Discuss some positive and negative aspects of such missions.

5. With the end of the Cold War, what was the continuing usefulness of NATO? Why should or should not the alliance continue to exist?

6. To what degree did the United States play the role of "world policeman" in the 1990s? What dynamics have increasingly forced the United States to assume this role? What role did, and should, allies play in this effort?

7. In what ways did the Army attempt to transform itself after the end of the Cold War, and why?

RECOMMENDED READINGS

Boot, Max. *The Savage Wars of Peace: Small Wars and the Rise of American Power.* New York: Basic Books, 2002.

Bourque, Stephen A. *Jayhawk!: The VII Corps in the Persian Gulf War.* Washington, D.C.: U.S. Army Center of Military History, 2002.

Brune, Lester H. *The United States and Post–Cold War Interventions: Bush and Clinton in Somalia, Haiti, and Bosnia, 1992–1998.* Claremont, Calif.: Regina Books, 1998.

Casper, Lawrence E. *Falcon Brigade: Combat and Command in Somalia and Haiti.* Boulder, Colo.: Lynne Reinner Publishers, 2001.

Kretchick, Walter E., Robert F. Baumann, and John T. Fishel. *Invasion, Intervention, "Intervasion": A Concise History of the U.S. Army in Operation UPHOLD DEMOCRACY.* Fort Leavenworth, Kans.: U.S. Army Command and General Staff College Press, 1998.

Schubert, Frank N., and Theresa L. Kraus, gen. eds. *The Whirlwind War: The United States Army in Operations DESERT SHIELD and DESERT STORM.* Washington, D.C.: U.S. Army Center of Military History, 2001.

Stewart, Richard W. *The United States Army in Somalia: 1992–1994.* Washington, D.C.: U.S. Army Center of Military History, 2002.

Other Readings

Baumann, Robert F., Lawrence A. Yates, and Versalle F. Washington. *My Clan Against the World: U.S. and Coalition Forces in Somalia, 1992–1994.* Fort Leavenworth, Kans.: Combat Studies Institute Press, 2004.

Bowden, Mark. *Black Hawk Down: A Story of Modern War.* New York: Atlantic Monthly Press, 1999.

Clark, Wesley. *Waging Modern War: Bosnia, Kosovo, and the Future of Combat.* New York: Public Affairs, 2001.

Fishel, John T. *The Fog of Peace: Planning and Executing the Restoration of Panama.* Carlisle Barracks, Pa.: U.S. Army War College, 1992.

Hillen, John. *Blue Helmets: The Strategy of UN Military Operations.* Washington, D.C.: Brassey's, 2000.

McDonnell, Janet A. *After* DESERT STORM: *The U.S. Army and the Reconstruction of Kuwait.* Washington, D.C.: U.S. Army Center of Military History, 1999.

Murray, Williamson, ed. *Army Transformation: A View from the U.S. Army War College.* Carlisle Barracks, Pa.: U.S. Army War College, 2001.

Owens, Dallas D. *A/C R/C Integration: Today's Success and Transformation's Challenge.* Carlisle Barracks, Pa.: U.S. Army War College, 2001.

Rudd, Gordon W. *Humanitarian Intervention: Assisting the Iraqi Kurds in Operation* PROVIDE COMFORT, *1991.* Washington, D.C.: U.S. Army Center of Military History, 2004.

Scales, Robert H. *Certain Victory: The U.S. Army in the Gulf War.* Washington, D.C.: Brassey's, 1997.

Swain, Richard M. *Lucky War: Third Army in* DESERT STORM. Fort Leavenworth, Kans.: U.S. Army Command and General Staff College Press, 1994.

14

THE GLOBAL WAR ON TERRORISM

September 11, 2001, started out as a beautiful day across most of the eastern United States. Blue skies and pleasant temperatures carried the hint of fall even as summer lingered. At 8:46 A.M. American Airlines Flight 11 slammed into the 96th floor of the 110-story North Tower of New York's World Trade Center, spewing out 20,000 gallons of aviation fuel that ignited in a firebomb nearly 2,000°F. As horrified Americans watched the unfolding tragedy on television, United Airlines Flight 175 slammed into the twin South Tower sixteen minutes later, creating yet another inferno on its 80th floor. Firefighters and police rushed to the rescue of what might have been upward of 50,000 employees later in the day. Soon hundreds and then thousands were streaming away from the doomed buildings and their neighbors. The 110,000 tons of steel, concrete, and impedimenta above the point of impact on the South Tower proved too much to bear by 9:59, and it collapsed from 110 stories to 150 feet of rubble. Within thirty minutes the North Tower collapsed as well.

At the Pentagon, crisis action teams were just standing up to deal with the emerging catastrophe when American Airlines Flight 77 roared into the western face of that squat building at 9:38 with somewhat less effect because of the Pentagon's formidable construction. Over the next several hours details would emerge of yet another plane, United Airlines Flight 93, which crashed under mysterious circumstances into a field in Pennsylvania. A total of 2,435 workers, 343 firemen, and 23 policemen died in the Twin Towers and another 125 employees and servicemen in the Pentagon.

Well before details became clear, Americans surmised that they had been attacked by a clever and ruthless adversary. A chilling story emerged: In a well-organized scheme each plane had been seized by a team of five (in one case four) terrorists armed with plastic weapons and purporting to be passengers. These imposters had overwhelmed the crews, substituted one of their own for each pilot, and flown into

Karzai reviews the troops at the first graduation of the Kabul Military Training Center, Afghanistan, July 23, 2002.

the Kandahar airport, Bagram Airfield, facilities in Kabul, and prisoner screening and holding areas. A deployable reserve was established as well. The facility with which Omar, bin Laden, and many of their adherents had eluded capture by encircling Afghan forces suggested the desirability of having tightly disciplined American ground forces to pursue critical targets. The newly allied Afghan warlords seemed receptive to having a modest number of Americans on the ground in Afghanistan pursuing diehard al-Qaeda while they themselves went about the business of consolidating their grip on the rest of the country.

On December 11, 2002, Hamid Karzai was sworn in as the Prime Minister of the interim government of Afghanistan during ceremonies held in Kabul. His ascendancy had the general support of both the people and the warlords—the concurrence of the latter having been the result of considerable negotiation. Over the next several weeks a UN International Security Assistance Force (ISAF) that would ultimately number about 5,000 soldiers from eighteen nations deployed into Kabul, while an American force of about that size fanned out to work the hinterlands looking for al-Qaeda. In seventy-six days of operations a few hundred American special operators and a handful of conventional units supported by 6,500 strike missions expending 17,500 munitions had provided the margin of reinforcement necessary for a Northern Alliance victory over the theretofore dominant Taliban regime. The Global War on Terrorism was by no means over, but at least terrorists were no longer safe in Afghanistan.

Global Operations

The speedy American victory in Afghanistan bolstered operations against terrorism worldwide. President Bush's administration clearly recognized that military operations would be only part, and perhaps a lesser part, of their ultimate success. Effective counterterrorism would require extensive diplomatic, financial, legal, public relations, and perhaps humanitarian efforts as well. Initiatives within each of these venues were already well under way when the fighting in Afghanistan began, but the overthrow of the Taliban generated intelligence and an atmosphere that reinforced the American hand in each of them. The overthrow also suggested or encouraged further military action.

American diplomatic efforts experienced an immediate ground-swell of sympathy throughout most of the world in the aftermath of the September 11 attacks, and numerous governments pitched in to help defang al-Qaeda. Operatives and fellow travelers were detained in Germany, Spain, Italy, and Great Britain. It turned out that a number of key figures in the attacks had important connections in the permissive and liberal environment of Germany, which cracked down with particular severity. Captured documents and prisoner testimony from Afghanistan facilitated the hunt. In Malaysia, captured materials enabled direct police intervention to break up a pending attack. Muslim nations like Pakistan, Tajikistan, and Uzbekistan took some risks in assisting the United States against the Taliban and went after their own potential terrorists energetically, recognizing that they had already "grabbed the wolf by the ears." Pakistan in particular made some spectacular arrests of al-Qaeda operatives bailing out of Afghanistan.

American operators in central Asia needed and got the tacit approval of Russia and China. These two regional giants had problematic Islamic extremists of their own and were gratified when Americans suddenly found much less to criticize concerning Russian operations in Chechnya or the Chinese handling of their western provinces. A major fraction of the al-Qaeda killed or captured in Afghanistan turned out to be Chechnyan in origin, reinforcing Russian views of that unruly province.

Even such previously hostile states as Iran, Syria, the Sudan, and Libya tacitly cooperated with the United States in a calculated sort of way. They seemed inclined to distance themselves from any appearance of affiliation with al-Qaeda after the ferocious American attack on those harboring them in Afghanistan.

In Indonesia and Saudi Arabia, historically tepid cooperation with U.S. counterterrorism efforts became suddenly energetic after further spectacular attacks in those two countries. In the case of Indonesia, over two hundred tourists succumbed to a car bombing in Bali. In Saudi Arabia, coordinated strikes on housing areas featuring foreign workers inflamed the government's ire. In dozens of countries around the world, operations against al-Qaeda and their fellow travelers increased, and the success in Afghanistan contributed in one way or another to that acceleration.

In addition to diplomacy, the United States pursued al-Qaeda in the financial realm. The 9-11 attackers seem to have been well funded, and al-Qaeda operations as a whole demonstrated considerable sophistication in raising money and bankrolling operations worldwide. Funding seems to have originated in bin Laden's personal fortune—he was scion of a wealthy Saudi family that had made a great deal of money in construction—but had grown well beyond that original source. Al-Qaeda had been a major financial backer of the Taliban regime and also may have profited from the drug smuggling so lucrative in otherwise impoverished Afghanistan. Much of al-Qaeda's money moved around in conventional financial channels, but much also moved through a shadowy network of telephone-connected loaners and creditors labeled Hawala. Captured documents and prisoner interviews from Afghanistan sharpened the American understanding of al-Qaeda financial transactions. Investigators uncovered, for example, a callous and cynical sale of stocks in anticipation of a drop in value when the World Trade Center was attacked. It also seemed that money donated to Muslim charities was diverted into terrorist hands, though the extent and foreknowledge of this remains a matter of dispute. In concert with other nations, the United States set about freezing or seizing known al-Qaeda assets and attempted to disrupt suspected sources of income. There is no way to confidently measure the extent of the damage thus done, but it seems to have been considerable.

The most lucrative source of intelligence from Afghanistan was from prisoners caught in the fighting. Their status and disposition, however, raised important legal issues. Conventions relating to prisoners of war had been designed with belligerent nation-states in mind. Upon achieving a treaty or peace, they could be repatriated to their nations. No nation sanctioned al-Qaeda, and strong arguments existed that they were simply criminals. If so, in what nation would they account for their crimes and against whose standard would they be judged? What was more, since the Global War on Terrorism was ongoing, could the United States not detain them until its conclusion—indefinitely?

Criminals in the United States are normally charged, afforded due process in defending themselves from a case that is made against them, and, if convicted, given a specific sentence. The United States was willing to turn over most of the prisoners to the Afghans or to their nations of origin for adjudication but decided to keep the most dangerous, knowledgeable, or influential under its own control. The Afghan allies were happy enough to oblige. The United States labeled these prisoners detainees and set about developing its own precedents for handling them. JTF–17 stood up in Guantánamo, Cuba, to house the detainees under circumstances that placed more emphasis on security than on amenities. Sufficient information did not exist to make a case against these individuals in the traditional forensic sense, and the right to confront witnesses who would then be in great danger was out of the question. If trials were to occur, they would be by military tribunal, for which there was some precedent from World War II. By 2003 some 660 detainees were housed in Guantánamo; 1,600 servicemen and women had been dispatched to secure them and exploit them for intelligence. Some of the intelligence drawn from the detainees proved invaluable and allowed timely apprehension of more suspects. The situation became even more complicated when alleged or potential terrorists were apprehended in the United States, the press in various countries of origin became aware of the nationality of their detainees, and the issues of individuals apprehended for violations of immigration laws became muddled with the issue of suspected terrorists.

The uncertain status of the Guantánamo detainees may have caused some public relations issues for the United States, but the far greater issue was to assure that a war against Islamic terrorists was not interpreted as a war against Islam itself. Within days of the September 11 attacks, President Bush appeared among American Muslim congregations to make the point that they too shared the common enemy of terrorism and that religion was not the issue. Educators and commentators went to some lengths to distinguish between the benign tolerance of mainstream Islamic traditions and contemporary extremists who were characterized as having hijacked a virtuous religion for their own evil purposes. Diplomats consciously courted Muslim counterparts to help them emphasize a spirit of cooperation against Islamic terrorism, and one Muslim nation after another demonstrated by its actions that it concurred. Even television and advertising got into the act. Popular shows such as "West Wing" and "Law and Order" aired episodes distinguishing evil terrorists from virtuous Muslims, and President Bush directly engaged a public relations firm to improve the image of America in the Muslim world. All things considered, the effort to separate Islamic terrorism from Islam itself seems to have gone reasonably well. Within the United States, relatively few hate crimes were perpetrated against Muslim citizens or visitors and nothing remotely resembling the abuse and incarceration of Japanese Americans in World War II emerged. Overseas, calls for *jihad* against Americans and Westerners gained relatively little momentum and produced truly dangerous circumstances sporadically rather than generally.

Counterinsurgency and counterterrorist doctrine had long held that there needed to be a carrot as well as a stick in conducting operations; the catch phrase, "draining the swamp," gained popularity among those envisioning a way ahead. The swamp described those countries or regions of the world where poverty, injustice, abuse, and instability drove people to desperation and to identification with the terrorists. Humanitarian intervention to ameliorate such circumstances seemed an appropriate way to drain the swamp. In Afghanistan itself, growing American troop strength afforded the opportunity to divert some efforts to humanitarian relief, and a civil affairs battalion was an important part of the force structure from an early date.

Perhaps even more important was the work done by the United Nations and nongovernmental agencies when the security environment was sufficiently permissive to allow them to go about their work. As the international, largely NATO, peacekeeping force matured in Kabul and an Afghan army and police force began to take shape, the security of efforts to refurbish the impoverished country became a primary emphasis. American forces shared their concern and energetically pursued Taliban and al-Qaeda remnants. A striking example of this kind of support to humanitarian relief was presented by the death of Mullah Satar. Satar, a relatively minor Taliban-sympathetic thug, shot and killed an Ecuadorian relief worker, a water engineer named Ricardo Munguia. This was the first overt case of an International Committee of the Red Cross employee in post-Taliban Afghanistan consciously killed for the good he was trying to do. In an operation best described as implacable, American special operators strained every intelligence resource available to reliably locate Satar and then gunned him and his adherents down during a spectacular air assault on the village of Safi during the night. Their message was clear.

Recognizing the critical diplomatic, financial, legal, public relations, and humanitarian aspects of the Global War on Terrorism, soldiers nevertheless discovered that there was ample ground fighting yet to do.

> As the international ... peacekeeping force matured in Kabul and an Afghan army and police force began to take shape, the security of efforts to refurbish the impoverished country became a primary emphasis.

In Afghanistan, the search for diehard al-Qaeda and Taliban continued, with a particular emphasis on the eastern mountains along the Pakistani border. Operation ANACONDA, conducted from March 2–19, 2002, proved particularly ambitious, challenging, and rewarding. Reports indicated a residual concentration of about 200 al-Qaeda and Taliban fighters congregating in the Shahi Kowt Valley, over a mile above sea level in rugged mountains proximate to Pakistan. (*Map 35*) When the allies attempted to sweep these remnants into a trap defined by helicopter-delivered American blocking positions in the mountains to the east that would pick off escapees from a major allied Afghan thrust from the west, major fighting ensued. It turned out that the al-Qaeda and Taliban fighters numbered closer to 1,000 in well-defended positions supported by elaborate cave complexes featuring huge stockpiles of arms and ammunition. Helicopters labored heavily in the thin mountain air, as did troops struggling to take the battle to the enemy across frozen, rocky ground.

Overcoming initial surprise and embarrassment, the allies piled on. Ultimately some 1,200 Americans; 2,000 friendly Afghans; and 200 Australian, Canadian, Danish, German, and Norwegian special operators were into the fight, supported by over 2,500 bombs. They killed about half their adversaries, while the other half seems to have exfiltrated to further mountain hiding places or into Pakistan. Warfare in eastern Afghanistan became a grim round of patrols and operations in the mountains to keep al-Qaeda and Taliban remnants off balance and under pressure while a new Afghan army was equipped and trained, relief efforts stabilized the economy and society, and Karzai's government established a grip. Occasionally, Americans and their allies were ambushed, sniped at, mortared, or rocketed; but the quality of intelligence available to the Americans improved over time and they ground their adversaries down, a few guerrillas or arms caches at a time.

Military success in Afghanistan inspired military efforts elsewhere. The most immediate need was to preclude Pakistan from becoming a refuge for guerrillas operating in Afghanistan. Particular risks existed in the so-called tribal regions, wherein the population was inclined to favor the largely Pashtun Taliban and the mandate of the Pakistani central government never ran strong anyway. The Pakistanis were very sensitive about visible American involvement in their country, yet the hundreds of miles of mountainous border was virtually impossible to police. Fortunately, the tribesmen were not particularly partial to the largely Arab al-Qaeda and the Pakistani hand could be reinforced by largely invisible assistance from American Special Operations Forces. Workable, cooperative cross-border arrangements emerged with time, and soon the Pakistanis were apprehending guerrillas in flight from the Americans and their Afghan allies.

Thousands of miles away in the Philippines, fanatic Abu Sayyaf Islamic militants seemed another dangerous source of potential terror. Hostile and separatist at least since the Moro Wars in the early twentieth century, Islamic extremists had waxed and waned in their defiance of central government over the years. Recently they had taken to piracy, theft, and kidnapping for ransom to fund their agendas and had acquired demonstrable links to international terrorism. Indeed, they were heavily implicated in a barely failed plot to simultaneously

Warfare in eastern Afghanistan became a grim round of patrols and operations in the mountains to keep al-Qaeda and Taliban remnants off balance and under pressure while a new Afghan army was equipped and trained.

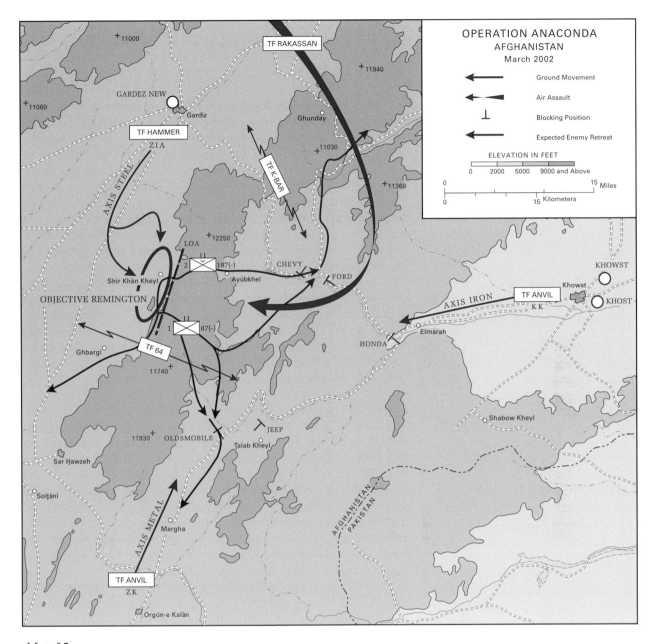

Map 35

destroy a dozen aircraft over the Pacific. Conscious of Filipino sensibilities, the United States undertook logistical, intelligence, and training support to the Philippine Army in its post–9-11 efforts to crush Abu Sayyaf. Combined "training" operations on a battalion scale in the midst of territory theretofore dominated by the Abu Sayyaf became an important feature of this renewed cooperation. Similarly, the U.S. Army and Special Forces greatly expanded their logistical, training, and intelligence cooperation with numerous Muslim nations such as Oman, Yemen, Djibouti, Indonesia, and Jordan to reinforce their hands against the mutual threat of terrorism. Most of these military-to-military relationships had already existed, and some were quite mature; but 9-11 lent them a special urgency insofar as the United States was concerned.

Back to Iraq

Since the liberation of Kuwait in DESERT STORM, Saddam Hussein's Iraq had remained a nagging threat to American security. Many expected Saddam to be overthrown in the aftermath of his overwhelming defeat, but in the absence of a sustained American military presence he had bloodily suppressed his internal adversaries and remained in power. Tens of thousands of Shi'ites and Kurds were murdered, and a police state already consciously modeled on that of Stalin became even worse. His internal brutality was matched by external belligerence; time and again he demonstrated against or bullied Kuwait, defied disarmament obligations under the terms of the cease-fire, and fired on allied aircraft enforcing a no-fly zone in northern and southern Iraq. He seems to have been involved in an attempt to assassinate President George H. W. Bush in 1993 and ultimately forced UN weapons inspectors out of the country in 1998. The new Bush administration expressed great concern that he would further develop weapons of mass destruction—he had already employed chemical munitions against the Kurds—and either use them himself or pass them along to international terrorists. Either prospect would be horrific.

Shortly after 9-11, Chief of Staff General Eric K. Shinseki had directed the Army to assume a wartime footing, with all other priorities being of lesser import. Every effort was made to bring units to full strength, and every division and cavalry regiment ascertained its preparedness to fight a war that had not yet been decided upon with a force list that had not yet been specified. War plans for Iraq came and went, and commanders likely to be involved war-gamed the plans separately and together. Key leadership was psychologically prepared and units physically prepared for Iraq even before they knew of a decision to go, and such in-theater investments as a state-of-the-art command and control facility in Qatar and a fuel farm on the Iraqi border furthered that preparation.

For all his bluster, Saddam's capacity for conventional warfare had dramatically declined since his invasion of Kuwait. UN sanctions and a weapons embargo had dried up his access to modern arms and spare parts. Rather than the 950,000 troops, 5,000 tanks, and 800 combat aircraft of 1990, he mustered 280,000 troops, 2,200 tanks, and virtually no combat aircraft in 2003. The equipment was poorly maintained and the troops demoralized. Postwar interviews suggest that discipline was maintained by fear. Iraqi soldiers tell of being tortured and abused and, if they deserted or went absent without official leave, of their families' being incarcerated or beaten. The regular army was in tatters, though the elite *Republican Guard* was somewhat better.

Hussein recognized his weakness and seems to have been inspired by America's Somalia experience in planning his way ahead should the allies attack. The regular army would be considerably reinforced by the irregular *Fedayeen* and by the *Special Republican Guard* operating as special operations forces. He would take maximum advantage of the urban terrain, ambush, surprise, and proximity to civilian targets.

Key leadership was psychologically prepared and units physically prepared for Iraq even before they knew of a decision to go.

480

Pickups modified with machine guns and RPGs, the Iraqi version of the Somali "technical," would allow for speedy movement and appreciable firepower. *Fedayeen* and Ba'athists hiding among the population would use terrorism to discourage cooperation with allied authorities. If the regular army could preoccupy units leading the allied advance, the *Fedayeen* could strike its vulnerable rear, increasing American casualties. If eighteen men killed in a Mogadishu firefight had precipitated an American withdrawal from Somalia, how much easier would it be to force a withdrawal from a challenge as complex as Baghdad?

In the aftermath of the 9-11 attacks, Americans were perhaps less averse to casualties than they had been; certainly, the stakes were higher. President Bush decided a regime change in Iraq was necessary, in part because of the potential threat of weapons of mass destruction in Iraqi hands but also because of potential Iraqi links with international terrorists, Iraq's continuing threat to the stability of the Middle East, and a sentiment that Saddam Hussein represented unfinished business. Not all of America's allies perceived Hussein as an imminent threat; many argued instead for granting more time to UN weapons inspectors whom Hussein, under pressure, had recently readmitted. Bitter wrangling ensued in the United Nations and elsewhere as the United States and Britain insisted on speedy intervention and other major powers declined to support such a notion. Perhaps most consequential, at the eleventh hour the Turkish parliament refused to allow the U.S. 4th Infantry Division (Mechanized) to move through Turkey en route to establishing a front in northern Iraq. This obviated a major feature of the preferred war plan, left the division's equipment out of play as it hastily transshipped from standing offshore from Turkey to Kuwait, and perturbed deployment schedules because the ships carrying 4th Infantry Division equipment were not available for other purposes for a prolonged period of time.

The theater commander, General Tommy R. Franks, and his ground component commander, Lt. Gen. David D. McKiernan, faced a quandary as combat operations became imminent. With approximately 200,000 ground troops available in theater at the time—as opposed to the 600,000 of Desert Storm—they did not enjoy massive and overwhelming ground combat force. With the Turkish option gone, their conventional ground attack would have to originate in Kuwait and progress 300 miles to Baghdad, and then perhaps 200 more to the vital oil fields around Mosul. The major headquarters that would control the fight were the U.S. Army V Corps and the U.S. Marines I MEF (Marine Expeditionary Force.) On hand in Kuwait they had but a single American heavy division, the 3d Infantry Division (Mechanized); an equivalent number of marines with some M1A1 tanks but including the awkward Amtrack as troop carriers; and a British force built up around the U.K. 1st Armoured Division including the 7th Armoured Brigade. Lighter forces included the 101st Airborne Division (Air Assault), one brigade of the 82d Airborne Division, the 11th Attack Helicopter Regiment, and a fistful of smaller units. This seemed a small force considering the challenges involved. The force did, however, have 1,600 combat aircraft in theater as compared to Desert Storm's 2,100, representing an air force proportionally much closer in size to that of the earlier war. Conventional wisdom held that combat operations would begin with a prolonged air campaign while the 4th Infantry Division made its way to Kuwait and then its newly freed shipping opened up a flow of follow-on heavy divisions.

General Franks examines a weapons cache that the 101st Airborne Division discovered in Najaf.

General Franks was not partial to waiting, and not just because to do so would mean operating in the terrible heat of the Iraqi summer. In his mind mass was firepower more so than troops; and, as we have seen, the widespread availability of inexpensive joint direct-attack munitions (JDAMs) had radically increased the effectiveness of his firepower. The Afghan experience convinced him that he could drive jointness to the lowest possible level and that a brigade supported by JDAMs could do what it had taken several to achieve before. What was more, the Iraqis were probably expecting a lengthy air campaign and perhaps anticipated time to redeploy their forces from northern Iraq to keep pace with the redeployment of the 4th Infantry Division. One of General Franks' contingency plans envisioned a rolling start, wherein he began the campaign with modest forces already on hand and fed in reinforcements as they arrived, if they were needed. Iraqi dispositions and circumstances did not suggest significant resistance much south of Baghdad, so why not sweep up relatively uncontested terrain with a lesser force and feed in further forces as they arrived?

Factors beyond JDAMs and strategic surprise argued for the rolling start. In effect the United States had already waged a prolonged air campaign. Time and again since DESERT STORM the Americans had reacted to Saddam's provocations by bombing Iraq. DESERT FOX in December 1998 had featured four intense days of air and missile strikes; and when retaliating for potshots at planes enforcing the no-fly zones, the Americans had taken the opportunity to further dismantle Iraqi air defenses and communications systematically. Over twelve years many of the purposes an air campaign might otherwise have served had already been achieved through these operations, called NORTHERN WATCH and SOUTHERN WATCH. American ground forces were acclimatized for operations in Iraqi and poised for a rolling start. Since DESERT STORM they had repeatedly sped into theater to defend Kuwait against Saddam's provocations and had developed a routine deployment and training program labeled INTRINSIC ACTION that rotated robust battalion combat teams through rigorous exercises in the Kuwaiti desert. American soldiers had long since figured out how to get the best results out of themselves and their equipment in this harsh environment. Most of the soldiers who would cross the line of departure had already been living in the desert for some time as diplomatic crises ebbed and flowed. Another argument for a rolling start lay in the memory of catastrophic damage retreating Iraqis had inflicted on Kuwaiti oil fields during DESERT STORM. If the coalition moved quickly enough on the ground this time, it could secure the nearby Rumaylah Oil Fields before Saddam Hussein could set them on fire. McKiernan gave his Marine Expeditionary Force an on-order mission to seize these oil fields within four hours of notification, and Special Operations Forces infiltrated to monitor and perhaps interfere with any attempts at demolition prior to the marines' arrival.

The final logic for the rolling start was fortuitous. Intelligence reports seemed confident that Hussein, his influential sons Uday and Qusay, and other regime leaders were in the same bunker at the same time and that the coalition knew where it was. The allies seized upon this opportunity to decapitate Saddam's regime with a single blow. Simultaneously, thirty-six Tomahawk Land Attack Missiles (TLAMs) hit the complex early in the morning on March 20. Unfortunately, later reports proved that the intelligence was faulty: Hussein and his sons were not in the bunker. Further combat operations followed immediately, and the main bodies of the 3d Infantry Division, 1st Marine Division, and U.K. 1st Armoured Division were rolling across the line of departure within twenty-four hours.

The 3d Infantry Division streaked up the west side of the Euphrates River toward Baghdad, blowing through light resistance to cover 200-plus miles into the vicinity of Al Najaf within twenty-four hours. (*See Map 36.*) During this same period the marines overran the Rumaylah Oil Fields, handily mopping up fragments of defenders and securing the facilities virtually unscathed. The British captured 750 dispirited defenders of Umm Qasr without much of a fight and set about preparing that port to receive humanitarian supplies. Far to the west, the Special Forces already had infiltrated to compromise Iraqi efforts to launch missiles from western Iraq into Israel; to the north, special operators in Kurdistan had laid groundwork to bring the Kurds in as a second front. Most of this drama and activity was televised worldwide by the virtue of embedded media correspondents traveling within units yet linked to their home stations by satellite technology. Their real-time, gripping, and sometimes breathless commentary added to the sense of momentum and success.

Unfortunately, the campaign did not stay easy. Many had thought that overwhelming American air strikes would so shock and awe the Baghdad regime that it would quickly fold with minimal ground effort. The Iraqis anticipated the allied advantage, surrendered control of the air from the beginning, hid much of their valuable equipment amidst the civilian populace where the allies were loath to strike, and pushed deep underground what command and control they could sustain. The allies were far too sensitive to world opinion to risk serious damage to civilian infrastructure and instead used spectacular firepower on selected government buildings and military facilities. The Arab world recoiled from footage of massive plumes of smoke over the fabled city of Baghdad and of hapless civilian victims of occasional errant munitions, when in fact little real damage was being done to the city or its citizens. Strategic bombing was also doing little real damage to Iraqi warfighting capabilities. The air power that would matter would be joint and in support of the ground advance.

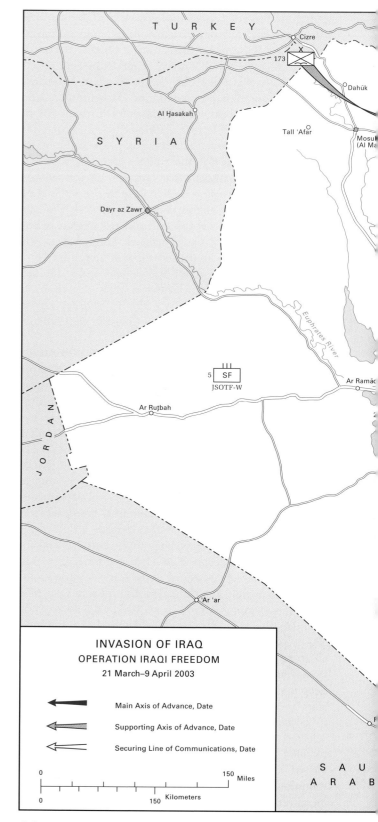

TURKEY

Cizre

173

Dahūk

Al Ḩasakah

Tall 'Afar

Mosu
(Al Ma

S Y R I A

Dayr az Zawr

Euphrates River

5 | SF
JSOTF-W

Ar Ramād

J
O
R
D
A
N

Ar Ruṭbah

'Ar 'ar

INVASION OF IRAQ
OPERATION IRAQI FREEDOM
21 March–9 April 2003

Main Axis of Advance, Date

Supporting Axis of Advance, Date

Securing Line of Communications, Date

0   150 Miles

0   150 Kilometers

S A U
A R A B

Map 36

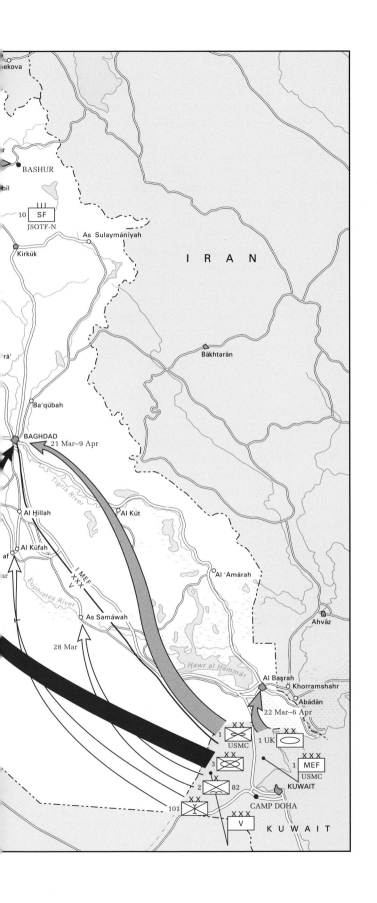

Ground troops soon enough found themselves in need of the advantages air power could bring. Although the Iraqi regular army quickly faded from view south of Baghdad, by desertion more so than through combat or surrender, *Fedayeen* and *Special Republican Guards* counterattacked with vengeance. Attacks against lead elements of the 3d Infantry Division seem almost suicidal in retrospect. Swarms of pickup trucks mounting machine guns and packed with light infantry raced to close with the Americans, only to be swept away by hurricanes of tank and Bradley fire. Ambushes more rationally sited amidst buildings and vegetation were still speedily shredded by phenomenal American gunnery, the product of thermal sights, state-of-the-art equipment, and years of training. The heavy armor of the M1A1 tanks was proof against almost any munitions in the Iraqi inventory, and the lighter armor of the Bradleys protected their crews from most. Shootouts with American armor inevitably went badly for the Iraqis.

Unfortunately for the Americans, their armor could not be everywhere and their rapid advance had exposed a lengthy supply line. While some *Fedayeen* were demolishing themselves fighting lead elements in and around Najaf, their brethren were having somewhat better results attacking trailing logistical assets around An Nasiriyah. One maintenance company became disoriented as they attempted to move through that enemy-held town and lost 11 killed, 7 captured, and 9 wounded in a chaotic gun battle. The Iraqis presented the prisoners on television for the world to see, and pictures of dead bodies showed on that media as well. Marines rushed in to assist in securing An Nasiriyah found themselves embroiled in stiff fighting with wily and ruthless opponents and took significant casualties as well. The *Fedayeen* and other irregulars routinely dressed as civilians, pretended to surrender and then opened fire, hid among civilians, attacked from ambush, and operated out of hospitals, schools, and mosques. They knew and exploited the American rules of engagement. As major fighting ceased, they persisted with sniping and encouraged suicide attacks against isolated American checkpoints.

March 24, 2003, was a discouraging day for coalition arms. The damage inflicted upon the ambushed maintenance company was becoming clear, and attacks along the elongated supply lines continued. An Nasiriyah in particular remained a hotly contested scene of carnage and confusion. The 11th Attack Helicopter Regiment attempted a deep

AMBUSH OF A CONVOY

The 507th Maintenance Company entered enemy territory unprepared for the type of combat it was about to face. On March 23, 2003, the company unwittingly drove through enemy positions at An Nasiriyah. So surprised were the Iraqi soldiers that they initially did not fire on the Americans and the 507th continued unscathed. Turning around, the lumbering column made its confusion obvious. The Iraqis, once fearful of American might, now saw easy targets. They began shooting; the surprised maintenance personnel fumbled with their weapons, with some jamming. The highway in An Nasiriyah became a gauntlet of fire. Sixteen Americans escaped, but eleven died and seven were captured in one of the costliest single combat incidents during Operation IRAQI FREEDOM.

attack on the *Republican Guard Medina Division* defending Karbala and overflew a mammoth air defense ambuscade of machine guns and shoulder-fired air-defense weapons coordinated by cellular telephones. Although all but one of the redoubtable AH–64 Apache helicopters made it out of the battle area, in one battalion only six of eighteen aircraft remained mission capable and in another only one. Weather reports anticipated the imminent arrival of a massive sandstorm, yielding several days of winds up to 50 knots and visibility measured in inches rather than miles. Such appalling weather conditions could negate American technical advantages and allow Iraqi attackers a close combat opportunity with American troops. Perhaps most troubling, Iraqi Shi'ites who had been so terribly abused during Saddam Hussein's regime did not rise to greet the allies as liberators but rather seemed to present an overall attitude of sullen indifference. Allied postwar plans depended heavily on Iraqi cooperation: If those most aggrieved with Hussein remained distant, what hope was there for an agreeable outcome? It was in this context of troubling surprises that V Corps Commander Lt. Gen. William S. Wallace made his now-famous remark that the Iraqis were "not the enemy we war-gamed against."

Wallace's remark was discouraging only to those who believed that wars are supposed to unfold as planned. Wallace's 34-year career included service as the Commander of the Operations Group and then Commanding General at the National Training Center, where he became acutely aware how often plans must change to accommodate a dynamic battlefield. His soldiers demonstrated that flexibility now. With respect to exposed logistics, within a few days V Corps drew on lessons learned in Vietnam and elsewhere—in some cases drawing on materials e-mailed from archives in the United States—to reconfigure convoys into a more defensible posture. Wallace resisted the temptation to redirect leading armored elements back into securing their own lines of communication and instead brought forward elements of the more lightly armed 101st

Allied postwar plans depended heavily on Iraqi cooperation: If those most aggrieved with Hussein remained distant, what hope was there for an agreeable outcome?

Sergeant First Class Paul R. Smith (1969–2003)

Sfc. Paul R. Smith of Company B, 11th Engineers, 3d Infantry Division, was awarded the Medal of Honor posthumously for his heroic actions on April 4, 2003, during Operation Iraqi Freedom. During an attack to clear a compound near Baghdad International Airport, his platoon was attacked by approximately sixty Iraqi insurgents. Sergeant Smith led his men from the front as they fought off the attackers with small arms and grenades. In a decisive moment, Sergeant Smith mounted one of his platoon's armored personnel carriers and in that exposed position directed .50-caliber machine-gun fire against the enemy until he was mortally wounded.

Right: *Low Visibility during a Sandstorm in Southern Iraq.* Below: Satan's Sandbox, *Elzie R. Golden, 2003.*

and 82d Airborne Divisions to deal with rear-area security. The 377th Theater Support Command pushed a hose-reel fuel system over fifty miles to the vicinity of An Nasiriyah, thus reducing the turnaround time for fuel-bearing trucks. This further capitalized upon a million-gallon fuel farm the Army had already quietly built up just short of the Iraq-Kuwait border. The 11th Attack Helicopter Regiment set about repairing or replacing shot-up aircraft, and their pilots conducted a video teleconference with the attack helicopter pilots of the 101st Airborne Division to discuss the innovative Iraqi defenses and to communicate lessons learned.

The 101st Division had more success with far less damage when their own opportunity for deep attacks came. The gigantic sandstorms did slow the American advance to a crawl and allowed some Iraqi *Fedayeen* and irregulars to get close, but these found the Americans as formidable close up as they had been at a distance. Even degraded thermal sights were better than the alternatives, and American gunners were quick on the trigger. American dismounts were well trained and organized, equipped with night-vision goggles, and heavily armed with automatic weapons. Perhaps most important, their newly improved Kevlar body armor was proof against fragments and munitions up through the ubiquitous 7.62-caliber round of the Iraqi AK–47. Dozens of American infantrymen who would have been fatally wounded in earlier wars remained in the fight. The close-in battles that did occur were lopsided in the favor of the Americans.

With respect to Shi'ite reticence, the British pioneered a go-slow technique around Basra that developed insights useful elsewhere. The allies had a free hand in the open desert and could surround populated areas to enter them at their own pace. It turned out that the Shi'ites were not so much hostile to the allies as they were frightened of a Ba'athist hard core in their own midst. The British gathered intelligence on the surrounded population, conducted nighttime forays to neutralize identified Ba'athists, and built the confidence of the Shi'ite remainder. Ultimately, the British, supported by the local populace, swept the Ba'athists out of Basra and entered the city as liberators. All things considered, the allies shifted their paradigm from the enemy that they had war-gamed against to the one they were actually fighting well.

Allied air power continued to hammer away at the Iraqis during all this adjustment. The rapid advance of the 3d Infantry Division (Mechanized) along the Euphrates and of the marines up the Tigris and between the rivers had drawn out the *Republican Guard* to defend the environs of Baghdad. They may have thought themselves concealed by the dust storm and by moving at night, but they were not. Satellites, unmanned aerial vehicles, and aerial reconnaissance detected their movements; Special Operations Forces and the leading ground forces established their front-line trace. Relentless air bombardment with PGMs seriously attrited the *Republican Guard* before it could achieve substantial ground contact with the Americans.

As vital as air power was to the advance from the south, it was even more instrumental to allied successes in the west and north. In the west, thinly supported Special Operations Forces quickly overran airfields and neutralized potential Iraqi missile strikes. Packing little organic firepower themselves, they depended heavily on aerial precision strikes to offset their shortcomings. In the north, the Air Force airdropped a reinforced battalion of the 173d Airborne Brigade, air-landed an M1A1 tank–equipped company team to support it, and then sustained this host and their Kurdish *Peshmerga* allies by air as well. Again much of the necessary fire support came from airborne PGMs. All these resources—tanks, paratroopers, *Peshmerga*, and PGMs—operated under the supervision of the handful of special operators already deployed in the north, inducing the Army's Vice Chief of Staff, General John ("Jack") M. Keane, to quip that it was like attaching a naval carrier battle group to a SEAL team. Operations in both west and north progressed well, while the climactic battle was shaping up in the south.

THUNDER RUNS IN BAGHDAD

Urban combat can bog down armies, and the campaign to seize Baghdad in April 2003 required audacity to prevent a slow, set-piece battle. The American Army mounted two armored raids, nicknamed Thunder Runs. First, on April 5 an armored battalion attacked swiftly up Highway 8 into Baghdad and then withdrew. Two days later an entire heavy brigade of Abrams tanks and Bradleys roared into downtown Baghdad and stayed, fighting off all counterattacks. These raids—armored vehicles speeding down highways—brought mayhem: tanks blasting thin defenses, suicidal assaults on armor, and vast expenditures of ammunition on suspected enemy locations. They were a key element in toppling the regime of Saddam Hussein.

By April 4 the 3d Infantry Division had battered its way through the fragmenting *Republican Guard* to seize Saddam Hussein International Airport. Meanwhile, the marines had continued up the Tigris to cut off Baghdad from the east. (*See Map 36.*) The following day the 3d Infantry Division dispatched a battalion task force on a raid into central Baghdad, taking advantage of the relatively open construction of major highways into the city. This foray turned into a spectacular media event as the tanks and Bradleys sped through town, blazing away to the left and right, destroying twenty armored vehicles, sixty-two trucks, and hundreds of troops while losing only four wounded in action themselves. Clearly, organized resistance was collapsing.

By April 7 the division had fought its way into central Baghdad to stay and the following day had closed to the Palestine Hotel in full view of the numerous international media who had set up operations there. The marines moved into the city from the other side, and the continuing rout of the Iraqis in the west and north completed the isolation of the now-fallen capital city. The campaign's cumulative casualties to that point were reported as 42 killed and 133 wounded for the Army, 41 killed and 151 wounded for the Marine Corps and 19 killed and 36 wounded for the British. On April 9 a tiny contingent of marines and a crowd of jubilant Iraqis pulled down the Saddam monument in the Shi'ite sector of Baghdad while breathless television commentary related the symbolism and decisiveness of the moment. It truly seemed that the war was over and a triumphant peace at hand.

Phase IV

Coalition planners had envisioned IRAQI FREEDOM as a multiphase operation, with Phase IV being the mop-up and reconstruction that followed the collapse of Saddam Hussein's regime. The conduct of Phases I through III had been mindful of Phase IV; collateral damage to the civilian infrastructure had been kept to a minimum. Graphic photos and film footage revealed smoke pluming out of precisely drilled military targets while civilian buildings surrounding them remained untouched. Psychological operations repeatedly made the point that the war was against Hussein's regime and not the Iraqi people. Unlike most other wars, there was no sudden flight of panicked refugees. The Iraqis stayed where they were and by and large had sufficient food on hand to last them for a week or so. Many thought that the Iraqis would greet the Americans as liberators and that Phase IV would involve a modest and expedient expenditure of resources. Unfortunately, these optimists underrated the resilience of the Ba'athist regime, the complexity of the Iraqi national identity, and the deplorable conditions in which Hussein had left his country.

There was no precise end to Saddam Hussein's regime, no surrender, no cease-fire, no treaty. There was not much formal capitulation at lower levels either. By and large the Iraqi Army deserted and went home rather than surrendering en masse. Regime adherents disappeared back into the population but retained the means to intimidate it through threat, arson, and murder. The coalition resorted to the attention-getting tactic of associating a different key regime figure with each card in a deck of cards: Hussein, for example, was the Ace of

Spades. In southern Iraq, the Shi'ites well remembered their abortive uprising against Hussein following Desert Storm and the massacres they blamed in part on America's failure to assist at that time. They were understandably wary of cooperating too soon; Ba'athist diehards would have to be rooted out and an expectation of personal security established before cooperation could be expected. In central Iraq, Sunni Arabs had received favored treatment from Saddam's regime; his personal power base had been heavily concentrated in Tikrit and other small towns north and west of Baghdad. (*See Map 37.*) Here, the number of his adherents was larger and their grip on the population more profound than in the south. Only the Kurds in the far north had already virtually extinguished the Ba'athists in their midst and enthusiastically welcomed the Americans as liberators.

Infantrymen provide security near an essential bridge crossing south of Baghdad.

The Iraqi national identity was both fragmented and complicated. Profound tensions had long divided Shi'ites, Sunni Arabs, and Kurds; such smaller minorities as Assyrians, Chaldeans, and Turks had their share of historical grievances as well. Iraqis were overwhelmingly Muslim, mindful of centuries of oppression by foreign powers, and wary of if not outright hostile to a sustained American presence. Ethnic and political ties extended well beyond their borders, producing additional potential for mischief. Iran's fundamentalist Shia government appealed to many Iraqi Shi'ites, who constituted about 60 percent of the population. A number of prominent Shia leaders had waited out the worst of the Hussein years in exile in Iran and now returned with organizations of followers intact. Kurds lived in Turkey and Iran as well as in Iraq, and those nations worried that a prosperous and autonomous Kurdistan might inspire their own minorities to further separatism. Ba'athists were dominant in Syria as they had been in Iraq, and armed men flowed back and forth across that porous and troubled border. Pan-Arab hostility to the West was also at play in Iraq, and popular international media networks like *al-Jazeera* put a spin on news that did not favor the coalition allies and what they were trying to accomplish. This attitude garnered support from some for the use of foreign mercenaries, zealots, and terrorists, first to defend Hussein's regime and then, when it fell, to carry on the fight on the part of Ba'athist diehards or in addition to them.

Coalition objectives depended heavily on convincing the Iraqis that they were better off with Saddam Hussein gone. This effort was compromised initially by the sorry state of the country's infrastructure. Hussein's regime had more in common with gangster-like extortion and extraction than it did with responsible government. Saddam had looted the country of billions of dollars and plowed much of that

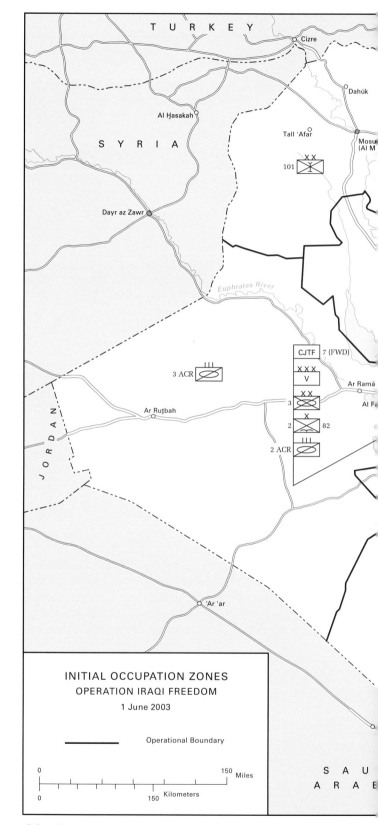

Map 37

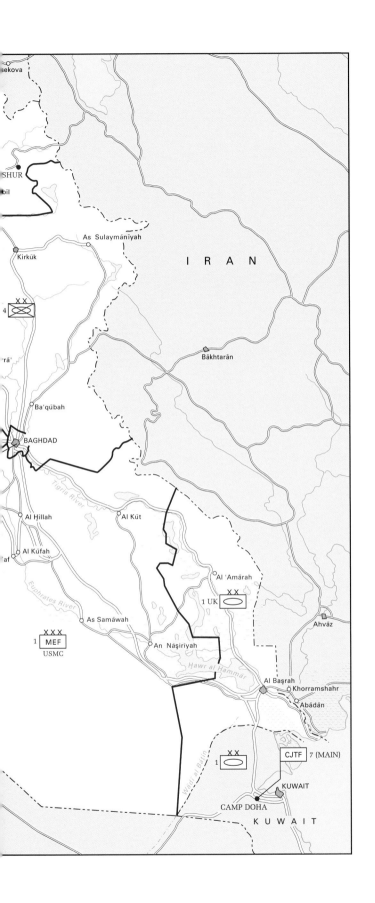

A soldier of the 3d Infantry Division scans the rooftops in Baghdad as part of a patrol to deter looting.

back into magnificent palaces for himself and his family. Much was simply stashed away, some in overseas banks and some in great bundles of money coalition troops found hidden in walls, under floors, or in basements. Given UN sanctions following DESERT STORM and Saddam's fiscal style, the black-market economy was in many cases more robust than the conventional economy. Saddam's adherents lived well, but most of the population lived in poverty. Routine recapitalization of oil-producing, electricity-generating, and transportation infrastructures simply did not occur, and there was not enough private investment to support a healthy economy.

Iraq's economic dysfunction manifested itself in the paroxysmal looting associated with the regime's fall. As Saddam's security apparatus collapsed and the allies proved too few and too distracted to police the country, impoverished masses saw their one clear chance to seize something—anything—for themselves. Palaces were stripped of furniture, doorknobs, and electrical wire. Hospitals were stripped of diagnostic equipment and medical supplies. Power-transmission lines were toppled and the copper and other metals in them melted down for resale abroad. Government buildings were left as empty shells. There was no particular rhyme or reason for most of the looting. It was a simple orgy of the dispossessed stealing anything that could possibly be used or sold. Some of the damage was more sinister, however. In power stations and fuel refineries, coalition forces found evidence of sabotage as well as looting. Regime diehards so wanted coalition efforts to fail that they were willing to inflict untold further suffering on the Iraqi people.

Looting and lawlessness quickly tarnished the allied victory. The breath-taking success of the attack from a rolling start left a relatively tiny force in the midst of a vast country. Further troops had not yet arrived. Fighting continued on a small scale, and the relatively few units on hand necessarily took some time to transition from a warfighting posture to a security posture. In the interval lawlessness continued, with much of it more organized, violent, and criminal than had been the case earlier. Ordinary Iraqi citizens found themselves terrorized by tales of robbery, car theft, rape, and murder, many of which were true. Even when reinforced, American troops could not be everywhere. As they spread out to secure schools, hospitals, banks, and traffic-control points, they made themselves increasingly vulnerable to sniping and ambush by diehard Ba'athists.

Fallujah, *Elzie R. Golden, 2004*

The original plans for postwar Iraq had envisioned a modest reconstruction effort under retired Lt. Gen. James ("Jay") Garner, the man who had supervised the reconstitution of Iraqi Kurdistan during Operation PROVIDE COMFORT. As the scale and intractable nature of the lawlessness, factional squabbling, and infrastructure collapse became clear, however, the need for a more comprehensive reconstruction effort became clear as well. Although some progress was being made, day after day the media reported electrical outages, fuel shortages, nonpotable water, crimes of violence, and attacks on American troops.

The Bush administration decided to upscale the reconstruction effort by devoting more resources and putting a prominent statesman favored by both the State Department and the Pentagon, L. Paul Bremer, in charge. Bremer determined early that half measures would not do and decided to totally disband the Iraqi Army and to ban a far larger proportion of Ba'athists from government employment than Garner had considered wise. Iraq would not merely be tinkered with; it would be rebuilt from the ground up. Whatever the long-term advantages of such a dramatic renewal, the short-term effect was leaving large numbers of soldiers unemployed and Ba'athists desperate. Many of these Ba'athists had blood on their hands and knew what their fate would be if they gave up local levers of power. These men were fighting for their lives. Others saw livelihoods slipping away and believed they had nothing to lose by joining the diehards.

Iraqis continued to attack American tactical units but had no more success than they had during the course of earlier combat. Even when isolated, Bradley platoons generated volumes of fire that lightly armed assailants could not withstand, and armored reinforcements were generally close at hand. The residual Iraqi resistance soon turned its attention to sniping at convoys. Since most supplies still flowed into central Iraq from far-off Kuwait, there was no lack of convoys to choose from. The RPG was the Iraqi weapon of choice. If the attackers could pick off a truck or two from a distance, they could hope to escape before retaliation followed. The Americans tightened their convoy procedures, embedded tactical vehicles, gravitated toward routes with open shoulders, secured key terrain en route, and rehearsed countermeasures. Potshots at armed convoys became riskier, with fewer of the attackers

Desert Boots, 2003

getting away. Convoy security did become expensive, however. Bradleys escorting convoys began to average 1,200 miles a month rather than the customary 800 miles a year and thus had to change tracks every sixty days rather than biannually.

Rationalization of the American logistical structure in Iraq inevitably led to elaborate base camps, logistical support areas into which supplies of all types would muster. These and other facilities became the targets of daring mortar attacks as Ba'athists attempted to lob a few rounds into a base camp and then flee into the darkness. Infantry companies deployed to secure the base camps played cat and mouse to hunt down the mortarmen. At Logistics Support Activity (LSA) ANACONDA north of Baghdad, one enterprising Bradley company commander was in pursuit of the source of a recent mortar volley when a helicopter overhead reported a puzzling thermal hot spot on ground from which rounds were thought to have come. Returning to that location, the company commander unearthed a recently fired mortar from the soft sand. The Americans had been attempting to apprehend a mortar party fleeing in a pickup truck or on foot with their weapon, when instead the attackers had fired their weapon, buried it, and then drifted off unarmed. A quick search of the area revealed ten men hiding in a chicken coop. The local farmer who owned the chickens did not know the men, whom the Americans quickly apprehended. They unearthed two more mortars in the course of the night.

Over time the preferred Iraqi method of attack shifted from direct fire and mortars, both increasingly dangerous to use, to improvised explosive devices. Often adapted from munitions or mines, these could be planted along roadways to detonate when run over or perhaps by remote control. A few men could employ such a device with relatively little risk to themselves. The devices were indiscriminant, however; as

Street Fight, *Elzie R. Golden, 2004*

the American soldiers became warier and their vehicles more protected, the victims were often innocent Iraqis.

As grim as the Phase IV combat could occasionally be, it did not approach previous guerrilla warfare in scale or intensity. Even in the seemingly embattled Sunni region north and west of Baghdad, only a tiny fraction of the resident manpower engaged in active hostilities. The proportion of the population actively hostile and under arms was at least two orders of magnitude smaller than the American experience in Vietnam or the Russian experience in Afghanistan. American casualty rates were correspondingly smaller as well.

Resistance proved more akin to terrorism than to guerrilla warfare as most envision it. Foreign terrorists flowed into the country to join the fight. Soft targets such as unprotected oil pipelines, refineries, water mains, and the unarmed Iraqis attempting to restore them became popular for the terrorists. Attempts to assassinate Americans guarding hospitals, banks, and schools transitioned to attacks on the Iraqi security personnel who eventually replaced them. Even UN relief workers, who often eschewed American protection, came under attack. The most egregious such attack was a truck-bombing of a UN compound on 19 August 2003 that killed at least twenty-three people, including Brazilian Vieira de Mello, the highly respected head of mission. The terrorists were determined to reverse whatever progress Iraq was making in the direction the coalition preferred, regardless of the suffering the Iraqi people would endure. The terrorists also aimed for purely civilian targets, both to reinforce a sense of insecurity and to promote trouble between the ethnic groups. Horrific suicide bombings of Shi'ite pilgrims and Kurdish well-wishers on respective religious holidays were cases in point.

President Bush had uneven results in attempting to garner international support for his efforts. As of October 2003 the British sustained a division in Iraq and the Poles, Italians, Spaniards, Ukrainians, and a few others each contributed yet another, coming to about 30,000 allied troops as compared to 146,000 Americans. To this add 60,000 Iraqis by that time assisting in coalition-sponsored security. Financial support was problematic, and Bush presented a bill for $87 billion to the U.S. Congress. Many nations did agree to forgive much of Iraq's foreign debt, removing a major obstacle to eventual recovery. Costs in lives and treasure proved contentious as a political issue, exacerbated by a failure to find the weapons of mass destruction so prominent in the original logic for the war. Nations not yet participating indicated an unwillingness to do so without a more substantial role for the United Nations in rebuilding postwar Iraq, yet there was no guarantee they would be forthcoming with troops and money even if that larger UN role was arranged. For better or worse, the United States had to continue the struggle or face incalculable international consequences.

The American response remained vigorous and attempted a balance between developing rapport with and support from the average Iraqi and smashing diehard Ba'athists and terrorists. Across most of the country, schools and hospitals were functioning normally within a few months. Local councils, some elected and some appointed, took on most aspects of local governance. Iraqi police and security guards progressed from coalition-sponsored training through joint patrols

Hussein Shortly after His Capture in Tikrit

497

General Schoomaker

with the allies to assuming full responsibility. With policemen back on the streets, the worst of the crime wave subsided. By September over 60,000 Iraqis were employed in coalition-sponsored security activities, and many local leaders had their own tribal or clan militias or contingents of personal bodyguards. American soldiers were happy when they no longer found themselves pulling guard in front of schools, banks, hospitals, and museums or enforcing traffic control or curfews—where they felt like sitting ducks. This freed them for other missions.

If the carrot was such nation-building activities, the stick was night-time raids to seize Ba'athist diehards and terrorist imports. With persistent coalition presence, intelligence improved as a population more confident in its own security became confident enough to inform. One by one, regime adherents identified on the deck of cards fell into coalition hands. Saddam's sons Uday and Qusay perished in a spectacular shootout. Foreign mercenaries were apprehended en route from the borders, flush with cash they had been paid to kill Americans. Tons of weapons and ammunition were uncovered and destroyed. On December 14, 2003, American soldiers pulled Saddam Hussein himself out of a tiny hole in which he was hiding near his hometown of Tikrit. They found valuable documents with him, and bit by bit the Ba'athist terrorist infrastructure was further disassembled and destroyed. Whatever Iraq's future, Saddam Hussein's regime was a thing of the past.

The capture of Saddam Hussein did not, contrary to some expectations, "break the back" of the by-now decentralized Iraqi insurgency. In fact, the extent of Hussein's influence in the growing insurgency was doubtful and the insurgency continued to gain strength even after his capture and execution. Each hopeful trend or development that seemed to portend increased effectiveness of the Iraqi government or decreased intensity of insurgent attacks was followed by renewed violence that continued to spiral out of control. While U.S. military and political leaders tried to move quickly to place more responsibility on an interim Iraqi government and its fledgling military and police forces, the ill-trained Iraqi forces failed time and again to step up to the mark. The drafting of a Transitional Administrative Law (TAL) in the spring of 2004 seemed a positive step; but the reluctance of the three major ethnic/religious groups in the country—Sunni Arab, Shi'ite Arab, and Kurd—to compromise on power sharing or even to agree on the nature of the proposed new government stymied all attempts at effective governance.

FUTURE COMBAT SYSTEM

The Future Combat System (FCS) was an unprecedented attempt to capitalize on emerging technologies and to develop and field the majority of a brigade-level unit's combat equipment as a single, integrated package. Its most visible component was a family of combat vehicles sharing a common chassis to reduce logistical and maintenance requirements. The main differences from the existing force were its highly integrated computer networks and unmanned reconnaissance platforms that were to provide the lightly armored force its early-warning and long-distance strike capabilities. The cost of the system, combined with the newly emerging requirements of the War on Terrorism, caused Congress to drop funding for the full program. However, the Army changed its focus and began applying "spinoff" technologies from the FCS to the force in an evolutionary rather than a revolutionary fashion.

The military situation in Iraq took a turn for the worse in March 2004 when four American contractors were killed in Fallujah, a Sunni insurgent stronghold, and their charred and mutilated remains were hung from a bridge for all to see. U.S. Marine and Army mechanized forces moved to clean out the city during Operation VIGILANT RESOLVE in April; but their initial success was frustrated when under Iraqi pressure U.S. Coalition Provisional Authority Chief Paul Bremer halted and withdrew U.S. units as they were on the verge of success. When ill-led and poorly organized Iraqi Army and police forces were ordered to Fallujah by their government to replace the U.S. units, they were completely unprepared for the reality of battle and most deserted the field. A second attempt to organize an Iraqi counterstrike, the formation of the "Fallujah Brigade," failed as well when it was infiltrated by insurgents and its leader, a former Republican Guard general, was arrested for war crimes committed during the 1991 Shi'a uprising. The result was an emboldened insurgency, safe within a new sanctuary, and an embarrassed and weakened U.S., Iraqi, and Coalition force seemingly helpless against it.

The enemy success at Fallujah seemed just one of the instances of the emergence of other factions that sought to capitalize on perceived U.S. weakness. That same month the radical leader of a Shi'ite faction, Moqtada al-Sadr, unleashed his militia—the self-styled Mahdi Army—in a series of attacks on U.S. forces. The militiamen seized radio and television stations, blew up bridges, and threatened numerous U.S. supply routes in their attacks on U.S. forces. Attempts to arrest some key followers of the fiery cleric and close down one of his newspapers failed, leading to greater violence and calls by him for a national "jihad" against the American "occupiers." In response, elements of the 2d Armored Cavalry Regiment pushed into Sadr City, a Mahdi Army stronghold in the northeastern, and poorest, section

STRYKER

In October 1999 General Eric K. Shinseki, the Army Chief of Staff, announced the creation of a prototype organization to pave the way for wide-ranging changes in Army doctrine, organizational design, and leader development. The Army selected a unit at Fort Lewis, Washington, the 3d Brigade, 2d Infantry Division, to convert to the new medium-weight design. On November 16, 2000, the Army announced that the medium-weight brigade would be equipped with a wheeled, third-generation light armored vehicle (LAV III) that the Canadian armed forces were acquiring. On February 27, 2002, the Army christened the medium-weight wheeled vehicle the Stryker after two unrelated infantrymen with the same last name who had each received the Medal of Honor. The 3d Brigade, 2d Infantry Division, deployed to Iraq in November 2003. The creation of the first Stryker-equipped brigade combat team, from inception to combat deployment, spanned a little more than four years.

of Baghdad. Units of the 1st and 2d Infantry Divisions, including the 2d Division's 3d Brigade equipped with the new Stryker combat vehicles, conducted operations to quell violence in An Najaf, Al Kut, and Karbala. But each time U.S. forces would complete an operation and drive off or kill the insurgents and move on to the next crisis spot, the resistance would reemerge behind them. The new Iraqi security forces were unable to hold what had been cleared by the U.S. military. This led to a series of frustrating "whack-a-mole" operations, so called after the popular amusement parlor game where a player hits the head of an emerging mole to "kill it," another appears, and then still another in seemingly endless succession.

U.S. efforts at pacifying Iraq—while simultaneously attempting to stand up an Iraqi government viewed as legitimate by its own people—at times suffered from self-inflicted wounds as dangerous as the insurgent attacks. It was important that the U.S. forces maintain their standing as an entity that was helping Iraq as a disciplined and ethical military. The U.S. posture in Iraq and around the world was certainly not helped when in April 2004 graphic photographs were released showing U.S. soldiers involved in abusing prisoners at the Abu Ghraib prison—a prison with an already notorious reputation as one of Saddam Hussein's torture factories. The detailed and disturbing photographs released to the world seemed to show U.S. soldiers physically and psychologically abusing prisoners. Further investigations highlighted a breakdown in authority and control within the prison and led to numerous charges and courts-martial. However, the damage was done: no matter how much the U.S. soldiers found culpable were punished, the images remained burned into the minds of the entire world.

It was soon apparent that all hopes of U.S. military and political leaders that the occupation could be quickly wrapped up and U.S. troops withdrawn by the end of the year were doomed to disappointment. The U.S. Army's V Corps, commanded by Lt. Gen. Ricardo S. Sanchez, was designated Coalition Joint Task Force–7 (CJTF-7) on June 15, 2003, and was the principal headquarters charged with the Iraq mission. But by mid-2004 the deteriorating security situation prompted the U.S. Central Command (CENTCOM) to create three new headquarters. In preparation for granting Iraq full sovereignty on June 30, CENTCOM redesignated CJTF-7 as Headquarters, Multi-National Force–Iraq (MNF-I), and temporarily placed General Sanchez in command. On July 1 Sanchez was replaced by General George W. Casey, Jr., who as a full general and former Vice Chief of Staff of the Army served to bring additional prestige, visibility, and clout to the position. Along with MNF-I, Casey had under him two new major subordinate commands: Multi-National Corps–Iraq (MNC-I) to handle the operational and tactical fight and Multi-National Security Transition Command–Iraq (MNSTC-I) to coordinate the training of Iraq's security forces.

One of General Casey's major goals in 2004 was to improve the security posture of the country enough so that the national elections, planned for December 2004 or January 2005, would be conducted with a minimum of violence. The ultimate legitimacy of the Iraqi government and the U.S. hope that such legitimacy would improve the chances for a speedy exit from the country depended on those elections running reasonably smoothly.

The experiences in the Balkans and Afghanistan and during IRAQI FREEDOM suggested the need to deploy smaller, nimbler, self-contained units—tactical and operational "small change"—to fit contingency circumstances.

Maintaining a sense of safety in Iraq, however, continued to be elusive. U.S. security operations, such as Operation Baton Rouge conducted in October by the 1st Infantry Division in the troublesome city of Samarra about seventy-five miles north of Baghdad, showed the degree to which the Sunni insurgents were dug in. Elements of the Big Red One fought a series of block-to-block, house-to-house fights in Samarra accompanied by a handful of poorly trained and equipped Iraqi soldiers. The division killed dozens of insurgents, discovered numerous caches of improvised explosive devices (IEDs), and captured many stockpiles of small arms. Yet Samarra continued to be a hotbed of insurgent violence even after what appeared to have been a successful operation. Again it proved impossible for the fledgling Iraqi security forces, in particular the venal and sectarian-dominated national police, to hold onto the gains made by combat operations.

After Samarra, U.S. forces turned their attention to the troublesome city of Fallujah, where the abortive Coalition offensive operation the previous April had seemed only to strengthen the insurgents. Now in Operation Al-Fajr (or The Dawn), called by U.S. forces Operation Phantom Fury, U.S. units and their Iraqi counterparts were determined to clear out the city. Beginning on November 8, two U.S. Marine regimental combat teams, each with an attached U.S. Army mechanized battalion, led the way into the city. Iraqi Army units, this time better prepared and led, were present to help secure the city once it was taken. The allies had instructed all noncombatants to leave the city before the attack in an attempt to reduce civilian casualties and have fewer civilians for the insurgents to hide behind. The combined-arms attack with helicopters, artillery, airstrikes, and armor slowly and methodically cleared out the city block by block. In the final phase of the operation, Iraqi Army and police established outposts, police stations, and security roadblocks throughout Fallujah and began slowly to allow citizens back in to start reconstruction. With approximately 2,000 insurgents killed and 1,200 captured at the cost

George W. Casey, Jr. (1948–)

General George W. Casey, Jr., Commander of Multi-National Forces–Iraq from July 1, 2004, to February 10, 2007, was a member of a distinguished Army family. His father, Maj. Gen. George W. Casey, Sr., Commanding General of the 1st Cavalry Division, had been one of the most senior officers killed in Vietnam when his helicopter crashed on July 7, 1970. The younger Casey was commissioned into the infantry through ROTC at Georgetown University in 1970 before embarking on a career that encompassed a variety of command and staff jobs including Commanding General, 1st Armored Division; Director of the Joint Staff; Vice Chief of Staff of the Army; and MNF-I Commander. Upon relinquishing command of forces in Iraq to General David H. Petraeus, General Casey returned to Washington in April 2007 to assume the position of thirty-sixth Chief of Staff of the U.S. Army.

of 70 Americans and 7 Iraqis killed, the city was liberated and no longer served as a sanctuary for the insurgents or as a base for their operations.

The promise of an improved security climate in Iraq seemed fulfilled with the peaceful and genuinely popular countrywide elections in January 2005. For the first time, Iraqis got a chance to vote and take charge of their own future. There were remarkably few security incidents as Iraqis guarded the polls with U.S. units generally out of sight in a backup role. Proud Iraqis, many shown on worldwide television brandishing their purple-inked forefingers as proof that they had voted, exercised their new franchise despite threats of violence and elected a slate of candidates for a national government. However, the boycott of the elections by the minority Sunnis—no longer the dominant political force in the country—and the mechanism of voting by slates of candidates rather than for individuals that skewed the vote toward religious party candidates were ill omens for the future.

Contrary again to all hopes and expectations, the nationwide elections in Iraq did not diminish the level of violence in the country or "defang" the insurgency. If anything, the elections seemed to isolate even more the Arab-Sunni minority. Al-Qaeda in Iraq, now led by a Jordanian terrorist named Abu Musaab al-Zarqawi, capitalized on their fears and began a systematic campaign to terrorize Shi'a Muslims in order to instigate them to conduct revenge attacks on Sunnis in an ever-downward spiral of violence. A few diehard Ba'athists continued their attacks, as well, in their attempt to turn back the clock. Added to this lethal mixture was the still-powerful Sadr whose Mahdi Army had not disbanded but had merely taken a lower profile after the rebellion had failed in April and was still strong in Baghdad and Basra. The militiamen had the advantage of being able to infiltrate the Shi'ite-dominated army and national police and use those official covers as they conducted their own terror attacks. In addition, with the Shi'ites in firm control of the government but the government itself only a shaky coalition, politicians of all parties hesitated to move against Sadr or oppose his followers because of the possible political consequences.

The need to stabilize Iraq while retaining as few troops as possible in that troubled country created a strategic dilemma both to those who wanted to leave Iraq quickly and to those who felt that the United States needed to stay and pursue a new strategy to "win." The result was a measure of strategic policy drift as General John P. Abizaid, the CENTCOM commander who had replaced General Tommy R. Franks in 2003, directed U.S. and Coalition forces to slowly withdraw from the cities into more easily defensible base camps with the goal of turning over more security functions, and even the administration of whole provinces, as quickly as possible to a slowly improving Iraqi government and army. This would, in time, perhaps allow U.S. forces to leave and in the short run minimize casualties. But in order to ensure that security was maintained, many military thinkers and policymakers foresaw that more U.S. forces were needed in Iraq. However, the stress and strain on the constantly deploying Army units made that politically and practically difficult.

The stress on the force, especially on the U.S. Army whose units, even when divided into the more numerous modular brigades, found themselves rotated in and out of Iraq with ever-decreasing time for training and "dwell-time" back at home station, had a powerful impact on any strategic plan. Enlistment rates were low, and ever-greater incentives were needed to maintain the end strength of the Army. A broken Army could not be expected to be effective in the long run in any attempt to stabilize Iraq. Yet "cutting and running," as some critics referred to it, might well damage the force and U.S. interests even more.

On the positive side, despite the fact that the War on Terrorism was the toughest test yet of the volunteer Army, retention rates continued high with over 100 percent of expected reenlistments being achieved year after year. Despite family strain, the continuing dangers of deaths or debilitating wounds, and the back-to-back rotations, the Army was still a well-trained and disciplined force capable of completing a mission that was clearly laid out for it. And in a departure from the national climate during the Vietnam War, the nation continued to provide moral support for the troops even while remaining divided by the policy that had launched them into Iraq in the first place.

Despite the continuing security challenges and under some pressure from Washington, General Casey began planning on drawing down the American forces in Iraq beginning in 2006. He planned to reduce the number of combat brigades in the country from fifteen to ten in the course of the year with the intent of forcing the Iraqis to shoulder more of the responsibility for their own security and governance. The U.S. presence could not be sustained indefinitely, and he and other senior Army leaders were fully aware of the strain on the Army as it faced back-to-back rotations into Iraq with the additional stress of having to maintain a small but important force level in Afghanistan, the Horn of Africa, and other locations around the world. All of his plans were put on hold, however, when the Golden Mosque at Samarra, one of Shi'a Islam's most holy shrines in a city that was still immersed in violence, was heavily damaged in an explosion on February 22 perpetrated by the terrorists of al-Qaeda in Iraq. Zarqawi's hopes of fomenting ethnic and sectarian strife seemed about to be fulfilled.

In the months following the bombing of the Golden Mosque, it appeared that Iraq was sliding into such a high level of ethnic violence and sectarian fighting that some commentators deemed it to be in a state of civil war, with the United States and other members of a dwindling Coalition caught in the middle. The violent sectarian cleansing of neighborhoods accelerated as Sunnis were driven from their homes by Shi'ites and Shi'ites from theirs by Sunnis in a paroxysm of violence and hatred. Internal refugees numbered in the tens of thousands while many of those who could afford to leave the country did so. According to some reports, over one hundred fifty bodies of dead Iraqis, murdered execution style, were being dumped on the streets of Baghdad every night to be discovered every morning. The spiraling level of violence did not seem to abate even when U.S. airstrikes killed Zarqawi, the leader of al-Qaeda in Iraq. Nor did it help when Iraq had its first regularly elected government put in place on May 20, 2006. The new prime minister, Nouri al-Maliki, the leader of a powerful Shi'ite faction who had spent years in exile in Syria and Iran, was viewed with great suspicion by the Arab Sunnis and seen by many outsiders as either a weak tool of the religious parties or a pawn of the Iranians.

Militarily the choices for the United States were few: withdraw as quickly as possible and let the Iraqis sort out their own problems (even if it meant a Shi'ite victory in a civil war with the possibility of increasing Iranian influence as a result) or increase the U.S. force level enough to make a dramatic difference in security levels throughout the country with the concomitant strain upon the already stressed force. The first strategy hoped that Iraqis would "step up to the plate" once they saw the U.S. forces leaving and further believed that U.S. forces were a part of the problem—an irritant that once removed would help preempt some of the claims of the insurgents that they were only fighting the "foreign occupiers." Increasing U.S. forces was the only other alternative, but not one without considerable risk.

The second strategy of a "surge" of forces relied upon the belief that a larger force, even if only slightly larger, could prove decisive if used properly. If the additional troops were committed to securing the people in accordance with counterinsurgency doctrine, the result might be a lull in the violence. This could provide the necessary "breathing space" for the new government of Iraq to make the political deals necessary to forge a more broad-based, national, representative government. Either way, the risks were great but the vital interests of the United States in the Middle East—regional security, protection of allies, and the free flow of essential oil—militated against a precipitous withdrawal. Such an exit in defeat from the region would shake the very foundations of America's leadership role in the Middle East with only terrorists and the states that sponsored them being the gainers. U.S. casualties remained relatively low but were on the rise in 2006. By the end of that year some 2,400 Americans, most of them Army, had been killed in action and over 20,000 had been wounded. Many had lost limbs or suffered severe head injuries from evermore powerful roadside bombs. The status quo was simply not the answer.

The Doctrine

The U.S. Army, one of the quickest militaries in the world to adapt to new battlefield conditions and adjust training, organization, and equipment to new circumstances, had not been complacent as the war shifted from conventional attack to security assistance to fighting an insurgency. In late 2005 and into 2006, the Army and Marine Corps teamed up to reenergize the doctrine necessary to prepare, intellectually and practically, for counterinsurgency operations in Iraq and Afghanistan. These operations reemphasized population control, police-like functions, information operations, and nation building. Both services had a long history of fighting such wars, especially the grueling struggle in Vietnam only thirty years before; but both had turned their backs on what they had learned from that conflict as soon as they could in order to focus on new competencies necessary to fight a conventional conflict in Europe. Neither service, despite a temporary surge in interest in low-intensity conflict in the 1980s, had retained the doctrinal focus or training commitment necessary to conduct counterinsurgency operations. Such operations were perhaps the most challenging of all missions to prepare for, given the emphasis on political negotiations, reconstruction activities, regional expertise, language skills, and other

David H. Petraeus (1952–)

General David H. Petraeus was commissioned into the Infantry from the U.S. Military Academy at West Point in 1974. In addition to the usual assignments of company and battalion command and schooling at the Advanced and Command and General Staff Officers Courses, Petraeus took the unusual step of earning a doctorate in International Relations at Princeton in 1987 with a dissertation entitled "The American Military and the Lessons of Vietnam: A Study of Military Influence and the Use of Force in the Post-Vietnam Era." Before taking command of Multi-National Force–Iraq in 2007, he served as the Commanding General of the 101st Airborne Division (Air Assault) in the opening days of Operation IRAQI FREEDOM; as the Commanding General of the Multi-National Security Transition Command–Iraq; and the Commanding General of the Combined Arms Center, Fort Leavenworth. From MNF-I, Petraeus was given command of U.S. Central Command in Tampa, Florida, in October 2008.

nontraditional military skills necessary for success. Even the U.S. Army Special Warfare Center and School at Fort Bragg, North Carolina, traditionally the Army center tasked to prepare to wage insurgencies and counterinsurgencies, had become dominated in recent years by special operations elements that conducted direct-action missions. Those more "glamorous" missions had received much of the attention and funding for the past decade. Those officers who saw the Iraq war turning into a protracted counterinsurgency fight, however, began to turn their minds and energies to writing a new doctrine that would capture their experiences, provide them an intellectual focus, and set in motion the training institutions to prepare the force for that mission.

In late 2006, Lt. Gen. David H. Petraeus of the Army's Combined Arms Center and Lt. Gen. James F. Amos, Deputy Commandant of the Marine Corps' Combat Development Command, put their signatures on a new Field Manual 3–24 (Marine Corps Warfighting Publication 3–33.5), *Counterinsurgency*, to provide the doctrinal basis for the reemphasis on this mission. Although not promulgated without controversy (some critics thought it overemphasized soft power and the nonmilitary aspect of operations and thus took the focus off the military's primary mission of warfighting and so-called kinetic, or strike, operations), the new doctrine was widely hailed as reflecting the reality of the struggle in Iraq. It returned the attention of the institutional and operational Army to those skills that had lain dormant for decades but were now needed to fight the continuing Global War on Terrorism in Iraq, Afghanistan, and other locations around the world.

This new counterinsurgency doctrine, together with a companion doctrine on stability operations published in 2009, gave the Army and Marine Corps the intellectual and training tools to prosecute the fight in

Iraq. But was it too late? Had the situation in Iraq by 2007 deteriorated so dramatically that no doctrine, however useful and thoughtful, and no Army, however skilled and battle tested, could retrieve the Iraqis from the headlong rush into civil war and chaos? Was the stress on the Army and its family members so severe that its recruitment and retention base would crumble and no longer be able to sustain the fight effectively even if ordered? Would the national resolve continue to back the troops in the fight as the complexity of the struggle only seemed to compound the lack of trust of many in the very rationale for the war in the first place? And even if the military was successful, would it be able to do what was necessary to help solve the critical political questions that had to be addressed in order to establish the basis for a free, independent, and stable Iraq? The very success of the long war in Iraq hung in the balance.

The Surge

The crisis in Iraq in 2006–2007 led to a number of critical military and political decisions. On February 10, 2007, the man who was one of the moving forces behind the new focus on counterinsurgency, General Petraeus, took command of Multi-National Forces–Iraq. He had testified in his confirmation hearings in favor of an increase, styled by some a Surge, of U.S. forces into Iraq. This would be the first necessary step to halt the slide into civil war, to provide the forces necessary for the exercise of a robust counterinsurgency strategy to restore a measure of stability and security for the Iraqi people, and to signal to Iraq and the region the resolve of the United States to finish what it had started. Although far from being the sole originator of the Surge idea, it was now General Petraeus who would be most closely identified with its success or failure. He believed that in a counterinsurgency campaign,

SPEC. ROSS A. MCGINNIS (1987–2006)

On December 4, 2006, while serving as an M2 .50-caliber machine gunner of the 1st Platoon, Company C, 1st Battalion, 26th Infantry, then Private First Class McGinnis was on mounted patrol with his platoon in Adhamiyah in Baghdad. An insurgent threw a grenade into the open hatch of McGinnis' HMMWV (high mobility multipurpose wheeled vehicle, commonly called a Humvee). Private McGinnis yelled "Grenade!" But then, perhaps realizing that the four other crewmates could not escape the vehicle quickly enough, McGinnis threw himself on the grenade. He absorbed most of the explosion but was mortally wounded while saving his comrades. He was awarded the Medal of Honor posthumously and promoted to specialist.

having "boots on the ground," ground units composed of well-trained, culturally aware soldiers, was the key to local security, building up the host nation's forces, and ultimate success.

The phased arrival of five additional Army combat brigades and two more Marine battalions, a total of around 30,000 troops, would provide the extra forces to help train more Iraqi units and begin a series of robust security operations. These operations, focused initially on the key population and political center of the country, Baghdad and its immediate suburbs, would help restore the confidence of the people that their lives and property would be secure. U.S. troops teamed with Iraqi units would man hundreds of small security outposts throughout the city to stabilize the situation. Then, a more carefully planned followup by Iraqi security forces to hold those areas and provide a permanent (and helpful) government presence would tip the balance permanently to the forces of stability.

The military operations surrounding the Surge of U.S. forces were, however, only one of the essential precursors of the main "battle": the battle for political reconciliation in Iraq without which no military gains would be truly permanent. All of the military aspects of the Surge—more troops on the ground, more trainers, more presence of U.S. and Iraqi forces in neighborhoods, more killed or captured terrorists, and more captured bomb factories—were important but could only shape the security conditions on the ground that made political success possible. They could not guarantee that success.

One of the important aspects of that Surge, however, was the renewed sense by all factions, and by all the countries in the region, that the United States was committed to finding a solution and was not about to abandon Iraq. This had, it appears, a positive effect on a number of factions previously opposed to the government who now determined it was time to switch sides and work *with* the government. This initiative, beginning in Al Anbar Province and thus picking up the nickname Anbar Awakening, saw a number of Sunni tribal leaders in the embattled province of Anbar to the west of Baghdad determine that they had had enough of interference in their local affairs by heavy-handed and violent al-Qaeda in Iraq and wanted arms to defend themselves. These predominantly Sunni tribes had previously supported the Hussein regime and thus were not trusted by the new Shi'ite-led government. However, even though it was a risk, the United States decided to support these tribes, pay them, and work to convince the Iraqi government to integrate them into their security forces in the future.

The Anbar Awakening and similar movements in nearby provinces held out the promise that Sunni tribes could fight back against al-Qaeda, maintain order in their provinces, and provide the confidence that they would not be cut out of future political settlements with the national government. Despite mistrust on both sides, this Awakening held out the promise of both security and political settlement, provided the government handled this opportunity well. While not a direct result of more troops in their province, the Surge did provide the necessary reassurance of continued U.S. support that made the Anbar Awakening possible, even if it could not guarantee its ultimate success. That lay in the hands of the Iraqi government.

Operations such as the long-planned Baghdad security plan went into effect in early February 2007 spearheaded by troops of MNC-I commanded by Lt. Gen. Raymond T. Odierno. The U.S. Army also faced the challenge of implementing the ambitious concept of bringing security to Iraq while absorbing the new troops of the Surge over a six-month period. As security gained by these troops and the Anbar Awakening spread to more areas, the Iraqi Army began to gain more confidence. The Maliki administration finally moved decisively against Mahdi Army strongholds in Baghdad and Basra in early 2008, and it began to look as if a strong national government that represented all the major parties in Iraq was at least possible. With the change of administration in the United States in early 2009 and President Barack H. Obama's decision to retain Secretary of Defense Robert M. Gates (who had replaced Donald Rumsfeld in December 2006), an Iraqi political solution and gradual withdrawal of U.S. troops became distinct possibilities. However, as force levels in Iraq slowly decreased, the other major front of the War on Terrorism, Afghanistan, began to be recognized by more national leaders as needing additional attention.

Back to Afghanistan

In early 2002 General Tommy R. Franks, Commander of the U.S. Central Command, established a new command to oversee operations in what appeared to be a relatively peaceful Afghanistan. General Franks and his staff were increasingly preoccupied with planning the impending invasion of Iraq. They hoped that a stronger command in Afghanistan would be able to maintain control of operations there while they devoted their attention to the preparation for the march to Baghdad. As things stood, the headquarters that commanded conventional forces in Afghanistan, Coalition Forces Land Component Command (Forward),

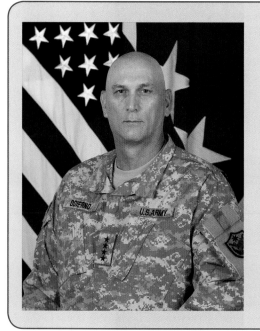

RAYMOND T. ODIERNO (1954–)

General Raymond T. Odierno was commissioned into the Artillery in 1976 at the U.S. Military Academy at West Point. He served in numerous command and staff positions during his career in Germany, Saudi Arabia, the Balkans, and the United States. He commanded the 4th Infantry Division in the early days of Operation IRAQI FREEDOM and the III Corps at Fort Hood and later in Iraq as it became the Multi-National Corps–Iraq in 2006. He took command of the Multi-National Force–Iraq from General Petraeus in September 2008.

was very small, being little more than an augmented division tactical command post of the 10th Mountain Division (Light).

To create a more capable headquarters, in May 2002 General Franks established Combined Joint Task Force–180 and placed it in the charge of Lt. Gen. Dan K. McNeill, Commanding General of the XVIII Airborne Corps. General McNeill formed the new headquarters around that of his own corps, which deployed from Fort Bragg, North Carolina, and augmented it with joint and Coalition staff and liaison officers. With a larger staff that incorporated international elements, General Franks hoped that CJTF-180 would be more capable of overseeing tactical operations while simultaneously taking control of an increasingly complex military and political situation at the operational level.

Taking charge of Combined Joint Task Force–180, General McNeill reorganized the command structure of his subordinate elements. The units of Maj. Gen. Franklin L. Hagenbeck's 10th Mountain Division, which were already in Afghanistan, continued operations against anti-Coalition forces as Combined Joint Task Force MOUNTAIN. That task force was replaced in June by units of the 82d Airborne Division. The Special Operations Forces units hunting for fugitive al-Qaeda and Taliban leaders—including Osama bin Laden and Mullah Omar—fell under the new Combined Joint Special Operations Task Force (CJSOTF). The Combined Joint Civil-Military Operations Task Force (CJCMOTF), comprised mostly of civil affairs units and individual augmentees, conducted humanitarian assistance missions in conjunction with international development and relief agencies.

Combined Joint Task Force–180 forces conducted a series of military operations to keep the Taliban off balance throughout 2002, 2003, and 2004. Typically, these efforts involved series of assaults conducted by heliborne company- or battalion-size units against small bands of insurgents that invariably suffered tactical defeats if they resisted. In August 2003, for example, Operation MOUNTAIN VIPER targeted anti-Coalition forces throughout Afghanistan with the aim of denying them sanctuary and destroying organized resistance. Operation MOUNTAIN RESOLVE followed in November and targeted Hezb-i-Islami Gulbuddin, a militia led by the Pashtun warlord Gulbuddin Hekmatyar, and other insurgent groups active in the mountainous region of the Hindu Kush near the border with Pakistan. The next month, by striking Taliban insurgents in Operation AVALANCHE, Maj. Gen. Lloyd J. Austin (who had replaced General Hagenbeck in command of the 10th Mountain Division) sought to set favorable security conditions for the grand assembly, or *loya jirga*, which would meet in January 2004 to frame a new constitution for Afghanistan. Operation MOUNTAIN BLIZZARD took place from January to March 2004, targeting anti-Coalition forces operating along the southern and southeastern border with Pakistan. A follow-on operation, MOUNTAIN STORM, began in March 2004. All these operations inflicted heavy casualties on the scattered insurgents and resulted in the discovery of hundreds of caches of weapons and ammunition. When the first units of the Afghan National Army began to operate alongside Coalition forces, they also helped to demonstrate early signs of the viability of Afghanistan's fledgling democratic government. However, the insurgents were resilient and used the terrain and nearby sanctuaries in Pakistan to keep up the fight.

The Afghan National Army was one of the first institutions established by the interim Afghan government, and it would soon become an important element of U.S. and Coalition strategy in Operation ENDURING FREEDOM. At first, in early 2002, the training of the Afghan National Army was the responsibility of the North Atlantic Treaty Organization's (NATO's) International Security Assistance Force (ISAF). During this stage, British and Turkish troops formed the recruits into *kandaks*, battalion-size units of about 600 soldiers. In 2002, the ranks of the Afghan National Army numbered between 2,000 and 3,000 volunteers. Initial plans called for five *kandaks* to report to a corps-level headquarters based in Kabul, but later plans expanded the size of the Army to more than 67,000 soldiers. Combined Joint Task Force–180 received the mission to take control of the training process and assigned it to the Combined Joint-Civil Military Operations Task Force. Later, CENTCOM established an Office of Military Cooperation–Afghanistan in Kabul to oversee training and to coordinate security assistance efforts under the command of Maj. Gen. Karl W. Eikenberry.

In July 2003, General Abizaid succeeded General Franks as Commander, U.S. Central Command. General Abizaid wanted to create a coherent and cohesive strategy by synchronizing the ongoing effort to build the Afghan National Army with other international efforts to create a police and judiciary for the Afghan government; to disarm, demobilize, and reintegrate armed factions and militias into civil society; and to confront a growing problem of narcotics production. Toward that end, he took steps to forge communications and working procedures between military commands and civilian agencies in Afghanistan. He also began work to establish a new command, initially named Combined Forces Command–Central Asia and then Combined Forces Command–Afghanistan, which would help ensure better cooperation with the Army's international and interagency partners.

Maj. Gen. David W. Barno assumed command of the new organization in October 2003 and immediately formulated a new strategy. The focus in Afghanistan thus shifted from counterterrorism to counterinsurgency. Identifying the Afghan people as its center of gravity, or decisive strategic focus, the approach sought to help win their allegiance to their new government by combining security and reconstruction actions into a coherent master plan. To build support for the approach, General Barno established close connections with U.S. embassy personnel and Afghan government leaders and began a public communications campaign directed at the Afghan people to emphasize the accomplishments of their own government.

The year 2004 began with signs of hope for the campaign in Afghanistan. Since Coalition forces had produced an unbroken string of tactical victories, General Barno wanted to follow them with more robust counterinsurgency and reconstruction operations, which he hoped would bring long-term strategic success. He lacked the forces at the time to implement such an ambitious plan; however, he had some reasons to be optimistic. The *loya jirga* that began in January 2004 approved an Afghan constitution on February 5 that created a new legal and political framework for the fledgling government. In April the Afghan National Army demonstrated its increased effectiveness when its troops quelled a revolt by militia in the Faryab Province located in the north of Afghanistan along the nation's border with Turkmenistan. Cooperation with Pakistan along Afghanistan's unstable southern border also seemed to be improving. Pakistani forces were engaging Taliban and other anti-Coalition forces in their own territory with greater frequency than before.

The situation in Afghanistan, however, was far from secure. The nation's President, Hamid Karzai, had an interim appointment to office, and it would take months to organize and carry out a national election. Determined to disrupt or prevent that election, anti-Coalition forces in Afghanistan were demonstrating an ability to learn from their tactical defeats at the hands of Coalition forces. Recognizing the futility of trying to meet Coalition troops in force-on-force engagements, for example, they had begun to adopt tactics from the rapidly escalating insurgency in Iraq, including the use of improvised explosive devices and later suicide bombers. Meanwhile, if the region near the capital of Kabul was relatively safe because of the strong presence of NATO forces, local governance and security were still uncertain for most Afghans.

This lack of security made it more difficult for the Afghan national government and the Coalition to begin the task of rebuilding a shattered nation still suffering from decades of Soviet occupation, civil war, and Taliban tyranny. To assist in rebuilding the nation, planners from U.S. Central Command, the Department of State, and the U.S. Agency for International Development established a number of Provincial Reconstruction Teams. These groups were composed of small units of troops (for security) augmented with civilian reconstruction, humanitarian assistance, and governance experts. These teams expanded in size and type over the next few years and increasingly included a greater number of teams organized and manned by NATO partners. By mid-2008 there would be twenty-six teams operating throughout Afghanistan, twelve under U.S. control and the rest under the command of various NATO partners.

New units continued to rotate in and out of Afghanistan as the various Coalition headquarters shifted names and focus over the next few years. Brigades of the 82d Airborne Division were replaced by similar units of the 10th Mountain Division; they in turn were replaced in quick succession by units of the 25th Infantry Division, the 173d Airborne Brigade, the 82d Airborne Division, and then elements of the 10th Mountain Division again. Marine, National Guard, and Army Reserve units augmented the Regular Army forces along with individual replacements from all services. Combined Task Force–180 was renamed Combined Task Force–76 in April 2004 to focus on the tactical fight while Combined Forces Command–Afghanistan remained committed to operational and strategic issues. Regional commands were set up in the south, west, and east to combine security with reconstruction responsibilities on an area-support basis. A series of operations followed in 2004 and 2005 (including LIGHTNING RESOLVE and LIGHTNING FREEDOM) focused on keeping the Taliban off balance, especially along the volatile border regions in Paktia and Paktika provinces in the eastern reaches of Afghanistan. Under General Barno's and later General Eikenberry's direction, CJTF-76 (called CJTF-82 in March 2007 and CJTF-101 in April 2008 as the unit headquarters shifted from division to division) synchronized the tactical operations with allied reconstruction and relief initiatives. On September 18, 2005, the soldiers of Combined Joint Task Force–76 replicated the previous year's electoral success by ensuring a largely peaceful parliamentary election.

By the end of 2005 it seemed as if the United States and its international allies had accomplished a great deal in Afghanistan. However, there were disturbing trends in the rugged mountains of the country. In 2006 and 2007 there were indications that the Taliban and its al-Qaeda allies, operating with relative impunity in the sanctuary of the border regions with Pakistan and well-shielded there by fellow Pashtun tribesmen, were determined to retake the initiative. A series of attacks on U.S., Afghan, and Coalition strongpoints and patrols drove up casualties and announced the resurgence of the insurgency. The insurgents gained much of their funding and support from the return of the illegal drug trade in opium and heroin, booming again after years of suppression. All U.S. and allied attempts at crop substitution programs, which attempted to wean farmers off the opium poppy, as well as stepped-up antismuggling campaigns, foundered on the remoteness of the fields and the lucrative nature of the crop.

The campaign for stability in Afghanistan was far from over. Much of the country remained beyond the control of Coalition forces. Many NATO units, handicapped by unique and often highly restrictive rules of engagement, were often unable or unwilling to suppress the resurgent Taliban even after assuming full responsibility for the restive Regional Commands South and East in 2006. President Karzai's government, although bolstered by two successful elections, could not provide consistent or effective governance in many of the provinces outside of Kabul; and Afghan military and security forces remained incapable of operating without foreign assistance. In addition, the endemic corruption of Afghan officials and police contrived to thwart all attempts by Coalition units to get the Afghan people to trust their own government. By late 2008 it seemed apparent to all that Afghanistan was continuing to suffer from endemic insurgency with increasing military and reconstruction efforts needed by the Western allies to prevent it from relapsing into a failed state. As Iraq seemed to quiet down by early 2009, the new administration of President Obama initiated a series of lengthy studies of strategic options and changed the U.S. command structure in Afghanistan as it wrestled with the cost of pursuing a counterinsurgency war in support of a weak Afghan government. Neither the administration nor its often weak and equally hesitant NATO allies saw a clear path to victory over a resurgent Taliban. Afghanistan, needing massive infusions of cash and international help, remained on the very edge of instability as 2009 began.

Transforming While at War

The campaign requirements of the Global War on Terrorism understandably had an effect upon Army Transformation. Generals Gordon R. Sullivan, Dennis J. Reimer, and Shinseki (in the first half of his tenure) had believed that they were in an interval between wars and that they had been afforded an opportunity to prepare for the next one. Operations in Latin America and the Balkans and security requirements around the globe needed daily attention, but the lion's share of their focus could be on the future. Prolonged campaigns in Afghanistan and Iraq forced current operations back into top priority, and new balances had to be struck if the Army was to maintain momentum toward transformation.

By the time General Peter J. Schoomaker became Army Chief of Staff in the summer of 2003, there already was considerable fluidity between the test-bed 4th Infantry Division (Mechanized) experimenting with the most modern digital technologies, the Interim Brigade Combat Teams anticipating Shinseki's Objective Force, and the larger army in the field. Appliqué versions of many of the advances were available to improve upon legacy equipment. Schoomaker's experience was grounded heavily in the Special Operations community with its marked ability to draw off-the-shelf technology for immediate use. Shinseki's Transformation Campaign Plan had, of course, been a forcing function to generate technology to draw upon, especially as more money became available in times of crisis. Believing the term Objective Force implied a neatness of time frames that would be impossible to sustain under wartime circumstances, Schoomaker dropped the use of the terms Objective Force, Interim Force, and Legacy Force in the favor of Current Force and Future Force, while maintaining most of Shinseki's program intact. The Army was no longer in an interval between wars, and technical advances would be applied as quickly as was practical. Development of the Future Combat System (FCS) would continue, but innovations intended for it would be applied to vintage vehicles as well, when practical.

The Operation Iraqi Freedom experience related by Lt. Col. John W. Charlton, Commander of Task Force 1/15 Mechanized Infantry, offers a graphic example of migrations of technology from selected units to the Legacy Force at large, in this case the 3d Infantry Division (Mechanized). Contractors had adapted the full-up Force XXI Battle Command Brigade and Battalion (FBCB2) digital system into a simplified version, called the BLUEFOR tracking system, and installed it in key leader vehicles throughout the division. As Charlton's task force first rolled into combat, he gave little attention to the small screen installed in his turret and instead relied on the old standby of 1:100,000 map sheets—thirteen of them mounted on 18x24-inch map boards with task force graphics superimposed.

This worked satisfactorily, even with interruptions when crossing from one map sheet to another while on the move, until the task force was drawn into an unexpected hot fight for the town of As Samawa. The 1:100,000-scale maps had no usable detail of As Samawa as an urban area; the task force had no overhead imagery of it either, since it had not intended to fight there. FBCB2, on the other hand, offered digital imagery allowing the viewer to zoom in and out and appreciate the streets in whatever scale. A few days later the task force was caught in the huge sandstorm south of Baghdad. With visibility near zero, vehicles with FBCB2 were nevertheless able to navigate through the sandstorm, following their own plot on the screen as they worked around obstacles and key terrain. For the rest of the campaign Charlton never used another paper map product. As the campaign progressed, such digital technology became so popular, pervasive, and generally used that the theater as a whole became concerned with lack of sufficient satellite communications bandwidth to accommodate all users. The experience nevertheless underscored the pace at which the current force could take advantage of developments intended for the future force.

Technology was not the only venue for transformation efforts, of course. Another was achieving an appropriate balance in the expectations of the reserve components. Since the Vietnam War, the National Guard and the organized reserve had increasingly transitioned from being an inventory of mobile units that could reinforce the active component in due course to being enablers that rounded out the active component's capabilities and were essential for its success from early in an operation. Since DESERT STORM, the reserve components had consistently deployed as an important fraction of every major mission and had even routinely assumed some overseas missions.

Since 9-11 large numbers had been called up for homeland security and for operations overseas, with the mobilization being particularly large and lengthy in support of Operation IRAQI FREEDOM. By September 2003, 144,000 National Guardsmen and reservists were on duty, with 28,000 of these mobilized for homeland security.

MODULARITY

To meet the force requirements of units constantly rotating to Iraq and Afghanistan, in September 2003 the U.S. Army began converting from an organization centered on divisions numbering from 10,000 to 18,000 soldiers to one based upon brigades totaling at most 3,900. Each division would create four separate brigades mixing combat, combat support, and combat service support in the same brigade to make each capable of independent operations. Each brigade was also "modular" in the sense that as many separate brigades as necessary for a particular mission could be plugged into any division headquarters. The means for doing this became known as *Modularity*, which the Army defined as a design methodology aimed at creating standardized, expandable Army elements capable of being tailored to accomplish virtually any assignment. The new units would be as capable as their predecessors, but they would also be able to transform to meet a broad range of missions. Over the fifteen months that followed, the service completed a design, tested it, and then deployed the first of forty-five new modular brigade combat teams to Iraq.

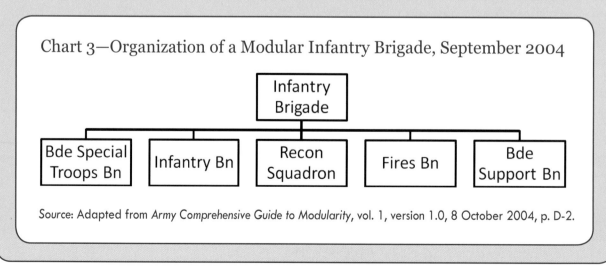

Chart 3—Organization of a Modular Infantry Brigade, September 2004

Source: Adapted from *Army Comprehensive Guide to Modularity*, vol. 1, version 1.0, 8 October 2004, p. D-2.

Manpower requirements in Iraq dictated a twelve-month tour actually in that country, more than doubling the six-month mobilization many had come to expect. Many reserve component soldiers were mobilized for two years. Not without a sense of humor, a number of reservists in Iraq made national television with a battle-weathered truck sporting the jaunty slogan, "One Weekend a Month—My Ass!!!" Clearly, the operational tempo was muddying the distinction between service in the active and reserve components. Soldiers who thought they had volunteered in cases of major national emergency now found themselves continually on call. The Army had to reexamine the force structures, roles, and missions of the reserve components if recruiting was to sustain itself in an atmosphere of trust.

The reserve components were challenged not only by the sheer numbers being called up, but also by departures from familiar systems whereby mobilizations and movements were managed and tracked. During the Cold War, contingency planning had been dominated by the expectation of gigantic slugfests in Central Europe and Korea. Comprehensive war plans identified the units involved in elaborate detail and gave each an appropriate mission. Courses of action were supported by an automated time-phased force deployment list (TPFDL) that assured an appropriate mix of combat, combat support, and combat service support units throughout a buildup and married deploying units and transportation in the most efficient manner. TPFDL was the apotheosis of detailed planning, and therefore a bit cumbersome: once initiated, it ran on like a vast and not particularly compromising machine.

The executors of IRAQI FREEDOM wanted more internal flexibility than TPFDL tended to allow. In some cases, for political reasons, they wanted force packaging to restrict overall force flow, accelerate the arrival of some types of units, decelerate the arrival of other types of units, and rapidly adjust deployment sequences as circumstances suggested. Enormous strides with respect to information management, the argument went, should enable far more flexibility with respect to force flow. Unfortunately, dramatic changes on short notice in the midst of a wartime deployment did not work well. The finite physical hardware of airlift and sealift could not morph as quickly as force packages could be redesigned; hasty reconfigurations typically did not allow for appropriate combat service support; and the imbroglio of not being allowed to move through Turkey put additional stress on an already challenged deployment. To many a guardsman and reservist, the result seemed to be chaos, with soldiers mobilized in accordance with the TPFDL waiting idly for weeks or months, rushing overseas only to find they had not been time-phased with the arrival of their equipment, or finding an imbalance between the scope of their mission and the resources available. The situation got worse when troops already away from their jobs and families for months awaiting deployment were told they would have to stay at least a year in Iraq to meet force requirements.

The inconveniences associated with the abandonment of TPFDL underscored another of Schoomaker's priorities, the development of more modular units. For generations the combined-arms framework of choice had been the division. The division had been the lowest level at which one had a robust representation of all branches and services assigned and could optimize the synergy of working them together. It was also the lowest level at which significant joint operations were feasible. This worked well when one's adversary was also a massive multidivisional force. The experiences in the Balkans and Afghanistan and during IRAQI FREEDOM suggested the need to deploy smaller, nimbler, self-contained units—tactical and operational "small change"—to fit contingency circumstances. Reimer and then Shinseki had experimented with alternate possibilities. The combined-arms framework of choice came to be the brigade combat team, a development that Schoomaker approved; this was intended to be nimbler than the brigade combat team of yore. Subordinate units would be trained to a high standard, and training would include the expectations of quickly mixing and matching units to achieve precisely tailored solutions at any point on the combat spectrum.

The notion of smaller, nimbler, highly trained units tracked with yet another transformation, unit manning. Since 1907 the U.S. Army had relied on individual replacements to keep units up to strength overseas and in turbulent or casualty-prone circumstances. The system had its advantages and disadvantages. Its critics argued that constant back-and-forth movement of unit personnel degraded unit cohesion and guaranteed a rapid loss of the value added by combat experience or training. A half-dozen times since World War II, the Army had experimented with systems featuring unit manning and rotation, wherein soldiers stayed together as a unit for a long time and deployed together, without success for various reasons. The emphasis on modularity, the nature and scale of recurrent deployments overseas, and improvements in airlift and sealift all seemed to argue for yet another attempt to make unit manning work. The smaller, nimbler, superbly equipped and painstakingly trained units of the transformed Army should profit from the further cohesion unit manning would bring.

Conclusion

By the end of 2008 the United States had been engaged in the Global War on Terrorism for just over seven years. During that time, broad preparations for a variety of possible post–Cold War operations focused quickly on specific adversaries and identified missions in Afghanistan, Iraq, the Horn of Africa, and the Philippines. At the same time, the Army could not afford to ignore continuing missions where the presence of U.S. headquarters and units were essential to maintaining worldwide U.S. commitments to peace and stability. U.S. Army units continued their watch in South Korea, manned a peace-keeping battalion in the Sinai, kept a corps headquarters and several brigades in Germany, sustained an active engagement policy in South America, and maintained an essential institutional training base in the United States, all with fewer than 550,000 active soldiers. The continual pace of operations in Iraq and Afghanistan would stretch the force to greater limits than expected as rotation followed rotation in the largest series of unit movements in Army history. The strain on families, the training base, recruiting, retention, equipment, and units continued throughout those years, with only a glimmer of hope at the start of 2009 that the pace might slow in the near future. The Army continued to evolve and transform itself into a more powerful force with new technology that could be ready for the next adversary while coping with the current ones. Expanding only slightly in size (from 485,000 in 2001 to nearly 550,000 at the start of 2009), the active force, powerfully supplemented by the strongest and most heavily deployed reserve and National Guard structure since World War II, was tested and tested again and proved up to its tasks. With no near-term closure in sight, transformation, modernization, and warfighting would have to go hand in hand as the Army continued to prepare itself for whatever missions the nation would ask of it.

DISCUSSION QUESTIONS

1. What impact did the events of September 11, 2001, have on the U.S. Army? How ready was the Army to respond to the initial challenges of the Global War on Terrorism? How does this war increase the need for joint operations?

2. What was the key to success in Afghanistan during Operation ENDURING FREEDOM? How did the small numbers of U.S. ground troops in Afghanistan achieve such a quick result, and what can we learn from that success?

3. To what extent was the invasion of Iraq justified by the Global War on Terrorism? What were some other reasons for our attack on Iraq, and how persuasive were they?

4. The rapid military success of Operation IRAQI FREEDOM was followed by the extensive involvement of the Army in peacekeeping, occupation duties, and nation building. To what degree are these appropriate roles for our Army?

5. To what extent does the Army role in the homeland security of the United States blur the lines of authority between strictly military and civic authorities in domestic affairs? What are some of the dangers of greater military involvement in such matters?

6. In what ways and how well did allies and alliances play in the Global War on Terrorism?

7. How has the Global War on Terrorism affected the continuing Army Transformation?

RECOMMENDED READINGS

Atkinson, Rick. *In the Company of Soldiers: A Chronicle of Combat.* New York: Henry Holt and Co., 2004.

Berkowitz, Bruce. *The New Face of War: How War Will Be Fought in the 21st Century.* New York: Free Press, 2003.

Brown, Todd S. *Battleground Iraq: Journal of a Company Commander.* Washington, D.C.: U.S. Army Center of Military History, 2007.

Fontenot, Gregory, E. J. Degen, and David Tohn. *On Point: The United States Army in Operation IRAQI FREEDOM.* Fort Leavenworth, Kans.: Combat Studies Institute Press, 2004.

Hoffman, John, ed. *Tip of the Spear: Small-Unit Actions in Iraq, 2004–2007.* Washington, D.C: U.S. Army Center of Military History, 2009.

Koontz, Christopher N., ed. *Enduring Voices: Oral Histories of the U.S. Army Experience in Afghanistan, 2003–2005*. Washington, D.C.: U.S. Army Center of Military History, 2008.

Reardon, Mark J., and Jeffery A. Charlston. *From Transformation to Combat: The First Stryker Brigade at War*. Washington, D.C.: U.S. Army Center of Military History, 2007.

Stewart, Richard W. *Operation Enduring Freedom: The U.S. Army in Afghanistan, October 2001–March 2002*. Washington, D.C.: U.S. Army Center of Military History, 2004.

Wright, Donald P., Timothy R. Reese, et al. *On Point II: Transition to the New Campaign: The United States Army in Operation Iraqi Freedom, May 2003–January 2005*. Fort Leavenworth, Kans.: Combat Studies Institute Press, 2008.

Other Readings

Briscoe, Charles, et al. *Weapon of Choice: U.S. Army Special Forces in Afghanistan*. Fort Leavenworth, Kans.: Combat Studies Institute Press, 2004.

Friedman, Richard S. *Advanced Technology Warfare: A Detailed Study of the Latest Weapons and Techniques for Warfare Today and into the 21st Century*. New York: Harmony Books, 1985.

Gordon, Michael, and Bernard Trainor. *Cobra II: The Inside Story of the Invasion and Occupation of Iraq*. New York: Pantheon Books, 2006.

Gunaratna, Rohan. *Inside al-Qaeda: Global Network of Terror*. New York: Berkeley Books, 2003.

Macgregor, Douglas A. *Transformation under Fire: Revolutionizing How America Fights*. Westport, Conn.: Praeger, 2003.

Robinson, Linda. *Tell Me How This Ends: General David Petraeus and the Search for a Way Out of Iraq*. New York: Public Affairs, 2008.

West, Bing. *The Strongest Tribe: War, Politics, and the Endgame in Iraq*. New York: Random House, 2008.

ABBREVIATIONS

AAF	Army Air Forces		FOA	field operating agency
ABDA	American-British-Dutch-Australian		FORSCOM	Forces Command
ACR	Armored Cavalry Regiment		FROG	Free Rocket Over Ground
AD	Air Defense			
AEF	American Expeditionary Forces		G–1	Personnel
AGF	Army Ground Forces		G–2	Intelligence
AMC	Army Materiel Command		G–3	Operations
AMSP	Advanced Military Studies Program		G–4	Supply
ARTEP	Army Training and Evaluation Program		G–5	Training
ASF	Army Service Forces		GHQ	General Headquarters
BAR	Browning Automatic Rifle		HAWK	Homing All the Way Killer
			HQDA	Headquarters, Department of the Army
CBI	China-Burma-India			
CCC	Civilian Conservation Corps			
CCS	Combined Chiefs of Staff		ICBM	intercontinental ballistic missile
CDC	Combat Developments Command		IRB	immediate reaction battalion
CENTO	Central Treaty Organization			
CIDG	Civilian Irregular Defense Group		JCS	Joint Chiefs of Staff
CINC	Commander in Chief		JRTC	Joint Readiness Training Center
CMTC	Citizens' Military Training Camp			
CMTC	Combat Maneuver Training Center		KATUSA	Korean Augmentation to the United States Army
CONARC	Continental Army Command			
CONUS	Continental United States		KMAG	Military Advisory Group to the Republic of Korea
CONUSA	Continental United States Army			
CORDS	Civil Operations and Rural Development Support		KP	kitchen police
COSVN	*Central Office for South Vietnam*		*KPA*	*Korean People's Army*
CPVF	*Chinese People's Volunteer Force*			
CS	combat support		LST	Landing Ship, Tank
CSS	combat service support			
			MAAG	Military Assistance Advisory Group
DCSOPS	Deputy Chief of Staff for Military Operations		MACOM	major Army command
			MACV	Military Assistance Command, Vietnam
DEW	distant early warning		MIS	Military Intelligence Service
DIVAD	Division Air Defense weapon (Sergeant York)		MLRS	Multiple-Launch Rocket System
			MRBM	medium-range ballistic missile
DPRK	*Democratic People's Republic of Korea*		MVA	Modern Volunteer Army
FEAF	Far East Air Forces		NATO	North Atlantic Treaty Organization
FEC	Far East Command		NSC	National Security Council
FMLN	*Farabundo Marti Liberacion Nacional*		NTC	National Training Center

OAS	Organization of American States	SEATO	Southeast Asia Treaty Organization
OPD	Operations Division	SHAPE	Supreme Headquarters, Allied Powers Europe
ORC	Officers' Reserve Corps		
OSS	Office of Strategic Services	SOG	Studies and Observations Group
		SOUTHCOM	Southern Command
PAC	Patriot Antitactical ballistic missile Capability	STRAC	Strategic Army Corps
		SWPA	Southwest Pacific Area
PAVN	*People's Army of Vietnam*		
PDF	Panama Defense Force	TDA	Table of Distribution and Allowances
PF	Popular Forces	TO&E	Table of Organization and Equipment
PLAF	*People's Liberation Armed Forces*	TOW	Tube-launched, Optically tracked, Wire-guided antitank missile
POA	Pacific Ocean Area		
PRC	People's Republic of China	TRADOC	Training and Doctrine Command
PROVIDE	Project Volunteer in Defense of the Nation		
		UMT	Universal Military Training
		UN	United Nations
RCT	regimental combat team	UNC	United Nations Command
RF	Regional Forces	UNPROFOR	United Nations Protection Force
ROAD	Reorganization Objective Army Division	USAREC	United States Army Recruiting Command
ROK	Republic of Korea	USAREUR	United States Army, Europe
ROTC	Reserve Officers' Training Corps	USARV	United States Army, Vietnam
SAC	Strategic Air Command (U.S. Air Force)	VOLAR	Volunteer Army
SAM-D	Surface-to-Air Missile–Developmental	WAC	Women's Army Corps
SAMS	School of Advanced Military Studies	WPB	War Production Board
SAMVA	Special Assistant for the Modern Volunteer Army	WSA	War Shipping Administration

MAP SYMBOLS

Function

Mechanized Infantry	
Psychological Operations Group	
Armored Cavalry	
Field Artillery	
Aviation	
Airborne	
Armor	
Air Assault	
Air Cavalry	
Infantry	
Special Operations Forces	SOF
Cavalry	

Size

Platoon	•••
Battery, Company, or Cavalry Troop	I
Battalion or Cavalry Squadron	II
Regiment	III
Brigade	X
Division	XX
Corps	XXX
Army	XXXX
Army Group	XXXXX

Examples

A Co, 4th Bn, 6th Infantry (Mechanized)   A ⊠ 4/6

1st Bn, 4th Psychological Operations Group   1 ▭ 4

2d Armored Cavalry Regiment   2ACR ⬭

41st Field Artillery Brigade   41 ⬭•

12th Aviation Brigade   12AVN ▭

82d Airborne Division   82 ⊠

2d Marine Division   2 ⊠
                                                       USMC

3d Armor Division   3 ⬭

101st Airborne Division (Air Assault)   101 ⊠

1st Cavalry Division (Vietnam)   1 ⊠

1st Cavalry Division (Post Vietnam)   1CAV ⬭

5th Infantry Division   5 ⊠

1st Corps   I

Special Operations Forces   SOF

Index